We have sought and obtained aid from too many sources to try to list them all here. We wish to express our indebtedness to the writers whose investigations and writings are referred to in the text, for the suggestions offered by Dr. Warren G. Findley, Coordinator of Educational Research, University of Georgia, and to Sr. M. Lucy Ann, C. S. A., who carefully read sections of the manuscript before publication.

K. C. G.
A. J. K.
A. S. M.

PREFACE

A textbook in educational psychology, like other textbooks, is limited in its aims and scope. It cannot provide solutions to the many individual problems that students of education will eventually encounter in their teaching activities. However, the writers have selected from the vast amount of information available sound and useful data on the learner and the educative process. They have sought to furnish the student with sound theories and to illustrate these theories with examples of the kinds of problems teachers face. The materials presented in this text should help teachers and prospective teachers to gain a clearer understanding of the nature of the learner, the learning process, personality adjustment and integration, and problems encountered in learning and personality development.

At the end of each chapter there is a list of selected readings intended to supplement the materials of that chapter. Each chapter also contains a number of problems and exercises that will facilitate the students' learning and utilization of the facts and concepts. Studying these exercises before reading the chapter will furnish the students an overview of the materials presented in the chapter, while studying them after completing the chapter will provide a basis for class discussion as well as a review. The suggested films in the appendix will extend the range of application of the ideas presented in the text.

The task of communicating through the medium of a textbook the concepts and theories of three educational psychologists about human development and the educative process is both a challenge and an opportunity. The accomplishment of this task was made possible through the continuous interchange of ideas, the careful selection of scientific data as a basis for the subject matter of the text, and the critical reading of the whole manuscript by each author. This textbook, therefore, has grown out of the cooperative effort of three authors with different backgrounds but with certain common conceptions about the major problems of educational psychology and similar viewpoints about the basic needs of teachers and prospective teachers. The writers have used the various materials in this text in their classes in educational psychology in an effort to assure that the content is readily understood and learned by the pre-service teacher and others interested in studying educational psychology.

CONTENTS

To

Linnea
Ann
Louise

EDUCATIONAL PSYCHOLOGY

Second Edition

KARL C. GARRISON
University of Georgia

ALBERT J. KINGSTON
University of Georgia

ARTHUR S. McDONALD
Marquette University

40539

 NEW YORK: APPLETON-CENTURY-CROFTS
DIVISION OF MEREDITH PUBLISHING COMPANY

EDUCATIONAL
PSYCHOLOGY

Edward E. Pino, District Superintendent
Reed Union School District
Belvedere-Tiburon, California

Through the application of the principles of educational psychology, man has been able to better understand and modify his physical and social environments

FIGURES

TABLES

PART I

Psychology in Education

CHAPTER 1

The Field of Educational Psychology

At birth the child brings his biological inheritance with him into the world, but characteristics of his biological heredity are not sufficient in themselves to enable him to develop harmoniously in a social culture such as ours. To aid him in acquiring the skills, information, concepts, and attitudes concerning his social heritage, American society has provided a variety of educational institutions to stimulate and nourish his development as he grows and learns.

Although the school is only one of a number of forces affecting the child's educational development, it has always been concerned with the teaching of certain aspects of the social heritage to growing boys and girls. Throughout the history of education, scholars have set forth challenging theories and viewpoints on the problems of growth and learning. The beginnings of educational psychology are to be found within these.

THE SCOPE OF EDUCATIONAL PSYCHOLOGY

A consideration of the scope of educational psychology should first attempt to answer the question, What is educational psychology? Many books have been written and many courses labeled *Educational Psychology* have been offered in college. A study of these will show that educational psychology is an area of knowledge, an application of methods and principles of psychology, and a field for continued study and research. The activities of educational psychologists are not confined to the laboratory and the writing of textbooks. Educational psychologists are also to be found in the clinic, the testing bureau, the office, and the classroom.

Scientific characteristics of psychology

Psychology, as a science, is concerned with observable human behavior, which it is its function to describe and explain. The psychologist

3

is interested in formulating fundamental principles of behavior. While the present status of psychology may appear to have emerged almost "full grown," closer examination shows its roots extend far into the past. Students of human behavior have recognized the operation of certain principles of behavior for many centuries. As a science, psychology evolved over a long period of time in close association with animal experimentation. It did not suddenly spring into complete functional existence as did Minerva, the Goddess of Wisdom, but developed gradually, first from philosophy and then from related fields of study.

  ◦ In the history of educational psychology, the classical studies of Thorndike, with animals as subjects, did much to furnish a basis for principles of learning in school situations. Through the use of animal subjects, the psychologist has been able to arrange more elaborate and better controlled situations for the study of learning and other behavioral activities than is possible with human subjects. The number of investigations conducted annually with animals, and the variety of problems being studied today, indicates their usefulness in furnishing scientific findings for educational psychologists.

Since psychologists are concerned with studying human behavior, interpretations are made within the context of the organism and the situation in which the behavior occurs. Concerning this Mussen states:

> The organism, or, in our case, the person, has a number of properties or characteristics. Because of these characteristics he behaves the way he does in the situation. On the other hand, it is equally valid to say that he behaves the way he does because of the characteristics of the situation. The same organism behaves differently in different situations; different organisms behave differently in the same situation. The behavior is, therefore, a function both of the characteristics of the person and the characteristics of the situation.[1]

The methods psychologists use for studying human behavior are essentially the same as those used by students in other areas of science. A given kind of behavior is observed and an attempt is made to relate it to the nature of the organism and to the situation. Sarah pinches her younger sister. The psychologist attempts to determine, on the basis of the observable factors, why Sarah pinched her younger sister. However, it is at this point that the psychologist's method of arriving at an explanation will most likely differ from that arrived at by laymen through day-to-day observations. The psychologist's observations are conducted more systematically, and frequently, over longer periods of time. The psychologist is more careful, not only in gathering data about the observations of Sarah, but also in interpreting the data and arriving at a more accurate explanation.

[1] Paul H. Mussen, *Handbook of Research Methods in Child Development* (New York: John Wiley & Sons, 1960), p. 20.

Aims of educational psychology

• Understanding, prediction, and control of behavior are the goals of psychology and educational psychology, as our study of the varied problems in educational psychology shall reveal. The materials of the chapters making up this book have been carefully chosen with these goals in mind. They may be thought of as sequential in nature: understanding must precede prediction, and control is largely a hit-or-miss proposition if it is not based upon relatively accurate predictions.

There are similarities in the work methods of all sciences. The individual confronted with a problem in educational psychology will depend upon precision, objectivity, controlled observations, and freedom from bias in the same manner as the individual seeking solutions for problems in geology, physics, or other sciences. There are different ways of studying difficult problems in educational psychology. How the educational psychologist studies a particular problem will depend upon the problem itself, his training, and his insight.

Since the adoption of the scientific method in psychology, a large body of knowledge has been assembled, increasing our understanding of problems in educational psychology. Certain principles have emerged which have been found effective in child development, learning, and personality adjustments. Although educational psychology is a relatively new science, its aims and content have become fairly well defined. The aims set forth by a committee into the late 40's are still appropriate today.

• Educational psychology is concerned primarily with the study of human behavior as it is changed or directed under the social process of education, and secondarily with those studies of processes that contribute to an increased understanding of how behavior is changed and directed through education.[2]

One of the major reasons we send a child to school, educators offer, is that training will enable him to solve problems more adequately and efficiently in later life. This notion is based on the theory of transfer of training, explained in Chapter 8. It should be pointed out, however, that some kinds of learning will make individuals less capable of solving problems. The student of educational psychology should be interested in acquiring the knowledge and skills that will enable him to solve problems more efficiently and that will equip him to guide others in the development of adequate and effective methods of solving problems, particularly in educational psychology. This aim will be most completely

2 Victor H. Noll, John E. Horrocks, and G. Lester Anderson, "The Function of the Division of Educational Psychology of the American Psychological Association: A Committee Report," *Journal of Educational Psychology*, Vol. 40 (1948), pp. 361-370.

Studying children in learning situations is an important part of the teacher education program.

realized in a teaching-learning situation where educational problems are studied, analyzed, and applied to classroom and other educational situations.

Subject matter of educational psychology

In the view of educators, particularly teachers, the educative process is a planned effort to guide boys and girls in the acquisition of certain skills, knowledge, and attitudes somewhat harmonious with their cultural heritage. The product of education refers to the changes in behavior that occur as a result of experience. The expanded school curricula, increased school attendance, improved teacher preparation, and broadened religious and community programs are a reflection of the needs of our society for better education of boys and girls—the citizens of tomorrow. The objectives of the homes, schools, churches, and other institutions reflect the social culture of the group, their aspirations and goals.

The subject matter of educational psychology is designed (1) to enhance and enrich the lives of the learners; and (2) to furnish students with the knowledge and understanding that will help them institute improvements in the quality of instruction. The subject matter includes the topics of growth and development, mental processes, learning, motivation, individual differences, measurement and evaluation, adjustments, guidance, and other aspects of behavior that appear in learning situations.

The divisions of educational psychology will depend on the emphasis given to the major topics as well as to the manner in which they are organized and combined. The major divisions recognized in this volume include the following:

1. The Child and His Development: The course of development. The nature of intelligence. Language and thinking. Socialization and its role.
2. Learning and the Educative Process: Learning and motivation. The learning of skills; Knowledge, understanding, and problem solving; Character development.
3. Evaluating Pupil Growth: Methods of pupil evaluation. Studying the individual child. Learning difficulties at school. Evaluating the results of instruction.
4. Guiding the Child: Personality integration. Adjustment problems of the child. Pupil-teacher relations.

SOURCES OF KNOWLEDGE AND UNDERSTANDING

In gathering and interpreting data useful to teachers and others concerned with its use, the task of the educational psychologist today is considerably more complex than it was several decades ago. Most of the data used by educational psychologists a generation or more ago were obtained from studies in the psychological laboratory. These materials were carefully interpreted and the results applied to learnings at school. However, there is today an increasing amount of materials available from other sources that have both a direct and indirect bearing on learning.

The experimental psychologist through his laboratory studies continues to supply valuable information on problems of learning and motivation. Because much of his work has been conducted with animals, the human factor has been eliminated, thus increasing the objectivity of his studies. However, in his efforts to screen out the different sources of error, he confines his studies to a very limited area, such as "The effects of olfactory cues upon learning" or "The effects of varying the intensity of a particular visual cue upon the behavior and learning of the chimpanzee." Because of this, it is difficult to apply the findings to a total learning situation characteristic of classroom learning. Nevertheless, studies of animal learning in laboratory situations have furnished valuable information about the learning process.

Clinical psychologists, psychiatric social workers, and counseling psychologists have also made important contributions to educational psychology. Much of their work may be classified as "clinical research"—case studies of individuals with learning or behavior problems. Although many of their concepts have not been tested by experimental methods, they have withstood the test of careful analysis and widespread usage during the last two or more decades. They have furnished useful information to educational psychologists on the various forces and conditions affecting the behavior of children, adolescents, and adults. The question arises, Are findings from emotionally disturbed children, adolescents, and pupils with special learning difficulties applicable to so-called normal children? Research studies show that there are no essential differences in the kinds of problems faced by children classified as emotionally disturbed. All children face problems, and all children display symptoms of emotional disturbances at times. The difference lies in the degree of disturbance that may be observed. Intensive clinical studies have yielded valuable clues to a better understanding of behavior problems in the classroom and elsewhere.

Another group of educators and psychologists has made use of tests and measurements in furnishing a better understanding of the learner and factors influencing the learning process. They have provided a wide range of measuring instruments useful in evaluation, diagnosis, and prediction, enabling us to treat different aspects of behavior statistically. For example, comparisons can be made between different groups, such as age or skeletal maturity groups, in intelligence, educational progress, anxiety manifestations, or other measurable traits. Through such measuring instruments and statistical procedures, such relationships as between intelligence and educational progress, or between anxiety and learning can also be obtained. The widespread use of measuring instruments has also enabled many experimental-minded teachers to participate in studies designed to improve classroom learning; and educational psychologists have used these instruments to gather objective data that have added considerably to our knowledge and understanding of learners and the relationship of various characteristics and conditions to learning.

Philosophers and educational theorists concerned with education have also made important contributions to educational psychology by challenging existing concepts and advancing new concepts on the educative process. This has led educational psychologists to re-examine existing theories and to conduct further studies dealing with the new concepts. These studies have led to important changes in the content and organization of the school curriculum and in educational methods.

PSYCHOLOGICAL PRINCIPLES AT WORK

The term psychology has come into common use. One hears the word used at the store counter, in the office, at the baseball game, and around the bridge table. Almost everyone familiar with the term considers himself an amateur psychologist. When the instructor reports the findings of some study, students frequently react with the expression, "Why, that's just plain common sense." A twenty-year-old college student reacted to a discussion of some problems connected with habit formation, "Why, I have known that all my life." This is, perhaps, to be expected. The subject matter of psychology is human behavior, and everyone has observed human behavior in many situations. Surely these personal observations are in a very large percentage of cases verifiable through experimental studies. However, the reason a formal science of psychology relying on experiments and a special vocabulary is necessary, is that everyday observations are frequently colored by subjective states, such as feelings and emotions, likes and dislikes. Only through careful observations scientifically conducted can we determine whether an everyday observation is dependable.

Science and common sense

There are those who would rely on what is termed *common sense*. We should be concerned with the source of what we refer to as *common sense*. Concerning this Barnett has stated: "But as Einstein has pointed out, common sense is actually nothing more than a deposit of prejudices laid down in the mind prior to the age of eighteen. Every new idea one encounters in later years must combat this accretion of 'self evident' concepts." [3]

Teachers have always had common-sense rules and principles to guide them in their activities, which they were sure were correct. We see this in the early reading primers and in the methods used in teaching reading. For example, common sense indicated that a child must first learn letters before he could learn words. Then, he must proceed to acquire a large word-reading vocabulary before he could be introduced to sentences. This was quite generally accepted as the correct and logical procedure to follow. In the *New England Primer* the alphabet was taught first, followed by letter combinations, such as *ab, ac, ad*, etc. This common-sense method of teaching reading continued until the reading process was scientifically studied. Careful observations showed that good readers do not notice each of the letters and syllables that make up a word, but take in whole words at a glance. The child, likewise, learns

[3] Lincoln Barnett, *The Universe and Dr. Einstein* (New York: William Sloane, 1952), p. 63.

G — As runs the Glass.
Our Life doth pafs.

H — My Book and Heart
Muft never part.

I — Job feels the Rod,—
Yet blefles GOD

K — Proud Korah's troop
Was fwallowed up.

L — L o t fled to *Zoar*,
Saw fiery Shower
On *Sodom* pour.

M — M o s e s was he
Who *Ifrael's* Hoft
Led thro' the Sea.

FIGURE 1-1.   Seventeenth Century Text Material. This page is reproduced from *The New England Primer*, Joel Munsell's Sons, 1887. The first notice of *The New England Primer* was an advertisement printed in an almanac of 1691.

to use cues such as outline, pattern, beginnings, and size to recognize words.

The results of scientific studies of the reading process brought about important changes in the method of teaching reading and in text ma-

A New Family

Dick and Jane went to the barn.

"See the four horses," said Dick.

"Look up, Dick," said Jane.

"Look up and see White Hen.

She wants to come down."

"Oh, White Hen," said Dick.

"We will come up and get you."

FIGURE 1-2. Modern Reading Material. The modern reader combines pictures with words and sentences.

terials, as shown in Figures 1-1 and 1-2. A study of the materials presented show that psychological principles are sound, perhaps in harmony with "common sense." The major task of educational psychology is not only to help learners acquire accurate and common-sense views about learning, growth, and adjustment, but also to discard inaccurate views that were regarded as "common sense."

Changed concepts of teaching and learning. Applications of scientific methods to problems of teaching and learning have brought about changed concepts of the teacher's role in the teaching-learning process. We must first recognize that learning is a complex process involving an interplay of mental and emotional processes by which the learner shapes his knowledge, attitudes, and feelings toward himself and others. It is the process by which the learner develops skills for meeting life's problems and reconstructing his environment. In these processes children need help and guidance. No clear-cut formula for helping children exists; however, concepts and principles will be set forth in subsequent chapters that should serve as a guide to those concerned with the teaching process.

The role of the teacher in the teaching-learning process is presented in chapter 19. Trow and others point out that the concept of the teacher as a professional educator has been gradually changing and expanding in American education.

It is obvious that the concept of what a teacher should do has changed over the years. To the Hoosier schoolmaster the matter was quite simple. He was the drill sergeant. The cadence of recitation was akin to the sound of marching feet. As master of the drill, he called the steps. This teacher also held the role of academic authority; not only did he choose the school experiences, but he was also revered as the great storehouse of information. His very person was the embodiment of learning, and he was categorically right. This fundamental instructional role has mellowed with the years. Now the teacher does not always have to know. He operates as an adult with superior knowledge, to be sure, but he serves more as a resource person explaining, telling, and demonstrating. His drill master's uniform has been changed for the Socratic garb, for his instruction is more concerned with fostering the student's power to think and reason. This major "informational role" of the teacher is often discussed and is perhaps quite well understood. But it should be understood that this role is not exclusively the property of the teacher. At times, especially when the content of the course falls within the experience of the students, the class members share or take over the instructional role. As we come to understand more the dynamics of the classroom, we realize the way in which the role is handled by the teacher has important effects on the total learning situation.[4]

Teacher-pupil relations. The way the teacher controls the children in the classroom is a product not only of her personal philosophy and attitudes, but also of the practices of her fellow teachers and expectations of the community in which the school exists. For the past decade considerable controversy has appeared over the best methods of instructing children. One group, representing an extreme traditional viewpoint, con-

[4] William Clark Trow, Alvin E. Zander, William C. Morse, and David H. Jenkins, "Psychology of Group Behavior: The Class as a Group," *Journal of Educational Psychology,* Vol. 41 (1950), pp. 322-338.

tends that the school program should be directed to helping children master certain basic skills and content. Adherents of this philosophy feel that the school should be so organized as to facilitate the child's acquisition of logically developed and arranged subject matter. In such a program the teacher naturally assumes an important position in the overall control and direction of the learning process. Most of the responsibility for the preparation, selection, instruction, and evaluation of learning rests with the teacher. On the other hand, proponents of the more progressive type of school program believe that learning is facilitated by a more integrative approach. They feel that the child should play an active role in setting goals and participating in their development. More consideration is given to the individual child's background of experiences, and the instructional units are developed around these factors.

It should be apparent that the controls exerted by any teacher will reflect the degree to which she adheres to either of these two points of view. The traditionally organized classroom demands that the teacher play a different role from that required of the teacher in a more progressive classroom. Since socialization develops through interaction, children studying under the more dominating and controlling teacher tend to have different social experiences from those studying under a teacher who furnishes them with more opportunities to participate in setting and developing their own goals. In general, the principles of child psychology favor pupil participation in goal setting and planning in activities where they are directly concerned, but the maturity and experiences of the children and the nature of the activity or problem must be taken into consideration. The democratically controlled classroom facilitates the personal-social development of the pupils by enabling them to assume greater responsibilities for self-direction and by providing a greater number of opportunities for social interaction with other pupils.

Psychology and classroom learning. The teaching-learning model presented in Table 1-1 shows the three variables involved in the teaching

TABLE 1-1. A Teaching-Learning Model

INDEPENDENT VARIABLES (TEACHER)	INTERVENING VARIABLES (LEARNER)	RESULTANT VARIABLES (LEARNER)
1. Linguistic behavior 2. Performative behavior 3. Expressive behavior	Attention, interests, memories, needs, attitudes, beliefs, associative mechanisms, inferences, and choices	1. Linguistic behavior 2. Performative behavior 3. Expressive behavior

situation.[5] They are (1) linguistic behavior, (2) performative behavior, and (3) expressive behavior. These variables are important in the course of teaching. The intervening variables are the processes involved in the pupil's learning. The resultant behavior can be observed and measured by the teacher, but it is more difficult to deal with the intervening variables. That is, he cannot observe interests, beliefs, needs, and inferences. These may be inferred from observations or from the pupil's responses. For example, the teacher is able to observe the interests and attention of the pupil from his overt behavior.

Although this model does not present a detailed picture of teaching, which would involve reviewing, testing, reciting, and different forms of teacher-pupil interaction, it does furnish a basis for studying the independent and resultant (dependent) variables found in a teaching-learning situation. By considering the different kinds of behavior manifested by the teacher and learner one can arrive at a better understanding and appreciation of classroom activities.

It should be pointed out that the school is not the only institution or agency through which children and adolescents learn. The home, church, playground, and community also provide many experiences out of which learning comes. So do communication media like television, radio, magazines, and newspapers. There are, however, some kinds of learning tasks that can usually be more readily learned through school experiences than through these other day-to-day experiences. Thus, the schools tend to emphasize certain kinds of learning tasks.

One of these tasks is the learning of relatively complex subjects that require guidance over long periods of time. One of the best examples of such a learning task is mathematics, which requires carefully organized lessons graded to increasing difficulty. By guiding pupils in these experiences over a long period of time, they learn to deal with relatively complex problems.

A second kind of learning task the school is concerned with is the student's acquisition and enlargement of concepts. Both form and color concepts are developed early in the child's life. The acquisition of language enables the child to acquire highly developed generalized concepts, such as an equation in mathematics.

A third kind of learning task, closely related to the acquisition of concepts, is the learning of principles, which furnish a basis for applying understandings to other situations. For example, scientific concepts and principles which explain the function and operation of the skin glands are not obvious to the individual who has only observed this in his own life. Neither is the principle of water purification and other sanitary

[5] B. Othanel Smith, "A Concept of Teaching," *Teachers College Record,* Vol. 61 (1960), pp. 229-241. The teaching-learning model presented in Table 1-1 is adapted from Smith's pedagogical model, page 234.

practices well understood by the ordinary observer. An understanding of the principles enables the learner to deal better with different situations and conditions involving the principle of water purification.

A fourth kind of learning task especially appropriate for the school involves teaching an appreciation and understanding of art, music, drama, literature, and historical events. Through school experiences pupils are given the opportunity to study selected examples of materials from these subjects and to get additional information essential for an appreciation of their experiences. In the appreciation of the arts, educational psychology has made important contributions to the development of a more functional curriculum.

A fifth learning task involves the teaching of attitudes and values. It is here that a coordination of the experiences at school with those at home, at church, and in the community get the best results. Ethical values and moral concerns appear daily in the lives of pupils at school. Character education must be an important function of the school, which can function effectively in guiding students in the evaluation of their attitudes and behavior on the basis of available information and accepted values. Spiritual values are acquired through guidance, experiences, and daily contacts with others. Teachers are constantly teaching values both through example and an instructional program. Special materials bearing on this subject are presented in chapter 11.

THE ROLE OF PSYCHOLOGY IN EDUCATION

Education is possible because humans can learn. The plasticity of the growing child makes it possible to begin an instructional program during the early years of life. However, it is evident to observers of human learning that much learning takes place outside of school. Mary and Henry have already acquired a culture, which they bring with them, when they enter school. It is not, however, the function of educational psychology to determine why Mary and Henry should be required to go to school and what the goals of the school should be. This responsibility lies with the social and educational philosophers of the present age. Once these goals are determined, the contributions educational psychology can make are numerous. The role of psychology in education is presented in the discussions that follow.

Psychology and educational theory

A careful reading of the history of education in the United States shows that educational psychology has continuously made significant contributions to the theory and practice of education. Before the turn of the century William James had published his *Talks to Teachers*. The importance of psychology is vividly presented as follows:

Everywhere teaching must *agree* with the psychology, but need not necessarily be the only kind of teaching that would so agree; for many diverse methods of teaching may equally well agree with psychological laws. . . .

But, if the use of psychological principles thus be negative rather than positive, it does not follow that it may not be a great use, all the same. It certainly narrows the path for experiments and trials. We know in advance, if we are psychologists, that certain methods will be wrong, so our psychology saves us from mistakes. It makes us, moreover, more clear as to what we are about.[6]

John Dewey, American philosopher and educator, is also closely associated with American educational theory in this century, and E. L. Thorndike, another American, is also widely noted for his pioneer studies in educational psychology. The contributions educational psychologists have made to teaching have been instrumental in furnishing a sounder foundation for educational theory and practice.

Educational psychology and contemporary practices

The vast amount of research conducted by educational psychologists and others continues to initiate important changes in the school curriculum and in instructional methods. Frequently, however, a considerable gap exists between theory and practice. Therefore, an important function of educational psychology is to help bring educational practice more clearly into line with the results obtained from educational research. Many educational practices today definitely result from the applications of the methods and findings of general and educational psychology to educational problems. These may be noted as follows:

1. The development of the psychology of learning has furnished a guide for evaluating methods of teaching.
2. Developments in motivation have made teachers more sensitive to the need for motivating classroom learning.
3. The increased understanding of transfer of training and mental discipline has continued to produce significant changes in the school curriculum and in methods of teaching.
4. Developments in child growth have made teachers sensitive to the problems children encounter at different stages in their growth. These developments have also caused teachers to focus their attention on all aspects of the child's development.
5. The development and use of a wide variety of measuring instruments have brought into focus individual differences. This has led to an increased interest in individualizing the educational program.

6 William James, *Talks to Teachers* (New York: Holt, Rinehart & Winston, 1920), pp. 7-11.

6. Developments in personality adjustment and mental hygiene have led to a re-evaluation of classroom control and discipline. Teachers are now more sensitive to the needs and the personal-social-emotional problems of the children they encounter in the classroom and on the playground. These developments have also shown the crucial role of constructive interpersonal relationships between teacher and children in creating good personal adjustment.

7. The development and widespread use of educational statistics have led to more accurate interpretations of test data as well as of other data bearing on problems in education. This has led to a refinement of educational practices and to continued educational progress.

Educational psychology and teaching. Three questions may be considered by the student of educational psychology. The first concerns the child or learner who is to be educated. The second deals with the educative process, while the third concerns man's need for specialized schooling in addition to the education he gets from everyday experiences. Materials bearing on the learner and the educative process are presented in chapter 2.

The school as an institution exists to guide children in the development of skills, subject matter, attitudes, and behavior patterns essential for effective living in a particular society. The teacher, therefore, has two major tasks: to help children learn as efficiently as possible the subject matter being studied, and to help them acquire those desirable personal and social behavior patterns. Where religious education is part of the curriculum, the teacher's function is to nurture the child in the proper relationship to God. Since children need the teacher's guidance to learn, and since teaching may be defined as a set of actions directed to pupils, an important aim of educational psychology is to help teachers acquire understandings needed to guide children in their educational development.

Teaching is based upon the concept that children can learn. Although many studies dealing with the learning ability of children at different maturational stages have been conducted, considerable theoretical differences exist about the relative importance of heredity and environment in learning. Despite numerous studies this problem is still unresolved. The viewpoint presented throughout this book, however, is that the child is a product of the interaction of the human organism and various environmental forces and conditions. This viewpoint emphasizes the role of both heredity and environment—not one to the exclusion of the other. Certain principles have emerged from this viewpoint, an understanding of which is essential for a successful educational program. They are summarized here:

1. Heredity provides the broad basic pattern and sets the limit to the development of the various traits, characteristics, and abilities of the human organism.
2. Within the limits and broad pattern set by heredity, the human organism develops.
3. The human organism is remarkably plastic, making it possible for individuals very similar in their native endowment to develop in diverse ways.
4. Although the human organism is remarkably plastic, it is dependent upon the experiences provided for its development.
5. The optimum development of the human organism can only be attained under favorable environmental conditions existing from the beginning of life.

Educational psychology and the needs of teachers.   A study of the teacher's task reveals something of his needs. Teachers cannot safely imitate others or depend upon trial-and-error in their teaching. It was pointed out two decades ago that "Good teachers will know how to select subject matter suitable to the children with whom they work, and how to present it in ways that will make it likely that it will be genuinely absorbed." [7]

A great many studies have been made dealing with the problems teachers encounter. One author summarized the results of thirty-one studies involving thousands of teachers—male and female, experienced and inexperienced, rural and urban—who listed their most pressing problems. This summary is presented in Table 1-2.[8] They show that problems of individual differences, teaching methods, discipline, motivation, directed study, organization of materials, classroom procedures, and many miscellaneous difficulties in the teaching-learning-testing process, rather than knowledge of additional subject matter were their main concern. An earlier study by Davis [9] showed that motivation, testing and evaluation, diagnosing and correcting difficulties, modes of presentation, and individual differences ranked among the five most frequently mentioned difficulties at the elementary, junior-high, and senior-high school levels.

[7] Commission of Teacher Education, *Teachers for Our Times* (Washington: American Council on Education, 1944), pp. 164-165.

[8] George E. Hill, "Teachers' Instructional Difficulties—A Review of Research," *Journal of Educational Research*, Vol. 37 (1944), p. 608.

[9] Robert A. Davis, "The Teaching Problems of 1075 Public School Teachers," *Journal of Experimental Education*, Vol. 9 (1940), p. 45.

TABLE 1-2.   A Summary of the Results of Thirty-one Studies of Teachers' Problems (*Hill*)

DIFFICULTY	NUMBER OF STUDIES IN WHICH DIFFICULTY WAS AMONG FIRST
1. Difficulties in providing for individual differences among pupils	19
2. Difficulties in teaching method	18
3. Difficulties of discipline, control, social development of the pupil	17
4. Difficulties of motivation, getting children interested, getting them to work	12
5. Difficulties in direction of study	9
6. Difficulties in organizing and administering the classroom	8
7. Difficulties in selecting appropriate subject matter	6
8. Lack of time during the school day for all the things that need to be done	6
9. Difficulties in organization of materials	6
10. Difficulties in planning and making assignments	5
11. Difficulties in grading and promotion of pupils	5
12. Inadequacy of supplies and materials	4
13. Difficulties in testing and evaluating	4
14. Personal difficulties of the teacher	4
15. Difficulties arising from conditions of work	3
16. Difficulties involved in diagnosing and correcting particular pupil difficulties	3
17. Difficulties in teaching reading	3
18. Difficulties in making plans for teaching	3
19. Difficulties in promoting desirable habits	3
20. Difficulties in securing study aids	2
21. Difficulty in securing pupil participation	2
22. Difficulty because pupils talk while others are reciting	2
23. Outside interruptions of class work	2
24. Miscellaneous problems mentioned in one study	40*

* These were most specific problems. Some were difficulties in teaching this or that subject. Others were rural school problems such as "only one pupil in a grade," or "too many grades in one room."

Teachers everywhere are confronted with tasks and problems having a common psychological basis. Some of these will be considered in the following discussions. We need to understand clearly how children learn and what the school, particularly the teacher, can do to foster these learnings. Every teacher should have a conscious, consistent set of principles and beliefs about how children learn.

In addition to understanding how children learn, teachers need knowledge and information about growth and the characteristics of children at different age levels. Closely related to this second need, to which educational psychology contributes, is the need for knowledge and skills involved in studying children. Varied techniques have been developed and made usable for studying school-age children. Through the use of these techniques teachers gain a better understanding of particular children.

A fourth need of teachers for which educational psychology attempts to provide assistance is to evaluate the outcomes of different learning procedures and programs. Teachers should be able to develop particular tools for their needs as well as make use of tools already available for studying the changes that have taken place in learners and for determining whether these changes are sufficient in amount and quality for each learner involved.

These needs require that students of education and teachers have an extensive working knowledge of the experimental findings and contributions of psychology to growth, learning, motivation, and adjustment of school-age individuals. Such knowledge furnishes the teacher with a basis for evaluating and trying out different techniques in learning situations. A method of teaching out of harmony with proved learning principles is unsound, a waste of time to the teacher, and unfair to the learner.

Psychology and educational research

The science of psychology has not yet reached the stage of maturity whereby it can present a unified, coherent, and generally acceptable set of principles of learning, motivation, and adjustment. However, scientific studies have furnished useful information to teachers and others concerned with guiding and motivating pupils in learning situations. Educational psychology has furnished teachers and students of education with the informational background and scientific methods for studying pupils and evaluating different educational practices.

This book incorporates recent research on problems dealing with children and adolescents in learning situations. Such research will provide us with additional information and encourage keener insight into many educational problems.

Problems and exercises are presented at the end of each chapter. They will require further reading, reflective thinking, and in some cases, a limited amount of research on your part. As students of educational psychology you should be alert to the problems presented and discussed in the text. They should furnish you not only with useful information, but should also help you to develop scientific attitudes and methods of solving educational and psychological problems. Successful teachers are always trying out new materials and techniques in their classroom activities in an effort to improve their teaching, and thus further the learning and adjustment of their pupils. They are participating increasingly in research projects as part of their educational activities.

SUMMARY

Psychology, as a science, is concerned with observable human behavior. Educational psychology is especially concerned with the application of methods and principles of psychology to human behavior in educational situations. The educational psychologist uses different methods in studying problems in educational psychology, the particular method he uses depending largely upon the problem being investigated.

The educational psychologist is not content to use common sense in solving problems. Only through careful observations scientifically conducted can we determine whether certain preconceived notions about growth and learning are dependable. The changed concepts of teaching and learning are in themselves evidence that many ideas based upon common sense were not sound. Thus, important changes have appeared during the past several decades in the content of the school curriculum and in methods of teaching.

The educational psychologist recognizes the importance of good pupil-teacher relations in the teaching-learning process.

Educational psychology as an applied science is not directly concerned with educational goals. The role of educational psychology in education may be summarized as follows: (1) to evaluate educational theories; (2) to study and evaluate contemporary practices in education; (3) to evaluate different methods of teaching in the light of established principles of learning and motivation; (4) to help teachers solve their personal problems; and (5) to furnish methods to help those engaged in the scientific study of problems in the general area of educational psychology.

Problems and Exercises

1. State in your own words the aims of educational psychology. Why is it important for the student of educational psychology to have a clear understanding of the aims of the subject?
2. Many books in educational psychology devote considerable space to a discussion of the results of animal experiments. How can the inclusion of results be justified?
3. Examine several recent textbooks for the amount of space given to each of the following areas: (1) growth and development, (2) learning, (3) evaluation and measurement, and (4) guidance.
4. Show how the reliance on "common sense" may lead to erroneous conclusions and generalizations.

5. Consider the problems encountered by teachers, listed in Table 1-2. What are the implications of these findings for the student preparing to teach? Interview one or more teachers relative to problems they have encountered. What do the results of your interview indicate?
6. Some teachers show great insight in their understanding of child behavior while others show very little insight. How would you account for the differences to be observed?
7. List several educational problems that might be investigated by the parallel group method of experimentation? How is this method different from the traditional laboratory method?
8. Some people have described teaching as an art. Do you find any evidence from this chapter or Chapter I to support such a notion about teaching? Is such a viewpoint incompatible with the idea presented in this chapter of educational psychology as a science?
9. What are some important changes that have taken place in the educational program during the course of the past thirty years? How would you account for these changes?
10. Study the teaching-learning model presented in Table 1-1. Show how these variables operate in a classroom learning situation.

Selected Readings

ANDERSON, G. Lester, "Nature and Methods of Educational Psychology," in *Educational Psychology*, 4th ed. Charles E. Skinner, ed. (Englewood Cliffs, N. J.: Prentice-Hall, 1959).

COLADARCI, A. P., "The Relevancy of Educational Psychology," *Educational Leadership*, Vol. 13 (1956), pp. 489-492.

CRONBACH, Lee J., *Educational Psychology*, 2nd ed. (New York: Harcourt, Brace, & World, 1963), Ch. 1.

LINDGREN, HENRY C., *Educational Psychology in the Classroom*, 2nd ed. (New York: John Wiley & Sons, 1962), Ch. 1.

McDONALD, Frederick J., *Educational Psychology* (San Francisco: Wadsworth Publishing Co., 1959), Ch. 2.

STEPHENS, J. M., *Educational Psychology: The Study of Educational Growth*, rev. ed. (New York: Holt, Rinehart & Winston, 1960), Ch. 1.

THELEN, Herbert A., and TYLER, Ralph W., "Implications for Improving Instruction in High School," *Learning and Instruction*, Forty-ninth Yearbook of the National Society for the Study of Education, Part 1, (1950), Ch. 12.

CHAPTER **2**

Psychology and
the Educative Process

The sciences concerned with human behavior, learning, and adjustment have advanced sufficiently to be of real service to those concerned with the educative process. The role of psychology in the education of individuals was stressed in the previous chapter. The human organism, unlike other organisms, is equipped by nature to acquire cultural patterns of behavior and to modify the existing culture in harmony with his needs. The function of the educative process is to promote or facilitate desirable changes in the organism. These changes are necessary if the individual is to function effectively in his environment. The emerging personality of the child, discussed in Part V of this text, is to a marked degree a product of varying educational influences, although the student of educational psychology should realize at all times that educational influences are limited by what the child inherits.

The student of educational psychology is faced with the task of applying the materials and methods of psychology to the education of individuals in the classroom and elsewhere. It is the purpose of this chapter to furnish the student with an understanding of (1) the relationship between the organism and his environment, (2) the learner in relation to the educative process, (3) forces influencing the educative process, and (4) the role of the teacher in the educative process.

THE ORGANISM AND HIS ENVIRONMENT

Since every child is born into a culture or perhaps, in a more exact sense, into multiple cultures, it is important to study the two forces and conditions affecting his growth and learning. The first deals with heredity. What does the child bring genetically into the world? The

23

second deals with the influences of his environment upon his development. Considerable controversy still exists over the influence of heredity and environment upon the growing child. Brief descriptions of the roles of heredity and environmental conditions upon the individual should give the student of educational psychology a better understanding of the developmental processes operating on the school-age child.

Genetic factors in development

The development of the individual begins with the fertilization of the egg cell. In this process of development the original fertilized ovum divides and subdivides until thousands of cells have been produced. From the moment of the fertilization of the egg cell, the new life is influenced by various environmental stimuli which help to mold the potentialities for growth and learning which are inherited from the parents. Regardless of how heredity is defined, psychologists agree that the genes play an important role in development. Geneticists have found that coded instructions for growth and development are inherited through the nuclei of egg and sperm when they unite to begin the history of the living organism. These instructions are then perpetuated throughout the organism's lifetime when cells divide and specialize. Thus, it may be said that the infant is patterned by both hereditary and environmental influences from the moment of birth. His inherited gene structure is an important determinant of the kind of biological potential with which he starts life. This inheritance will be important in determining the extent to which his abilities and characteristics emerge later in interaction with his environment.

Considerable research has been carried on in an effort to ascertain the relative importance of heredity and environment. Much of this research has employed the co-twin method—an attempt to control the influence of heredity by selecting identical twins for study. Since heredity is thus assumed to be constant, the environment becomes the variable and any differences appearing in the twins are ascribed to environmental influences. In other studies, particularly those with animals, the physical and physiological environments are held as constant as possible, and the effects of differences due to heredity are observed. A number of studies have utilized siblings and identical twins who were reared apart to determine the effect of environmental forces. Although such studies have furnished useful information about the roles heredity and environment play in the individual's development, they have oversimplified the operation of these forces and have implied that they operate independently in the child's development.

The influence of heredity. Although authorities fail to agree on the relative amount of influence the biological inheritance exerts on the development of a given individual, it is commonly agreed that the individual's inheritance sets limits within which he can achieve his potential.[1] The influence of heredity may be noted in the baby's general characteristics. He is born tall or short, with a narrow or broad body build, small or large ears, and blue-gray or dark eyes. The different combination of genes from his parents determine, in the main, his general physical appearance at birth.

We do not expect the child who is mentally or physically handicapped to perform like the child who is not handicaped. We do not expect many children with musical talent to develop into Beethovens, but simply, to develop within their limits. This does not mean that the child with average musical talent cannot learn to participate in musical activities; he can develop within the limits set by his heredity. Exploiting his full potentiality would enable him to take part in a wide range of musical activities.

Interaction of heredity and environment. Environment has sometimes been regarded as a passive place in which an individual's behavior and growth occurs. Such a view regards the environment as a setting for behavior and growth, rather than as an active stimulating agent. The child enters into a world of people, things, ideas, attitudes, and values. He grows and develops according to certain fundamental principles set forth in Chapter 3. The type of adult he becomes will depend upon the interaction of various environmental influences upon him as a living and maturing organism. Although American culture offers children born into it both differences and similarities in opportunities, family life, neighborhoods, religious beliefs, discipline, social strata, attitudes, and values, an identical background for two children is not found even in the same family with identical twins. Each individual's environment is as unique as his individual self because he not only responds selectively to the forces within him and about him, but he also gives those constantly selected elements a particular interpretation colored by his past experiences, his organic make-up, his specific needs, and the level of his maturational development.

The most widely recognized principle involving the operation of heredity and environment upon the individual is that there is continuous interaction between the two factors. The tendency of early investigators to ascribe a certain per cent of the individual's development to heredity and a certain per cent to environment met with many difficulties. It became apparent to many researchers concerned with such problems that

[1] For a relatively complete discussion of the influences of heredity and environment on behavior see A. Anastasi, *Differential Psychology* (New York: Macmillan Co., 1958), Chap. 5; A. Anastasi, "Heredity, Environment, and the Question 'How?'," *Psychological Review*, Vol. 65 (1958), pp. 197-208.

the two forces are so closely related that behavior and growth could not be separated or exclusively classified under either one of the two categories. Functional development is an outgrowth of the interaction of the organism with its environment. The hereditary "determiners" of the genes cannot function unless environmental forces are able to play their roles. Kallmann states:

> Environment influences are vital, and after conception they gain coequality with those arising from heredity. However, only within the limits set by the genetic constitution of the organism can external factors have an effect on the dynamics of physiologic functions and interactions. Beyond these limits no power plant exists for generating behavioral potentials.[2]

The failure of a typical first-grade child in the United States to identify a television set from a simple descriptive definition is likely to be an indication of mental inferiority, while such a failure among typical six-year-olds from the villages of India would indicate their lack of opportunities to learn about television sets. One's selection of elements in his environment and his reaction to them will be affected by varying conditions of either heredity or environment. The hard-of-hearing child will fail to respond to the differentiation of tonal qualities present in certain pieces of music, while the child with a very limited rural background will reveal a very superficial understanding of farm crops.

The early sociocultural environment.   The child is born into a home where specific forms of social behavior are practiced and where certain cultural behavior patterns are manifested. Socialization and cultural behavior patterns, then, may be said to begin at birth. It is worthwhile for the teacher to realize that the child acquires ways of responding in social situations as a result of his experience. His readiness for school and the learnings introduced at school will depend in large measure upon his earlier sociocultural experiences.

Children in every society must learn to behave according to certain expectations. They must learn what to say and when to say it; what to wear on different occasions; what to believe; and how to respond to the actions of others. Eventually society determines which characteristics and behavior are to be positively reinforced, which to be shunned or avoided, and which to be merely tolerated. The typical child learns to operate physically, psychologically, and socially within the culture into which he is born and reared. Learning the accepted ways of behaving makes the child a functioning member of his society. This learning process begins at birth and continues throughout one's life. Members of a group tend to adopt similar cultural patterns, giving them a national or religious

[2] Frank Kallmann, "The Genetic of Human Behavior," *American Journal of Psychiatry*, Vol. 113 (1956-57), p. 496.

Children's knowledge of the physical and social world is expanded through carefully guided instruction.

character. Those who have visited different cultures and studied how the socialization of children is accomplished are often amazed at some of the child-rearing practices they see. Some of these practices may seem cruel to the outsider.[3] Yet, like those in our own society, they must be judged in terms of the total environmental setting and the general objectives and philosophy of that society.

The expanding physical environment. During infancy, childhood, and adolescence the individual's physical environment continuously expands as he gains strength and agility, knowledge, and meaningful complex skills. Similarly his social environment expands as he moves from the home to school and other formal and informal community agencies and institutions. The most obvious expansion of the child's environment is in

[3] Ruth Benedict, *Patterns of Culture* (Boston: Houghton Mifflin, 1934).

27

his range of physical stimulation. Environment for the newborn child
is limited to his crib and other places where those caring for him take
him. As he learns to walk and talk he is able to move around, thus expanding his physical environment to many areas in and around the home.
At the kindergarten and on the playground he comes into contact with a
larger environment, providing him with a wider range of stimulation.
Entrance into kindergarten is a significant stage in his personal and
social development, since it carries him beyond the home and the supervision of his parents.

Until the child enters school he is largely concerned with people,
objects, and activities around the home. Entrance into school brings him
into contact with different adult figures and many other children of his
own age. Induction into school also furnishes him with opportunities for
learning skills and acquiring information which increase his span of
interests and activities. He is now called upon to learn to read, to write,
to recite events, and to deal with a variety of numerical problems.

The expanding social environment. The normal infant is endowed
with potentialities for development. He comes equipped in such a way
that he could develop any one of a number of personalities. Of the
environmental factors affecting the developing personality, the most
influential are the social and cultural forces that surround him from birth.
The social factors include the types of relationship he forms from
repeated association with people. The significant cultural factors consist
of the values and judgments people have applied to conditions and behavior.

For most children the home furnishes the main stream of their social
activities before they enter school. Entrance into school brings the child
into contact with a new adult, the teacher, who plays an important role
in his development. The importance of the teacher-pupil relationship is
given special consideration in chapter 19. The child also comes into
contact with children from varied backgrounds. As he develops further he
will most likely become involved in other groups—Sunday school, Scouts,
clubs, and neighborhood gangs. Each of these groups affects, for better
or worse, the socialization of the child. Materials bearing on the influences
of these groups on the socialization of the individual child are presented
in subsequent chapters.

MATURATION AND LEARNING

The development of the individual results partly from an intrinsic
maturing of abilities, characteristics, and structures, and partly from experience. The term *maturation* has been used by geneticists for many
years to designate the stage of development during which a germ cell

becomes mature. The term was borrowed and made popular in psychology largely through the efforts of Gesell. He states: "Maturation may be defined as the net sum of the gene effects operating in a self-limited life cycle. Here lies an important key to his constitutional individuality."[4]

Any behavioral change resulting from experiences may be regarded as the product of learning. Many of the characteristics we identify as *human* stem from learning, and all facets of development are affected by learning. The complexity of the human organism and the integrated patterns of behavior which characterize the individual at all stages in his development make it difficult if not impossible to evaluate the exact influence of learning. An example illustrating this may be useful. Child psychologists constantly encounter difficulty in differentiating those changes in the behavior of the young child primarily due to maturation and those due to learning. Parents, for instance, frequently speak of the child who "learns to walk." Although the phrase "learning to walk" is commonly used to describe the development of motor skills involving locomotion, it is likely that maturation plays a more important role than learning. It is equally true, however, that learning plays some part in the child's early attempts to master this skill. We encounter similar difficulties in describing the mastery of such tasks as talking, throwing, handwriting, and other similar activities.

The nature of learning

The question may be raised: What is learning? Unfortunately, many definitions may give the reader oversimplified concepts. Like the problem of defining electricity, it may be more fruitful at this stage of our thinking to describe the concept rather than to define it. The child is born equipped with the potential to mature, to grasp, and to learn, at different age levels, the language, ways of behaving, attitudes, and values of his culture. We should also realize that he is born with potentials for reorganizing and remolding many aspects of his culture in harmony with changed conditions and needs. Any view of the child as a product of culture must also consider him as the product of biology. We must remember that through the years, it is the biological man that has developed the culture into which the child is born.

Many individuals and agencies contribute to teaching the child the cultural patterns of his social group. Through maturation and learning the child is capable of acquiring a culture. The term *enculturation*[5] is used to describe the process whereby the child is taught the cultural ways society expects him to follow. The process of enculturation requires the

[4] Arnold Gesell, "Developmental Pediatrics," *The Nervous Child*, Vol. 9 (1952), p. 225.
[5] M. J. Herskovits, *Man and His Work* (New York: A. A. Knopf, 1948), pp. 40-41. The anthropological meaning and use of *enculturation* is here presented.

child to adjust his innate biological characteristics to the prevailing cultural practices in his society. *Homo-sapiens* are the only biological group that have developed a culture requiring each newborn member to modify his biological characteristics according to rather highly specialized cultural ways. It is through the educative process that the individual organism is molded to fit into a particular culture and to function effectively as a member of that culture.

Differences in maturation

Children of the same age and grade differ considerably in their maturational level; hence, this becomes an important factor to reckon with

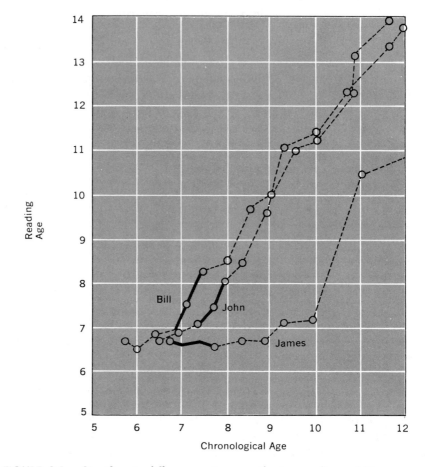

FIGURE 2-1. Significant differences in growth in reading ability appear among children similar in reading ability at age six (*Olson*)

in evaluating a child's growth and readiness for a learning experience. Many children who enter school at the age of six are too immature to begin reading or to understand the other educational tasks which confront first grade children. Various growth curves show that some children develop more rapidly than others. This has been illustrated by Olsen [6] in growth curves for reading. As Figure 2-1 indicates, James, John, and Billy may show approximately the same reading ability at the age of six years. However, significant differences appear with further educational growth. These differences among them may best be accounted for by variations in motivation, intelligence, maturation, and environmental stimulation.

Studies show further that a group of boys or girls will vary considerably in their physical development. Such differences, for example, are reflected in their interests, social development, strength, pulse rate, and motor performances. Individual differences have important educational implications if the various children of a class are to benefit from instruction or if they are to be stimulated toward the learning tasks they face. Long before the principle of readiness was postulated, teachers had discovered that children at each developmental level were able to master certain skills or knowledge, but unable to master others. The modern elementary-school teacher spends considerable time preparing children for instruction in various types of skills and subject matter. The concept of readiness is perhaps best exemplified by instructional procedures in reading.

The significance of maturation. Learning and maturation are closely interwoven in all aspects of the child's development. This may be noted in the development of language, motor, and social skills. The co-twin method was used by Gesell and Thompson [7] in studying the influence of early practice or exercise on motor development during childhood. This method makes use of identical twins, one of whom becomes the control subject while the other becomes the experimental subject.

In this study, beginning at the age of forty-six weeks, one twin (twin T) was given training in stair-climbing, while the other twin (twin C) was given no such training. After six weeks of training, twin T climbed the stair case in twenty-six seconds. At the beginning of the fifty-third week, twin C was given training in stair-climbing. At this time she climbed the stair case in forty-five seconds, but after two weeks of training she was able to climb it in ten seconds. Thus, twin C rapidly reached an achievement level as high as that attained by twin T, primarily because of her advanced maturation when she began the stair-climbing.

[6] Willard C. Olson, "Experiences for Growing," *Journal of the National Education Association*, Vol. 36 (1947), p. 502.

[7] Arnold Gesell and Helen Thompson, "Learning and Growth in Identical Twins: An Experimental Study in the Method of Co-twin Control," *Genetic Psychology Monographs*, Vol. 6 (1929), pp. 1-124.

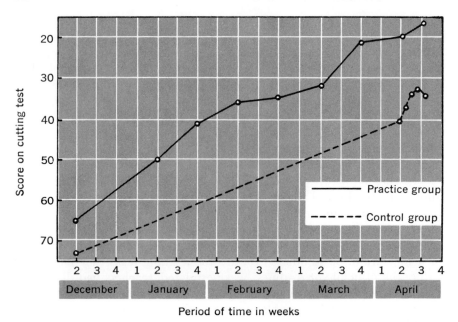

FIGURE 2-2.   Mean Learning Curve for Two Groups in Cutting (*Hilgard*)

Practice group trained for 12 weeks between 2nd week in January and 2nd week in April. Control group trained for one week between 2nd and 3rd week in April.

Similar results have been obtained with infants in studies dealing with manipulating cubes, cutting with scissors, language development, memorization, and the like. In an experiment reported by Hilgard [8] two groups of fifteen children each were matched by chronological and mental age, sex, and initial ability in three skills—buttoning, cutting with scissors, and climbing. One group, the practice group, trained for twelve weeks; a second group, the control group, received no training during the twelve-week period, but was given four days of training immediately following the twelve-week period. Tests were given both groups at the beginning and end of the twelve-week period, and at the end of the four-day period immediately following the twelve-week training period. The mean learning curves for the two groups in cutting are shown in Figure 2-2. These curves indicate that both groups improved throughout the twelve-week period, even though the control group was not practicing. The control group showed marked improvement during the four-day practice period following the twelve-week period.

These studies show that progress in learning depends upon the

[8] J. R. Hilgard, "Learning and Maturation in Pre-school Children," *Journal of Genetic Psychology*, Vol. 41 (1932), pp. 36-56.

maturation of the learner, as well as the kinds of experiences he has had. Readiness for learning motor skills, like readiness for other learnings, depends upon maturation and experience, among other factors. The effects of training in the learning of a motor skill will be most beneficial when it is introduced at the time the learner has reached a sufficient level of development enabling him to profit from such training.

FORCES INFLUENCING THE EDUCATION
OF A HUMAN BEING

In the life-long process of education the individual develops or changes according to his needs or according to the nature and level of his choices. The influences in an individual's environment may be consciously planned and formulated, or may be subconsciously pressuring and informal. The community in which he lives offers many informal agencies of education, like social organizations, clubs, camping groups, jobs, religious organizations, the movies, and television. As we have pointed out, these influences may be positive and enabling or negative, inhibiting, and crippling.

In our American culture the most important formal agencies of education are the home, the church, and the school. There is an increased awareness of the need for every agency of education, formal and informal, to cooperate in educating the personal, social, intellectual and moral aspects of the student so that he will be better equipped to participate as a useful and effective citizen in a democratic society.

The home

The *family* is a social unit existing for the procreation, guidance, and education of the newborn child in his growth toward maturity. A favorable home environment that guides the growing child in an atmosphere of love and affection is well equipped for this task. How the child integrates into the family unit, the emotional climate, attitudes, values, aspirations, and emotional maturity of the family members, especially the parents, are strong influences in the child's education. These influences begin even before birth and continue beyond the period of the child's maturity. By the time the child is of school age he has acquired important attitudes, values, and habits that have a bearing on his adjustments at school and elsewhere. Although the school should not attempt to supplant the home, it is frequently called upon to supply many elements essential to the healthy growth of children that are not supplied in certain homes. Some children will need special attention and consideration; some will need affection and acceptance; others will require successful experiences; still others will need friends of their own age. All these needs will be met, to some extent at least, in a good school situation.

The most important social, political, or educational organization is the family. Lessons are acquired in the home during the early years which affect the whole individual throughout his life. Every competent and experienced teacher realizes the important role parents play. The convictions presented by Stella Center, arising from her experiences in her Reading Center, are shared by most experienced educators.

Early . . . it becomes unmistakably clear that I had to know the parents as well as I knew the students. I could, except in very rare instances, count on the parents' affection for their children and an earnest desire to promote the children's welfare. Convinced of my sincere interest in the boys and girls, parents were willing to listen to reports on diagnoses and analyses of children's difficulties that were often as disturbing as a surgeon's report must at times be.[9]

The school

In more complex societies like ours, children need to learn more complex skills and need to acquire a greater amount and variety of knowledge than would normally be required through the informal activities at home and in the community. However, children in our society still rely upon their parents and family for much of their learning, particularly emotional habits of childhood, good personal relations, attitudes toward conditions, objects, and persons in their immediate environment, and ways of behaving.

In the United States the education of the child is a joint responsibility of the family and the school. Entrance into school plays an important role in the child's conception of himself as well as of the world about him. It further implies that he has matured sufficiently to benefit by the program of instruction at school. Before one can determine the role of the school in the educative process, he must first consider the function of the school in modern society. Its primary task is to assist children and adolescents by providing experiences, guidance, instruction, and discipline in learning facts, skills, attitudes, and habits essential for them to function effectively as members of the society in which they live.

In America the schools transmit the cultural heritage through the language arts, the curriculum, teaching, and such mass media as books, radio, and television. The discovery of this heritage and experiences in it are means and aids to personal fulfillment and enrichment, and to social and civic effectiveness. The school is concerned essentially with each learner, the whole child, accepting him with his individual endowments, personal experiences, unique reactions, and particular rate of develop-

[9] Stella S. Center, *The Art of Book Reading* (New York: Charles Scribner's Sons, 1952), pp. 295-296.

ment. In cooperating with other agencies and institutions it guides him in his growth toward maturity so that he will be able to function more effectively and attain greater satisfaction from daily living.

The church

To be effective in his relations with others, a mature person with an integrated personality needs to have his knowledge and understanding, emotional habits, attitudes and values, ideals, and moral concepts unified into a consistent philosophy of life, which will then be reflected in his self-concept, self-realization, self-expression, self-restraint, and in his relationship with the universe, his neighbor, and his God. The American way of life and American democracy is built on the Judaeo-Christian tradition and religious values which have been the fundamental principles of Western civilization for peoples of many different cultures and traditions for nearly twenty centuries.

In a sense, therefore, the church can be considered an important agency in the educative process. While growing and learning, the child may have been instructed in basic religious beliefs and may have been trained in the formation of behavior patterns consistent with these beliefs. But as he matures, he must make, and should be guided in making, objective judgments and choices in incorporating beliefs, ideals, and values into his own life patterns and guiding philosophy. In the process of developing, each person must also develop his own conscience, moral values, and habits of action. He needs guidance and practice in appraising his own conduct, and he needs opportunities for making rational choices between alternate courses of action. From infantile automatic responses, the first real choices may be tentative, but conscious control will become habitual and confirmed through successful practice. This is implied in the statements by Cox and Duff:

> It is not experience alone that educates, but experience analyzed for its meaning, refined by good thinking (and feeling) in such a way that the individual is prepared to act better (more wisely) in the future. It is not mere activity that begets character, nor on the other hand is character achieved, alone by contemplation. It is built out of progressive, continuous analysis and synthesis of related actions and reactions.[10]

Other community agencies

The wide range of cultures existing in our society—from community to community—complicates the problems children face in their development. They must assimilate the culture of their family and church or religion. However, many forces operate in any community to affect the

[10] Philip W. Cox and John C. Duff, *Guidance by the Classroom Teacher* (Englewood Cliffs, N.J.: Prentice-Hall, Inc., 1942), p. 44.

education of the members of that community. Some of these forces operate through organized agencies; others operate in an informal and unorganized manner.

Scouting organization. The scouting organizations and the Camp Fire groups are examples of agencies organized for specific developmental influences. These organizations seek to help the growing child develop his potentialities in socially desirable channels. They emphasize the sanctity of promises and the obligations of youth to prepare for a worthwhile place in the adult world. At the same time, these groups utilize youth's interest in organized play and field activities to provide beneficial social experiences. It is noteworthy that these organizations were among the first to be suppressed by Communist governments.

Geographical-social organizations. Although the neighborhood is an example of an informal geographical-social organization, it exerts a powerful influence on the child. Neighborhood mores, taboos, and biases are internalized by children, and at the same time, the beliefs and values of the neighborhood, especially where school districts are small, shape the practices of the classroom to some extent. The school cannot ignore the neighborhoods which it serves. It must aid the child in coming to terms with himself wherever conflicts exist between values learned in school and the neighborhood biases.

Playgrounds and teen centers are often geographical organizations that also exert a powerful influence on those who participate in their activities. In some deprived areas, the playground provides children with their only opportunity for play and group experiences. In these cases, the "law of the playground" (although informal or even unsanctioned by society) may govern the child's course of development more than the values which the school seeks to inculcate.

There are other agencies, both formal and informal, which serve educational purposes. These groups range from secret societies to formally organized extracurricular activity clubs. Such groups fulfill the need of teen-agers for their own "society" in which they may work through the developmental processes of association with each other. These agencies thrive best in a setting where the needs of children and youth are not being adequately met by existing institutions. Additional materials bearing on these agencies and conditions affecting the educational development of growing boys and girls will be found in subsequent chapters.

THE TEACHER AND THE EDUCATIVE PROCESS

We have already pointed out that many agencies are concerned, either directly or indirectly, with the educative process. The school as an institution exists to guide children in the development of skills, subject matter, attitudes, and behavior patterns essential for effective living in a particular society. The school situation involves (1) pupils, (2) teachers, (3) teacher-pupil relationships, and (4) ideas or problems. Teaching may be defined as a system of actions directed toward pupils, the learners.

The teacher and educational objectives

If the learner is central in the educative act, educational objectives can best be thought of in terms of the changes we would like to see take place in him. Therefore, what the educative act will accomplish depends on the teacher's objectives. He may wish to cover so much subject matter, or he may require his students to write so many term papers. On the other hand, he may work for certain kinds of changes or learnings in his pupils. Educational objectives should be formulated in terms of the behavior changes desired, and the educational approaches by which these objectives will most effectively be achieved. Materials and methods should be chosen with these objectives in view. Without clear, comprehensive, and fairly specific statements of objectives, the teacher will overlook some important educational goals.

The teacher and learning experiences

Teachers need to remember that the heart of all education is learning, and that their role is to guide and stimulate pupils. The teacher needs to know the conditions which make for effective learning, and must be able to apply these conditions in the classroom. He must have an understanding of the characteristics of children and adolescents, and of the principles of learning. The successful teacher is able to bring to bear his understanding of the principles of learning to a specific classroom situation.

From a psychological point of view it might be stated that the function of the teacher in the learning environment is to (1) elicit the desired behaviors or responses, (2) reinforce these responses, (3) help the learner to integrate these into previous learnings, and (4) overcome or eliminate undesirable forms of behavior or responses. There is no mechanical device or magic formula for achieving these aims. Educational psychology is not concerned with providing the teacher with magic tricks or gadgets for helping him with his teaching. Each child in the classroom has had a variety of experiences, and on the basis of his concepts, attitudes, and previous learnings, he interprets his environment and new experiences encountered at school and elsewhere. The function of the learning experience in the classroom is to help the child broaden his existing concepts, develop new skills, acquire changed or new attitudes, and reorganize his existing behavior. The teacher can do this best when he guides the child in his learning through the process of *realization* so that he integrates new learnings into existing patterns of behavior.

Teacher evaluation of results

Special attention is given in Chapter 14 to methods teachers use in evaluating the results of instruction. *Evaluation* is an important aspect of the educative act. Without it the teacher will be unable to determine the extent to which his objectives are being reached. The process of evaluation is complex, since it is very difficult to evaluate the results of learning experiences involving, as they must, personality changes and character formation. Considerable research has been completed and much more is now in progress dealing with various aspects of this problem. Teachers should constantly keep in mind objectives that have been set forth and use a variety of means for evaluating behavioral changes.

The errors teachers most frequently make may be listed as follows: (1) relying wholly on some simple evaluating device; (2) failing to make continuous evaluations, but waiting until the end of the school term for one lengthy measurement; (3) evaluating behavior changes which have little or no reference to the objectives set forth; and (4) failing to evaluate the behavioral changes that have been listed as the desired ones and for which learning experiences have been provided.

Interpersonal relations

Experienced teachers are aware that the quality of the interpersonal relations in the classroom markedly affects the learning and behavior of their pupils. Much teaching takes place somewhat silently across a bridge of feelings embedded in favorable interpersonal relations between teacher and pupils. One of the most frequent complaints young teachers make is that they failed to learn how to deal with such problems as discipline during their professional training programs. No teacher-training program can adequately anticipate the variety of behavior problems that will appear during the course of a year in a typical classroom. Emphasis, instead, will be given in subsequent chapters to understanding child behavior, problems of motivation and learning, the importance of understanding the individual child, and the importance of a favorable emotional climate in the classroom.

Learning is much more than a matter of books and school subjects. Children and adolescents are likely to see it in terms of how well they get along with teachers. Accordingly, learning depends upon the relationship teachers build with their classes. When discussing a subject, pupils express what they think of the teacher. A good teacher makes a subject interesting; a poor one makes it dull or disliked.

Based on data gathered from 450 seventh-, eighth-, and ninth-grade pupils, Tiedeman [11] found that the autocratic, domineering teacher is most disliked. The use of ridicule, sarcasm, or nagging ranked next in the characteristics pupils disliked. Other disliked characteristics frequently mentioned are unfairness, favoritism, impatience, lack of clarity, and unreasonableness. The way teachers conduct themselves often has more influence on children than what teachers say. Other studies have also shown that the classroom personality of the teacher has a definite influence on the achievements of pupils.[12] These will be discussed in Chapter 19 with teacher-pupil interrelationships.

SUMMARY

The educative process is a highly individual series of changes occurring in the human being in numerous aspects of his growth and development throughout his life. The educative process is utilized by every society to prepare its growing members for intelligent, active, fruitful participation in adult, personal, and social life. Not every society, however, provides that education which allows the growing child to realize his potentialities as fully as possible. This process of realization is the goal of American education.

In the complicated, civilized society of modern America, the process of education involves many agencies and forces. Formal agencies, such as the home, the church, and the school, have active and definite roles to play in the formal education of the whole child in his need for guidance, direction, and instruction in all aspects of his developing powers. Other agencies and forces, formal and informal, organized and fortuitous, also play educational roles. These agencies may exert beneficial or harmful influences on the child, depending on their relationship with the home, school, and church as well as on the nature of their activities. The effectiveness of each of these agencies in the favorable development of the child will be enhanced by the interrelation and cooperation of all in close psychological relationship to the emerging personality of the child.

Throughout a child's development the factors of growth and learning, heredity and environment operate and interact continuously. Individual development is most facilitated in learning climates in which the teacher (or other educational leader) is forcefully presenting an idea or principle within the context of the cultural tradition and within the sphere of the learner's developmental readiness. The learner is required to be challenged in a teacher-pupil-idea interplay.

---

[11] Stuart C. Tiedeman, "A Study of Pupil-Teacher Relationships," *Journal of Educational Research,* Vol. 35 (1942), pp. 231-248.

[12] See L. Berkowitz and R. M. Lundy, "Personality Characteristics Related to Susceptibility to Influence by Peers and Authority Figures," *Journal of Personality,* Vol. 25 (1957), pp. 306-316.

In a confused, changing world with its shrinking boundaries and narrowing margins for permissible errors, the social aspect of the educative process is not only cultural but intercultural, compelling us to look on all men as neighbors and brothers. Our attitudes, interests, values, and ideals need widening, deepening and heightening to spiritual and moral dimensions if we are to contribute anything in a world where men yearn for the recognition of those values that make them truly human.

Problems and Exercises

1. What are the major manifestations in the process of development? Of what value to the teacher is an understanding of the developmental process?
2. Discuss the implications for teaching of the concept of continuous interaction between heredity and environment.
3. What is the significance of the fact that a child is born into a particular culture?
4. Consider the functions of the schools in relation to culture. Show how the educative process is influenced by culture.
5. What is the role of psychology in the educative process?
6. Name three formal agencies of education in American culture.
7. What are four important functions of the teacher in the learning environment?
8. List several errors in evaluation commonly made by teachers.
9. Ask two or three of your friends (not in education courses) to list 5 qualities characteristic of teachers they liked most and 5 qualities characteristic of those they disliked most (or liked least). Compare your list with those personal qualities mentioned in this chapter and Chapter 19.
10. Mr. Brown is beginning his first year as a high school teacher. To evaluate his class in American History his plans are:

   a. to give two long (200-question objective test) tests, one at the end of each semester.
   b. to require two 3,000-word papers from each student, one at the end of each semester.
   c. to evaluate oral responses daily for quality and aptness.

He plans no other written work and intends to give no other tests (except weekly oral quizzes).

Discuss his evaluation procedures. What outcomes do you expect if this plan is put into effect? How might his plan be improved?

Selected Readings

BRUNER, Jerome S., *The Process of Education* (Cambridge: Harvard University Press, 1961), Ch. 1, 3.

CRONBACH, Lee J., *Educational Psychology,* 2nd ed. (New York: Harcourt, Brace & World, 1963), Ch. 2.

KEARNEY, Nolan C., *Elementary School Objectives* (Russell Sage Foundation, New York, 1953).

LINDQUIST, E. F., "Preliminary Considerations in Objective Test Construction,"

Educational Measurement (Washington: American Council on Education, 1951), Ch. 5.

MARTIN, William E. and STENDLER, Celia Burns, *Child Development: The Process of Growing Up in Society* (New York: Harcourt, Brace & World, 1953), Ch. 9.

MEAD, Margaret, *The School in American Culture* (Cambridge: Harvard University Press, 1951).

PRESSEY, S. L., ROBINSON, F. P., and HORROCKS, J. E., *Psychology in Education* (New York: Harper & Row, 1959), Chs. 1-3.

SMITH, Henry P., *Psychology in Teaching*, 2nd ed. (Englewood Cliffs, N. J.: Prentice-Hall, 1962), Ch. 1.

TYLER, Ralph W., "Educability and the Schools," *Elementary School Journal,* Vol. 49 (1948), pp. 200-213.

PART II

The Child
and His Development

CHAPTER 3

The Course of Development

Development suggests that changes take place in children from year to year. An understanding of these changes is extremely important to those who guide growing boys and girls. Closely related to development is the concept *readiness,* important in educational planning. The readiness of the learner is central to such questions as: "At what age should formal number work be introduced?" or "When should state history, as a subject, be presented in the junior-high school program?" It should be pointed out, however, that not all children of a particular age will be ready to begin formal number work at the same time. This makes it necessary for the teacher to do some educational planning to meet individual needs.

This chapter and subsequent chapters are designed to give the student of educational psychology an understanding of developmental processes and patterns. Such an understanding should serve as a basis for evaluating readiness for learning. Data of average childern at different ages will be presented to show the students something of how changes occur in growth. However, the student must realize at the outset that readiness for any learning experience involves all the characteristics affecting his responses to the situation, some of which can be accelerated through a well-planned educational program while others cannot.

SOME PRINCIPLES OF GROWTH

As the child emerges from one developmental period into another we may observe certain changes. Studies show that these changes tend to follow fairly well-defined principles. These are here referred to as principles of growth. The most obvious change that takes place in children is in their physical growth, although growth is not confined to size. It includes changes in complexity, proportion, and qualitative character-

istics as well. Furthermore, the term *growth* is not confined to physical
changes in structure or form, but applies also to behavior and achievement. We speak of growth, for example, in language skills, motor skills,
social skills, and emotional responses.

Detailed investigations that have been made of the same individual
from infancy through adolescence have furnished useful information
about the nature of growth. These studies provide the basis for the
formulation of certain principles of growth.

Growth, a continuous process

The various stages of life are often divided into different periods,
largely for convenience in studying the different developmental stages.
However, this has led many people to look upon growth as periodic rather
than continuous. There is evidence from longitudinal studies of individual
children that growth tends to follow a pattern—certain forms of behavior
tend to precede other forms of behavior. We may observe this best in the
pattern of motor development, where the complexity of behavior grows
gradually and continuously. This is well illustrated in the results of the
study by McGraw showing, in Figure 3-1, the early developmental phases
leading to creeping and crawling.[1]

It can be stated as a fundamental principle that each stage in an
individual's development is an outgrowth of an earlier stage, not a mere
addition to it. We may observe an illustration of this principle with
speech, which evolves from the cries and gurgling sounds of infancy, and
with the growth of reading and arithmetic abilities.

The rate of growth is not even.   Although growth is described as
continuous, specific aspects of growth do not occur at the same rate at
different times. The psychological growth of a given pupil is also uneven.
His state of maturation at a particular time will vary with the different
characteristics or abilities being tested. This uneven development is
illustrated in Figure 3-2. Although growth for all pupils is far from even, it
is more uneven with some pupils.

This unevenness of growth has important implications for those
concerned with the education of children and adolescents. At a given
age there will be differences in the degree of maturity of various traits and
abilities. Individual growth curves for height, weight, strength, motor
coordinations, writing, and reading ability show plainly that the growth
rate is marked by fluctuations.

Children differ in rate of growth.   Although children tend to follow
a somewhat similar pattern in their development, each child grows at his

[1] Myrtle B. McGraw, *Growth: A Study of Johnny and Jimmy* (New York: Appleton-Century-Crofts, 1935), p. 70.

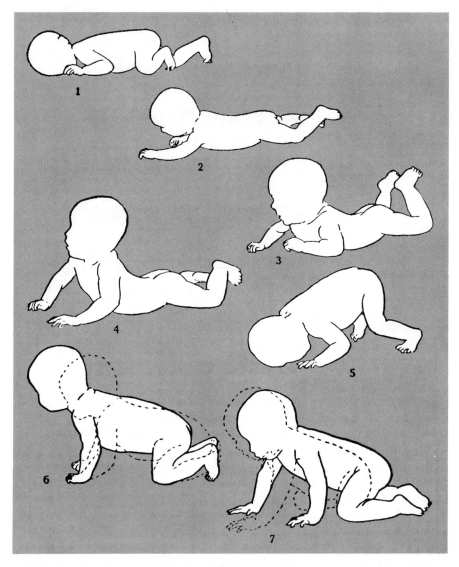

FIGURE 3-1. Phases In The Development Of Crawling And Creeping In An Infant

1. Newborn crawling movements. 2. Less activity in lower extremities; begins to hold head up. 3. Increased control over movements of head and shoulder girdle. 4. Marked development in upper part of body; pelvis rests on the surface. 5. Conflict in action of pelvic and shoulder regions; when pelvis is raised, head and shoulders are lowered. 6. Rocking movements; maintains abdomen above surface. 7. Associated creeping movements.

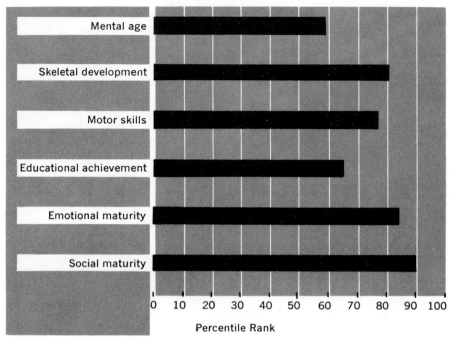

FIGURE 3-2.   A Profile Of The Maturity Of One Pupil In Several Areas Of Growth. Note the superiority in social and emotional maturity.

own unique rate. The growth rate of each individual is affected by many forces both within and without the body, making prediction of growth very difficult. Some of the major factors affecting growth and learning will be discussed in subsequent chapters.

It is important for teachers to understand individual differences in growth rate. Parents, likewise, should realize that such differences are normal and that one child's deviation from another should not be a source of disturbance. The timing of the growth spurt, which takes place around the beginning of adolescence, will vary considerably with individuals of the same sex. The failure of teachers and parents to recognize these differences in the rate and timing of certain growth features is often a source of misinterpretation and faulty guidance.

All growth is interrelated.   Although we speak and write of physical growth, mental growth, emotional growth, and other aspects of growth, we should realize at all times that it is the total child who is growing. The interrelation of growth has received considerable attention in recent years as a result of the great amount of research that has been conducted on the different aspects of the growth of children and adolescents. The organismic viewpoint emphasizes the harmony and interrelation of the growth of component parts of the individual. Thus, the organism is conceived of as a closely knit community, growing and functioning as a unit rather than in a nonrelated way.

The growth of the child as a unified whole may be very well illustrated by his growth in the ability to creep, crawl, and walk. In the average child, this growth will be accompanied by changes in interests, attention span, mental outlook, and social behavior. Furthermore, it can be shown that changes in interests and social behavior are closely related to growth in language and motor coordination. The interrelation may also be observed in educational achievement. The results of a study by Tilton [2] show that diagnostic and remedial activities that fail to consider the total growth of the child are ineffective in producing permanently improved achievement.

The individual passes gradually from one stage to another in his learning and maturation, preserving a patterned integration throughout life. In other words, growth and learning are patterns rather than isolated events affected by addition of minute increments to separate parts. Learning and development do not take place in a piecemeal fashion with unrelated items appearing at different periods and later becoming fashioned into unified patterns. The entire child is involved in learning to read and swim. The child's emotional nature, social self, and physical self are involved, along with the intellectual self, in the acquisition of reading and writing skills. This concept is most important for those who would direct the learning of children, and for this reason will be given further attention in later chapters on learning and personality adjustment.

Physical Development

Fundamental to the degree to which the child will develop as a personal and social being is his pattern of physical growth. Modern conceptions about children and the function of the school, make it imperative for teachers to understand the relationship between physical growth and social and academic achievements. Genetic studies of children from birth to maturity have furnished valuable information about the course of physical development and its relation to readiness for learning.

Growth in height and weight. The most readily observed type of growth is size. Most of the early studies used the cross-sectional method for gathering data on height and weight. Generally, such studies determined the measurements of a large number of boys and girls and calculated the average height and weight for each age level and sex. A chart was then constructed and the results regarded as group norms. A parent,

---

[2] J. W. Tilton, "An experimental effort to change the achievement test profile," *Journal of Experimental Education,* Vol. 15 (1947), pp. 318-323.

teacher, or nurse presumably could weigh and measure a youngster, compare the figures with the appropriate age and sex norms on the chart, and thus determine the amount of variation from the average.

Height-weight charts derived from measurements of children are only valid when applied to children with comparable genetic and environmental backgrounds. Studies show that children from superior environmental backgrounds are on the average taller and heavier than children of the same genetic stock reared in an inferior environment. Furthermore, the enormous variation in the rate of children's growth makes it impossible to judge the desired weight of a child in terms of general averages. Differences in body build must also be considered. In general, teachers should not be seriously concerned with the height-weight ratio of a child unless he deviates significantly from other children of his age and body build.

Growth curves. Increased interest in child study has brought about many long-time studies. Investigators have made use of repeated measurements on the same children to plot individual growth curves for height, weight, and other physical measurements. While this method may not appear to have immediate value, such measurements over a long period of time have furnished valuable information about the different factors affecting growth. It should be noted, however, that individual differences in the appearance of certain characteristics tend to be obscured when averages are used. This is shown in Figure 3-3, where the average growth curve is rather smooth while the individual curves are uneven.[3]

Individual growth curves have been secured and studied for a large number of boys and girls. Conclusions drawn from these studies may be listed as follows:

1. Growth is very rapid from birth to the age of two or two and one-half years.
2. Growth continues at a

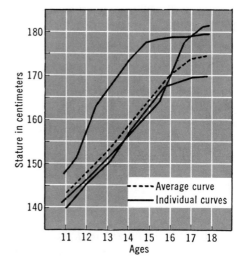

FIGURE 3-3. Comparison Of Average And Individual Curves For Growth In Stature (Meredith)

[3] Howard V. Meredith, "The Rhythm of Physical Growth," *University of Iowa Studies in Child Welfare*, Vol. 11 (1935), No. 3, p. 112.

diminishing rate through the kindergarten and early elementary-school years.

3. About two years prior to the advent of puberty an accelerated rate of growth may be noted.
4. Following the advent of puberty there is a gradual and continuous deceleration of the growth rate.
5. The shape of the growth curves for the sexes is very similar, with girls maturing one and one-half to two years earlier than boys.

Variations in the growth pattern occur frequently and tend to increase with age. The excessive variability found among some children may be explained partly by hereditary factors, partly by their food and health habits, and partly by general health conditions. Concerning nutrition and growth, Peckos states: "As long as a child eats adequately and maintains a steady gain in weight and height, there need be no concern over comparison with children of different stock and build." [4] However, the importance of physical development and health in relation to school readiness and school achievement must be reckoned with in educational planning.

Anatomical development. The child's bones differ from those of the adult in proportion, shape, composition, and even number. During the growth period, they contain more water and less mineral matter than adults' bones. Children's bones are also more vascular, permitting a large quantity of blood to flow through them with the nutritive elements needed at this stage of growth. This condition, however, also makes the child more susceptible to bone diseases from infection.

X-ray pictures of the bones of children show the bony structure at different ages, the development of the ends of the bones, the relative size of the different bones, and the development of the ligaments and their attachments to the bony structure. The space between the ends of the bones is in an inverse ratio to the age of the child. Data thus obtained may be used in two principal ways. (1) They may be computed in terms of age units and thus may be used to evaluate the child's skeletal age, and (2) they may be computed in terms of age units and may be used to evaluate the child's total development obtained from combining measurements of different aspects of his growth.

It will be recalled that the relationship of growth in one part of the body is correlated with growth in other parts. We observe this in the close relationship between anatomical and sexual development. Furthermore, evidence suggests that the anatomical development of children furnishes a basis for determining their general physical development and

[4] Penelope S. Peckos, "Nutrition during Growth and Development," *Child Development,* Vol. 28 (1957), p. 280.

for predicting their mature size. Bayley concludes from her studies at the Institute of Child Welfare, University of California, that

> When expressed as per cent of a child's eventual natural size, his growth is seen to be closely related to the development and maturing of his skeleton . . . It appears that growth in size is closely related to the maturing of the skeleton. At a given skeletal age we may say that a child has achieved a given proportion of his eventual adult body dimension. Consequently, mature size and skeletal age are known.[5]

THE DEVELOPMENT OF MOTOR ABILITIES

Motor development is contingent upon the individual's use of his physical equipment and cannot be separated from physical development. Neither can it supersede the maturation of physical structure, a fact frequently overlooked in the educational program since the school has often concerned itself primarily with those activities that involve intellectual attainments.

Pattern of motor growth

Motor growth follows the same principles and patterns as other aspects of growth. Certain motor abilities are acquired at an early age and are learned in a relatively short time, while others are acquired at a later stage of maturity. The sequence of achievements through which a child moves as he acquires the ability to walk alone or to reach, grasp, and manipulate an object with his fingers illustrates many important phases of development. The acquisition of the ability to walk alone, for instance, is only one part of a larger, continuing process of motor development. As soon as the child learns to walk, he begins to incorporate elements of walking into larger and more complex patterns of motor behavior. Through maturation and practice he gradually develops better balance and a smoother gait. With increased maturation, practice, and training we can expect more specific-less generalized motor patterns to emerge.

According to the developmental trend the large muscles are the first muscular groups the child is able to coordinate and to use in varied activities. Many of the preschool activities and games which involve the manipulation of large objects are based on this developmental trend, and may be noted in the block-building activities of the preschool child, the use of large crayons by the kindergarten child, and manuscript writing with single strokes for beginning pupils. The better coordinated movements are further interrelated with other aspects of the child's develop-

---

[5] Nancy Bayley, "Skeletal Maturing in Adolescence as Basis for Determining Percentage of Completed Growth," *Child Development*, Vol. 14 (1943), pp. 44-45.

ment; they emerge as a result of the maturation of certain physical characteristics, the development of the individual as a whole, and learning.

The behavior pattern involved in throwing was studied by Wild.[6]
Thirty-two carefully selected children, a boy and a girl at each six-month
age level from two to seven years and at each age level from seven to
twelve years, were used as subjects for the study. A definite relationship
existed between older children and better timing and mechanical means
for throwing. These changes were closely related to physical growth and
development at all ages. Maturational factors were apparent, especially
during the early years, and largely accounted for the basic type patterns
of throwing. Learning, especially after age six, greatly influenced the
pattern of skill. Training and practice during the school years are to a
marked degree responsible for differences in the pattern of motor growth
of boys and girls at these ages, although differences in maturation and
body build should not be overlooked.

Growth in motor abilities. A decrease in reaction time with age has
been observed by a number of investigators. Using the *Miles Reaction
Board,* Goodenough [7] reported the speed of reaction to a predominately
auditory stimulus of subjects ranging in age from three and one-half years
to adulthood. There was a marked decrease of reaction time with age;
however, the reduction of useless accessory movements and the decreased
bodily tension were even more marked. This decreased speed of reaction
and reduction of useless accessory movements is important in the development of a number of skills requiring speed and precision.

Tests of strength, motor coordination, and flexibility during childhood reveal a constant and continuous increase with age. Relative strength
has been expressed in terms of a *physical fitness index quotient.* Age and
sex standards for elementary-school children show that there is a
pronounced growth in strength during this period, so that the child of
twelve is two or three times as strong as he was when he entered the first
grade. Large muscle skills, involving the use of the arms or legs, predominate. A recognition of this is important in guiding school-age boys
and girls in their motor achievement and development. However, there is
no best age to start the teaching of such motor skills as use of the hammer,
scissors, and other tools. Among children of any particular age, there will
be considerable differences in readiness and skill.

Results from different tests of motor performances of adolescents by

[6] Monica R. Wild, "The Behavior Pattern of Throwing and Some Observations
Concerning Its Course of Development in Children." Reprinted from *The Research
Quarterly,* Vol. 9 (1938), pp. 20-24.

[7] Florence L. Goodenough, "The Development of the Reactive Process from
Early Childhood to Maturity," *Journal of Experimental Psychology,* Vol. 18 (1935),
pp. 431-450.

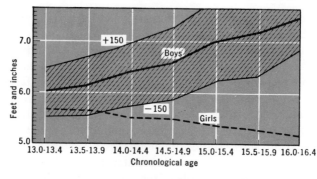

FIGURE 3-4.   Comparison Of Boys And Girls On
The Broad Jump

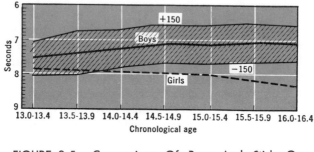

FIGURE 3-5.   Comparison Of Boys And Girls On
The Fifty-Yard Dash

Espenschade,[8] show that the different traits do not develop at the same rate. The average score for boys on the broad jump shows considerable development after age thirteen, while the average for boys on the fifty-yard dash at age thirteen (see Figure 3-5) is almost as high as the average for the sixteen-year-old group. A gradual and continuous decrease in these abilities among girls is indicated by the curves presented in Figures 3-4 and 3-5. These activities are quite vigorous, and competition is less keen among girls where strenuous physical activities are involved. Their lack of motivation, combined with differences between boys and girls in body build, seem to provide a sound explanation for the continuous decline in these activities among girls after age thirteen.

Interrelations of motor growth.   It is a common observation that boys and girls who excel in one sport tend to be proficient in, and often-

[8] Anna Espenschade, "Motor Performance in Adolescence," Monographs of the *Society for Research in Child Development*, Vol. 5 (1940), No. 1.

times excel, in other sports. This relationship between different motor skills has led some to point out that there is a general factor present which may be regarded as potential ability or talent and that the amount will vary considerably among individuals in the same age group. There is much evidence for this in a study of the relationship between strength and other developmental traits. Significant correlations have been reported between strength of grip and such developmental traits as height, weight, physiological development, skeletal age, and interest in motor activities.[9]

The results of a study by McCaskill and Wellman [10] conducted with preschool children offer evidence that a close interrelationship of different motor abilities appears at an early age. The tests devised for this study were given to 98 children from two to six years of age. The activities were ascending and descending ladders and hopping, skipping, jumping, balancing on path and circle, ball-throwing, ball-catching, and ball-bouncing. The scores for the different activities were combined into common categories as shown in Table 3-1. Correlations obtained between these categories were positive and statistically significant, indicating an

TABLE 3-1. Correlations Between Scores on Various Motor Achievements of Preschool Children (*After McCaskill and Wellman*)

MEASURES CORRELATED	BOYS		GIRLS	
	NUMBER	CORRELATION	NUMBER	CORRELATION
Total Group				
Steps and ladders with ball activities	50	.54 ± .10	48	.72 ± .06
Steps and ladders with hopping, skipping, etc.	50	.69 ± .07	48	.79 ± .05
Ball activities with hopping, skipping, etc.	50	.69 ± .07	48	.47 ± .96
Younger Group (26 to 53 months)				
Steps and ladders with ball activities	16	.40 ± .21	29	.66 ± .10
Steps and ladders with hopping, skipping, etc.	16	.72 ± .12	29	.72 ± .09
Steps and ladders with hopping, skipping, etc.	16	.69 ± .13	29	.75 ± .08

[9] Harold E. Jones, *Motor Performance and Growth* (Berkeley and Los Angeles: University of California Press, 1949), Chap. 2.

[10] Carra L. McCaskill and Beth L. Wellman, "A Study of Common Motor Achievements at the Preschool Ages," *Child Development*, Vol. 9 (1938), pp. 141-150.

interrelationship of these abilities even at this early age. This study also revealed sex differences: boys were superior in the steps, ladder, and ball activities; girls were superior on hopping and skipping. Boys engage more frequently in activities involving climbing and ball throwing, while girls are more concerned with hopping, skipping, and jumping rope. This furnishes some evidence for the influence of practice on sex differences in motor skills.

PERCEPTION AND CONCEPTUAL DEVELOPMENT

Man's knowledge of the external world and his relationship to it is obtained through sensory experiences. His sensory impressions are organized, differentiated, and integrated into past impressions through the developing central nervous system. Little is known about the complex operation of the perceptual processes and no attempt will be made here to review the research bearing on this. The functional effects of sensory experiences and the nature of the perceptual processes are better understood. An understanding of these is important to teachers and others concerned with the educational process. Sensations and perceptions have been roughly differentiated by Thompson as follows:

1. *Sensations* are primitive activities resulting from contacts with physical stimuli and mediated by the sensory organs with little, if any "interpretation" by the central nervous system.
2. *Perceptions* are the results of interactions between sensory impressions and data "interpreted" within the matrix of present neurological processes, current motivating conditions, and a variety of other psychological variables.[11]

Importance of sensory and perceptual development

The sense organs have at times been referred to as "the gateways to the mind." Without the sense organs man would have no way to interpret his world. One has only to observe the deaf or blind person to realize the importance of a single sensory function in the life of an individual. People like Helen Keller, without vision or hearing, are able, under optimal conditions, to interpret their world through the other senses. Such individuals cannot visualize the colors and forms about them or hear the sounds coming from various sources. An optimal condition necessary for any interpretation such individuals give is a highly developed nervous system. Perceptual development, as implied in the definition quoted from Thompson, necessitates a central nervous system with integrative or "interpretive" abilities. Without such a nervous system the individual would

---

[11] George G. Thompson, *Child Psychology*, 2nd ed. (Boston: Houghton Mifflin Company, 1962), pp. 317-318.

learn little about his external world, even though his sense organs were unimpaired.

The nature and role of concepts. Concepts have been described by Thompson as "verbally identifiable and more-or-less stable abstractions (constructed from experience) which serve man in his psychological adjustments to a particular environment." [12] The child's concepts of the world in which he lives and grows consist of the ideas he associates with the things about him. These ideas are classified into special categories or classifications and are especially useful in communication and problem-solving. Perhaps the most clearly defined concepts used in our civilization are those found in mathematics. Here we note that the term *square root* stands for a number of antecedent operations and can be applied in many situations or problems.

Development of some common concepts. There is evidence that form discrimination develops during the early years of life. As early as the first two months of life consistent preference for visual patterns was noted by Fantz.[13] However, the acquisition of language is essential for the development of more highly organized concepts. Gellermann [14] compared the relative ability of chimpanzees and two-year-old children in discriminating triangularity *per se*. The selection of the correct form gave the subject access to a food box. The results showed that two-year-old children are able to discriminate triangular forms better than chimpanzees. Gellermann further observed that children used gestures and words in formulating the problem. The ability to verbalize principles would seem to give them a significant advantage in formulating problems like the one in this study.

Individual differences in apperceptive responses of 77 preschool children to 15 pictures were studied and analyzed by Ames.[15] She noted (1) a tendency to interpret the visual stimulus first by form and later by activity; (2) a tendency to interpret the visual stimulus at first concretely or literally, with a slow development toward more subjective interpretation; (3) a tendency to first interpret the stimulus in terms of a primitive unanalyzed whole, with a gradual development of the capacity to enlarge the whole and to increase the detail; and (4) a tendency toward some degree of self-identification with the picture stimuli. In an

[12] *Ibid.*, p. 318.

[13] R. L. Fantz, "Pattern Vision in Young Infants," *Psychological Record*, Vol. 8 (1958), pp. 43-47.

[14] L. W. Gellermann, "From Discrimination in Chimpanzees and Two-year-old Children: I Form (triangularity) *per se*," *Journal of Genetic Psychology*, Vol. 42 (1933), pp. 3-27.

[15] Elisabeth W. Ames, "Individual Differences in Apperceptive Reaction: A Study of the Response of Preschool Children to Pictures," *Genetic Psychology Monographs*, Vol. 23 (1941), pp. 319-385.

experiment reported by Sigel [16] seven-, nine-, and eleven-year-old children were asked to classify 20 toys varying in color, form, texture, and
representation. Those things that were similar in one way were to be
placed in one pile, while those that were alike in other ways were to be
placed in another pile. They were told to make as many piles as they
wished. The seven-year-olds classified the toys by *perceptual* characteristics such as the use and structure of the object or its geographical location. The eleven-year-olds grouped the objects by their *conceptual* characteristics such as living, nonliving, furniture, and metal. These findings
are summarized in Figure 3-6.

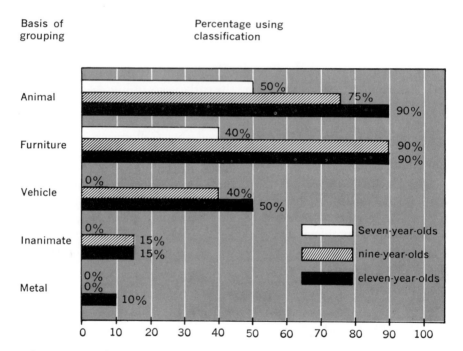

FIGURE 3-6.   The Percentage Of Children In Three Age Groups Identifying
Classification Of Toys. (Adapted from I. E. Sigel, "Developmental Trends in
the Abstraction Ability of Children," *Child Development*, Vol. 24 (1953), p. 138.

The nature of causal thinking of children at different age levels has
been studied by a number of investigators. The findings of a study reported by Mogar [17] offer positive evidence that children within the age
of five years and four months to twelve years can induce laws about

[16] I. E. Sigel, "Developmental trends in the abstraction ability of children," *Child
Development*, Vol. 24 (1953), p. 138.
[17] Mariannina Mogar, "Children's Causal Reasoning About Natural Phenomena,"
Child Development, Vol. 31 (1960), pp. 59-63.

natural phenomena from repeated observations of a phenomenon and can explain the event in terms of these laws. The importance of age as a correlate of the adequacy of a child's explanation was clearly shown. This supports the view that there is a significant relationship between the child's chronological age and his level of causal reasoning.

The growth of memory ability

The development of memory ability represents an important aspect in the child's growth, since this enables him to adjust his behavior to objective stimuli not within his immediate environment. We may observe this with the child who stops crying when he hears footsteps. Children improve in their ability as they grow older, so that by the time they are two years old they may be expected to remember, for a considerable length of time, people and things that have impressed them.

During the first two years, memory is stronger for persons and objects than for situations. In the years from three to six, persons and objects in situations become important factors in the child's memory. The speed with which children acquire a vocabulary and a fund of understanding indicates that the growth of memory ability is rapid during the preschool and early school years. In this connection memory may be classified as *immediate* memory and *delayed* memory. Learning may be said to occur as a result of delayed memory ability—another indication of a child's readiness to learn to read and spell.

The development of delayed memory ability is used in various forms in the measurement of intelligence. The *Stanford Revision of the Binet Tests of Intelligence*, as well as recent revisions of the Binet tests, have also made use of immediate memory ability in measuring intelligence. The increase with age in the capacity for repeating digits is shown in Table 3-2. These are standards for the different ages taken from the *Terman-Merrill Revision of the Binet Tests, 1937*.

THE DEVELOPMENT OF NEEDS

The developmental tasks appearing at different ages are closely related to the development and satisfaction of certain needs. The task of acquiring an appropriate sex role during early adolescence is not achieved in a short time. This is an outgrowth of developments related to the appropriate sex role during early stages of growth. This task is also closely related to the satisfaction of the need for independence from home ties and the need for affection. The need theory furnishes a useful device for describing the dynamics of behavior involved in the attainment of the different developmental tasks. According to this theory behavior patterns evolve from efforts to satisfy needs. This theory, however, has been

The mental growth of boys and girls is enhanced through a challenging educational program at school and elsewhere

TABLE 3-2. The Development of Immediate Memory Ability for Digits

REPEATING DIGITS IN ORDER GIVEN		REPEATING DIGITS IN REVERSE ORDER	
YEARS AND MONTHS	NUMBER OF DIGITS	YEARS	NUMBER OF DIGITS
2.6	2	7	3
3	3	9	4
4.6	4	12	5
7	5	Superior	
10	6	adult (I)	6
Superior			
adult (II)	8		
Superior			
adult (III)	9		

challenged by a number of students of psychology as being too inclusive. White [18] has proposed the term *competence* to describe such behavior as grasping, crawling, walking, attention and perception, language and thinking, and manipulation—all of which promote an effective interaction of the organism with his environment. This is made into a motivational concept. The activities in the service of competence are conceived of as motivated in their own right. Such activities are given special consideration in motivation and learning.

Any attempt to classify the common needs of human beings meets with many difficulties. There are probably as many lists of needs as there are psychologists who have attempted to develop these lists. The reason for the difficulty in developing a fairly complete list of needs is that human variability, even in a common culture, is so great that the need satisfaction takes many forms.

System of needs

There are some needs common to all people. These have been referred to as physiological needs, like the need for food and rest. There are other needs common to individuals of a given culture and needs that grow out of the unique characteristics and features of the individual's development. Similarity in needs other than physiological among individuals is due primarily to similar environmental backgrounds and experiences. Variability is due mainly to different environmental backgrounds and experiences.

The student will find a very complete list of needs in the study by Murray.[19] A more limited but clearly defined list, described by Maslow,[20] classifies needs in the following categories from the most basic to the least basic:

1. Physiological needs: hunger, thirst, and rest
2. Physical security or safety needs: protection from injury
3. Needs for affection and belongingness
4. Self-esteem needs and the need for independence, self-respect, and social approval
5. Self-actualization involving achievement and the fullest development of one's potentialities

A limited list, especially applicable to American culture, is given by Cronbach.[21] His list includes (1) need for affection, (2) need for

[18] Robert W. White, "Motivation Reconsidered: The Concept of Competence," *Psychological Review*, Vol. 66 (1959), pp. 297-333.

[19] H. A. Murray, *Explorations in Personality* (New York: Oxford University Press, 1938).

[20] A. H. Maslow, "A Theory of Human Motivation," *Psychological Review*, Vol. 50 (1943), pp. 370-396.

[21] L. J. Cronbach, *Educational Psychology* (New York: Harcourt, Brace & World, 1954), pp. 99-112.

approval from authority-figures, (3) need for approval by peers, (4) need for independence, and (5) need for self-respect. No attempt is made here to present a detailed list of needs. The major needs that appear common to most, if not all cultures will be described, especially as they appear in the American culture.

Need for affection. Close affectional ties with a few persons form the basic satisfactions of most people in our culture. The home is especially well suited to furnish these satisfactions. However, there are a few people who are forced to work out some substitute for the warm home and family situation. Sometimes the child from a rejecting home will find a favorable substitute in the teacher. Certainly the teacher should be on the alert for such children. The need for affection, and the values to be derived from it, may best be described as a two-way affair. This may be observed in the reactions of the infant child to cuddling by the mother. The child early responds with affection to those adults who care for him and give him affection.

Child specialists emphasize the importance of giving the small child the needed attention and affection during such routine processes as feeding, elimination, and preparation for rest or sleep. The weaning or toilet training period, especially, may be a source of confusion and difficulty for the infant, but if he emerges from this training satisfactorily, he usually retains his feelings of security in the parents' affectional relations. The birth of another baby brother or sister may upset this feeling, if the parents fail to give the older child the needed attention. There is evidence from many studies to support the view expressed by Menninger: "Among the basic requirements for healthy development of personality probably the most difficult lesson that every child needs to learn —and many adults should, but have not learned—is how to love and be loved." [22]

Need for independence. The child begins life completely dependent upon others and for a longer period of infancy than for any other form of life. However, if the constancy of the growth principle is to operate the child must be given increased independence and responsibility with each advanced level of maturity. The child appears to develop independence from the association, in his experience, of his behavior with tension reduction when he is successful in the manipulation of elements and forces in his environment. The development of independence has been described as follows:

The infant's crying and struggling when in a state of need may be the basic response pattern of what appears later in life as "acting when he is in

[22] William C. Menninger, "Mental Health in Our Schools," *Educational Leadership,* Vol. 7 (1950), p. 520.

a state of need" or *taking initiative*. For this to be associated with drive reduction, the parent must withdraw sufficiently from his frequent helping response to the child's vocal and motor reactions when he is in a state of need and permit the child to manipulate the non-human environment successfully.[23]

It is during the adolescent years that boys and girls establish close relationships with others and develop increased independence from family ties. Achieving independence does not mean that dependency is completely eliminated. There is established with growth a new dependence-independence relationship. Personal and social growth are accompanied by increased responsibility and independence along with a greater recognition of one's dependence upon his family, upon people outside the family, and for American children brought up in a religious atmosphere, upon God.

Need for approval. Very early in life the child learns that the approval of his behavior by others is pleasurable, while disapproval of his behavior is unpleasurable. Thus, the individual early develops the desire and need for approval from others, especially from adults who are in a position to exert authority over him. During the early years of life the child develops rather definite attitudes toward authority-figures. If he succeeds in reaching a particular goal by resorting to temper tantrums, he acquires the appropriate emotional habit patterns to achieve his purpose.

The attitudes toward authority-figures and peers the child acquires at home are also carried to school. If he has acquired a favorable attitude toward rules and self-discipline he will tend to display these attitudes at school. If he thinks of parents and parent-figures as tyrants, he will regard his teachers as tyrants to be dealt with. The process of developing attitudes toward authority-figures is a continuous one, and the attitudes the child brings to school will be modified by his experiences with new authority-figures. The need for the approval of the parent, teacher, and others in authority is a developmental need. The satisfaction of this need has an important bearing on the child's adjustment at school.

The school-age child not only has the need for the approval of authority-figures, he also has a need for the approval of his classmates. This is commonly referred to as the need for peer approval; the need to be liked and included in the activities of his peers. This need includes the need for belongingness, since approval tends to bring with it an acceptance by the group in their activities. This acceptance pattern of behavior will change as the nature and age of the group changes. During the preschool years race, social position, and sex are markedly unimportant

[23] Emanuel K. Beller, "Dependency and Independence in Young Children," *The Journal of Genetic Psychology*, Vol. 87 (1955), p. 26.

in the child's acceptance behavior pattern. Growth and learning bring about important changes in the child's acceptance pattern and in the role he plays in the group.

The acceptance of the child by his peers depends on his ability to do things that have prestige value in his group. The boy who is able to bat a ball a long distance is likely to be accepted by his peers in American culture, since this achievement has prestige value among school-age children. The child who makes good grades may receive the approval of his peers if this has prestige value among them. It has been observed that activities and abilities having prestige value in one group may have little prestige value in another group. The lower-class boy may win the approval of his peers by fighting and using profanity, while this is likely to be frowned upon by boys from a middle-class culture. The influence of different groups on the values, ideals, and accepted behavior patterns has been presented in a colorful manner by Lynes [24] in his descriptions of American adults divided into *lowbrows, middlebrows,* and *highbrows.* There is a significant element of truth in the portrayal of these *brows.* Their influence on the needs, values, and behavior patterns of children has been recognized by teachers and others at all times.

Need for self-esteem. The need for self-esteem may be thought of as the need for personal worth, or feeling that one is a worthy member of the group. One of the most common and serious personality problems is that frequently referred to as an *inferiority complex.* Children who feel inadequate are not only unlikely to succeed, but are unlikely to exert their best efforts. Healthy personality development requires that the individual not only know himself, but also accept himself. The orthopedically handicapped child must recognize his limitations and accept them without apology to the self or to others. Self-esteem does not mean a conceited or self-centered attitude. Considerable research has been conducted on the relationship of the individual's self-concept to healthy growth and personality adjustments. These studies have shown that a favorable attitude toward the self contributes to educational achievement, good mental health, and the attainment of the developmental tasks referred to earlier in this chapter.

The child's attitude toward himself is a result of (1) the successes he has had in reaching the goals set for the self, and (2) the attitudes others have taken toward him. The first of these involves the need for achievement; the second involves the need for approval. No single failure and no single social incident where approval is lacking will destroy a child's feeling of personal worth. Continuous failure at different tasks will surely have an adverse effect upon the child's feeling of worth. The

[24] Russell Lynes, "Highbrow, Lowbrow, Middlebrow," *Harper's Magazine,* Vol. 198 (1949), pp. 19-28.

child suffering from such failure needs guidance and reassurance. Teachers should remember, "There is no such thing as a poor learner, when the materials and methods are geared to the child's abilities and needs."

The child who meets social disapproval at every turn also acquires a changed attitude toward the self. In the past minority groups have often developed unfavorable attitudes toward themselves because of the roles they have been forced to play. To speak of a child as "not succeeding this time," is quite different from speaking of him as "a failure." To refer to a girl as "no good," is quite different from politely pointing out that "she has misbehaved." The goal should be to guide the child toward the development of a healthy self-concept in which he feels adequate to meet certain goals and demands, and feels capable of improving his behavior patterns.

DEVELOPMENTAL TASKS

In addition to physical and mental development, the stage of development for a child may be observed in the developmental tasks with which he is confronted. Developmental tasks consist of those major common tasks that face all individuals of a group or sub-group in a particular society. These tasks differ somewhat among communities or across religious and socioeconomic lines within a given community. Concerning their nature and importance Robert J. Havighurst writes:

A developmental task is a task that arises at or about a certain period in the life of the individual, successful achievement of which leads to his happiness and to success with later tasks, while failure leads to unhappiness in the individual, disapproval by society, and difficulty with later tasks.[25]

A summary of specific tasks, according to developmental stages and broad areas of behavior and adjustment, is presented in Table 3-3 for four stages of development—early childhood, late childhood, early adolescence, and late adolescence. By reading down each of the four columns the reader can determine the specific tasks designated for each of the four developmental stages. The kindergarten teacher and the first-grade teacher will find most of the children of their grade levels in early childhood. The majority of fourth- and fifth-grade boys will still be in late childhood, but a large percentage of girls will have reached early adolescence by the sixth grade.

The developmental tasks given for late adolescence are largely in terms of middle-class American culture. One may note this from a comparison of these developmental tasks with the middle- and lower-class

---

[25] Robert J. Havighurst, *Human Development and Education* (New York: Longmans, Green, 1953), p. 2.

TABLE 3.3 Important Developmental Tasks of American Children and Adolescents

TASK	EARLY CHILDHOOD	LATE CHILDHOOD	EARLY ADOLESCENCE	LATE ADOLESCENCE
Achieving an appropriate dependence - independence pattern	Establishing one's self as an independent being, while remaining emotionally dependent	Growth in self identification. Accepting one's physical characteristics, aptitudes	Establishing independence from adults in self identification and emotional independence	Establishing one's self as an independent person. Making own decisions
Achieving an appropriate affectional pattern	Learning to give and share affection	Forming friendships with peers on sharing basis	Accepting one's self as a person worthy of affection	Building a strong affectional bond with another person
Achieving a sense of belonging	Learning to interact with others of a group	Establishing peer loyalty and identification	Accepting and adjusting to special groups	Accepting an adult role in the group
Acquiring an appropriate sex role	Learning to identify the self with male or female roles	Identifying with peers of the same sex	Learning one's role in heterosexual situations	Becoming attached to a member of the opposite sex. Preparing to accept one's future sex role
Developing intellectual skills and concepts	Forming simple concepts of social and physical reality	Developing concepts essential for everyday living	Developing intellectual skills and concepts essential for individual and group participation	Developing intellectual skills and understanding for assuming civic responsibility
Developing conscience, morality, and a set of values	Emergence of conscience —distinguishing right and wrong	Acquiring moral concepts and elementary values	Acquiring values and moral concepts as guides to behavior	Acquiring standards and ethical concepts. Acquiring a philosophy of life

66

family expectations of adolescents, shown in Table 3-4. In the late adolescent period many young people leave school to work, while others remain in high school to graduate. Parents of middle-class adolescents expect their children to remain in high school, and a very large percentage of these parents expect their teen-agers to go on to college after graduating high school. Most adolescents from middle-class American culture place a relatively high premium on education and social prestige. Thus, the developmental tasks, shown in Table 3-3, relate to the expectations of adolescents from middle-class homes.

The role of the sex drive, emerging as a strong drive during the adolescent years, may be observed in the developmental tasks of late adolescence. The close ties of affection and understanding with someone of the opposite sex appears. This feeling of casting off the close emotional

TABLE 3-4. Differences in Middle- and Lower-Class Expectations of Adolescents

MIDDLE CLASS	LOWER CLASS
a. Children are expected to finish high school.	a. Parents do not especially care whether children finish high school.
b. It is emphasized that marriage be postponed until an education is secured.	b. Marriage will likely be early, with a family responsibility.
c. Children are given an allowance, but frequently encouraged to save money.	c. Children are allowed to spend what money they have as they wish.
d. An interest in school grades and graduation from high school is stressed.	d. Graduation from high school and good grades are not especially important.
e. Aggression must be controlled; children are discouraged from fighting.	e. Boys, especially, are encouraged to fight for their rights.
f. Children are taught respect for law and policemen.	f. Children are taught fear of law and policemen.
g. Tact is essential in dealing with social situations.	g. Honesty and frankness are used in dealing with social situations.
h. Emphasis is placed on education, so they may maintain their social position or move upward socially.	h. Stress is placed on getting a job and accepting financial responsibility.
i. Good manners and correct English are emphasized.	i. Little emphasis is placed on good manners and correct English.

ties of the home and sharing affection with someone else is a developmental aspect of growing up, and is important as a preparation for marriage. Marriage is often delayed by adolescents from the middle-class, although important changes have appeared within recent years in the attitudes of young people and adults toward marriage and home making.

SUMMARY

Development has been described as change. Change results from the interaction of the organism and his environment. The changes that occur among children over a period of time follow certain principles. Some of these principles are (1) growth is a continuous process; (2) children differ in rate of growth; and (3) all growth is interrelated.

It is emphasized in this and subsequent chapters that the child grows as a unitary whole, and that physical growth is closely related to other aspects of growth. Variability in physical growth is a result of hereditary factors, living conditions, diet, and general health conditions. The roles of maturation and learning may be observed in all aspects of growth.

The development of memory ability is an important aspect of mental development, which is affected by schooling. Factors such as curiosity, emotional independence, and eagerness to learn are also positively related to mental development. However, growth potentials are inherited.

Children in a given culture are faced with somewhat common developmental tasks. In Western culture these involve (1) an appropriate dependence-independence pattern, (2) an appropriate affectional pattern, (3) a sense of belonging, (4) an appropriate sex role, (5) intellectual skills and concepts, and (6) conscience, morality, and a set of values. Differences may be noted in the nature and operation of these developmental tasks among middle- and lower-class families.

Closely related to the developmental tasks are developmental needs. Needs common to all people have been referred to as physiological needs, although certain psychological needs appear well-nigh universal. Many lists of needs have been described by different students of educational psychology. Those we have described in this chapter are (1) need for affection; (2) need for independence; (3) need for approval; and (4) need for self-esteem. Motivation and personality integration are dependent in large measure upon the manner and extent to which the individual is successful in satisfying these needs in socially approved ways.

Problems and Exercises

1. Observe a group of twelve-year-old pupils. What do you find relative to individual differences in physical development? What do you find rela-

tive to sex differences? How would you account for the differences between the largest and smallest girl or boy of the group?

2. Illustrate the interrelation between the physical, motor, mental, and social development of some school-age child or adolescent of your acquaintance.

3. Miss Martin, a first-grade teacher, makes very little effort to teach reading to about one-third of her pupils. However, she provides them with a variety of rich experiences. How would you account for her action?

4. What is meant by the term *intelligence quotient?* How would you account for the effects of schooling on the intelligence quotient?

5. What is meant by the term *developmental tasks?* Study the developmental tasks presented in Table 3-3. Show how the role of maturation is involved in the attainment of certain developmental tasks.

6. What is meant by the statement, "The developmental tasks given for late adolescence are largely in terms of middle-class culture"?

7. What is meant by the term *system of needs?* What are some needs common to all people?

8. Examine several classifications of needs. What appears to be common to these different classifications? Why is an understanding of the child's needs important for the classroom teacher?

Selected Readings

CRONBACH, Lee J., *Educational Psychology,* 2nd ed. (New York: Harcourt, Brace & World, 1963), Ch. 4.

FRANDSEN, Arden N., *Educational Psychology* (New York: McGraw, 1961), Ch. 3.

HAVIGHURST, R. J., *Human Development and Education* (New York: Longmans, 1953).

JERSILD, Arthur T., *Child Psychology,* 5th ed. (Englewood Cliffs, N. J.: Prentice-Hall, 1960), Chs. 2, 4, 5, & 6.

LINDGREN, Henry C., *Educational Psychology in the Classroom,* 2nd ed. (New York: Wiley, 1962), Ch. 3.

McDONALD, Frederick J., *Educational Psychology* (San Francisco: Wadsworth, 1959), Ch. 11.

MOULY, George J., *Psychology for Effective Teaching* (New York: Holt, Rinehart, & Winston, 1960), Ch. 3.

OLSON, Willard C., *Child Development,* 2nd ed. (Boston: Heath, 1959), Chs. 2-7.

PRESSEY, Sidney L., ROBINSON, Francis P., and HORROCKS, John E., *Psychology in Education* (New York: Harper & Row, 1959), Chs. 2-6.

WOODRUFF, Asahel D., *The Psychology of Teaching,* 3rd ed. (New York: McKay, 1951), pp. 161-181.

CHAPTER 4

Intelligence

The great promise and needs of the age we live in require the full development of our human resources. Although schools are concerned with the development of the whole child, special emphasis is given to his intellectual attainments. This means that every individual should be trained, through self-realization, to the full development of his abilities—abilities which must first be identified. To aid in this task, many different tests have been developed that can give teachers an understanding of the wide range of abilities their students possess.

This chapter is especially concerned with intelligence, methods of appraising intelligence, mental growth, and the uses of intelligence tests in the educative process.

THE MEANING OF INTELLIGENCE

Before examining the psychological tests that are available for measuring intelligence, let use examine the major theories of the nature and manifestations of intelligence.

Perhaps no term in psychology is so generally used with functional meaning and yet is so difficult to define operationally as the term *intelligence.* Many authorities advance the concept that intelligence is synonymous with learning ability or that it is what intelligence tests measure and make little effort to define or describe it further. Since there is no common agreement about what constitutes intelligence, the theorists may well be arranged on a scale according to their belief in intelligence as a *unitary* characteristic or as an aggregate of highly *specific* abilities.

Binet, among the earliest investigators who believed intelligence to be a unitary characteristic, described intelligence as directness of thought, capacity for making adaptations, and auto-criticism. Others have described intelligence as the ability to adapt to new problems or situations.

In a sense intelligence, as used in psychology, has no absolute meaning, since it is frequently defined to suit the needs and philosophy of the student defining it. Terman early defined it as "an individual's ability to carry on abstract thinking. . . ." [1] Goddard defined it as "the degree of availability of one's experience for the solution of immediate problems and the anticipation of future ones." [2] One of the most complete definitions of intelligence is Wechsler's. He states that "Intelligence is the aggregate or global capacity of the individual to act purposefully, to think rationally, and to deal effectively with his environment." [3]

Spearman's two-factor theory.   At another extreme of the scale is Spearman.[4] He postulated that there is a general factor, *g*, underlying all mental functions and a multitude of factors, *s*, specific to given tasks. According to Spearman, individual differences in intelligence depend upon the extent to which individuals of a given group possess factor *g*. A child's ability to learn science would, according to this theory, depend upon the quality of his *g* and of his *s* factors in dealing with the different problems in science. Thus, two pupils may differ in the amount of *g* as well as in the specific *s* factors involved in the learning tasks. It is possible, then, for a person superior in *g* to be inferior in learning a given task because of his inferiority in the *s* factors involved in the performance of such a task. However, since the general factor permeates all tasks, it would be most unlikely that a person inferior in *g* would be especially capable in the learning of a specific task.

Thorndike's multi-factor theory.   At the other end of the scale Thorndike [5] maintained that intelligence is made up of all the many specific abilities involved in intelligent behavior. Based upon research evidence and usefulness, Thorndike classified intelligence as *abstract* (ability to deal with ideas and symbols), *mechanical* (ability to deal with mechanics and things), and *social* (ability to deal with people). The correlation between tests of these three categories, however, tends to be high because common elements are involved. Tests of abstract intelligence correlate highest with scholastic achievement. This may well be accounted for by the abstract nature of much school work.

---

[1] Lewis M. Terman, *Measurement of Intelligence* (Boston: Houghton Mifflin Co., 1916), p. 42.

[2] H. H. Goddard, "What is intelligence?" *Journal of Social Psychology*, Vol. 24 (1946), pp. 51-69.

[3] David Wechsler, *The Measurement of Adult Intelligence*, 4th ed. (Baltimore: Williams and Wilkins Co., 1960), p. 7.

[4] Carl E. Spearman, *The Abilities of Man: Their Nature and Measurement* (New York: Macmillan, 1927).

[5] E. L. Thorndike, in the symposium, "Intelligence and Its Measurement," *Journal of Educational Psychology*, Vol. 12 (1921), pp. 123-147, 195-216.

Thurstone's theory of primary mental abilities. Somewhere between these views is a middle-of-the-road view proposed by Thurstone.[6] According to Thurstone there is no general factor, but rather, intelligence is made up of a number of *primary mental abilities.* Intelligent behavior results from the operation of certain primary abilities essential for the performance of a given task. Thurstone attempted to identify these primary factors. On the basis of intensive studies, he constructed the *Chicago Primary Abilities Test.* This test offers a profile of the individual's ability on each of the primary factors. For example, Alice may have a

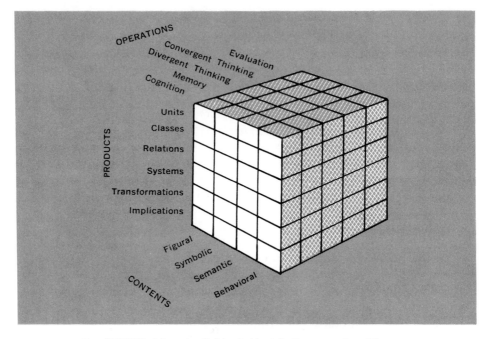

FIGURE 4-1. A Cubical Model Representing The
Structure Of The Intellect *(Guilford)*

composite score on the test less than that of Grace, but she may have considerably more of one of the abilities than Grace, making it possible for her to excel on tasks requiring that special ability.

Guilford's structure of the intellect. Guilford [7] recently has expanded the theories of Thurstone and Spearman based on further factor

[6] L. L. Thurstone and Thelma G. Thurstone, "Factorial Studies of Intelligence," *Psychometrics Monographs* (1941), No. 2.

[7] J. P. Guilford, "Three Faces of Intellect," *The American Psychologist,* Vol. 14 (1959), pp. 469-479.

analytic studies. He has classified the factors of intellect according to (1) the kind of process or operation performed by the individual, (2) the kind of material or the content involved, and (3) the kinds of products involved. He has developed the conceptual model shown in Figure 4-1 to help explain his theory.

Manifestations of intelligence

As we can see from the different concepts of intelligence there is no general agreement among theorists concerning the nature of intelligence. Instead, in each case, the measure of intelligence is actually based upon the ability of the individual to function in a certain test situation. Thus, our measure of the thing we call intelligence should be correlated differently with different criteria of intelligence. To arrive at a more accurate and useful understanding of the problem of measuring intelligence, we should first distinguish between intelligence as an inherited potential ability, and intelligence as measured by intelligence tests. Actually, the only intelligence we know anything about is that manifested in some performance or on some intelligence test. Intelligence as an inborn ability is, to a large degree, an abstraction, and is not directly subject to measurement. It can only be inferred from one's responses in test situations. Whereas motor ability is inferred through specific tests such as running, throwing, and jumping, mental ability is inferred from the child's performance on specific tests such as vocabulary, following directions, interpretation of pictures, and detecting similarities and differences. Furthermore, such intelligence is the product of the interaction between innate intelligence and environmental stimuli.

THE MEASUREMENT OF INTELLIGENCE

Binet's tests of general intelligence are especially important because of their influence in stimulating and guiding students in other countries in the development of instruments for measuring intelligence of pre-school and of school-age children.[8] Binet gave little consideration to theories concerning the nature of intelligence, but proceeded empirically to determine the kinds of tests that would distinguish between criterion groups of children.

One of Binet's most significant contributions was the development of the mental age concept. It had long been recognized that older children were able to do certain tasks, solve certain problems, or think more rationally than younger children. In developing his scale, Binet attempted

[8] Joseph Peterson, *Early Conceptions and Tests of Intelligence* (Yonkers-on-Hudson: Harcourt, Brace & World, 1925). A rather complete account of the early history of intelligence testing is here presented.

to measure these mental abilities as children grew older. The concept of mental age will be described more fully later in this chapter.

Individual tests of intelligence

Binet's scale of 1905 passed through a process of revision and culminated in a set of performance standards for each age from three to fourteen years. The revised age scale was translated into English by Goddard (1910, 1911) and revised for use with American children. The best known American revision of the *Binet Tests* is the *Stanford Revision of the Binet Tests* by Terman which appeared in 1916. For more than two decades this remained a standard instrument for use in clinical psychology, psychiatry, and educational counseling. A further revision of this scale was published by Terman and Merrill in 1937.[9] It was standardized on more than 3,000 cases and was extended to be useful for testing individuals of all ages from very young children to adults and superior adults. The test items for age nine are listed to give a general idea of the nature of the entire test.

Age 9

1. Makes a drawing to indicate how a piece of folded paper in which a hole has been cut would look when unfolded.
2. Detects absurdities in verbal statements.
3. Reproduces designs from memory.
4. Gives a word which rhymes with certain other words.
5. Tells how much change would be left after certain transactions.
6. Repeats four digits reversed.

The Binet Test was again revised in 1960 with certain modifications based on accumulated experiments with the 1937 scale (see 1960 Manual). The basic concept remains the same but Forms L and M have been combined to provide more testing on performance items.

The Wechsler Intelligence Scale for Children (WISC) provides both verbal and nonverbal scores and subtests in each category. This test has been widely used in school situations. The correlations obtained between the results on this test and those obtained from the *Stanford Revision of the Binet Tests* have been sufficiently high to warrant its acceptance and widespread use.[10]

The Wechsler Adult Intelligence Scale (WAIS) was developed to test the intelligence of adolescents and adults. It includes the following category of subtests: information, comprehension, arithmetic, similari-

[9] Lewis M. Terman and Maude M. Merrill, *Measuring Intelligence* (Boston: Houghton Mifflin Co., 1937).

[10] James B. Stroud, Paul Blommers, and Margaret Lauber, "Correlation analysis of WISC and Achievement Tests," *Journal of Educational Psychology,* Vol. 49 (1957), pp. 18-20.

ties, vocabulary, picture completion, picture arrangement, block design, object assembly, and digit symbol. On both the WISC and the WAIS profiles of the individual may be obtained from the scores on the several subtests. In addition the batteries yield verbal, performance, and full-scale IQ's. The correlations between the verbal and performance scales and among the subtests indicate that they measure both common and differential mental functions.

Group tests of intelligence

Although intelligence scales such as the Stanford-Binet and the WISC yield valuable information about the intelligence of individual children, a real need developed for group tests which could be quickly administered, scored, and interpreted. Group tests of intelligence, modeled after those employed during World War I, filled this need. Today, group tests are widely used in the schools for studying pupils, identifying those with special abilities, or locating those with special handicaps. Group tests tend to be of two major types: omnibus tests that include many different items which differentiate among children, and special tests based upon the theory that intelligence consists of predominantly separate abilities.

The California Test of Mental Maturity is an example of an intelligence test constructed on the theory that intelligence consists of many relatively independent variables. The diagnostic profile of an eleven-year-old pupil presented in Figure 4-2 shows the kind of items it contains.[11] The profile score was designed to correlate a pupil's scores, and thus indicate his relative strengths and weaknesses in measured degrees on a mental age scale.

Many group tests have been devised for studying the intelligence of children. While most of these are verbal, efforts have been made to develop tests that would eliminate the advantage of a high degree of verbal ability. The Goodenough *Draw a Man Scale*,[12] in which a child is simply instructed to draw a man, is an example of such a test. Figure 4-3 shows four drawings and their mental age equivalents. This test represents an early attempt to measure intelligence by nonverbal types of tests.

The *Davis-Eells Test of General Intelligence or Problem-Solving Ability* [13] is a group test of general intelligence for grades one through six. Intelligence here is defined as problem-solving ability. The authors attempted to select test items or problems that would eliminate such factors as cultural background, socioeconomic status, reading level, or other in-school instruction. The test items deal with a variety of prob-

---

[11] Published by California Test Bureau, Los Angeles, California.

[12] Florence L. Goodenough, *Measurement of Intelligence by Drawings* (Yonkers-on-Hudson: Harcourt, Brace & World, 1926).

[13] Published by Harcourt, Brace & World (Yonkers-on-Hudson, New York, 1952).

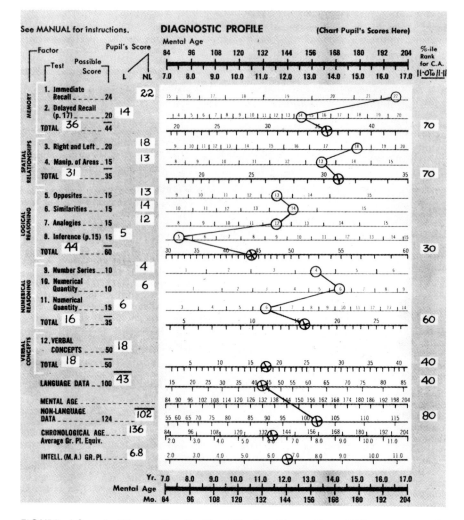

FIGURE 4-2. A Diagnostic Profile Of An Eleven-Year-Old Boy On The
California Test of Mental Maturity, Elementary, 1957 Edition

lem areas and closely parallel real-life problems. The items consist of
pictures accompanied by verbal materials to be read to the pupils by the
teacher or person administering the test. Figure 4-4 shows a sample item
of this test.

Because of the variety of test items and test content it becomes very
difficult to compare the validity of different intelligence tests. Studies
consistently show a high correlation between results from group tests and
those from individual tests. Individual tests probably have their greatest

FIGURE 4-3. Drawings-Of-A-Man And Their Mental Age
Equivalents

FIGURE 4-4.   A Problem-Solving Item From The Davis-Eells
Test Of General Intelligence. The person taking the test is
to decide which boy is starting to get across the water the
best way (Yonkers-on-Hudson: World Book Company, 1952).

advantage in testing (1) preschool children, (2) exceptional children, and (3) children with learning, guidance and emotional difficulties.

Indices of intelligence

The *mental age* and *intelligence quotient* (IQ) are scores widely used in evaluating the level of a child's intelligence. The term *mental age* designates the score earned by average children of given chronological ages. If a particular child earns a score equal to that earned by average seven-year-olds, his mental development is then considered comparable to that of a seven-year-old. He is then said to have a mental age of seven years.

In 1912, Stern, a German psychologist, suggested that if mental age, as determined by a test, were divided by chronological age the quotient would be relatively constant throughout life. For example, if a child of four has a mental age of five, the quotient obtained by dividing the mental age by the chronological age is 1.25 ($5 \div 4 = 1.25$). Then, if at the age of eight he has a mental age of ten, the quotient obtained by dividing mental age by chronological age again is 1.25 ($5 \div 4 = 1.25$). Stern called this the "intelligence quotient" or the I.Q. In practice this quotient is multiplied by 100. A normal IQ would thus be 100 ($4 \div 4$). A mentally superior child would, of course, have an intelligence quotient significantly more than 100 and a mentally inferior one would have an IQ significantly less than 100.

MENTAL GROWTH

Problems concerning the characteristics of mental growth have attracted the attention of many psychologists over the past several decades. The earliest studies of this problem were based on a mass of data gathered by the cross-sectional method. Subject to serious limitations, the cross-sectional method has been replaced by many studies conducted by the longitudinal method, which makes use of repeated tests on the same group or groups of individuals.

Mental growth curves. Among the studies that have used the longitudinal method of gathering data is the early study by Freeman [14] with pupils from the Laboratory Schools of the University of Chicago. In order to compare the mental growth of different ability groups 122 children were selected for whom there were available repeated measurements from ages 11 to 16. These children were divided into three groups, based upon the mean of their scores at ages 12, 13, and 14. The average mental growth curves for these three groups are presented in Figure 4-5.

[14] Frank N. Freeman, "Intellectual Growth of Children as Indicated by Repeated Tests," *Psychological Monographs,* Vol. 47 (1936), No. 212, pp. 20-34.

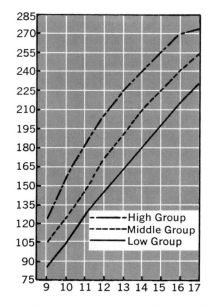

FIGURE 4-5.   Mean Intelligence Test Scores Of Three Groups Of Pupils With
Consecutive Tests From 11 to 16 Years *(Freeman)*

These children are labeled high, middle, and low groups only in relation
to each other, since the children of the Laboratory School have an average
IQ of 115. These curves show that each group retains its relative position
from one age to another. There are, however, wide individual variations
in the rate of mental growth.

One must be careful about generalizing too freely from group data.
As we pointed out in Chapter 3, children differ in their rate of growth.
Because a child develops slowly we must not conclude that he is mentally
inferior. Neither should it be assumed that he is mentally superior if he
develops rapidly. The rate of a particular child's mental growth will
depend upon a number of factors, some of which are (1) the child's pattern of development, (2) nutrition and health conditions, (3) psychological and social forces in his environment, and (4) the kind of test used
in evaluating mental growth.

Stability of mental growth.   The problem of the stability of mental
growth has been given considerable attention by educational psychologists, an issue referred to as *the constancy of the intelligence*

quotient. The central problem is whether an adverse environment will lower the IQ, or whether a superior environment will raise it.

The concept one holds of intelligence has an important bearing on the problem of the stability of the IQ. Certainly we cannot hope to raise the level of one's inherited potentialities. Furthermore, it is not possible to measure inborn capacity. However, intelligence test scores may be obtained on individuals based upon the number of exercises or problems they are able to complete in a given period of time.

Individual age curves of intelligence test scores have been plotted by Bayley.[15] These curves furnish useful information about the nature and stability of mental growth during childhood and adolescence. She concluded from the data gathered that only one-fifth of the 48 children studied had maintained approximately the same relative position through-out the first nine months. Some had successive periods of rapid and slow growth; others displayed a much greater regularity in their growth.

A longitudinal study of 140 children with frequent and periodic measurement of IQ's by Sontag, Baker, and Nelson [16] indicates that no constant increment of change in IQ is to be found in the majority of cases. The pattern of retest correlation of IQ at one age with IQ at other ages was similar to that found by earlier investigators of this problem. A characteristic noted in the individual curves of smoothed IQ was the idiosyncratic nature of the patterns of change. This may be noted in Figure 4-6. Some individuals had periods of gain in IQ followed by a loss, others had periods of loss in IQ followed by a gain, while others showed a different pattern of change. It appears from the results of this study that the extent of childhood IQ changes has generally been under-estimated previously. The median amount of IQ change reported in this study was 17.9 points, with 62 per cent of the children changing more than 15 IQ points some time during the course of their mental develop-ment from the age of three to the age of ten. The investigators conclude:

. . . Accelerative and decelerative rates of mental growth did not appear to be related to any specific areas of ability as measured by the differences in performances on the different types of items. Rather, there appeared to be general acceleratory-deceleratory factors present regardless of a child's area of special competence.[17]

Age of cessation of mental growth. Closely related to the problem of the mental growth of different abilities is the age of cessation of mental

[15] Nancy Bayley, "Consistency and Variability in the Growth of Intelligence from Birth to Eighteen Years," *Journal of Genetic Psychology,* Vol. 72 (1949), p. 189.

[16] Lester W. Sontag, Charles T. Baker, and Virginia L. Nelson, "Mental Growth and Personality Developments: a Longitudinal Study," *Monographs of the Society for Research in Child Development,* Vol. 23 (1958), No. 2.

[17] *Ibid.,* p. 54.

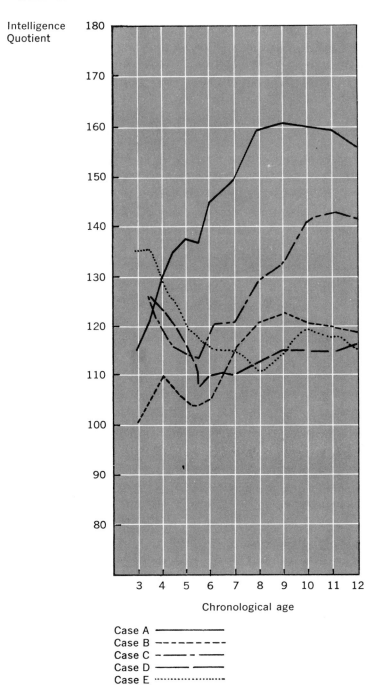

FIGURE 4-6. Changes In IQ Of Five Individuals From Age Three
To Age Twelve (Adapted from Sontag, Baker, and Nelson)

growth. When individual tests are repeated from year to year an increase in ability is usually found, especially during the growing years. The question may be raised, At what age does this increase in intelligence test scores cease? It was pointed out earlier that the pattern of mental growth is not identical for all individuals. Likewise, the age of cessation of mental growth will vary with different individuals.

It is possible that the apparent cessation of mental growth discussed previously may be due primarily to differences in experience during the adolescent and early adult years which are not measured equally by traditional tests. Some substantiation of this possibility may be noted in the tendency for further development of the tested intelligence of young adults who remain in school or who are employed in work which places a premium on learning and thinking. Adults who leave school or who discontinue their education do not appear to continue to develop mentally at a comparable rate. Comparisons of army classification scores of World War I and World War II soldiers show that World War II soldiers were significantly superior to their World War I counterparts. The best explanation for this difference would seem to be the greater amount of schooling World War II soldiers had.

Husén [18] found that the children of a Swedish town who remained in school the longest registered the greatest gain in IQ throughout the adolescent years. The need for achievement seems to be related to continued mental growth.

The age at which individuals cease to grow in intelligence has been estimated to vary from thirteen and a half-years to some time in the twenties. Freeman and Flory [19] reported results from the Chicago growth study in which tests were administered to several hundred children over a period of years. Most of the subjects were retested at the age of seventeen or eighteen years. Some were later tested in college. A composite of four standardized tests consisting of (1) vocabulary, (2) analogies, (3) completion, and (4) opposites were used. Growth curves drawn from the raw scores showed that mental development continued well beyond the ages of seventeen or eighteen years. There was also some evidence from these mental growth curves that the children of average ability might continue intellectual growth to a somewhat later age than those of superior ability. However, in all likelihood, this results from the failure of the average environment to present opportunities for stimulating the superior pupil to grow at an accelerated rate. This presents a challenge to teachers to provide a more enriched environment to

[18] T. Husén, "The Influence of Schooling upon IQ," *Theoria*, Vol. 2 (1951), pp. 61-88.

[19] F. N. Freeman and C. D. Flory, "Growth in Mental Ability as Measured by Repeated Tests," *Monographs of the Society for Research in Child Development*, Vol. 2 (1937), p. 116.

stimulate the intellectual curiosity and thus the mental growth of the superior pupils.

The results of the study reported by Freeman and Flory are substantiated by data presented by Bayley.[20] Thirty-three subjects of the Berkeley growth study took the *Wechsler Bellevue Intelligence Scale* at 16, 18, and 21 years of age. The results indicate that intellectual functions continue to improve through 21 years and probably beyond. The gains occur at all levels of intelligence found in the sample. There are indications, however, that some individuals reach their top capacity by 16 to 18 years, while others may still be growing at the age of 24 or 25 years.

Factors related to mental growth

Many studies have been conducted on the relationship between mental development and various aspects of the child's hereditary constitution and environmental circumstances. The problem of the relative importance of heredity and environment constantly appears in the evaluation of results. This problem is further related to IQ changes, discussed earlier in the chapter. The notion of a constant IQ has gradually been abandoned as a result of the avalanche of studies showing IQ changes. Some of the most important factors affecting the nature and rate of mental growth will be presented in subsequent discussions.

Hereditary factors. Certain fundamental principles of heredity operate in producing the individual child, a product of the interaction of heredity and environment from the very beginning of life.

Sontag and others noted that "close genetic relationships tend to have somewhat similar patterns of mental growth."[21] Although children with deficiencies in intelligence may be found in all cultural levels and often are offspring of families with normal or superior ability, a high percentage of feebleminded and borderline children are found among certain families with histories of mental deficiency.

It should be pointed out, however, that not all children regarded by their teachers as mentally inferior are actually inferior, although their mental responses may be on the level with those of a mentally inferior child. There is a difference between children whose potential mental abilities are extremely low and those who are functioning on a very low plane. Some conditions, listed by Grace Arthur, that can lower the reaction level of an individual to the feebleminded level in spite of a normal intellectual endowment include the following:

1. Physical handicaps such as impaired vision, impaired hearing, and im-

[20] Nancy Bayley, "Data on the Growth of Intelligence Between 18 and 21 Years as Measured by the Wechsler Bellevue Scale," *Journal of Genetic Psychology*, Vol. 90 (1957), pp. 3-15.

[21] *Op. cit.,* p. 134.

paired mechanisms for motor coordination that interfere with academic learning and with success on some scales for measuring intelligence.

2. Brain injury which occurred at birth or from later accident that interfered with some kinds of intellectual activity but not with others.

3. Severe early illness that delayed but did not prevent mental development.

4. Delayed speech that extends far beyond normal limits, but has not prevented development of nonverbal abilities.

5. Intellectual idiosyncrasies that act as special intellectual disabilities until they are diagnosed and given appropriate treatment, and frequently are confused with general mental deficiency.[22]

Relation between physical and mental development. The problem of the relationship between physiological and anatomical structures and mental development has received the attention of a number of investigators. The significant increase in stature among American children, assumed to be the effects of improved standards of living, is evidence of the changes that may occur within a generation. Evidence of the influence of genetic factors on individual differences in mental ability has been presented in a comparison of intelligence in children of different degrees of genetic similarity. Identical twins are presumed to have the same genetic characteristics. To the extent that such twins are more alike in intelligence than siblings, hereditary influences are implied. Comparisons have also been made between children of different degrees of kinship but from a somwhat similar sociocultural background. It has been pointed out, however, that twins are from an identical environment and that environmental factors may have been the influential forces. In an attempt to overcome this likelihood, comparisons have been made between identical twins reared together and identical twins reared apart. Also, comparisons have been made between siblings reared together and siblings reared apart. If the greater resemblance in intelligence of identical twins persists despite the separation, the role of heredity becomes more clearly established. Burt [23] has presented the following correlations in support of genetic influences:

Identical twins reared together .... .925
Identical twins reared apart .... .876
Siblings reared together .... .538
Siblings reared apart .... .517
Unrelated children reared together .... .269

Evidence has also been presented showing that a superior environment produces an increased mental growth. Thus, many factors that

[22] Grace Arthur, "Some Factors Contributing to Errors in the Diagnosis of Feeblemindedness," *American Journal of Mental Deficiency*, Vol. 54 (1950), p. 497.

[23] C. Burt, "The Inheritance of Mental Ability," *American Psychologist*, Vol. 13 (1958), pp. 1-15.

produce superior development for one aspect of growth will likely produce superior development for other aspects. Most studies, however, have failed to eliminate such factors as age, cultural differences, schooling, and other environmental factors in their attempt to answer the question of the relation between mental and physical growth. Bersch, Lenz, and Maxwell obtained intra-pair correlations between intelligence and height of two groups of twins. The investigators conclude:

> For both the German and the Scottish twin samples the intra-pair correlations between physical and mental measurements are of the order of zero. This is compatible with the hypothesis under investigation, namely, that there is no intrinsic biological relation between physical and intellectual development and that the observed tendency for more intelligent children to be better developed physically is a function of common environment.[24]

Personality and IQ change. It was pointed out earlier that measured intelligence is a sample of an individual's behavior. It depends not only upon the possession of an aggregate of neural structures that make certain mental operations possible, but also upon the extent to which the individual is motivated to perform them. A number of investigators [25] have hypothesized about the effects of personality differences on changes in IQ. Sontag [26] and others suggest that the changes in IQ levels reflect what may well be termed "learning to learn." The question has been raised, Are there certain motivational factors in the child's personality that may affect his performance in tests as the *Stanford-Revision of the Binet Tests?* In an attempt to answer this question the investigators used seven-point rating scales in making judgments of a number of personality factors. A comparison of the personality ratings made at age six of the children who gained most in IQ with that of those who lost most in IQ showed that the *emotional independence from parents* personality rating was a significant factor. Concerning the analysis at age ten they state:

> . . . The analysis of the ratings made at age 10 resulted in a large number of scales discriminating significantly between subjects who gained and subjects who lost in IQ during the elementary school years. Independence, Aggressiveness, Self-Initiation, Problem-Solving, Anticipation, Competitiveness, and the two scales having to do with scholastic competition all appeared to be related clearly to an accelerated pattern of IQ change during this period. The ratings made on the basis of these significant scales were all highly intercorrelated, suggesting that a common dimension of personality could explain the

[24] O. F. Bersch, W. Lenz, and J. Maxwell, "The Correlation between Mental and Physical Growth in Twins," *British Journal of Educational Psychology*, Vol. 31 (1961), p. 267.

[25] D. H. Stott, "Interaction of Heredity and Environment in Regard to Measured Intelligence," *British Journal of Educational Psychology*, Vol. 30 (1960), pp. 95-102.

[26] *Op. cit.*, pp. 89-143.

results obtained at this age. The referent behaviors of these scales suggested the achievement motive as a common dimension.[27]

It appears that guilt-free curiosity, likely to characterize the child who has gained a relative degree of emotional independence from his parents, and opportunities for exploration, may have a beneficial effect upon mental growth during the early years. The child who is emotionally dependent upon his parents during the preschool years would likely develop behavior patterns not conducive to "learning to learn." During the elementary-school years the IQ of the child who is motivated through a high need for achievement, or who has been taught many skills at home, will likely be accelerated. Other studies suggest that freedom from rigid personality structure enhances "learning to learn."

It might also be appropriate to emphasize that there usually exists a difference between the child's functional level of intelligence and his potential ability. Often very bright children have emotional difficulties which may prevent them from utilizing their potentials optimally. Similarly other children who might be less well endowed have developed habits and goals which motivate them toward learning and make them more secure in dealing with learning problems. Since intelligence tests tend to measure either directly or indirectly the child's achievements, this group of children often do fairly well. In the case of the boy who kept house, described later, it should be emphasized that intelligence tests merely select certain types of achievements for determining intelligence. Personal and social developmental patterns which are different from "the norm" often are not considered. Psychologists constantly urge teachers and parents to regard intelligence as being merely one of many important factors in dealing with children.

The social-class structure.   There are many studies to support the hypothesis that the cultural level of the home has an important bearing on the intelligence test scores children make. In administering individual intelligence tests, the writers have observed that the type and quality of language responses of children from homes differing in social-cultural level vary considerably. The language responses of twins are often strikingly similar. Recently twins were asked by one of the writers, as part of a test, why they would rather ride in an automobile than on a bicycle. Each responded individually that "if it rains you will get wet while riding a bicycle."

One of the writers recently had a fourth-grade boy referred to him for testing. The boy's teacher and the principal of his school believed that the boy was below average in intelligence. The writer discovered that the boy had a low-normal IQ but in addition assumed responsibilities in

[27] Sontag *et al., op. cit.,* p. 137.

the home far beyond those of the average child of his age. The boy's mother had deserted the family and his father, who drove a truck, was away from home a great deal. This eleven-year-old boy managed the household, did most of the cooking, and practically all of the family shopping. In responsibility and practical intelligence this pupil was far advanced over most of the children in his grade, but his intelligence test performance was not consistent with his personal and social achievements.

Continued exposure to differential environmental conditions found in different socioeconomic groups favors the development of certain abilities, but it discourages the development of other abilities. The tasks to be learned at school are usually more closely related to the stimulating forces and educational background of the middle-class child than of the lower-class child. Consequently, middle-class children tend to excel on these tasks. This was shown in an early study by Freeman, Holzinger, and Mitchell.[28] The results of one of these studies are summarized in Table 4-1. A rating scale was used for appraising the foster homes, taking into

TABLE 4-1.   Influence of the Quality of the Foster Home on Change in IQ of Foster Children (*After Freeman, Holzinger, and Mitchell*)

FOSTER HOME RATING	NUMBER OF CASES	IQ BEFORE PLACEMENT	IQ AFTER 4 YEARS	GAIN
Good	33	95.2	100.5	5.3
Poor	41	88.0	88.1	0.1

account the neighborhood, size and comfort of the building, general conditions of the building, reading matter in the home, educational level of the parents, congeniality, and character of the foster parents. The children were tested before being placed in the foster homes and again four years later. The table shows that the children from the foster homes rated good registered an average gain of 5.3 in IQ, while those from the homes rated poor, registered no significant gain.

Comparisons of rural and city children yield results favorable to the city child. The most plausible explanation for this is the greater cultural advantages offered by the urban environment. Smith [29] noted that urban

[28] F. N. Freeman, K. U. Holzinger, and B. C. Mitchell, "The Influence of Environment on The Intelligence, School Achievement and Conduct of Foster Children," *Twenty-seventh Yearbook of the National Society for the Study of Education*, 1928, Part I, pp. 103-217.
[29] Paul M. Smith, *Personality Characteristics of Rural and Urban Southern Negro Children*. Ed. D. Dissertation, Indiana University, 1958.

Negro students in Southern segregated schools were significantly higher in intelligence test scores than were rural Negro students. Urban students, however, seemed to come from homes of slightly higher socioeconomic status with a higher educational status than did rural students.

A detailed analysis of the many items making up most intelligence tests reveals a cultural bias in favor of the urban child. Such bias may be expressed, for example, in a test item that asks, What should you do if on your way to school you suddenly realize that you may be tardy? The urban child who walks to school will generally recognize that he should run or walk faster. The rural child who travels by school bus will likely be perplexed because there is actually little or nothing he can do in such a situation. This bias no doubt accounts for many of the differences frequently found in the intelligence test scores of rural and urban children.

Evidence has also been presented to show that group tests tend to favor upper-middle-class urban children rather than lower-class urban children. This may account, in part, for differences frequently found in intelligence test scores between these two groups. Teachers and others who interpret the results of intelligence test scores should be aware of these relationships and take them into account wherever pertinent.

Influence of schooling. Although many studies have reported a significant relation between intelligence test scores and school achievement, there have been few experiments dealing with the effects of schooling on the IQ. The results of studies bearing on this problem are somewhat conflicting. Substantial evidence indicates that children from substandard home conditions benefit most from nursery-school and kindergarten experiences, while those from favorable home environments benefit least. In a study of the effects of nursery-school attendance, Olson and Hughes [30] studied children from average or superior home environment. They found that nursery-school children from such home backgrounds did not differ significantly in their mental growth from non-nursery-school children from similar home backgrounds. An environment which provides for mental stimulation and opportunities for mental development in harmony with the child's maturational level tends to promote optimum mental development. It thus appears that the improvement of an environment beyond a certain point may be of little value in contributing to mental growth.

The question may be raised, What constitutes a superior environment? An allied question is, Will an environment that is superior for one child necessarily be superior for another child? What constitutes a

[30] W. C. Olson and B. O. Hughes, "Subsequent Growth of Children With and Without Nursery-school Experience," *Thirty-ninth Yearbook of the National Society for the Study of Education,* 1940, Part II, pp. 237-244.

superior environment is difficult to describe, except in very general terms. It has already been suggested that an environment which provides for mental stimulation and optimum opportunities for mental growth might be regarded as a very good environment. Since children differ in needs and in abilities, it seems most likely that an environment providing stimulation for one child may actually frustrate another. This may be observed among a group of fourth-grade pupils in their spelling or writing activities. The child who is motivated to spell so that he may be able to write a composition about his summer vacation at the beach will find the learning experiences more meaningful and challenging than the child who is impelled to spell or write merely to satisfy the teacher.

Intelligence and bilingualism. Many studies have been conducted on the problem of the relation between intelligence and bilingualism. In general these studies have supported the hypothesis that children from homes where a language other than English is spoken are at a disadvantage on intelligence tests. Here again, one should be careful in arriving at conclusions about the cause of low intelligence test scores among such children, since it is difficult to obtain reliable estimates.

In the study by Darcey [31] of the effect of bilingualism upon the measurement of the intelligence of preschool children, 106 monolingual and 106 bilingual children were matched for age, sex, and socioeconomic status. Two individual intelligence scales were administered to each child of the two groups. The 1937 *Revision of the Stanford-Binet Scale, Form L* was used as a verbal test and the *Atkins Object-fitting Test, Form A* was used as a nonverbal measure of intelligence. Some of the conclusions from this study are summarized by Darcy:

1. There were significant differences between the mean IQ's achieved by the monolingual and bilingual subjects on the *Stanford-Binet Scales.* These differences were consistently in favor of the monoglots when divided according to age and sex and also when the age groups and sexes were combined.
2. Conversely, when the differences in the mean IQ's were determined for both language groups on the *Atkins Test,* significant differences in favor of the bilingual group were found. . . .

Since a large number of children may be bilingual, those concerned with measuring their intelligence should bear these facts in mind.

The *Jenkins Non-verbal Scale of Mental Ability* was used in a study of bilingualism and nonverbal intelligence reported by Lewis.[32] Sixteen

---

[31] Natalie T. Darcey, "The Effect of Bilingualism Upon the Measurement of Intelligence of Children of Preschool Age," *Journal of Educational Psychology,* Vol. 37 (1946), pp. 21-44.

[32] D. G. Lewis, "Bilingualism and Non-verbal Intelligence: a Further Study of Test Results," *British Journal of Educational Psychology,* Vol. 29 (1959), pp. 17-22.

The Psychological Corporation

Arthur Point Scale Of Performance Tests, Revised Form II. The *Arthur Point Scale of Performance Tests* provides a means of measuring the abilities of deaf children, those suffering from reading disabilities, those with delayed or defective speech, and the non-English speaking. It is primarily nonlanguage in nature.

primary schools in the areas predominantly Welsh-speaking or English-speaking were selected to secure a wide range of linguistic background. The children were divided into four equivalent groups, except for the language feature. The characteristic features of the four groups were as follows:

Group 1. The language in the home is entirely Welsh.
Group 2. The language in the home is varied, and in no case is Welsh always spoken.
Group 3. The language in the home is varied, with no Welsh spoken by one of the parents.
Group 4. The language of the home is English, and in almost all cases Welsh is never spoken by the child.

The mean scores of the groups, together with the standard deviations on the *Jenkins Non-verbal Scale of Mental Ability*, are presented in Table 4-2. The results show an orderly decrease in intelligence test scores

TABLE 4-2. Mean Intelligence Test Scores for the Four Groups (*Lewis*)

GROUP	MEAN	STANDARD DEVIATION
1	33.30	16.37
2	38.36	15.95
3	38.94	16.26
4	40.98	17.69

with an increase in bilingualism. The over-all differences between the four groups are statistically significant. The results support those of an earlier study by Morgan.[33] There is evidence from Morgan's study that the retardation of bilingual children may result, in part, from the time limit imposed on certain tests. It may well be that bilingual children, required to make a choice between two languages, tend to be slightly slower in solving problems and are thus penalized on all time tests.

SUMMARY

What constitutes intelligence has challenged the thinking of educational psychologists and has encouraged intensive study and research. Although psychologists are not in complete agreement about the essential nature of intelligence, intelligence tests have furnished considerable information about how it functions at different age levels. The various studies of mental growth agree that growth is rapid during the preschool period. Most of the intelligence tests designed for school-age children make use of language. Thus, mental growth has been closely identified by some students of child development with language development.

The child's mental ability, as measured by intelligence tests, is undoubtedly influenced by many factors. The respective influence of heredity and environment can never be completely separated, a fact perhaps less important than the ways in which they interact. Heredity seems to set forth the broad limits within which mental growth must take place, while environment is influential in determining the manner and extent to which certain abilities might be developed. In a complete evaluation of a child's mental ability at a particular age level, it is essential that performance tests as well as language tests be used.

Studies of the upper limit of mental growth are not wholly in agreement about the time the growth of intelligence ceases. It appears that

[33] E. R. Morgan, "Bilingualism and Non-verbal Intelligence: a Study of Test Results." Pamphlet No. 4. Collegiate Faculty of Education, Aberystwyth (1957).

the child's environment operates throughout life and may have a beneficial effect at almost any age in increasing his scores in specific situations.
The mental growth of different functions will not be uniform by any
means. Much controversy has taken place regarding the constancy of
the IQ. Again, studies are not wholly in agreement. The various studies
reported during the past two decades have offered considerable evidence
that environmental factors as well as the individual's emotional and
physical conditions have an important bearing on the stability of the IQ.
Mental growth curves must take into account these factors along with the
dynamics of the individual child.

Problems and Exercises

1. Collect several definitions of intelligence. What do you find in common
   in these different definitions? What are some significant differences?
2. Look up further data on the development of intelligence tests. What was
   the nature of the early tests? Point out any differences noted between
   the views of early investigators and those of today.
3. What are the advantages of the group tests? What are some of their disadvantages?
4. Describe the general nature of the mental growth curve. How is this related to the principle that all growth is interrelated?
5. Look up the meaning of the term, "IQ." What factors affect the "constancy of the IQ"?
6. How would you account for the differences in the pattern of growth of
   the different mental functions? What are the educational implications of
   these differences?
7. Discuss the role of heredity in mental growth. How has this been studied?
   What are the educational implications of the results or conclusions of
   the studies dealing with this problem?
8. What is meant by the dynamics of mental growth?
9. What conclusions are presented relative to personality and IQ changes?
   How is this related to the dynamics of mental growth?
10. How does the social-class structure affect mental growth? What can the
    schools do to meet the problem of the slower mental growth of children
    from underprivileged areas?
11. How is schooling related to mental growth? What bearing would this have
    on the cessation of mental growth?
12. What conclusions are presented relative to the influence of bilingualism
    on mental growth? What are the educational implications of the findings
    bearing on this problem?

Selected Readings

GOODENOUGH, Florence L., "The Measurement of Mental Growth in Childhood," L. Carmichael, ed., *Manual of Child Psychology*, 2nd ed. (New York:
John Wiley & Sons, 1954), Ch. 8.

JERSILD, Arthur T., *Child Psychology*, 5th ed. (New York: Prentice-Hall, Inc.,
1960), Ch. 17.

JORDAN, A. M., *Measurement in Education* (New York: McGraw, 1953), Chs.
14 & 15.

MILLARD, Cecil V., *Child Growth and Development in the Elementary School,* rev. ed. (Boston: D. C. Heath, 1958), Chs. 6-8.

OLSON, Willard C., *Child Development,* 2nd ed. (Boston: D. C. Heath, 1959), Ch. 5

PRESSEY, Sidney L., ROBINSON, Francis P., and HORROCKS, John E., *Psychology in Education* (New York: Harper & Row, 1959), Ch. 3.

REMMERS, H. H., and GAGE, N. L., *Educational Measurements and Evaluation,* rev. (New York: Harper and Bros., 1955), Chs. 8 & 9.

RUSSELL, David H., *Children's Thinking* (Boston: Ginn & Co., 1956), Ch. 2.

SEIDMAN, Jerome M., *The Child: A Book of Readings* (New York: Holt, Rinehart & Winston, 1958), pp. 250-275.

SMITH, Henry P., *Psychology in Teaching,* 2nd ed. (Englewood Cliffs, N. J.: Prentice-Hall, 1962), Ch. 6.

THOMPSON, George G., *Child Psychology* (Boston: Houghton Mifflin, 1952), Chs. 6 & 10.

WECHSLER, David, *The Measurement of Adult Intelligence* (Baltimore: The Williams and Wilkins Co., 1960), Ch. 1.

CHAPTER 5

Language and Thinking

The language of a society is one of its most important distinguishing characteristics; it is a vehicle for communication, expression, self-realization, and is perhaps our most peculiarly human characteristic. The acquisition of the language of one's culture is an important factor in socialization. It is also through language that a child learns about many aspects of his culture. The scope of language includes speaking and comprehending vocalizations, reading, and writing. Emphasis in this chapter is given to the development of language, influences affecting this development, and the interrelations of language and thinking.

The previous chapter defined intelligence and presented materials dealing with the measuring of intelligence, the nature of mental growth, and the uses of intelligence tests. Since language development and mental development are so closely linked, attention will first be given in this chapter to the variety of mental abilities that may be observed among children and adults.

VARIETY OF MENTAL ABILITIES

Intelligence tests are at best only samplings of certain mental abilities. The fact that correlations between scores obtained from different tests are far from perfect indicates that different tests may be measuring different mental abilities. Intelligence test makers have succeeded, however, in developing tests that furnish a good sampling of abilities important for success in school. Group intelligence tests may well be labeled *scholastic aptitude tests*. In other words, the discrimination value of a good intelligence test is sufficient to enable the teacher or other educator to discriminate, within limits, between those children who are most likely to succeed at school and those who are not.

Complexity of mental development

Mental development, the complexity of which is indicated by the *Primary Mental Abilities Test*, includes the development of memory abilities, attention and concentration, judgment, imagination, concept formations, creative abilities, and other aspects of the mental processes. It also includes the thinking and thought processes Piaget emphasized in his studies.[1] We may see this complexity in the healthy infant of three months. His ability to observe, change expressions, and adapt to changed environmental conditions are evidence of mental activities.

During the preschool years a child's complex mental development is evidenced by the wide range of mental activities he exhibits in his language, play, social behavior, and thought processes. His growing attention span also furnishes additional evidence of his development. Jersild has suggested that during this period the child develops into a thinking creature. Materials presented later in this chapter on language development, vocabulary growth, and thinking ability during the preschool and early years support this belief.

Varieties of mental development. Most tests of mental ability attempt to measure a number of different abilities. Samples of tests of mental development by Buhler, by Bayley, and by Gesell for young chil-

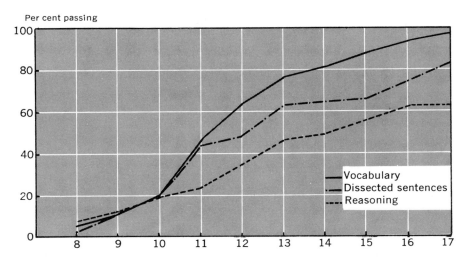

FIGURE 5-1. Growth In Three Mental Abilities—Vocabulary, Dissecting Sentences, and Reasoning *(After Conrad, Freeman, and Jones)*

[1] Jean Piaget, *The Language and Thought of the Child* (New York: Harcourt, Brace & World, 1926).

dren reveal the complex variety of mental abilities that appear in young children, especially by the time they reach kindergarten and school age. There is evidence from a number of studies that individual differences in different mental abilities increases with age. We may note this from an examination of children in three mental abilities—vocabulary, dissecting sentences, and reasoning—shown in Figure 5-1.[2] The rapid growth in vocabulary throughout late childhood is here shown, while there is a much slower development of reasoning ability. The development of reasoning ability depends upon a combination of factors and conditions with training and experience playing an important part. It seems likely that special abilities may be more influenced by training than the general ability described by Spearman. Thus, where training in tasks requiring special abilities is involved, one would expect individual differences between these abilities to increase with age. Subsequent materials dealing with the development of language and thinking will throw additional light on this problem.

Not only do children grow mentally at different rates, but the developmental pattern of different functions is also different. The growth curves of three of the eleven tests of the *Wechsler Intelligence Scale for Children,* presented in Figure 5-2,[3] show the general trend and pattern of mental growth during the elementary-school years. These curves show roughly the proportion of fifteen-year mental maturity attained at the different ages. The early rate of mental growth for digit span is faster than that for the other processes studied. By seven and a half years of age, the average child has reached a level of maturity in this ability not reached in the other mental functions until the age of nine and a half and ten and three-quarter years. The continuous development of vocabulary from age five to fifteen shows how important language becomes as the child grows toward maturity.

Language and intelligence. The development of language approximates the development of intelligence and is usually regarded as one of the best indices for evaluating intellectual growth and development. The intimate relationship of language achievement to intelligence is exemplified in a study by Clymer.[4] He used Stanford-Binet mental ages as a criterion for comparing two groups of fifth-grade students.

[2] H. S. Conrad, F. N. Freeman, and H. E. Jones, "Differential Mental Growth," *Yearbook of the National Society for the Study of Education,* Vol. 43 (1944), Part I, pp. 164-184.

[3] D. Wechsler, "Intellectual Development and Psychological Maturity," *Child Development,* Vol. 21 (1950), pp. 49-50.

[4] Theodore Clymer, "A Study of the Vocabulary of the California Test of Mental Maturity, Elementary, Language Section," *The Eighteenth Yearbook of the National Council on Measurements in Education,* 1961, pp. 125-135.

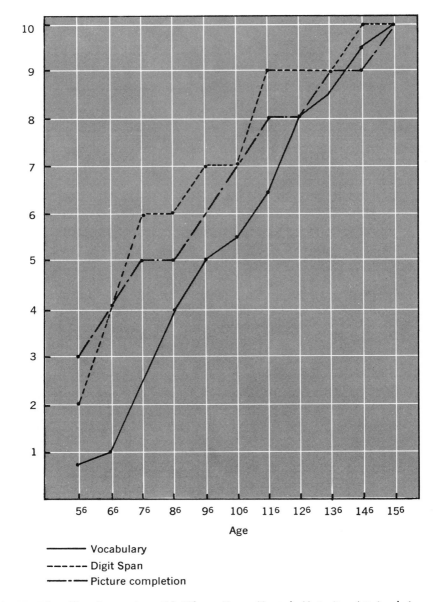

Vocabulary
Digit Span
Picture completion

FIGURE 5-2. The Proportion Of Fifteen-Year Mental Maturity Attained in Different Mental Functions At Various Age Levels *(After Wechsler)*

The *low* Binet group had an IQ of 92.7 while the *high* Binet group averaged 133. Both groups were administered the language section of the *California Test of Mental Maturity.* The results, presented in Figure 5-3,

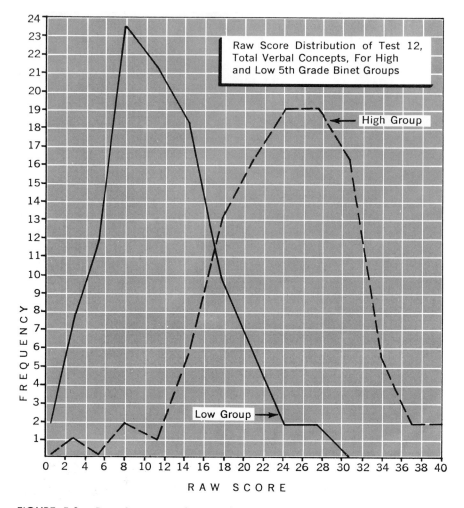

FIGURE 5-3. Raw Score Distribution Of Test 12, "Total Verbal Concepts" For
High And Low Fifth Grade Binet Groups *(Clymer)*

illustrate the differences in total verbal concepts found in the two groups.

We may note a further indication of the relationship of language to group intelligence tests from an examination of materials included in a group intelligence test. Some language items from the *California Test of Mental Maturity*, listed in Table 5-1, show that the affective use of words is very important to the person taking the test. The verbal tests correspond closely with the types of work required of students in the academic school program. Thus, one would expect language test scores, group intelligence test scores, and school achievement to be related.

TABLE 5-1. Verbal Test Items from the *California Test of Mental Maturity*

Tickets to a show cost 10 cents. Jim bought 2 tickets. How much did he pay for them?

alarm—blame, signal, address, comfort

Jack runs faster than Harry.
Bert runs faster than Harry.
Which is the slowest of the three?
Bert—Jack—Harry

The name of the story read to you a while ago is—
The Guide
A Summer's Outing
In the Rockies
The Pack Train

Language development in early childhood

Acquisition of speech. Babbling is a form of vocal activity which is produced voluntarily, but without involving significant meaning or associations. Generally the age of babbling is between the third and twelfth months, although many infant sounds that resemble babbling continue after the first birthday. Babbling is a form of play involving sound, and occurs during periods of contentment, especially when the youngster is alone. Because it is not associated with particular objects, people, or situations, it cannot be thought of as real speech. With maturation and practice the infant increases the variety of sound combinations and acquires increased variations in speech and inflections. Thus, the babbling sounds take on a sort of word-naming tone. When others give attention to these sounds, the infant tends to use them in a greater variety of situations, including social situations.

The process by which the infant moves from babbling to naming is unknown. It has been speculated that his mother may say the proper word often enough so that he begins to discriminate the proper sounds, and by trial and error succeeds in reproducing them. The recognition he receives from making a sound meaningful to others probably serves to reinforce his efforts. Thus, it is likely that imitation and conditioning play important roles in the acquisition of language. Parents and siblings in their normal conversation repeat many words which the infant hears and imitates.

The period between the ages of twelve and eighteen to twenty months is usually regarded as the period of speech readiness. During this time, even though they usually lack oral language, most children are able to communicate many of their needs and desires to other members of the family. The ability to articulate is not so well developed at this age. One investigator found that she was able to understand only 26 per cent of the vocalizations of children eighteen months of age, whereas at two years of age this had increased to 67 per cent.[5] Growth in comprehensibility and accuracy of pronunciation is shown in Figure 5-4. The accuracy of pronunciation lags far behind that of understandable responses.

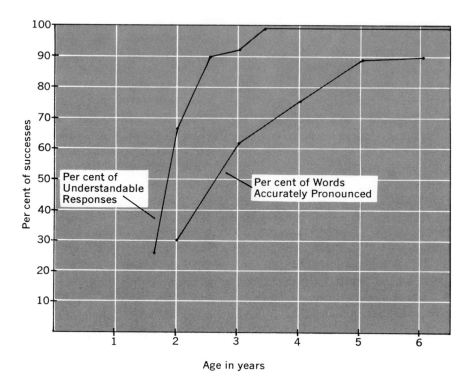

FIGURE 5-4.   Growth In Comprehensibility And Accuracy Of Speech (Data from McCarthy)

Children at this age need encouragement to talk and good models to imitate. Criticism of a child's pronunciation, or unwillingness to listen to a child trying to talk are detrimental to his language and mental development. One of the authors knew a young woman who asked her pediatrician when her child would learn to talk. In discussing the question with her the pediatrician elicited the information that the mother

[5] Dorothea McCarthy, *The Language Development of the Preschool Child.* Institute of Child Welfare Monograph Series, No. 4 (Minneapolis: University of Minnesota Press, 1930).

rarely spoke to her child because she felt he wouldn't understand what was being said. A normal child's failure to talk during the period of speech readiness may lead to behavioral maladjustments. Since talking is an important way of expressing feelings and needs, frustrations and emotional disturbances may result from its delay. Except in cases of mental deficiency or auditory difficulties, delayed speech generally stems from a lack of opportunity to learn to talk, and a lack of motivation; it is often symptomatic of poor or faulty parent-child relationships. It has been found that children who lack language models develop incomprehensible "private speech."

The amount and kinds of language the child possesses at various ages, such as the number of words in his vocabulary, his ability to utilize complete sentences, his preponderant use of various types of words, and his grammatical usage, have been measured. These studies have thrown light upon the development of the child's oral language.

The speech of young children varies from that of adults both in quantity and quality. Strauss and McCarus [6] offer a possible explanation. They state that the language of the child—much of which is developed between the ages of one and three years—consists in naming and labeling his activities for retention as he verbalizes his percepts. On the other hand, the adult uses language to communicate. For communication to be effective, ideas must flow two ways; but the child is really only concerned with himself, so language does not represent communication in the adult sense.

Vocabulary development. During the past twenty-five years, a number of studies have been made to determine the size and quality of the vocabularies of both children and adults. Unfortunately, there is a great variation in the findings of these studies. Differences in sampling procedures and in methods employed for obtaining data probably account for the different results. Analyses of various types of writings, such as themes or letters, tend to yield somewhat different word-counts than those obtained from oral conversations. Similarly, variations in scoring and in interpreting results account for some differences. When a child is very young, it is possible for us to count all the words he uses. Later, when his vocabulary is rapidly increasing, we must use other methods. Then problems relating to eliciting responses (the use of word lists or pictures), the acceptability of the responses (whether to accept synonyms, explanations, or illustrations), and the extent of the child's understanding (the child may be able to use the word or recognize it only when it is in context), make the study of vocabulary development difficult.

Generally, studies of vocabulary development reveal a consistent

[6] T. A. Strauss and E. McCarus, "The Linguist Looks at Aphasia in Children," *Journal of Speech and Hearing Disorders,* Vol. 23 (1958), pp. 54-58.

growth in vocabulary with age. Smith [7] studied 867 pupils in grades one through twelve. Her results revealed a fairly steady growth of vocabulary from grade one through twelve. At all grade levels overlapping of

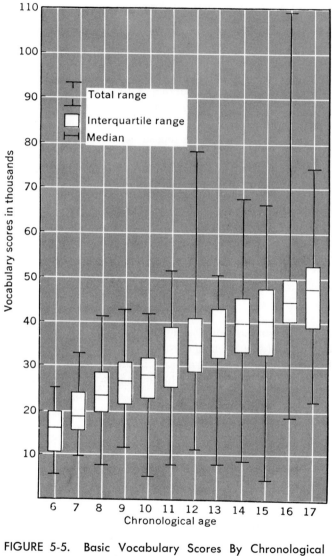

FIGURE 5-5. Basic Vocabulary Scores By Chronological
Age Groups (Smith)

[7] M. K. Smith, "Measurement of the Size of General English Vocabulary Through the Elementary Grades and High School," *Genetic Psychology Monographs*, Vol. 24 (1941), pp. 311-345.

vocabulary was noted. Figure 5-5 shows the basic vocabulary scores she obtained for various chronological age groups.

Seashore [8] used a vocabulary test consisting of 89 items in which pictures were used to give the child an opportunity to display his knowledge of words. The test was given individually to 117 children ranging in age from four to ten years. The following estimates of vocabulary size were based on the results of this study:

Age 4	5,600 basic words
Age 5	9,600 basic words
Age 6	14,700 basic words
Age 7	21,100 basic words
Age 8	26,300 basic words
Age 10	34,300 basic words

Sentence development. Before the age of two, the child generally uses one word to do the work of an entire sentence. By the time he is three and one-half years old, sentences average between four and five words, and by five years the average is between five and six words.[9] Hahn [10] found that sentence length varied with the situation. When her first graders were talking before their peers in a show-and-tell lesson, their sentences averaged 10.4 words; but when these same children were conversing with an adult, the average length was slightly less than seven words. Templin [11] examined 50 remarks made to an adult by boys and girls who ranged in age from three to eight years. The results were similar to those of other studies and revealed that a general tendency exists for the number of incomplete sentences to diminish in the child's conversation as he grows older. Table 5-2 shows this decreasing trend in the use of incomplete sentences, along with an increasing trend in the use of compound and complex sentences for the children from five to eight years old.

Qualitative differences in children's speech. It has been suggested previously that there seem to be certain qualitative differences in the speech of young children and adults. Usually the child does not develop fluency in all aspects of language at the same time. During the preschool period the child tends to learn the names of objects and persons first.

[8] Robert N. Seashore, "A New Light on Children's Vocabularies," *School and Society*, Vol. 66 (1947), pp. 163-164.
[9] Florene M. Young, "An Analysis of Certain Variables in a Developmental Study of Language," *Genetic Psychology Monographs*, Vol. 23 (1941), pp. 473-479.
[10] E. Hahn, "Analyses of the Content and Form of the Speech of First Grade Children," *Quarterly Journal of Speech*, Vol. 34 (1948), pp. 361-366.
[11] M. C. Templin, *Certain Language Skills in Children* (Minneapolis: The University of Minnesota Press, 1957), pp. 74-104.

TABLE 5-2. Mean Percentage of Total Remarks in Each Sentence Construction Category (*Templin*)

TYPE OF SENTENCE	CHRONOLOGICAL AGE			
	FIVE	SIX	SEVEN	EIGHT
Functionally complete but structurally incomplete	17.2	9.8	9.0	9.4
Simple without phrases	35.8	38.2	34.1	31.5
Simple with phrases	16.8	20.7	22.8	21.3
Compound and complex	8.7	10.8	11.1	15.0
Elaborated	8.1	11.9	13.4	13.2
Incomplete	12.6	8.6	10.5	9.5

Thus his speech patterns contain a greater number of nouns than verbs.

The lack of pronouns and the preponderance of nouns in the speech of the very young child is quite noticeable. However, pronouns, particularly *me* and *my,* appear with increasing frequency as the child develops a concept of self. By the time the child enters the kindergarten, his use of the various parts of speech approximates that of adults.

There is an increased growth in the size and quality of words in a child's vocabulary with new experiences at school. Feifel and Lorge [12] examined the responses of 900 children ranging in age from six through fourteen years to the vocabulary test of the *Revised Stanford-Binet Test of Intelligence.* The children averaged slightly above 100 IQ, except for those on the fourteen-year level. The children's definitions were studied for their completeness and quality. It was found that children at the age of six and seven years gave the use and descriptive type of response the most frequently. For example, the word *orange* would be defined as *something to eat.* An explanation type of response was rarely used at this age.

The use of explanation-type responses increased slowly and continuously until the age of thirteen, while demonstrational and illustrative responses declined during the 12, 13, and 14 year period. The synonym, although seldom used by six- and seven-year-olds, also became more evident throughout the following years. This may be attributed to the growth of vocabulary and the ability to symbolize things and events in terms of opposites and similarities (see Figure 5-6). This study illustrates the close relationship between language development and mental development. As children mature mentally they become better able to deal with abstract concepts, to use the many word-symbols of their language that make the formation of abstract concepts possible.

[12] H. Feifel and I. Lorge, "Qualitative Differences in the Vocabulary Responses of Children," *Journal of Educational Psychology,* Vol. 41 (1950), pp. 1-18.

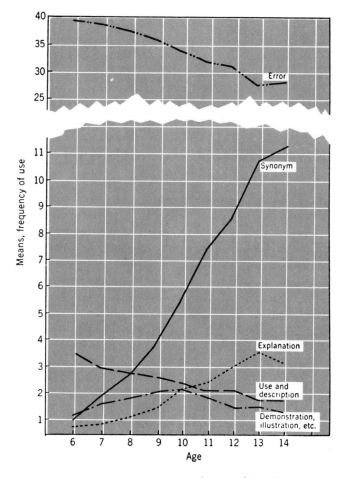

FIGURE 5-6.   Mean Frequency Of Use Of Five Language
Categories By Age *(After Feifel and Lorge)*

Grammatical errors.   The development of language is also determined by the degree to which children at various age levels commonly
employ grammatically acceptable speech patterns. Measures of this aspect
of linguistic development tend to be somewhat less precise than the
procedures described previously. Davis [13] points out that when we appraise a youngster's speech we should consider not only the frequency
with which he incorrectly uses a certain construction, but also the number of times such a construction occurs in a specific sampling. Templin [14]

[13] E. A. Davis, "Accuracy Versus Error as a Criterion in Children's Speech,"
Journal of Educational Psychology, Vol. 30 (1939), pp. 365-371.
    [14] *Op. cit.,* pp. 98-99.

disregarded the relative frequency of the various constructions; instead, she reported the number of times a specific error occurred in 1000 words. In her study the use of *got* for *have* was the most frequent error for all ages. The disagreement between the verb and subject ranked second on the six-year level and third on the eight-year level. Colloquialisms and slang ranked third for six-year-olds and second for eight-year-olds. All errors, except those of colloquialisms and slang, decreased with age. In a study published twelve years prior to Templin's, Carlton and Carlton [15] found that seven kinds of errors made up approximately two-thirds of the total number of errors normal children make. These included the use of double subjects, failure of the verb to agree with the subject in number and person, wrong verb, misuse of *sort of* and *kind of*, confusion in the use of adjectives and adverbs, wrong verb forms, and general redundance. When these errors were compared with those made by children in 1909, it was found that the types of error changed with the times. Double negatives and the use of *ain't* were the two most frequent mistakes children made some three or four decades ago. Inasmuch as the language itself is also affected by cultural patterns, socially acceptable linguistic forms, words, and structure have changed during the period encompassed by the studies.

Studies of grammatical usage not only reveal the developmental characteristics of language but also indicate the popular speech patterns of the subcultural group of which the individual is a member. Teachers often fail to recognize that ungrammatical speech is learned just as grammatical speech is learned. Such studies, however, are valuable in revealing the commonly employed language of certain segments of society and may serve to focus the teacher's attention on the discrepancies which might exist between commonly accepted language standards and the language patterns of certain of her pupils.

The functions of language. Although the number and kinds of words children use may be of interest to students of educational psychology, the question of why and how the child uses language is more significant to an understanding of the dynamics of child behavior. The appearance of Piaget's *The Language and Thought of the Child* presented an analytical approach to a study of the functions of the child's language in his development. Piaget was primarily interested in studying the child's development as a basis for understanding his thought processes. He recognized two types of speech in the child's language—egocentric and socialized speech.

Piaget emphasized the importance of egocentric speech in the child's

[15] T. Carlton and L. E. Carlton, "Errors in the Oral Language of Mentally Defective Adolescents and Normal Elementary School Children," *The Journal of Genetic Psychology*, Vol. 66 (1945), pp. 183-220.

development. Through egocentric speech, according to Piaget, the child "does not bother to know to whom he is speaking nor whether he is being listened to. . . . He does not attempt to place himself at the point of view of his hearer." [16] On the other hand, in socialized speech the child addresses his hearer and tries to influence him or exchange ideas with him. Piaget distinguishes five kinds of socialized speech: (1) adapted information, (2) criticism, (3) commands, requests and threats, (4) questions, (5) answers.

The relation of language and thinking

The symbols children and adolescents most frequently use in thinking are words. The use of words in creative thinking and problem solving will be discussed in chapters 10 and 11. The close relationship of language and thinking was emphasized by Piaget. Other investigators have also recognized this close relationship, although there is considerable disagreement about the extent and nature of this relationship.

The nature of thinking. The role of experience in thinking has been emphasized by many students of education and psychology. What is the nature and content of our experience when we are faced with a problem? We can distinguish two kinds of elements in our experience when we are in a problem situation. First, there are objects in our immediate environment such as doors, furniture, books, and the like. Second, there are images of objects that are not in our immediate environment but which we recall from previous experiences. These were recognized by Dewey in his explanation of thinking in the infant's early experiences.

. . . As soon as the infant begins to *expect* he begins to use something which is now going on as a sign of something to follow; he is, in however simple a fashion, judging. For he takes one thing as *evidence* of something else, and so recognizes a relationship. Any future development, however elaborate it may be, is only an extending and refining of this simple act of inference. All that the wisest man can do is to observe what is going on more widely and more minutely and then select more carefully from what is noted just those factors which point to something to happen.[17]

A typical example illustrating this thought process is the student's observation that the teacher has had a projector brought into the classroom and is about to get a movie screen in proper position in the front of the room. One student may say, "I think we are going to have some pictures shown today." Another student, however, having observed the

[16] *Op. cit.*, p. 9.
[17] John Dewey, *Democracy and Education* (New York: The Macmillan Company, 1916), pp. 163-178.

projector more carefully, states, "Yes, but I think it will be slides rather than a movie." In this illustration inferences are made, based upon the application of past experiences, to objects and conditions in the classroom environment.

The role of words. There are some who hold that the nature and content of thinking bears very little relationship to the nature and content of language. Such a view emphasizes the importance of imagery. The following excerpt from a letter by Einstein to Hadamard furnishes an account of Einstein's thought processes as he himself describes them.

> The words of the language, as they are written or spoken, do not seem to play an important role in my mechanism of thought. The psychical entities which serve as elements in thought are certain signs and more or less clear images which can be "voluntarily" reproduced and combined . . . this combinatory play seems to be the essential feature in productive thought—before there is any connection with logical construction in words or other kinds of signs which can be communicated to others. . . . Conventional words or other signs have to be sought for laboriously only in a secondary stage, when the above mentioned associative play is sufficiently established and can be reproduced at will.[18]

According to this view, the development of a child's thinking and language go along together without a close interrelationship. The acquisition of new words helps him to better communicate his thoughts. Thus, language is a convenient means of communicating thought to self and others.

On the other hand, a number of linguistic studies have been conducted supporting the view that as thought turns from imagery into language it is molded by linguistic forces. Anthropological studies indicate that the nature of a culture affects and is affected by its language. The extent to which language and thinking interact is not clear. However, since language is used to express thinking, there will inevitably be a correspondence between the two. This has been observed by many students of child development and has important implications for the teacher.[19] The child from a substandard cultural environment will probably be seriously handicapped in his language development. Thus, he will find it difficult to express himself in words as well as children from better environmental circumstances. Guidance in reading, televiewing, and in other activities where he will encounter a wide range of words should help him to develop a larger vocabulary.

[18] J. Hadamard, *Psychology of Invention in the Mathematical Field* (Princeton, N.J.: Princeton University Press, 1949).

[19] David Krech and Richard S. Crutchfield, *Elements of Psychology* (New York: Alfred A. Knopf, 1961), p. 473.

Developmental stages in thinking. Most attempts to define developmental stages in thinking will draw on the studies of Piaget. Although most students of child development do not distinguish the different stages as clearly as Piaget did, they recognize his important contribution to our understanding of the language and thought of children.

According to Piaget the language and thought of the child are aspects of the cognitive process. The intellectual development of the child can best be understood through his language and thought processes. In this account he described three levels of intellectual development: (1) sensory-motor activity; (2) egocentric thought and language; and (3) rational thought.[20]

The first, or sensory-motor activity level, is the period during which the infant explores his world, and comes to deal with it as something apart from the self. At this stage he learns that symbols are closely related to the objects and happenings around him. He gradually learns that his world includes others and that he must learn to adjust to their activities. The world, however, is still interpreted largely in terms of the self. Piaget describes language during this period as egocentric, although during early childhood, the child's speech passes from the initial stage of egocentricity to a stage of social egocentricity.

The third stage emerges during the seventh to eleventh years. At this time the child is capable of rational thought, while prior to this stage the child was largely egocentric and incapable of logical thought. There is evidence that, with mental maturity and added experience, logical thought increases while more elementary and egocentric thought diminishes. However, attempts to separate stages as clearly as Piaget did meets with many difficulties.

Preschool children frequently display rational thought in their attempts to solve complex problems within their level of ability. Materials bearing on this will be presented in chapter 11. Studies by Deutsche [21] revealed that different types of explanations of causal relations were offered by students at different age levels. The results of her study suggest that the child's thinking cannot be sharply distinguished from adult modes of thought, although certain types of thinking predominate during childhood and decline during late childhood and adolescence. Other types of thinking, such as logical thinking, tends to increase during the school years.

Interplay of thinking and feeling. A number of early studies of child development show that the intellect lags far behind the emotions

[20] Jean Piaget, *Factors Determining Human Behavior* (Cambridge: Harvard Univity Press, 1937).

[21] Jean M. Deutsche, *The Development of Children's Concepts of Causal Relations.* University of Minnesota Child Welfare Monograph, 1937, No. 13.

during early childhood. More than any other person Piaget systematically presented the view, in his studies, that sustained thinking and problem-solving during childhood lag behind more primitive types of mental and emotional activity. We pointed out earlier that Piaget classified the child's language as largely egocentric. According to early studies by Piaget it is only after the age of seven or eight that the child begins to grow conscious of his reasoning activities. Thus, Piaget saw little evidence of an interplay of feelings and intellectual awareness in which logic and understanding are used.

Later studies have revealed that the child's intellect does serve at a relatively early age to give him a better understanding of himself and the world he lives in. These studies suggest that self-awareness, self-deception, reasoning, and socialized speech develop gradually from a feeble beginning during infancy. These ways of thinking and communicating develop in accordance with principles of maturation and learning suggested in chapter 3. Although egocentricity is marked during early childhood, it is also present to a lesser degree during adolescence and adulthood. Likewise, the feeling states appear early in life, but not in full-grown fashion. Emotional development follows the same growth pattern as other aspects of development, but no age of the child's development can be classified exclusively as an emotional stage, egocentric stage, or logical stage.

Imagination and critical thinking. The development of imagination and critical thinking keeps pace with other aspects of the child's development. The early imagination of the child is sometimes reflected in fantasy, often regarded by adults as lies. The imagination of children is further reflected in art, poems, stories, games, and spontaneous expressions. Although there is a growth in the ability of the child to think critically, we must not assume that imagination and critical thinking develop and function in a void. The interpretation an elementary-school child gives to a picture or behavior act will be determined not only by his mental development but also by his previous experiences with the elements presented in the picture or behavior act. This was observed by one of the writers with a seven-year-old boy who for the first time watched two men take honey from a hive of bees. The boy asked, "What do they use smoke for?" "Well, won't that make the bees sick?" "How did the bees get the honey into that box?" "Where did they carry it from?" "How do the bees carry the honey?"

You will note from this example that the boy was depending upon his language and experiences to think critically.

Imagination at all stages of the child's development will be limited by his experiences. This does not mean that all children with similar experiences will display the same type or amount of imaginativeness. The maturity, mental ability, social climate of the home and school, and sensory abilities will influence the development of imagination and critical thinking. The child also needs guidance and training in critical thinking.

Factors influencing language development

As is true with all aspects of child growth and development, the rate and extent of language development are the result of numerous factors. The close relationship between mental growth and language has been discussed previously. At present, verbal tests and vocabulary tests are among the most reliable and valid measures of intellectual ability available. In using the Stanford-Binet Scale with children, for example, the psychologist usually administers the vocabulary section first because it helps him to determine the approximate basal age of the child. Language development, however, is also affected by maturational factors, which affect the child's general development, and by such environmental factors as the educational level of the child's parents, the sociocultural level of his home, and the parent-child and child-child relationships to which he has been exposed. Some of these factors are discussed in the following pages.

Maturation. The importance of maturation to learning was emphasized in chapter 3. In language, as in motor skills, training at appropriate maturational levels is beneficial. Strayer,[22] using identical twins, found that a maturational advantage of as little as five weeks had a definite influence on the relative effectiveness of vocabulary training. The twin whose practice was delayed not only learned more easily, but also had a pattern of response that was more mature. Many of the studies we have discussed previously also reflect maturational influences. The studies of Young, Hahn, and Davis reveal a developmental pattern of language usage and structure which undoubtedly is affected by maturation.

First grade teachers have recognized the importance of maturation in language learning as demonstrated by their extensive use of *reading readiness* measures. Almost all first grade teachers employ grouping techniques so that they can adjust their instructional methods to children of varying degrees of maturity.

Sex differences. Sex differences in language development may be related to maturation. Girls tend to develop language facility more rapidly than boys during the preschool period. This more rapid development has two noteworthy features. Girls tend to vocalize at an earlier age and also seem to progress more rapidly in total language develop-

---

[22] Lois C. Strayer, "Language and Growth: The Relative Efficiency of Early and Deferred Vocabulary Training Studied by the Method of Co-Twin Control," *Genetic Psychology Monographs,* Vol. 8 (1930), pp. 209-319.

ment than boys. By the time they enter the first grade, girls tend to have greater fluency and to possess larger vocabularies than boys. Girls also tend to enunciate more clearly and distinctly, make use of a greater number of words, and employ longer sentences when speaking. This observed language advantage is thought to be indicative of a more advanced reading readiness and has led some educators to conclude that this factor is a basic reason why more boys than girls have difficulty in mastering fundamental reading skills during the primary grade period.

McCarthy summarized the results of a number of studies, each of which compared the mean length of responses, which she judged to be the best single index of the linguistic ability of boys and girls. She discovered that in the 64 comparisons, 43 favored the girls, 3 were identical for each sex, and 18 favored the boys. McCarthy concludes that "Whenever groups of boys and girls are well matched in intelligence and socioeconomic background, and when the situation in which responses are recorded does not tend to favor the interests of one sex or the other, there appears slight differences in favor of girls." [23]

It is difficult to determine the exact extent to which the language superiority of girls remains apparent throughout the total developmental period. Generally it appears that at all age levels girls tend to have greater verbal facility than boys. Not all studies, however, have substantiated this generally held belief. In McCarthy's summary there were 14 comparisons with children who were five and a half years of age or above; of these, seven favored boys. One study,[24] in which written and tape-recorded oral language activities of fourth-, fifth-, and sixth-grade pupils were studied, little sex-based differences were found. It was concluded that the slight sex differences found at these grade levels represented a manifestation of boy-girl competition rather than actual sex differences in language.

It seems likely that sex differences in language ability tend to decrease with age, although girls appear to maintain a slight advantage throughout their lives. It may be that maturational factors account for these conditions during early childhood, and that cultural factors play a role in helping them to maintain a superiority in a somewhat lesser degree during the adolescent and adult periods.

Environmental factors. Many environmental factors appear to influence the language development of children. Most of these factors affect the child's opportunities for learning language. The child who is brought up in a home where the language he hears is limited to simple communi-

[23] Dorothea McCarthy, "Language development in children," in L. Carmichael, *Manual of Child Psychology*, 2nd ed. (New York: John Wiley & Sons, 1954), p. 577.
[24] Tondow Murray, *A Study of the Oral and Written Language of Children in the Fourth, Fifth, and Sixth Grades in Various Social Situations*. Ph.D. dissertation, University of Southern California, 1953.

The language development of children is stimulated by creative activities of a cooperative nature such as those involved in the use of the Whopper Blocks

cation about rather concrete ideas or objects, does not have many opportunities for learning words or expressions that are more abstract. If the language his parents employ is grammatically incorrect, or loaded with slang and colloquialisms, the child naturally will learn these speech patterns.

Irwin [25] compared the language development of children whose parents were engaged in professional or managerial positions with that

[25] O. C. Irwin, "Speech Development in the Young Child: Some Factors Related to the Speech Development of the Infant and Young Child," *Journal of Speech and Hearing Disorders*, Vol. 17 (1952), pp. 269-279.

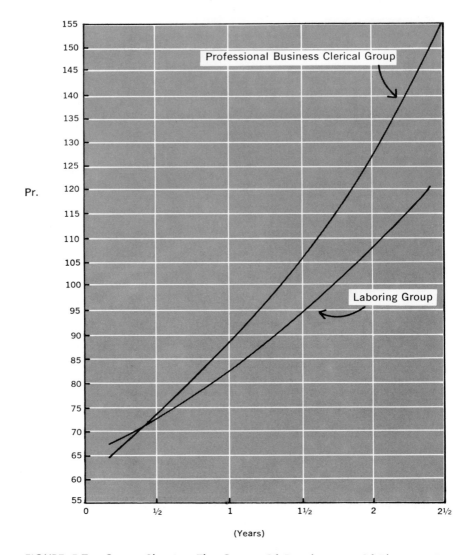

FIGURE 5-7. Curves Showing The Course Of Development Of Phoneme Frequencies During The First Two And One Half Years Of Life In The Speech Of Infants Reared In Homes Of Different Vocational Status

of children whose parents were employed at lower-status occupations. At an early age significant differences in their speech production were noted. These findings are illustrated in Figure 5-7. Irwin felt that parental stimulation was an important variable in the language development of children in the six- to thirty-month age group.

Similar results were found in an earlier study which compared the language of children from diverse social groups. For a period of time the nursery school at the University of Georgia was run as a Federal Emergency Relief Project. During this time the customary tuition fees were discontinued and only children from families on relief were admitted. Young [26] compared language records made for 74 of the nursery school youngsters, half of whom attended when tuition was charged and half of whom attended later. The tuition group surpassed the relief group in every aspect of language analyzed. These findings were verified by another study [27] of young children in which it was noted that those from a high socioeconomic status communicated in longer units with a greater variety of words. Schulman and Havighurst [28] found that such differences persisted even after a considerable amount of schooling. They administered vocabulary tests to 16-year-olds; the results indicated differences for the various socioeconomic levels.

It is interesting to speculate whether such differences result from fundamental differences in the language spoken in the children's homes, or whether they result from the different child-rearing attitudes or adult-child practices found at various social levels. Generally, the child from a higher socioeconomic home has greater opportunity for free oral expression and interaction with his mother and father than does the lower-class child. Probably a number of factors are related to these findings: there are fewer cultural opportunities in the homes of the less financially and socially fortunate; there are fewer activities and opportunities for travel, and fewer materials such as books, magazines, and pictures to evoke more elaborate speech patterns. Also, examples of good speech are less apt to be available in the home. What effect will improved standards of living have on the language development of children from the lower socioeconomic groups in the future? Will the increasing availability of television and other mass media of communication also affect their language development? These are interesting questions for speculation.

Ordinal position in the family. Children learn language through contacts with other people. If relationships with parents are important, it would seem to follow that contacts with other children may also be important. Unfortunately, additional study is needed before the exact effects of sibling relationships can be established. Some studies have indicated that the language development of twins is somewhat slower

[26] Florene M. Young, "An Analysis of Certain Variables in a Developmental Study of Language," *Genetic Psychology Monographs,* Vol. 23 (1941), pp. 3-141.

[27] Fred Rosenthal, "Some Relationships Between Sociometric Position and Language Structure of Young Children," *The Journal of Educational Psychology,* Vol. 48 (1957), pp. 483-497.

[28] M. J. Schulman and R. J. Havighurst, "Relations Between Ability and Social Status in a Midwestern Community: IV. Size of Vocabulary," *Journal of Educational Psychology,* Vol. 38 (1947), pp. 437-442.

than that of singletons, but few investigations have been concerned with other sibling relationships.

In an early study [29] of the language development of twins, 20 pairs of twins were tested yearly from ages two to five. On the average it was found that twins began to talk one month later than their older brothers and sisters and also revealed a slight but somewhat consistent retardation in their language development during the preschool period. Another study [30] that included children between the ages of five and ten supported these results. However, by the age of nine and a half years, twins from the upper occupational groups had practically overcome their handicap, while those from the lower occupational groups were still inferior in their development.

Evidence is still scanty regarding the rate of language development for only children as compared with that of children in other ordinal positions within the family. We may speculate that the younger child has a greater opportunity to learn because of contacts with an older sibling who has mastered speech. However, some evidence shows that the oldest child may develop at a faster rate. The study by Sears and others [31] indicated that first-born children, particularly boys, are given special attention by their mothers. This attention results in considerable instruction and mature verbal stimulation which leads to greater word understanding. Some evidence also indicates that an only child may develop language faster than the child with siblings. The same explanation given above may account, in part, for this advantage. It is likely, however, that socioeconomic and other factors enter the picture as well. A higher percentage of only children are generally found in homes of higher socioeconomic levels than at lower socioeconomic levels. Children with siblings usually develop some portions of a "private language," comprehensible only to themselves.

Lack of reinforcement. Additional information concerning the effects of environmental conditions such as institutional living upon language development has been obtained in studies by Goldfarb.[32] He found a marked difference in the ability to make speech sounds, in the intelligibility of speech, and in the level of language orientation between

[29] E. J. Day, "The Development of Language in Twins: I. A Comparison of Twins and Single Children," *Child Development,* Vol. 3 (1932), pp. 170-199.

[30] E. J. Day, "The Development of Language in Twins: II. Their Resemblances and Differences," *Child Development,* Vol. 3 (1932), pp. 298-316.

[31] R. R. Sears, J. W. M. Whiting, V. Nowlis, and P. S. Sears, "Some Child Rearing Antecedents of Aggression and Dependency in Young Children," *Genetic Psychology Monographs,* Vol. 47 (1953), pp. 135-236.

[32] W. Goldfarb, "Infant Rearing and Problem Behavior," *American Journal of Orthopsychiatry,* Vol. 13 (1943), pp. 249-265; —————, "Effects of Psychological Deprivation in Infancy and Subsequent Stimulation," *American Journal of Psychiatry,* Vol. 102 (1945), pp. 18-33.

those youngsters who spent the first three years of life in an institution and those who, at an early age, were placed in a foster home. Scores from tests administered seven months after foster home placement to children between six and eight years of age, and repeated at adolescence, indicated that the children institutionalized until the age of three remained deficient in language ability years later. Since only a few children were involved in this study, and since those placed in foster homes at an earlier age had higher intelligence ratings, it is difficult to determine how much of the retardation was caused by the institutional environment. However, other studies tend to confirm Goldfarb's findings. Moore [33] compared the language abilities of orphanage and nonorphanage children of the same chronological and mental age. Her findings showed that the nonorphanage group was superior in all aspects of language tested.

Bilingualism. The effects of bilingualism upon language development have been studied by several investigators. Generally, it has been found that children from homes in which two languages are spoken tend to be retarded in the rate and extent of their development in either language when they are compared with children brought up in monolingual homes. Some investigators assume that these findings may result from the bilingual children's tendency to intersperse words from both languages in their speech and confuse the grammar and syntax of one language with the other language. It is more probable, however, that early bilingualism is conducive to superficial linguistic production.

Smith [34] studied a group of bilingual children ranging in age from approximately three years to six and a half years. She gave the children English and Chinese vocabulary tests in an effort to compare the development of bilingual and monolingual children. Although the parents of these bilingual youngsters were somewhat more successful, the children's vocabulary in neither language approximated the norm for the monoglots of the same chronological age. When the vocabularies were combined for each child, however, the scores, on the average, were almost as high as the norms and two-fifths of the individual ratings exceeded the norms. When duplicate meanings were deleted, the group average fell to about 80 per cent of the estimated norm and only one-sixth of the individual children exceeded it. Smith concluded that it would appear unwise to start any but superior well-adjusted children in learning two languages during early childhood or pre-school years. It has been found

[33] J. K. Moore, "Speech Content of Selected Groups of Orphanage and Non-Orphanage Pre-School Children," *Journal of Experimental Education,* Vol. 16 (1947), pp. 122-133.

[34] Madorah E. Smith, Measurement of Vocabularies of Young Bilingual Children in Both the Languages Used, *Journal of Genetic Psychology,* 1949, Vol. 74, pp. 305-315.

that bilingual children tend to be handicapped in their performance on intelligence tests. This was noted by Anastasi and Cordora [35] in their investigation of the effects of bilingualism upon the intelligence test performance of 176 Puerto Rican children enrolled in grades six through eight. It is likely that the slower development of vocabulary previously discussed may account in part for these findings. Cultural differences may also play an important part.

Speech disorders

Speech is produced by the movements of the organs of articulation, that is, the jaws, lips, tongue, and soft palate. Any failure of these organs to make the correct movements may result in an articulatory defect. A child's speech is closely associated with his aspirations, his attitudes, and his feelings, and the way they interact on his development. Speech is part of his general behavior pattern and can never be separated from the *self*. Anything that affects a child's well-being may also affect his speech. Thus, the child who is having difficulty with his speech may also be struggling with other problems. Since successful personal and social development is dependent, in part, upon normal speech development, a discussion of the more common speech disorders should prove helpful to prospective teachers.

Types of speech disorders. Problems of speech disorders may be roughly divided into two groups: (1) those found among children with limited or distorted speech; and (2) those present among children who stutter. It is evident that disorders of speech may result from such organic defects or conditions as cleft palate, cerebral palsy, nasal obstruction, muscle paralysis, and laryngeal difficulties. Speech and language disorders have been classified by Karlin as follows:

1 Delayed speech—retardation in acquisition and use of words
2. Articulary disorders—the distortion, omission, and substitution of consonant sounds
3. Voice disorders—the absence of voice or abnormal production of the qualities (intensity, pitch, or melody) of voice
4. Cluttering—rapid speech, associated with slurring and distortion of sounds
5. Stuttering—disorganization of the rhythmic flow of speech
6. Aphasia—disorders of linguistic symbolization [36]

Immature speech. Kindergarten and first-grade children frequently substitute one sound for another. This may be observed with the child

---

[35] Anne Anastasi and Fernando Cordora, "Some Effects of Bilingualism upon the Intelligence Test Performance of Puerto Rican Children in New York City," *The Journal of Educational Psychology,* Vol. 44 (1953), pp. 1-19.

[36] Isaac W. Karlin, "Speech- and Language-Handicapped Children," *Journal of Diseases of Children,* Vol. 95 (1958), p. 372.

who substitutes *w* for *l* and *r*. Instead of *run* he says *wun*, and instead of *log* he says *wog*. The normal process of maturation, along with correct examples, will usually remedy this. Davis has presented the ages at which most children are able to articulate certain sounds. *S's* and *Z's* are listed at two age levels because difficulties in correctly articulating these sounds frequently appear among eight-year-olds when they lose their front teeth.

3.5 years:	*b, p, n, w, h*
4.5 years:	*t, d, n, g, k, ng, y*
5.5 years:	*f, v, s, z*
6.5 years:	*zh, sh, l, th* (as in then)
8.0 years:	*s, z, r, wh* [37]

Roe and Milisen [38] noted that substitutions characterize the faulty speech of children from grades one to six. They state, "Children up to the fourth grade do make improvements in articulation of individual consonant sounds without formal speech practice."

Lisping. Lisping is frequently found among preschool children and among those in the lower grades. It includes the inability to pronounce certain letter sounds or combinations of letter sounds, as well as a tendency to omit, transpose, or make slurring sounds. Such speech is the most characteristic feature of baby talk and is found in a greater or lesser degree among very young children. When it persists beyond the age of five or six years, the condition may be looked upon as a special speech difficulty. The frequency of this condition decreases rapidly in the upper grades of the school. Garrison and Force state:

The undue persistence of lisping may be attributed to (1) lack of practice in the proper use of the articulatory organs, due to bad models in the child's language environment; (2) weakness of the auditory centers; (3) incomplete development of the speech organs; (4) anatomical abnormalities of teeth, lips, tongue, jaws, soft or hard palate, nasal or pharyngeal cavities, etc.; or (5) a general deficiency of the motor centers.[39]

The child's ability to articulate consonant sounds accurately and distinctly furnishes a partial basis for judging his physical, mental, and emotional maturity. By the time a child is three and a half years old he

[37] Irene Poole Davis, "The Speech Aspects of Reading Readiness," *Newer Practices in Reading in the Elementary School,* Seventh Yearbook, Department of Elementary School Principals, National Education Association, 1938, pp. 282-289.

[38] Vivian Roe and Robert Milisen, "The Effect of Maturation Upon Defective Articulation in Elementary Grades," *Journal of Speech Disorders,* Vol. 7 (1942), pp. 37-50.

[39] Karl C. Garrison and Dewey Force, *The Psychology of Exceptional Children* (New York: The Ronald Press, 1959), p. 288.

Special Education Department
Charlotte-Mecklenburg County Schools

Many children with speech problems are given special help by teachers trained in this work

should use the sounds *m*, *p*, *b*, and *w* correctly and consistently in words. Children in the kindergarten and lower elementary grades derive satisfaction, as well as develop speech skills, by listening to and imitating the sounds of the things about them. A trip to the country or to the zoo brings them into contact with the sounds animals make: the *moo-moo* of the cow; the chirping of the bird—*peep, peep, peep;* the barking of the dog—*bow-wow, bow-wow;* and the buzzing of the bee—*b-z, b-z-z*. Certain objects in the environment produce sounds whose imitations require much skill, as the ticking of the clock—*tick-tock, tick-tock,* the buzzing sound of the airplane—*b-z-z-z, b-z-z,* and the ringing of a bell—*ting-a-ling, ting-a-ling.*

Stuttering. A child's speech reflects his emotional and personality characteristics. We observe this with children who stutter. Such children repeat speech sounds rapidly and compulsively under muscular tension. The entire body functions in the act of stuttering, not just some discrete phase of it, like the speech apparatus. It usually has its onset between the ages of two and four, and frequently, experiences in this period have a deep seated effect upon the individual and keep the stuttering in force. It differs from lisping in that it frequently increases, at least up to the age of ten or eleven years, from grade to grade.

Studies bearing on the incidence and causes of stuttering have produced some interesting and worthwhile results. In the first place, statistical evidence shows that stuttering tends to run in families. That some children of a family, where one of the parents is inclined to stutter, develop the tendency to stutter while others from the family do not indicates that imitation alone is not a sufficient explanation for the onset of stuttering. It appears safe to conclude that there is an hereditary constitutional condition present in some individuals that enables them to develop the habit more readily than the average person.

It seems unlikely, however, that a child would develop the habit if his general environment were completely satisfactory. Moncur [40] concludes that a syndrome of environmental factors precipitate and aggravate the stuttering condition. They are parental domination, overprotection, oversupervision, the setting of excessive standards of performance, and adverse criticism. Such conditions tend to produce nervous tension likely to set off the beginnings of stuttering.

Speech defects and mental retardation. It was suggested in the previous chapter that a close relationship exists between mental growth and language growth. Studies of speech defects among mentally retarded children show that the incidence of such defects is considerably higher among them than among children of average intelligence. According to Gens,[41] 70 to 75 per cent of institutionalized mentally deficient children have some kind of speech disorder. The articulation profiles of 209 mentally retarded school children from 7 years and 3 months to 17 years and 5 months in eighteen classes in Kern County, California, were studied by Russell.[42] The IQ range of the group was from 40 to 79, with a mean of 65.5. A matched group of children showed a greater incidence of errors typified by indistinct sounds. This may be accounted for by their larger vocabulary and inability to pronounce certain words in their vocabulary. In the case of vowel errors Russell noted that there were approximately four times as many distorted sounds among the retarded than among the matched group. No significant sex difference in articulation errors were noted, although the mean number of errors was slightly higher for the

---

[40] J. P. Moncur, "Parental Domination in Stuttering," *Journal of Speech and Hearing Disorders,* Vol. 17 (1952), pp. 155-165.

[41] George W. Gens, "Speech Retardation in the Normal and Subnormal Child," *The Training School Bulletin,* Vol. 48 (1952), pp. 32-36.

[42] Hugh K. Russell, *Articulation Profile of 209 Mentally Retarded Children.* Seminar in Special Education Report, San Francisco State College, 1952.

boys. The mentally retarded children also showed a significantly greater number of consonant errors than did the matched group of children.

SUMMARY

Language development during the preschool years furnishes a clue to the child's intellectual development. The development of comprehensible speech, in particular, is rapid during this period. Language development is not only important in learning, but it is also important for the child's socialization and thinking. The social development of the child may be noted in certain changes in language behavior. The five- and six-year-old is quite egocentric compared to the eight- and nine-year-old. The young child defines words by the use or description of the objects they symbolize. The explanation type of response grows until the child is 13 or 14 years of age.

There is a high correlation between the various language abilities. This has important implications for the teacher concerned with guiding pupils in the language arts. The importance of maturation and experience in language development is emphasized throughout this chapter. The language development of girls, particularly the length of response, exceeds that of boys, although this difference appears to decrease with age. Home conditions, including bilingualism, have an important influence upon language development.

Language concepts and symbols play an important role in both cognitive and connotative thinking at all age levels. The number and extent of an individual's vocabulary as well as the number and variety of associations he has with each word are positively correlated with a number of abilities. The exact nature of such relationships is not thoroughly understood at present.

Anything that affects the child's well-being will also affect his speech. Thus, a close relationship exists between favorable home conditions and freedom from speech disorders. Generally, speech continues to improve gradually and continuously up to the fourth grade. Studies indicate a low negative relationship between intelligence and speech defects, and also indicate that children with speech defects tend to be retarded in their school work. With age, the frequency and types of speech errors found among preschool and elementary-school children change. From six to eight years of age, for example, errors in the production of nasals, fricatives, and semivowels decrease markedly. Speech problems, particularly stuttering, appear to reflect the child's emotional and personality characteristics; a close relationship exists between these conditions and the child's feelings of insecurity or rejection.

Problems and Exercises

1. Trace the development of language during the preschool period. What factors in the child's environment affect his language development?
2. What is the relation between language and intelligence? Why, then, is language not a safe index for judging a child's intelligence?
3. How is language related to thinking? Cite an illustration to show how thinking would be seriously affected by an inadequate vocabulary.
4. What effect do you feel the mass media such as television and radio have upon the language development of the preschool child? Of the fourth-grade child?
5. What are the major speech difficulties among first-grade children? Just when should a speech difficulty be considered serious?
6. Consider a stutterer with whom you are familiar. Under what conditions does the individual tend to stutter most? Would you regard the individual as a nervous type? What explanation, if any, do you offer to account for his stuttering?
7. Do you believe that a second language should be taught to elementary school children? At what grade level should it be taught?
8. What percentage of instructional time do you think should be devoted to each one of the language arts at the first grade level, the fourth grade level, the sixth grade level, and the eighth grade level?
9. What are some possible explanations for the high correlation between measures of intelligence and language ability?
10. How can a teacher help a bilingual student to improve his language?

Selected Readings

HURLOCK, E. B., *Child Development* (New York: McGraw, 1956), Ch. 6.

McCARTHY, Dorothea, "Language Development in Children," in L. Carmichael, ed., *Manual of Child Psychology*, 2nd ed. (New York: John Wiley & Sons, 1954), Ch. 9.

MARTIN, W. C., and STENDLER, C. B., *Child Behavior and Development* (New York: Harcourt, Brace & World, 1959), Ch. 15.

MILLARD, C. V., *Child Growth and Development* (Boston: D. C. Heath, 1958), Ch. 7.

PEEL, E. A., *The Pupil's Thinking* (London: Oldbourne, 1960).

RUSSELL, David H., *Children's Thinking* (New York: Ginn & Co., 1956).

SMITH, Henry P., *Psychology in Teaching*, 2nd ed. (Englewood Cliffs, N. J.: Prentice-Hall, 1962), Ch. 11.

THORPE, Louis P., *Child Psychology and Development* (New York: The Ronald Press, 1955), Ch. 7.

YOUNG, Florene M., "Language Growth and Development," in K. C. Garrison, ed., *Growth and Development* (New York: Longmans, Green & Co., 1952).

CHAPTER 6

Socialization and Its Role

The development of the individual as a social creature proceeds apace with the development of his status as an independent person, distinct from others. Interwoven with the growing child's earliest experiences, and intimately related to his security and survival, are close ties with others, especially the adult members of his family. As he matures, he becomes conscious of himself as a separate being; the quest for independence evolves, and he begins to assert himself.

The developmental tasks of learning to get along with others and learning an appropriate sex role appear relatively early in life. They become more important when the child enters school, and take on added meaning and increased importance during late childhood and adolescence.

SOCIAL DEVELOPMENT

The social development of the child, like other aspects of development, proceeds from the interaction of the organism with his environment. Although the readiness of the organism is the first requisite to social interaction, children must still learn to be socially responsive and interactive. The wide differences among children and adolescents contribute significantly to the range of social behavior in any school-age group. These differences flourish under the influence of democratic practices. The teacher, to be effective with pupils, must recognize these differences if she is to guide each individual in his growth and learning according to his unique abilities and traits.

The biological nature of man

All humans belong to one biological family although several distinct races exist. The differences among the races such as blood type, rate of maturation, and psychological needs are not important physiologically. Although we may observe important differences among school-age pupils, far more important are the similarities among them appearing even during infancy.

All normal infants whine when they are hungry and depend upon others for food. No race differences are discernible in maturational pattern, brain pattern, or in the time when puberty or adolescence is reached. Upon this common inheritance of brain structure, man has developed a consciousness of self, social customs, an advanced culture, and a complex civilization. However, the average person does not always recognize this commonality of man. It is certainly present in the findings of scientific studies and in the normal precepts of religious teachings which emphasize the brotherhood of man.

The nature of the group

The nature of man leads to the formation of groups, a type of human relationship most useful for study. Group activities play an important role in the lives of boys and girls because through such activities are many of their needs satisfied.

We can distinguish two kinds of human relationships, *primary* and *secondary*. Primary relationships are the deeply involved ties the individual forms with his family. In former agrarian societies, most of the individual's relationships were primary. The people with whom the child lived, played, attended school, went to church, and visited were his kinfolk, his neighbors, and others he knew intimately.

Secondary relationships are those in which people are brought together in a common activity; their interest in each other are limited largely to the activity they are involved in as a group. Because populations in the United States are more mobile than ever before, secondary groups have become important, and their study will prove useful to us.

Since the nature of man leads to the formation of groups, the child must learn to adjust to varying secondary groups largely in terms of what each member of the group expects or demands of him. Certain forms of behavior may be tolerated or even expected in one group situation, while unacceptable in others. The problem of learning to adjust to groups with different expectations and demands makes growing up difficult for the child.

Roles and social behavior. In describing the social development of the child, the sociological concept of *status* and *role* are helpful. Status refers to the place an individual occupies in a particular system at a particular time. Closely related to one's status are the different roles one must learn. Society judges an individual's behavior in terms of the appropriateness of his role behavior. Role refers to the sum total of the cultural patterns associated with a particular status.[1] Such factors as age, sex, and family relations determine the individual's status; since each status is associated with a role, the individual's behavior is learned on the basis of his statuses. The individual's behavior is also judged by society's expectations of what that behavior should be. In modern society an elementary-school child is expected to behave respectfully to an adult, merely because he is younger and less experienced. Children and adolescents who are disrespectful of their teachers fail to play their roles properly. Boys are expected to be somewhat more unruly or aggressive than girls; if they are not, parents tend to worry about them. On the other hand, overactive, aggressive girls are regarded as tom-boys and their behavior tends to be discouraged.

From infancy throughout life, the individual learns to play certain roles. Parents, teachers, other adults, and children tend to judge the growing person according to his success in mastering these roles. When the child or adolescent successfully plays the role expected of him, his behavior is reinforced. When he does not meet the role expectancies, his behavior is discouraged. These experiences have an important bearing on the child's development of a *self-concept*. In the home the child may be the center of attention; he may dominate others, and may form an idea of himself as the center of most activities. In his social relations outside the home, however, he may find himself avoided and rejected by other children. Thus, he withdraws from group activities and assumes a different role from that in the home.

A child develops social roles in activities outside the home by the way he interacts with other children. If he wins leadership and prestige roles and plays them successfully, his confidence is enhanced and leadership characteristics are developed. The experience of participating in group activities and being evaluated by others have a powerful influence on his developing self-concept, the social roles he plays, and the aspirational level he develops. This has been noted in studies of children and adolescents.

Susie's family lives in a six-room house. She is seven years old, has an older sister and a younger brother, and sleeps in the room with her older sister. Susie plays well with the other children of her grade (grade 2). She is inclined to suggest the games to play and knows how a number of different games are played. The other children accept her leadership, and she is resourceful enough to provide many suggestions for the group. She likes to sit by Tom, and this seems to please him, since Susie is regarded by the group as a leader. Susie realizes that she has considerable prestige with her group, and plays her role well.

[1] Ralph Linton, *The Cultural Background of Personality* (New York: Appleton-Century-Crofts, 1945), pp. 76-77.

As children develop physically, mentally, emotionally, and socially they are faced with the task of adjusting their behavior; old roles are modified or abandoned, and new ones must be mastered. Much of the child's self-concept stems from his success in mastering appropriate role behavior.

Sex identification. An important factor in the development of the child's self-concept is his ability to identify with his sex. A boy must learn to think of himself as a male if his behavior is to be appropriate. Similarly, a girl must see herself as a female if she is to assume her appropriate sex-roles. Thus must children identify with their own sex long before they enter school. Katcher [2] investigated the ability of four-, five-, and six-year-old children to discriminate sex differences. He used a series of colored pictures which permitted the children to determine sex by their hair style, clothing, breasts, and genital organs. He found that errors in discrimination decreased with age and that there were no significant differences between the ability of boys and girls to discriminate sex differences. Interestingly, he found that clothing, hair style, genitals, and breasts, in that order, made for ease in identification. This study tends to illustrate that young children often respond to sex symbols in identifying sex.

An independent study by Pauls and Smith [3] also indicated that children tend to learn both their own sex roles and what parents expect of them at an early age. An investigation by Rabban [4] explored the influence of social class upon the identification with one's sex role among nursery and lower-elementary-school children. Diverse groups of children differentiated by occupational and community characteristics were studied. Pairs of toys were validated for use as cultural media invested with sex-appropriateness. The results show that boys are more clearly aware of sex-appropriate behavior than girls in both middle-class and working-class groups. Also, boys and girls of the working-class group are earlier aware of sex-role pattern than are boys and girls of the middle-class group. Concerning age differences Rabban concludes:

(a) Three-year-old boys and girls of both groups show incomplete recognition of sex differences and as a group are unaware of any appropriateness of sex-typed objects.

(b) The fourth and fifth years are periods of growth in clarification of sex role for working class boys, while the sixth year is particularly significant for middle class boys.

[2] Allan Katcher, "The Discrimination of Sex Differences by Young Children," *Journal of Genetic Psychology,* Vol. 87 (1955), pp. 131-143.

[3] Lydia B. Pauls and W. D. Smith, "Sex-role Learning of Five-year-olds," *Journal of Genetic Psychology,* Vol. 89 (1956), pp. 105-117.

[4] Meyer Rabban, "Sex-role Identification in Young Children in Two Diverse Social Groups," *Genetic Psychology Monographs,* Vol. 42 (1950), pp. 81-158.

(c) Working class girls accept the sex-appropriate patterns by six years of age, but middle class girls do not fully acquiesce to the definition of appropriate sex-patterning even by the eighth year, when all other groups have accepted the social expectations.[5]

Consciousness of group membership. Very early in the child's life, group membership begins to function. Favorable attitudes are established toward certain groups while unfavorable attitudes are established toward other groups. It has been pointed out that small children are largely free of prejudices. Certainly no child inherits the prejudices of his parents through the germ plasm. Two questions may be considered about prejudice toward other groups among children and adolescents: When does prejudice toward other groups appear? How is this prejudice acquired?

A study reported by Radke-Yarrow [6] sheds some light on the first question. Using a questionnaire, she obtained responses from adults about the beginning of their prejudice toward certain minority groups. She concludes, from studying their responses, that during early childhood (seven- and eight-year-olds in her study), they begin to feel the minority status of these groups. Increasingly, with advancing age, children begin to see their affiliation with one group, while a gap gradually develops between them and certain other groups.

Prejudice toward other groups is learned and is not different from other learnings. It is perhaps more complex and more subtle than much of the learnings involving motor skills and understanding. It seems likely that much prejudice has its roots in stereotyped concepts regarding the role and status of different subgroups. Prejudice frequently reflects basic personality characteristics, illustrating further the unity of character and personality. This was observed in the findings of one study in which children who were most fearful, least confident and secure, and more suspicious of others displayed the greatest intolerance toward Negroes and Jews.[7]

Awareness of race. Several studies have indicated that children in America become aware of racial differences at a relatively early age. Stevenson and Stewart [8] used tests to determine children's ability to discriminate physical differences between Negroes and whites. The tests also elicited attitudes toward race. A group of 125 white and 100 Negro

[5] *Ibid.*, p. 141.

[6] Radke-Yarrow, M. J., "Developmental Changes in the Meaning of Minority Group Membership," *The Journal of Educational Psychology*, Vol. 44 (1953), pp. 82-101.

[7] Dale B. Harris, "Children's Ethnic Attitudes: Relationships to Certain Personality Factors," *Child Development*, Vol. 21 (1950), pp. 83-91.

[8] Harold W. Stevenson and Edward Stewart, "A Developmental Study of Racial Awareness in Young Children," *Child Development*, Vol. 29 (1958), pp. 399-409.

children between three and seven years of age were tested. They found a rapid increase with age in the ability to discriminate among the children of both races. White children tended to develop discrimination at a younger age than Negroes, and Negroes tended to assign negative roles to Negro children more frequently than whites assigned such roles to white children. It seems likely that these findings reflect differences in past learning and experiences of the two groups of children.

Cooperative behavior. Most of the play of two- and three-year-old children is parallel play, with few indications of true cooperation. With increased maturity cooperative play appears, especially when the child has had opportunities to be with older children. Cooperative group activity is rarely understood before the child is six or seven years old. Of course, there is more cooperation among friendly groups than among those less friendly.

As children grow, cooperativeness and the ability to play together without supervision increases. Leadership characteristics are evident even among kindergarten children, the roles of leader and follower varying with the situation. Cooperative behavior improves as the child advances through the elementary-school grades. The nature and extent of cooperativeness at a given age will depend on the maturation and experiences of the child, and the social climate of the particular situation.

Competition versus cooperation. The relative influence of a competitive and a cooperative social climate upon the behavior and performance of children was studied by Stendler, Damrin, and Haines.[9] The children's behavior in painting a classroom mural was compared when they worked for a prize and when they worked cooperatively to create a mural which, if judged satisfactory, would bring a prize to each member of the group. It was observed that during cooperative activity, there was relatively more friendly behavior, more mutual help, and more sharing of ideas and materials. On the other hand, during the competitive activity, there was relatively more unfriendly behavior, obstruction of the work of others, and general refusal to share materials.

Although many teachers and adults believe that competitiveness is part of man's hereditary nature, it is important for us to recognize that research findings fail to support this belief. Those who have visited among the Eskimos or Australian aborigines are often amazed at their lack of competitiveness. Mead [10] has pointed out that members of cer-

---

[9] Celia B. Stendler, Dora Damrin, and Aleyene C. Haines, "Studies in Cooperation and Competition: I. The Effects of Working for Group and Individual Rewards on the Social Climate of Children's Groups," *Journal of Genetic Psychology,* Vol. 79 (1951), pp. 173-197.

[10] Margaret Mead *et al.,* *Cooperation and Competition Among Primitive Peoples* (New York: McGraw, 1937).

tain tribes in New Guinea are strikingly noncompetitive in their relations with each other. It is interesting to note that in the study by Leuba [11] rivalry was found among all children born in the United States, where competition is part of the social structure from the first year of life. No signs of rivalry were observed in the foreign-born children's performance. Furthermore, it has been noted that a child might be highly competitive in one group and quite cooperative in another, depending largely upon the demands and structural composition of the particular group.

It appears likely that the tendency for children to compete or cooperate arises not only from their learning and experiences, but is also intimately related to their self-concept, attitudes, and needs. The child who has unsatisfied needs for love and affection will likely be less able to cooperate than the child who is secure. The parent and teacher should focus attention upon the individual—John or Sally—rather than compare him with others.

The development of social compliance. Little attention has been given to the question of how social compliance or noncompliance develops in children, and the role of parents, teachers, and peers in this development. One study of this question involved 50 children from three through eight years of age. [12] The children were studied in two separate groups. A younger group of 20 children, three, four, and five years old were enrolled in the Fels Experimental Nursery School during the regular school year. A second group of 30 children six, seven, and eight years old attended the Fels Day Camp in early summer after the regular schools had closed.

During the Nursery School and Day Camp sessions, the children's interactions with peers and teachers were carefully observed, and rated on a rating scale entitled, *Compliance with Commands and Suggestions From Others.* This scale measured the frequency and enthusiasm with which each child acceded to the demands and suggestions of other persons. Each child's social behavior was also available from the pooled judgments of two observers.

The findings from this study showed that the degree of social compliance was not a function of either sex or intelligence at the ages studied. At the nursery school age it was noted that children's compliance with their mothers at home correlated significantly with their compliance toward adults. However, this was not so for peer-compliance.

[11] Clarence Leuba, "An Experimental Study of Rivalry in Young Children," *Journal of Comparative Psychology,* Vol. 16 (1963), pp. 367-378.

[12] Vaughn J. Crandall, Sonya Orleans, Anne Preston, and Alice Rabson, "The Development of Social Compliance in Young Children," *Child Development,* Vol. 29 (1958), pp. 429-443.

By Day Camp age the magnitude of compliance had become more generalized and consistent across situations (from home to Day Camp) and people (from adults to peers). We may observe this in the correlations presented in Table 6-1, showing the relationships of children's compliance toward mothers and their social compliance at the Fels Institute.

TABLE 6-1. The Relationships of Children's Compliance Toward Mothers in the Home and Their Social Compliance at the Fels Institute (*Crandall, Orleans, Preston, and Rabson*)

GROUP	PERSONS INTERACTED WITH AT THE FELS INSTITUTE	CORRELATION
Nursery School	Peers	.21
Nursery School	Adults	.37
Day Camp	Peers	.51
Day Camp	Adults	.60

The question may be raised, Why do some children show more compliance than others? This study showed that the attitude of the mother towards compliance was important, especially among the Day Camp children. The investigators conclude: "By early grade school age, mothers' socialization attempts do seem to affect their children's general social compliance; before, they do not—or at least there is no evidence in the present study that they do." [13] In general, maternal rewards for compliance predicted the children's social compliance outside the home better than did maternal punishment for noncompliance. The role of learning is clearly revealed in this and other studies involving compliance. This study also suggests that reward is superior to punishment in the acquisition of compliant behavior, although the role of punishment in developing compliance among children of school age cannot be overlooked. Punishment may appear in many different forms, and may come from parents, teachers, other adults, and peers. As the child develops throughout the elementary-school years the influence of those outside the home, particularly peers, becomes greater in producing compliant behavior.

Social-sex development. It was once believed that the child was nonsexual and that the sexual urge or drive remained dormant until the time of the glandular changes signifying the appearance of adolescence. It is now generally recognized that sex feelings as well as sex drives have their beginnings early in life. This recognition has brought about a

[13] *Ibid.*, p. 441.

Sex differences in interests and activities are frequently insignificant
among seven-year-olds

Sex differences in interests become more pronounced during
late childhood

changed attitude toward the social-sex development of children. The modern school attempts to direct the child's growth in his understanding of sex differences and sex feelings, rather than assume an attitude of censorship toward all ideas, feelings, and actions related to sex.

The manner in which a preadolescent reacts to sex situations will depend largely upon the attitudes he forms during his earlier years. Thus, there will be important differences in the social-sex pattern found among preadolescents with different backgrounds of experiences. The preadolescent is faced with a number of developmental tasks in his social growth. He must learn to get along with his peers and must assume an ever-increasing responsibility for the solution of his problems. He must resolve conflicts that emerge between the teachings at home, at school, and among his peers, and must learn to play his sex-role as a part of his preparation for adolescence.

The beginning stage of dating. One of the basic developmental tasks adolescents must learn is to get along with members of the opposite sex. When the teen-ager has his or her first date the parents begin to realize that their son or daughter is actually growing up. The majority of boys and girls have their first formal date on such occasions as school picnics, school parties, movies, and church activities. Sometimes the first date is complicated by advice from parents or teasing from peers. The first date is often a cooperative activity, involving members of cliques of the opposite sex. Parents and teachers should realize that this is an important step in the transition from childhood to adolescence. Some characteristics that frequently appear in connection with first dates are shyness, fear of doing the wrong thing, fear of saying something the other person won't like, and overcautiousness.

Dating practices vary with culture and social class. There is, however, a widespread tendency for youngsters in urban areas to "go steady" —date one person exclusively. In some high schools it is estimated that two-thirds of the students go steady, despite objections voiced by parents, teachers, ministers, priests, and other adult leaders. Three objections have been raised to the custom of going steady. First, it is pointed out that keeping company with the same person of the opposite sex frequently leads to sexual intimacies. The Roman Catholic church in particular emphasizes this danger, especially with immature youngsters. The second objection relates to the developmental task of learning to get along with members of the opposite sex. The teen-ager needs contacts and social experiences with different members of the opposite sex to learn more about them and to be able to make sound decisions about marriage at a later date. Third, going steady at an early age is likely to lead to an early marriage and interfere with the further educational growth of the teen-agers. Concerning this Burchinal concludes from a study of this problem, "Girls who married prior to high school graduation, on the average, started dating and going steady at an early age, had more steady boy friends, and felt that they had been in love with a larger number of dates and steadies than the control groups of nonmarried secondary school-age pupils." [14] The higher divorce rate among those who marry early indicates further that such marriages are not based upon a sound foundation.

Going steady occurs mainly because of group pressure, or for the social approval and prestige it gives. Socially ambitious mothers, in particular, are anxious for their daughters to be popular and to enjoy the prestige that having a desirable date conveys to their mind. Going steady also guarantees the girl a date for any social function she may attend. Teen-agers give two reasons for going steady. First, they feel they are in love and prefer each other's company to the exclusion of others. Second, they need the assurance that they will have a date. "It makes me feel secure," is their argument, and besides, "everybody does it."

The role of the family

Studies of early home influence on the personal and social adjustments of children and adolescents have furnished considerable evidence that satisfactory adjustments are closely related to the extent basic needs for affection, security, status, and belongingness are met during the early years of life. Families which do many things together, where everyone participates in the varied home activities, produce well-adjusted and happy children. Children reared in such homes tend to catch the spirit of the home and develop good dispositions and favorable outlooks upon life. On the other hand, parents who display habits of selfishness, and who are unable to accept their children as unique personalities may well hinder their personal and social adjustment, and consequently, their outlook and disposition.

Influences of the family. A study by Carlson [15] had for its hypothesis that parental attitudes would, in part, determine aspects of the child's self-concept and social status. Forty three sixth-graders completed a questionnaire specially designed to furnish descriptions of the self and the ideal self. Their mothers and fathers completed the same questionnaire. The findings confirmed expected interrelationships among children and parents in their self-acceptance, social orientation, and peer status.

Children's roles tend to become specialized in large families, whereas the only child becomes the center of attention in a large percentage of single-child families. The specialization of roles found in large families

[14] Lee G. Burchinal, "Adolescent Role Deprivation and High School Age Marriage," *Marriage and Family Living*, Vol. 21 (1959), p. 384.
[15] Betty Rae Carlson, *Parent-Child Relationship and the Self Concept of Children*. Ph.D. Dissertation, University of Michigan, 1958.

is a natural outcome of the division of responsibilities and actvities made necessary by the size of the family. Bossard and Boll point out that, "very early in life, a child acquires a special personality, which comes to be recognized by the family members as well as by other persons subsequently." [16]

Koch [17] noted that children more frequently listed members of their own sex as preferred playmates and best friends. Also, where a child's sex was different from his siblings, he tended to prefer playmates of the opposite sex. Among children with siblings of the same sex, the preference was more frequently for playmates of the same sex. Preference for friends and playmates of the same sex tended to increase as the age difference between the child and his sibling increased.

Parental authority patterns. Almost all children are dependent upon their parents to some degree. During the long period of infancy, parents succor the child, furnish the necessities to sustain life, and provide most of the affection and emotional support the child gets. As the child develops physically, emotionally, and socially, he becomes less dependent upon his parents for the satisfaction of his needs. Some children become more independent earlier than other children. Although a number of factors are important in determining the development of independence in children, the child-rearing attitudes and practices of the parents seem to be very important.

The effects of domineering and autocratic parents on the personal-social development of children have been studied by a number of investigators. The results of a number of these studies have been summarized by Radke.[18] He noted that the following behavior characteristics frequently appeared among children from domineering and from autocratic homes.

DOMINEERING PARENTS	AUTOCRATIC PARENTS
Quarrelsome	Don't get along with other children
Uncooperative	Noncompliant
Tense	Emotionally unstable
Bold	Uninhibited
Disinterested	Inconsiderate
Undependable	Insensitive
Shy, submissive	Nonrivalrous
Polite	Unpopular
Self-conscious	

[16] James H. S. Bossard and Eleanor S. Boll, "Personality Roles in the Large Family," *Child Development,* Vol. 26 (1955), p. 71.

[17] Helen L. Koch, "The Relation in Young Children between Characteristics of Their Playmates and Certain Attributes of Their Siblings," *Child Development,* Vol. 28 (1957), pp. 174-202.

[18] M. J. Radke, *The Relation of Parental Authority to Children's Behavior and Attitudes* (Minneapolis: University of Minnesota Press, 1946), p. 103.

In a more recent study Gough, Harris, and Martin [19] found that children from homes where parents expected prompt and unquestioning obedience, were more prejudiced against other groups of people than children from homes where parents assumed a more democratic attitude toward their children.

Parental expectations. A real problem exists for the child from the lower-class family who often must adjust to the middle-class standards and ways of behaving imposed by the school and teacher. Children, however, face the problem of living up to the expectations of their parents, who sometimes overestimate and often underestimate their children's capabilities. Langford and Alm [20] compared the judgment of a group of parents with the feelings of their twelve-year-old children regarding their self and social adjustments. They found that parents tended to underestimate their children's feelings about self adjustment in areas like self-reliance, sense of personal worth, feelings of belonging, and freedom from nervous tension. Similarly, the parents tended to overestimate their children's feelings about social adjustment in areas like adherence to social standards, extent of social skills, freedom from antisocial tendencies, and compliance in family and school relations.

Establishing independence—the task of emancipation. The child should become increasingly more independent as he grows toward maturity. However, the task of emancipating himself from home ties is more difficult than this statement implies. The following factors and conditions complicate the task of equipping and guiding the child and adolescent toward greater independence:

1. Parents' hesitation in giving up their control.
2. Parents' failure to guide the child and adolescent in developing habits of responsibility.
3. The existence of small families whereby much attention is centered on each child.
4. The prolongation of economic dependence on the home.
5. The attitudes of parents toward adolescent behavior and parental controls.

Learning to let go means, for the adolescent, throwing off childhood habits of dependency with the security that accompanied these habits. His emancipation from almost complete supervision to independence should be a gradual process, begun during childhood by the parents

[19] H. G. Gough *et al.,* "Children's Ethnic Attitudes: I. Relationships to Certain Personality Factors," *Child Development,* Vol. 30 (1959), pp. 83-91.

[20] Louise M. Langford and O. W. Alm, "A Comparison of Parent Judgments and Child Feelings Concerning the Self Adjustments and Social Adjustments of Twelve-Year-Old Children," *Journal of Genetic Psychology,* Vol. 85 (1954), pp. 39-46.

and developed through planned education for *initiative* and *responsibility*. With the adolescent caught between new urges and old habits, one cannot help but realize the need for sympathetic understanding and wise guidance by parents and adult leaders.

What then are some desirable procedures to follow in guiding a growing child into a socially adequate and responsible youth? This is not a simple question; neither is there a simple answer. That habits of independence should begin in childhood has already been suggested. With further development, responsibilities and privileges should be increased. The adolescent should be brought to realize that with freedom goes responsibilities. The growing child will need more spending money, which can be increased as he grows older. Again, the adolescent should be given greater freedom in selecting his friends. The parents can function effectively here through early training in ideals; for the present situation they can provide encouragement and a favorable setting for desirable friends whom the child has chosen. The adolescent wants greater freedom, for example, in buying his clothes or in doing his Christmas shopping. The family budget will, in itself, tend to put a limit on the amount of spending money the adolescent may have. Also, his ability and opportunity to earn money is a factor to be considered. Too close supervision on how the money is spent tends to create tensions and annoyances which largely defeat the purpose of an allowance.

Not only are parents inclined to thrust their ideals and way of life upon their children, but they may lay out certain educational and vocational plans and try to make their teen-agers conform to them. Sometimes such plans represent the parents' unfulfilled desires, or the parents' wish to enhance their position with their associates and friends. The vocational plans of the adolescent should be made by the adolescent himself, with the aid, of course, of parents, teachers, and other adults who may be able to help him make a sound vocational choice. Parents may also have certain ideas about what their children should study, and sometimes force them to study particular subjects without explanation. It is in matters of advice that parents can best serve. To the extent that parents use reason and understanding based on fairness and truth, and control their emotions and feelings, their advice becomes sound.

The role of the school

The education and training of children appears to be a function of all societies regardless of how primitive or how civilized they are. In the more highly civilized societies like the United States, the school becomes an important institution. Its influence is felt either directly or indirectly, from infancy throughout a major part of one's life. Its importance as a socializing agency stems from the fact that upon reaching school-age, the child spends more of his waking hours at school than at any other place.

Effects of nursery-school training. The importance of the early childhood years on the personal-social development of the child has been emphasized by educators, psychologists, and others who have worked with children. The results of an intensive investigation by Van Alstyne and Hattwick [21] bear out the importance of early adjustments in relation to subsequent adjustments in the elementary school. They conducted a follow-up study of 165 elementary-school children who had had nursery school training. They noted that children classified as well-adjusted in nursery school were also classified as well-adjusted in the elementary school, while those classified as poorly adjusted in the nursery school were classified as poorly adjusted in the elementary school.

The early findings on the effects of nursery-school attendance and later school adjustments are further supported in more recent studies by Bonney and Nicholson. They conclude from their studies that ". . . if early socialization experiences are going to possess significant carry over values into subsequent years they probably will need to be of a particularly high quality-level in reference to interpersonal rapport between the pupils and their adult supervisors and also in regard to adequate provision for meeting the varying needs of individuals." [22]

Entrance into school. Entrance into school has many implications for the child: he comes into contact with new adult authorities such as his teacher and principal. Prior to school entrance, his contacts with peer groups have also been very limited. Stendler and Young [23] interviewed the mothers of children entering first grade to discover the effects of school entrance on their children. Their findings may be summarized as follows:

1. In general children look forward to beginning first grade; they regard this as an important stage in growing up.
2. Upon entering school children show evidence of significant changes in their self-concept. They begin to feel more important.
3. Upon entering school children's behavior tends to improve in traits like responsibility, helpfulness, good humor, and independence.

[21] Dorothy Van Alstyne and L. A. Hattwick, "A Follow-up Study of the Behavior of Nursery School Children," *Child Development*, Vol. 10 (1939), pp. 43-70.

[22] Merl E. Bonney and Erite L. Nicholson, "Comparative Social Adjustments of Elementary School Pupils With and Without Preschool Training," *Child Development*, Vol. 29 (1958), p. 132.

[23] Celia B. Stendler and Norman Young, "The Impact of Beginning First Grade upon Socialization as Reported by Mothers," *Child Development*, Vol. 21 (1950), pp. 241-260.

4. Most mothers reported no change in their children's attitude toward their authority and importance as compared to the teacher's.
5. In general first-grade children like school; their greatest task of adjustment is in social relationships.

The teacher as an authority-figure. Because she is an important adult authority-figure, the classroom teacher is perhaps the most important influence in the school-age child's social development outside the home. Generally, the child assumes his parents to be the first authorities on almost every phase of life, and he probably has not questioned the validity of their judgments or standards of behavior. When he enters school, however, he is confronted with a new adult authority-figure and finds that he must modify and adjust his behavior to meet her expectations. Often, his teacher has somewhat different standards; she may reward behavior which may not be rewarded at home, or may punish him for behavior which is either rewarded at home or goes unnoticed.

Instead of being the only child, or one of a few, making demands upon his mother or father, he finds himself one of a group of twenty-five or more in a relationship with his teacher that is likely to be less familiar or less close than with the adults at home. If he is older than his siblings and has been accustomed to having his needs gratified immediately he now finds he must often wait his turn. His self-concept undergoes certain modifications and the process of socialization is further developed.

Teacher-pupil relationships. The relationships which develop between pupil and teacher are important indicators of the adjustment of both the child and the adult. Let us, however, consider the effects of these interactions upon individual pupils at different grade levels. Important for the child in the socialization process is learning to modify his behavior so that it meets the expectations of others. This concept of self in a given role may either coincide with or differ from the role expectations of others. An individual will be judged effective in the performance of a given role when his self-concept matches or coincides with what is expected of him by others.

The classroom group represents a social-interaction unit as well as a learning unit. The social role of the teacher remains that of the group leader, although leadership activities appear within the group. The social roles of the pupils making up the group change from time to time and with different learning situations.

Throughout his life the child will learn to play various roles according to the standards and patterns of his culture. The teachers are representatives of different aspects of the cultural pattern in which he lives and learns. When he behaves according to their expectations he is rewarded—considered a phase of reinforcement of certain learnings. When he fails to behave as expected, his behavior is not rewarded.

Socialization, as a result of teacher-pupil relationships, is frequently made difficult because of two conditions. First, the teacher's behavior standards are not wholly consistent, nor in complete agreement with the standards of adult-authority figures outside the school. Second, the interactions of the child with his teachers reflect his previous learning. If he has been overprotected and sheltered at home, he will strive for a similar relationship at school. If he has learned to function within the sphere of a rigid or autocratic atmosphere at home, he will encounter difficulties in a freer, more permissive school atmosphere.

Many children encounter difficulties in school because of their family backgrounds. Since the majority of public school teachers come from middle-class backgrounds, their attitudes and standards of behavior tend to reflect such cultural conditioning. Thus, children from the lower-class often encounter difficulty in adjusting their behavior to the standards imposed by the teacher. The problems may involve differences in religious practices. Children and adolescents whose standards of behavior or dress vary from those of their teachers and peers will find the problems of socialization at school difficult. These problems are intensified during the adolescent years and are closely related to social maladjustments. Such students frequently drop out of school.

Influence of peers

The child's social reactions to other children lag behind his social reactions to adults. However, the social interactions of children are extremely important to their personal-social development.

Early childhood. There is no evidence that infants seek social contact on any particular plane with other infants during the first year of life. Friendly contacts, when they do appear, are limited to smiling, looking, and grasping at each other. After the first twelve or fourteen months the infant begins to shift his attention from the play materials to his play-partner, frequently an obstacle to him in getting play materials. Maudry and Nekula[24] noted, however, that the 19-month-old infant displays more interest in his playmates. At this age the play is personal with little effort made toward cooperative play. After the age of 19 months, children exhibit an increased social orientation in each other's presence. The early social relationships in the home have an important bearing on the social behavior during the preschool period.

The versatility of social interaction with playmates increases be-

[24] Maria Maudry and Maria Nekula, "Social Relations Between Children of the Same Age During the First Two Years of Life," *Journal of Genetic Psychology,* Vol. 54 (1939), pp. 193-215.

tween the second and fifth year. This increase may be observed in the more cooperative nature of social interactions. The youngest children tend to engage either in solitary or in parallel play; older children tend to engage in either associative or cooperative play. At this age boys and girls pay little attention to intellectual differences, physical characteristics, or even sex differences in their social activities. Children at this age are always ready to include others of the same age, physical development, and sociability in their activities. Friendships during the preschool years often show some unique characteristics. The newcomer to the group tends to attach himself to some person who gives him some attention or displays friendliness toward him. At this time, a gradual transition from egocentricity to an increased cooperation and socialization takes place.

Late childhood. By the age of eight the child has, to a marked degree, moved away from close ties with his mother to membership in larger groups composed of his peers—school class, Cub Scouts, religious group. The personal-social developmental tasks become increasingly important during the elementary-school period.

Increased social participation brings with it more opportunities for social conflict. This was observed by Landreth.[25] She reported that 75 per cent of the situations that cause crying in the nursery school involved conflicts between children. The social reactions at a later age involve quarreling, pouting, negativism, and outright fighting.

It was suggested earlier that social participation furnishes opportunities for children to satisfy needs not ordinarily satisfied through other avenues. Elementary-school children form gangs in situations where their needs are not being adequately met through existing agencies. A study of the home conditions of elementary-school gang members usually shows a general lack of supervision or actual neglect. Older gang members establish admission requirements, rules of conduct, and set particular goals. Thus, the group tends to act as a unit. The gang behavior of elementary- and junior-high-school children and adolescents often leads to juvenile delinquency. This may be observed in the behavior of the following junior-high-school gang:

The gang consisted of seven boys twelve, thirteen and fourteen years of age. They came from middle-class homes and lived in the same general area of a city of 60,000. They had a special hideout in a wooded territory, referred to as "The Tiger's Den." The Leader of the gang was a fourteen-year-old boy with average or slightly above average intelligence but with a poor scholastic record. The gang plotted activities against their teachers, which grew more serious during the course of the school year. They were also guilty of minor

25 Catherine Landreth, "Factors Associated with Crying in Young Children in the Nursery School and in The Home," *Child Development*, Vol. 12 (1941), pp. 81-97.

acts of mischief in the neighborhood and in an adjoining neighborhood. They were on one occasion apprehended by a policeman for stealing fruit from a fruit stand. Although the gang did not enter into more serious activities, it could well have done so had not one of the parents become aware of the situation and taken steps with some of the other parents to guide the boys into more acceptable activities, particularly camping during the summer.

Social acceptance. To understand a child one must know how well he is accepted by others, especially his peers. Although a teacher or parent may be able to watch children at play and gather some ideas about how well a particular child is accepted by his peers, they may acquire a mistaken notion about how children actually feel toward each other.

The opinions children and adolescents express about each other furnish us with insight into the behavior patterns that make for acceptance and status within their group. The sociometric technique is an attempt to make use of these opinions in securing an objective method for studying social acceptance. These opinions have been gathered through pupils' choices and through the use of a *Guess Who* type of test. These methods yield reputational scores for the different pupils. They are discussed more fully in Chapter 14.

The sociogram has been used to show the personal-social cliques found among children and adolescents. The sociogram in Figure 6-1 is of a fifth-grade class of girls who were asked to choose the two girls they liked best in their grade. According to this sociogram, Patricia is especially popular with a group of five girls. Those not chosen by any one are sometimes referred to as *isolates*. The alert and understanding teacher will recognize the needs of these girls and take steps to help them make better social adjustments.

A study reported by Gronlund [26] was designed to determine the generality of sociometric choice. Sixth grade pupils were given five sociometric choices for seating companions, work companions, and play companions. The sociometric-status scores of pupils were correlated between the choices of seating companions and play companions, between play companions and work companions, and between seating companions and work companions. These correlations furnish a basis for conclusions concerning the generality of sociometric status in each classroom group. The means and standard deviations of the 240 correlation coefficients resulting from an analysis of 40 sixth-grade classes are presented in Table 6-2. The data of this Table reveal a fairly high degree of generality of sociometric status over all three criteria for both boys and girls, the mean correlations ranging from .76 to .89. Generality is

[26] N. E. Gronlund, "Generality of Sociometric Status over Criteria in Measurement of Social Acceptability," *Elementary School Journal*, Vol. 56 (1955), pp. 173-176.

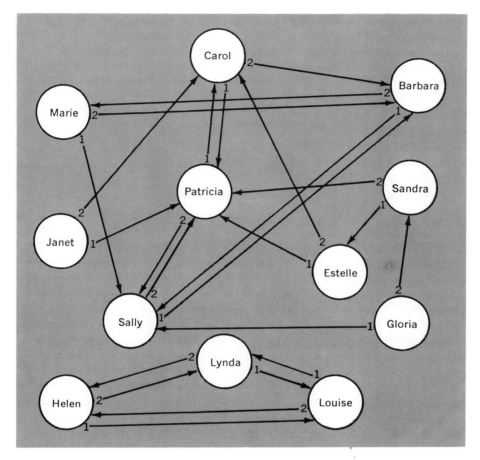

FIGURE 6-1. Simple Sociogram Showing First And Second Choices Of Twelve
Girls From A Fifth-Grade Class

TABLE 6-2. Means and Standard Deviations of 240 Correlation Coefficients of Sociometric-Status Scores Based on Choices
of Companions

	BOYS		GIRLS	
CHOICES CORRELATED	MEAN CORRE-LATION	STANDARD DEVIA-TION	MEAN CORRE-LATION	STANDARD DEVIA-TION
Seating and play	.80	.13	.76	.11
Play and work	.76	.12	.76	.11
Seating and work	.86	.09	.89	.07

highest with seating companion and work companion. The correlations suggest that sociometric choices are somewhat general.

Importance of peers.   At no time is the peer group so important to the individual as during the teen years. The peer group provides the teen-ager with a sense of belongingness at a time when conflicting loyalties, identifications, and values make him unsure of himself. Within the peer group the adolescent can acquire the status often denied him in the adult world—a status which is predictable and based upon values he can understand, and expectations he can fulfill.

The peer group enables the teen-ager to gain social recognition through his personal qualities and achievements, something he cannot get through most formal educational programs. Dating patterns, athletic contests, and other activities build a clear-cut sex role into the self-concept of the adolescent. The boys assert maleness in athletics and the girls compete for prestige through dating and other social activities. In these ways the peer group, far more than the formal school program or even the home, defends the individual through the security of group membership against the uncertainties of adolescence.

Attaining a satisfactory role.   It has already been suggested that peer activities furnish teen-agers opportunities to attain a better understanding of their sex role. This is a very important developmental task adolescents face. The insecure or rejected adolescent finds social development a most unpleasant undertaking, and may try out various adjustment methods in an effort to solve his problems. Studies of adolescents have revealed several important facts about their relation to their peers:

1. The adolescent desires the approval of his peers.
2. The importance of peer approval increases as the individual reaches and grows into adolescence.
3. Preadolescents and adolescents like to imitate their peers or those slightly older than themselves.
4. Good peer relations during preadolescence are perhaps the best assurance available for good peer relations during adolescence and postadolescence.
5. Early adolescence is accompanied by the formation of cliques. These cliques play an important part in satisfying certain needs of adolescents.

Peers versus the home.   Because teen-agers frequently find in their peer groups the sympathy and understanding they cannot find at home, peer involvement becomes an extremely important socializing force. The greater the cohesion and solidarity of the peer group, the greater the extent to which it will take over the role of the family in the socialization of growing boys and girls.

The family and the peer group expect conformity to their ways of behaving. If the teen-ager departs very far from expected ways of behaving, he is likely to be punished, one way or another. In the family group he will most likely be scolded; in the peer group he may be left out or expelled from the group. In a situation known to one of the writers, a teen-age girl was isolated from her peers because of her firm attachment to the religious teachings of her parents and church—teachings which prevented her from studying or attending movies on the Sabbath. She was described by her peers as "narrow" and "fanatic," and was virtually without friends among her age-mates. This was an extreme case; ordinarily the group achieves conformity to its ways by effectively creating a climate of opinion which gently coerces the teenager into acceptance of the group's ideas and ways of behaving.

Unless the parent's standards have become his own, the peer group's definition of situations becomes more important to the teen-ager than those of his parents. He is playing the role for the teen group— by the teen-group's standards; thus, success and failure is judged by teen standards rather than by the standards of parents, teachers, or other adult leaders. This means that parents today have only 12 to 14 years in which to give the child experiences in making decisions about personal and social development.

Involvement in community activities

The growing child lives and learns in his total environment. His behavior patterns and personality development cannot be understood apart from the cultural background in which he lives and learns. As he grows into and through adolescence, his social world broadens. The family group furnishes the major environmental stimulation during the early years. During the preadolescent years the play groups and gangs furnish considerable stimulation. With further growth the social environment broadens so as to include many secondary groups, with the larger cultural pattern of the community exerting an ever increasing influence.

Formation of groups and gangs. Teen-age boys and girls are particularly interested in forming groups, societies, gangs, and clubs. These appear most frequently among heterogeneous groups, such as those found in the large modern high school. Scientific investigations show that as a rule the members of a gang are likely to be of about the same level of intelligence. They usually come from within a limited geographical area and are very apt to be neighborhood affairs. Individuals are affected by the behavior patterns of the gang, and tend to influence the formation of behavior patterns in others by their activities. The group is generally quite similar in its desires, likes, and dislikes; there is considerable social uniformity in its attitudes and ideals. Loyalty to different members of the group reaches a high pitch and may even surpass the loyalty established earlier to such ideals as honesty and truthfulness. It is at this point, in particular, that the teachings at school, in the church, and elsewhere should function.

The structure and behavior of a gang is molded in part through its accommodation to the life of its members. The groups in ghettos, in suburbia, along a business street, in the small town, or in an industrial village vary in their interests and activities not only according to the social pattern of their respective localities, but also according to the layout of the buildings, streets, alleys, recreational facilities, and the general topography of their environments. These conditioning factors within which the children and adolescents live and develop furnish a setting within which gang behavior operates. So marked is the influence of such factors as bodies of water, hills, and plant life in determining the location and character of activities, that in some cities delinquent gangs have been classified on this basis.

It is well for teachers and other adult leaders to realize that gangs represent the spontaneous effort of boys and girls to create a society for themselves where none exists adequate to their needs. They derive from such associative experiences satisfactions they do not get under the conditions the adult society imposes—the thrill and zest of participation in activities involving a common interest. The gang functions with reference to these conditions in two ways: it offers a substitute for what society fails to give; and it provides relief from suppression and unsuccessful activities. It fills a gap and affords an escape. The formation and behavior patterns of gangs furnish a good basis for judging the effectiveness of community and institutional, educational, social, and recreational programs for children and adolescents.

Social-class influences. Many factors in the socioeconomic class group a child belongs to affect his emotional and social development. Some of these factors can be called cultural, since no clear line can be drawn between socioeconomic and cultural influences. Habits of cleanliness, good manners, and tidiness are much more difficult to acquire in a home where ignorance reigns and sanitation is largely unknown. In homes where good manners are of little consequence and financial conditions make it impossible for children to participate in activities with other children of the community, social and emotional development are likely to be retarded. Children in more favorable socioeconomic circumstances are encouraged to be tidy, to display good manners, and to attend school regularly. These differences leave their imprint on the child's emotional and social development.

Social-class influences are reflected in parents' attitudes toward school and in their expectations of their children's educational and social de-

The telephone gives the adolescent a closer relationship with other teen-agers who have the same interests and problems

velopment. This is clearly revealed in a study reported by Stendler.[27] Interviews were held with mothers of first-grade children prior to the child's entrance to the first grade and after he had been in school approximately two months and had received his first report card. An analysis of the results of these interviews showed significant social-class differences. A child's chance of attending preschool decreases as one goes down the social ladder. Parental expectations for their children also become less ambitious as one goes down the social scale, although half of the lower class mothers expressed a desire for their children to finish high school. This contrasts quite sharply with the percentage of lower class children who actually finished high school at the time this study was made. Upper class children were more often taught the alphabet, nursery rhymes, and writing or reading before entering the first grade. Also, middle and upper class parents showed greater concern over school attendance and report cards. Evidence shows that such anxieties and concerns affect the growth and behavior of children and adolescents.

Social-class influences become more pronounced when the child

[27] Celia Burns Stendler, "Social Class Differences in Parental Attitudes Toward School at Grade 1 Level," *Child Development*, Vol. 22 (1951), pp. 37-46.

enters junior-high school. These influences may be observed in the cliques children form, the social activities they pursue, and even in the curriculum pattern. The intra- and interdating patterns of teen-agers closely parallel the clique patterns. In one study of sixteen-year-olds the population was divided into five social-economic classes.[28] A study of dating patterns showed that 61 per cent of the dating was between boys and girls of the same class; 35 per cent between boys and girls of adjacent classes; and 4 per cent between boys and girls separated by an intervening class. There was no dating between members of the polar (extreme) classes. The schools must be cognizant of this condition, if they are to develop an effective social and recreational program. Socialization is made easier when there is increased social solidarity, although this does not lead to a better understanding between individuals from different socioeconomic groups.

Membership in minority groups. As individuals become affiliated with different groups in school and elsewhere in the community, they may develop conflicting loyalties. This is especially true for members of minority groups, since the larger and more inclusive community organizations and agencies are likely to foster ideals and attitudes dominated by the majority element. For children and adolescents from minority groups, adjustment is difficult because it is fraught with more opportunities for conflicts. For example, the attitudes, beliefs, and behavior patterns of teen-agers of Greek-born parents, living in a family culture that is largely Greek but located in a third-generation German neighborhood, would be in conflict with those of other children in the community. Unless the minority group, through family and church, furnish an idealistic and functional program for adolescents, serious conflicts are likely to appear.

Discrimination and hostility directed toward minorities is a major concern of the church, school, and other social institutions. Studies of the formation of attitudes toward racial and religious groups illustrate the principles of learning presented in Chapter 6. These studies also reveal some of the unsolved problems of our society. The nature and cause of prejudices will vary with different groups. Prejudices are likely to be found in some degree in most communities throughout the United States. A child growing up in a town where considerable prejudice exists against him as a minority group member, will feel the effects of this prejudice with injurious consequences for his self-concept as well as his concept of others.

Children who are members of the majority group tend to take on the prejudices of the majority group. Frequently teachers and other adult leaders share many of these prejudices. Those who do not are likely to run into difficulty with the members of the community. In discussing a

[28] A. B. Hollingshead, *Elmtown's Youth* (New York: John Wiley & Sons), 1949, p. 339.

controversial problem, a teacher will feel safe only when he assumes the prejudices of the power-structure of the community. Thus pupils sometimes have their prejudices reinforced by the institutions of the community, including the schools and churches. Some evidence suggests, however, that education contributes to the development of favorable attitudes toward minority groups.

Leisure activities and socioeconomic status. A number of studies have shown that different socioeconomic groups in the United States have different cultures, although these cultures share a common culture including language, political attitudes, interest in sports, food habits, and the like. Thus, one will find groups of teen-agers culturally alike in some ways and culturally different in other ways. An interesting question relating to the interests of adolescents is, What is upward social mobility?

An outstanding feature of the activities of upper-class children and youth is their relative exclusiveness. They attend summer camps where the cost would exclude the major portion of children. They travel to resort areas and stay at hotels patronized by a select group. Often they attend school where only boys and girls from homes like theirs are to be found. They are in many ways protected from the rough edges of life which children from the lower class constantly stumble against. However, they frequently lack the close association with their parents, characteristic of the life of lower-class children.

While the activities of upper-class children and adolescents tend to be exclusive, those of the middle class may best be described as selective. Middle-class children and adolescents are required, because of financial considerations, to use public facilities. They are usually found in the public schools, the public parks, and other public areas. However, a selective process is continuously operating among middle-class children and their parents. The parents try to choose the parks, the playground areas, and the forms of entertainment on the basis of middle-class culture and values. Middle-class parents, especially in modern suburbia, tend to be more discriminating and put greater pressure upon their children to achieve and move ahead socially than do lower-class parents. In suburbia success is usually defined as "moving ahead," failure, as not moving ahead. Parental anxieties and pressures are very great among middle-class families, creating many difficult problems for teen-agers unable to fulfill parental expectations.

The activities of lower-class children and adolescents are generally confined to the areas around which they live. They pursue those activities available to them in nearby playgrounds and sand lots. Welfare services are usually welcomed. Unprotected from the difficulties of life, the boys especially engage in athletic competition and depend upon physical strength and stamina. There is frequently little parental supervision, and usually, few parental barriers to their growth in responsibility.

These differences, although not rigid, are important. The socialization of many lower-class children frequently presents a difficult problem, especially when teachers fail to recognize the nature of parental and peer pressures. The problem of the school is not to attempt to stamp out the influences of the early background experiences, but to enrich these experiences with a variety of worthwhile cultural experiences. This is done by creating a favorable climate for learning and continuously reinforcing the learnings at school.

SUMMARY

The social development of the child follows the principles of development set forth in Chapter 3. The wide differences found among children are a result of heredity, maturation, social experiences, and the dynamics of the individual. From infancy throughout life, the individual learns to play certain roles. An important phase of socialization is learning to play the expected role. Learning to play the sex role, class role, and the role based upon parental expectations appears early in life.

We have emphasized the influence of the family in the adjustments of children and adolescents. Parental authority patterns, parental expectations, family prejudices, and family values influence the child's socialization. Entrance into school is a milestone in the socialization process. Nursery-school training and kindergarten experiences have a bearing on the child's school adjustments. Teacher-pupil relations become very important as the child progresses in school. During the preschool period there is a gradual transition from egocentricity to socialized forms of behavior. Social participation furnishes opportunities for the satisfaction of needs not met at home. During the teen years the importance of peers reaches its peak. Peer activities at this stage furnish the individuals concerned with opportunities to attain a better understanding of their sex roles. Frequently, teen-agers find in their peers the sympathy and understanding they are unable to find at home.

Socialization is affected by all aspects of the environment. The socioeconomic status of the home, proximity to playmates, opportunities for participation in activities outside the home, the mores and customs of the community, and the leisure activities of the children have important bearings on the nature of socialization.

Problems and Exercises

1. What is meant by role? Consider some teen-age child of your acquaintance. What is his role with his peer group? What is his role at home? Why are these frequently very different?

2. What are some things or conditions that affect a teen-ager's role in his group? Illustrate by some example of your acquaintance.
3. Have someone in the class play the role of a member of a minority group. How is this likely to affect his socialization?
4. What is meant by "consciousness of group membership"? Does this have any relationship to role? How?
5. Trace the social-sex development of children from early childhood through the teen years. How is this related to maturation? To home influences? To the customs and mores of the community?
6. Compare the role of the family and the role of peers in the socialization of the child.
7. Study the behavior characteristics Radke noted among children from dominating and from autocratic parents. Do your observations tend to agree with the findings of Radke? Cite examples.
8. What difficulties did you encounter in establishing independence? How can the school help the adolescent establish greater independence, especially when home conditions tend to impede this developmental task?
9. What are some of the socialization difficulties of the child coming from a home where opportunities for socialization have been very limited? Show how good teacher-pupil relations can help such a child.

Selected Readings

ANDERSON, Harold H., and ANDERSON, Gladys L., Social development, in *Manual of Child Psychology*, 2nd ed. Leonard Carmichael, ed. (New York: John Wiley & Sons, 1954), Ch. 19.

CRONBACH, Lee J., *Educational Psychology* (New York: Harcourt, Brace & World, 1963), Ch. 13.

GARRISON, Karl C., *Growth and Development*, 2nd ed. (New York: Longmans, Green & Co., 1959), Ch. 12.

JERSILD, Arthur T., *Child Psychology*, 5th ed. (Englewood Cliffs: Prentice-Hall, 1960), Ch. 6.

MEAD, Margaret, *The School in American Culture* (Cambridge: Harvard University Press, 1951), p. 48.

PRESSEY, Sidney L., ROBINSON, Francis P., and HORROCKS, John E., *Psychology in Education* (New York: Harper & Row, 1959), Ch. 6.

STONE, Joseph L., and CHURCH, Joseph, *Childhood and Adolescence* (New York: Random House, 1957), Ch. 8.

PART **III**

Learning and the Educative Process

CHAPTER 7

Learning and Motivation

The school is especially concerned with those phases of a child's development that can be greatly affected by experience. The task of the teacher, that of guiding and motivating learners, is not simple. Each child is unique; he brings to the learning situation his hereditary equipment along with all that has happened to him in his life. He arrives at the learning scene with certain concepts about himself, about others, and about the different elements making up the learning situation. The teacher must realize that the same learning task is perceived differently by each child.

The learner is the central element in the educational process, described in Chapter 1. Too often learning is looked upon narrowly as acquiring skill in reading, writing, arithmetic, and other school subjects. Learning, however, is much broader than this. Children and adolescents acquire attitudes, values, likes and dislikes; they learn appropriate sex roles; they develop habits of selfishness or unselfishness, honesty or dishonesty, and courage or cowardice.

Pressey, Robinson, and Horrocks offer the following definition of learning: "Learning is an episode in which a motivated individual attempts to adapt his behavior so as to succeed in a situation which he perceives as requiring action to attain a goal." [1] Cronbach offers a brief and precise definition stating that "learning is shown by a change in behavior as a result of experience." [2] Hilgard, on the other hand, presents a relatively complete definition:

Learning is the process by which an activity originates or is changed through reacting to an encountered situation, provided that the characteristics

[1] Sidney L. Pressey, Francis P. Robinson, and John E. Horrocks, *Psychology in Education* (New York: Harper & Row, 1959), p. 232.
[2] Lee J. Cronbach, *Educational Psychology* (New York: Harcourt, Brace & World, 1954), p. 47.

of the change in activity cannot be explained on the basis of native response tendencies, maturation, or temporary states of the organism (e.g., fatigue, drugs, etc.).[3]

It should be noted that these definitions emphasize the role of experience. They also point to the importance of the activity of the organism in relation to environmental forces or conditions. This concept of interaction was emphasized throughout the earlier chapters of this book and will be emphasized again in subsequent chapters.

THEORETICAL EXPLANATIONS OF LEARNING

In attempts to understand, predict, and control learning, three major theories or schools of thought have emerged: the conditioned-response theory, the trial-and-error theory, and the Gestalt or insight theory. These theories tend to represent the particular investigator's point of view, and grew out of studies of some aspect of the total learning situation in which it occurred. Some are interested in the initial aspects of learning; others are interested in problems related to improvement; still others are interested in transfer and generalizations, while some are interested in the dynamics or motivational aspects of learning. In order that the student may better understand these learning theories and how they apply to learning activities, examples of each kind of learning are here presented.

Learning by conditioning

The conditioning method has been widely used in the study of both animal and human learning. Learning as a result of conditioning can be thought of as associational learning: when two or more stimuli are presented in close succession, either stimulus can eventually elicit the original response. When a child enters school for the first time, he enters into a new situation where things are likely to seem strange to him. He may have feelings of fear or anxiety. If the teacher greets him warmly and helps him feel secure in his new environment he will be favorably conditioned toward school situations where the teacher or perhaps other teachers are involved. In such a case one trial or one day of school experience may be sufficient for the learning.

The word *reinforcement* is frequently used in connection with experimental studies of conditioning. If the first-grade child who smiles when she is greeted by the teacher receives a nice hug from the teacher or warm greetings from her classmates, the warm response she makes to the teacher-school situation will be strengthened. Conditioned responses

[3] Ernest R. Hilgard, *Theories of Learning* (New York: Appleton-Century-Crofts, Inc., 1956), p. 3.

occur in classroom situations, whether or not the teacher has planned for them. In a teaching situation one should not lose sight of the original stimulus and the desired outcome. The development of literature appreciation, a desired goal in high-school English, will not occur in a classroom situation where threats and sarcasm are used as stimuli. Neither will this occur when some extrinsic reward is substituted for the desired goal of appreciation.

Learning by trial-and-error

Many educational psychologists do not attempt to make a clear-cut distinction between conditioning and trial-and-error learning so far as the basic principles are concerned, but there are important differences in the arrangement of the learning activities. The conditioned response depends upon reinforcement while trial-and-error depends upon a reward in terms of the attainment of a goal. Both the trial-and-error theorists and the conditioned response theorists emphasize association as the basis of learning.

One of the earliest experimental studies of animal learning shows something of what has been termed blind trial-and-error problem solving.[4] A hungry cat was placed in a closed cage with food just outside the cage. The cat could get out of the cage by pulling a string extending from the door latch to a position inside the cage within his reach. The motive or drive was hunger, the goal was the food just outside the cage, and the solution was to pull the string that would release the door.

When the cat was placed in the cage he tried many ways to get to the food, repeating some ways many times. The cat finally (apparently by accident) pulled the string, thereby opening the door. The problem was solved; he was able to reach the food. The question then was, Did the cat know how he had solved the problem of opening the door? The next time he was placed in the cage, he again made many false or incorrect moves, except that he didn't repeat them as often. The apparently accidental solution to the problem came sooner than in the first trial. This was also true for subsequent trials. Finally the cat pulled the string as soon as he was placed in the cage.

Problem solving of a trial-and-error nature frequently appears on the human level. Miller and Dollard[5] have presented a rather dramatic description of trial-and-error learning by a six-year-old girl. The girl was brought into a room where candy was hidden under the bottom edge

[4] See E. L. Thorndike, *Animal Intelligence* (New York: Macmillan Company, 1911).

[5] N. E. Miller and J. Dollard, *Social Learning and Imitation* (New Haven: Yale University Press, 1941), pp. 14-16.

of the corner book on the lower shelf of a four-foot-long bookcase containing books of similar color and size. She was told that she may eat the candy if she were able to find it. The descriptive account of her activity is an illustration of trial-and-error behavior.

Learning by insight

The Gestalt or field theory of learning, advanced by Koffka in 1924, makes use of insight as a basic principle.[6] The Gestaltists explain learning in terms of modifications that take place in response to meaningful patterns or configurations. For example, when the learner is confronted with a new problem, he draws upon the patterns of his past experiences to help him understand the new situation. Learning, according to this theory, takes place through the reorganization of old terms permitting one to grasp significant relationships in the new problem. When these relationships are perceived the learner is said to have achieved *insight* into the problem. According to the Gestalt psychologists, the important changes constituting learning are perceptual and cognitive.

Much of the child's problem-solving learning in school can be explained by this theory. The child's early perception of the meaning of a printed word is in terms of a pattern or configuration. The process of identifying the meaning of words in reading, of understanding concepts in science and social science, of solving problems in arithmetic, and of grasping meanings in the practical arts or achieving a satisfying pattern in creative arts may be explained as insightful learning.

Perhaps the most commonly used criterion for the presence of insight in problem-solving is the suddenness with which the solution appears. Yet, there is good evidence that insights often appear for one aspect of a problem, while not appearing for other aspects. A boy confronted with the problem of constructing a dog house may study certain details, bring to bear his observations of other dog houses, and gather useful information from the library. All of these experiences are beneficial to the appearance of insight into the problem. Furthermore, he may grasp the solution of how to construct the door or some other part of the dog house before he comprehends completely the pattern for the entire structure. Thus, the individual may acquire partial insight into a problem, although learning is not complete until some solution has been reached that allows the learner to achieve his goal.

Learning as habit formation and understanding

Contemporary learning theories seem to agree upon the meaning of learning. Furthermore, they are generally in agreement upon the variables

[6] See K. Lewin, "Field Theory and Learning," *The Psychology of Learning,* pp. 215-242. Forty-first Yearbook of the National Society for the Study of Education, Part II, 1942.

that must be considered in any theory of how learning takes place. They recognize two general elements in any learning situation: (1) the state or condition of the learner at the time, and (2) the particular situation with which the learner is confronted. Learning is not a passive process, but takes place to the extent that the learner is actively striving toward a goal or the solution of a problem. There are some who would divide learning into various kinds; others conceive of all learning as following the same basic principle. The disagreements among psychologists about how learning occurs take place primarily at the abstract level. However, an area of common ground exists, based upon results of experimental studies, which can give the student a good understanding of the nature of learning, factors and conditions that make for efficient learning and retention, the fundamental principles of transfer, and effective methods of study.

It appears that there are variations or gradients in learning, from what is primarily blind trial-and-error method to a creative attack on a problem for which there is no ready-made solution. It is within this realm that the various theories or explanations of learning have operated. There are some who regard problem-solving and reasoning as trial-and-error learning involving symbols. Certainly we may observe trial-and-error behavior in problem-solving. Note this as a student tries to get the answer to an algebraic problem, especially in his early attempts to solve the problem. There are others who would explain problem-solving as an attempt to bring together and to organize possible responses from many experiences in the solution of a problem. Again, it may be noted that one draws upon his past experiences in his attempts to solve a problem. One's understanding will depend largely upon past experiences with the problem situation. Thus, habits and understanding grow out of experiences. They are learned. Materials bearing on the acquisition of habits and understanding will be presented in subsequent chapters.

Learning as reorganization

Learning as a reorganization of experiences has two aspects, one dealing with the transformation which produces the new patterns and the other with the stabilization and consolidation of this new organization. The latter phase is one of *fixation* and *precision;* the former is one of *differentiation* and *integration*.

The responses of the infant child are diffuse and undifferentiated. When the baby learns to distinguish his mother from others, and reacts to her differently from others, differentiation may be said to have occurred. At a later stage the growing child learns to distinguish the house from the garage, the chair in the house from the couch, and a school from a church. Differentiation may be thought of as an essential stage in learning. It is also the process whereby a feature or detail of an original pattern emerges to becomes a new or particularized pattern. Through differentiation the student of botany is able to identify different types of plant life which fall within a large classification. The importance of differentiation in learning may be observed with the college professor of English literature or electrical engineering who can't distinguish the different kinds of shrubbery growing around his house. It is important for the teacher to realize that undifferentiated behavior occurs during the early stage of the learning process, and that differentiated behavior develops through guidance and experience.

Integration is the process whereby more or less discretely perceived things or actions become more closely related or organized into a meaningful pattern. For example, when one learns to play the piano he organizes the movements of the hands and fingers into a new structural pattern of movements. Also, when the child learns to read the sentence, "I have a pet dog," integration takes place bringing together the various letters and words making up the sentence into the newly perceived pattern. The teacher should realize that much of the learning at school involves continuous integration of less organized elements into larger and better organized response patterns.

Fixation and precision may be thought of as the later stages of learning. At one time repetition was thought to be the central factor in fixation and precision. Although Thorndike early proclaimed this as an explanation of learning, at a later date, under the influence of an avalanche of studies, he refuted this explanation. There are perhaps many teachers who still look to repetition as the primary means of teaching and learning. While repetition alone does not seem to affect the learning of new response, it is a means by which certain conditions appear persistently, and these conditions, closely related to the learning process, are responsible for learning.

The importance of goals has been emphasized by recent students of learning. Learning is regarded as an active process whereby the responses of the organism are directed toward certain goals. The attainment of these goals is satisfying to the organism and produces a relief from the tension involved in the efforts to reach the goal. Thus learning involves attentive responses directed towards certain goals. A repetition of this persistent attention is important in the differentiation, integration, and fixation of certain responses. However, the repetition of the response alone is not important. It appears rather that through successful reactions there is a change in the tension system which was created through certain conditions, needs, or goals. These tension-reducing reactions produced by the successful performance of the act are linked with differentiation, integration, fixation, and precision.

THE ROLE OF MOTIVATION

It has been suggested that learning as well as remembering is affected by numerous factors. The child's rate of development, physical health, previous experiences, and mental ability are recognized as important factors affecting his learning. During recent years more attention has been given to the motives or set of the individual faced with a learning task. It is well recognized by successful teachers that a pupil's motivation is essential for effective learning. Since motives are revealed in many ways and are often subtle, it is frequently very difficult for the teacher to understand them. Two children may attempt to complete their arithmetic assignments for entirely different reasons. Also, two children may give entirely different expressions to similar motives. This may be observed by the different techniques children use to get attention. One may be boisterous but not especially disorderly, while the other may resort to mischief and disorderly conduct. To understand a pupil's motive for studying, cooperating, and displaying initiative is most important. However, the teacher must also be able to direct these motives to develop desirable habits and useful skills among her pupils.

Drives to behavior

According to the drive theory, brought forth by Woodworth in his *Dynamic Psychology* in 1918 and elaborated by Dashiell in his *Fundamentals of Objective Psychology* in 1928 "all behavior is motivated." Thus, psychologists introduced the term *drive* to answer the question of what motivates organisms to become active. Organisms have been conceived of as driven, first by primary, inner stimuli which arise from homeostatic imbalance or needs. The restlessness of the baby is a result of the need for sleep or food. The "showing-off" of the adolescent in the presence of members of the opposite sex is a result of inner stimuli arising from the sex drive. The organism is also driven by various forms of intense and painful external stimulation. These two forms of stimulation arouse an inner state of excitement which has been referred to as drive.

The idea that the organism is inactive unless stimulated by homeostatic need or painful stimuli or conditioned stimuli has been challenged by a number of psychologists.[7] Play among young children occurs most frequently when they are comfortable, well-fed, and rested. The occurrence of either homeostatic need or strong external stimulation stops play and turns the child or adolescent to activities calculated to relieve such stimulation. It has been shown that hunger and thirst limit the exploratory activities of rats. It has been further demonstrated that monkeys will

[7] J. McV. Hunt, "Experience and the Development of Motivation: Some Reinterpretations," *Child Development,* Vol. 31 (1960), pp. 489-504.

learn to disassemble a three-device puzzle with no other drive or reward present than the privilege of disassembling it. Piaget, a French psychologist, has pointed out how the child repeated such performances as pulling up in his crib, standing, and cooing. Such evidences of spontaneous behavior, not resulting from stimulation by homeostatic need or painful stimuli, have led some psychologists to use the term *curiosity* or *exploratory behavior.* Hunt has suggested that we should give up the ancient Greek idea that living matter is inert substance to which motion must be imparted by extrinsic forces. He has presented the view of the "thermodynamic conception of living things as open systems of energy exchange which exhibits activity intrinsically and upon which stimuli have a modulating effect, but not an initiating effect." [8] In this connection White proposed the term *competence.* The behaviors based on competence motivation are described as follows:

> The behavior that leads to the building up of effective grasping, handling, and letting go of objects, to take one example is not random behavior produced by an overflow of energy. It is directed, selective, and persistent, and it is continued not because it serves primary drives, which indeed it cannot serve until it is almost perfected, but because it satisfies an intrinsic need to deal with the environment. [9]

These activities in the service of competence are conceived of as motivated in their own right. This motivation is designated by the term *efficacy,* and the feelings produced referred to as feelings of efficacy. Such behaviors as attention and perception, language and thinking, exploration and manipulation are thought of as motivated in their own right—they produce feelings of efficacy.

This view has important implications for the teacher and the learner. When the learner is furnished opportunities to explore, has a rich variety of materials to explore, such as a good library or laboratory, and has the background of experiences to understand some of the things he is exploring, learning will result even when no need to avoid painful stimulation or to relieve homeostatic imbalance exists. Every successful teacher makes use of curiosity in teaching.

The nature of motives

The view that activity is intrinsic in living tissue does not eliminate the role and importance of needs and stimulation by homeostatic need or painful stimulation. Terms which have been used somewhat synonymously with motives include *drives, needs, purposes,* and *impulses.* Some of these are largely a result of physiological states or conditions, while others

---

[8] *Ibid.,* p. 493.
[9] Robert W. White, "Motivation Reconsidered: The Concept of Competence," *Psychological Review,* Vol. 66 (1959), p. 318.

grow out of cultural conditions and demands. Hunger and fatigue are motives which are based upon the physiological needs of the individual. Cooperation and competition, as motives, are closely related to cultural forces. The motives resulting from cultural forces are sometimes very puzzling to the teacher, since different subcultures develop different motives. A motive once aroused leads to action. It is in this connection that we think of motives as drives. The nature of the resulting action will depend upon a number of factors, such as (1) the nature of the individual, (2) the environmental situation, (3) the nature of the motive, and (4) the strength of the motive.

The drive or motivating aspect of learning puts the emphasis upon the organism rather than upon the environmental stimulus. It is the *whole* organism which selects certain types of responses to an environmental situation. The view that behavior is purposive rather than mechanical has an important bearing on the teaching and guidance of children. The motives of the teacher are also important. Rogers states: "Science has its meaning as the objective pursuit of a purpose which has been subjectively chosen by a person or persons. . . . Consequently, any discussion of the control of human beings by the behavioral sciences must first and most deeply concern itself with the subjectively chosen purpose which such an application of science is intended to implement." [10]

The modern teacher regards behavior as a result and seeks the causes. Maladjustments, aggression, and hostile behavior are learned ways of responding to special situations or problems. The behavior and learning of the child can be more successfully guided when the motivational forces are understood. Concerning the action of the individual as a dynamic organism displaying purposive behavior, Rogers states further:

> If we choose to utilize our scientific knowledge to free men, then it will demand that we live openly and frankly with the great paradox of the behavioral sciences. We will recognize that behavior, when examined scientifically, is surely best understood as determined by prior causation. This is the great fact of science. But responsible personal choice, which is the most essential element in being a person, which is the core experience of psychotherapy, which exists prior to any scientific endeavor, is an equally prominent fact in our lives.[11]

Learning as goal-seeking behavior

One should not conclude from the statements quoted from Rogers that teachers and others have no place in helping the learner set goals. However, it is the learner who chooses one goal rather than some other goal. There is considerable agreement among psychologists that goal

---

[10] Carl Rogers, "The Place of the Person in the New World of the Behavioral Sciences," *Personnel and Guidance Journal*, Vol. 39 (1961), p. 448.

[11] *Ibid.*, p. 451.

Portland (Oregon) Public Schools

Learner involvement is important in the educative process. Pupils learn best in situations where there is a favorable climate for learning and where they are motivated by worthwhile goals.

relationships are learned. It appears that most of the rewards and punishments in life are not innately rewarding or punishing, but develop their characteristics as a result of experience. Thus, the child's motives develop and change with new learnings.

Learning can best be thought of as an active process, not a passive one. This was noted in an early investigation of memorization. Poppelreuter [12] found that if he, as a learner, maintained a purely passive attitude while observing a series of nonsense syllables, he learned little even after fifty repetitions. Many investigators have shown that the amount of learning which takes place through the repetition of certain experiences is directly related to the attention a learner gives to the task.

Goals and purposes are essential if the learner is to maintain a high degree of attention to the learning task. The nature of learning, as an

[12] W. Poppelreuter, "Nachweis der Unzweckmässigkeit der Bebräuchlichen Assoziationsexperimente," *Zeitschr. f. Psychol.*, Vol. 61 (1912), pp. 1-25.

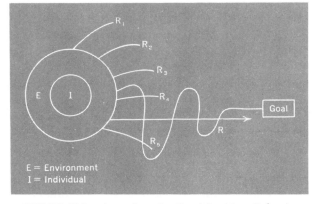

FIGURE 7-1.   Learning As Goal-Seeking Behavior

active process whereby the learner strives to attain certain goals, is shown in Figure 7-1.[13] The responses of the learner in his efforts to reach a particular goal may be thought of as trial-and-error in nature. They are labeled R_1, R_2, R_3, R_4, etc. The learner operates within a particular setting referred to as his environment. In his goal-seeking behavior, perhaps efforts at solving an arithmetic problem or hitting a ball, he draws upon his storehouse of past experiences. Some of these responses are likely to be irrelevant to the attainment of the goal, but as learning proceeds some responses are modified or eliminated, reducing the variability of the responses until the appropriate response is selected. This was described earlier in connection with the process of differentiation and integration.

Multiple goals.   Most acts of behavior cannot be adequately explained as directed to a specific goal. The fourth-grade child completes an assignment in arithmetic not only to satisfy his desire to finish the assignment, but also to please his teacher, to please his parents, to compete successfully with his classmates, and perhaps still other reasons. In drawing and painting a house, a third-grader may be motivated by an acquired and remote goal to become a well-known artist someday. The drawing of the house may be quite rewarding to the child if it meets with the teacher's approval. However, the motive for drawing the house may go far beyond the goal of satisfying the teacher. There is certainly more involved than simply drawing and painting a house.

Remote goals.   As the school-age child advances toward maturity, he performs an increasing number of tasks for remote goals. Remoteness

[13] Figure 7-1 is adapted from Anderson and Gates, "The General Nature of Learning," *Forty-ninth Yearbook of the National Society for the Study of Education, Part I, Learning and Instruction* (Chicago: Univ. of Chicago Press, 1950), p. 17.

may be a relative term. It may refer to benefits at the end of the day, the end of the week or month, the end of the year, or when the individual is fully grown. The child who draws and paints a house because she wants to grow up to be an artist like her aunt, is being motivated by a remote goal. Of course this does not mean that immediate or less remote goals are not operating.

Sometimes the pupil may be aware of the far-away goals without consciously realizing their operation. This appears, in particular, when there are immediate, attractive goals as motivating forces or conditions. Foresight or long-time goals are learned through planning ahead and continuously thinking in terms of future wants as well as present desires. With maturity pupils should be encouraged and guided into placing more emphasis upon long-time as well as immediate goals. There is evidence from American cultural patterns that middle-class children tend to give greater weight to remote goals than lower-class children. This idea was discussed in Chapter 3 in connection with parental expectations of children.

Anxiety and learning

Attitudes have an important effect upon one's learning and behavior. A learner may approach a learning task indifferently, passively, negatively, or eagerly. There is evidence from many sources that self-direction involving a desire to learn facilitates learning. There is, however, the problem of the effects of the learner's anxiety on the learning of a particular task. The investigation by Palermo [14] and others attempted to determine the relationship of anxiety in children to performance in complex learning situations where one or more competing incorrect responses were dominant. The learning task of the subjects involved turning off different colored lights by buttons arranged on a panel connected to the lights. The subjects were instructed to learn which button turned off each light and were told that if an error was made correction would be allowed.

The subjects consisted of 36 fourth-grade pupils selected on the basis of extreme scores on the children's form of the *Taylor Scale of Manifest Anxiety*. Anxiety scores for the nonanxious groups range from three to eleven and for the anxious groups from twenty-three to thirty-three. The results, presented in Figure 7-2, showed that on each block of trials the nonanxious subjects made fewer errors than the anxious subjects. It appears that in difficult learning situations where the dominant response is not correct, anxious subjects show inferior performance to nonanxious subjects.

Using 180 students in introductory psychology classes as subjects,

[14] David S. Palermo, Alfred Castaneda, and Boyd R. McCandless, "The Relationship of Anxiety in Children to Performance in a Complex Learning Task," *Child Development*, Vol. 27 (1956), pp. 333-337.

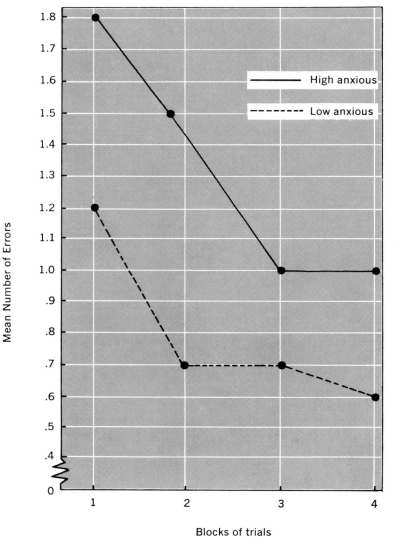

FIGURE 7-2. Error Curves For The Anxious And Nonanxious Subjects Plotted In Blocks Of Five Trials *(Palermo, Castaneda, and McCandless)*

Sarason [15] noted that high motivation instructions were detrimental for high-anxious groups of students and facilitating for low- and middle-anxious groups. The motivation of individual pupils should vary with their anxiety level. It would seem that the best motivation conditions for a high anxiety group would be those where no further reference is made

[15] Irwin Sarason, "Effect of Anxiety, Motivational Instructions and Failure or Serial Learning," *Journal of Experimental Psychology*, Vol. 51 (1956), pp. 253-260.

to success. On the other hand, the best motivation conditions for the low-anxiety group would be those in which the subjects are given additional stimulation. This is another example of how the child's perception of the school and teaching situation affects his functioning on a wide variety of intellectual tasks related to the classroom.

Level of aspiration

Anxiety, when directed toward a relatively remote goal, has an important bearing on learning. This may be noted with a child's aspirational level. Various studies involving children's aspirational level show wide individual differences in their statements about goals and aspirations. The influence of past experiences involving success or failure on a particular task may be noted in the level of aspiration pattern for the task. This was noted by Sears [16] in a study of the aspiration level of children in the fourth, fifth, and sixth grades. The evaluation of their past experiences of success or failure was based upon their achievement in reading and arithmetic. The tasks used for determining the level of aspiration were also derived from reading and arithmetic.

The results of the study by Sears showed that self-confident, successful children react to the level of aspiration situation in a similar way, whereas unsuccessful children, lacking in confidence, may adapt one of a variety of behavior patterns in such a situation. The levels of aspiration set by these children were apparently influenced by the cultural pressure to excel and to continue to improve. A subject who has failed in the past, generally has performed at a level considerably below that of most other pupils. He has probably felt the cultural pressure to improve more than children in the success group. These cultural forces exert pressure on him to list a higher level of aspiration than he can reach as an acknowledgement of his intention to reach a desirable goal. Thus, for the child with past experiences of failure, the expressed aspiration level may be a goal he recognizes as desirable for him to reach rather than one he actually expects to reach.

We must not confuse a child's level of aspiration with his goal, although they are closely related. A child will not have a level of aspiration for all tasks, although he may have definite goals. In order to develop a level of aspiration he must have some idea of the difficulty of the task and of his own ability to learn or perform it. For most individuals the level of aspiration will represent a compromise between their own evaluation of their ability to perform or learn a task, and their desire to achieve a high level of performance. The child's level of aspiration is also very unstable when he faces the performance of new tasks; but in

16 Pauline S. Sears, "Levels of Aspiration in Academically Successful and Unsuccessful Children," *Journal of Abnormal and Social Psychology*, Vol. 35 (1940), pp. 498-536.

the performance of familiar tasks, to a degree at least, he has already learned what level of difficulty he will be able to reach on the basis of his ability and the effort which he is likely to expend. This level which he finds he can reach is most important in determining his level of aspiration. Furthermore, there is evidence that an individual's level of aspiration will drop if he fails and rise if he succeeds. The amount of failure or success necessary to change one's level of aspiration will vary considerably from individual to individual and from one situation to another. It is perhaps a good indicator of such characteristics as determination and persistence.

It has already been suggested that the nature of the task and the general expectations of what constitutes success and failure in its performance influence the level of aspiration an individual sets himself. Thus, cultural pressures from the home influence the child's aspirational level.

Parental anxieties can have ill effects upon children. So can parental ambitions that are out of harmony with the interests and abilities of their children. Children from an impoverished environment also often fail to develop goals and aspirational levels in harmony with their potential abilities. The teacher of these children should be careful in evaluating or criticizing their work, lest they come to feel that they can't do the task. Continuous failure at the high school and college level may lead to a level of aspiration lower than is needed for a realistic approach. Parents and teachers should motivate students to set themselves realistic levels of aspiration. Such motivation would not be based upon an absence of failures. Continuous success does not prepare the child for possible failures; neither does it encourage the child to attempt tasks that are challenging and that might lead to failure.

Factors affecting goal-setting and aspiration level.   Since goal-setting and aspiration level are very important in the motivation process, it is worthwhile to consider the factors affecting them. We have already discussed the role of success and failure. Expectation of further success will have a beneficial effect upon aspirational level, while expectation of failure in future performances will have a detrimental effect. There are other factors, not directly related to the task, that affect a learner's aspirational level. First, a task may appear so complex or difficult to him that he sees no reason to set a goal or to hope to succeed at it; on the other hand, the task may be so easy that it fails to challenge him at all. Third, insecure people frequently set themselves high goals in order to attain a feeling of success, even though they realize they will be unable to reach them. Fourth, a learner may have a low aspirational level to protect himself from possible failure. By setting a goal he knows he can reach, he takes no chance on failing. Fifth, the teacher and other adult figures sometimes influence the learner's level of aspiration. In this connection, teachers should be careful to see that the learner can achieve the goals he sets himself. Closely related to the influence of the teacher is that of peers. Most children will tend to set themselves goals not too far from those set by other members of their group.

THE USE OF INCENTIVES

Parents and teachers use a variety of incentives to control behavior and direct learning. Many studies of the effects of different incentives have been made during the last two or three decades. The results of these studies show that some incentives have considerable value, some have limited value, and some may actually be detrimental to the learning process. However, it is very difficult to generalize since the effects of a particular incentive may vary from individual to individual. Thus, many factors must be taken into consideration in attempting to evaluate these results.

Rewards

Rewards, one of the most frequently used incentives, serve as reinforcements to goal-seeking behavior in learning. Reinforcement has been found to be effective in stimulating the individual to greater effort and increased achievement. Concerning the use of reinforcement in learning Symonds states:

> . . . It is generally agreed that reinforcement is most effective the closer the reward or reinforcement is, in time, to the response which is to be learned. The most effective reinforcement is one that follows the response in a matter of seconds. . . . Also reinforcement is more effective if the response to be learned is simple, clear-cut, and not imbedded in a mass of concomitant responses.[17]

In a study by Abel [18] the effects of different incentives on children's learning of a sensori-motor skill were investigated. She used a finger-type maze of the pattern shown in Figure 7-3. Groups of nine- to ten-year-old boys of approximately average intelligence were given a variety of rewards after their attempts to traverse the maze without error. The subjects were separated into five groups. Group I received no reward; Group II received a material reward, a penny after each trial; Group III received a verbal reward, "good," "very good," and the like; Group IV

---

[17] Percival M. Symonds, "What Education has to Learn from Psychology. V. Learning is Reacting," *Teachers College Record*, Vol. 59 (1957-58), p. 98. Bureau of Publications, Teachers College, Columbia University.

[18] L. B. Abel, "The Effects of Shift in Motivation upon the Learning of a Sensori-motor Task," *Archives of Psychology*, Vol. 29 (1936), No. 205.

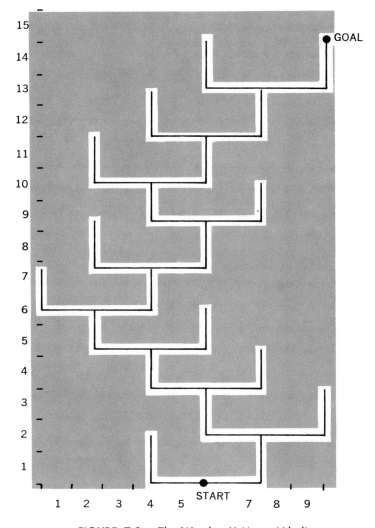

FIGURE 7-3. The Warden U Maze (Abel)

was promised 25 cents; and Group V received a combination of these at different periods of the learning.

All groups showed some improvement, although the group with no reward showed the least. Abel noted that the verbal reward, when repeated more than three or four times, begins to lose its effectiveness. It was also noted that a child need not actually attain the goal-object to stimulate him to increased effort. It is unlikely, however, that a material reward would continue to stimulate individuals to increased effort, if the goal-object were never reached.

The use of rewards may have some value to a few pupils who win while frustrating all the others who lose. A prize for the best reader or speller in class will likely become a contest between two or three pupils. There are also other important drawbacks to the use of rewards in school learning. Some are (1) rewards must be increased periodically to maintain a high level of performance; (2) pupils tend to work for the reward rather than the major goal; (3) learning efficiency falls off rapidly when rewards are eliminated. Other incentives to learning are just as effective without the likelihood of relegating learning to a secondary place.

Achievement motivation.   The child's interests in learning activities may be termed achievement motivation. This may be observed in the third-grade pupil's intense interest in working arithmetic problems or the seventh-grade pupil's interest in collecting and classifying leaves or butterflies.

Individual differences in achievement motivation may be noted among preschool as well as school-age children. This is frequently an important motivational force in the educational process. The achievement need, like many other needs, is a product of social learning and reinforcements which children have experienced. As children experience satisfactions and rewards for their achievement, their achievement motive tends to increase. Approval from teachers and parents, favorable report cards and other indicators of achievement serve to reinforce the learning. When learners have been operating for some time under low or unchanged stimulation an increase or change in stimulation reinforces learning. Berlyne [19] noted that when rats were stimulated with increased variety, they spent more time exploring their environment. Teachers have continuously observed that achievement motivation is reinforced by changed classroom procedures or by the introduction of new or different elements into the learning situation.

The influence of praise.   It has already been suggested that pupils vary widely in their response to a given incentive or motivating device. In one study fifty fifth-graders were asked to work for thirty seconds crossing out certain letters as fast as they could. After doing the work the pupils, divided into two groups, were given a mark of either P or G. They were told that P meant they had done poorly while G meant they had done well. Another group of fifth-graders was used as a control group. These pupils received no report on the quality of their work.

[19] D. E. Berlyne, "The Arousal and Satiation of Perceptual Curiosity in the Rat," *Journal of Comp. Physiol. Psychol.*, Vol. 48 (1955), pp. 238-246.
[20] George G. Thompson and C. W. Hunnicut, "Effects of Repeated Praise or Blame on the Work Achievement of Introverts and Extroverts," *Journal of Educational Psychology*, Vol. 35 (1944), pp. 257-266.

The scores of all three groups improved appreciably on the second day and slightly thereafter. The groups were equal at the beginning of the study. The scores of the three groups on the final test were as follows:

Group P 21
Group G 20
Group C 15

The results indicated that the groups praised or criticized made greater improvement. A further analysis of the results showed that some pupils responded better to praise while others responded better to criticism. Out-going, active, self-assured pupils respond better to criticism, while worried, sensitive, withdrawn pupils respond better to praise. Sometimes it is not so much what is said as the way it is said. Children's interpretation of what was meant by the adult or person who praises or criticizes will have a bearing on the results. If a warm friendly relationship exists between teacher and pupil the results will be very different from what they would be in a cold indifferent relationship. All this points to the danger of generalizing too widely about the effectiveness of a particular motivating device. The use of praise or blame should depend on the nature of the pupil, the pupil-teacher relationship, and the situation at the particular time. The effect on the pupil must be evaluated in terms of his total behavior rather than in terms of his immediate performance. Praise, in general, is better than blame.

Punishment

Punishment has been described by Symonds as "something that hurts inflicted by one person on another." [21] An application of this definition to the needs of an individual suggests two general types of punishment: to withhold the satisfaction of a need from a child, and to inflict pain or abuse. The child who needs activity but is required to stay indoors illustrates the first type. Corporal punishment or some form of ridicule illustrates the second type. Punishment, according to these definitions and descriptions, may be regarded as forms of frustration imposed by one individual upon another.

These types of punishment have wide implications when applied to the activities of parents and teachers in their attempt to motivate children and adolescents. Failure to attain one's level of aspiration is a sort of self-punishment, since it results in an infliction of pain on the self. The second term of the following pairs of terms may be regarded as punishment: acceptance-rejection, success-failure, praise-blame, reward-punishment. It should be noted, however, that punishment can-

[21] Percival M. Symonds, "What Education has to Learn from Psychology, III. Punishment," *Teachers College Record*, Vol. 57 (1955-56), p. 450. Bureau of Publications, Teachers College, Columbia University.

not be thought of completely in terms of the stimulus applied to an individual. For a student, failing in music may be a means of reaching the goal of discontinuing music lessons, which he dislikes. Animal experiments bearing on the effects of punishment reveal that (1) punishment inhibits the behavior in process when the punishment was administered, (2) punishment may actually produce other undesirable behavior, and (3) punishment spreads its influence both in terms of the stimuli and the responses.[22]

Investigations of the effects of punishment on people have not always yielded similar results. This may be attributed largely to differences in the nature and intensity of the punishment. There is considerable evidence that mild punishment has little or no direct inhibitory effect, while moderately strong punishment temporarily inhibits certain forms of behavior. Severe punishment may be a sufficiently traumatic experience to permanently inhibit the behavior act.

Punishment and anxiety. The relation between punishment and anxiety may be observed with a school youngster who was not allowed to participate in some group activity because of his previous rebellious behavior. The next day, displaying anxiety, he realized that he must exercise more self-control or he would again be denied the opportunity to participate in group activities. The spread of anxiety to varying cooperative situations is one of the most important outcomes of punishment. The extent to which the effects of punishment will spread to other similar situations will depend largely upon the mental and emotional development of the subject and the manner in which the punishment is administered.

It was suggested earlier that the severity of punishment has a bearing upon its effects. When punishment is so mild that little anguish or pain results, anxiety is also mild. In such situations punishment has little effect upon behavior other than to furnish information as a guide to behavior. When punishment hurts, anxiety may be a motivating force for inhibiting and for withdrawal behavior. When punishment is so severe that the anxiety aroused is intense, responses may be panicky and disorganized.

The motivating effect of punishment depends to a marked degree upon the anxiety produced. Thus, when punishment is sufficiently severe to hurt, the resulting anxiety may interfere with learning but may serve to control or direct behavior. Threat of failure or low grades in school may be an important motivating force for the pupils with reasonably high aspiration levels. One experiment compared threat of failure, which

22 R. L. Solomon, L. J. Kamin, and L. C. Wynne, "Traumatic Avoidance Learning: The Outcomes of Several Extinction Procedures with Dogs," *Journal of Abnormal and Social Psychology,* Vol. 48 (1948), pp. 291-302.

produces insecurity, to reassurances of promotion as motivating procedures.[23] The gains made on the *Stanford Achievement Test* of groups of second and fifth graders periodically threatened with failure were compared with groups reassured that they need not have any fear of being promoted. In both grades the nonthreatened groups made greater gains than the threatened groups, although the differences were not statistically reliable. The ill-effects of insecurity have been emphasized by psychiatrists as well as by clinical psychologists. Thus, it appears that threatening pupils with failure has little to offer the teacher in the elementary school.

The role of competition

It has often been assumed that competition with others is the most desirable form of motivation. Thus, schools have often relied upon contests, school marks, and other individual rewards based upon winning or doing better than others of their group. While no one can deny the presence of these motivating factors, the wisdom of their widespread application is questionable. All too often John or Sally is compared with others in his class or grade. The parent and teacher should focus their attention upon the particular individual rather than compare him with others. John, who doesn't get along in industrial arts, is not necessarily doing poorly when we consider his work in relation to his motivation and development.

Perhaps the most serious criticism that can be raised against reporting pupils' progress is the ill-effects produced in the competitive atmosphere of the middle-class home. Many parents seem unable to understand why their sons or daughters do not make as good grades as their friend's or neighbor's son or daughter. As we pointed out in Chapter 6, competition may produce some undesirable by-products. These must be taken into consideration in any evaluation of the relative merits of competition and cooperation as motivating devices.

The role of interests

Interest and achievement. Anyone who has worked with children or adolescents in some constructive undertaking in which they have an intense interest will attest to the dynamic energy they seem to release. Evidence from scientific studies points to a positive relationship between interest and school achievement. A study by Dean [24] of the relation of children's preference of school subjects to their achievement showed that high achievers in reading, arithmetic, spelling, and language in the fifth

[23] H. J. Otto, "An Attempt to Evaluate the Threat of Failure as a Factor in Achievement," *Elementary School Journal*, Vol. 35 (1935), pp. 588-596.

[24] S. E. Dean, "Relation of Children's Preference to Their Achievement," *Elementary School Journal*, Vol. 51 (1950), pp. 89-92.

grade tended to express preference for these school subjects to a greater degree than did the low achievers. Likewise, a study by Sheldon and Cutts [25] showed that good readers showed a superior interest in social studies, science, music, and reading as an out-of-school activity.

The implications of findings dealing with interests and achievement for the classroom teacher are clear. Methods of teaching that appeal to the interests of the learner are much more likely to be effective than methods that do not. It should be pointed out that every school child has some interests. If the teacher can determine these interests and find some means of relating the materials of the school program to them, his task will be easier and pleasanter, for himself and for the learner.

Interests and goals. The importance of goals as motivating forces was discussed earlier in this chapter. Success is recognized as an important motivating force. To succeed at a particular task may be one's immediate goal. One study [26] with college students as subjects supported the hypothesis that persons in whom the motive to succeed is stronger than the motive to avoid failure (1) more often select tasks of intermediate difficulty, (2) work for a longer time on the final examination, and (3) get higher scores on the final examination.

Learning results from action directed toward the attainment of a goal, thus satisfying a need. This may be noted in a comparison of the learning activities of two high-school girls, Frances and Joan.

> Frances, a high-school student from Portland (Oregon) is studying Spanish. She has heard her teacher and others speak of Spain and the Spanish-speaking people in different parts of the world, but she was not especially interested and paid little attention to what was said. She never expects to travel to a country where the Spanish language is generally used, and sees no particular need for this in connection with her future vocational and marital goals—to get a job as a clerk in a department store. She is not interested in Spanish, although she is not adverse to taking it.
>
> Joan, a classmate of Frances, is also studying Spanish. She expects to be an exchange student with a girl from Mexico City. She has been reading about the customs of Mexico, and looks forward to spending some time as an exchange student in Mexico City. Spanish fits nicely into her plans. She even burdens her parents and younger brother with Spanish words at home. Her interest in Spanish is an outgrowth of needs related to her goal to study in Mexico City.

The role of learning. It has already been suggested that learning is enhanced when the learner is interested in the task to be learned. Joan

---

[25] W. D. Sheldon and W. C. Cutts, "Relation of Parents, Home, and Certain Developmental Characteristics to Children's Reading Ability," *Elementary School Journal,* Vol. 53 (1953), pp. 517-521.

[26] John W. Atkinson and George H. Litwin, "Achievement Motive and Test Anxiety Conceived as Motives to Approval Success and Motive to Avoid Failure," *Journal of Abnormal and Social Psychology,* Vol. 60 (1960), pp. 52-63.

had little trouble giving her attention to the study of Spanish. However, it should be noted that Joan's interest in Spanish was acquired. It developed out of her experiences with her teachers, from reading about Mexico City, and from other experiences in which the Spanish language and expectations about the self were involved.

Interests are learned as any other learnings. The child who has spent a pleasant summer vacation in the White Mountains of Vermont will show an increased interest in mountains and the things he associates with them. An educational policy of utilizing existing interests in promoting learning may be somewhat misleading, however. Certainly any sound learning procedures will attempt to develop more interests. The experiences of the boy at camp should promote an increased interest in the out-of-doors and the things he associates with the out-of-doors. The experience of the girl in a civics class should lead to an increased interest in community activities and government.

The nature of the learner's experiences may be observed in the interests manifested at school and elsewhere.

The role of learning in the development of interests cannot be over-emphasized. And, although curiosity in the form of exploration appears early in life, the child's interests in the world of objects and events will depend primarily upon his experiences and ability to understand and interpret his world. This does not mean that a child must understand the complete operation of all elements of his environment. A ten-year-old girl may not understand many things about the play life of Navaho Indian children, but she may display a rather keen interest in this as a result of her trip through Arizona and Utah or from actions and things she has seen on television. There may have been aspects of their play life that were meaningful and significant to her, and these may have aroused her interest and curiosity about other aspects of Navaho Indian culture.

Knowledge of results. Closely akin to achievement motivation is knowledge of results. The learner attains satisfaction not only from reaching a goal, but also from recognizing that progress is being made toward attaining that goal. A boy who is trying to gain weight will be motivated to eat a well-balanced diet, and will be further motivated if he can note, from time to time, the progress he is making in gaining weight. This form of motivation is built upon the notion that "Success breeds success." Success in making progress toward one's goal is one of the most important motivating forces for the individual, and one of the most important reasons why he should be informed from time to time about the progress he makes. The value of knowledge of results is borne out in a study reported by Bouchard.[27]

Superior performance on arithmetic problem exercises was achieved by a group of children given both knowledge of correct answers and information that other sixth graders were taking the same test. The knowledge of success at different stages in learning reinforces the aspirational goals as a motivating device.

Samples of pupils' work kept over a period of time are not only valuable in evaluating growth but are useful as motivating and diagnostic instruments. A sample of handwriting or spelling secured at the beginning of the year can be a basis for encouraging the pupil, if it is used later in the year to reveal progress. The use of handwriting charts, art models, and other materials which are well-nigh perfect are often discouraging for the elementary-school child, since the comparisons between his work and the model are most unfavorable to him.

The advantage of knowledge of results as a motive is that the student is competing with himself rather than with a large group of individuals. His chances of succeeding are exceedingly good and this creates interest. Knowing how he has progressed will help him to set realistic aspirations and goals. Another advantage of this method of motivation is its availability. Any teacher can use this method merely by seeing that work samples and other related evaluative materials are kept over a period of time which need not be long. The pupil may be able to note progress from day to day in his ability to do arithmetic problems, to read, or to spell. In mechanical work, art, and the acquisition of facts or information, he is often able to note progress over a relatively short period of time, even without samples and tests. This may be observed from statements

[27] John B. Bouchard, "An Exploratory Investigation of the Effect of Certain Selected Factors upon Performance of Sixth-Grade Children in Arithmetic," *Journal of Experimental Education*, Vol. 20 (1952), pp. 105-112.

he makes about his work. Where such progress is noted there is most likely to be an increased interest in the learning activity.

Guiding learning at school

The school was described in Chapter 2 as an agency of society in which teachers are occupied guiding, instructing, and disciplining children and adolescents toward full, integrated human maturity in all aspects of their nature according to their capacity. The role of the teacher in the educational process has been emphasized. It is to guide and stimulate the learner in the acquisition of skills, information and attitudes.

The teacher and the learning situation. The primary purpose of curriculum improvement is to furnish a basis for better learning experiences. It should be borne in mind, however, that a curriculum is merely suggested materials. The most impressive array of printed materials will be of little use if the teacher does not use them for the improvement of learning experiences. The teacher who understands the characteristics of a democratic society, the nature and needs of his pupils, the learning process, and the curriculum experiences appropriate for the different maturational levels, will endeavor to guide the children toward the goals of self-realization and social development.

The responsibility of the teacher for guiding the learning of children is based upon the following fundamental axioms:

1. The child, as a total being, is the central factor in any school program. His presence in school furnishes the sound basis for an educational program.
2. Learning in school cannot be divorced from learning at home and in the community.
3. Learning activities at school should concentrate on behavior changes which can best be produced through experiences in a school environment.
4. Learning in school should be most concerned with behavior changes directly related to the desired goals of education.

The value of guidance. Evidence of the value of guidance may be observed in connection with such motor skills as swimming and dancing or in more complex coordinations such as those involved in writing. The child left to himself in learning to write, will likely develop the ability to copy letters and words, although it is quite unlikely that he would develop the rhythm and precision in making the letters and words that would be attained through guidance.

The results of an early experiment by Woodrow [28] revealed that specific instruction directed toward good methods of study are helpful. The gains of three groups of pupils who used different forms of mem-

[28] H. Woodrow, "The Effect of Type of Training Upon Transference," *Journal of Educational Psychology,* Vol. 18 (1927), pp. 159-172.

orizing over a period of four weeks and five days were compared. One group was given no training or practice but was merely given a test at the beginning and at the end of the experiment. A second group practiced memorizing poetry and nonsense syllables without explanation or a discussion of methods to be used in memorizing. They spent 177 minutes in this activity during periods averaging 22 minutes in length held twice a week. The third group spent the same amount of time in the activity except that their time was divided between actual practice in memorizing and in listening to an exposition of the technique of memorizing. The results presented in Figure 7-4, show that the third group (training group) far surpassed either of the other groups on gains made in memorization during the course of the experiment.

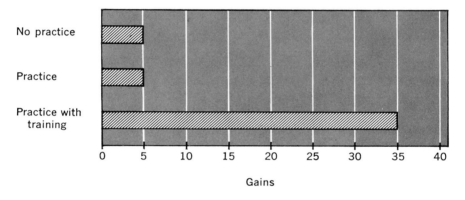

FIGURE 7-4. Average Gains In Memorizing By Three Groups Of Pupils In Different Forms Of Memorizing Over A Period Of Four Weeks And Five Days (Woodrow)

The purpose of a study by Kittell,[29] with 132 sixth-grade pupils as subjects, was to determine the relative effects of the amount of direction to learning for transfer to differing situations and to learning for retention. Each of three groups was supplied with minimum, intermediate, and maximum amount of direction during learning on the discovery of principles determining solution of multiple-choice verbal items. The results showed that sixth-grade pupils did benefit from guidance. However, both the maximum and minimum amount of guidance was as effective as an intermediate amount. The results of this study suggest that teachers should aid pupils in the discovery of principles by suggesting meaningful relationships on which pupils may base their discovery and by providing opportunities for them to discover principles.

[29] Jack E. Kittell, "An Experimental Study of the Effect of External Direction during Learning on Transfer and Retention of Principles," *Journal of Educational Psychology*, Vol. 48 (1957), pp. 391-405.

Learnings are never isolated experiences. When James or Marie learns that the first letter of important words such as names of cities is to be capitalized or that three multiplied by ten makes thirty, facts and skills other than those involved in the lesson being taught are learned simultaneously. James and Marie are learning from the attitude displayed by the teacher, from their interaction with other pupils, and from the total school environment. They also tend to fit the new learnings into previous learnings. This produces important changes in previously learned materials. It is in this respect that learning is not a matter of simply adding to what was previously learned; instead it involves a reorganization of previously learned ideas, skills, habits, and attitudes.

There is also considerable incidental learning that takes place in every classroom. Pupils learn from the examples set by their teachers and classmates. This view will be stressed in a later chapter dealing with character formation. The emotionally unstable teacher tends to have an adverse effect upon the development of good emotional habits among pupils. There is also evidence that the influential and liked teacher tends to pass on to pupils any religious, racial, or other prejudices they have. For example, the science or mathematics teacher gives examples to amplify ideas presented. The examples may actually have more meaning and be more significant to the pupils than the mathematics principle being taught. The teacher brings his experiences and attitudes to the classroom and these are passed on to the pupils. Pupils are influenced by all the forces of the classroom, and these influences may be quite widespread.

Distribution of practice. The most desirable spacing of practice in learning has received the attention of a number of students of educational psychology. The question is, Is it better to practice a task without interruptions, or are frequent rest intervals beneficial to learning and retention? In general, different studies of learning both verbal and motor skills have favored some distribution over no distribution of practice. However, the advantage of distributed or massed practice depends upon a number of factors.

Long practice periods of repetitive activities such as writing, spelling, memorizing literary selections, and the study of arithmetic computations are likely to lead to boredom or loss of interest and thus to inefficiency in learning. For such activities shorter practice periods with reasonably long rest intervals are likely to give the best results. Several cautions should be observed before too wide generalizations are made from these and somewhat similar findings. There is a time interval beyond which there is no increased efficiency. Again, the efficiency of a particular distribution of practice is conditioned by the maturity of the learner. It seems likely that both too long work periods and too long rest intervals, alike, may adversely affect the learning of immature learners.

Three important variables are involved in the distribution of practice. These are (1) the length of the practice period, (2) the length of the rest period, and (3) the manner in which the rest period is used. The length of the practice and rest period should not only vary with the maturity of the learner but also with the nature of the materials being learned and the stage of the learning. On a complex problem the early practice periods should be of longer duration, with the length of the time interval increasing as the learning progresses. Menefee [30] noted that a class in sociology meeting two hours a day for a single quarter learned more than a class meeting one hour per day for two quarters. It seems that most of the advantage of distributed practice lies in some distribution over none; however, the length of the work period should vary directly with the complexity of the materials being learned and the maturity of the learner.

Whole versus part methods. The whole method of learning has been set off as a type of learning in contrast to the part method. That this notion is not entirely accurate may be observed from a consideration of what constitutes the *whole*. This is a relative term. The whole might be an entire book; it might be an arithmetic problem; it might be a unit in science; or it might be a poem to be memorized. Learning by whole refers to considering the entire unit each time. Thus, in learning a poem, the learner would study through the entire poem each time, rather than one line or sentence before going on to the next line or sentence.

From the many scientific investigations bearing on the effectiveness of the whole and part methods of memorizing verbal materials, no universal conclusions favoring either approach have emerged. The whole method of learning should not be set off as a type of learning in contrast to the part method. A careful consideration of what constitutes the whole reveals that this is a relative term. To the first grade teacher a single sentence may be treated as a unit or whole. At a later stage a story from the first or second grade reader may be thought of as a whole, or a special group of arithmetic exercises may be treated as a whole. The science teacher may consider a special unit on light as a unit or whole.

Although no clear-cut results have been obtained from comparisons of these methods of learning, there is considerable evidence that a relatively short unit with a unifying thread of meaning or unifying pattern is learned more effectively when studied as a whole. The superiority of one method over the other will be conditioned by such variables as, (1) the nature of the materials being learned, (2) the maturity and intelligence of the learner, (3) the experiences of the learner with the materials or skills being learned, and (4) the learning habits which characterize

[30] S. C. Menefee, "Distribution of Effort in Studying Sociology," *School and Society,* Vol. 48 (1938), pp. 243-245.

the learner. When the content is very long, some subdivisions into smaller units is often helpful. For many individuals, and especially children, the learning of the task part by part or in small units results in better motivation.

Ten experiments on whole and part learning were reported by Jensen and Lemaire.[31] Six of these dealt with the memorization of poetry, two with chemical information, and two with directions about typing. The averages for the whole method of learning were superior in all six of the experiments involving poetry. No significant differences appeared for the typewriting learnings, while conflicting results were obtained for memorizing chemical information. The investigators conclude: "Where either method of memorizing is prescribed, or where the child is left to choose his own method, a significantly large percentage will be handicapped." No simple formula can be advanced which gives the superiority of one method over the other. The teacher should select units that are meaningful and within the individual's capacity, rather than divide the materials into isolated meaningless parts to be learned.

Meaningful experiences. The selection and direction of experiences is an essential part of the teaching process. This was suggested in Chapter 1. A collection of unrelated and meaningless experiences will result in little pupil growth. Artificial motivation will not be necessary to enlist children's interest in science or other materials if the teacher will relate the materials to be learned to the children's experiences. Often young children are challenged by ideas that appear commonplace or even dull to the teacher or adult. It is only when the teacher is able to view the universe from the learner's point of view as well as his own, that he is able to enlist the interest and best efforts of the pupils.

Investigations in educational psychology have furnished useful data showing that meaningful materials are learned more readily than meaningless materials. Students in educational psychology were used as subjects in a study of retroactive inhibition and facilitation in the learning of meaningful materials.[32] (The term *retroactive inhibition* has been used to designate interference exerted by new materials that are learned on the retention of previously learned materials.) The learning material consisted of a passage of approximately 1700 words on the history, sacred literature, doctrine, and ethical teachings of Buddhism. The interpolated materials, introduced 24 hours after the initial learning, consisted of a 2100 word comparative essay on Buddhism and Christianity. The results

---

[31] M. B. Jensen and Agnes Lemaire, "Ten Experiments on Whole and Part Learning," *Journal of Educational Psychology,* Vol. 28 (1937), pp. 37-51.

[32] David P. Ausubel, Lillian C. Robbins, and Elias Blake, "Retroactive Inhibition and Facilitation in The Learning of School Material," *Journal of Educational Psychology,* Vol. 48 (1957), pp. 334-343.

indicate that in learning meaningful materials the interpolation of materials somewhat similar to but not identical with the original learning task does not result in retroactive inhibition, but produces as much retroactive facilitation as identical repetition of the learning material. It appears, therefore, that retroactive facilitation occurs when the interpolated material enhances the discriminability of the learning task.

Motion pictures and television have been found useful in enriching the experiences of students at all grade levels. They aid in bringing to the attention of students, concretely and realistically, materials that are taught as abstractions in a conventional way. The use of these media is rapidly becoming an integral part of the educational program. However, television and other audio-visual aids are not substitutes for good teaching. These devices are most helpful in the hands of capable teachers. In the hands of poor teachers they are of little value.

The use of teaching machines. Although the use of teaching machines is a relatively recent innovation in teaching, there has already developed considerable research on their use. Pressey showed a multiple-choice testing and teaching machine at the 1924 American Psychological Association meeting. The following decade saw little progress in the use of such machines. Pressey's [33] 1950 study of over 1000 students used multiple-choice questions with self-scoring punchboards to supplement the instruction in educational psychology. The purpose as stated was to make more efficient use of the teacher's time.

In contrast to Pressey, Skinner [34] developed machines which required the student to compose his responses rather than to select them from a set of alternatives. Also, the student was put through a carefully designed sequence of steps, each so small that (in theory, at least) each student can always take every step. The sequence continuously moves the student closer to the end-product behavior desired. This is in accord with Skinner's emphasis on reinforced conditioning in which the subject is rewarded after he makes the correct response.

This application of technology to education has been termed *auto-instruction* or *self-instruction*.[35] In discussing instructional technology, the following definitions are useful:

Teaching machines: a device which presents to the learner bits of lesson material in small sequenced pieces. It presents a question about each bit and informs the learner immediately of the correctness of his answer. It may

[33] S. L. Pressey, "Development and Appraisal of Devices Providing Immediate Automatic Scoring of Objective Tests and Concomitant Instruction," *Journal of Psychology,* Vol. 29 (1950), pp. 417-447.

[34] B. F. Skinner, "Teaching Machines," *Science,* Vol. 128 (1953), pp. 969-977.

[35] J. D. Finn, "Technology and the Instructional Process," *Phi Delta Kappan,* Vol. 41 (1960), p. 371.

keep electronic records of his learning attempts, his progress, and the zeal with which he works.

Program: a logical ordered learning sequence with thousands of carefully selected bits of lesson material. Cues, prompts, and hints may be used to aid the learner. A two- or three-track program can be designed to further individualize learning. Programs are the heart of the auto-instructional process.[36]

The following distinctive features are claimed for auto-instruction:

1. Each student is continuously active in purposeful learning procedures.
2. Each student is immediately aware of the correctness of his response, and is informed of the correct answer if his response was wrong.
3. Each student proceeds at his own pace.
4. The teacher is freed for special instruction with students needing individual or small-group teaching.

A variety of self-instructional devices have been developed. These include:

1. multiple-choice apparatus and "self-scoring answer sheets"
2. apparatus requiring student constructed responses
3. programmed books, requiring same type of student response as teaching machines
4. complex programs for use with or without machines, such as "scrambled books," mechanical tutors, and computers.[37]

Experiments suggest that machines can be produced which *sense* the characteristics of the student as he studies. It is claimed that these machines will automatically adjust presentation of the programmed materials to fit the student's individual needs.

Enthusiasts claim that the new media can illustrate, discuss, analyze, present content, form concepts, build generalizations and even systematically prescribe areas for continued student inquiry in an automatic classroom.

On balance, however, auto-instructional technology presents the the teacher with two major problems: (1) how to control automation so that the proper objectives of education are served and the human (learner) remains central in the process, and (2) the lack of learning theory, especially with respect to humans, which underlie the media. It will be remembered that an earlier chapter pointed out that the ideal educational climate consisted of one leading to realization resulting from an interplay of forces among the teacher, student, and the idea under

[36] S. L. Pressey, "Review of Teaching Machines," *Contemporary Psychology,* Vol. 6 (1961), p. 186.

[37] Simon Ramo, "A New Technique of Education," *Engineering and Science,* Vol. 21 (1957), pp. 17-22.

consideration. The danger exists that unwise use of automated instructional devices may, in effect, take the teacher out of the learning situation. Lifton's [38] studies have indicated that the end-product of removing the teacher is either failure of the educational effort or a move closer to "thought reform."

SUMMARY

The learner is the central element in the educational process. This notion was emphasized in Chapter 2 and has continuously been restated. The teacher's task is to guide the learner and to stimulate him in his learning activities. Learning has been defined in this chapter as an active process whereby the learner strives to attain a goal or goals which have significance for him. One of the teacher's central problems is to provide students with experiences which will help them attain meaningful and significant goals at successive stages in their growth and learning.

Motivation is essential for learning. The motivational cycle must have its beginning within the individual, although the teacher has the responsibility of guiding the learner in the development and modification of needs. The importance of goals and aspirations as motivating forces has been stressed. Anxiety when directed toward a goal has an important influence on behavior and learning. Closely related to aspiration and anxiety are the interests of the individual child. There is frequently a wide difference between the goals perceived by the teacher and those perceived by the pupils. For example, the teacher may ascribe a pupil's interest to the appeal of the subject matter, while the actual interest is to keep up with some other member of the class.

A variety of incentives are used at home and at school to control and direct learning. A variety of rewards are used by teachers, one of the most frequent being marks or grades. Studies show that these are not equally effective for all pupils. Several important drawbacks to the use of rewards have been presented. Also, the widespread use of competition may actually deter learning for many pupils. There is some evidence that praise may be more effective for most pupils, although certain pupils seem to respond better to reproof. The effects of punishment will depend largely upon the anxiety produced. A comparison of threat of failure with

[38] Robert J. Lifton, *Thought Reform and the Psychology of Totalism* (New York: W. W. Norton & Co., 1961). Thought reform, according to Lipton, relies on an organized blend of energetic and ingenious psychological techniques used in a perverted manner to produce changes in man. Its two basic elements are: (1) confession, exposure, and renunciation of past and present evil (real, fancied, or suggestive), (2) re-education—the remaking of a man in the totalitarian image by means of a series of intellectual, emotional, and physical appeals, in an atmosphere of coercion, aimed at social control and individual change.

security as motivating forces shows that threat of failure has little to offer as a means of motivating most pupils.

Problems and Exercises

1. Look up several definitions of learning. How does the teacher's concept of learning influence the instructional program? Can you illustrate your answer?
2. Give an illustration of learning that involves *insight*. How is trial-and-error behavior involved in learning involving insight? Illustrate.
3. Consider some learning activity from some recent experiences of yours. Show how *differentiation, integration,* and *fixation* were involved.
4. Illustrate from an example of your own experience the role of practice or repetition in learning.
5. What are the implications for teaching of the statement, "Motivation on the part of pupils is essential for effective learning"?
6. Why are motives resulting from cultural forces frequently very puzzling to the teacher? Illustrate this in the case of some learning experience with which you are familiar.
7. Show how the classroom behavior of the third-grade child is an outgrowth of multiple goals. Why is it important for the teacher to be aware of the operation of these goals?
8. How is anxiety related to learning? To one's aspirational level? What are some factors or conditions that determine the aspirational level of a pupil?
9. Compare the effectiveness of praise and reproof or punishment in learning. What difficulties do you encounter in making such a comparison?
10. How would you account for the fact that investigations of the effects of punishment of the child upon learning have not always yielded similar results? What are the major values of punishment in the educational process?

Selected Readings

COLE, L. E., and BRUCE, W. F., *Educational Psychology* (New York: Harcourt, Brace & World, 1950), Ch. 14.

DEESE, J., *The Psychology of Learning* (New York: McGraw, 1958), Ch. 5.

FRANDSEN, A. N., *How Children Learn* (New York: McGraw, 1957), Chs. 2-3.

HILGARD, E. R., *Theories of Learning*, 2nd ed. (New York: Appleton-Century-Crofts, 1956), Chs. 1, 14.

KINGSLEY, H. L., and GARRY, Ralph, *The Nature and Conditions of Learning*, 2nd ed. (Englewood Cliffs: Prentice-Hall, Inc., 1957), Ch. 1.

MOWRER, O. Hobart, "Learning Theory: Historical Review and Re-interpretation," *Harvard Education Review*, Vol. 24 (1954), pp. 37-38.

PRESSEY, S. L., ROBINSON, F. P., and HORROCKS, J. E., *Psychology in Education* (New York: Harper & Row, 1959), Chs. 7-8.

SMITH, Henry P., *Psychology in Teaching*, 2nd ed. (Englewood Cliffs, N.J.: Prentice-Hall, 1962), Chs. 7, 8, 9.

SWENSON, Esther L., *et al.*, *Learning Theory in School Situations* (Minneapolis: University of Minnesota Press, 1949).

THOMSON, Mehran K., "Motivation in School Learning," *Educational Psychology*, 4th ed., Chas. E. Skinner, ed. (Englewood Cliffs: Prentice-Hall, Inc., 1959), Ch. 16.

CHAPTER **8**

Learning for Retention
and Transfer

The assumptions underlying education and teaching today, as they have been throughout the history of education, are that what is learned will be useful in future learning as well as in the solution of everyday problems. All educational efforts aim at learnings which can be recalled and transferred to new situations. Although some of these new situations are met within the school, far more are met in later life after school has been completed. Indeed, many of the situations which the learner will encounter cannot be foreseen, like the consequences of the depression of 1929 upon the economic structure of the nation and the application of atomic fission and fusion to industry and civil life. Ultimately, of course, educational interests in transfer are pointed to later life situations which the learner will meet. Teachers, therefore, are concerned with the amount and type of transfer which may be expected from learning experiences in school.

RETENTION AND FORGETTING

The ability to recall is a great asset to living and to learning, although remembering cannot be equated with learning. Memory may be defined as

. . . a present response bearing a relationship to the past because its stimulus has a previously learned relationship with other experiences. The term "recall" is a very apt designation for memory, for in remembering an event, you re-call it, that is, you name it again. Nothing is ever remembered without a present sign, which arouses a present response determined by past learning. The present symbol may be very gross and obvious or it may be subtle and difficult to identify.[1]

The ability to forget is likewise an important and useful asset to living, for it assuages the painful and unpleasant as well as frees the mind for attention to more significant matters. Consequently, many studies have been made to determine the nature of retention and forgetting in relation to formal learning.

The studies of Ebbinghaus [2] are important not only because they represent the earliest studies in the general field of learning, but also because they present materials bearing on the nature of forgetting. Ebbinghaus constructed and used for the first time nonsense materials in a learning and retention experiment. His results showed that after a one-hour interval following the initial learning it required 45 per cent as much time to relearn lists of nonsense syllables as in the original learning. After an interval of twenty-five hours, it required 79 per cent as much time to relearn the syllables. Thereafter the increase in the amount of time required to relearn the syllables increased progressively with an increase in the time interval (although at a slower rate).

Many subsequent studies have illustrated this tendency to forget rapidly material of low meaningfulness. Figure 8-1 shows a typical curve of forgetting. Note the great amount of forgetting which occurs within the first twenty four hours after learning nonsense material.

Later studies, however, have suggested that such curves are inapplicable to more meaningful material properly taught. Highly meaningful learning may be retained indefinitely with little, if any, forgetting. The rate of forgetting is a function of a number of factors like: (1) thoroughness of initial learning; (2) relevance of learning to personal needs and concepts; (3) influence of time intervening; (4) character of activity following the initial learning; and (5) physical and psychological health of the person at time of learning and time of recall.

Sterrett and Davis [3] concluded from an extensive review of investigations on retention of learning at various school levels that differential retention was to be expected. They found that, at the elementary school

[1] L. F. Shaffer and E. J. Shoben, Jr., *The Psychology of Adjustment* (Boston: Houghton Mifflin, 1956), pp. 141-142.

[2] H. Ebbinghaus, *Memory: A Contribution to Experimental Psychology*, trans. (New York: Teachers College, Columbia University, 1913).

[3] M. D. Sterrett and R. A. Davis, "The Permanence of School Learning: A Review of Studies," *Educational Administration and Supervision*, Vol. 40 (1954), pp. 449-460.

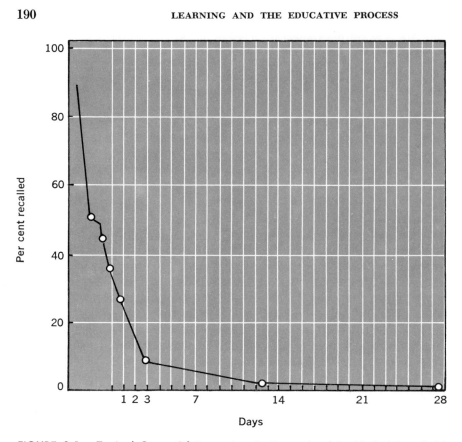

FIGURE 8-1. Typical Curve Of Forgetting As Determined By Verbal Recall Of
Words Learned

level, skills which were used during the vacation period, such as reading, showed a gain during the vacation. There was a difference for history studies: easier material showed a gain on the retest while there was a loss for difficult material. Advanced arithmetic learning was more easily lost than were the fundamental operations.

At the secondary school level, the investigators found a definite loss in mathematics and science during vacations. The amount of loss varied with the different kinds of material and was lowest in the area of general information and application of facts.

For college studies, the review of research indicated that there was "highest retention in United States history, ancient history, and geometry whereas the lowest retention was in physics, chemistry, and Latin . . . The greatest loss (for science) appears to be in technical information with little loss in ability to apply principles to new situation."[4]

    [4] *Ibid.*, pp. 455-456.

Other investigators have found, however, that elementary school children make better scores on tests measuring arithmetic ability which are administered weeks and even months after termination of instruction. The explanation seems to lie in the amount of *meaningfulness* in the instruction. When the children understand fully what they are doing, experience success instead of frustration, they learn to enjoy "playing" with numbers and so continue to learn by themselves.

Influences in forgetting

It has been suggested by psychologists that the curve of forgetting is influenced by several factors, four of which may be listed as follows: (1) non-use of the learned material, (2) retroactive inhibition, (3) reorganization of knowledge, and (4) psychologically motivated forgetting.

We commonly observe and experience *forgetting through disuse* in all learning in school and elsewhere. The early studies of Ebbinghaus showed that there was a very rapid rate of forgetting during the days immediately following the initial learning. Almost all studies of this problem have verified the general results he obtained. As we have pointed out earlier in this chapter, these investigations have been mainly concerned with relatively meaningless material. Recent studies have shown that meaningful structure is the most important factor in preventing forgetting. Clusters of facts organized around concepts, general principles, and molar statements are remembered far longer than details, single facts, and isolated specific rules.

The implication for retention is that during the early days following the learning, materials should be reviewed to reduce the amount of forgetting through disuse. Further, spaced reviewing should be provided, and students should be brought to see material as an organized body of meaningful concepts.

Retroactive inhibition. Retroactive inhibition is the interference exerted by new material on the retention of previously learned materials. There will be considerable forgetting of materials learned in history if the student immediately turns to a study of his psychology lesson without carefully reviewing what he had read in his history assignment. It is not mere disuse that causes ordinary forgetting. Learning of new materials seems to interfere with the recall of earlier responses, particularly if they are not reinforced or reviewed.

Swenson draws the following general conclusions from a review of the literature bearing on this aspect of forgetting:

It seems in general that the conditions contributing to the construction of well-organized patterns of knowledge and skill are those for which retroactive inhibition is at a minimum. Previous experience, meaningfulness of material, intelligence, and general maturity seem to result in such reduction of inhibitory effects. On the other hand, retroaction tends to increase under conditions contributing to disorganization or confusion of original and interpolated learning materials.[5]

Reorganization. Learning as a reorganization of experiences is a factor both in learning and forgetting. The phases of differentiation and integration described in Chapter 7 suggest this. Much forgetting is due to inattention and inadequate initial learning. When the student must utilize such imperfectly learned material he *reorganizes* his response in the form of a regular and consistent interpretation.[6] Such responses will resemble objects or concepts familiar to the student. They will be more regular, more consistent, and less involved than their original counterparts of which they are the imperfectly remembered productions.[7]

Psychologically motivated forgetting. This well-known phenomenon enables us to forget unpleasant experiences or tasks which we may find threatening. An unconscious defense mechanism, it may even influence the acquisition of complex *initial* learnings. A number of carefully controlled studies have found positive evidence that repression is a cause in selective forgetting. Summarizing, Shaffer and Shoben conclude that "if an event is in disagreement with your social evaluation of yourself and especially if it represents a derogatory appraisal, it will arouse conflict and anxiety. One way to adjust to such a threat is to forget it, or to distort it into agreement with your self-evaluation based on the social standards you have learned." [8]

Thoroughness of learning. Retention is influenced by the thoroughness of the initial learning. One's retention of Mother Goose rhymes learned as a child and repeated many times after the materials were originally learned illustrates this. (Other factors are also present, such as mnemonic aid from rhyming and pleasurable associations with parental affection.) Continued practice and repetition of material to be learned is referred to as *overlearning.*

This problem was studied in an early experiment by Krueger [9] in which monosyllabic words were memorized by different groups of

[5] Esther Swenson, "Retroactive Inhibtition: A Review of the Literature," *University of Minnesota, Studies of Education,* No. 1 (1941), p. 56.

[6] Frederic C. Bartlett, *Remembering: A Study in Experimental and Social Psychology* (New York: Macmillan, 1932).

[7] A. Burton and R. Tueller, "Successive Reproduction of Visually Perceived Forms," *Journal of Genetic Psychology,* Vol. 58 (1941), pp. 71-82.

[8] Shaffer and Shoben, *op. cit.,* p. 234.

[9] W. C. Krueger, "The Effect of Overlearning on Retention," *Journal of Experimental Psychology,* Vol. 12 (1929), pp. 71-78.

subjects. The words were presented by means of a memory drum at the rate of two seconds per word. When a subject was able to anticipate correctly all the words in a list during a single presentation there was 100-per-cent learning. To obtain 150-per-cent learning the presentations were continued until the number of trials equalled one half of the number required for the 100-per-cent level; while 200-per-cent learning was considered to have occurred when the presentations were continued an equal number of times taken for the 100-per-cent learning.

Results for the three degrees of learning are presented in Figure 8-2. These retention curves show that retention increased in direct relation to the amount of overlearning; however, there was not the corresponding increase in retention from 150-per-cent to 200-per-cent learning as there was from 100-per-cent to 150-per-cent learning. The results suggest that overlearning by at least 50 per cent is highly desirable in order to

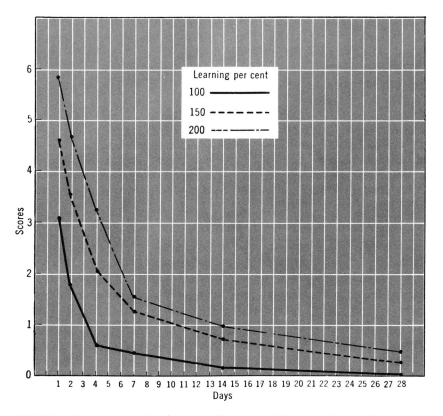

FIGURE 8-2. Average Verbal Recall Scores Obtained For Different Degrees Of Overlearning Monosyllabic Nouns

increase retention, but that there is a point beyond which overlearning is uneconomical.

Special features of memory and forgetting

Educators concerned with the problems of recall and transfer must consider what brain mechanisms are involved. Neurologically, what determines memory or enhances its power? What prevents or inhibits its function? Gerard summarizes the evidence currently available:

. . . we face one great problem: how does experience alter the experiencing nervous system? How do nerve impulses running along nerve fibers and across synapses change the ease with which subsequent impulses may follow and sometimes even alter the path which they are to follow; what and where is the memory trace?

Not all incoming messages leave a lasting trace, or even a brief one. At one extreme are single "unforgettable" experiences—a close brush with death on the highway or a sudden shaft of sunlight in the forest. . . .

At the other extreme are the experiences which leave no permanent trace —for example, the vivid experiences of a dream, often related to some sensation, that evaporate when one wakes. Extended interactions of a person under the influence of alcohol or narcotics or light anesthesia or hypnosis may be totally erased when he returns to normal. Other actions may appear to be forgotten but can be recovered by appropriate manipulation. The memory gap for events preceding a concussion is usually absolute. But the loss of memory associated with a violently unpleasant experience can often be overcome by drugs or hypnosis or psychotherapy. One effect of aging, especially among those with arteriosclerosis, is loss of recent memory. Such a person may carry on a complex set of activities, including an important conversation, and yet forget the entire episode as soon as it is completed. Clearly, the physiological state of the neurons is important for fixing experiences, whether jarred or drugged, young or old.

More subtle differences in state are also involved, ones that can be most simply described in terms of attention. Happenings to which one is "paying attention" are more likely to be noted and remembered than those not attended to. The schoolboy, asked unexpectedly to tell the meaning of a passage he had just read aloud in class, who blurts out, "I don't know. I wasn't listening," is a good example . . . Clearly, the level of attention and the pattern of activity of various brain regions at the time of the experience are also important in determining how well the message is received and how permanently it is fixed in the mind.

These examples exhibit again the components of all neural behavior— the units or neurons on the one hand and, on the other, the ways in which they interact, by fiber nets, electric fields, or chemical concentrations. A nervous system after it has stored a given memory must be different from what it was before it received it, in the properties of some neurons or in their patterns of interactions.

For example, when one spot on the exposed brain of a conscious human is stimulated by electric shocks (a necessary procedure in connection with some brain operations), a given episode from his past may unwind, as if a movie reel were being projected, so long as the stimulation continues. If the electric stimuli are stopped and restarted, the memory also starts again at the beginning. If a nearby spot is stimulated, a different memory unfolds . . . [Further] . . . learned behavior in, say, a rat can be abolished by cutting out a part of the brain . . . [But] that same rat may later relearn the same behavior even though the part of his brain that originally stored it is missing. And extensive damage to an animal or human brain may produce no detectable memory loss. It is clear, then, that memories cannot be simply *deposited,* each on its own spot or neuron.

Perhaps, then, a memory is some continuing activity—a trapped nerve message running round and round a particular set of loops formed by neurons with fibers synapsing on one another . . . It can be tested simply by stopping all neuron activity for a period and observing whether memories are abolished. Any brain difference depending only on *patterns of impulse travel* should be eliminated when the travel stops. In order to test this theory, rodents are taught some performance and then given a vigorous electric shock across the brain, which discharges all neurons at once and blocks all messages temporarily; or are made to hibernate at freezing temperatures, which stop all brain messages. When they recover from the shock or the cold they remember perfectly well.

. . . If the shock is given some hours after the trial experience . . . it has no influence on learning or remembering. But if it is given only a few minutes after the trial, the animal never does learn. Time must elapse between having the experience and fixing it in the brain . . . Other experiments suggest that this fixation time may well be occupied by nerve messages running round and round a neuron chain. Something like a hundred thousand circuits could be traveled in the time available, and it is quite conceivable that only after enough passages have been made is a permanent change left behind in the neurons or synapses . . . Perhaps, then, incoming messages do not simply enter the nervous system and either fade out or emerge to produce immediate effector responses. It is possible that they may also reverberate for a longer or shorter time and so leave more or less enduring changes in the brain itself.

. . . Many such [experimental] findings show that messages may reach an appropriate region of the brain and lead to partial but incomplete consequences. . . . If the incoming message starts to reverberate but is cut off too soon, full awareness does not develop. And the cutoff could come about in many ways—by the setting up of suppressing or inhibiting messages that feed back to the incoming path and block it, for example, or by the failure of facilitating or reinforcing responses.[10]

Research indicates that whatever is not in consciousness is probably electronically stored in the brain.[11] Meaningful associations have been found to be helpful in retrieving (*recalling* or *remembering*) this *stored* information. Therapy, hypnosis, drugs, physiological approaches, and the force of psychological interrelationships can also be used to aid in its

[10] R. W. Gerard, "The Brain: Mechanism of the Mind," in *An Outline of Man's Knowledge of the Modern World,* Lyman Bryson, ed. (Garden City, N.Y.: Doubleday & Co., 1960), pp. 79-82.

[11] See Wilder Penfield and Lamar Roberts, *Speech and Brain-Mechanisms* (Princeton: Princeton Univ. Press, 1959).

recall. Fatigue, illness, anxiety or other bodily disturbances which upset the homeostasis of the brain tend to interfere with retention.[12]

Educational implications of retention. The various studies concerning learning and retention point to the following conclusions and implications for education:

1. The retention of materials learned or habits acquired is significantly affected by the extent to which the materials and habits are fully integrated into previously learned materials.
2. The rate of forgetting is most rapid during the period immediately following the learning. Spaced reviewing should be provided to reduce such forgetting.
3. Retention will be significantly affected by the purposes and goals of the learner. Consequently, a special effort should be made to relate habits, skills, and knowledge acquired to the learner's goals, needs, and purposes.
4. Overlearning is directly related to retention. There is, however, an optimum point of learning and overlearning which should be taken into account by the teacher. If this point is exceeded, learning and retention tend to diminish. This, of course, varies with different individuals and different types of learnings.
5. Retention is affected by the nature of the activity immediately following the learning. This interference exerts an important consequence in all study and learning situations.
6. Reviews and additional practice may cause the learner to retain erroneous concepts and faulty habits. Consequently, the learner should be guided in eliminating wrong responses before they become definitely fixed.
7. The physical and psychological condition of the learner are important determinants of learning and retention. Fatigue, anxiety, and illness significantly affect the amount learned as well as the ability to recall.

Evolution of transfer theories

Theories of learning and transfer. Transfer of learning is a problem of major concern to the educational psychologist and to teachers alike. Just as retention refers to the extent and duration of remembering what has been learned, so transfer refers to the nature and amount of use that is made of previous learning—especially the learning acquired in the school program—to new learning situations. The findings of research studies in connection with the prevalent learning theories will be important to teaching practices for the transfer of learning. The very existence of an educational system implies that learning can be transferred to new situations and problems. However, it is the extent of the transfer

[12] Albert D. Biderman and Herbert Zimmer, eds. *The Manipulation of Human Behavior* (New York: John Wiley & Sons, 1961). This book carefully reviews experimental evidence regarding the amount of voluntary or forced recall which might be induced by drugs, psychophysiologic response measures, hypnosis, physiologic and sensory deprivation, and interpersonal influence. It also examines their effect on brain functioning in general.

and the manner in which it takes place that is a matter of psychological and educational concern.

Formal-discipline theory. The classical curriculum of the nineteenth century was built upon the idea that the student should study Latin, Greek, logic, and mathematics because of their value in training the mind. According to the doctrine of formal discipline, the study of mathematics quickens the mental faculties so that they are powerful in meeting any and all mental tasks. The real value of a subject, such as mathematics, then, is that it is difficult. From the formal-discipline viewpoint, the study of difficult materials strengthens the mind, just as exercise with heavy weights strengthens the muscles. The study of logic, similarly, would train the student to deal with all problems in an orderly manner and with profound insight.

The theory of formal discipline had an important influence on the high school and college curriculum in the nineteenth century. Some of this influence apparently still exists today in American schools although it is masked under such terms as *mastering the humanities, intellectual discipline,* and *mental discipline.* Much of European higher education is still based upon the doctrine of developing the higher mental abilities through the use of the classical, academic program. In his discussion of reforms in educational systems being carried out in Europe, Elvin points out that "the argument for maintaining [scholastic] standards has got mixed up with the arguments for and against certain traditional subjects of study." [13]

At the end of the 19th century, William James [14] tested the theory that mental exercise enabled the mind to perform better. He practiced learning sections of *Paradise Lost* for exercising memory. Then he tested his improvement on a section of Victor Hugo's poetry. (He had previously established a base time on another section of Hugo.) The results of his experiments and those of his students led to the conclusion that practice in memorizing did *not* improve the memory.

In the period that followed James' report the mental measurement movement got under way and various tests were developed for measuring mental abilities. Thorndike and Woodworth reported experiments on transfer in the estimation of areas, lengths, and weights along with the results of training in various forms of observations and perceptions. The results of these studies indicated varying possibilities of transfer—sometimes positive, sometimes negative, and frequently near zero. These investigators summarized the results of their studies in the following

[13] Lionel Elvin, "An Introduction to Reform in West Europe's Post-Primary Education," Lionel Elvin, *Phi Delta Kappan,* Vol. 43 (1961), pp. 50-53.

[14] William James, *The Principles of Psychology* (New York: Holt, Rinehart & Winston, 1890), p. 667.

statement: "Spread of practice occurs only where identical elements are concerned in the influencing and influenced functions." [15]

Here we note the first use of the widely used phrase *identical elements.*

Theory of identical elements. These and other researches led Thorndike to conclude:

> Training the mind means the development of thousands of particular independent capacities, the formation of countless particular habits, for the working of any mental capacity depends upon the concrete data with which it works. Improvement of any one mental function or activity will improve others only in so far as they possess elements common to it also. The amount of identical elements in different mental functions and the amount of general influence from special training are much less than common opinion supposes.[16]

Thus, the doctrine of identical elements held that transfer could occur from one learning to another only so far as the two functions had elements in common. As the similarity decreased there was usually a falling off in the amount of transfer. Conversely, the amount of transfer would increase in proportion to the number of identical elements contained in both situations.

Thorndike defined identical elements as those "mental processes which have the same cell action in the brain as their physical correlate." [17] Thus, there were "thousands of particular independent capacities each of which must be developed by itself" if they are to be developed at all. Each "one ability is improved by the exercise of another only when the neurones whose action the former represents are actually altered in the course of the exercise of the latter."

The theory of identical elements as stated by Thorndike presupposes *neural grooves* or neural synapses along which reactions move and nerve cells change to *fix* memories for transfer. In this concept, Thorndike anticipated some of the findings of neurologists but was handicapped by the erroneous assumption of medical researchers of the period that complex functions had "centers" in the cerebral hemispheres. Modern research has found that the cerebral hemispheres do not have specific pathways associated with such mental activities as *abstraction, cognition, integration, reason,* or the like. Instead, the brain has a maze of potential paths over any of which the complex patterns of activity associated with the

[15] E. L. Thorndike and R. S. Woodworth, "The Influence of Improvement in One Mental Function upon the Efficiency of Other Functions," *Psychological Review,* Vol. 8 (1901), pp. 247-261, 384, 395, 553-564. Quotation from p. 250.

[16] E. L. Thorndike, *Principles of Teaching* (New York: A. G. Seiler, 1906), p. 248.

[17] E. L. Thorndike, *Educational Psychology* (New York: Columbia University Press, 1913, II), p. 359.

highest intellectual functions may be established. Thus, recent research has found that when any part of the cerebral hemisphere is damaged, none of the highest integrative activities are entirely lost, but the capacity to perform all is impaired to a greater or lesser extent depending on the severity of the damage.

An often cited example of transfer of training based upon apparently identical elements is the effect of learning to spell orally upon the ability to spell the same words in writing. Although the cues on which the subject depends are said to be common, *written* and *oral* spelling, in fact, depend on intricate, complex and *differing* associative learnings.[18] This example is presented as a sample of the type of misconception which sometimes leads teachers into difficulty. (It should be noted, however, that the misconception is *not* that of the proponents of the theory of identical elements, but is based on the seemingly logical identity of spelling operations.)

The theory of identical components did not confine transfer to highly detailed segments or merely to extremely narrow items. This theory, while denying, for instance, that target practice would improve one's power of concentration, temperament, or observation, would affirm that certain methods, skills, and attitudes learned in the course of target practice would carry over to another activity to the extent that the two activities and the total situations have important characteristics in common. What, then, are some of the responses, according to this theory, which may transfer? The method of keeping the eye carefully focused upon the target may carry over to hitting a baseball or even to catching a ball. Also, the development of a reasonable amount of assurance and confidence may carry over into another activity. What is carried over, from the viewpoint of identical elements doctrine, is *not* an improved memory *faculty* or *power* of reasoning, but *methods* of attack, ideas, and *attitudes* which may be *beneficial* or *harmful* to the performance of another act. For instance, to the extent that they are similar, previous knowledge learned in algebra may provide cues to the solution of other problems. Historical information may make the reading of certain pieces of literature more meaningful.

A study by Gagne' and Foster,[19] bearing on this, was designed to determine the influence of the practice of certain subordinate activities of a complex skill upon the learning of the total skill. Different amounts

[18] See David H. Russell, "Auditory Abilities and Achievement in Spelling in the Primary Grades," *Journal of Educational Psychology*, Vol. 49 (1958), pp. 315-319. Donald Durrell also discusses the influence of visual and auditory perception in written and oral spelling in *Improving Reading Instruction* (New York: World Publishing Company, 1956), pp. 279-283.

[19] R. M. Gagne' and H. Foster, "Transfer of Training From Practice on Components in a Motor Skill," *Journal of Experimental Psychology*, Vol. 32 (1949), pp. 47-68.

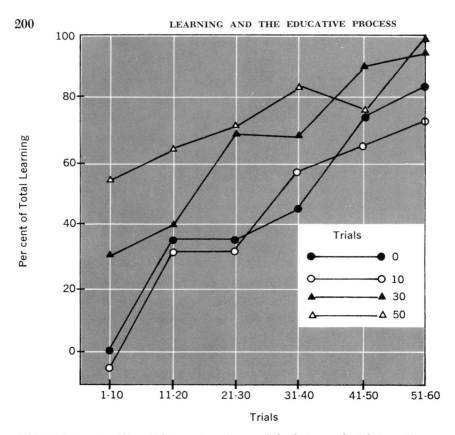

FIGURE 8-3.   Per Cent Of Learning Accomplished By Each Of Four Groups With Different Numbers Of Preliminary Training Trials And Six Stages Of Practice On The Final Task

of training were given to separate groups of subjects on an initial task which was a part of a total skill involving four different manual reactions. Following the initial practice each group learned the total skill to a high degree of efficiency. The degree to which different amounts of practice on the subordinate parts contributed to the learning of the total skill is shown in Figure 8-3. These data show that there is a definite transfer from the subordinate to the total performance. It is evident, however, that the most efficient method of training for any given level of performance, in terms of number of trials to learn, is that which begins with the total motor skill without preliminary practice on the subordinate parts.

Generalization theory and transfer.   The theory of generalization was early projected by Judd [20] as an explanation of transfer. In his ex-

[20] C. H. Judd, "The Relation of Special Training to General Intelligence," *Educational Review*, Vol. 36 (1908), pp. 36-37.

periment two groups of boys were given practice in shooting at a target beneath water. In one situation the target was submerged twelve inches under the water, while in the second situation it was placed four inches under the water. One group was taught the theory of refraction of light by water while the other group was given no explanation. When the depth of the target was changed, the group which had been taught the theory of refraction of light showed a significant superiority over the other group. Judd explained this superiority as the result of applying a principle learned in one situation to the performance of a task in a different situation. Thus, he places emphasis upon human intelligence which enables an individual to understand and apply to specific situations principles and meanings acquired in previous situations.

Hendrickson and Schroeder [21] repeated the experiment in 1940, attempting to duplicate as nearly as possible the work of Judd. The investigators used 3 groups however. As in the Judd experiment, the control group received no explanation. Group A received an elementary explanation of the theory of refraction. Group B received the same explanation with the addition of a sentence specifically calling attention to the fact that changing the depth of water changes the amount of refraction. Both experimental groups learned more rapidly than the control group. Group B learned more rapidly than Group A. The researchers found that, as did Judd, knowledge of theory facilitated transfer. They also concluded, however, that 1) knowledge of theory was helpful in making the original adjustment to the learning situation and that 2) the definiteness and completeness of theoretical information had a direct effect on both initial learning and transfer. (See Figure 8-4.)

The theory of generalization has received support from many other investigations. An experiment reported by Swenson [22] was concerned with this problem. Three groups of second-grade children learned 100 addition facts by three different methods:

In method D the addition facts were arranged in order of difficulty and repetitive drill was the principal procedure followed.

In method X the addition facts were grouped by the size of the sum (all the combinations with the sum of 8 were grouped together, etc.), and the children were allowed to verify the newly presented fact prior to the drill process.

In method G the addition facts were grouped by generalization, and the children were guided in discovering the generalizations rather than having them given self-made.

Tests were administered to the groups at intervals during the period of the experiment and at the end. These tests included addition facts not

[21] Gordon Hendrickson and William H. Schroeder, "Transfer of Training in Learning to Hit a Submerged Target," *Journal of Educational Psychology*, Vol. 32 (1941), pp. 205-213.

[22] *Op. cit.*

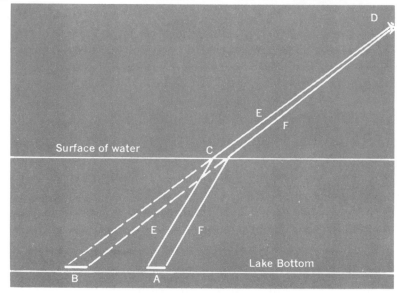

FIGURE 8-4.   Illustration Of Light Refraction In Water

Explanation of refraction as provided for group A

Everything we see is visible because light comes from it to our eye. Objects under water, when seen from above, do not appear in their true positions. Thus, in the diagram, the rock at A seems to be at B.

This deception is caused by the refraction or bending of the light beam ACD at the surface of the water. The light rays are bent because light moves faster in air than it does in water. The side of the beam marked E escapes from the water before the side marked F reaches the air. Therefore side E gets ahead of side F and the ray of light is actually bent.

We are not used to light rays being bent. Consequently, we suppose that the stone lies in a straight line from our eye, and we make the mistake of thinking that it is at point B.

Additional explanation for group B

It is easy to see from the diagram that the deeper the lake, the farther the real rock A will be from the image rock B.

taught, more complex addition problems, and subtraction facts. The results of these tests showed transfer in the case of all three groups. Group G (in which the addition facts were grouped by generalizations) made the greatest gain, while Group D (the drill group) showed the least gain. A tendency was noted for retroactive inhibition to occur more frequently and in greater amount among the children taught by the drill method than among those who were guided in formulating generalizations.

Beginning, therefore, with the writings of Judd and continuing with significant experiments into the 1930's, it was suggested that considerable transfer may result from applications of general principles. These studies opened the way for educators to project the possibilities for increasing the transfer value of particular school subjects. Successful teachers have based their teaching on this principle, thus increasing the transfer value of the materials taught. Concerning this Symonds has stated:

. . . Of primary importance is experience with the materials that permits a child to make reactions toward the material; but merely telling the child the principle without giving him an opportunity to react to it is sterile. The greatest gain is made by organizing the materials, directing attention to them, and the like, so that children are helped to react to the principle and hence to discover it. One should not expect them to discover, unaided, principles in science, mathematics, and language that it has taken the best thinkers of all ages to discover.[23]

These findings reveal that, in the period following Thorndike's explication of the theory of identical elements, the propositions advanced by Thorndike were too narrowly interpreted in their applications to all learning.

Transposition theory and transfer. Transposition theories describe the process of using understanding of the inner structure of a problem situation to aid in dealing with variations of the situation later encountered. Such theories are sometimes called *patterns of experience.*

Among several theories of transfer emphasizing patterns of experience, one of the best known is the Gestalt theory, set forth by Max Wertheimer and others. Wertheimer's precepts were evolved over a number of years.[24] A "gestalt" is a whole "the behavior of which is not determined by that of its individual elements but where the part-processes are themselves determined by the intrinsic nature of the whole." Thus, according to this theory, to learn is to form or to complete a Gestalt—a pattern or configuration which has *meaning.* According to this viewpoint, the learner responds as a unified and integrated organism to the total stimulus—a pattern or structure. In a discussion of how learners transfer mathematical learnings to the task of finding the area of a parallelogram, Wertheimer points out that a number of mental operations are involved:

1. There is *grouping, reorganization, structurization,* operations of dividing into sub-wholes and still seeing these sub-wholes together, with clear ref-

[23] Percival M. Symonds, "What Education Has to Learn from Psychology. VII. Transfer and Formal Discipline," *Teachers College Record,* Vol. 61 (1959), p. 44.

[24] A compilation is contained in M. Wertheimer, *Productive Thinking,* rev. ed. (New York: Harper & Row, 1959).

erence to the whole figure and in view of the specific problem at issue . . .

2. The process starts with the desire to get at the inner relatedness of form and size. This is not a search for just any relation which would connect them, but for the nature of their intrinsic interdependence . . .

3. Outstanding relations of this kind—sensible with regard to the inner structural nature of the given situation . . . play a large role here . . .

4. There is the feature of the functional meaning of parts, e.g., the characteristically different meaning of the two terms entering into the multiplication, a feature decisive for the productive solution and for any real understanding of the formula.

5. The entire process is one consistent line of thinking. It is not an and-sum of aggregated piecemeal operations. No step is arbitrary, ununderstood in its function. On the contrary, each step is taken surveying the whole situation. [25]

Thus, according to this theory, transfer will take place to the extent that the learner recognizes significant relations in two situational patterns. In poetry, for instance, a particular rhythm may be repeated even though the lines differ in length and have no words in common.

There is some similarity between the transposition and the identical elements doctrines. This is found in the common emphasis of both doctrines on the importance of generalizing or carrying over ideas and principles from an old to a new pattern. They also agree in that both stress the necessity of understanding the *inner relatedness* of the wholes. The main difference between the doctrines lies in the basis of equivalence. The transposition doctrine may be regarded as a theory which emphasizes generalizations involving patterns. Furthermore, the identical-elements theory is *atomistic* in approach whereas the transposition theory is *holistic*.

There are a number of studies which indicate that the learner must recognize previously encountered common elements found in new situations before transfer can take place. Maier [26] has suggested that when previous experiences help one in solving a new problem, it is because the problem contains an element of relationship to which the person has already reacted.

It will be recalled that, according to the doctrine of formal discipline, the learning of certain materials, such as mathematics or logic, strengthens the faculties of the mind—particularly the reasoning faculty. Thus, the theory held, the learner would develop an increased reasoning power applicable to all situations. When research cast doubt on the validity of this doctrine, it was discovered that situations containing *common elements* elicited transfer. Later research, however, failed to substantiate

[25] *Ibid.*, pp. 41-42.
[26] Norman R. F. Maier, "Reasoning in Humans: The Mechanism of Equivalent Stimuli in Reasoning," *Journal of Experimental Psychology*, Vol. 35 (1945), pp. 349-360.

some of the theories held by educators who narrowly interpreted the propositions of Thorndike. While transfer of training was found to involve identical elements, experiments showed that mere identity was not enough. The individual must recognize, as a result of memory or meanings established, the existence and relevance of identities. It is at this point that the theory of identical elements referred to in the early studies by Thorndike, and the theory of generalization, referred to in the studies by Judd, tend to fuse into a unitary theory based upon *subjectively observed identical elements*. The form of awareness which reflects these functional relations may also be called *patterns of experience*.

Current concepts and interpretations of transfer theories. Careful study of research and modern experiments have indicated that, in addition to similarity of content, and appropriateness of methods of instruction or guidance, the amount of transfer will depend upon the ability of children to generalize and upon the intelligence of the children. It has also been shown that the attitude or mental set of the learner has an important influence upon transfer. It might be stated as a fundamental principle that a favorable attitude toward learning a task and desirable learning procedures will tend to produce a superior amount of transfer from one learning task to another.

An experiment by Ulmer may be cited to illustrate this. In a carefully controlled investigation, Ulmer [27] demonstrated that when geometry was taught so that emphasis was given to the application of principles to nongeometric situations, marked gains on general reasoning tests occurred; whereas, when no such emphasis was given the gains on reasoning tests were only slight.

Katona contrasted the results of rote learning by memorization with the results of learning by understanding, drawing three generalizations:

1. The advantage of learning with understanding does not necessarily appear in the original learning because learning with understanding may take a longer time than rote learning.
2. Retention after meaningful learning tends to be greater than retention after learning by rote memorization.
3. Transfer of learning to new tasks is greater from meaningful learning than from learning related tasks by rote.[28]

In distinguishing between senseless and meaningful learning, Katona asserted that if a pupil learns a procedure by rote without understanding

[27] Gilbert Ulmer, "Teaching Geometry to Cultivate Reflective Thinking: an Experimental Study with 1239 High School Pupils," *Journal of Experimental Education*, Vol. 8 (1939), pp. 18-25.

[28] George Katona, *Organizing and Memorizing* (New York: Columbia Univ. Press, 1940).

why or how it works (senseless learning), he will be unable to vary it appropriately for use in a similar situation.

In an investigation with 60 high school students which was designed to test Katona's generalizations, Hilgard and his colleagues found:

1. Considerably more time was required to teach the learning tasks initially to the *Understanding* Group than to the *Memorization* Group.
2. Overnight retention was equal for both groups, although many retention errors were made even after this short interval. Tests of retention through relearning favored the Understanding Group.
3. Transfer to a task requiring simple transposition showed that the Understanding Group achieved—to a marginally statistical significance—greater success than the Memorization Group.
4. Transfer to three tasks requiring problem-solving all favored the Understanding Group by statistically significant amounts.[29]

These findings, although failing to substantiate Katona's assertion that students who learn by understanding would retain more than those who learned by rote, substantiated his conclusions that understanding is superior to rote memorization in learning for transfer.

Bruner summarizes the changing conception of how transfer is achieved:

. . . Virtually all of the evidence of the last two decades on the nature of learning and transfer has indicated that, while the original theory of formal discipline was poorly stated in terms of the training of faculties, it is indeed a fact that massive general transfer can be achieved by appropriate learning, even to the degree that learning properly under optimum conditions leads one to "learn how to learn." These studies have stimulated a renewed interest in complex learning of a kind that one finds in schools, learning designed to produce general understanding of the structure of a subject matter . . . The often unconscious nature of learning structures is perhaps best illustrated in learning one's native language. Having grasped the subtle structure of a sentence, the child very rapidly learns to generate many other sentences based on this model though different in content from the original sentence learned . . . How can [a necessarily limited exposure to materials to be learned] be made to count in [students'] thinking for the rest of their lives? The dominant view among men who have been engaged in preparing and teaching new curricula is that the answer to this question lies in giving students an understanding of the fundamental structure of whatever subjects we choose to teach. This is a minimum requirement for using knowledge, for bringing it to bear on problems and events one encounters outside a classroom—or in classrooms one enters later in one's training. The teaching and learning of structure, rather than simply the mastery of facts and techniques, is at the center of the classic problem of transfer.[30]

[29] Ernest R. Hilgard, Robert P. Irvine, and James E. Whipple, "Rote Memorization, Understanding, and Transfer: An Extension of Katona's Card-Trick Experiments," *Journal of Experimental Psychology*, Vol. 46 (1953), pp. 288-292.

[30] Jerome S. Bruner, *The Process of Education* (Cambridge, Mass.: Harvard Univ. Press, 1961), pp. 5-6, 8, 11-12.

Such transfer (i.e., the mere mastery of facts and techniques), of course, is not desirable but it is an illustration of how transfer of learning does occur in all aspects of life. Such transfer of learning, however, can be consciously guided by the teacher, in many instances, so that it increases the pupil's ability to utilize his potentials constructively as he develops toward maturity in aptitudes, interests, attitudes, and the manifold other aspects of personality.

Personality factors affecting learning and transfer

Each type of response that can be learned can be transferred under the right conditions, and each learning experience becomes a part of one's personality, for good or ill.

Learnings which are not adjustive often transfer from the initial experience to others where they handicap or injure the learner. As we have already pointed out, anxiety has a potential for generalization so that anxious feelings may become attached to other situations similar in some element to the original anxiety-arousing stimulus. Recent investigations have shown the tendency of anxiety-arousing cues to inhibit memory and restrict creative thinking.

Attitudes and transfer of learning. A learner may approach a learning task in many ways—indifferently, ambivalently, positively. Attitudes, the person's desire to learn, and his level of aspiration are major factors in his readiness to learn.

Kersh concluded from his research that:

. . . the superiority of the discovery procedure over procedures of learning with external direction is not adequately explained in terms of "meaningful learning." The results of this experiment suggest that when the learner is forced to rely on his own cognitive abilities, it is more likely that he will become motivated to continue the learning process or to continue practicing the task after the learning period. Consequently, the learning becomes more permanent and is more effectively transferred than when the learner is not so motivated.[31]

Attitudes may also reinforce incidental learning initially occurring without any intent on the part of the person to consciously master the task. Skinner points out how this many happen:

. . . behavior [of an organism] at the moment of reinforcement and during the period preceding reinforcement is part of the stimulating environment, aspects of which acquire control over subsequent behavior. To take a very simple example: if an organism is characteristically responding at a high rate

[31] Bert Y. Kersh, "The Adequacy of 'Meaning' as an Explanation for the Superiority of Learning by Independent Discovery," *Journal of Educational Psychology,* Vol. 49 (1958), p. 292.

at the moment of reinforcement [as might occur under the set of a favorable or facilitating attitude] behavior at that rate becomes an optimal stimulating condition, comparable to the presence of the reinforced stimulus in a discrimination, and the probability of further responding is therefore maximal.[32]

Teachers may *lessen* readiness for reasoning and ability to transfer learning instead of increasing it by encouraging the pupil to accept uncritically rules of procedure to learn techniques without understanding the underlying principles, to memorize formulae, or to proceed in a stereotyped way in approaching learning tasks. The pupil often develops a rigid attitude, and becomes set to react in a certain way. This helps him as long as each new learning task is like the preceding one, but hampers him whenever a task is different.

In an investigation of the effects of such a set, Luchins [33] used water-jar problems in which the pupil was required to obtain a specified amount of water using only empty jars and their total capacities as measures (e.g.: if you have a 9 quart jar, a 3 quart jar and a 1 quart jar, how can you get exactly 5 quarts of water?) By working many problems using all 3 jars during the training sessions, Luchins created a set in the pupils to use combinations of three water jars. Consequently, many pupils were not able to solve simpler problems involving only two jars, such as, How can you get exactly 6 quarts of water?

In an investigation using an adaptation of Luchins' water jars problems, Ackerman and Levin [34] found that pupils trained in alternative problem-solving methods solved more problems correctly, offered a greater variety of solutions to the problems, and persisted longer in working on problems which they were unable to completely solve than did a like group of sixth graders who had been trained in only one problem-solving procedure.

In another study which presented students with a variety of problems which could not be solved by just one attack, Schroeder and Rotter [35] showed that flexibility in the attack on problems is something that can be learned and that such a learned behavior pattern had transfer possibilities. Students who developed an attitude of flexibility experienced success whereas those who had a rigid approach failed.

These studies suggest that a teacher, by emphasizing a variety of alternative learning approaches and by encouraging his students to seek

[32] B. F. Skinner, "Reinforcement Today," *American Psychologist*, Vol. 13 (1958), p. 96.

[33] Luchins, A. S., "Mechanization in Problem Solving," *Psychological Monographs*, Vol. 54 (1942), No. 6.

[34] Walter I. Ackerman and Harry Levin, "Effects of Training in Alternative Solutions on Subsequent Problem Solving," *Journal of Educational Psychology*, Vol. 49 (1958), pp. 239-244.

[35] Harold M. Schroeder and Julian B. Rotter, "Rigidity as Learned Behavior," *Journal of Experimental Psychology*, Vol. 43 (1952), pp. 141-150.

out possibilities for additional applications of the principles learned, will help them to develop attitudes facilitating transfer.

The influence of set on learning and retention. The influence of set on the learning and retention of concepts was investigated by Reed [36] with 51 college students as subjects. The materials used in the experiment consisted of 42 cards, each of which had four unrelated English words on the face and a nonsense syllable on the reverse side. One group of students was instructed to learn only the names on the cards (the nonsense syllables). The other group was instructed to learn both names and meanings (English words) associated with them. The results from this study revealed that a *set* to learn meanings as well as names yields a much higher rate of learning and a greater degree of retention than does a set to learn names only. Also concepts logically formed are learned more quickly and are better remembered than those illogically formed.

The individual who has a set to *learn* a problem in arithmetic is more likely to see relationships and form logical deductions than one merely set to *memorize* a formula. This problem, furthermore, is closely related to *meaning*. For example, the concept *justice* is learned more readily when it is closely related to activities and experiences in the home and school. As the early studies of Hartshorne and May [37] suggest, abstract concepts like *justice* and *honesty* are more readily transferred (i.e. put into action in specific situations) if they are learned meaningfully. Thus, the transfer of conceptual learning is enhanced by ways of learning which make it meaningful and significant to the pupils. The researchers concluded:

This experiment has added strong support to the contention of Katona and Hendrix that independently derived principles are more transferable than those where the principle is given to the student.[38]

In another experiment with college students, Birch and Rabinowitz found that prior experience of a narrowly specific kind with a potentially useful tool for problem solving effectively prevented students from perceiving the instrument as an object to be used in completing an assigned task. They concluded that:

. . . what appears to be important for problem solving is not that an individual's performance is dependent upon past experience per se, but rather

[36] Homer B. Reed, "Factors Influencing Learning and Retention of Concepts. The Influence of Set," *Journal of Experimental Psychology*, Vol. 36 (1946), pp. 71-87.
[37] Hugh Hartshorne and Mark May, *Studies in Deceit* (New York: Macmillan Co., 1928).
————, *Studies in Service and Self Control* (New York: Macmillan Co., 1929).
[38] G. M. Haslerud and Shirley Meyers, "The Transfer Value of Given and Individually Derived Principles," *Journal of Educational Psychology*, Vol. 49 (1958), p. 296.

that *different kinds* of experience are differentially effective in influencing the content of problem-solving behavior. Our results therefore are in accord with those of Katona, who found that *how* and *what* an individual learned and not simply *whether* he learned determined the amount of positive transfer effect that occurred in subsequent learning.[39]

Birch and Rabinowitz further pointed out that their findings suggested two kinds of learning which affect problem solving and influence transfer of learning. One kind was described as consisting of broad, nonspecific, general notions about objects or methods. This type, facilitating the acquisition of meaning, provides the "repertoire of experience essential for productive thinking." The second type involves the perception of objects or methods of procedure in specific, limited, functional ways. This second type of thinking interferes with problem solving and so with transfer of learnings.

The learning and retention of concepts. Studies of concept formation by Smoke show wide individual differences in ability and manner of learning concepts. According to Smoke,[40] some subjects appear to learn little or nothing from negative instances while others found negative instances instructive. Later investigations have indicated that, in general, ability to formulate concepts and to transfer them increases with maturation, but that wide variations among children of the same chronological age exists.

Studies have indicated that there is no uniform way or method for learning concepts. Neither is there any one best method. Each individual tends to arrive at his goal by his own method. Reed, however, points out from his observations of concept formation that there are some steps which frequently occur. These are designated as follows:

> first, a period of doubt and orientation;
> second, a period of search and trial solution;
> third, a period of evaluation and checking.[41]

The *retention of concepts* will depend on such factors as thoroughness of learning, meaningfulness, and intent to remember. The now classic studies of Ebbinghaus, referred to earlier in this chapter, revealed that meaningless materials are poorly retained. The retention of meaningful concepts and nonsense materials at different levels following the initial learning is presented in Table 8-1.

[39] Herbert G. Birch and Herbert S. Rabinowitz, "The Negative Effect of Previous Experience on Productive Thinking," *Journal of Experimental Psychology,* Vol. 41 (1951), p. 125.

[40] Kenneth L. Smoke, An Objective Study of Concept Formation," *Psychological Monographs,* Vol. 42 (1932), pp. 1-43.

[41] *Op. cit.,* p. 84.

TABLE 8-1.   Percentage of Retention for Consistent and Inconsistent Concepts and Nonsense Materials *

GROUP	KIND OF CONCEPT	MEAN PERCENTAGE OF RENTENTION AFTER		
		ONE WEEK	THREE WEEKS	SIX WEEKS
4	Consistent	97.6	95.6	96.0
	Inconsistent	95.4	91.2	89.2
5	Consistent	97.3	95.0	
	Inconsistent	94.2	89.5	
6	Nonsense syllables			
	Ebbinghaus	25.4	22.8**	18.2**
	Radossawlejevitch	49.3	38.0	16.3**

* After Reed
** Interpolated from the curve

Even though the materials in the experiment by Ebbinghaus were learned to the *second* errorless reproduction, while those in Reed's experiment were learned only to the point of *one* errorless reproduction, an enormous percentage of concepts were retained by subjects in Reed's experiment. It is also of interest that consistent concepts are retained better than inconsistent ones.

The use of examples.   In teaching concepts of a broad and abstract nature which have great practical importance in most life situations, too often the general principle is presented with few or no examples of specific applications to different concrete situations meaningful to the child or youth. Such teaching will have little significance to the pupil and will result in *verbalism* which McKee has defined as:

. . . [the ability] to recognize the form of a printed word or group of words as a symbol that he has seen before and to think, speak, or write the pronunciations for which that symbol stands without understanding clearly and correctly what the symbol means in the setting in which it is used.[42]

McKee asserts that verbalism is "rampant in our schools at most educational levels and in most fields of learning." The acceptance of verbalism in the place of understanding of concepts results in the most absurd errors by the child. Studies of pupils' knowledge of the pledge of allegiance (used to aid in developing loyalty to American ideals) indicate an unfortunate substitution of rote mismemorization for understanding. Mistakes such as the following were found:

[42] Paul McKee, *The Teaching of Reading in the Elementary School* (Boston: Houghton Mifflin, 1948), p. 56.

Edward C. Pine, District Superintendent Reed Union School District, Belvedere-Tiburon, California

Retention and transfer of learning are facilitated by a meaningful learning situation which makes the activity significant, personal, and useful to the pupils

I pledge the legions to the flag of the United States and to the legions for which it stands, one nation individual with liberty and justice for all.[43]

Similar mistakes have been observed in rote mislearning. The oft-cited "lead us not into Penn Station" rendering for "lead us not into temptation" is another example of the lack of understanding of concepts. Spiritual and moral concepts are understood only to the extent that they are integrated meaningfully and personally into the total behavior patterns of the pupils through application to numerous, varied, specific situations. Concepts of this type become practically meaningless when they are taught as certain rules to be memorized or when they are parroted in ritualistic and misunderstood fashion. This statement and the research cited above *does not imply* that positive values will not be realized from meaningful affirmations of loyalty through thoughtful

[43] A. C. Moser and B. B. David, "I Pledge a Legion," *Journal of Educational Sociology,* Vol. 9 (1936), pp. 436-440.

renditions of the Pledge of Allegiance or that spiritual values will not ensue from prayerful recitation of prayers, statements of creeds, and formalized principles of doctrine. Such verbal expressions will have value, however, in the proportion that they are truly understood and accepted. Behavior will be affected only as transfer to specific situations can be achieved.

Learning and transfer in relation to emotional responses.   Teaching and guiding for growth toward emotional adequacy and maturity (concepts discussed at length in Chapters 17, 18, and 19) will facilitate transfer of learning in a broader spectrum of experience. Such transfer involves conscious and planned educational efforts in the school in cooperation with the home, the community, and the church to insure adequate emotional adjustment and transfer of adjustive emotional learnings.

Thus, emotional development involves maturation, change, diversification, integration, and increasingly more appropriate regulation of responses in the intellectual, motor, and emotive spheres. Each person has capacities for many different kinds of emotional experiences. As he develops, external and internal forces bring these capacities into use. In a good educational environment, the interpersonal relationships favor growth toward constructive self-regulation of these emotional capacities and their use in the service of the individual.

Much comment has appeared in recent years concerning the use of conditioning to produce emotional changes in humans. Experimental studies have shown that humans can be conditioned to respond to stimuli with certain emotional reactions, such as anger, fear, and hope. But, because conditioning is peripheral in nature and because human functioning is complex, it is unlikely that this process plays more than a minor role in emotional development.

Schneiders points out, however, that:

The situation is different with respect to *learning.* Modification and differentiation are integral aspects of the learning process; and we may safely suppose that the individuation of emotional responses is due both to the maturational processes described earlier, and to learning which functions as a complementary agent to maturation. In fact, all differentiation of this sort is a result of the combined influence of these two factors. Thus, in a very real sense, the child learns embarrassment, shame, pride, and similar emotional responses; that is, these responses become gradually differentiated out of a mass emotional excitement through the combined effects of many different factors, of which learning is the most significant . . . By way of summary, then, we can say that the conditions of emotional health and adjustment include: (1) adequate physical well-being; (2) adequate intellectual development, and the growth of a wholesome concept of self; (3) healthy expression of the basic human needs, and the reduction of damaging frustrations; (4) development of personal integration and self-control; (5) good social and moral development; (6) wholesome and expanding interpersonal relations; and (7) the application of conditioning, training, and other learning procedures in a way to ensure healthy emotional growth.[44]

Motivation and purpose in retention and transfer. The importance of the learner as a dynamic force in the learning situation is recognized by the educational psychologist. It has been noted repeatedly that learning is not a passive process, but takes place in proportion to the extent that the learner is actively directed toward a goal or the solution of a problem. Needless to say, many characteristics of the learner affect the efficiency of his learning, retention, and transfer of such learning into life situations. But, none of these is as basic as the dynamic nature of the learner himself. This, together with an effective learning situation and interest, makes education personal, significant, and meaningful to a human being.

Such constructs as *set, purpose, goal-setting, will-to-learn,* and *personal involvement* are not only basic aspects of the learner's dynamic nature but they are basic factors in learning for retention and transfer. Teachers should understand that teaching proposes how these constructs aid learning and transfer. Intent to remember and belief that one can remember (a realistic level of aspiration) facilitates retention. A study by Ausubel and others,[45] however, showed that the *time* of formulating an intent to remember is important in affecting transfer. They found that intent to remember, when formulated after learning, had little effect on retention.

Effective habits and skills basic to retention and transfer of learning. Difficulties in retention and transfer of learning may be due in large part to poor study procedures. It has been found, moreover, that many superior students achieve well *in spite of* poor study habits but that they could learn more effectively and economically if they used better study techniques.

There is ample proof that individuals, left to their own devices, will not usually develop the best study and work methods nor utilize the most effective learning skills.

In an early study, Pressey [46] investigated the performance of 31 pairs of probation students carefully matched as to intelligence, academic record, age, and sex. One of each pair (31 students) was given

[44] Alexander A. Schneiders, "Emotional Development in Children," *Education,* Vol. 78 (1951), p. 222.

[45] David P. Ausubel, S. H. Schpoont, and L. Cukier, "The Influence of Intention on the Retention of School Materials," *Journal of Educational Psychology,* Vol. 48 (1957), pp. 87-92.

[46] S. L. Pressey, *Research Adventures in University Teaching* (Bloomington, Ill.: Public School Publishing Company, 1927).

special training in study methods for the probation term while the other 31 students received no such training. Seventy per cent of the academic grades for the probation term received by the trained group were above the D level while only 34 per cent of the grades of the untrained group were above that level. More than half of the untrained group (16) left college at the end of the probation term while only nine of the trained group left college.

In the same study, Pressey compared the study habits of college students with good academic records with the study habits of students with poor records. He found 18 study habits which distinguish good students from poor ones. These are shown in Table 8-2.

Summarizing the results of recent research on study approaches, Robinson concluded:

> . . . In brief, the average and superior student in high school and college is inefficient in his reading and study skills; he tends to excel other students in grades mostly because of differences in intellectual ability and not because of better reading and study methods . . . .[47]

Harlow[48] concluded from his research with formation of learning sets that "learning to learn efficiently" changes the learner from a creature that seeks to adapt to a constantly changing environment by trial and unguided manipulation to one that adapts by hypothesis and insight. He also concluded that learning how to learn is a more important factor in most learning tasks than making correct responses in the presence of certain stimuli.

Thus, the problem for teachers is to determine where learners are in relation to their study techniques and to help them develop those study procedures and methods which will enable them to achieve in accordance with their potential abilities. Previously cited research suggests that both *good* and *poor* students (on the basis of academic performance) need such guidance.

The following principles will help teachers attain this goal as well as help them facilitate their own studying.

1. *Intend* to remember. Such an intention creates a mental set facilitating recall.
2. Clearly outline your purpose for study. Having a definite purpose in mind focuses attention on whatever will achieve this purpose.

[47] Francis P. Robinson, "Study Skills for Superior High School Students in Secondary School," *Reading Teacher*, Sept., 1961, pp. 29-33.

[48] H. F. Harlow, "The Formation of Learning Sets," *Psychological Review*, Vol. 56 (1949), pp. 51-65; H. F. Harlow and J. M. Warren, "Formation and Transfer of Discrimination Learning Sets," *Journal of Comparative Physiological Psychology*, Vol. 45 (1952), pp. 482-489.

TABLE 8-2. Study Habits Which Distinguish Poor College Students From Good Ones

HABIT	CORRECT ANSWER	PER CENT OF GOOD STUDENTS EXCEEDING POOR STUDENTS
1. Are you usually tired when you get up in the morning?	No	36
2. Do you usually study every day in the same place?	Yes	36
3. Do you frequently skip graphs or tables in your textbook?	No	40
4. Do you frequently make simple charts or diagrams to represent points in your reading?	Yes	40
5. When you find a word in your reading that you do not know do you usually look it up in the dictionary?	Yes	32
6. Do you usually skim over a chapter before reading it?	Yes	28
7. Do you usually have trouble getting the meaning of a chart or table?	Yes	28
8. Do you keep your notes from one subject together?	Yes	32
9. Do you usually take your class notes just as rapidly as you can write?	No	32
10. Do you usually take lecture notes in outline form?	Yes	28
11. Do you usually take your notes on reading in outline form?	Yes	28
12. Do you usually have difficulty expressing yourself in written work?	No	56
13. Do you usually have difficulty making complete sentences when you write?	No	28
14. Do you sit up late the night before an exam studying?	No	40
15. Do you often write an answer to a question and then find that it is the answer to some other question on the exam?	No	32
16. In preparing for an exam do you try to memorize the test?	No	28
17. Do you frequently try to analyze your work to find out just where you are weak?	Yes	36
18. Do you frequently use facts learned in one course to help you in some other course?	Yes	28

3. Organize your reading around meaning. Survey the material quickly to discover its general arrangement. Study then with the general plan in mind, relating the details to the major ideas.

4. Study actively. Relate your reading to your beliefs, your knowledge of present practices, your expectations. Note contradictions as well as concurrence. Make notes in your own words.

5. Practice using your reading and study material in new situations. Make up problems and solve them. Visualize practical examples which represent concrete forms of theory which you have studied.
6. Schedule your study time. Study in the most suitable place available. Begin your work at once. Take breaks when your attention begins to wander.
7. Establish vivid impressions by making associations with meaningful experiences, by visualizing actual examples in your mind, by making brief, clear notes.

Summarizing the results of recent research conducted by himself and his associates, Klausmeier reported:

Given the same material to learn, the less intelligent pupils forget more than do the more intelligent, mainly because the less intelligent do not acquire it so well or do not understand it fully. But when the material is appropriate to each child's achievement level, there is no difference in retention among children of low, average, and high intelligence . . . The results from all the research are clear: namely, material which is meaningful and acquired at a fairly high level of mastery is retained well.[49]

Degree of learning in retention for transfer. The degree of initial learning in relation to adequacy of understanding and mastery was discussed earlier in this chapter. It has been pointed out that inadequate initial learning is often the cause of faulty retention and inappropriate transfer. As previously mentioned, thoroughness of learning may be observed in one's retention of Mother Goose rhymes learned as a child and repeated many times after the materials were originally presented. In general, too, motor skills are retained better than fact or even principles from history and science. This is so, in part, because one series of muscular motions acts as a confirming cue (that is, their consequences are immediately seen) for ensuing series. Furthermore, in the learning of a motor skill, such as typing or swimming, one is required to continue practicing after the initial learning in order to reach a certain minimal degree of proficiency. Continued practice beyond the point necessary to perform an act successfully for the *first time* after undergoing a learning experience is called *overlearning.* This essential factor in the mastery of skills will be discussed in the next chapter.

Certain investigators have suggested that if verbal materials were practiced to produce a somewhat similar degree of proficiency attained in motor skills, they would be retained and transferred with the same degree of appropriateness, providing, of course, that the experiences following the learning were equally beneficial or facilitative to retention and transfer. These experiences should include confirming situations

[49] Herbert J. Klausmeier, *Learning and Human Abilities: Educational Psychology* (New York: Harper & Row, 1961), pp. 367-368.

which enable the learner to know immediately that he is right or wrong (analogous to the confirmation experienced by a proper set of muscular actions mentioned above).

Educational practices which lead to interference and faulty reorganization may be causes which prevent adequate transfer. Teachers who permit verbalism, fail to vary learning activities, and do not ascertain that pupils have mastered learnings will have difficulty with transfer to other situations. Both interference and reorganization through partial recall impede retention and inhibit transfer. The best way to improve retention is to insure that the original learning is meaningful and thorough. Later rehearsals and examinations must also be meaningful and thorough. Teachers should also avoid large blocks of similar learning activities.

The degree of similarity need not *necessarily* result in retroactive inhibition interfering with retention. It may rather be a positive factor in transfer of what has been retained in a new or subsequent situation. Thorndike's identical elements and Judd's generalization doctrines are basic to this aspect of retention and transfer. The identical elements or similarity of the subject matter, however, will not transfer automatically. The *student* must perceive the likeness or the possibility for transfer. The teacher, of course, should be clearly aware of the similarity and of the possibility of transfer and *guide* the learner to discover or understand the common relationships also. Besides actual similarity, there are the basic similarities of relationship or structure discussed earlier in this chapter. The research findings in regard to the superiority of discovery will be helpful in guiding the teacher in using methods of instruction and choosing teaching procedures which will maximize transfer.

Methods of instruction and transfer. Although some transfer may be expected to occur in most learning, the teacher must not assume that transfer is automatic. He must be aware that the extent of retention and its transfer is in large measure due to the teaching approaches. If the maximum amount of transfer is to occur, the efforts of the teacher must be directed to this goal. The *goals* of the teacher are most important in determining the nature and the amount of transfer. If the major goal of the history teacher is the acquisition of historical facts, the teacher will most likely teach and test for such factual information. The results will likely be a transfer of information to somewhat similar material. (Recall, too, that research has shown that little of this factual information will be retained long.)

If the teacher teaches "subject matter" and does not help learners to discover meaningful principles and patterns of concepts in accord with their individual differences and needs, there may be *no* retention but much transfer of the *negative* kind. This may happen with the teacher who insists on meticulous examination of grammatical usage in works by great literary figures or who concerns herself with details of poetry or drama. Students develop aversion to literature under these conditions.

On the other hand, if the problem approach is used, one might well expect transfer to the solution of somewhat similar problem situations. Again, if the teacher stresses understanding of civic responsibility and provides opportunities for specific application of related principles, transfer will most likely occur in out-of-school behavior. The maximum transfer will occur in either case, when the learner's attention is directed so that he can see the relationship between the experiences in the classroom and those outside the school. The maximum transfer will also occur when he has become personally involved in the relationships through active participation in the learning, and when he has helped to set his goals or has been able to make personal choices in the learning situation. Meanings, understanding, applications, and worthwhile attitudes should be aspects of the goals in teaching.

When a subject is meaningfully taught to consciously provide for retention beyond the time of the final examination and is taught to facilitate transfer for effective living with the learner cooperatively working with the teacher toward a common goal, then one can expect the material to be more readily learned and retained. Increased transfer results from good learning procedures. Retention and transfer are subject to the same laws of learning discussed in Chapter 7.

SUMMARY

The major aim of educational efforts throughout history has been to provide learning experiences which would enable pupils to cope better with life situations outside the school. Therefore, the amount and type of transfer that occurs was a major concern of teachers.

A number of areas of learning were mentioned which involved not only the school but other agencies of society. The nature of retention and causes of forgetting were discussed with an examination of the *types* of learning which were best retained. Special features of neurological research were discussed which offered an explanation of educationally significant phenomena associated with recall and understanding. Educational implications of retention were pointed out.

Because of its great importance, many theories have been devised to explain the operation of transfer of learning and to guide teachers in selecting instructional procedures thought to provide the greatest transfer. These theories and the research underlying them were surveyed. It was stressed, however, that the solution to the problem of transferring learning experiences rests with the teacher.

Problems and Exercises

1. What were the major findings of early experiments on transfer of learning? What criticisms have been offered of these studies? Are these criticisms justified?

2. How is intelligence related to transfer? What bearing does this have on the school program for gifted children? Upon the guidance program in general?

3. Show how good learning principles, introduced in earlier chapters, will improve transfer of learning.

4. A popular article in a newspaper asserts that "Every experience which a person has is forever imprinted on his brain." Comment on this statement on the basis of the explanations for recall and forgetting given in this chapter.

5. All pupils in grades 4, 5 and 6 at an elementary school are required to write an essay on 'Why Neatness is Important." The winner will receive a badge labeled "The Neatest Boy (Girl) in School" and a prize of $5. The winner must wear this badge for two weeks.) The school principal explains to the parents that preparing the essay will not only be valuable in giving the pupils practice in writing but will also make them neater in schoolwork and at home.

   Comment on the contest and on the probable reactions of the pupils. In the light of this chapter and your experience, how much transfer should the principal, the teachers, and the parents expect?

6. John, a 9th grade student, was asked to stay after class to talk to his teacher about a disciplinary infraction. John forgets to report and goes to the library to study. What explanation of forgetting might be applicable here?

7. A sixth grade teacher teaches American history in a strictly chronological fashion. Her pupils learn "all the important dates." Daily, she cites names of places or events. The pupils are expected to respond with the correct dates. Her weekly tests require pupils to list happenings chronologically or to make tables of events and personalities in correct time sequence. If the pupils are tested two years later, how much retention can be expected for historical dates? At this time, how much transfer would there probably be on a test measuring understanding of the causes of historical events, the importance of occurrences, and the interrelationships of political, economic, and military activities? Explain your answer.

8. A research study showed that some teachers scored high on a test measuring recall of statements of educational psychology (e.g.: Much forgetting is caused by retroactive inhibition. T. F.) These teachers, however, scored very low on a test measuring understanding of procedures to use with students with various types of learning difficulties (each student's case was fully described and appropriate actions were requested). What does this indicate about the type of educational psychology instruction received by these teachers? What principle in this chapter does it illustrate?

9. Teachers A and B in Stopgap High School used two different procedures in teaching elementary French during the school year.

   Teacher A stressed formal grammar and composition, giving tests twice a week on grammatical rules and translation of English sentences into French. She required her students to memorize lists of vocabulary words and tested them on these words 3 times a week. Twenty-five per cent of total class time and 50% of the time spent on outside assignments was devoted to translating English sentences into French. (These exercises were composed of isolated sentences.) Forty per cent of total class time and 20% of outside work was spent on grammatical drills and exercises. The remaining time was devoted to reading French passages silently with occasional oral practice.

Teacher B began the school year with French conversation and easy selections in French which the students read in class, receiving help from the teacher on words which they could not guess from context. Grammatical principles were developed only as need for them arose from the reading or speaking situations. Thirty per cent of the total class time was spent in listening to the teacher speak French (telling stories, giving directions, commenting on the high school news, etc.) and 20% was devoted to student reactions (in French) to the teacher's conversation. Eighty per cent of outside assignments and 40% of class time was spent in reading French articles and stories and reacting to them. Weekly tests consisted of answering questions on the content, meaning, and interest of selections written in French (no written translation into English was required) and on commenting on the meaning and use of certain selected words.

In what respects will the retention of the students of Teacher A differ from that of Teacher B? If the final examination is a standardized test measuring the students' ability to *read*, understand, and react to selections written in French, which students will be likely to do better? Which teacher's students are more likely to be interested in continuing study of French? Why? On a trip to France, which teacher's students would best be able to use their language learnings? What kind of transfer will one teacher's procedure encourage which will not be present in the students of the other? (Discuss both Teacher A and B here.)

Selected Readings

BRUNER, Jerome S., *The Process of Education* (Cambridge: Harvard University Press, 1961), Ch. I.

CRONBACH, Lee J., *Educational Psychology*, 2nd ed. (New York: Harcourt, Brace and Co., 1963), Ch. 10.

HILGARD, E. R., *Theories of Learning* (New York: Appleton-Century-Crofts, 1956).

KLAUSMEIER, H. J., *Learning and Human Abilities: Educational Psychology* (New York: Harper & Row, 1961), Ch. 30.

McGEOCH, J. A., and IRION, Arthur I., *The Psychology of Human Learning.* 2d ed. (New York: Longmans, Green and Co., 1952), Ch. 9.

MURSELL, James L., *Psychology for Modern Education* (New York: W. W. Norton and Co., 1952), Ch. 10.

SORENSON, H., *Psychology in Education*, 3rd ed. (New York: McGraw-Hill, 1954), Ch. 17.

SAWREY, J. M. and TELFORD, C. W., *Educational Psychology* (Boston: Allyn and Bacon, Inc., 1958), Ch. 4.

SKINNER, B. F., *Science and Human Behavior* (New York: Macmillan Co., 1953).

STEPHENS, J. M., *Educational Psychology*, rev. ed. (New York: Holt, Rinehart & Winston, 1951), pp. 455-469.

CHAPTER 9

The Learning of Skills

We have shown that the learner is constantly seeking to actualize his innate capacities by making more adequate responses to reality. The habitual level of his responses produces the changes in him which we call learning. Just as there are many abilities which naturally develop as a part of the growth and development of man's nature, so there seems to be no upper limit to the abilities which man can choose to develop or which he can be guided and motivated to develop. There are, of course, boundaries set by his native constitutional endowment, but these remain an unknown quantity throughout life; they can only be approximately inferred by samples of behavior.

The refinement or perfection of an ability to do or perform something is a *skill*. Skills do not develop singly or in isolation but as integral parts of the individual's total development. Skills are developed like other learnings and follow the principles of learning, discussed in Chapter 7.

The acquisition of motor skills begins in an elementary form so early in the child's life that it is identified as an integral part of the total growth process. Furthermore, such skills are at all times interrelated with all other aspects of growth. And, although we speak of different kinds of learning and growth, it should be emphasized that all growth and learning tend to follow certain general principles discussed in the previous chapters. Some of these principles, however, may be more readily observed in some kinds of learning. The importance of maturation, experience, motivation, and related habits and experiences may be observed in the acquisition of motor skills and meanings.

THE NATURE AND CHARACTERISTICS OF HUMAN SKILLS

Skills of doing or performing are apparent in all aspects of the school program, although they are usually more in evidence in extra-curricular and vocational activities. Ragsdale [1] groups motor activities and skills into three broad categories: object-motor activities, language-motor activities, and feeling-motor activities.

A *skill* is a facile and automatic form of response to a stimulus or cue. Skilled performance, thus, involves the effective differentiation of cues and the continual correction of errors through feedback. As learning progresses, fewer cues are required and feedback becomes smoother and better integrated.

Patterns of action skills

Motor skills have form, internal organization, rhythm, precision, force, and coordination. The particular pattern developed by an individual will depend upon a number of factors, such as (1) maturation, (2) body build, (3) past experiences, (4) constitutional characteristics, (5) readiness, which includes motivation and the will to learn, and (6) exercise and guidance. Thus, skills are not fixed for an individual; neither are they similar in pattern for all individuals. Each person has his own particular rhythm and form. We see this with children jumping rope. One child may assume a posture almost completely upright while another child remains stooped. There may also be variations in the movements of different parts of their bodies. To perform best each individual will develop the form most appropriate for his ability and constitutional characteristics, although there are general features which may be regarded as good form, while others may be regarded as bad form. Since all children are, however, biophysical organisms, there will be limits within which each child will tend to operate.

The task of the teacher is to determine the essentials of good form. Certainly there are some techniques of moving the lips and tongue which have been found best for producing distinct sounds. There are methods of movement and coordinations which are useful to the person in learning to bat a ball. Furthermore, certain motor coordinations are dependent upon previous learnings. The child who has not learned to skip will find it difficult, if not impossible, to acquire certain dance skills. Such a learner may have to practice essential movements before he can progress in the particular dance he wishes to perform. These preliminary, basic skills essential to the development of the new skills are aspects of readiness to learn a skill.

Object-motor activities or manipulative skills

This category of motor activities includes the use of tools in household and industrial pursuits, manipulation of materials like wood,

[1] C. E. Ragsdale, "How Children Learn the Motor Types of Activities," *Forty-ninth Yearbook of the National Society for the Study of Education, Part I, Learning and Instruction* (Chicago: University of Chicago Press, 1950), Chapter III.

The whole body is involved in the acquisition of motor skills such as those involved in playing baseball

metal, and fabrics, the use of measuring and recording devices, and the manipulation of objects used in sports and recreation like balls, fishing materials, and swings. Most of these activities call for judgment, understanding, and a period of learning. The extent to which they require these components varies with the nature and complexity of the particular activity.

The development of manual-tool skills will depend upon a number of factors, among which may be listed (1) the maturity of the learner, (2) the organization of the units of work, (3) the complexity of the learning task, (4) the learner's motivation, and (5) the kind of instruction and guidance. Manual-tool activities should be an important part of the elementary-school program and should be closely related to other aspects of the school program. They should also be closely correlated with work in the fine arts. Good design should be carried over in the making of a baby crib or a home for a pet rabbit. Tools and procedures should be carefully chosen with regard to their functional use and the maturity and experience of the pupils.

Language-motor activities and communication skills

The language-motor activities include movements of the speech organs, movements of the eyes in reading, and the movements in hand-writing, telegraphy, commercial arts, and mechanical drawing. Special consideration will be given here to the vocal skills, writing skills, and reading skills.

Vocal skills. A consideration of problems involved in speech, oral reading, and singing reveal that there are certain common elements. The child's speech begins with babbling sounds some of which are early understood by the mother. Growth in comprehensible speech continues until by the age of three approximately 90 per cent of the child's remarks are understandable.[2] The ability to articulate the words correctly, how-ever, lags far behind. Even at the beginning of first grade, a rather large number of words are incorrectly pronounced. Most children will outgrow this faulty pronunciation which is called baby talk. Too much attention, indeed, may aggravate the speech difficulty rather than correct it. With children who persist in lisping or stuttering, the teacher should seek the help of a specialist who, besides considering treatments, may suggest special exercises the teacher can administer.

Oral reading is recognized today as an important part of a well-balanced program in the elementary school. In addition to the values obtained in auditory acuity and discrimination, work in oral reading may be developed to provide for individual motivation, benefits that can accrue from group dynamics, and desirable personal and social develop-ment. Needless to say, correct articulation is essential for successful oral reading. This ability alone, however, is not sufficient. The child must also have mastered the fundamental skills requisite to reading and must have carefully guided experience in oral reading. It is important for the teacher to realize that successful oral reading does not just happen, but proceeds from developmental learnings in a whole complex of motor, cognitive, and affective skills and abilities.

Observers have noted that children spontaneously produce melodic fragments at an early age.[3] These are marked by a lack of semitone steps, and appear with all kinds of rhythmic formations. One study on the ef-fects of systematic training on the singing ability of children who were severely lacking in pitch-discrimination ability indicated that such a

[2] See Dorothea McCarthy, "Language Development in Children," in L. Car-michael, ed., *Manual of Child Psychology*, rev. ed. (New York: John Wiley and Sons, Inc., 1954).

[3] William Stern, *The Psychology of Early Childhood* (New York: Henry Holt and Co., 1926).

disability can be corrected significantly by training.[4] The nature of this training, however, must harmonize with maturational level of the child. Specialized instrumental training at too early an age will only produce meager results, and may condition the child against such musical experiences. The same amount of time and effort given at an early age to the singing of folk songs, songs involving games, and the like, produces better results, since such training makes use of childhood interests and involves simpler muscular skills.

Writing skills. The skills developed in learning to write are based on previously acquired movements and abilities. Readiness in writing is determined in part by the extent to which these movements and abilities are developed, and in part to the motivation of the subject. Thus, maturation, practice, and motivation are factors which contribute to readiness for writing instruction as they do to the learning of any skill. In a study reported by Ames and Ilg [5] the spontaneous pencil and paper behavior of approximately fifty children was observed at each six-month age period from three through six years of age. This behavior was carefully analyzed to determine the normal course of the development of writing. Most of the subjects were enrolled in some sort of preschool program, which might have influenced the results.

Much the same developmental sequence occurs in all subjects. This had been earlier noted by Hildreth in a study in which she presented a detailed gradient of stages in writing from three through five years of age.[6] The development at age three, for instance, shows a tendency toward horizontal lines with some systematic up-and-down writing through five years when the first name is often printed (although with occasional reversals and letter malformations). Some of the writing gradients for six-, seven-, eight-, and nine-year-olds noted by Ames and Ilg have been listed as follows:

Six Years

Circle is now drawn counterclockwise, starting at the top.

Letters are printed usually large and somewhat irregular.

Words are printed by some children at this age. Some reversals of single letters or word order of letters may appear.

Numbers from 1 to 20 or higher usually appear. Sometimes numbers are written upside down.

[4] Manuel Wolner and W. H. Pyle, "An Experiment in Individual Training in Pitch-Deficient Children," *Journal of Educational Psychology*, Vol. 24 (1933), pp. 602-608.

[5] Louise B. Ames and Francis L. Ilg, "Developmental Trends in Writing Behavior," *Journal of Genetic Psychology*, Vol. 79 (1951), pp. 29-46.

[6] Gertrude Hildreth, "Developmental Sequences in Name Writing," *Child Development*, Vol. 7 (1936), pp. 291-303.

Seven Years

Words: The majority are now able to write, although an appreciable number prefer to print. The printing is now smaller and more regular.

Names: The majority are now able to write their given name and surname. A minority will still print their names.

Numbers: There is an increase in the numbers written, with the figures now written smaller and in rows.

Eight Years

Words: The majority write single words, printing being seldom used. Important individual differences in writing skill are discernible. Reversals seldom appear.

Names: Nearly all write both their names well spaced, and small letters other than the initial letter of each word. Important variations in style of writing appear.

Numbers: Figures are much smaller and better spaced.

Nine Years

Words: Writing is smaller, neater, lighter, more even and slanted, though some still write straight up and down and about one-third still have very irregular letters. Letters are now much better proportioned.

Names: The beginnings of individual style appear, with sex differences being observed. Letters are more evenly made and more correctly proportioned.

Numbers: Writing of numbers is now small and well formed.

The student should realize that the above writing gradients represent *typical* performance at these ages. At each age, there will be wide individual differences. Furthermore, there will be wide overlapping between the poorest performances at one age and the best performances of a much younger age so that some six-year-olds will perform better than some nine-year-olds.

Eye-movements in reading. The early activities involved in learning to read furnish a splendid illustration of the close relationship between motor and verbal learning or between ocular and interpretive factors. During the early stages of reading the child must develop the habit of focusing the eyes on the left side of the page and work from left to right as he swings them back to the left side of the page after each line is completed.

As the person reads, his eyes progress along the line in a series of eye stops (*fixations*) and quick movements (called *saccadic movements*). Seeing occurs only during the fixations which last a fraction of a second each. Most people have reverse eye movements (*regressions*) interspersed with their forward movements.

Studies have shown that beginning readers make more fixations per line, more regressions per line, have longer durations of fixation, and

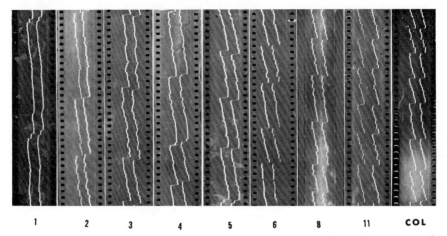

The above graphs show characteristic performances for the various grade levels. As the average pupil advances academically, his pattern reflects fewer fixations to the line, indicating a broadening of the span of recognition; shorter duration of fixation, indicating a more rapid reaction to the reading material; and a more rapid rate of reading. In general, the pattern becomes more regular and uniform, reflecting an increase in overall organization.

From Grade Level Norms for the Components of the Fundamental Reading Skill, S. E. Taylor, H. Frackenpohl, and J. L. Pettee, EDL Bulletin no. 3

FIGURE 9-1. The Maturation Of Reading Skills

evidence less organization in their characteristic patterns of eye movements than do mature readers. The graphs shown in Figure 9-1 show characteristic performances at the different grade levels.[7] As the average pupil advances academically, his pattern of eye movements shows fewer fixations per line, indicating a broadening of the span of recognition. There is also a shorter duration of fixation and fewer regressions per 100 words as shown in Figure 9-2. In general, with advancing grade level, the pattern becomes more regular and uniform, reflecting an increase in overall organization.

Faulty habits in basic reading skills are often related to the psychomotor aspect of the reading skills. Although the first five or six grades are considered crucial for the development of desirable eye-movements and good reading skills, recent studies and expert opinion have identified constellations of skills that can be developed only at higher levels of maturity and as clusters built upon the basic skills of the elementary grades. Teachers, therefore, must understand the complexity of the skills they teach, like reading, if they are to see the need for seqeunce in development and if they are to realize the importance of well-

[7] Stanford E. Taylor, Helen Frackenpohl, and James L. Pettee, "Grade Level Norms for the Components of the Fundamental Reading Skill," *Research and Information Bulletin* No. 3, Educational Development Laboratories, 1960.

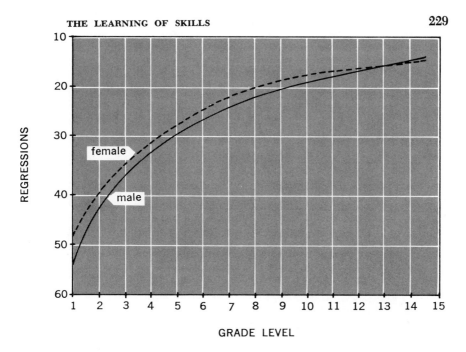

FIGURE 9-2. Norms For Males And Females For Regressions Per 100 Words

developed preliminary skills for more mature performance. (See Figure 9-3.)

Feeling-motor activities or affective abilities

The feeling-motor activities have also been referred to as manual-esthetic coordinations. These activities should not be thought of as functioning apart from vocal skills, manual-tool coordinations, and other perceptual-motor learnings. We have already suggested that manual-tool coordinations should be closely related to certain fine-arts activities. For example, creative dancing and the playing of musical instruments—regarded as manual-esthetic coordinations—involve the attitudes and feelings of the individual who practices them. The purpose of such activities is not primarily to communicate ideas and thoughts, but to express one's feelings, ideas, and values. Furthermore, through musical activities, the learner is able to express either his mood and feelings or the mood and feelings of the composer.

Teaching children to sing simple songs in unison should be the beginning of music instruction, and should continue to be a large part of the music program. Music reading may be successfully introduced in the early elementary grades if such experiences are connected with music games and songs the children have already learned together. Some types of songs that have been suggested for children are festival songs, Mother

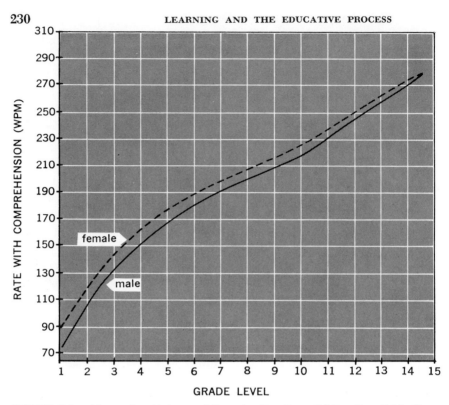

FIGURE 9-3.   Norms for Males and Females For Rate Of Reading With Comprehension, Words Per Minute

Goose songs, lullabies, songs about animals and birds, Christmas carols and hymns, and songs about children in other lands. Besides singing, many schools are making good use of radio programs, television instruction, and phonograph records to develop appreciation of rhythm and music. Rhythm bands, dancing, dancing and skipping to music, and special school programs furnish means for developing motor-esthetic coordinations and motivating the work in music.

There is little systematic knowledge pointing to just when the average child is ready to learn to *sight-read* or to play a musical instrument. This type of readiness will be influenced by such factors as intelligence, musical aptitude, musical background, and motivation. Individual differences exist, but they are probably no greater than in other areas of education. However, inadequate cultural environment and exposure to substandard quality of performance and expression or to low-caliber programs may prevent an individual from developing the proper readiness. Worse still, they may create undesirable tastes and faulty appreciations and insights which will need unlearning before adequate development of skills, appreciation, and motivation can actually take

The acquisition of complex skills in music is a result of a number of factors including potential ability, motivation, practice, and training.

place. Today children can be exposed to the undesirable and the unrefined almost constantly, even in the home.

Easy-to-play instruments afford opportunity for enjoyment and may be useful in the development of esthetic-motor coordinations and a greater appreciation of music. The use of rhythm instruments at school need not be restricted to the lower elementary grades. It has been observed that such Latin American instruments as the claves, maracas, and bongo drums appeal to the interests of teenagers. Such instruments can be made by the students and can be used in a variety of learning situations to develop an increased understanding of music, to further enjoyment, and to develop esthetic-motor skills.

Through art activities children may develop a greater appreciation of the world about them and increased esthetic-motor coordinations. The elementary-school art program usually includes the graphic and industrial arts. This is an integral part of the elementary-school program. Through art activities the child is given the opportunity to explore the world about him and to relate this to his inner world of feelings, wishes, and understandings. If he is permitted to explore without too much adult interference and without the harsh imposition of adult standards, he will show an intense interest in art and will grow in self-expression, motor-esthetic coordination, and in increased appreciation of his surroundings at home, at school, and in his community. In all the variety of complex skills which confront boys and girls in the educative process, the teacher or director is fundamental. She guides them, through wholesome experience and practice, to insightful learning and positive growth.

Higher-level skills. Although we may characterize some skills as higher-level skills, it should be pointed out that most people with good ability do many things only moderately well chiefly because they lack motivation. Consider Ralph, a ninth-grade pupil with above average ability but with a low motivational index for school activities. Ralph is satisfied with a passing grade and manages to study sufficiently to make such a grade. Buswell and Kersh [8] studied how 499 high-school and college students solved six types of problem in practical arithmetic. The students were instructed to think aloud and their recorded remarks were carefully studied. It was found that frequently, capable students failed to solve the practical arithmetic problems for several reasons. Apparently, their failure to discriminate relevant materials, their poor planning procedures, and their confusion were among the factors responsible.

Similar evidence of inefficiency was noted in an earlier study by Symonds in which the problem-solving processes of teachers was studied. He concludes from his study that "teachers are not able to clearly formulate their problems, nor are they able to work out clearly thought-through solutions to them. It would be more correct to speak of the process as one of emotional adjustment to personal difficulties than of problem solving." [9]

Factors affecting the learning of skills

The relationship between maturation and learning is clearly evident in the acquisition of motor skills. Through the influence of maturation the child is brought to the most favorable time to learn, and through his motor-learning experiences, properly timed with maturation, he is able to achieve the optimum degree of efficiency in motor skills.

Learning as integration of skills. In the development of motor skills there is progress not only from more generalized to more spe-

[8] G. T. Buswell and B. Y. Kersh, "Patterns of Thinking in Solving Problems," *University of California Publ. Educ.,* Vol. 12 (1956), pp. 63-148.

[9] P. M. Symonds, "How Teachers Solve Personal Problems," *Journal of Educational Research,* Vol. 38 (1945), pp. 651-652.

cialized forms of activity, but also from specialized to more inclusive activities that serve to integrate other operations. Thus, it is to the child's advantage to learn the basic motor skills as early as possible. In many performances, children will concentrate for a time on establishing a simple level of skill, then move on to a higher level. At various stages of their progress they will combine such skills with others which were practiced independently at an earlier stage. When mastery of the new larger skill is achieved, the different operations involved may be subordinated to the more complex task. Development proceeds both from wholes to parts and from parts to larger wholes, just as the act of running is combined with the act of catching a ball when a child makes a "running catch" in softball.

Many motor tasks not only require complex motor coordination, but also involve increased attention span or difficult mental processes which increase the learning difficulty. This augments the necessity for spaced practice among elementary school children.

Growth in motor ability. The sequence of increasingly complex skills mastered by a child is part of a larger, continuing process of motor development. Walking, running, sliding, climbing, hopping, and more intricate skills develop as a result of maturation and practice.

A study of the motor development of nearly 2,000 children from two to seven years of age showed that climbing stairs, low inclined planks, packing boxes, jungle gyms, and the like were well established as skills at three years of age in half of the children.[10] After this age there was a steady increase in climbing ability. During the early stages it was noticed that climbing up was somewhat easier than climbing down. No difference was observed in the case of accomplishing these tasks after they were once mastered.

Skill in hopping on one foot, skipping, and jumping may be developed during the preschool years if children have the opportunity to practice these skills. Gutteridge reports that 42 per cent of her group of three-year-olds rated well at jumping, while 72 per cent were rated skillful at four and a half years of age. Skipping is a skill that few children can do at four years of age. At five a relatively large percentage are able to skip, while by the age of six most children are able to do so. The ability to hop on one foot develops more slowly, although the majority of children are able to hop by the time they are six years of age. Even at this age the range of ability to hop is very wide.

As the body develops and changes, new motor learnings are needed. The change in the amount and distribution of weight makes it necessary for the growing boy and girl to make new adjustments in maintaining

[10] M. Gutteridge, "A Study of Motor Achievement of Young Children," *Archives of Psychology*, No. 244 (1939).

balance. Furthermore, the development of motor coordination does not keep pace with the rapid growth of the limbs of the body. Thus, by age twelve, a girl's arms and legs have about reached the length they will have at maturity. Consequently, she finds herself breaking dishes and displaying awkwardness in many situations. This clumsiness in motor activities, in light of the fact that she has previously developed considerable confidence in her ability to perform certain motor skills, is most disconcerting, especially if adults laugh at her.

The *Lincoln-Oseretsky Motor Development Scale*, consisting of 36 items, was developed and standardized by William Sloane.[11] This scale represents an extensive revision of Oseretsky's original scale, designed to measure motor development of school-age boys and girls. Its normative data, obtained from over 700 children between ages 6 to 14, show a continuous increase in motor ability with age.

It appears that gross motor skills develop largely as a result of maturation while complex motor skills depend upon practice, especially after the child has reached the elementary-school age.

Sex differences. A comparison of the scores of boys and girls on the *Lincoln-Oseretsky Motor Development Scale* shows no consistent sex difference favoring either sex. A study by Jenkins [12] of the motor achievement of children of ages five through seven in running, jumping, hopping, and accuracy of throwing yielded results favoring boys, who were slightly larger during this period of growth. On the other hand, Carpenter [13] has presented data on the ability of children six to nine years of age to accurately hop on a hopscotch pattern. The results of this study favor the girls. Carpenter attributes this to the greater amount of practice girls have in this particular skill.

Physical growth and motor performance. The first-grade teacher is concerned with gross motor performances of the children. A knowledge of the sequence of development in gross motor performances and the relationship of this phase of the child's development to physical growth will be useful to her in guiding the child during the early school years. A study reported by Seils [14] deals with the relationship between the physical growth and maturity of primary school children and their pro-

[11] William Sloane, "The Lincoln-Oseretsky Motor Development Scale," *Genetic Psychology Monographs*, Vol. 51 (1955), pp. 183-252.

[12] Lulu M. Jenkins, *A Comparative Study of Motor Achievement of Children Five, Six, and Seven Years of Age*. Teachers College, Columbia University, Contributions to Education No. 414 (1930).

[13] A. Carpenter, "Tests of Motor Educability for the First Three Grades," *Child Development*, Vol. 11 (1940), pp. 293-299.

[14] LeRoy G. Seils, "The Relationship between Measures of Physical Growth and Gross Motor Performance of Primary Grade School Children," *Research Quarterly*, Vol. 22 (1951), pp. 244-260.

ficiency in performing certain gross motor activities. An analysis of the data in terms of each grade level showed that the mean performance for both boys and girls becomes higher at each grade level, although the correlations between the gross motor skill performances and age, height, and weight were low. A positive relationship was found between gross motor skill performance and the results of a measure of maturity. When one considers the varied factors which influence motor skill performances, this relationship between skeletal maturity and gross motor performances, although not great, appears more significant.

Certain skills were selected by Lachtaw [15] as basic to performance in many motor activities for grades four, five, and six. These skills were running, jumping, throwing and catching, striking, and kicking. Selected tests to measure these skills were given to a group of 67 boys and girls in grades four through six. The results of the study tended to corroborate those of Seil's. The relationship between age, height, weight, and performance as measured by these tests was relatively low. Height and weight factors in general showed a lower relationship to performance than did the age factor for both boys and girls. It appears from this study that experience and maturation are significant factors in the development of more complex skills.

Importance of maturation. Experiments with music training show that preschool children can profit from certain types of training.[16] Studies conducted at the University of Iowa show the effectiveness of early training upon the development of singing ability and interest in music. Groups of nursery-school children were given intensive help in the use of the singing voice for an average of ten minutes daily for forty periods. The control group was given no intensive training, but did participate in the music activities of the nursery school program. There was an accelerated development at all age levels in the singing ability of the children given the intensive training. This accelerated development was paralleled by an increased interest and desire to participate in musical training. The results of the study indicate quite clearly that singing ability and musical interest can be stimulated and accelerated through a training program that emphasizes individual as well as group performance and gives special attention to children who need voice and ear training.

An important question about perceptual-motor development is, How early can we begin to teach a child a skill and expect to see improvement beyond that which would result from maturation and general practice?

[15] Marjorie Lachtaw, "Measuring Selected Motor Skills in Fourth, Fifth, and Sixth Grades," *Research Quarterly,* Vol. 25 (1954), pp. 439-449.

[16] R. L. Updegraff, L. Hertiger, and J. Learned, "Part III. The Effect of Training on Singing Ability and Musical Interest of Three-, Four-, and Five-year-old Children," *Studies in Preschool Education, University of Iowa Studies in Child Welfare, New Series,* Vol. 14 (1938), pp. 83-131.

Dusenberry [17] studied this problem with 56 children as subjects, ranging in age from three to seven years. Two groups of twenty-eight children each were carefully equated. One of these groups was given practice and instruction in ball-throwing twice a week over a period of three weeks, while the other group was used as a control group.

The children were found to vary greatly in the way they threw the ball. In general the boys made better use of their bodies than did the girls and had more advance arm and hand movements in executing the throwing. As we can see from Table 9-1, both the practice and control groups made gains in average throwing scores from the initial to the final test. There is, however, a significant difference in the gains of the trained group over those of the control group. The boys improved more in distance-throwing skills than the girls with the same amount of training. Radical changes in style of throwing were sometimes accompanied by power performance. The most marked change in throwing style due to training, however, was found in stance. This is noteworthy for those concerned with guiding children in the development of skills. The importance of good form in the development of simple motor skills is indicated by the results of this study.

TABLE 9-1. Differences Between Beginning and Final Throwing Averages

GROUP	THROWS IN FEET		GAINS	
	INITIAL	FINAL	FEET	PER CENT
Trained (Boys)	24.0	30.0	6.0	25
Control (Boys)	23.5	26.5	3.0	12.8
Trained (Girls)	16.3	18.4	2.1	12.7
Control (Girls)	15.7	16.0	.3	2.1

There is some evidence, however, that training given at too early an age is largely ineffectual in promoting the development of motor skills. This is shown in a study by Hicks.[18] Children from two and a half to six years of age were given eight weeks of training in throwing a ball at a moving target. Such training produced no greater gains in the skills than were produced in the control group through structural maturation and

[17] Lois Dusenberry, "A Study of the Effects of Training in Ball Throwing by Children, Ages Three to Seven." Reprinted from *The Research Quarterly*, Vol. 23 (1952), pp. 8-14. Copyright, 1952, by the American Association for Health, Physical Education, and Recreation, Department of the National Education Association, 1201 Sixteenth Street, N.W., Washington 6, D.C.

[18] J. A. Hicks, "The Acquisition of Motor Skill in Young Children," *Child Development*, Vol. 1 (1930), pp. 90-105.

general practice. There are skills which should be delayed to permit the child to mature sufficiently to acquire the best methods of performing them. The gains to be derived from deferred practice, however, do not continue indefinitely. For example, training in motor skills needed to perform acrobatic dancing cannot be delayed too long. Such delay may be more detrimental than helpful.

Also, the younger child is at an advantage in learning foreign languages. Penfield and Roberts [19] point out that the child's brain has a specialized capacity for learning language. This neurophysiological ability diminishes with the years. Also, the child experiences a direct psychological urge which immensely facilitates foreign language learning. His primary motivation is satisfaction of his curiosity and not mastery of a new language.

Experiences in the schools of Europe and America have shown that, after a certain age—10 or 11—the child approaches a second language by using the already mastered symbols of his own language. He tries to use his own verbal units and thus speaks with an accent. Furthermore, the youth who begins learning a second language during his teens or twenties employs the linguistic units already learned during the period of vocabulary expansion. He therefore *translates* the symbols of the foreign language into his own and then derives meaning. The young child does not do this. He employs the foreign language units directly to get meaning.

Thus, if easy and natural pronunciation together with facility in use is the goal of modern language instruction, such instruction should begin during the early elementary years in classroom situations *where no other language is spoken* for the time being. The impetus then will not be to collect words, nor to acquire language, but to learn about interesting things, to play games and to read pleasant stories. Penfield and Roberts point out that evidence suggests that those who learn more than one language in early childhood find the learning of later additional languages easier.

The neurologists also suggest that speech is not the only new skill which is more easily and accurately acquired in childhood. Learning the piano and violin and learning to ski also come into this category.

In this connection a comment from Pearson is interesting:

. . . Perhaps definite instruction in the specific skills of various games—batting, catching, and pitching in baseball; stance, swing and putt in golf; tennis strokes; techniques of basketball, bowling, boxing, wrestling, swimming, dancing, fishing, hockey, whatever game the individual selected would accomplish more toward the development of coordination and rhythm than the usual

[19] Wilder Penfield and Lamar Roberts, *Speech and Brain-Mechanisms* (Princeton, New Jersey: Princeton University Press, 1959), Ch. XI.

physical training of the gymnasium, and it would also enable the child to learn a recreational sport which he would continue in adult life.[20]

One should not oversimplify the factors involved in the acquisition of skills, however. The dynamics of the individual child operate at all stages and in all aspects of his development. One six-year-old child will persist in a skill-developing activity in spite of difficulty and failure while his classmate with equal maturity and opportunity for learning gives up quickly. Materials bearing on the role of emotions and motivation on behavior and learning will be presented in subsequent chapters.

In general, it may be stated as a fundamental principle that beyond the early years most of the differences in learning complex skills—especially the higher initial scores—are a result of the wide range of experiences and differences in motivation. Where gross motor skills involving the large muscles are concerned, differences in strength at different age levels give a significant advantage to older children. Also, the older individual has greater ability to sustain attention and follow directions in the performance of complex motor skills.

Learning the task as a whole.   It has been noted earlier that learning is usually more efficient when the learner grasps the major relationships. The whole, when understood, gives meaning to the parts. After one has gotten the general pattern of the plan of a city, such as Washington, D.C., it is easier to learn the location of important buildings and parks in that city. Thus, formal training on specific items of a task may be very helpful in overcoming a specific difficulty.

Although experimental results favor the whole method of learning, they are not sufficiently conclusive to permit a simple and generalized statement of the relative efficiency of the whole and part methods in the learning of skills. Even when applied to specifically perceptual-motor skills, the results vary from person to person. There is some evidence that the more capable students are likely to do better with the whole method. Certainly the size of the unit to be learned should vary with the capacity of the learner. This was noted in a study by Lemke [21] of motor-esthetic learning. His study was concerned with children's improvement in playing the violin through instruction in phrasing. The importance of distinguishing the rhythmical phrases in the interpretation of music is analogous to the value of punctuation and accentuation in written and oral expression.

Two groups of intermediate-grade children were used in Lemke's

[20] Gerald H. Pearson, *Psychoanalysis and the Education of the Child* (New York: W. W. Norton and Company, 1954), p. 239.

[21] Leo Lemke, "Improvement in Playing the Violin through Instruction in Phrasing," Ph.D. Thesis (University of Michigan, 1949). The fundamental basis of music interpretation is phrasing or the grouping of notes.

study. The experimental group was given instruction in phrasing three periods a week for ten weeks, while the control group was given no such instruction. The experimental group was given the task of perceiving and executing this smallest unit, in contrast to a larger measure of unit which beginners are usually taught. The experimental group showed marked improvement over the control group—improvement which was reflected not only in phrasing but also in tone, time, pitch, and technique. The conclusions drawn from this and other studies bearing on the whole-part method of learning may be summarized as follows:

1. No one method is superior for all learners or for all tasks. The length and complexity of the task may make learning by the purely part method superior in some instances to learning by the whole method.
2. In general, students should be oriented to the problem before practicing special details.
3. The size of the learning unit should be influenced by the maturation and capacity of the learner.
4. In complex perceptual-motor tasks or complicated skills, special attention should be given to difficult parts.
5. The learner's attention should be focused upon the task as a whole and the perceptual cues rather than upon special movements to be made.
6. Attention should be given to the total performance of the task, leaving "the rough edges" to be smoothed out later in additional practice.

The effects of practice. To be effective, practice must be sufficiently long for the learner to identify cues and make discernible progress on the task. Further, practice must be so arranged that there is a *minimum* lapse of time between cue and response and between the response and reinforcement. The learner must know when his response is correct.

The importance of adequate spacing of practice is a fundamental principle of learning. This is most important in acquiring skills.

Research findings at the present time do not support a simple definitive decision to mass or to distribute practice solely on the basis of categories of verbal or motor learning. A more workable distinction lies between *serial* (verbatim) and paired-associate types of tasks. A distinction must also be made for idea learning which is in a separate category (underlying both serial and paired-associate tasks). Evidence suggests that distributed practice is better in verbatim *learning* than in paired-associate learning. Massed practice, on the other hand, produces better *retention* for serial tasks than for paired-associate tasks.

In general practice periods should be short and well spaced at first, but not so short that the learner will be unable to grasp the act as a unit. In the precision stage, practice periods may be longer and more numerous. A study by Fulton [22] attempted to compare the effect of placing emphasis on speed and accuracy in the initial stages of a training period of a ballistic movement. Results obtained from the comparison of two equated groups given fifteen training periods at the rate of two a week revealed no significant differences in speed of strokes at the end of training period. However, the group which emphasized speed developed greater accuracy than the group which made accuracy the primary aim. This finding is in accord with other studies which indicate that the correct order of emphasis in teaching skills should be technique first with speed and accuracy being achieved as the result of control.

The importance of practice in the development and fixation of a skill will also depend upon the motivation of the learner. Practice, as mere repetition, may create unfavorable attitudes toward a task and may thus act as a barrier to the development of a high state of efficiency. We can see this with the student who finds practice periods in typewriting unpleasant. He will not reach as high a level of performance as he could were he adequately motivated. This is one of the potential dangers in overlearning. When practice is carried to the point where it is distasteful to the learner, or when it is carried on in a mechanical, repetitive fashion, efficiency in learning will be adversely affected. The value of overlearning is largely dependent upon the motivation of the learner and the optimal distribution of practice time.

Guidance in the acquisition of a skill

Skills are learned by practice. It has been noted that at certain maturation levels in human development, there are developmental tasks whose practice gives the child such satisfaction that the mere repetition of the activity seems to be an end in itself until the task-skills have been adequately mastered. This is almost naturally achieved before the child will get the opportunity to practice the next sequence of skills. At the same time there is usually a naturally motivated "teacher" in a parent or family member who constantly motivates and demonstrates by talking to the child, praising, and illustrating. This practicing takes place in natural life situations and is purposeful. The same principles should be observed in the more formal settings where skills such as writing, reading, swimming, skating, and typing are taught.

Of paramount importance is the teacher or instructor. He must not only know the whole constellation of the skills involved with their clusters of sub-skills but he must be able to demonstrate the correct pattern of performance, not only in its entire, smooth performance, but also in its

[22] Ruth E. Fulton, "Speed and Accuracy in Learning a Ballistic Movement," *Research Quarterly,* Vol. 13 (1952), pp. 30-36.

individual and involved parts. Furthermore, he must be able to observe the student's weaknesses and strengths as he practices, and he must be able to capitalize on the student's strengths to aid him in overcoming his weaknesses. The instructor has the responsibility to know the best methods of teaching the skills and how they can be best practiced.

Evidence of the value of guidance. Evidence of the value of guidance may be observed with the learning of such motor skills as swimming and boxing or in the more complex coordinations like those found in typewriting. An individual left to himself in learning to swim will likely develop some stroke similar to that referred to as the dog-paddle, whereas a capable swimming instructor would guide him in the learning of a

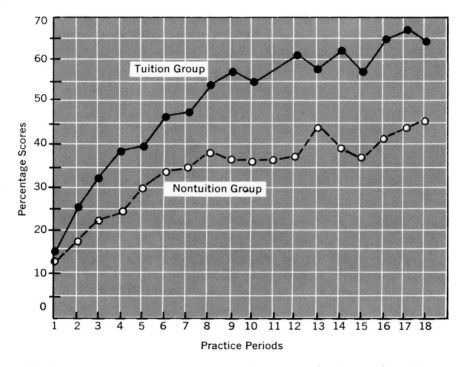

FIGURE 9-4. Daily Average Percentage Scores For The Two Archery Groups

more efficient stroke such as the crawl. The person who teaches himself to swim may also develop undesirable fears of the water which will inhibit smooth muscular coordination regardless of the stroke which he ultimately develops. The cramped style of typing known as the hunt-and-peck system will be replaced by a "touch" system under the guidance of a capable instructor.

One of the most complete studies of this problem was conducted by Dorothy Davies [23] with two groups of college girls. The members of one group were given regular and systematic instruction in the techniques of archery while the members of the second group practiced archery under the observation of the experimenter but without instruction. At the start of the experiment, the two groups were considered to be equally capable of acquiring skill in archery. The term of the experiment comprised eighteen practice periods during which arrows were shot and scores recorded. The average learning curves of the two groups, presented in Figure 9-4 show a sharp initial rise in performance from the first to the eighth or ninth practice periods.

The instructed group was given instruction prior to the first trial and was superior in performance to the noninstructed group from the very beginning. This superiority increased throughout the course of the experiment. The results of this study support the conclusion that instruction in techniques of performing a complex skill aids the learner in achieving the skill and in developing a higher level of proficiency. The educational implications of this study are clear. They may be summarized as follows:

1. Teaching a skill takes advantage of the learner's capacity for intellectual analysis of the problem and thus increases the rate of learning.
2. Instruction tends to prevent the learner from early falling into a set pattern below his potentialities.
3. Through instruction the learner's attention is directed to more adequate techniques than those which he has probably been using. Thus the learner is guided and stimulated in favor of better techniques. This enables the learner to reach a higher level of proficiency.
4. Through instruction the teacher promotes the growth of the learner's intellectual insight into the nature of the skill and into the factors related to success.

Positive versus negative guidance. One may observe positive guidance in the development of such a skill as handwriting.

Handwriting as a sensorimotor skill involves muscular coordination. Thus, the development of writing skill will follow the same general course as the development of other sensorimotor skills. The muscular skills involved in good handwriting develop as a result of maturation, practice, the absence of pressure, and the elimination of incorrect habits

---

[23] Dorothy R. Davies, "The Effect of Tuition upon the Process of Learning a Complex Motor Skill," *Journal of Educational Psychology,* Vol. 36 (1945), pp. 352-365.

of movements. The emphasis sometimes given to the full-arm movement tends to freeze motor behavior at the second or third grade level because it does not allow the child to make use of smaller muscles that develop with increased maturation. Also, writing difficulties may be ignored in the emphasis frequently given to speed in writing. The abandonment of mechanical and meaningless drill was perhaps good, but the failure to provide a more useful method has been unfortunate. The acquisition of writing skill must include certain sound precepts present in the learning of other skills. Some of these are:

1. The presentation of a reasonably good demonstration or model
2. Practice under supervision
3. Freedom from stress and pressure
4. Guidance in self-diagnosis and self-appraisal of the skill
5. Consideration of maturity
6. Drill or intensive practice when needed

An instance of negative guidance in teaching handwriting is the practice of pointing out special errors to the learner and instructing him to avoid them. When the emphasis is upon avoiding errors which were previously made, there is negative guidance. An emphasis upon making *correct* movements is regarded as positive guidance.

A study by Holodnak was designed to compare the effectiveness of positive and negative guidance in the learning of mazes by children.[24] Sixty-four children ranging in age from six to ten years were used as subjects in maze learning. Positive guidance consisted of informing children whenever a correct response was made; while negative guidance consisted of informing them when an incorrect response was made. The results of the study are presented in Table 9-2. On all three criteria, errors, trials, and time, the learning with positive guidance was superior to the learning with negative guidance. The difference in favor of positive guidance was greatest with the youngest, the six-year-old group. It is also worth noting that the performance of girls surpassed that of boys with respect to the criteria. These results are in harmony with those of other experimenters using mazes and other simple skill tasks.

The use of models and demonstrations. Demonstrations by the instructor or audio-visual material (charts, TV, films, slides, etc.) showing the nature of a skill or some of its aspects enables the learner to perceive the task as a whole. To be successful in performing a skill, the learner must know, in general, what is to be done and how it is to be

[24] Helen Barbara Holodnak, "The Effect of Positive and Negative Guidance upon Maze Learning in Children," *Journal of Educational Psychology*, Vol. 34 (1943), pp. 341-354.

TABLE 9-2. A Comparison Between Positive and Negative Guidance

	POSITIVE GUIDANCE			NEGATIVE GUIDANCE		
	ERRORS	TRIALS	TIME	ERRORS	TRIALS	TIME
Boys	27.07	12.34	283.87	36.78	16.93	395.52
Girls	24.71	11.06	265.20	29.40	12.63	315.97

done. Demonstrations are valuable devices in the introduction of new materials and techniques. On the secondary-school level visual aid materials may be most useful. The value of such devices, however, will depend upon the extent to which the learner has been prepared for them, the motivation of the learner, the clarity of the demonstration, and the instructional procedures following the demonstration. The work should be organized in such a way that it proceeds from simpler to more complex materials and problems. It should always be organized within the scope of the learner's maturation and experiences.

Essentials in guidance. The first requirement of one who guides another in the learning of a skill is knowledge of the characteristics of a good performance. For example, the teacher of archery should first of all be an expert in archery himself and know how the learner can best acquire such a perceptual-motor skill.

Much of the current criticism of instruction in handwriting stems from the fact that, although the skill improves with practice during the elementary school years, it rapidly declines during the later school years. Reasons for this rapid decline may be ascribed to (1) absence of guided practice, (2) lack of social pressure, (3) less favorable conditions for writing, and (4) increased demand for writing in the upper grades resulting in an emphasis on speed.

Certain precautions should be observed in the guidance of acquisition of skills. Pupils should be given opportunities to try out different techniques, to explore (and sometimes err). The instructor should keep in mind that a particular form or method is not applicable to all situations or to all people. Guidance, however, should be introduced before the learner has acquired habits or skills that will interfere with his progress in the attainment of increased proficiency.

Motivation is most important in learning skills. The problem of motivation is, however, simpler in predominantly perceptual-motor learning than in predominantly verbal-abstract types of learning. In the former, the learner can see the results of his efforts more readily; he can also set up more specific goals, factors tending to make it easier for him to recognize his deficiencies. Those who guide children should keep criticism to a minimum in the early stages of such learnings, lest the learner develop a hypercritical attitude toward his performance. The learner needs encouragement. Self-confidence is most important if he is to make the optimum progress in the acquisition of skills.

A study by West [25] tested the merits of nonsense, word, and sentence materials as vehicles for the development of skill in typing.

Nonsense materials have been widely used to train each finger to strike the keys assigned to it. For example, the left index finger is used for the sequence *frf*. In order to assess the influences of word length as a factor, one set of word materials was restricted almost entirely to words of three to five letters long while another set included words covering greater lengths, averaging 0.5 letters more per word.

West found that word and sentence materials were superior to the nonsense materials. He lists the chief factors which may account for this superiority as:

(a) the greater allowance for individual differences in ability to attempt stroking habits of a higher order, (b) the absence of possible interference from earlier practice on sequences which do not exist in the language, (c) the greater variety of responses allowed by the practice and (d) the higher levels of attention, concentration, and interest.[26]

Certainly the use of words and sentences agrees with those principles of learning which stress meaningfulness of material, distributed practice, learning by larger units involving the coordination of various muscles of the fingers, and the acquisition of skills in the way they are to be used. This type of material also lends itself to sustaining a higher level of motivation.

The most serious mistake teachers make in guiding the esthetic development of the child is to place great emphasis upon factual knowledge or to expect expert performance. We may note this in the development of music appreciation. If the emphasis is on the names of composers, their biographies, and the dates of their various achievements, many learners will find the experiences very dull. Also, if the emphasis on learning to play the piano is upon *do, re, me,* and the correct finger and hand movements, there will be little in such experience that challenges the interests and the needs of the individual learner. There is good evidence that when children are guided in expressing their feelings through the dance or music, learning is enhanced.

In general, the elementary schools have been more successful than the secondary schools in teaching the arts. Elementary teachers are more

[25] Leonard J. West, "An Experimental Comparison of Nonsense, Word, and Sentence Materials in Early Typing Training," *Journal of Educational Psychology,* Vol. 47 (1956), pp. 481-489.

[26] *Ibid.,* pp. 488-489.

committed to methods which place emphasis on the individual child rather than specific skills or units of subject matter. A few, however, have at times confused creativeness with freedom of action. It should be pointed out that creative work must be motivated and directed. The way the teacher directs the work and his understanding of the methods of guiding growth in skills and techniques will determine whether the learner's activity is an expression of himself or a mere mechanical response to the teacher's instructions. Adult patterns or standards imposed upon immature learners will almost certainly destroy their interest, initiative, and creative desire.

SUMMARY

The broad categories of motor skills are presented in this chapter: object-motor activities, language-motor activities, and feeling-motor activities. Object-motor activities include the use of tools and are an important part of a modern elementary school program. The language-motor activities include movements of the speech organs, drawing activities, reading, and other perceptual-motor movements involved in the use of language. These make up a fundamental part of the school program and are basic to the intellectual and social development of the pupils. Feeling-motor activities do not operate to the exclusion of these other motor skills. In these activities, however, the attitudes and feelings of the individual are clearly related to his expressed activities. Readiness and sound principles of learning are applicable to these learnings as well.

There is good evidence that most children are not given training in the different skills commensurate with their abilities and needs. The guidance of the child's development in perceptual-motor skills should be an integral part of the school program. Principles of learning, discussed at length in Chapter 7, are applicable to the acquisition of these skills. These principles include:

1. The choice of activities in harmony with the maturational level of the learner.
2. Setting forth purposive learnings and goals.
3. Organizing activities and learning experiences in relation to the needs, interests and aspirations of the learner.
4. Providing opportunity for the child to explore besides guiding him in his activities.
5. Keeping criticism, especially autocriticism, to a minimum.
6. Integrating the perceptual-motor learning with other aspects of the child's development—providing for the all-around development of the child.

Problems and Exercises

1. Give an example to show how specific training is dependent upon the stage of maturation of the individual learner. What fundamental principle is involved here?
2. What factors should be considered in planning practice periods for perceptual-motor learning?
3. Cite evidence from your own experience and observations which tend to refute the general supposition that girls are inherently inferior to boys in the acquisition of perceptual-motor skills.
4. A second grade teacher plans to spend 20% of time allotted for reading on exercises to increase speed. Discuss this procedure in the light of this chapter.
5. A high school teacher urges her students to "widen their fixation span so that they 'devour' words—5 or 6 to each fixation." Discuss this in the light of the chapter and Figure 9-2.
6. Advocates of foreign language instruction in the early elementary grades assert that young children learn foreign languages more readily than older children. Is this true under all conditions? If not, under what conditions would the assertion be true? Why is it true? Why isn't it true?
7. How do the motor abilities of the adolescent differ from those of the elementary-school child? Be specific.
8. A high school typing teacher plans her schedule so that students practice typing letters and take timed tests once a week. The rest of the week they work on their own material under their own planning. Discuss this procedure.
9. In the light of this chapter, what are some shortcomings of the common procedure of "cramming"?
10. Differentiate *positive* and *negative* guidance. Evaluate the merits of each.

Selected Readings

CRONBACH, Lee J., *Educational Psychology*, 2nd ed. (New York: Harcourt, Brace and Company, 1963), Ch. 12.

GATES, A. I., *et al.*, *Educational Psychology*, 3d ed. (New York: The Macmillan Co., 1948), Ch. 13.

LAWTHER, John D., "Learning Motor Skills and Knowledge," in C. E. Skinner, ed., *Educational Psychology* (Englewood Cliffs, N. J.: Prentice-Hall, 1959), Ch. 18.

MILLARD, Cecil V., *Child Growth and Development in the Elementary School Years* (Boston: D. C. Heath and Co., 1951), Ch. 5.

PENFIELD, W. and ROBERTS, L., *Speech and Brain-Mechanisms* (Princeton: Princeton University Press, 1959), Ch. 11.

RAGSDALE, C. E., "How Children Learn the Motor Types of Activities," *Learning and Instruction*, Part I, *Forty-ninth Yearbook of the National Society for the Study of Education* (Chicago: University of Chicago Press, 1944), Ch. 3.

STEPHENS, J. M., *Educational Psychology* (New York: Henry Holt and Co., 1951), Ch. 12.

CHAPTER **10**

Acquisition of Knowledge and Understanding

As we have already discussed, maturation and experience play important roles in helping children and adolescents understand the world of which they are a part and in helping them deal with new situations as they arise. In the course of development the child becomes increasingly aware of various objects, persons, and situations through which his experiences develop; these experiences tend to arouse mental activity which produces learning. By the time he enters school he has acquired many meanings and has already learned to deal with many simple and concrete problems.

ACQUIRING MEANINGS—THE NATURE OF MEANING

It has already been suggested that by reacting to a particular situation or condition we acquire a meaning. We see a child crying and we ask, "What is the trouble?" Through our past reactions we have learned that children frequently cry when they are in trouble, especially when they are hurt. The lists of meanings acquired will vary with individuals and with the nature of their experiences. They are many in number and relate to all phases of life. The general structure of an experience is easier to learn when the materials making up the structure are meaningful. Thus, existing meanings are beneficial in acquiring new meanings.

There is considerable evidence, based upon experiences as well as scientific investigations that children learn to read, write, and solve arithmetic problems better when they are confronted with meaningful and vital materials. Children in the second grade learn to spell such words as Easter, Christmas, and Santa Claus—words meaningful and significant in their lives. The word *play* will be recognized more readily

248

than the word *plot,* because it is more meaningful to them. Words have meaning because of the individual's experiences with what they stand for. They are in themselves abstractions. They are symbols that may be repeated by rote, or that may be learned in connection with particular objects, situations, or conditions. It is possible, however, for a particular word to have different meanings for different people, because their experiences with the thing the word symbolizes differ.

There are endless degrees of meaning involved in an ideational learning task or situation. This is illustrated in the pictured diagram.

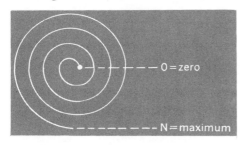

At the center, near the zero point, is the learning task, well-nigh meaningless. The meager knowledge that Alaska is one of the fifty states making up the United States is not far from the zero point, while an understanding of its location, history, resources, climate, and people would be represented somewhere nearer the outer-rim of the circle. The illustration is intended to show that one's knowledge and understanding grows gradually from the beginning point near zero.

There is perhaps no limitation placed on the meaning attached to a particular stimulus-object or situation. Any limitation would result from the native ability, dynamics, and experiences of the learner. Furthermore, there is nothing to determine to what degree a particular learning task should be learned. Just how much should one learn about Alaska? How much knowledge does one need about the true meaning and significance of the information in mathematics that six plus four equals ten? Simple facts learned in arithmetic are seldom learned beyond the point of the arbitrary associations acquired. Teachers need to reckon with the problem of how far on the continuum of meaningfulness should be the goal in the learning of different tasks. Certainly materials regarded as very important to the learner should be learned more thoroughly and be made more meaningful than less important materials.

The development of meanings

There are two widespread misconceptions about the development of meanings which should be carefully considered. In the first place some people are inclined to identify all meanings with words. This is probably the result of the meanings they acquire at school. Certainly books, lectures, and class discussions are important in the development of meanings. Modern education, however, takes advantage of other media for the development of meanings, and meanings have important bearings apart from words. The child experiences running, jumping, and climbing;

Visual aids and related devices are useful in the present day educational program. Materials are made more meaningful and motivation is heightened when these are correlated with other phases of the teaching program

studies of deaf children show that meanings are not absent, even though the acquisition of words may be. The second misconception consists in thinking of the acquisition of meanings as separate and distinct from all other kinds of learning. This arises from attempts to divide learning into several main types. Such divisions may be practical and convenient, but are not in harmony with the conception of learning presented in earlier chapters. All these types of learning are clearly interrelated. For example, consider the meaning of the word *knife*. Such a meaning will incorporate all of one's experiences with a knife, including motor activities involving its use and attitudes acquired toward a knife.

Differentiation and integration are clearly discernible in the formation of meanings. In the development of the meaning of *knife* the child develops the ability to distinguish between a knife and other objects. Integration is accomplished as the child comes to understand the function of the knife and incorporates this understanding into his total knowledge and understanding.

It should be emphasized that all meanings grow out of experiences. Words encountered in listening and reading have meaning in accordance with our experiences. Children who have had only one meaning of a word find it confusing when the word is given a different meaning. For example, the word *pitch* may have a single meaning for the schoolboy engrossed in baseball, but confuses him when he encounters it in music. An important task in the teaching of meaning is to make sure that there is no gap between the experiences of the child and the words he encounters in the textbook and classroom.

Importance of cues.   One of the features involved in learning is that cues are established which affect one's response to a situation. At first the individual responds to the whole object, such as an airplane. After experiencing various situations involving airplanes he is able to respond to some specific aspect of the situation as if it were the whole pattern. The pattern (cue) may be the propellors or the noise of the airplane as it moves through the air. This reduction of the necessary stimulation to that of some single part of it is the essence of *perceptual learning.* These parts of the situation which provoke the meaningful response are termed cues.

These meanings develop in a gradual and somewhat orderly manner. This was noticed in a study reported by Weinstein.[1] A battery of open-ended questions relating to the United States flag was devised and administered to elementary-school children. A correlation of .76 was found between age in months and total score on the interview schedule. No significant sex differences were observed on the over-all interview performance. Ten-year-old children identified the flag with patriotism and loyalty to the United States. By the ages of eleven and twelve children identified the flag not only with people but with special conditions and historical events when the flag was displayed. Here we note the flag as a symbol of loyalty, country, patriotism, and a national body of people with a history.

Firsthand experiences are valuable, especially during the early stages of learning. Realistic, direct apprehension of insect life, the grocery store, or the post office is useful motivationally, and can help children to learn quickly through direct sensory experiences. Meanings developed at this level can then be enriched and extended through language symbols used in thinking and communication. After children acquire these richer and more generalized meanings, a return to firsthand experiences offers an excellent means of testing the ideas being formulated.

Contrived experiences are useful for guiding individuals in learning

[1] Eugene A. Weinstein, "Development of the Concept of Flag and the Sense of National Unity," *Child Development,* Vol. 28 (1956-57), pp. 167-174.

those things where actual experiences are too cumbersome and time consuming. These may be set up in the classroom or laboratory, and can be changed by the teacher to meet specific needs and conditions. Teaching machines make use of carefully planned and continuously reinforced experiences to teach specific meanings or ideas. The laboratory method is prominent in the use of contrived experiences. In one school children studied the effects of diet by using white rats as subjects. One group was fed an adequate diet, while the other group was fed an inadequate diet. Such an experience involving the experimental approach to the solution of a problem enlists the pupils' interests and points up realistically the value of an adequate diet. Through a process of generalization involving communicative language the learners generalize the results obtained to situations in their own lives.

Experiences with symbols are essential for learnings of an abstract nature as well as for complete learning which would involve generalized experiences. Progress in this direction can be made with relatively young children when firsthand experiences and contrived sensory experiences are included.

CONCEPT FORMATION

A concept may be defined as a way of grouping an array of objects or events in terms of certain characteristics that distinguish this group from other objects or events. By grouping together things or events that have common characteristics one is able to (1) reduce the complexity of the situation, (2) identify more clearly the objects or events, (3) make more meaningful the learning experience, and (4) relate objects and events in the special grouping.[2]

Experiences of every kind help the child to understand the nature and functions of the people and things in his environment. He learns that books are to read, that certain tables are used to eat on, and that other tables are used for other purposes. The particular meaning he attaches to each object or person results from the influence these have upon his needs, interests, and total personality. The young child who has had many pleasant experiences with a pet dog and has learned to pet it and play with it will have different perceptions of dogs than the child who has been brought up without firsthand experience of a dog. Both the number and type of concepts which a child has are important for further learning. The child's readiness to learn certain tasks and the understanding he acquires from instruction are in part dependent upon the concepts he has previously formed.

[2] Percival M. Symonds, "What Education Has to Learn from Psychology, VI. Emotions and Learning," *Teachers College Record,* Vol. 60 (1958), pp. 9-22.

Acquiring concepts

Concepts are acquired as the result of the interaction of sensory impressions, past experiences, intelligence, and the interests and goals of the individual. A child who has had an opportunity to sense a variety of things, to go many places, and to be with a number of people of different backgrounds will be set to look for similarities and differences, while the youngster who is not encouraged to explore and not included in the group when company is around will lack experience in using his senses and find himself handicapped even when new experiences are available. Concerning the acquisition of concepts Kingsley and Garry state:

> Concepts are developed by the enrichment of experience, by the differentiation of details and by the synthesis of these details into a structural unity. The process of comprehension proceeds from vague gross impressions to clear-cut distinctions and from a poverty of association to an abundance.[3]

The child's ability to hear, see, feel, smell, and taste determines the things he will be able to respond to in his environment. If hearing is impaired, there will be difficulty in associating sounds with written words. Those who are nearsighted miss much that happens at a distance, while those who are farsighted have difficulty in understanding relationships that depend upon the observation of those minute details we encounter in reading, writing, and number work. The learner's physical equipment, especially during the preschool and early school years, is very important in concept development.

Importance of experience. It has been emphasized that a wide range of experience is essential for the formulation of concepts. The results of scientific studies bearing on this problem indicate clearly that actual experience on the part of the preschool- and elementary-school child is essential for concept formation. However, vicarious experiences are useful at all stages in the growth and extension of concepts. Pictures, illustrations, and models help to enlarge concepts. They are also useful in making more concrete ideas and relationships implied in language. Individuals do not readily acquire concepts by merely meeting words in context. Rather, it appears that at all age levels the building of concepts necessitates a certain amount of actual experiences.

The growth and extension of concepts requires experience. However, even with experience a certain level of maturity is needed. Immature reasoning is illustrated by this example. A child had a variety of flowers in a bouquet. An adult passerby asked how it happened that so many different kinds of flowers bloomed at the same time. The youngster replied, "I suppose they were all planted on the same day."

[3] H. L. Kingsley and R. Garry, *The Nature and Conditions of Learning.* Englewood Cliffs, N. J.: Prentice-Hall, Inc. (1957), p. 388.

Concepts develop in sequential order. We may note the sequential order of concept-development in the development of time concepts. Uka [4] studied the development of time concepts of elementary-school children. He found that some concepts develop early, some show a slow start with a sudden spurt, some develop gradually over a relatively long period of time, and some have their beginnings near the age of six. Figure 10-1 shows this growth in understanding of the following problems related to time:

(15) What day comes before Friday?
(22) In what month is Christmas?

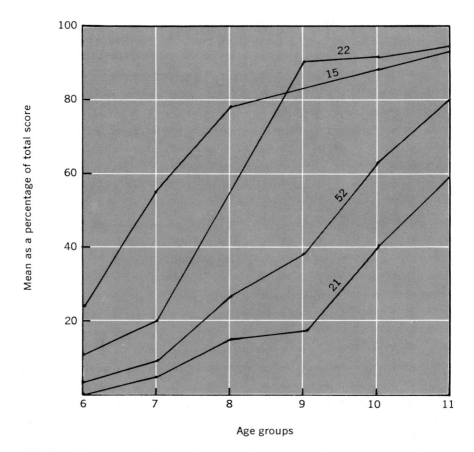

FIGURE 10-1. Growth Curves Showing The Nature Of The Growth Of Certain Time Concepts *(After Ngwobia Uka)*

[4] Ngwobia Uka, *Sequence in the Development of Time Concept in Children of Elementary School Age.* Ph.D. Dissertation, University of Southern California, 1956.

(52) How long does the summer last?
(21) Name the months of the year.

There was a significant relationship between the level of the intellectual ability of the pupils and the development of time concepts. The development of time, space, and number concepts closely correlate with other aspects of the child's intellectual development. These developments also reveal the sequential nature of concept development.

The principle of the sequential order of the acquisition of knowledge and understanding is apparent in science, social studies, and problem-solving activities. Materials dealing with the acquisition of concepts at school are presented later in this chapter.

The extension of concepts is a gradual and continuous process, as suggested in the case of growth of meaning. It might be described as a linear and progressive growth from

simple responses _____ to _____ complex responses;
undifferentiated responses _____ to _____ differentiated responses;
discrete responses _____ to _____ systematic responses;
rigid responses _____ to _____ flexible responses.[5]

Acquisition of concepts in relation to transfer. Subjecting a child to a great amount of specific, unrelated data does not help him to form concepts. The child should be guided in discovering that trees, weeds, and flowers are basically the same. They are all living things that require water and nutrition, and are referred to as different forms of plant life. If more of the stress in teaching were placed upon principles and relationships which give meanings to isolated facts, the application of such facts would be more readily made. Such a view favors the procedure employed in many schools of presenting materials in organized topical units. Pupils who are taught in terms of complete understanding and who are able to perceive the relations between things are better able to appreciate and understand what they encounter in new experiences, thereby extending the scope of what is often referred to as transfer.

The pupil who has learned only certain isolated items in a whole field has nothing with which to bind them together. It is at this point that Gestalt theory, referred to in Chapter 7, is important. This theory has shown that one cannot arrive at a clear understanding of a part unless the part is regarded as an integral functioning unit in a structural pattern. For example, the child cannot understand the isolated parts of the hands of a clock except as he sees these as functioning parts of the whole

[5] K. F. Scheussler and A. L. Strauss, "Study of Concept Learning by Scale Analysis," *American Sociological Review*, Vol. 15 (1950), pp. 752-762.

structure of the clock. We may observe the role of experience and the gestalt in one example with people from the southeastern part of the United States. Their concept of the beach is both a place for playing in the water and the sand itself. Such a concept may differ from another person's who may come from an area where clam digging is the principal activity at the ocean beach. Transfer of concepts depends upon experience, maturity, intelligence, and the manner in which particular concepts are learned. It was emphasized in Chapter 8 that the teaching-learning procedure is very important in connection with all aspects of transfer.

Effectiveness of reinforcement. The importance of reinforcement in learning was emphasized in Chapter 6. Reinforcement should also be helpful in the acquisition of concepts. A study by Carpenter [6] dealt with the effects of varying amounts of reinforcement upon concept formation. He divided 92 college students into four groups and had them learn a set of concepts, using blocks of assorted shapes, sizes, colors, and heights. Four schedules of reinforcement were used. The reinforcement consisted of statements made by the experimenter: "That's right" or "That's wrong." The following indicates the amount of reinforcement for each group:

Group	No. of Students	Per cent of correct trials reinforced	Per cent of incorrect trials reinforced
I	23	25	
II	23	50	
III	23	100	
IV	23	100	100

The effects of different degrees of reinforcement are shown graphically in Figure 10-2. The curves show that the group that was most frequently reinforced made the greatest progress in acquiring the concepts. The notion that concept formation does not benefit from reinforcement was not supported by the results of this study. The greatest benefit came during the early stages of the learning process. However, the student should not conclude that the same results would apply to the learning of concepts under different conditions. Carpenter concluded:

. . . But this study suggests together with what is already known that the teacher may find profit in: (1) Being certain that the desired response is per-

[6] Finley Carpenter, "Conceptualization as a Function of Differential Reinforcement," *Science Education,* Vol. 38 (1954), pp. 284-294.

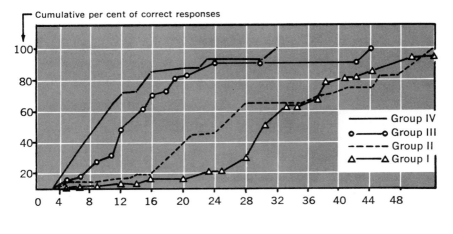

Cumulative per cent of correct responses

Number of trials

FIGURE 10-2.   Cumulative Per Cent Of Subjects Reaching Criteria By Groups As A Function Of The Number Of Trials *(Carpenter)*

formed before assuming that learning has occurred. (Far too often teachers seem to operate on the assumption of "osmosis" and that this absorption of knowledge will guarantee sufficient transfer to the level of application.) (2) Noting the various responses that compose a skill, act, or complex behavior, and making sure that ample reinforcement is contiguous with them instead of rewarding only end results. This suggests that we focus attention upon the behavioral processes instead of only products.[7]

The use of symbols.   The use of symbols in concept formation is an important feature of the modern school program. By classifying events symbolically man is able to study their relationships and to reason and think about things and events that are far distant in time or space. We sometimes assume that, unless a child can verbalize a concept, it has not been learned. This assumption is consistent with the educational practice so frequently observed of having children memorize and define the concepts that are being learned. Experimental evidence as well as general observations show that individuals can respond to elements in their environment without being able to define the characteristics of the discriminations they make. One of the writers who made the acquaintance of a mechanic who did poorly in school revealed considerable mechanical insight and skill at "do-it-yourself" tasks, even though he could not name the various mechanical parts that were being assembled. Carpenter's experiment involving conceptualization showed that of the 72 subjects who were able to operate the materials in a manner indicating that they had

[7] *Ibid.,* p. 293.

learned the concepts, only 18 per cent were able to verbalize the characteristics of the concepts.

Why then are individuals who have learned a concept unable to define it? The explanation offered by Carpenter appears to answer this question.

> . . . The simplest explanation is that the non-verbal learning required establishment of different responses than the verbal learning and that it is not necessary to expect 100 per cent transfer from one to another. Also, there was no systematic reinforcement of verbalization during learning. But it is quite possible that Ss verbalized implicitly such that reinforcement was *sometimes* associated with the correct response.[8]

Concepts are enlarged and extended when children are taught to classify familiar things into categories, such as trees, animals, fruits, furniture, rivers, and mountains. The use of symbols makes it easier to group objects and events into categories. Concepts of color, size, and shape may be developed through games in which these play an important role. The child needs guidance in the development of concepts, while reinforcement will contribute to the efficiency of the learning process. On the basis of a review of the literature bearing on concept formation Vinacke has presented some fundamental principles. Some of these are here presented.

1. Performance proceeds from simple or easy to complex or difficult, and the ability to deal with given kinds of tasks improves as the child becomes older.
2. There appears to be no intellectual processes which emerge sharply at a given age.
3. Increasing ability corresponds more closely to an even, regular progression than to discrete stages.
4. Concrete and abstract conceptual performance develop simultaneously, even though they may develop at different rates.[9]

Growth in understanding

The number and type of concepts which an individual child has learned profoundly affects his success or failure in future learning tasks. Without adequate concepts the child will be unable to understand or comprehend many of the learning tasks he faces. When concepts are inadequate or inaccurate they have an adverse effect upon the interpretation of pictures, reading materials, and other educational experiences. A story about fishing, for example, where the words *perch, cast, line, rod,* and *hook* are used, have entirely different meanings for children un-

[8] *Ibid.*, p. 292.
[9] William E. Vinacke, "Developmental Changes in Thinking," *Education*, Vol. 77 (1957), pp. 318-322.

familiar with fishing terminology. *Perch,* used as a noun in the story, may be a verb to them. The word *cast* may mean a group in a play; *line,* what you draw on a piece of paper to indicate direction or distance; *rod,* a mathematical term; and *hook,* a verb rather than the object which becomes attached to the fish. A number of studies have illustrated the relationships between children's learning in the classroom and the types of concepts they have acquired.

Concept of time. Concepts related to time are developed over a period of years. Five-, six-, and seven-year-olds think of time in terms of what they do. If asked, "What time is it?" they may respond, "Time to eat." Similarly the days of the week and the seasons are known by the activities associated with them. Many second graders can tell time but seem not to use it as a guide to work or play. Bradley [10] studied the ability of elementary-school children to understand ordinary time words and to develop a concept of the universal nature of the time scheme.

The results indicate a gradual and continuous growth in understanding "time" words throughout the elementary-school period. By the age of five years, distinctions between the present, past, and future seem to have been established. The first "time" words used after this stage were those referring to natural phenomena and personal activities. In general, the ability to understand the conventional time scheme and to use particular time words appeared later than was generally believed. Nine- and ten-year-olds were able to comprehend a long period of years. Twelve- and thirteen-year-olds could answer questions which were mainly concerned with duration. The principle of a sequential order of the acquisition of time knowledge was apparent in this study.

Uka [11] devised a testing instrument consisting of 60 items for measuring time concepts of elementary-school children. This was administered to 346 elementary-school pupils, six to eleven years of age. Consistent and progressive growth in time concepts was noted throughout the age range studied. There were noticeable mean differences between the total scores of boys and girls at each age level in favor of the girls. This is shown in Figure 10-3. The most difficult time concepts were those dealing with time duration; less difficult were those showing time extension and time order. The simplest time concepts were those related to the children's personal experiences, indicating further the importance of personal experiences for the development of understanding. On the whole there seemed to be a speeding up of the growth of time concepts in children between the ages of ten and eleven.

[10] N. C. Bradley, "The Growth of the Knowledge of Time in Children of School-age," *British Journal of Psychology,* Vol. 38 (1947), pp. 67-78.

[11] Ngwobia Uka, *Sequence in The Development of Time Concepts in Children of Elementary School Age.* Ph.D. Dissertation, University of Southern California, 1956.

Abstract concepts are more readily learned when pupils have the opportunity
to test them in a tangible manner

There was a significant relationship between the level of the intellectual ability of the pupils and the development of time concepts. This is indicated by the correlations presented in Table 10-1. The test correlated highly with grade placement and school progress in arithmetic and reading for the eleven-year-olds. Arithmetic ability and a knowledge of the tenses seemed to be important factors in the formation of time concepts.

Concepts related to size, distance, and direction. The child's understanding of size, distance, and direction is fairly well established by the time he reaches the primary grades. The average kindergarten youngster responds correctly to such words as *in, on, up, at, down, behind, in front of, under, big, middlesized,* and *small.* His ability to judge size, however, becomes increasingly inaccurate as the difference between the size of the articles judged decreases.[12] Upon entering school the youngster can estimate small distances rather accurately. Greater distances require more

[12] M. E. Thrum, "The Development of Concepts of Magnitude," *Child Development,* Vol. 6 (1935), pp. 120-140.

TABLE 10-1.   Correlation Between Scores on the Time Concept Test and Certain Measures of Intellectual Development (*After Uka*)

INTELLECTUAL DEVELOPMENTAL FACTORS	AGE GROUPS	N *	r **
Gates Primary Reading Test	6	39	.50
California Test of Mental Maturity			
Intelligence Quotient	10	43	.70
Mental Age	10	43	.79
California Achievement Test			
Grade Placement	11	70	.73
Arithmetic	11	70	.80
Reading	11	70	.77

*N—number of cases.
**r—correlation.

experience and maturity. A child who receives training in judging size and distance in relation to instruction in arithmetic has better concepts than those who do not have this advantage. Generally a six-year-old can distinguish between the left and right sides of his own body, but he is unable to distinguish another person's right or left until he is approximately two years older.[13]

Perception for depth is poorly developed in the six-year-old when he enters school. The immature child may be observed placing his cup very close to the edge of the table. He incorrectly estimates the height of things. This may account for some of his accidents and awkwardness. He may be seen to give a big step downward when a small step is sufficient, or to jump from a high place thinking that it is not so high.

There is a constant and continuous increase in the verbalized manifestations of the sense of space by children. Words like *in, on, up, at,* and *down* are frequently used. He is able to understand directions in which space words are used. Thus, *Place the ball behind the chair* has meaning for the six-year-old. However, his perception of space and distance is almost completely limited to his concrete experiences. A more abstract concept of space, such as that used in studies of maps, the globe, or reading matter develops slowly during the elementary school years.

Number concepts. One of the contributions of the nursery school and kindergarten is to furnish children with many favorable opportunities for the development of number concepts. Through association with

[13] Arnold Gesell and Frances L. Ilg, *Child Development* (New York: Harper and Row, 1949), pp. 442-443.

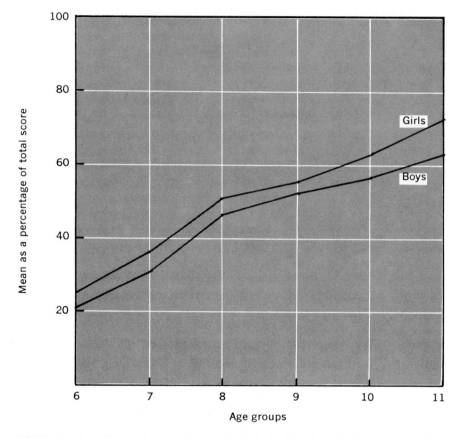

FIGURE 10-3.   Comparison Of Boys And Girls On The Total Score For Test
Of Time Concepts (Ngwobia Uka)

other children and through work with different things where numerical
terms are used, meanings are gradually developed. Many opportunities
are available for stimulating the growth and clarification of number
concepts. The children working at a particular table or on a special
problem are counted; glasses for orange juice are counted; the number
of chairs needed are assembled, and many other situations arise which
call for simple number combinations. Later, in the primary grades, experiences are provided to extend the concepts related to the use, value,
and interrelationship of numbers.

Brotherton, Read, and Pratt [14] tested children's knowledge of indeterminate number concepts through their application of such terms as

[14] D. A. Brotherton, J. M. Read, and K. C. Pratt, "Indeterminate Number Concepts II, Application by Children to Determine Number Concepts, *Journal of Genetic
Psychology,* Vol. 73 (1948), pp. 209-236.

hardly, few, several, and *many* to actual groups of symbols. Three groups of youngsters were used: those in grades two and three, six and seven, and ten and eleven. A reliable increase was noted in the precision with which these concepts were used from grades two and three to grades six and seven, but little progress was found between the six and seven, and the ten and eleven grade groups. This seems to indicate that the precise use of these concepts is well established by the sixth and seventh grade level.

Concepts of causal relations. An important aspect of children's thinking is that related to cause-and-effect. The very young child accepts many things he observes without considering their cause. Few things appear extraordinary. At the nursery or kindergarten level, the child seems to assume that some one thing, generally a person, is responsible

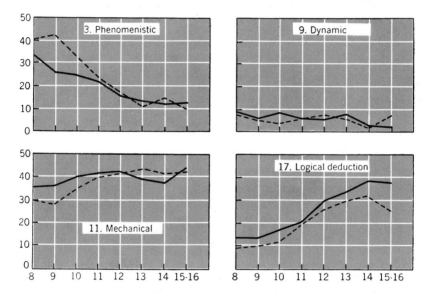

FIGURE 10-4.   Percentage Of Answers On Form I and Form II Of Causal Relations Questions Falling Into Several Classifications, According To Age
(After Deutsche)

for the object or situation he observes. As the child progresses through school, he improves in his understanding of why many things happen as they do. Deutsche [15] analyzed the causal thinking of children ages eight through fifteen years by means of questions and experiments and found that there was steady improvement from year to year. Concepts related to

[15] Jean Marquis Deutsche, *The Development of Children's Concepts of Causal Relations* (Minneapolis: The University of Minnesota Press, 1937).

cause, it was found, did not develop by stages but by a gradual process. In other words, the answers a child gave could not be classified as a single type; instead, some were adequate while others indicated a considerable lack of understanding. Figure 10-4 shows in graphic form the percentage of responses that fall under phenomenistic, dynamic, mechanical, and logical deduction. Responses listed under phenomenistic decreased with age while those listed under logical deduction increased. In this study ability to answer questions seemed to be more closely related to school experience than to either chronological or to mental age level.

Nass [16] noted that the causal responses of children to questions concerning physical causality were significantly influenced by (a) personality differences, (b) the contact which they have had with the agency of causation of the phenomena, and (c) the wording of the question or statement. The nature of the causal thinking of withdrawn children was significantly less mature than that of normal children. Questions about phenomena whose causal agents are not accessible to actual experiences yielded significantly more nonnaturalistic responses than did those questions about phenomena whose causal agents are more readily experienced. Also, questions worded so as to suggest certain solutions tended to yield responses in harmony with the suggested solutions. Since elementary-school children are generally quite suggestible, one would ordinarily expect the wording of questions to have an important influence on the children's responses.

Arithmetic learning.   Our knowledge of the nature of learning leads to the conclusion that there must be order and sequence in the development of mathematical concepts. It has already been pointed out that a learning program in arithmetic must consider the readiness of the learners. Arithmetic learning is systematic. Consider for a moment how best to learn to count, add, and multiply. The elements of addition are based upon counting, and an understanding of multiplication includes a recognition of its relation to addition. Where the learning program does not follow a proper sequence, rote learning generally results.

An experiment conducted by McConnell [17] with second-grade pupils as subjects compared the results of teaching addition and subtraction facts by drill methods and by what was claimed to be methods leading to the discovery of generalizations. The drill group at the end of the experiment was significantly superior in speed and accuracy while the

[16] Martin L. Nass, "The Effects of Three Variables on Children's Concepts of Physical Causality," *Journal of Abnormal and Social Psychology*, Vol. 53 (1956), pp. 191-196.

[17] T. R. McConnell, "Discovery versus Authoritative Identification in the Learning of Children," *University of Iowa Studies in Education*, Vol. 9 (1934), pp. 13-62.

discovery and generalization group surpassed in transfer and maturity of manipulation.

Experimental and control groups of children, aged 10 years and three months upward, were used in a study by Middleton [18] of the effects of systematic teaching of number combinations. Each child in the experimental group had daily practice using special systematically compiled sheets of number combinations, while the children of the control groups received regular practice for the same period daily in similar basic number combinations by methods usually adopted by the classroom teacher.

The experimental method "proved significantly superior in addition, multiplication, division, and mechanical arithmetic, and there appears to have been some transfer to problem arithmetic. For the brighter children (E. A. and C. A.) the value of the experimental method for subtraction is less marked." These results emphasize the extent to which children's ability in mathematics depends on a thorough grasp of the basic number combinations. Work activity accompanied by errors leads to unfavorable attitudes toward mathematics and to poor achievement.

Considerable effort has been made toward the improvement of arithmetic problem-solving procedures. Some of the major causes of difficulty in problem-solving are: (1) mental immaturity or mental defects; (2) reading disabilities (especially with reading problems); (3) lack of experiences involving numerical relations; (4) insufficient experiences in solving simple arithmetic problems; (5) lack of skill in the fundamentals; (6) poor teaching; (7) carelessness; and (8) lack of motivation. Schaff [19] has emphasized the desirability of a realistic approach to teaching problem-solving in arithmetic. Many of the suggestions he offers aim at correcting the causes for the disabilities. The teaching of problem-solving to students should induce (1) an understanding of number and number relations, (2) an understanding of mathematical relations as functions, such as time, rate, distance, etc., (3) an ability to visualize what is wanted, (4) an improved vocabulary, (5) the ability to discriminate between relevant and irrelevant material, (6) the ability to analyze the steps to be taken in solving the problem, (7) an ability to estimate the likely answer, and (8) habits of checking the answer.

Science learning. Children enter school with six years of knowledge and experience about their physical environment. They seek answers to questions about the forces and materials of the physical universe that

[18] I. G. Middleton, "An Experimental Investigation into the Systematic Teaching of Number Combinations in Arithmetic," *British Journal of Educational Psychology,* Vol. 26 (1956), pp. 117-127.

[19] W. L. Schaff, "A Realistic Approach to Problem Solving in Arithmetic," *Elementary School Journal,* Vol. 46 (1946), pp. 494-497.

have important bearing on their lives. The teacher should help the child to interpret the forces and materials of his environment as his mental horizon grows and expands.

Children should be encouraged to explore and to have experiences which will help them increase their understanding of scientific methods and different scientific concepts. Rudman [20] found that children placed science topics among the top-ranking categories in their reading interests. Although the child's curiosity about happenings in his environment appears early, the learning of science in the elementary grades must be paced. A scientific concept is never completely mastered at any one level of the child's development. A new experience should become a part of the total learning process. Such experiences inside and outside the classroom should become integrated into a total meaningful pattern.

Social studies learning. The grade level at which different geographic facts and concepts are taught will depend to a large extent on the geography or social studies curriculum for a particular school. However, it is reasonable to expect that all geographic concepts and skills need to be reinforced and sometimes retaught from grade to grade. A geophysical relief globe has been found useful in teaching various phases of social science. It will be helpful to the teacher in introducing new ideas, reviewing concepts and skills already developed, and in reinforcing other learnings at all grade levels.

Concept building in the social studies is based upon the ability of the textbook and the teacher to make both historical and contemporary peoples and places seem real to the pupils. Movies, dramatizations, and television may be used effectively for this purpose. Correct concepts in globe and map reading should not be overlooked. The teacher must guide the pupils in correctly interpreting materials shown on globes and maps. They must see the blue on the map as oceans, the irregular lines running through the land areas as rivers, and the darker brown areas as mountains. After the pupils have learned to read meaning into a map, an enlarged aerial map of the community may be studied. Pupils are particularly interested in locating familiar points—places where they have lived or visited.

Eskridge has presented a comprehensive list of developmental principles applicable to the growth in understanding geographical terms in grades four to seven. These are:

1. Growth in understanding proceeds through an increase in the number of different kinds of meanings.

[20] Herbert C. Rudman, "The Information Needs and Reading Interests of Children in Grades IV through VIII," *Elementary School Journal*, Vol. 55 (1955), pp. 502-512.

2. Growth in understanding proceeds through an increase in general information.
3. Growth in understanding proceeds through a substitution of basic for associative and comprehensive meanings.
4. Growth in understanding proceeds through a development of comprehensive meanings.
5. Growth in understanding proceeds through a reduction of errors of various types; important types are those due to (a) confusion of terms having similar sounds, (b) confusion of positions, (c) application of old meanings to new situations, and (d) "other causes." [21]

SUMMARY

The materials of this chapter consist of important learnings that take place both in and out of school. We have stressed the role of experience and the importance of maturation in the acquisition of meanings and in the development of concepts. The child in our society acquires many cues that enable him to respond more effectively to elements present in his environment. The growth and extension of concepts is gradual and continuous, proceeding from the simple to the complex, from the undifferentiated to the differentiated, from the discrete to the systematic, and from the rigid response to more flexible responses.

The use that a pupil makes of a learned concept will depend in large measure upon the way it was learned and the extent to which the concept is integrated into other learnings. Significant and positive correlations appear between the acquisition of concepts of time and related concepts and intellectual development. Concepts need to be reinforced and enlarged as the individual pupil moves from grade to grade.

Problems and Exercises

1. In what ways is a concept more than a word and more than mere meaning? Illustrate.
2. What are some of the major difficulties encountered in the teaching of moral concepts? What are some sources of confusion to the learner?
3. What are some essentials in the learning of number concepts? What are some of the major difficulties involved?
4. Show how *differentiation* and *integration* are involved in acquisition of a concept.
5. Show how the use of symbols is important in modern educational programs.
6. How would you account for the findings by Deutsche relative to concepts of causal relations? What are some educational implications of these findings?
7. What are some of the major difficulties encountered in teaching social science concepts? What are some sources of confusion to the learner?

[21] T. J. Eskridge, *Growth in Understanding of Geographical Terms in Grades IV to VII.* Duke University Researches in Education, No. 4, Duke University Press (1939), p. 63.

8. Show how the ability to generalize depends upon experience. Upon maturation.
9. Discuss the proposition that "generalization is an active process."
10. What are some aids to science learning in the elementary schools? What are some difficulties encountered by elementary-school children in the learning of science?
11. What is meant by the interrelatedness of learning? Show how this operates in connection with science and social studies materials.

Selected Readings

BURTON, W. H., *The Guidance of Learning Activities,* 2nd ed. (New York: Appleton-Century-Crofts, Inc., 1952), Chs. 10-14.

CRONBACH, Lee J., *Educational Psychology,* 2nd ed. (New York: Harcourt, Brace & World, 1963), Ch. 11.

FRANDSEN, Arden N., *Educational Psychology* (New York: McGraw-Hill, 1961), Chs. 7-9.

GATES, A. I., *et al., Educational Psychology,* 3rd ed. (New York: Macmillan Co., 1948), Ch. 13.

Learning and Instruction, Part III, *Forty-Ninth Yearbook of the National Society for the Study of Education* (Chicago: University of Chicago Press, 1949).

LINDGREN, Henry Clay, *Educational Psychology in the Classroom,* 2nd ed. (New York: John Wiley & Sons, Inc., 1962), Chs. 8-9.

RUSSELL, D. H., *Children's Thinking* (Boston: Ginn and Co., 1956).

SKINNER, Chas. E., ed., *Educational Psychology,* 4th ed. (Englewood Cliffs: Prentice-Hall, Inc., 1959), Chs. 18-20.

TROW, William C., *Educational Psychology,* 2nd ed. (Boston: Houghton Mifflin Co., 1950), Chs. 10-16.

CHAPTER 11

Creative Thinking
and Problem Solving

Creative expression and problem-solving behavior appear among all age groups and among children with varying degrees of intelligence. It has been suggested that every child has "an inborn creative spirit." We can observe this in their play—make-believe, fantasies, and other imaginative activities that occupy an important place in the child's mental life. Even before he can fully express himself in words, a child may be able to play an important role in pantomime. Through his imagination he is able to solve problems that he cannot easily deal with otherwise.

Maturity and experience play an important role in the child's ability to discriminate relevant from irrelevant factors in causal relations. Ausubel and Schiff [1] found significant and progressive increases with age in children's ability to learn a relevant causal sequence and to inhibit the learning of an irrelevant causal sequence in a teeter-totter problem. The authors concluded that among children the ability to learn a relevant causal relationship (i.e., that the side of a teeter-totter which is farthest from the fulcrum will fall) is a function of age. This was a challenging problem for kindergarten and third-grade children. However, sixth-grade children were able to master it directly without any errors. Parallel results were obtained with respect to children's ability to resist the learning of an irrelevant causal relationship. Creative expression and problem-solving at an early age involves fewer verbal generalizations and is confined to concrete and personal things from the child's immediate environment.

[1] David P. Ausubel and Herbert M. Schiff, "The Effect of Incidental and Experimentally Induced Experience in Learning of Relevant and Irrelevant Causal Relationships by Children," *Journal of Genetic Psychology*, Vol. 84 (1954), pp. 109-123.

THE NATURE OF CREATIVE EXPRESSION

The idea, frequently expressed, that creative ability is related to the activities of gifted individuals results perhaps from one's conception of what constitutes creative expression. The notion of what constitutes creative expression may best be understood from an examination of behavior involving creativeness. A little girl at play was recently observed by one of the writers. She was gathering blocks left over from some recent construction and placing them parallel to each other in two rows about eight inches apart. She later constructed two small make-believe houses near the parallel rows of blocks. Upon questioning the little girl it was learned that she was constructing a railroad, and two railroad stations.

The little girl had relatively recently been on a trip by train to see her aunt. This trip had no doubt made quite an impression on her, and this furnished the dynamics for her activity. There is discernible in the play of this little girl some of the important characteristics of creative expression. These include the following:

1. Prolonged attention related to some absorbing experience.
2. Heightened motivation to discover, test, or interpret for one's self the meaning related to the experience.
3. Expressive behavior resulting from the heightened motivation.
4. Variations in behavior as an outgrowth of experimentation to discover ways of expressing one's self.
5. Tension reduction through successful experiences in creating ways of expressing one's self.

Applied to the play life of the typical six-year-old, any activity into which children enter wholeheartedly will probably have some characteristics of creative expression. Creative activity may take place through a great variety of media. The kindergarten child who uses bright blue tempera (a paint) to portray his family, the first-grade child who makes up a silly jingle to sing, and the third-grader who plays cowboy all are demonstrating creative expression. Likewise, the dramatic "skit" of the sixth graders may be the creative product of several pupils. Not all school activity is, or should be, creative, although the various aspects of school life should furnish opportunities for creativeness. As in problem-solving, thinking is also involved in creative behavior. Through the process of thinking, the learner will grasp new relationships, give a new interpretation to a problem or fact, or improve creatively existing conditions or standards. In this connection it should be pointed out that the learner must discover before he can create.

Children, as they develop, seek to explain the world, particularly aspects of the world they live in. Out of a wide variety of experiences the learner discovers the nature of the physical world and the culture in which he lives. Such a discovery is essential for creativeness.

Factors influencing creative expression

Various factors in the child's physical and social environment affect the extent and nature of his creative expression. The principles of growth and learning applicable to other aspects of the child's growth and learning are also applicable to creative ability. Important differences may be noted in the creative ability of children of the same age level. Also, the same child will vary in his creative expression from one situation to another.

It has already been suggested that the creative expressions of the child will be limited by the extent to which he has discovered the physical and social world he lives in. Creative expression cannot take place without ideas and thoughts, and ideas and thoughts are not nourished in a vacuum. Since creativeness involves a new interpretation and a reorganization of experiences, the wider the experiences and the greater the wealth of ideas and thoughts, the greater may be the creative activity.

A second factor influencing the creative expression of the child is environment. Environments which furnish the child an opportunity to express himself and encourage him to do so while supplying media in harmony with his interests and abilities is most important. In the elementary school considerable use is made of paints, crayons, drawing paper, scissors, paste, blocks, and the like.

Closely akin to the second factor, and perhaps part of this factor, is a condition or situation which stimulates creative expression. An attractive room with good pictures and other materials furnishes a good setting for creative expression. A bird, goldfish, flowers, window curtains, and other materials in the room will likely add to the stimulating effect. The children should be encouraged in their efforts. In some cases a display of their products may be stimulating. However, the best motivation will be a feeling on their part that they are growing, that they are reaching a goal—a feeling of accomplishment.

A fourth factor influencing creativeness is the social climate. Where the child does not feel inhibited, he will be freer to express himself. Criticism from the teacher and others in such a manner as to lead to loss of interest and confidence is extremely harmful. If the child comes to feel that he can't do acceptable work, he will stop trying. There is nothing more harmful to creative expression than the feeling of inadequacy. It is at this point that an understanding teacher is most important.

Self-expression versus imitation. It has already been suggested that many forms of creative expression are observable in the activities of children. On one occasion, a first grade child, when requested to draw a man, drew a house with one window and one door. When the teacher asked where the man was, the child replied, "He was behind the window, but he has gone away." The understanding teacher will take advantage of such a situation to direct the growth of creative ability, rather than to discourage it by demanding stylized responses in activities. The beating of the tom-tom by Frank may show all the characteristics of creativeness when he is allowed to beat out the frenzy of an Indian war-dance or the fury of the approaching storm.

Self-expression may be contrasted with imitation. In self-expression, the child's responses are on the level of his own ability and age, motivated by his own feelings and ideas. This does not mean that there is no place for suggestions and guidance from others. It has been observed that considerable help may be given the child in his creative efforts through suggestions from the group—perhaps truer in creative activities than in most other forms of behavior.

In imitation, the child's responses are patterned. For example, the teacher may have the children draw some picture hanging on the wall or may have them write a short story, furnishing them with all the data and requesting them to put the facts together. In these activities there is little opportunity for self-expression. Lowenfeld [2] has presented the following contrasts of self-expression and imitation:

Self-Expression	Imitation
Expression according to child's own level	Expression according to strange level
Independent thinking	Dependent thinking
Emotional outlet	Frustration
Freedom and flexibility	Inhibition and restriction
Early adjustments to new situations	Going along set patterns
Progress, success, happiness	Leaning toward others, dependency, stiffness

Emotional release through creative activities. Many students of child psychology have emphasized the importance of furnishing children with favorable emotional outlets. The inmost self of children, which they often have difficulty expressing in an adult-dominated environment, is often released through creative activities. Such was the case of Louise.

[2] From Viktor Lowenfeld, *Creative and Mental Growth.* Copyright 1947 by the Macmillan Company and used with their permission.

On the playground Louise frequently quarreled and had temper outbursts. She was described by the playground supervisor as "a ball of fire." However, in her art activities (clay modeling and painting) another self appeared. These products depicted a child with considerable originality, and with the orderliness and quality characteristic of the poet.

Aesthetic appreciation. The development of the ability to accomplish things regarded as worthwhile is accompanied by the building of an appreciation of similar things created by others. Thus, appreciation develops as a result of growth in creative expression, and may be regarded as one of the values to be derived from growth in creative expression. The purpose of appreciation is enjoyment. Many teachers lose sight of this in their teaching and often miss the close relationship to be found between the development of certain skills and the appreciation of the aesthetic elements involved in the products.

There are common as well as specific problems involved in the acquisition of aesthetic appreciation. Studies show that the transfer of appreciation from one area to another is not automatic. If the art instructor wants the pupils to increase their appreciation of the dance or music he must relate the classroom activities in art to the dance or music. There are certain fundamental principles in common, but the pupils need to be guided in seeing and understanding these common fundamental principles.

The traditional grading system presents one of the most frequently observed barriers to training for aesthetic appreciation. This, perhaps, results from the relative difficulty involved in evaluating growth in aesthetic appreciation. It is much easier to measure a pupil's ability to recite a poem or name the principal characters in a play than to measure his aesthetic appreciation of the poem or play.

If we are interested in increasing a pupil's appreciation for fine arts or music we must keep appreciation as an important objective and make use of learning procedures designed to develop appreciation. Aesthetic appreciation involves both emotional and intellectual development. An intellectual understanding of the conditions under which a song was written or a painting produced may be most important in the development of appreciation among more mature pupils. However, this intellectual information alone is insufficient. The development of appreciation for the poem includes increased understanding, a feeling tone, and in many cases a sharpened imagery of the situation. Actual experiences in writing poems, use of visual aids, dramatizations, good oral readings, and group projects in writing are useful in the development of the components making up what is termed *aesthetic appreciation.* The beginning point for teaching the pupil to appreciate things encountered in his physical or social environment is a social climate that does not interfere with creative expression. Also, a teacher who has developed aesthetic appreciations and who is able through sound learning principles to lead others to develop aesthetic appreciation, will significantly affect the learning and development of aesthetic appreciation among her pupils.

Guiding the child in the development of creative ability

The motivation of creative expression. The fundamental principles of motivation and learning are as applicable to the development of creativeness as they are to other aspects of the child's growth and learning. Creative expression does not appear in a vacuum; neither does it appear without motivation and effort. Students of psychology have emphasized the value of the fine arts in satisfying basic needs. Likewise, the creative expressions of children through drawing or other media have been found useful in studying the personality dynamics of individual children.

There are many opportunities available for creativeness in motor and language skills. The dance, dramatics, and writing as media for creative expression are frequently used in the modern school program. The language arts offer one of the best mediums of expression for the intelligent school-age child. However, all school-age children should be encouraged and stimulated to express themselves through the language arts as well as through other media. Stimulation may be provided by having children relate certain aspects of their experiences—how they spent the summer, what they would like to do during the Christmas holidays, and the like. The children may be asked to respond to such propositions as:

What I would like to do when I grow up.
What I would do if I had lots of money.
What I would like to do next summer.

Atmosphere for creativity. We have already pointed out that creative activity does not take place in a vacuum. Neither does it occur in an atmosphere that places too much restriction on behavior. A suitable atmosphere for creativity will be characterized by certain conditions, some of which are here described.

First, the child must feel that he is accepted. Such a feeling will best develop in an atmosphere where teachers and others in authority recognize and respect the uniqueness of each child's personality. Closely related to this need for acceptance on the part of both teachers and pupils is the feeling of personal worth which grows out of a recognition that what he is doing is a worthwhile contribution.

Second, a child needs to feel secure. Children who are inhibited, who feel insecure, or who are not interested in the activities at hand are not likely to display creative thinking. Gillilies [3] presents a good description of how one teacher, by gaining the confidence of a group of underprivileged children, was able to secure their participation in creative dramatics. Preparation for creative dramatics includes such activities as guided reading and listening to other children's stories. It is also dependent upon the proper set or attitude which can only be secured in an atmosphere where the children feel that they are wanted and are part of the total group. Studies of the dynamics of child behavior show various causes underlying security; however, there is no substitute for an inner-contentment fostered in an atmosphere where the individual is not inhibited through fear of severe censure or disapproval.

Third, the child does his best creative efforts in an atmosphere of freedom. The child who is told what, when, and how to do something will not have the opportunity to exercise his own initiative or give expression to his own feelings and ideas. This does not mean that guidance is necessarily a barrier to self-activity. When guidance is presented in a democratic spirit of helpfulness it becomes a source of encouragement to the child. Parents and teachers have the responsibility for providing opportunities for children to act on their own purposes toward satisfying the need for self-expression. The parent or teacher who sets an example for the child through his own creative activity need not expect the child to be inspired to duplicate this effort or activity. Control and direction, whether they are by example or by teaching, will inhibit self-expression and destroy originality and creativeness.

The danger of stereotyped procedures. Educators are becoming more aware of the deleterious effects of unimaginative or stereotyped school work. Also, there is an increased recognition of the importance of creativeness in the lives of growing boys and girls. Educational psychologists have recognized, since the early teachings of William James and others, that stereotyped procedures in school tend to produce stereotyped products. We can see the results of these stereotyped procedures in the drawings of children who are taught to imitate rather than to express themselves. We discussed this earlier in the chapter. We also pointed out that stereotyped procedures may evolve as a result of imitation of things observed on television or heard on the radio. The extent to which children will develop stereotyped procedures will depend largely upon how teachers and others who guide them in their educational growth proceed.

Problem solving

Master teachers have constantly interspersed the learning experiences of their students with problem-solving. However, despite the vir-

[3] Emily P. Gillilies, "Crosses and Knives," *Childhood Education*, Vol. 23 (1947), pp. 382-387.

A favorable emotional and social climate is essential for optimum creative expression

tues claimed for the problem-solving approach to teaching and learning, most teachers rely upon memory procedures and recitation because first, most of the studies in problem-solving—conducted in laboratories—have limited application in the classroom. Second, the results of these studies have not been presented to students of education in a form useful for classroom teaching. Two yearbooks of the National Society for the Study of Education have devoted considerable attention to this problem, and have had some worthwhile effects.[4] The student of educational psychology will find the materials of these yearbooks useful. A study of problem-solving behavior, steps involved in problem-solving, and the problem-solving behavior of school-age children should give the student of educational psychology better insight into the role of problem-solving in learning at school.

[4] National Society for the Study of Education. *The Psychology of Learning.* Forty-first Yearbook, Part II. Chicago: University of Chicago Press, 1942; ————. *Learning and Instruction,* Forty-ninth Yearbook, Part I. Chicago: University of Chicago Press, 1950.

Thinking and problem-solving. The role of language in thinking was emphasized in Chapter 6. Many early writers assigned to the "mind" the function of thinking. There are many people today who merely assign thinking to the mind without offering any explanation of what they mean by mind or how thinking is carried on by the mind. On the human level, thinking and problem-solving are so closely related that it is well-nigh impossible to conceive of problem-solving behavior without some consideration of the thought processes. Children as well as adults constantly encounter problems which demand clear thinking.

Problem-solving behavior is here regarded as those activities an individual pursues in trying to reach a goal or solution to a problem. The problem situation may vary in complexity from a child's attempts to stack two or three blocks to a scientist's calculations of space and time relationships. Differences in the complexity of problem situations have contributed to different explanations of problem-solving behavior. At least two processes appear to be common in all these explanations. These involve (1) an analysis of the goal, and (2) an analysis of the situation.[5]

Analysis of the goal. The nature of a problem situation features a goal to be attained, but the individual concerned has not figured a way of attaining the goal. Sometimes the learner suggests solutions before he understands what the goal is. This may result from failure to understand the problem or from the development of faulty habits in problem-solving. Certainly the development of students as problem-solvers is one of the most important functions of the school. Many learning experiences are so arranged that students are given training in solving problems similar to the kinds of problems they are likely to meet later. The elementary-school child who learns to use the dictionary is learning a problem-solving technique that will likely be useful on many occasions. The boy who learns to follow directions carefully in the physics laboratory is learning a technique of problem-solving that will be most useful in many aspects of life. The first step in any problem is for the pupil to have a goal and to grasp an understanding of the problem. This requires careful thinking.

Analysis of the situation. The problem-solving process requires the individual to analyze the situation. This may be thought of as the second step, if an analysis of the goal is regarded as the first step. By analyzing the situation the learner determines some of the things he must do to solve the problem. Logical analysis of the problem-solving situation usually involves a series of steps which we will describe later.

Experiments in human problem-solving. Many experimental studies of problem solving, both with animal and human subjects, have

[5] See K. Duncker, "On Problem-Solving," *Psychological Monographs*, 1945, No. 270.

appeared during the past several decades. The results furnish the basis for our learning principles including problem-solving processes. A problem used in studying human ability is shown in Figure 11-1.[6] A lighted candle is placed some distance from the subject, who is instructed to use the articles shown under A to blow out the candle. The solution is shown under B.

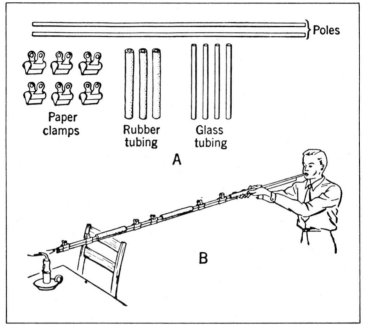

Paper clamps   Rubber tubing   Glass tubing

A

B

Poles

FIGURE 11-1. Maier's Candle-Blowing Problem

Subjects were to blow out a candle some distance
away by using the "tools" shown under A. Solution
is shown under B.

Trial-and-error, insight, and careful analysis all may be used in trying to solve the problem. Even the intelligent student may resort to trial-and-error in the earlier stages, but he will, however, analyze the problem, talk to himself about possible solutions, and make use of insight as it appears. He would make very few blind trials and would not likely continue to repeat errors.

In another study Maier[7] gave "hints" to a group of subjects who had been unable to solve the problem shown in Figure 11-2 in ten minutes. In this problem the subject was instructed to tie the two cords to-

[6] N. R. F. Maier, "An Aspect of Human Reasoning," *British Journal of Psychology*, Vol. 24 (1933), pp. 144-155.

[7] N. R. F. Maier, "The Solution of a Problem and Its Appearance in Consciousness," *Journal of Comparative Psychology*, Vol. 12 (1931), pp. 181-194.

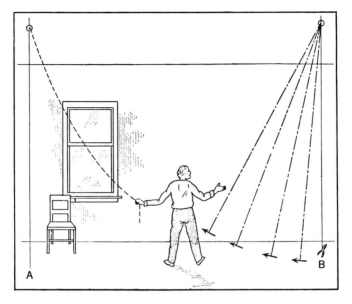

FIGURE 11-2. Maier's Two-Cord Problem

gether. The distance between the cords was too great to enable the subject to reach one while holding the other. The only solution was to tie a weight (a pair of pliers was placed nearby on the floor) to one cord and start it swinging like a pendulum. Then, while holding the other cord, he could grab the swinging cord in the near phase of the swing.

The hints given to 61 subjects who were unable to solve the problem in ten minutes were as follows:

HINT 1. In walking past one of the cords, the experimenter "accidentally" brushed against it and started it swaying.
HINT 2. The experimenter handed the subject the pair of pliers and told him that the problem could be solved with the use of the pliers.

With these hints, 62 per cent of the subjects were able to solve the problem within a time limit of thirty minutes. A control group of 55 subjects, who had also been unable to solve the problem in ten minutes, received no hints or additional assistance. Only 20 per cent of them were able to solve the problem in the additional time limit. Apparently the hints were useful in directing the attention of the subject to information needed for the solution of the problem.

The two problems just described could be solved by overt trial and error with a minimum of symbolic function. However, symbolic behavior appeared in the solution of the problem, especially in the solutions by superior subjects. Many problems in life and at school necessitate considerable symbolic function. Such problems are sometimes referred to as "pencil and paper problems."

In his excellent studies of problem-solving, Karl Duncker [8] used a problem dealing with regulating the pendulum of a clock during temperature changes. The subjects were instructed as follows:

> In order for a clock to go accurately, the swings of the pendulum must be strictly regular. The duration of a pendulum's swing depends, among other things, on its length, and this in turn on the temperature. Warming produces expansion and cooling produces contraction. Temperature changes produce changes in the length of the pendulum and thus affect the speed of the clock's operation. How can the rate of the pendulum be kept constant during temperature changes.

It was a "pencil and paper" problem and no materials were offered for actual experimentation. There were many proposals, illustrated in Figure 11-3, some of which showed a comprehension of the problem and others which did not. Proposals *a* and *f* show no comprehension of the problem. Proposal *d* is the customary solution, but *b*, *c*, *e*, and *g* all

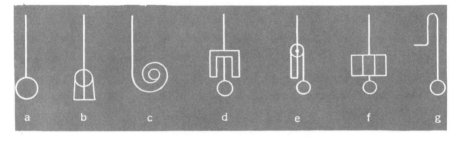

FIGURE 11-3.   Proposals For The Solution Of The Pendulum Problem

embody the same functional value, although differently constructed. From results obtained in experiments involving this and other problems, Duncker concluded that problem-solving is essentially a process of reformulating or restructuring the problem.

Problem-solving among school-age children. Concrete, direct experiences are important to the school-age child's problem-solving activities. However, as he grows older there is a significant increase in his ability to state a problem in words and to verbalize its solution. An important difference between the problem-solving behavior of younger and

[8] Karl Duncker, "On Problem Solving," translated by L. S. Lees, *Psychological Monographs*, Vol. 58 (1945), No. 5.

older children is that the older children recognize the problem as a problem, whereas the younger children tend to emphasize the objects used in the problem rather than the problem situation. This was apparent in a study reported by Heidbreder[9] in which the problem was to find a small celluloid doll concealed in one of two boxes. The children were to solve the problem by responding to different clues, such as the design at the top of the box. Heidbreder noted that three-year-olds were concerned only with obtaining the doll from the box, that some four-year-olds appeared to react to the problem as such, and that children six to ten years of age definitely responded to the problem as a problem.

Using a problem box built by Parcy Taska, Hensley[10] compared the problem-solving ability of bright and dull children and the methods they used. Criteria for selecting the subjects were: (1) chronological age, (2) mental age, (3) sex, (4) level of intelligence, and (5) no apparent emotional disturbance. The younger groups (approximately seven years of age) were superior to the older groups (approximately twelve and one-half years of age) of the same mental age in number of problems solved. A comparison of subjects of the same mental age but varying in chronological age revealed a significant difference in the number of solutions with verbal generalizations, indicating that younger subjects are superior to older subjects with similar mental age in verbal generalizations. This is important to teachers of bright and dull children.

Thinking and problem-solving abilities do not develop in a vacuum. Children need guidance in the development of problem-solving ability. There are many opportunities for developing such ability in the classroom. Some conclusions about problem-solving among elementary-school children are:

1. Much of the problem-solving activities of preschool children involves the manipulation of concrete objects in the environment.
2. Increased language development is an aid to problem-solving. There is a positive relation between language development and growth in abstract problem-solving ability.
3. The use of trial-and-error in children's problem-solving activities varies with the nature of the problem and the intellectual development of the child.
4. Children are often impetuous in their problem-solving, jumping from an awareness of the problem to a solution without careful testing of the information and data available.
5. There is some evidence that children often solve subordinate

[9] Edna Heidbreder, "Problem Solving in Children and Adults," *Journal of Genetic Psychology,* Vol. 35 (1929), pp. 522-545.
[10] Horace Gene Hensley, *A Comparative Study in Problem Solving of Bright and Dull Children.* Ph.D. Dissertation, University of Oklahoma, 1957.

parts of problems before integrating them into the total problem.
6. With age, there is an increase in problem-solving ability, both in accuracy and speed.

Barriers to problem-solving. A study reported by Kersh was designed to test the idea that learning by independent discovery is superior to learning with direction, because it is more meaningful. Based on retest data and reports from the subjects Kersh concluded

> . . . the superiority of the discovery procedure of learning over procedures of learning with external direction is not adequately explained in terms of "meaningful learnings." The results of this experiment suggest that when the learner is forced to rely on his own cognitive capacities, it is more likely that he will become motivated to continue practicing the task after the learning period. Consequently, the learning becomes more permanent and is more effectively transferred than when the learner is not so motivated.[11]

An important barrier to the development of problem-solving ability and to the solution of a problem is lack of motivation. Because of lack of motivation, both attention and practice are likely to be limited.

Students frequently acquire attitudes which are barriers to critical thinking. The following incident in an education class illustrates how prejudice limits clear thinking. The instructor was discussing problems and methods involved in teaching respect for rules and, particularly, the law. In the midst of the discussion a student raised his hand and said, "But, don't you think that each state should have the right to run its own schools?" This was the first mention of states rights or the public schools, but the student's attitudes were so strong that they colored his thinking on related areas and interfered with his concentration upon the problem being discussed. A second barrier to critical thinking, closely related to the first, is the complete dependence upon authority. Students accustomed to the autocratically managed classroom are likely to be more dependent upon their textbook, the teacher, or some other source of authority than students trained in a freer classroom atmosphere. Students should be guided in evaluating materials being studied in light of their experiences, previously learned materials, and other available evidences. They should be taught that people frequently differ in their interpretations of what they observe and of what they read. Thus, different interpretations sometimes occur in textbooks. They should be taught, however, that scholars are "truth-seekers," and that they should be continuously interested in trying to learn the truth from all available sources. If the teacher is going to be effective in training students to be

[11] B. Y. Kersh, "The Adequacy of Meaning as an Explanation for the Superiority of Learning by Independent Discovery," *Journal of Educational Psychology*, Vol. 49 (1958), pp. 282-292.

"truth-seekers," he must first of all be one himself. Teachers tend to pass on to their students their prejudices and ineffective methods of solving problems.

A third barrier to good problem-solving is a lack of a relatively systematic method of attacking the problem. Poor geometry students—relying almost completely upon trial and error—frequently start trying to work out a solution to the problem before they have carefully analyzed it. Some science students begin a laboratory experiment before they have secured a good understanding of the problem and procedures to follow in the experiment. It is here that teaching as guidance can be very effective.

A fourth handicap to problem-solving is rigidity in thinking. This rigidity may be a result of previous experiences in which pupils are taught to perform a problem in specific ways. This may result in negative transfer when the subject attempts to apply the same method to a different problem. This was noted in an experiment reported by Birch and Rabinowitz.[12] The problem consisted of Maier's cord experiment, described earlier. Twenty five students were divided into three groups, a control group and two experimental groups. The results showed that specific prior experience limited the perception of object properties and made the experienced materials less available as aids to solving problems.

A fifth barrier to problem solving is the learner's lack of confidence. A person who has continuously failed in solving science or mathematics problems will not likely approach a new problem with a feeling that he will be able to solve it. Teachers need to guide students not only in problem-solving techniques but also in the successful solution of problems. This procedure would take advantage of success as a motivating force and of reinforcement as a means of aiding the learning process.

Guiding the learner in the problem solving process

The question may be asked, What schoolroom procedures will teach pupils how to solve problems most effectively? The answer will be found in the application of the principles that have been presented in this chapter and in previous chapters to problem-solving in the classroom. The preceding chapters have emphasized that learning is a product of behavior. What is learned depends upon what is done. Therefore, school procedures must consist in guiding the child in the correct methods of mastering what we teach as well as in content. If we want him to be able to solve problems after he gets out of school, he must be given the experience of solving problems while he is in school. More attention in

[12] Herbert G. Birch and Herbert S. Rabinowitz, "The Negative Effect of Previous Experience on Productive Thinking," *Journal of Experimental Psychology*, Vol. 41 (1951), pp. 121-125.

education should be given to the *problem-solving method*. The schools must be concerned with *how to do* as well as with *what others have done*. It is important for the junior-high-school pupil to learn how his ancestors built their houses and earned a living more than a century ago; but it is equally important for him to learn how he is going to solve the problems of the future.

The problem-solving process. A number of investigations have been concerned specifically with how people go about solving problems. Experimental studies dealing with the nature of problem-solving by humans suggest that people use a variety of methods which can be roughly grouped into three categories: (1) trial-and-error behavior; (2) insightful behavior; and (3) analytical behavior.[13] These three methods are not qualitatively different, but may be arranged on a continuum; subjects shift from one method to another quite readily during the problem-solving process. The individual attempting to solve Maier's two-cord problem may first resort to trial-and-error behavior. Insight may be noted when the individual observes the pair of pliers, not as a tool to hold objects, but as an object to be made into a pendulum bob. The learner will likely analyze the problem at different times during the problem-solving process. This tends to furnish him with ideas or hypotheses that become the bases for new or revised ways of attempting to solve the problem.

The results of studies suggest two kinds of learning that may be useful in problem-solving. The first of these involves the acquisition of certain broad, non-specific notions about the object, situation, or method experienced. We see this with the child who gains experiences in mounting insects. A second type of learning is one in which the pupils take general ideas and convert them into more limited functional characteristics. The pupil who spends much time and effort mounting butterflies illustrates this. The learning involved in the mounting of butterflies may be of such rigid pattern that it interferes with other activities in nature study or science involving different kinds of insect life. If pupils are to become efficient problem-solvers they must be taught to vary their methods of dealing with problems in harmony with the nature of each problem encountered.

The results of studies reported by Luchins suggest that repetition may exert harmful influences on the individual's ability to solve problems, especially problems requiring originality. Luchins' experiments showed that even young children can learn several methods of solving problems within their grasp. He concludes: "This suggests that a means of combining the possible blinding effects of repetition is to teach more than one thing in a given lesson and to allow practice in more than one

[13] Richard E. Gross and Frederick J. McDonald, "Classroom Methods III. The Problem-Solving Approach," *Phi Delta Kappan,* Vol. 39 (1958), pp. 259-264.

response in a given practice period." [14] Such experiences would give the pupils the feeling of being creative, the satisfaction of understanding something of the formulation of problems, and better understandings of different methods useful in solving problems.

Essentials in the problem solving process. Considerable psychological research has been concerned with how students solve problems. Dewey's analysis of the stages of the problem-solving process has had an important influence on the thinking of many educators. Other investigations have also dealt with how people solve problems. The result of these investigations indicate that the problem-solving process involves four essential functions: (1) an orientation function—understanding of the nature of the problem; (2) an information gathering function; (3) an hypothesis-formation functions; and (4) an hypothesis-testing function. Although these processes are identifiable in most problem-solving situations, they do not necessarily appear in this sequential order. For the teacher to demand that the learner always follow this sequential order would not contribute to creative thinking, important in difficult problem situations.

Educational psychologists are concerned with the problem's influence on the problem-solving process and the influence of the characteristics or the problem-solver on the problem-solving process. In the solution of simple problems, the child depends upon obvious cues present in the immediate environment; in the solution of more difficult problems hypotheses are likely to be set forth and tested. Investigations show that the more complex the problem the more apparent the differences appear in the problem-solving process.

One of the differences to be noted between intelligent and unintelligent problem-solving behavior is the degree of accuracy each kind of behavior attains in evaluating possible solutions. The intelligent subject is more likely to "think a possible solution through" and to foresee whether it will work. This does not mean, however, that intelligence is synonymous with good problem-solving ability. The ability to imagine a possible solution to a problem grows out of training and experience, and not simply out of superior intelligence. Basically it is clear thinking that involves reasoning. The effectiveness of reasoning will depend upon innate mental ability, the amount of information at hand, and the extent to which good habits of thinking are applied to the problem at hand.

Creating the problem. The first essential in guiding the child in the development of problem-solving ability is to guide him in the recogni-

---

[14] A. S. Luchins and Edith H. Luchins, *Rigidity of Behavior* (Eugene, Oregon: University of Oregon Books, 1959), p. 530.

tion of problems. This can be done by raising one or more thought questions of interest and concern to the pupils. Such a question should not be one that can be answered by repeating something that may be read from some assigned source, although this is highly important for certain types of problem-solving. The problem should call for clear thinking and insight, the outgrowth of knowledge and understanding. The problem may be to determine an effective Christmas program, to invite parents to the school program, or to decorate the schoolroom for Halloween.

Whatever the nature of the problem, it must be adapted to the experience and maturational level of the pupils. Also, while the teacher may suggest the problem, it is not a real problem for the pupils until they accept it and are motivated to find a solution to it. The teacher's question should be designed to set off a chain of suggestions from the pupils. Unless these questions appeal to the interests and curiosity of the children so that they have a felt desire to solve the problem, they are ineffective. Thus, it takes the teacher's skill, initiative, and originality to provide thought-provoking questions that will challenge the interests and abilities of the pupils.

Understanding the problem.   Once the problem is stated, the next step in its solution is for the pupils to understand it. Sometimes, when pupils fail to make headway with a problem, teachers frequently admonish them with the words, "you aren't thinking." Actually, the pupils may be thinking intensely, but perhaps, not on the problem, nor in the way the teacher wants. A problem not clearly understood, or one vaguely defined leads to mental fumbling. Thus, it is very important from the beginning that pupils have a clear idea of what the problem is. To assure this, pupils may be asked to repeat the problem. The teacher may also feel the need to point out some significant aspects of the problem that they are overlooking. Sometimes a well directed question to the pupils will help them to clarify the problem.

There are times when children and adolescents must be urged to "stick" to the problem or to "keep on the subject." Without such guidance irrelevant materials are likely to be introduced, and may lead to a discussion far afield from the problem under consideration. Clear thinking about a problem depends ultimately upon seeing the relationship between the relevant facts leading to a solution of the problem. This, in turn, is dependent upon a clear understanding of the problem.

Gathering information about the problem.   On problems where the relations between the different elements are not clear, the child resorts to trial-and-error behavior. Children ordinarily need more trials and make more errors than adults in solving problems, although their thinking and reasoning processes are generally similar to those of adults. While reliance upon trial and error is justified, the solution to the problem will not be found through "blind" trial-and-error behavior. Problem-solving is a goal-seeking process in which the individual knows what he is looking for and is aware of the solution when he finds it. If the problem falls within a field where the pupils have much information, they can arrive at a solution by recalling relevant information about the problem. When the problem situation contains aspects of problems with which the children are familiar, relations are more apparent and insight appears.

In many cases the pupils will need additional information before attempting to solve the problem. They should be encouraged to use their past experiences in seeking additional information about the problem. The teacher should guide the pupils in becoming acquainted with sources of information and in how to use such sources. He may suggest that they contact certain people, visit certain places, write to authorities, or make a trip to the police station, court house, hospital, or factory to get the information they need. He may suggest library source material and the librarian's help may be enlisted. The development of problem-solving ability will not take place automatically. The traditional school curriculum, although rich in facts, often failed to help students apply the information learned to actual problem situations.

Seeking and evaluating suggestions for the solution of problems. Language and symbols provide the means for solving most of the problems students encounter at school, although actual experiences are often essential. The good teacher will not give the student answers, but will guide him in seeking possible solutions. Pupils should be encouraged to do their own thinking. It is out of such thinking, fumbling, and reconstructing that insight usually appears. The teacher can best guide the pupils by directing their attention to important elements in the problem that have been overlooked.

Sometimes the pupil will get off on the wrong path or lead. At this point he should be encouraged to reexamine the problem to see if that approach will lead to solution. He should be encouraged to vary his attack on the problem. Because pupils sometimes give up very quickly, they should be urged to try different approaches once or twice more. If they are very discouraged, they should be permitted to drop the problem and return to it later. After a period of rest, they may be able to return to the problem with new zeal and perhaps with new ideas.

An evaluation of the solution of a problem requires that the learner have the problem clearly in mind. Failure to understand the goal one is striving for may lead to an inadequate or incorrect evaluation. Guessing does not, in itself, solve problems. Neither do "blind" trial and error attempts. An evaluation of the solution requires a critical and open-minded attitude which grows through maturation, experiences, and careful guidance in suspending judgment and maintaining an open-minded attitude.

Group dynamics in problem solving. Studies indicate that group situations have an important bearing on learning and problem-solving. Group solutions to problems tend to be superior to individual solutions. A friendly group situation seems to contribute to the solution of problems, particularly those requiring originality. Heise and Miller [15] noted that the success of group activity in problem-solving was dependent upon the channels of communication in the group, the nature of the problem, and the stress or tension of the total situation. It was further noted that problem-solving was most efficient where communication was unrestricted, and least efficient where there was one-way communication among all pairs.

A study reported by Hudgins [16] was designed to test the hypothesis that problem-solving experiences in a group improve individual ability more than does individual experience. The subjects of the study were 128 fifth-grade pupils. In the first phase of the study the pupils worked on arithmetic problems in subgroups of four students; in the second phase the pupils solved the problems individually. The results of the study did not substantiate the hypothesis that group problem-solving behavior was superior to the individual behavior. It appears that any problem-solving superiority present in small groups will depend upon the efforts of the most able member of the group to communicate his knowledge and understanding to others of the group.

The question of the superiority of group versus individual problem-solving behavior must be considered in terms of the needs of pupils and the nature of the problems involved. Too much emphasis on group methods may be wasteful in terms of developing competent individual problem-solvers. Furthermore, much "group work" in school is actually work by one individual, usually the one considered most able in the area, since the students' problem is to secure a passing mark. Some characteristics of a classroom that promotes problem-solving behavior are:

1. Teacher-pupil planning
2. Thought questions and effective discussion procedures
3. Good techniques for presenting data, such as blackboards, bulletin boards and reports
4. Cooperative effort in projects involving group-problem solving

[15] G. A. Heise and G. A. Miller, "Problem Solving by Small Groups Using Various Communication Nets," *Journal of Abnormal and Social Psychology*, Vol. 46 (1951), pp. 327-335.

[16] Bryce B. Hudgins, "Effects of Group Experiences on Individual Problem Solving," *Journal of Educational Psychology*, Vol. 51 (1960), pp. 37-42.

5. Discussion, debate, criticisms, and suggestions
6. An emotional climate of friendliness, cooperation, and the sharing of ideas

Experiences basic to successful problem-solving. It was pointed out in chapter 10 that concepts grow as a result of experiences. For instance, the child evolves a set of concepts related to fairness, to family life, or to safety. These groups of concepts guide his thoughts and constitute a useful frame of reference; they are also essential for solving problems. Unless the child has had some experience or experiences that furnish meaning, he will be confused and unable to find solutions to problems. His inability to understand terms and his failure in reasoning often stem from his lack of experiences. In these circumstances, exhortations by the teacher to "think" will be quite futile. Home and school should therefore strive to furnish him with a variety of experiences using pictures, radio, television, stories, pets, toys, books, excursions, opportunities to explore, answers to questions, and contacts with persons from different backgrounds.

As long as life moves along familiar channels where no new demands are made on the individual, habit is sufficient. However, when the individual is faced with a goal he cannot reach without special help or consideration, habit is insufficient and he is faced with a problem. Thinking seems to occur when the individual, confronted by a problem, endeavors to find a solution based upon relevant past experiences. In this connection language is very important. Even the preschool child tends to verbalize while attempting to solve a relatively complex problem. This verbalization increases with age.

SUMMARY

Creative ability and problem-solving behavior appear early in the child's development. Creative behavior is characterized by free expression. Some characteristics listed for creative expression are: (1) prolonged attention around some absorbing experience; (2) heightened motivation related to the experience; (3) expression, involving problem-solving behavior.

Certain conditions have been found helpful in the development of creative expression, while some of the methods used in the homes and schools present hazards or obstacles to the development of creativeness. Opportunity for experimentation, freedom of choice, heightened motivation, and guidance in the form of encouragement and a minimum of suggestions are helpful in the stimulation and growth of creative ability.

Although optimum conditions may be provided for the growth of creative ability, it should be stated again that training and practice cannot transcend maturation. This is clearly shown in studies involving drawing and rhythm activities in the first, second, and third grades.

Thinking and problem-solving abilities do not develop in a vacuum. Children need guidance in the development of problem-solving ability. Many opportunities for problem-solving behavior appear in the classroom. The problem-solving process seems to involve four essential functions: (1) an orientation function; (2) information gathering function; (3) an hypothesis-formation function; and (4) an hypothesis-testing function. People do not follow the same sequential order in the problem-solving process.

Lack of motivation has been discussed as a significant barrier to the development of problem-solving ability. A second barrier that may impede critical thinking is the learner's attitudes. Such attitudes may stem from deep-seated prejudices or from reliance upon authority for the answer to all problems. A third barrier is a relatively systematic method of attacking problems, while a fourth barrier is rigidity of thinking. Lack of confidence is given as a fifth barrier. Guidance of the learner in the problem-solving process should be directed toward helping the individual overcome these barriers. The *how* in learning becomes very important in the development of problem-solving ability. The nature of the group situation also has a bearing on problem-solving. However, too much emphasis on group methods may be wasteful in terms of developing competent individual problem-solvers.

Problems and exercises

1. What are the major characteristics of creative expression? Give illustrations of these in connection with creative expressions of the six-year-old child.
2. What are some of the major barriers frequently present in the school program to the development of creativeness?
3. Observe a group of school-age children in their play activities. What evidences do you observe of creativeness? Do you note that some children display more creativeness in play than do others? What are some of the special characteristics of those children that display a considerable amount of creativeness in play activities?
4. Observe a group of school-age children in art, music, or dramatic activity. Do you find evidences of creativeness in the activities observed? What are some things the teacher of art can do to promote creativeness?
5. Look up several definitions of problem-solving. From these definitions try to arrive at a definition of your own. Why is it important for you to have a relatively clear notion of the meaning of problem-solving if you are to help others in problem-solving activities?
6. Show how thinking and problem-solving are closely related.
7. Study the conclusions presented about the problem-solving of elementary-

school children. Show how many adults frequently use the method employed by children in their attempts to solve problems.

8. Consider some problem with which you are acquainted, one that is meaningful and significant to you. Show how trial and error, insight, and careful analysis all may be used in trying to solve the problem.
9. Study the barriers to problem-solving. Show how each of these may operate in the solution of a social, political, or religious problem.
10. What are some important things the teacher should keep in mind in guiding learners in solving problems?
11. Teachers often lament the fact that the older children show less spontaneity and imagination than do the younger children. Does this signify that creativity has been inhibited? If not, how would you account for the observations of these teachers?

Selected Readings

BURTON, W. H., *The Guidance of Learning Activities,* 2nd ed. (New York: Appleton-Century-Crofts, Inc., 1952), Chs. 12-14.

HILGARD, E. R., *Introduction to Psychology* (New York: Harcourt, Brace and World, 1953), Ch. 14.

KINGSLEY, H. L., and Garry, Ralph, *The Nature and Conditions of Learning,* 2nd ed. (Englewood Cliffs: Prentice-Hall, Inc., 1957).

PRESSEY, S. L., Robinson, F. P., and Horrocks, J. E., *Psychology in Education* (New York: Harper and Row, 1959).

RUSSELL, David H., *Children's Thinking* (Boston: Ginn and Co., 1956).

SKINNER, Charles E., ed., *Educational Psychology,* 4th ed. (Englewood Cliffs: Prentice-Hall, Inc., 1959), Chs. 11, 12.

SMITH, Henry P., *Psychology in Teaching,* 2nd ed. (Englewood Cliffs, N. J.: Prentice-Hall, 1962), Ch. 5.

THORNDIKE, Robert L., "How Children Learn the Principles and Techniques of Problem Solving," in *Learning and Instruction.* Forty-ninth Yearbook of the National Society for the Study of Education. Chicago: University of Chicago Press (1950), Part I, Ch. 8.

CHAPTER 12

Character Education

The Hebraic words, "Train up a child in the way he should go and when he is old he will not depart from it," illuminate the one aim of education that has persisted throughout the ages—the formation of character. When we consider the function of education as the preparation of children for adulthood and membership in the group, community, or state, this is easily understood. The importance of religious and moral training was recognized in the teaching of the church, and is fostered today in different religious educational programs.

The problem of character education is not new. It was regarded as important in early colonial schools, and was closely identified with religious instruction. It has received special attention during the last few decades, sometimes under the title, *Moral and Spiritual Values*. Such terms have been introduced in public education in order to escape a religious connotation; however, the character education movement has usually been ill-defined both as to objectives and directions. Some people have looked upon character as something distinct and separate from intelligence, knowledge, or emotional development. Character is evidenced in behavior, and behavior cannot be detached from intelligence, knowledge, and level of maturity. This is implied in the definition offered by Neumeyer:

As a moral quality, character is the sum and organization of traits, attitudes, and habits oriented with reference to an objective standard of conduct. It is the phase of personality that conditions or determines the course of action in a situation requiring choices in terms of moral values.[1]

Frequently character, morality, and ethical behavior are used interchangeably. Although hard and fast boundary lines between these con-

[1] Martin H. Neumeyer, *Social Problems and the Changing Society* (New York: D. Van Nostrand Co., 1953), p. 169.

ceptual areas cannot be drawn, certain distinctions should be made to help the student better understand their genesis and growth.

Morality is concerned with conformity to certain standards as a guide to behavior. Character may or may not involve such conformity. According to Jones character is a more dynamic and a more inclusive concept. He states:

> In character development much more attention is given to volitional factors and to individual creativeness in the realm of goals to be achieved than is true in moral or ethical growth. If we add to morality the ability to reconstruct one's values and the volitional powers sufficient to direct conduct progressively toward such evolving values, then we have character. . . .[2]

THE DEVELOPMENT OF MORAL BEHAVIOR

Moral development has two phases: (1) the development of moral behavior, and (2) the development of moral concepts. It is well known that moral knowledge does not *necessarily* insure moral conduct consistent with it. One reason for this is that habits are formed through practice. It is far easier to teach one what is good behavior through verbalization than to be one of the "doers." Also, one's behavior is motivated by many factors other than his moral knowledge. Social pressures, reaction to peers, family attitudes, attitudes toward self, personal desires, and many other factors operate to affect a child's behavior.

How moral behavior is learned

In a list of environmental factors influencing moral behavior, the most important, for most children, is the home. From the period of their first perceptions they look first of all to their parents for guidance by precept and example. A child gets his first impressions in the home—and these impressions are made during the life-period when the foundational habits and moral attitudes are being formed. Undoubtedly, a good home is the greatest asset, and a bad one the greatest liability. Havighurst and Taba [3] have described three ways that character is learned. These are:

> through reward and punishment
> through unconscious imitation
> through reflective thinking

[2] Vernon Jones, "Character Development in Children—An Objective Approach," *Manual of Child Psychology,* in L. Carmichael, ed., 2nd ed. (New York: John Wiley and Sons, 1954), p. 781.

[3] Robert I. Havighurst and Hilda Taba, *Adolescent Character and Personality* (New York: John Wiley and Sons, 1949), pp. 6-7.

Learning to behave according to certain standards follows the same principles of learning as do other forms of learning. Evidence from many sources shows that teaching a child dogmas, creeds, or rules of conduct is insufficient. If he is to develop good moral habits he must be guided in the development and practice of such habits. Rewards for good conduct and reproof or punishment for undesirable conduct may be effective means for developing such habits. Studies of honesty among children have shown that young children must learn moral behavior in specific situations; such learnings are later integrated into a unifying concept. Thus, the development of moral behavior consists of acquiring habits which are integrated into a unifying concept. It is in this unifying process that fundamental moral concepts and beliefs present in most religious teachings may be very effective.

It is well known that children tend to develop habits similar to those practiced by their parents and others with whom they are closely associated. This may be closely related to reward and punishment. The child discovers that he is rewarded when he follows their wishes and behaves as they do. By imitating their behavior he secures their approval. The habit of imitating tends to carry over outside the family. The child may imitate another child, his older brother or sister, his teacher, or even some character in the movies, comic books, or on television.

The development of moral behavior is closely related to the satisfaction of needs. The boy or girl at school who feels insecure with the group will behave differently in response to the demands of the group than will the boy or girl who feels secure. The explanation of deviant behavior should not be oversimplified. This is illustrated in the case of Harry, a sixth grader.

Harry has a record of lying and stealing from the time he entered Willow School in the second grade. Mrs. Weaver, a teacher of the old-school of thought blames the lack of discipline in the home for Harry's dishonesty. Miss Hart, who recently completed a course dealing with the mental hygiene of the school child, talks of Harry's needs that are not being met at home or at school. The principal, who is well acquainted with Harry's father, asserts that Harry is just like his father. The explanations, though somewhat different, are alike in that the three recognize that Harry's dishonesty is a form of learned behavior.

The emergence and development of conscience. In popular language conscience is thought of as a self-directive and self-censoring agency. There has, however, been much general speculation about its emergence and its dependability as a guide. The child during the early years behaves in accordance with his biological nature and the standards and rules of living set by adults, usually his parents. As he attains increased maturity he develops inner standards which serve him as guides for action. The term *moral needs* has been used to designate these internal standards or the "voice of conscience." [4] Psychoanalysts have referred to these internal standards as the *superego*, represented in the person by the mores and standards of the parents, other adult associates, peers, and the culture and teachings of the society in which he lives.

There is considerable evidence from psychoanalytical studies that much of one's behavior is governed by inner forces not present in the conscious mind. Many of the impressions, feelings of guilt, and anxieties which govern behavior lie deep within the unconscious part of the mind frequently referred to as the subconscious. It is important, then, that children, during their developmental years, have affection, security, and effective guidance which can contribute to the favorable development of inner standards both at the conscious and subconscious levels.

Growth in moral behavior. Depending upon both maturation and experience, the individual acquires the behavior pattern of his culture gradually. Moral behavior here is based upon social sanctions rather than authority. Such a concept of moral behavior does not lead to stability of morals and is not in harmony with the viewpoint of well-established religious groups, although the behavior of members of different religious bodies is influenced to a marked degree by the sanctions of peers and neighbors.

It is important for the growing individual to acquire certain standards as guides if he is to live a harmonious life. These standards furnish him with boundaries, limits, and freedoms in his behavior. It was pointed out earlier that when a child lives up to the standards set by his parents he is praised. Since praise is closely associated with affection and security, these basic needs are supplied. We may note this with Sally. At the age of five Sally assumes responsibility for putting away her dolls and other play things. She is praised by her parents for accepting this responsibility. This sense of responsibility grows so that by the time Sally enters school she is capable of assuming responsibility for taking care of her wraps, books, and other things which she takes with her to school. If this behavior is reinforced at school, Sally will grow in responsibility in harmony with the principles of growth and learning set forth in earlier chapters. With guidance Sally can easily be trained to assume responsibility in a wide range of activities, including behavior outside the home and school. Transfer of training principles, described in Chapter 8, operate with habit patterns as well as with facts and principles.

Ugurel-Semin [5] reports a study of sharing conducted with 291 children between the ages of four and sixteen attending the primary school

---

[4] Wesley A. Smith, "Conscience and Conflict: The Moral Force in Personality," *Child Development,* Vol. 28 (1957), pp. 469-478.

[5] R. Ugurel-Semin, "Moral Behavior and Moral Judgments of Children," *Journal of Abnormal and Social Psychology,* Vol. 47 (1952), pp. 463-474.

of Istanbul. It was noted that the selfish tendency, at its height among children between the ages of four and six, gradually diminished thereafter. There was a slight tendency for children from large families to be more generous than those from small families. One of the most complete studies of moral development in the child is that by Piaget [6] who endeavored to interpret the child's concepts of moral rules. In one study 150 children between the ages of six and twelve were told stories involving a conflict between obedience to parents and a sense of justice and were requested to solve the conflict. There was a continuous and steady decline with advancing age in the choice of solutions based upon obedience to parents. Thus, only five per cent of the eleven-year-olds favored the solution "obedience to parents," while 95 per cent of the six-year-olds chose this as a solution. From studying the rules of play and moral judgments pertaining to stories, Piaget presented two moral systems: (1) coercive pressure resulting from rules, and (2) free cooperation and respect for the rules based upon mutual understanding. The expansion of moral judgment from specific situations in the home to situations outside the home is gradual, occurring as a result of maturation, training, and a wide range of experiences.

Moral concepts and the beginning of moral judgment

The child's development of the sense of self, standards of behavior, and patterns of feelings develop out of the social atmosphere at home, in the neighborhood, and later, at school. His early concepts of what is right and wrong are closely identified with the things his parents permit and forbid. In the closely knit home the young child associates right and truth with the statements from his parents. As he matures and becomes a member of larger groups, rules and moral judgments become less rigid and authoritarian. The feelings and needs of the group are given increased consideration. Also, with increased mental and educational growth the child is able to make a more critical analysis of rules earlier accepted without questions or doubt. This is sometimes a disturbing condition for parents and teachers.

The expansion of a child's moral concepts may be noted in the development of his concept of justice. The child's concept of justice, like other concepts, is a product of learning. It will vary with age, intelligence, social-class status and other factors affecting learning. A study by Durkin [7] dealing with this problem involved second-, fifth-, and eighth-grade pupils from middle-class Protestant homes of a midwestern community. The children were tested by means of story-situations and questions. The

[6] Piaget, Jean, *The Moral Judgment of the Child* (New York: Harcourt, Brace and World, 1932).

[7] Delores Durkin, "Children's Concepts of Justice," *Child Development,* Vol. 30 (1959), pp. 59-67.

kinds of responses given to the question of what a child should do if hit by another child are presented in Table 12-1. These results indicate a relationship between chronological age and concepts of justice. The older children showed more concern for mitigating factors in the situation. The answers to the question do not support the notion that reciprocity increases with age. This was perhaps related to the middle-class culture represented by the homes of the children studied.

TABLE 12-1.   Responses by Children to the Question of What a Child Should Do if Hit by Another Child (*Durkin*)

KIND OF RESPONSE	NUMBER OF CHILDREN GRADE		
	2	5	8
Tell authority person	15	13	27
Return identical aggression	8	15	7
Other	(5)	(10)	(4)
Ignore aggression		6	1
Withdraw from situation	3		
Have aggressor apologize		2	
Tell aggressor to stop		2	
Exclude aggressor from play	1		
Do nothing			1
Undecided	1		

Discrepancies between moral concepts and moral behavior.   When Mrs. Weaver asked Harry "Didn't you know it is wrong to steal?" Harry answered "Yes." However, the knowledge that it was wrong did not keep Harry from stealing. Abstract knowledge of what is right and wrong does not keep children from doing what is regarded as wrong when particular situations arise in which they are tempted. The extent to which such knowledge will function will depend upon the nature of the teachings, opportunities to practice the right behavior under favorable conditions, and the degree of the temptation. There is evidence from many sources that the bright child at school is more honest in the performance of educational tasks than the average or dull child. The best explanation for this is that the bright child does not feel the need to cheat in order to excel in school tasks, whereas average and dull children are quite likely to feel such a need.

Often moral concepts conflict with each other. The child hears about love and the brotherhood of man at church, but sees hate and distrust practiced against certain national, racial, or religious groups at home or some other place. He also finds that behavior frequently does not harmonize with teachings. He hears his parents, teachers, and others proclaim the desirability of honesty and truthfulness as ideals, but notes that these ideals are not practiced in many of their personal relations with others. He finds it difficult to distinguish between *dishonesty* and behavior classified as *tact*.

In a study by Wolfenstein [8] boys and girls between the ages of five and sixteen were asked to tell a story about a "good boy (or girl)." An analysis of the stories showed important age and sex differences. The young children seemed to relate *goodness* with gratification, while older children related it to postponement of gratification leading to future reward. Boys' themes often expressed a conflict between moral values and ego integrity, e.g., between suppressing aggression and the maintenance of one's masculine characteristics. That is, "one should stand up and fight" when attacked, even though this may be in conflict with a moral code against fighting or aggression.

Developing a sense of trust and responsibility. It was pointed out earlier that habits of responsibility are not developed passively through exhortations and formal teachings. If a child is to develop a sense of trust and responsibility he must be trusted to take care of himself and to accept certain responsibilities. In this complex age in which the individual is faced with many problems and hazards, many parents and teachers are likely to overprotect their children. Children of seven or eight years of age may be carried to school by their parents, even though they live only three blocks from the school. They may be very carefully supervised on the playground and not allowed to swing high or do any appreciable amount of climbing. One eight-year-old was heard to say, "The way you treat me about crossing the street you must think I want to get killed." Hazards at home, school, and on the streets must be recognized and dealt with, else the already high accident mortality rate among children will become higher. It is better for these hazards to be dealt with as a group enterprise in which each child is made to feel that he is largely responsible for his own safety as well as partially responsible for the safety of others.

Inadequate protection which leads to fear or actual harm tends to destroy a child's confidence in himself as well as in others. Working mothers frequently leave children to shift for themselves after they get home from school. Children need guidance and protection along with the opportunity to assert their independence. The amount of responsibility a particular child can accept will depend upon a number of factors including constitutional characteristics, maturation, and experience. How-

8 M. T. Wolfenstein, "A Developmental Study of Children's Fantasies about Moral Problems: II. Conceptions of 'Goodness,'" *American Psychologists,* Vol. 5 (1950), pp. 304-305.

ever, it is safe to say that adolescents who were not given opportunities to develop habits of responsibility during the preschool and early elementary school years are ill-equipped to assume responsibility as teenagers. The preschool and early elementary-school child needs an adult in the background to furnish him with the needed security for developing a sense of trust in himself as well as in others.

Trust, then, can be built or broken by too much protection or too little attention and guidance. Excessive expectations also fail to build a sense of trust or tend to destroy such a sense once it has been established. There is always a danger that a parent or teacher will expect too much of the child who displays a high degree of responsibility. They may expect the child to perform at a high level all the time. If he fails to complete an assignment or otherwise fails to live up to expectations he is reprimanded and made to feel that he has failed. No child, adolescent, or adult can perform at a peak level all the time. Even the most responsible adults express misgivings about their ability at times.

A sense of trust and responsibility can best be built during the early years by (1) recognizing individual differences among children, (2) recognizing the maturational level of the individual child, (3) providing an emotional climate of affection and security, and (4) giving the child the controlled freedom needed for satisfying his need for independence and status.

The role of discipline

Although discipline is an old and universal problem, one finds conflicting claims and viewpoints about it. The word *discipline* is derived from a Latin verb signifying *to learn.* Certainly discipline is usually related to learning. The behavior of children and adolescents is not always in accord with what adults expect. Thus, they are steered into certain preferred ways of behaving through a system of rewards and punishment. Punishment in particular has come to be closely identified with discipline. Because of negative connotations of the word, it is also sometimes called "setting limits." It is related to "giving the child the controlled freedom needed for satisfying his need for independence and status."

The wholesome function of discipline. Although discipline seems to be essential in the rearing and training of children, it is not always successful. If the outcomes of discipline are to be judged successful or not, one must consider its function. Havighurst [9] described three wholesome uses of discipline. The first is *to teach the child that the world responds in an orderly fashion to his actions.* The only kind of control

[9] Robert J. Havighurst, "The Functions of Successful Discipline," *Understanding the Child,* Vol. 21 (1952), pp. 36-37.

one can achieve over his world is to predict what will happen as a result of his actions. He does this when he burns his finger on the hot stove, or hurts his bare feet on sharp pebbles, or mashes his finger with a hammer. He also learns to predict punishment from his parents when he does certain things. There is a need for orderliness and consistency in these punishments, such as occurs from touching the hot stove. Inconsistent discipline, by which the child is punished one day and not the next for the same act, leaves the child confused about what will happen to him. It is only through consistent discipline that he learns of a moral orderliness in the world.

A second wholesome function of discipline is *to teach the child a reasonable degree of social conformity*. Through discipline the child is taught to dress himself each morning, not to expose certain parts of his body, to keep clean, to speak kindly to others, to behave at school, to cooperate in team activities, and to respect the property of others. Too rigid discipline, frequently related to overprotection, may lead to complete social conformity and a lack of initiative and originality or to rebellion. A certain amount of social conformity is essential for social interaction. However, to insist upon complete social conformity just for the sake of conforming destroys all semblance of independence and may lead to personal maladjustments.

A third wholesome function of discipline suggested by Havighurst is *to help the child develop self-control and self-discipline*. Through wholesome discipline the child is taught to substitute *inner* for *outer* controls. It was pointed out earlier that conscience as an inner controlling force emerges in situations early in life in which certain forms of behavior are referred to as good, while certain other forms of behavior are referred to as bad. It is during the preschool years that punishment from those he loves for doing that which he has been told is wrong helps him to develop a conscience which acts as an inner voice. Havighurst states: "A balance of consistent punishment with a good deal of affection on the part of parents seems to be the only formula for the development of self-control and self-direction." [10]

Discipline and character. It has been emphasized throughout this chapter that discipline is closely identified with character formation. The attainment of psychological needs calls for certain restraints, the ultimate goal of which is self-restraint. Care must be taken, however, not to thwart self-initiative in efforts to develop self-restraint. There are some who claim that if children were taught to obey under a system of rigid controls, they would, by some miraculous device, develop self-restraint for all situations. The learning of self-initiative and self-restraint are active

[10] *Ibid.*, p. 37.

processes which can only be learned in specific situations through individual effort. Through guidance such learnings can be generalized to a variety of situations.

The development of self-control can only take place in situations where children and adolescents are given opportunities to practice self-control, not in situations where all controls are imposed upon them. Some conclusions and generalizations about the role of discipline in character development are as follows:

1. True discipline is a learning process designed to establish certain preferred ways of behaving.
2. The end result of discipline should be increased self-control.
3. Consistency of discipline, not severity, is important in the development of character.
4. Through discipline the individual learns that there are certain rules and regulations that must be followed.
5. Through guidance the individual can be taught that certain behavior patterns are associated with punishment while others are associated with approval and rewards.

Attitudes, ideals, and values

Education is both directly and indirectly concerned with the molding of character and personality—a process through which individuals take on the attitudes, ideals, and values of the society of which they are a part. These are extremely important to the goals of education. The purposes and goals of man are not in themselves subject to scientific investigation. They represent the aspirations and needs of man.

The development of attitudes. Attitudes relate to situations around which we have constructed behavior patterns and built up various concepts and feelings. The child, born and reared in a social world, is continuously subject to ever-changing social stimuli. Socially, he tends to become what his environment makes him. Attitudes are often tinged with emotions, and may be displayed in emotional as well as in rational behavior. Evidence, based on observations of children, shows that the fundamental pattern of many attitudes is laid down during the preschool years. The source of these attitudes lies primarily in the culture of the home. Attitudes toward father, mother, brother, and sister are learned largely through the behavior patterns encountered in the home environment.

It was pointed out in Chapter 6 that the individual's attitude toward the *self* and others is determined largely by the attitude others take toward him. Thus, at an early age he acquires some rather definite notions about *self* and others like him. The socioeconomic status and cultural level of the home have a tremendous influence upon the child's attitudes. This was observed in a study by Dolger and Ginandes [11] of the attitudes toward discipline exhibited by children from different socioeconomic and cultural groups. Children were selected from two schools in New York City which differed widely in their educational philosophy and in the socioeconomic and cultural status of the pupils. The attitudes of the children regarding the action to be taken against Jimmy, a problem-child six years of age, were studied. The children were also interviewed concerning disciplinary measures appropriate for ten situations involving problem behavior.

Important differences in the attitudes of these two groups of children toward appropriate disciplinary measures for specific types of problem behavior were noted. The children from low socioeconomic backgrounds were more inclined to hold the individual child responsible for the misbehavior and they were more concerned with his punishment than were the children from the high socioeconomic and cultural backgrounds. The latter group of children seemed to comprehend an environmental basis for such conduct. The low socioeconomic status group expressed the opinion that a truant officer should see that the child who played "hookey" from school is punished; while the other group of children were inclined to account for the misconduct on the basis of an unhappy home or unhappy school life or some other factor largely beyond the control of the individual child. The children from the low socioeconomic group frequently referred to reform schools, truant officers, and correction homes in connection with the serious offenses. The children from the high socioeconomic levels did not reveal familiarity with these guardians of the law. These differences in the attitudes have an important bearing on the needs and nature of guidance that should be provided for children and adolescents.

The development of intergroup attitudes. Of the attitudes developed by children and adolescents, perhaps the most important are those which they develop toward other persons, especially as members of the different groups which make up their society. These are referred to as intergroup attitudes. Such attitudes determine the extent to which an individual can work with others on common problems or toward a common goal and are very important in group planning and group action.

Children bring their prejudices to school with them, a reflection of the attitudes of their parents and others with whom they have been

---

[11] Laura Dolger and Janet Ginandes, "Children's Attitude Toward Discipline and Related to Socioeconomic Status," *Journal of Experimental Education,* Vol. 15 (1946-47), pp. 161-165.

closely identified. Contacts with a particular group during childhood also affect the child's prejudices. However, such contacts alone are insufficient for the development of desirable intergroup relationships, especially when home or other influences have adverse or opposing attitudes. The schools face a difficult problem in combating prejudices. How, then, can teachers deal with prejudices formed at home and reinforced by other forces or conditions in our society? Certain principles and methods have been found effective in building desirable and healthy group attitudes in school-age children. Martin has set forth four principles which if applied by the skillful teacher should lead to the development of desirable intergroup attitudes. These are:

Principle I: That program is most desirable which accepts the child as he is and provides recognition of accepting behavior on the part of each child toward every other child.

Principle II: That program is most desirable which leads to an understanding on the part of children of the reason why different people live as they do.

Principle III: That program is most desirable which fosters interaction among representatives of different groups, with every representative being given equal status.

Principle IV: That program is most desirable which makes it possible for each child to achieve success, but not at the expense of others.[12]

The development of ideals. Ideals and values differ from attitudes in their ever-present, imperative nature. Ideals are sometimes regarded as broad guiding principles of behavior, which tend to give stability and direction to one's life. During the early years of life ideals emerge and tend to pass through an elementary formative stage in harmony with the child's innate equipment and the environmental forces playing upon him. It is during this period, when ideals are being formed, that conscience begins to appear as a vital force in behavior. The child's experiences at this stage are rather narrow and his ideals, very elementary, involving mainly the welfare and pleasure of the ego. As we look upon the socializing process as one of growth and development, so must we consider the process of acquiring ideals in the same way, especially during the expanding and developing period of life beginning with the early stages of adolescence. Ideals are thus dependent upon maturation and experience. Where the child's experiences have been quite limited, ideals tend to be narrow; where the child's experiences have been fuller and more inclusive, ideals will be broader in scope.

Ideals, like attitudes, are taken up from the milieu in which the child

[12] William E. Martin, "Some Ways to Develop Desirable Intergroup Attitudes in Children," *Journal of the National Education Association*, Vol. 43 (1954), pp. 219-220.

lives and learns. Consider the case of Don, who comes from an upper middle-class home. His father is a horticulturist and spends considerable time weeding his lawn and caring for the flowers and shrubbery. Therefore Don, like his father, appreciates the beauty of well-kept lawns, blooming flowers, and nice shrubbery. The home, church, and other institutions of our society have, as one of their major objectives, the development of desirable attitudes and ideals in boys and girls. This can best be done if the efforts are coordinated and the influences appear early in the lives of these boys and girls.

Values—their meaning and importance.   Any attempt to completely separate attitudes, ideals, and values would be misleading. Values refer to what we regard as important rather than what we know about something. Each individual develops his own system of values, and these are especially important in relation to morals and character. The meaning and nature of values may best be understood from a brief description of six main types, presented by Spranger.[13] These six types are (1) the *theoretical*—individuals who regard theories and knowledge the all-important thing; (2) the *aesthetic*—one who places a high premium on beauty, as in art; (3) The *economic*—one who cherishes things because of their material value; (4) the *social*—one who is influenced largely by social prestige and social factors; (5) the *political*—the individual who has a strong desire to control or to have power; and (6) the *religious*—the person who finds joy and satisfaction in his relationships with the whole of life's experiences and purposes for living. These values have been modified and organized into measurable tests, and considerable research has been conducted dealing with the nature and importance of values.

Lecky [14] has postulated that after values are integrated into the personality they act as barriers to the acceptance of new ones which might be in opposition to them. From the point of view of mental hygiene this is important. Without the feeling that something is important the person lacks the drives and stability essential for a life of happiness and success. Four prevailing sets of conditions are set forth by Leckey: (1) new values that are in opposition to those already accepted by the individual may be rejected; (2) new values may be so modified that they are no longer in opposition to the accepted values; (3) new values that are in opposition to old values may be ignored and thus not incorporated into the value system; and (4) old values may be modified in such a way that the new values are incorporated into the total value-system.

[13] E. Spranger, *Lebensformen* (translated into English under the title, *Types of Men*) (Halle, Germany: Niemeyer, 1928).

[14] P. Lecky, *Self-consistency* (New York: The Island Press, 1945).

Building sound values. The development of desirable moral concepts and sound values does not proceed in a vacuum. Neither are these developments unrelated to the mental-social, emotional, and physical development of the individual. The case of Connie bears this out.

This is the first year Connie has attended Pine Street School. The father is somewhat shiftless, and seems unable or unwilling to stay on one job very long. The mother, at the time of the encounter with Connie, had a job in a nearby hosiery factory. The family lives in a small house composed of four rooms. Connie, who is thirteen years old, sleeps with her younger sister in one room, while the parents sleep in another. Connie is in the eighth grade and seems to be doing satisfactory work in school. She likes friends and recognition which she gets because of her physical prowess. Her home and neighborhood are unimportant to her, and she is ashamed to have her friends visit her at home. She values highly the attention she gets from her classmates and the encouragement she gets from her teacher. Her science teacher, who came from an underprivileged background, seems to understand Connie and Connie is very fond of her. Connie's associations with her have had a significant influence upon her values and moral standards. The influence of her school associations may also be observed in her social and mental development. These influences have raised Connie's aspiration level to where she plans to finish high school and then go into training for the career of a nurse.

Children need to live and grow in an environment which fosters the development of sound values as a basis for their actions. The modern school, emphasizing the development of the whole child, is concerned with his spiritual development. Moreover, the child is exposed to a variety of values from many sources in the environments of the home, school, church, and neighborhood. Some of these are wholesome; others are less wholesome and sometimes unwholesome, depending partially, upon the interpretation given to them. The teacher has the responsibility of accepting the value patterns which the child brings to school and guiding him in the attainment of those values cherished and decreed as worthwhile by the society of which the individual and the school is an integral part.

Conditions affecting character development

Many useful studies have been conducted bearing on the relationship of various cultural forces and conditions upon the moral growth and character formation of children and adolescents. Also, a variety of devices have been used for studying the behavior of children in situations involving cooperation, competition, generosity, honesty, persistence, self-control, prejudices, and anxieties. Studies in anthropology and psychology have furnished much information about the contributions of biological and cultural factors to the development of character. Materials from some of these studies are included in the subsequent discussions of conditions affecting moral growth and character formation.

Importance of good family relations. It has already been pointed out that attitudes, ideals, and values are absorbed early in life. The foundations of character development, shown in Figure 12-1, are provided by these early home influences. The optimum condition prevails when the home, church, school, other community institutions, and certain conditions operate harmoniously in the education of the growing individual. However, the beginning point is an emotionally secure and harmonious home environment.

Conscious formulation of knowledge and understanding, attitudes and values, and social relations harmonious with ethical teachings at home, church, school, and other character-building institutions

Broad social experiences involving good human relations combined with sound ethical practices and teachings

Development of favorable attitudes toward self, others, and the physical and social world

Desire to be approved by family; taught good human relations involving others

BIRTH in an emotionally secure and harmonious home environment

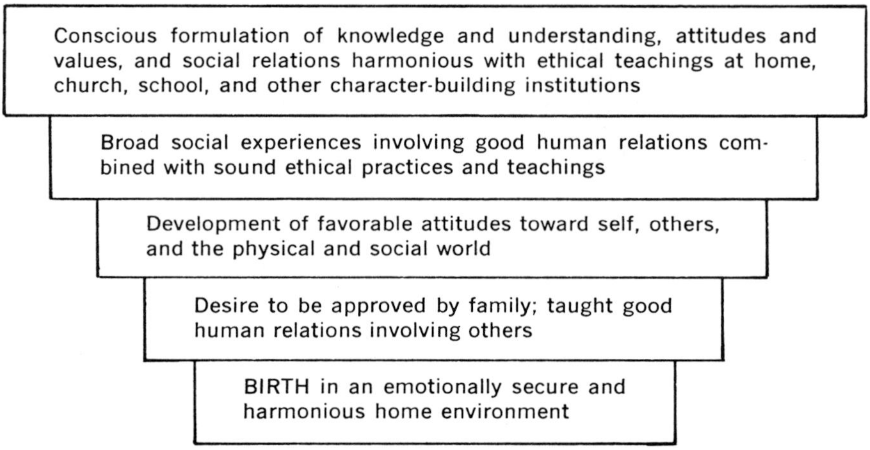

FIGURE 12-1.   A Schematic Presentation Of Character Development As Affected By Favorable Forces And Conditions

When the individual is rewarded for a display of unselfishness at home, he is likely to display this behavior at school and in other social situations. It might be stated as a general principle that those social behavioral responses which are accepted and rewarded at home will be generalized to social responses outside the home. The manifestations of these responses are generally labeled *character traits*.

In one study bearing on this a *Family Relations Questionnaire* was administered to 105 ten-year-olds.[15] The questionnaire included six important aspects of parent-child relations: (1) trust and security in parents manifested in sharing confidences, (2) opportunities for self-expression, (3) parent recognition of the child's play and work activities, (4) parent-child sharing in play and work, (5) parent's sacrifice of own interests for welfare and security of children, (6) family solidarity and mutual loyalty.

[15] A. W. Brown, J. Morrison, and G. B. Couch, "Influence of Affectional Family Relationships on Character Development," *Journal of Abnormal and Social Psychology,* Vol. 42 (1947), pp. 422-428.

The reputation of the children was measured by several kinds of tests administered to teachers, youth-group leaders of the community, and peers, all of whom were well acquainted with the children. On the basis of these results each child was assigned scores on five character traits: honesty, moral courage, friendliness, loyalty, responsibility. These scores were assumed to measure the child's moral behavior in social situations, with high scores indicating high moral principles and behavior in accordance with these principles. Correlations were obtained between each of the five character traits and scores on the *Family Relations Questionnaire*, with the following results:

Affectional parent-child interactions and honesty .... .65
Affectional parent-child interactions and moral courage .... .51
Affectional parent-child interactions and friendliness .... .71
Affectional parent-child interactions and loyalty .... .69
Affectional parent-child interactions and responsibility ..... .79

Social stratification and moral standards. The moral standards of the child are influenced by the special group to which the family belongs. Different social groups adhere to different moral standards, and these have their impact upon the child during infancy and early childhood. The family's economic condition will affect the size of the house, the amount of play space available, the amount of traveling the family can do, the leisure-time and recreational pursuits of the family, and the clothes and spending money provided for the children.

Children from the lower socioeconomic status are subjected to more authoritarian and punitive treatment than those from the middle and upper socioeconomic groups. However, children from middle-class homes are likely to be more closely supervised, and their education and future, likely to be of more concern to their parents. The lower cultural-level parents regard certain types of behavior inherently wrong rather than harmful because of the consequences. An important reason why many upper-middle and upper-class parents don't want their children to go to certain schools is that they don't want them to talk and behave like children from the lower class or from slum areas.

The results of scientific studies show ways in which children from different socioeconomic groups tend to differ in their behavior, although such differences will not be found in all cases or even in all communities. There are wide variations between individual families of the same socioeconomic status as well as between different socioeconomic groups. It is important for the teacher to understand variations within each group as well as the broad differences between groups. Too often children from the lower socioeconomic group are stereotyped by their teacher and by parents of children from middle and upper socioeconomic groups.

The role of religion.   The various religions set forth certain fundamental beliefs and practices which have an important influence on the
lives of children, adolescents, and adults. The degree to which religious
training and experiences will affect the lives of children and adolescents
will depend upon the extent to which the religious teachings are grounded
in the lives and teachings of the adults responsible for the rearing and
training of the children. It was emphasized earlier that children learn both
from example and precept. Teaching will be ineffective when examples
are out of harmony with what is being taught. It should be emphasized
that if the church is to be effective in character training, the teaching must
follow the fundamental principles of learning set forth in educational psychology. For maximum transfer to occur, the teaching must also generalize
to daily living situations.

A young child brought up in a religious atmosphere is likely to connect ideas of right and wrong with the idea of God as one who rewards
for good behavior and punishes for bad behavior. The small child's concept of God is, like other concepts at this stage of maturity, concrete. The
idea he has of God as he develops will depend upon the concepts he acquires during the period of maturation and learning. A study reported by
Bradshaw [16] indicates that this idea of God as one who rewards good behavior and punishes bad behavior persists among a large percentage of
children into adolescence. This may be noted in the results presented in

TABLE 12-2.   Religious Beliefs of Children and Adolescents (*After Bradshaw*)

STATEMENT	AGE	PER CENT WHO SAID TRUE	PER CENT WHO SAID FALSE	PER CENT WHO SAID DO NOT KNOW
Good people would go to heaven	11–12.11	68	14	18
	13–14.11	54	19	27
	15–16.11	45	20	35
God will punish you if you are bad	11–12.11	45	40	15
	13–14.11	38	49	13
	15–16.11	38	35	27
Bad people go to hell	11–12.11	33	34	33
	13–14.11	38	49	13
	15–16.11	15	39	46

[16] J. Bradshaw, *A Psychological Study of the Development of Religious Beliefs
in Children and Young People.* M. Sc. Thesis, London University.

Table 12-2. It should be emphasized again that the results one would find in answer to the questions proposed in Table 12-2 will depend upon the nature and intensity of the teachings as well as upon the maturation and learning of the children and adolescents concerned.

A study reported by Woodward [17] indicated that the interrelation of religion with family activities influenced parental treatment of children. Religious parents who are active in doing things with their children at church and elsewhere are likely to exert, both consciously and unconsciously, a positive religious influence on their children through storytelling, reading materials, the practice of certain rituals, references to God's will and love, and church attendance. On the other hand, religious parents who are domineering may send their children to Sunday School or other religious functions, while displaying little real concern over their religion. Such parents may also scold and punish their children and use religious threats, such as, "The devil will get you if you misbehave," or "God won't love you if you do that." A child with a religious background of threats and punishment will look upon God as a punitive person watching for acts of guilt, while the child who looks upon God as one of love and forgiveness will not likely develop a sense of guilt and insecurity.

The role of the school. The school is in many cases the only place where some children are furnished the opportunity for learning certain middle-class motivational patterns. This may be noted in the lower-class children's cultural behavior related to dating, physical aggression, and manners. The notion that the boy who displays good manners and is considerate of others is a "sissy," sometimes held by boys from lower-class culture, is not in harmony with the teachings and practices found in our high schools. Through contact with children from different socio-cultural backgrounds, the individual child learns that there are different ways of doing things and that some of these ways are preferred by their teachers. Thus, the school is an important force in the moral and character development of individual children. The teachings at school are most effective when they are reinforced by the teachings in the home and other social institutions.

In our attempt to impress the principles of justice and fair play upon growing boys and girls, we must be continuously aware that "actions speak louder than words." Pupils are aware of every deed and word, even of the inflections in the voice. The importance of the teacher as a personality on the attitudes, ideals, and values of children is generally recognized. This may account for the public's concern over the moral concepts and behavior of teachers.

[17] L. E. Woodward, *Relations of Religious Training and Life Patterns to the Adult Religious Life* (New York: Bureau of Publications, Teachers College, Columbia University, 1952).

The Reed Elementary School, grades 5-8—Reed Union School District, Belvedere-Tiburon, California

Good physical facilities at school or elsewhere help to create an emotional climate favorable to desirable character development.

Opportunities for increasing ethical understanding appear in teaching most, if not all the subjects of the school curriculum. For example, in the geography class the teacher can introduce the students to the lives of great explorers who exemplified the best in man. This may be followed by outstanding examples of people today who continuously strive to help their neighbors and others in time of need and stress. Literature, history, science, and religion are filled with examples useful for ethical guidance and exploration.

Essentials in moral and ethical training

We can give moral instruction in either of two ways or in some combination of these ways. Children can be taught to "internalize" certain ideas, beliefs, and ways of behaving without reference to the reasons that lie behind them. We may conceive of moral education here as, "This is not to reason who . . . ," and use memory, drill, and hidden motives as means of instilling moral beliefs and acts. Another way would be to use reason along with all moral teaching. These two methods should not be considered mutually exclusive. It would appear that since moral teachings should be introduced at all stages of life, the methods used and concepts presented should depend upon a number of factors including the maturity of the child, his mental ability, his educational level, his emotional and social development, and his religious background.

Need for cooperative effort. Most acts of behavior cannot be adequately explained by a single factor or condition. The teen-ager who persists in damaging property at school or at church is motivated by a number of reasons. It may be comfortable for parents and the church to blame the movies, television, schools, or present day entertainment for the juvenile delinquent. The fact remains, however, that many basic habit patterns and attitudes are formed early in life. This idea was emphasized earlier in this chapter. Second, the church has a responsibility to help in meeting the needs of growing boys and girls, especially needs that are not adequately met by the home, school, and other community agencies. This, of course does not mean that meeting spiritual needs is not the primary function of the church. Third, the school must recognize that its function extends beyond that of teaching the three R's and certain prescribed content materials. This is being recognized more and more by schools all over the country. To cite one example, the New York City Board of Education, which after more than a year of study and hearings from different groups, adopted in the fall of 1956 a guiding statement for the teaching of moral and spiritual values. The statement as finally adopted stated that religious education is not the function of state-supported schools. It says, "However, it is the function of the schools . . . to support the efforts of the home and church in building good character in our children." The concepts presented in the home, on the playground, in school, and at church are often too unrelated to have any great functional significance. The program of the church is in so many cases too far divorced from other interests of the child, and the materials presented are too archaic to have any meaning for him in present day living. What seems to be needed is a positive approach to morals. Or, as Fleege states, "It would seem that too much emphasis has been placed on impurity and not enough on purity. The virtue has been left in the shadow while the failings have been paraded across the stage." [18]

Religious education. The present attitude in our society of the role of religion in education can be described as (1) an increasing recognition of the importance of spiritual values and the role of religion in the development of these values, and (2) confusion as to how religion can be integrated into a total educational program for the development of boys and girls. Some would ask, "Why should education be concerned with religion?" A number of reasons may well be offered to answer this ques-

[18] U. H. Fleege, *Self-Revelation of the Adolescent Boy* (Milwaukee: Bruce Publishing Co., 1944), p. 286.

tion. Perhaps the fact that Western civilization is imbedded with the philosophy, teachings, and traditions of Judeo-Christian religion is itself a sufficient reason. One of the reasons given by Van Dusen should furnish an adequate answer to the question. He states: "Religion has to do with the most elemental, the most universal, and in the end *the most important issue of human existence*—its origin, its nature, its meaning and purpose, its destiny, especially with the determination and inescapable events which mark and move each person's life—birth, love, parenthood, death." [19]

The increased delinquency today, in spite of improved standards of living and increased education, presents a real challenge to educational, religious, and civic-minded leaders. Much of the character-building work is too artificial and too highly organized to be effective. The level of character development frequently remains on a conforming or "fair play" basis, referred to in Table 12-3. Character building that does not take into consideration the importance of the education of the emotions will be largely ineffective, lacking dynamic force essential for helping others without the promise of a reward or some fair return for help rendered. In this connection the emotions have been aptly described as "the modes of physiological integration through which we meet relatively critical situations." Character based upon the desire to conform and to please others will lack the strength and dynamics needed to lead the individual to a full social and spiritual development.

Self-governing activities. It has been emphasized that self-control is not developed through the memory of rules of conduct, although these may serve as goals. Boys and girls should be given opportunities to plan and execute behavior. They will need guidance at all levels of their development. Such guidance should be in harmony with their maturation, background of experiences, the difficulties of the problems concerned, and the goals to be attained. Self-governing youth groups at the school and in community institutions may be very effective in the development of civically-oriented boys and girls. Youth activities of some sort or another are sponsored by all the major religious bodies in the United States. Although the importance of their work is difficult to estimate, evidence shows that where active community help and institutional supports are lacking, delinquent behavior flourishes.

Through self-governing youth activities needs of adolescents are frequently satisfied that are not being adequately satisfied through ordinary community programs. Through these activities adolescents are able to find a positive place in the institutional and community life as junior citizens. If the home, school, church, and other community institutions are successful in building up sound values and in leading the individual into

[19] H. P. Van Dusen, "What Should be the Relation of Religion and Public Education?" *Teachers College Record*, Vol. 56 (1954), pp. 3-4.

TABLE 12-3. Factors Related to Different Levels of Character Development

	HOME	PEERS AND FRIENDS	RELIGIOUS EDUCATION
Amoral	Neglected home; parents without consistent standards	Lack of standards	No religious influence
Selfish	Selfishness practiced in home; lack of standards rejection by parents	Considers what is best for self; no consideration for welfare of others	Child taught self-concern without consideration of others
Conforming	Emphasis upon social conformity; taught the rules of justice and fair play	Enjoys peers; feels need for their love and approval. Willingness to do his part	Emphasis upon getting along with others; standards based upon a fair exchange
Critical– Conscientious	Emphasis upon specific standards; generosity supplants duty and fair play	Feels secure with peers; doesn't feel necessity to conform in behavior contrary to standards	Emphasis upon standards based upon religious teachings
Social-spiritual –conscientious	Emphasis upon consideration of others; recognition of Will of God	Secure with peers; guided by desire to help others, without consideration of rewards	Guided by spirit of love of God and fellow man; practices compassion and forgiveness in daily living

313

the development of worthy ideals, teen-age boys and girls will not be seriously affected by undesirable movies or television programs. Television and movies are in themselves neither good nor bad. They are used both for educational purposes and emotional outlets, to intensify feelings and to suggest outlets for needs not satisfied by other media.

SUMMARY

The importance of character education has been recognized throughout the ages. Frequently this has been referred to as moral training, religious education, and training in ethical ideals and principles. Certain distinctions have been offered in this chapter. The importance of experiences in the development of character has been emphasized. It is generally recognized that moral concepts, attitudes, ideals, and values are outgrowths of experiences.

Modern concepts of child training lay stress on the fact that morality is not developed by rules, creeds, dogmas, or the establishment of specific amounts of punishment for various acts of mischief. This does not mean that these have no value in training children. Rules and creeds cannot be judged apart from the institutions and conditions in which they appear. The emotional climate and teachings in the home, school, church, or elsewhere are extremely important factors affecting the results to be attained from rules, creeds, rewards, and punishments.

The function of discipline in child training has too often been misunderstood. Too often discipline is administered in an atmosphere tinged with fear and hate, and the child fails to understand the relationship between discipline and the behavior related to such discipline. Parents and teachers recognize the negative aspect of discipline, but often fail to realize that there is a positive aspect. The ultimate purpose of discipline is (1) to furnish the child a guide to follow, and (2) to establish self-control. A problem frequently encountered is that of conflicting standards. When the standards of the home, church, school, and other institutions affecting the lives of children and adolescents are harmonious, character building is much easier. The role of religion in character building is very important, both directly and indirectly, in the lives of the great majority of children and adolescents.

Problems and Exercises

1. Look up several definitions of morals. What are some different ways of regarding morals? How are morals related to character?
2. List several moral concepts. How are moral concepts related to moral behavior? How are moral concepts acquired?
3. Discuss the role of rules, creeds, and religious education in character development. What are some essentials if these are to be effective?

4. What are some problems created by conflicting group membership? Can you suggest ways to help meet some of these problems.
5. What should be the function of discipline in relation to character development? List mistakes frequently made by parents and teachers in administering discipline.
6. Study Figure 12-1. Give illustrations to show how broadening experiences and maturity affect character development.
7. Show how the interrelation of parental activities and religious beliefs and practices affect character development.
8. Show how the teacher functions in the child's acquisition of attitudes, values, and ideals.
9. Point out social class differences in moral behavior. How would you account for any differences noted?
10. Interview one or more school-age boy or girl and note their attitudes toward adult authority figures, the church, and the school. Are the inferences and conclusions presented in this chapter in harmony with observations from your interview?

Selected Readings

CRONBACH, Lee J., *Educational Psychology,* 2nd ed. (New York: Harcourt, Brace & World, 1963), Ch. 18.

Educational Policies Commission, *Moral and Spiritual Values in the Public Schools.* Washington: Educational Policies Commission, 1951.

HURLOCK, Elizabeth B., *Developmental Psychology,* 2nd ed. (New York: McGraw-Hill Book Co., 1959), pp. 108-110, 154-156, 307-309, 356-359.

JONES, Vernon, "Character Development in Children—An Objective Approach," in L. Carmichael, ed., *Manual of Child Psychology,* 2nd ed. (New York: John Wiley and Sons, 1954), Ch. 13.

MARTIN, William E., and STENDLER, Celia B., *Child Behavior and Development,* rev. ed. (New York: Harcourt, Brace & World, 1959), pp. 406-410, 429-432.

MILLARD, Cecil V., *Child Growth and Development in the Elementary School Years,* rev. ed. (Boston: D. C. Heath and Co., 1958), Ch. 12.

PECK, R. F., HAVIGHURST, R. J., COOPER, Ruth, LILIENTHAL, J., and Moore, D., *The Psychology of Character Development* (New York: John Wiley and Sons, 1960).

POWERS, Francis F., "Social Development," in Chas. E. Skinner, ed., *Educational Psychology,* 4th ed. (Englewood Cliffs: Prentice-Hall, Inc., 1959), Ch. 12.

RUSSELL, Ivan L., "Development of Attitudes, Interests, and Values," in Chas. E. Skinner, ed., *Educational Psychology,* 4th ed. (Englewood Cliffs: Prentice-Hall, Inc., 1959), Ch. 12.

SMITH, Henry P., *Psychology in Teaching,* 2nd ed. (Englewood Cliffs: Prentice-Hall, Inc., 1962), Ch. 5.

PART **IV**

Evaluating Pupil Growth

CHAPTER **13**

Methods of Pupil Evaluation

Is Billy "ready" for formal reading instruction? How much does Jack really know about our social studies unit? How can I help Sally improve her computational skills? Why is Joseph so slow in getting down to work? Why does Matthew have trouble with spelling? Many questions similar to these are being asked by teachers daily. The many techniques of measurement and evaluation available today help to provide them with answers. Measurement and evaluation techniques also help to answer questions like, Does the class understand the functions of base five in arithmetic? Have I taught this unit so that the children really understand it? How do the various members of the class compare in reading ability? Is my class doing as well as they should? Can I safely assume that my pupils have mastered the skills and abilities I have taught so that I can build on this knowledge in future lessons?

MEASUREMENT AND EVALUATION

College students often become confused when they encounter the words *measurement* and *evaluation* in their reading. Often they tend to use one term when they mean the other. Although measurement and evaluation are, or should be, closely related, each is different. Measurement, essentially one aspect of evaluation, pertains to the process by which the teacher assigns a given rank or other numerical value to a particular pupil characteristic. Reliable and valid measuring instruments generally provide one important basis for the evaluation of a pupil's success in learning.

Evaluation

Evaluation usually is thought of as the process by which a teacher brings together information from a number of different sources for the purpose of making judgments about a particular pupil or group of pupils. Whereas measurement often is limited to an attempt to appraise a single pupil characteristic, such as reading ability or arithmetic achievement, evaluation seeks to combine a number of reliable and valid measures of various traits or characteristics so that the teacher can best judge the over-all potentiality or rate of development of a student.

Measurement

Measurement techniques may represent all degrees of refinement. Some measures are so gross as to be of little value; others may be so complicated in design and function as to be impractical for ordinary classroom use. During the last thirty years there has been an increasing tendency to quantify measurement instruments and to make them more precise. Greater reliability, validity, and usefulness have resulted. Thorndike and Hagen describe the following four points along a scale leading to greater precision and quantification of measurement.

1. *Either-or.* A pupil is either a boy or a girl. A man is single, married, widowed, or divorced. A student is enrolled in the college preparatory, commercial, or general curriculum.
2. *Qualitatively Described Degrees.* Thus, a pupil may show "normal speech," "slight stuttering," "stammer," "marked stutter," or the pupils in a class may be characterized as "quiet and relaxed," "slightly fidgety," or "tense and restless."
3. *Rank in a Group.* Thus, a series of graded tasks scored by uniform standards enables us to find who does best and who does worst on reading comprehension, arithmetic problems, or spelling. The rest of the group can be arranged in order from best to worst.
4. *Amount, Expressed in Uniform Established Units.* A boy weighs 56 pounds, is 45 inches tall, is 6½ years old.[1]

Ideally the teacher employs measuring tools which are sufficiently refined and precise to accomplish her purposes. In some cases merely describing a child's behavior will be sufficient. In others, merely establishing a pupil's rank within the class group will suffice. Generally, however, quantified instruments are needed to describe and interpret the more complex aspects of pupil behavior. Thus, teachers must know how to construct, employ, and interpret the more highly refined instruments for measuring and evaluating pupil behavior.

The characteristics of pupil evaluation. Throughout this text it has been emphasized that the human being functions in a unified way. It follows then that educational measurement and evaluation can not be

[1] Robert L. Thorndike and Elizabeth Hagen, *Measurement and Evaluation in Psychology and Education* (New York: John Wiley and Sons, 1961), p. 11.

limited merely to a determination of how well a pupil can read or how much Latin or arithmetic he knows. Rather, evaluation must be concerned with many aspects of the child's growth and development if it is to prove helpful in stimulating and guiding him. A well-rounded program of evaluation should be concerned with each of the following areas:

1. The physical and motor development of the individual child
2. The degree to which he has mastered the basic tools and skills required for successful study
3. His achievements in the various content areas
4. His mental ability
5. His special abilities and aptitudes
6. His personal-social adjustments.

It must be recognized that because certain areas of human behavior are more difficult to study than others, evaluation and appraisal are not always readily accomplished. Schools, for example, have always accepted the responsibility for determining the extent to which pupils have mastered the instructional content. Similarly, for several generations, teachers have assigned marks and grades which were indicative of pupil achievement in the various content or subject matter areas. During this century, however, the trend has been to broaden the emphasis and nature of pupil evaluation. This trend has served to shift a great deal of the emphasis from the mere comparison of students to a systematic and continuous study of the individual from year to year and from educational level to educational level. One salutary effect of this trend has been the development of continuous, all-school programs of evaluation which provide for an increased number and variety of instruments and procedures.

Although most of the better programs of evaluation stress the central role played by the classroom teacher in the administration of tests and the utilization of test results, many other school personnel are concerned with pupil evaluation. For example, the school principal may use the results to evaluate the effectiveness of the curriculum and other aspects of the instructional program. The counselor may employ the pupil's cumulative record, including the results of teacher-made and standardized tests, to help the pupil achieve more satisfactory educational adjustment and to make suitable vocational plans. The pupil also benefits from a systematic program of measurement and evaluation. Tests not only serve to motivate the pupil in the learning situation, but also help him to determine the progress he has made toward the goals he has established. In short, it permits self-evaluation. Inherent in a good evaluation program are the following:

1. Evaluation includes all the means available for collecting information about a pupil's knowledge and understanding, attitudes and values, and behavior patterns.
2. Evaluation should be largely concerned with the growth of each individual, rather than with comparisons of the different members making up the group.
3. Evaluation is an important aspect of the teaching-learning process. It should be carried on continuously.
4. Evaluation is both qualitative and quantitative—descriptive statements about a pupil's attitudes and behavior furnish useful information about the nature and extent of his growth toward maturity.
5. Evaluation is concerned with the total personality—knowledge, interests, attitudes, beliefs, behavior patterns, etc.
6. Evaluation should be a cooperative process involving pupils, teachers, and other adult leaders especially concerned with the guidance and education of the individual members making up the group.

The importance of including the student in evaluation is often overlooked. One could even argue that because much of what the pupil learns most readily stems from his perceptions of the situation and his own motivations, the most important evaluations are those made by the child.

It should be apparent that no one will ever be able to know everything about another individual. Even the most skillful and painstaking teacher will not be able to discover all of the factors which influence a pupil's behavior. In actual practice she merely samples the behavior of her students and tries to make judgments based upon the characteristics she observes and the interpretations she makes in the light of her training and experience.

Characteristics of a good measuring instrument

It should be recognized that any test is actually a sampling of behavior. It is assumed that the sample of behavior obtained from a test or appraised by a measuring device is a true sample of the individual's behavior. However, it is not always so. One's reaction at any time will depend upon a number of factors including the kind and amount of stimulation, the environmental setting, the mental and emotional state of the individual, and the motives operating within the individual. Furthermore, the nature of the reaction to be measured is important. An effective method of measurement in one field may be ineffective in another. The method of measurement must be governed by the nature of what is measured as well as by the instruments available and the objectives of such measurements.

Sources of errors in measurement. Whenever one individual tries to appraise or evaluate the behavior of another, error is likely to result for a number of reasons. A teacher may be attracted to one pupil, and less attracted to another. If so, she is more likely to see worth or "good behavior" in the pupil she likes and may be less likely to recognize his "weaknesses." Similarly, she may see "poor behavior" in the pupil she dislikes. Some times the instrument we use to appraise behavior is not sufficiently precise and refined for our purpose. For example, a principal may decide that a teacher is a poor disciplinarian because he happened to see some pupils misbehaving in the school cafeteria. The misbehavior may not be typical of the class, although the principal may assume that it is. Another source of error may grow from the inconsistencies of human behavior. No one is "always good" or "always bad." Again, no one performs with the same efficiency each day. Many of us are like the little girl in the nursery rhyme, "When she was good she was very very good, and when she was bad she was horrid." At various times we reveal different patterns of behavior.

In an effort to recognize the extent to which errors of this type enter into the appraisal of behavior, measurement specialists employ such concepts as validity and reliability.

Validity. Measurement specialists commonly use the term *validity* to describe the degree to which a test measures what it is designed to measure. It should be readily apparent that the validity or truthfulness of any test varies according to the use which is made of it. A test of mathematics designed for use with fifth-grade pupils may be valid. When the same test is used with college students it may have less validity, depending upon how the results are used. If the test is to predict future ability to do college mathematics the test would probably prove to be too easy to predict success or failure effectively. Validity then is specific. It applies to a specific use with a particular group under certain prescribed conditions and circumstances. Many teachers and college students rather naively assume that any test which has been shown to be valid for use in one situation is valid for use in any situation. As our discussion shows, validity is not merely a characteristic of the test, but also of the use to which it is put.

A number of interesting problems arise for the classroom teacher in relation to the concept of validity. If the measurement involved is a standardized test, the teacher must be concerned with the *curricular validity* of the instrument. Suppose, for example, that the teacher selects a standardized test that presumes to measure the achievement of pupils in American history. A number of conditions must be satisfied if the test is to be valid as a measure of the achievement of the pupils in the teacher's classroom. First, the content of the test must closely approximate the content of the specific course. Suppose, for example, that the teacher's guide extends only from the Colonial Period through the Civil War, while the test extends from the American Revolution to the beginning of the twentieth century. Obviously, the test would fail to measure part of the class's achievement, while measuring their achievement in something it had not been taught. Similarly, the test should approximately reflect the amount of instructional time spent in learning a given topic or group of topics if it is to be a valid measure. If the teacher spent almost two-thirds of the semester teaching the history of America prior to the Civil War and one-third of the semester teaching later phases, the test should reflect this emphasis. On the other hand, if the test has been selected by someone merely to determine how much American history the members of the class know rather than to evaluate the outcomes of instruction, the test may be valid. Most likely, the test results would reveal that the pupils know more about the earlier phases of American history than they do about the later phases. In this situation, the use of the test for this purpose would seem justifiable, and the results, valid.

Many standardized instruments as well as teacher-made tests fail to measure pupil achievement in the broad developmental goals and objectives deemed desirable. Although many educational objectives are extremely complex and difficult to measure, failure to appraise progress toward them tends to limit the validity of many measures of achievement. There is also a tendency among many teachers at all grade levels to overemphasize a pupil's ability to memorize facts and details in evaluating his work and to underemphasize the more important ability to ingest principles, generalizations, and wholesome attitudes.

Publishers of standardized tests often correlate the performance of a group of students on a test with such indices as previous grades, other standardized tests, and similar criteria of performance. This procedure affords some knowledge of how the test relates to other measures of behavior and is known as *statistical validity*. Many school counselors and classroom teachers study the standardized instruments they use to determine the statistical validity of the instruments in the local situation.

As we can see from the previous discussion, the concept of validity is probably the most essential concept in any form of measurement. The validity of a test, whether it is standardized or teacher-made, group or individual, subjective or objective, is the *sine qua non* of evaluation.

Reliability. If the teacher is to make judgements about a student, based on test performance, he must be fairly certain that the sample of behavior he has obtained is reliable or consistent. Measurement specialists employ the term *reliability* to indicate the degree of *consistency* of a measure, or the degree of precision with which the test measures whatever it is measuring. Note that we assume that the score a pupil obtains on a given test is an efficient measure of his knowledge or ability. We assume, for example, that if we test the pupil's knowledge of science, his relative standing would be similar if we remeasured it the next day or the next week. We would be suspicious of any test in which students who scored high one day scored low on the same test the next day. Standardized test authors usually spend considerable time determining the reliability of their instruments. Classroom teachers, however, tend to take the reliability of their measures for granted.

A number of factors function to lower the reliability of any measure of human behavior. First, it is likely that errors arise from the instrument itself. For example, if we take a simple twelve inch ruler and measure an object that is twelve and one-half inches long, we find that we either have to estimate the length of that portion which is longer than the ruler, mark the place where the ruler ends and then measure it, or use some other object whose length we know and add to this sum twelve inches. In this case our ruler, as an instrument, lacks the precision to do what we want. Another source of error in measurement may arise from the nature of the characteristic being measured. Human behavior is sometimes inconsistent or atypical. All of us have experienced days when we feel that we are not functioning up to "par." Other days we feel are good days and we think we are at our best. If our test results are to be regarded as valid samples of behavior, we must be able to show that the observed performance would be consistent if samples were obtained many times. Rarely, however, is an identical test given repeatedly to a class of pupils. The classroom teacher who devises an algebra test tends to assume that the results she obtains are reliable indications of the performance of each child in the class. All teachers, however, can cite children whose test performance is erratic. If John scored 90 on the first weekly test and 20 the second week, which score is a more reliable measure of his knowledge and performance? Rarely does a student, for example, compose a series of compositions or essays which possess the same degree of excellence. One essay may be excellent in content, grammar, and spelling; the next essay may not be, perhaps because he feels the pressure of time or lacks interest in the topic, or any number of other reasons. This then, is the problem of reliability. Generally the classroom teacher obtains additional samples of the student's performance so that over a period of time she can make judgments about a pupil's typical performance. In most test situations, particularly in the use of standardized tests in the schoolroom, the test is merely utilized once and its reliability assumed.

Test specialists have developed a number of procedures to determine the reliability of measuring devices the most common of which are 1) test-retest; 2) equivalent forms; and 3) split-half. The test-retest method simply involves administering the test to a group and then at some later date or dates, readministering the test. The performance of each pupil is studied, usually by correlation methods. If pupils who performed well on the first test tend to maintain their positions on other retestings, we assume that the measure is consistent. The test-retest method is valuable where the effect of improvement through practice from previous testings is minimal. It also has the advantage of being a more realistic measure of the consistency of test performance.

Sometimes the authors of a test develop two or more forms of a test which are presumed to be equal in difficulty and content. In such cases reliability is determined by judging pupils' performance on the different equivalent forms of the test. If the relative achievements of a group of pupils is approximately the same on each form of the test, the instrument is thought to be reliable. At times it is deemed impractical to employ either the test-retest method or the equivalent forms method for determining reliability. The test developer then resorts to the split-half method. This method furnishes an indication of the internal consistency of a test by dividing it in half and analyzing pupils' performance on each part of the test. Essentially this technique separates the instrument into two parts and seeks to determine the consistency of the whole. Usually alternate items are employed in the division.

An elaborate and full discussion of these procedures for determining the reliability and validity of testing devices is outside the scope of this text. The interested student should consult any of the standard texts dealing with educational or psychological measurement for additional study. The above discussion, however, should serve to emphasize that judgments made by school personnel must be based on valid and reliable measures if they are to be meaningful. Validity and reliability are essential to all forms of measurement and evaluation, whether they are used to judge the academic progress of pupils, to determine their potentialities for future achievements, or to gain insight into their behavior.

Usability.   A third factor to consider is the usefulness of any measure in a particular situation. The cost of the test, the time required to administer and score the test, the time required to interpret the test results, the amount of knowledge and skill required to understand the measures, and similar practical considerations are factors in a measure's usability.

Standardized tests come in many forms. Some are quite expensive, while others are relatively cheap. In most schools a decision has to be made concerning the cost of a test in relation to the value to be derived from it. Some tests require several hours of testing time; others require merely twenty or thirty minutes. Teachers and principals must face the problem of disrupted schedules, time lost from the instructional program, and similar concerns in selecting an instrument. Some tests have elaborate scoring procedures which increase the possibilities of error in scoring. Others can be more readily and accurately scored by teachers with minimal skills in handling tests. In all testing procedures the advantages and disadvantages of a given instrument should be analyzed and the decision to employ a given measure made, in part, on the basis of usability.

Usability also is a factor in the evaluation of instruction in teacher-made tests. For example, junior-high and high-school teachers often must decide whether the time advantage gained in the construction of an essay examination is offset by the time such tests require to score and by the difficulties they present. Similarly, most teachers feel that they cannot give as many tests as they want because their time is limited. Even the form of a test is affected by practical considerations. In some schools little or no clerical help is available to teachers who want to duplicate test materials. Such teachers often rely on essay tests written on the chalkboard or read to the class. Luckily such schools are becoming less common, and most teachers can expect to have facilities which will enable them to make decisions based on more important considerations.

CLASSIFICATION OF TESTS

The new teacher is often confused by the number and variety of tests available. On the other hand, schools sometimes select tests for use before they have thoroughly investigated what is available. Test specialists and publishers also seem to classify their tests in different ways so that it is difficult for the unsophisticated to search out the type of instrument they want.

It may be convenient to think of tests as classifiable into two categories, by the methods or procedures of testing, and by the objectives or purposes of testing. The student will find that almost every test will fit into both categories, yet each classification provides a convenient frame of reference to help him compare one test with another in terms of the characteristics of a good measuring instrument discussed previously.

Classifications based on methods of testing

Various methods have been developed and employed in testing pupils, and the competent teacher will make use of several of them in arriving at a more accurate appraisal of the students. Their use, however, should depend largely on the purpose of the testing. Since the methods we shall describe are not exclusive, one will find considerable overlapping.

Individual and group tests. Tests are sometimes classified according to the number of persons who can be examined by a single examiner at any given time. As may be expected, an *individual test* can be administered to one pupil at a time. During the testing period the examiner establishes a suitable working relationship with the examinee, called *rapport,* and records the answers given to test questions or observes the examinee's success or failure in performing the various tasks on the test. Usually the individual test requires more skill and understanding in scoring and interpreting than does a group test. Among the more common individual tests are the *Stanford-Binet* and the *Wechsler Intelligence Scales,* employed to determine the mental ability of pupils. Such personality measures as the *Rorschach Ink Blot Test, Thematic Apperception Test,* the *Blacky Pictures,* and similar clinical instruments are also good examples of individual tests. Each of these instruments requires special training if the results are to be reliable and valid. Generally they are not used by the classroom teacher unless she has had special training. Some individual tests, however, are designed for use by the classroom teacher. A number of diagnostic reading tests such as the *Durrell Analysis of Reading Difficulty,* and the *Gray Standardized Oral Reading Paragraphs,* are commonly employed by classroom teachers.

Group tests, as the name implies, are designed to be administered to more than one person at a time. An entire class or a group of classes may be examined in a single testing session, providing for a considerable saving in time. Group tests are now available for appraising almost every facet of human character. Mental ability tests, academic achievement tests, and personal-social adjustment tests at various grade levels have been made available for use in schools.

Speed and power tests.   Another classification of testing instruments is related to the time conditions under which the measures are made. Speed tests are those which impose specific time restrictions so that almost all persons taking the test are unable to complete it. Power tests, on the other hand, provide generous time limits and are designed to provide a somewhat broader measure of the depth and breadth of an examinee's knowledge. Speed tests are built upon the premise that quick reactions and rapid responses to test tasks are important indices of pupil knowledge and ability. It is thought that those who complete more items correctly in a given time also have a greater depth and breadth of ability and knowledge. A number of mental ability and aptitude tests are speed tests, but the trend in achievement and scholastic aptitude testing appears to favor more generously timed instruments.

Standardized and teacher-made tests.   A standardized test is so designed that it must be administered and scored under standard conditions. The user of the test is supplied with a testing manual which prescribes in detail the specific methods to be employed in administering and timing the test. Similarly, scoring procedures are spelled out so that the examiner does not have to make judgments concerning the correctness or weighting of answers. Generally the standardized test is published by a company which specializes in testing or by a text book publisher. The best instruments have been tried out under a number of circumstances and the reliability of the device, studied. The publishers of the test typically furnish the test user with *norms* so that comparisons can be made of any student's performance with that of an appropriate population. Norms will be discussed in more detail later in this chapter.

Teacher-made tests, on the other hand, are usually not so carefully prepared or studied and do not provide a comparable norm group for purposes of comparison. They are usually constructed by classroom teachers for their personal use in evaluating the learning or behavior of their students. Teacher-made tests will be discussed in detail in Chapter 14.

Objective and subjective tests. A somewhat older classification of tests, less frequently used now, is based upon the scoring procedures employed in correcting the instrument. The objective test, designed with answers keyed to each question, requires little or no personal judgment to score. Its real advantage lies in largely eliminating the personal biases and judgments of the scorer. Thus greater reliability is achieved; for no matter who marks the test, the student will receive the same score. Objective tests may also be quickly administered, although they usually require considerable time to construct. Because answers generally consist of single words, phrases, or numbers, some writers call it a short-answer test. Typical examples of this kind of instrument are alternate response tests, matching tests, and multiple-choice tests.

Subjective tests, on the other hand, differ because they usually require the scorer to use judgment in interpreting and weighting responses to test questions. The popular essay examination, widely used in high school and college, is a good example of the subjective test. The teacher must ascertain whether each answer is sufficiently correct or partially correct, and whether answers are pertinent and well-phrased so that a pupil receives maximum credit for his work. Often such decisions are difficult. The less commonly used oral examination also represents a subjective testing procedure. These factors will be discussed in more detail in the next chapter.

Performance and paper-pencil tests. Another classification is sometimes based upon the nature of the testing materials and the tasks imposed on the examinee. Most classroom teachers utilize paper-and-pencil tests which simply require a test-answer sheet, composition paper, and pencil or pen. Most of the popularly used standardized tests and almost all of the examinations used by teachers of academic subjects are of this type. Certain characteristics, however, may best be evaluated by the use of objects and equipment. Counselors often measure a student's manual dexterity by peg boards and similar devices. In other tests, students may be asked to place objects in various slots, assemble parts of familiar ob-

The *Bennett Hand Tool Dexterity Test,* useful for evaluating skill with hand tools

jects, or otherwise perform a given task. Typing teachers, physical instructors, art and mechanical drawing teachers, and industrial arts instructors often use performance tests in evaluating student progress. Counselors and school psychologists also employ performance tests in vocational counseling.

Classification based upon the objectives and purposes of testing

The previous discussion has dealt with classification schemes based upon the methods employed in testing and measurement. Another commonly used system of classification is based upon objectives of measurement as they relate to the traits or characteristics being appraised. Thus the student will find authors who talk about intelligence tests, aptitude tests, personality tests, interest inventories, and achievement tests. The following discussion will describe briefly some of these major test groups.

Achievement tests. Previously in this chapter it was pointed out that teachers have always evaluated the extent to which pupils have benefited from the instructional program. Achievement tests are designed for this purpose—to determine the progress pupils make toward the goals and objectives of the curriculum. The achievement test measures the present ability of the child or the extent of his knowledge in a specific content area. Some achievement tests measure a pupil's mastery of skills, such as reading and arithmetic tests. Others like chemistry, history, or literature are designed to measure the extent of knowledge and understanding the student possesses. Figure 13-1 illustrates typical achievement test items designed to evaluate an intermediate grade pupil's ability to

TEST 3 — SECTION C

DIRECTIONS: Work these problems, using the space to the right of each problem for your work. Write your answer on the line to the right.

1. Jack has 5 apples. His sister has 3 apples. How many apples do they have together?

_____ _____ 1

2. A farmer had 14 horses. He sold four of them. How many horses did he have left?

_____ 2

FIGURE 13-1. Sample Items Taken From The Arithmetic Section Of The California Basic Skills Tests (Grades 4, 5, 6, 1954 Edition California Test Bureau, Inc.)

handle arithmetic concepts. Figure 13-2 shows sample items of a social study test which measure a child's knowledge of geography. Note that in both cases the test items require more than simple rote learning for successful handling.

At present a number of excellent achievement-test batteries are available for use in pupil evaluation. The achievement-test battery typically consists of a series of subtests designed for joint use, and furnish a comparative picture of a child's achievements in various content areas. Usually the test batteries are available for different grade levels so that they provide a basis for an integrated testing program. Common norms are also generally available. As a result the year to year growth and development of pupils can be systematically studied. Another major advantage of

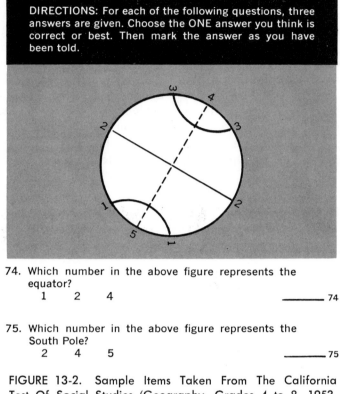

DIRECTIONS: For each of the following questions, three answers are given. Choose the ONE answer you think is correct or best. Then mark the answer as you have been told.

74. Which number in the above figure represents the equator?

    1   2   4   _____ 74

75. Which number in the above figure represents the South Pole?

    2   4   5   _____ 75

FIGURE 13-2. Sample Items Taken From The California Test Of Social Studies (Geography, Grades 4 to 8, 1953, California Test Bureau, Inc.)

the test battery is that it provides a teacher with a readily understood picture of each child's comparative achievements in the several academic areas. The teacher can then plan for additional diagnostic testing and remedial teaching both for the total class and for individual pupils. Figure 13-3 illustrates a profile of a fourth grade pupil's abilities and achievements as measured by one such achievement test battery.

Mental ability tests. Different authors and publishers employ the terms mental ability, scholastic aptitude, or intelligence to describe measures for determining a student's intellectual level. Generally, there is agreement that intelligence is positively related to an individual's ability to learn, but as we pointed out in Chapter 4, there is no commonly accepted definition of intelligence. As we may expect, any test of mental ability reflects the author's beliefs regarding the nature of intelligence, and the results obtained by one test may differ considerably from those obtained with a different test. If, for example, Test A emphasizes verbal

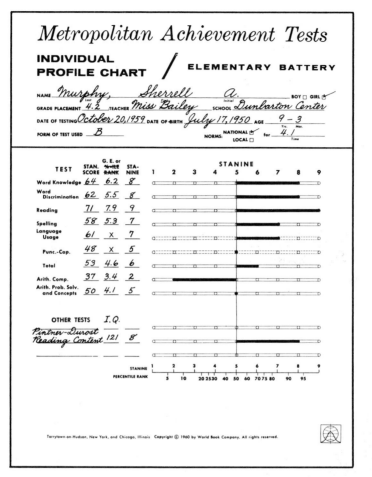

FIGURE 13-3. Individual Profile Chart Of A Fourth Grade Pupil On The Metropolitan Achievement Tests (Copyright, Harcourt, Brace and World, Inc., 1960)

factors in intelligence and Test B emphasizes reasoning and quantitative manipulation, the results achieved by a given pupil may be quite different. Similarly, some tests furnish merely a single score which often can be interpreted as an Intelligence Quotient. On the other hand, a test constructor who believes in a factored theory of intelligence is likely to develop an instrument which gives a number of scores and provides for a profiling of abilities. Again, some tests provide the user with verbal and quantitative scores. In all cases, the purposes of the testing will be most important in making decisions about which test to use. One further word of caution should be noted. All tests in this category reflect the previous learning of the examinee. Since we are unable to probe the depth and breadth of an individual's intelligence, we ascertain how much he has learned compared to his peers and predict future intellectual development and achievement on this basis. Despite progress in public education, not all children have environments which provide for equal opportunities to learn. Furthermore, a paper-and-pencil test of intelligence is likely to be influenced by a child's reading ability. The child's motives, interests, and emotions may also affect his test scores adversely. The wise teacher always interprets intelligence scores cautiously and in the light of other data about the child.

Examples of different types of items employed to measure mental ability are shown in Figures 13-4 and 13-5. Note that the items shown

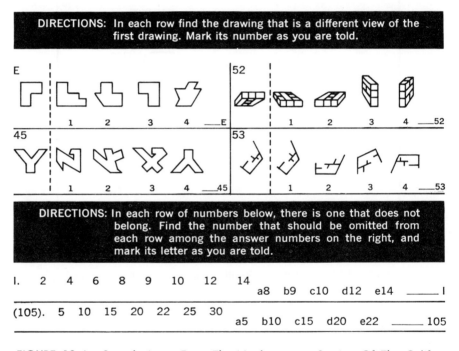

FIGURE 13-4. Sample Items From The Nonlanguage Section Of The California Test Of Mental Maturity (Elementary Edition, 1951)

in Figure 13-4 do not depend upon a knowledge of verbal or language ability, but upon the child's ability to deal with relationships between geometric forms or numbers. On the other hand, items in Figure 13-5 require greater language and reading ability for successful response. Both language and nonlanguage measures are helpful to teachers and counselors in understanding a pupil's strengths and weaknesses.

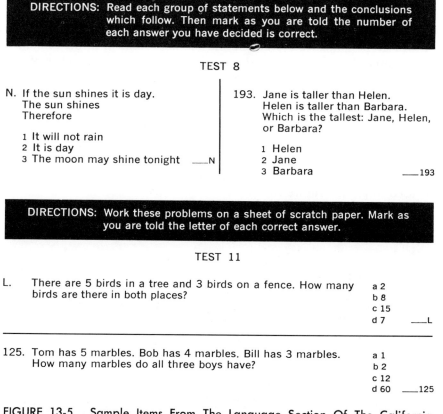

DIRECTIONS: Read each group of statements below and the conclusions which follow. Then mark as you are told the number of each answer you have decided is correct.

TEST 8

N. If the sun shines it is day.
The sun shines
Therefore

1 It will not rain
2 It is day
3 The moon may shine tonight   ___N

193. Jane is taller than Helen.
Helen is taller than Barbara.
Which is the tallest: Jane, Helen, or Barbara?

1 Helen
2 Jane
3 Barbara   ___193

DIRECTIONS: Work these problems on a sheet of scratch paper. Mark as you are told the letter of each correct answer.

TEST 11

L.   There are 5 birds in a tree and 3 birds on a fence. How many birds are there in both places?
a 2
b 8
c 15
d 7   ___L

125. Tom has 5 marbles. Bob has 4 marbles. Bill has 3 marbles. How many marbles do all three boys have?
a 1
b 2
c 12
d 60   ___125

FIGURE 13-5. Sample Items From The Language Section Of The California Test Of Mental Maturity (Elementary Edition, 1951, Copyright by California Test Bureau, Inc.)

Aptitude tests. An aptitude test actually measures the present existing knowledge or ability of an individual and uses these findings to predict his future success in some specific occupation or educational program. Although we have described tests of scholastic aptitude as measures of mental ability, we should recognize that usually they are used to predict a student's success or failure in a higher educational program. The scholastic aptitude test, for example, is commonly used by the high-school counselor to help a student estimate his chances of successfully completing the required educational programs in a specific occupation or profession. Such measures often provide sub-tests, such as quantitative and verbal reasoning, memory, and vocabulary. The counselor can help a pupil analyze his own strengths and weaknesses in terms of the requirements of his educational and vocational plans.

Other aptitude tests seek to identify the individual's potentiality for functioning in mechanical, clerical, artistic, musical or other areas. Usually a number of aptitudes are needed for success in a given occupation, and in all cases certain personality factors are involved. As a result of the growth in the guidance movement and the improvement in personnel selection procedures in industry during this century, a vast number of aptitude measures have become available and are widely used. Figure 13-6 illustrates items included on the *Test of Mechanical Comprehension*. The items measure a student's knowledge of various principles of mechanics. Generally the child with greater knowledge of mechanics will have greater success in work or study involving such knowledge than those who lack such understanding. Like many aptitude measures it is assumed that an individual's present abilities, compared to those of other students, can be used to predict future success.

FIGURE 13-6. Test Items From The *Test of Mechanical Comprehension*, Form AA (George K. Bennett, The Psychological Corp., 1940)

Measures of personality. Numerous measures have been developed for appraising various aspects of personality. Similarly, a number of titles are used to describe such instruments. They may be called tests, scales, inventories, blanks, or something else. After the student has read the materials in Part V of this text, he will better understand the difficulties encountered in attempting to sample these areas of human characteristics and behavior. Generally, measures of personality may be regarded as having two types of purpose. The first seeks to gain some insight into the personal-social adjustment of the individual or to assess his characteristic behavior in normal situations. Such measuring devices as the *Bernreuter Personality Inventory, Gordon Personal Inventory, Bell Adjustment Inventory,* and *Mooney Problem Checklist* are examples of this type of instrument.

The second type of instrument seeks to ascertain the motivating factors regarded as determinants of behavior. Such devices provide an organized and systematic method of recording an individual's preferences in certain situations, his likes and dislikes to a variety of objects or activities, his value-judgments and motivations. Such measures are widely employed by counselors in helping students plan future educational and vocational programs. The *Kuder Preference Record* and *Strong Vocational Interest Blank* are widely used in schools and guidance centers and are excellent examples of interest measures. The *A-S Reaction Study* and the *Study of Values* are examples of tests which reveal certain motivating conditions which presumably lead the individual to certain types of behavior in different situations.

It should be recognized that because of its complexity, personality is extremely difficult to measure. Most psychologists believe that personality must be studied in terms of its total structure and the reactive patterns of the organism. Projective methods and clinically oriented personality inventories have been developed for this purpose. These have been found useful for the study of the individual child and are described in Chapter 15. Generally the training and responsibilities of the class-teacher do not provide an adequate background or suitable conditions for the use of clinically designed measures of personality.

STANDARDIZED AND TEACHER-MADE TESTS

Much of the philosophy and basic characteristics of measurement and evaluation which have been discussed previously has applied equally to the standardized and teacher-made test. Both must be valid, reliable, and usable if the desired outcomes are to be achieved. Similarly, both standardized and teacher-made tests can be either performance or paper-and-pencil measures. They can be either objective or subjective, short-answer or essay, although in practice almost all standardized tests are objective in design. Both types of measures can be constructed for use either as group or individual tests, as speed or power tests. The student may ask, How then do standardized tests really differ from the teacher-made test? A few differences were suggested in the earlier part of this chapter and the following discussion will amplify these points.

Teachers' concern with tests. As an educator the teacher is concerned with such questions as, Are the students making progress in the direction of the goals appropriate to a particular learning situation? If so, how much progress is being made? What is the evidence that progress is being made? Thus, the teacher is faced with the task of obtaining evidence relative to progress being made by pupils appropriate to a particular learning situation. The securing of accurate data on the progress of pupils is not easy. After data about student progress have been obtained, the teacher is faced with the task of interpreting the data.

Raw scores. The difficulty of presenting meaningfully the results obtained from an educational test can be illustrated by a pupil's score on a science test given by the teacher. The teacher may determine the pupil's score by the number of items that were correctly answered or by the per cent of the total number correctly answered. Either score is meaningless, if other information is not available. For example, if there are fifteen exercises and the pupil answers ten of them correctly, his score would be $66\frac{2}{3}$ per cent correctly answered. The teacher may also consider this in terms of the actual number of items correctly answered, which is 15. This would be the raw score, that is, the quantitative amount correctly performed. In this case the pupil is credited with one point for each item correctly answered. The teacher may prefer to give the pupil two or more credits for each item correctly answered and provide less credit for items only partially answered. In this circumstance a larger raw score is obtained and recorded by the teacher.

When the teacher examines the scores of the different members of the class he may find himself grappling with uncertainties. Is this a good score? He further notices that the average score is 14. Then, is the score of 15 really a score above the average? If the score is above the average, How much above the average is it? On another test consisting of 50 items the student makes a score of 35, answering 70 per cent of the items correctly. Can we say that this is a better score than the score of 15 made on the first test? These and other questions relating to raw scores contribute to difficulties and uncertainties in interpretation.

The construction of standardized tests. The standardized test does not evolve out of a local setting in a short period of time. It is usually constructed by a specialist or a group of specialists working as a team.

Usually the specialist or team knows test construction thoroughly and is familiar with the subject area or behavioral characteristics being measured. In constructing the test, considerable care goes into the writing of each item to avoid ambiguity. The test is then tried out with various groups representative of the population with which it will be used. After the preliminary instrument has been tried out it is studied and modified in the light of this experience. The developers of the test, for example, ascertain by trial whether their instructions for administering and scoring the test are adequate. Studies also are made which furnish evidence of the reliability and validity of the test items as well as of the total instrument itself. These experiences help to determine the standards or conditions under which users of the test will operate. Few classroom teachers have the time to develop their tests to this degree; if they were to attempt it they would find that they would lose much valuable instruction time.

Norms. Perhaps the most significant difference between the standardized and teacher-made tests lies in the furnishing of *norms*. Norms actually represent scores attained on the test by given groups of individuals. By comparing the score a student makes on a given test with a comparable norm group, the teacher gains more understanding of that student's relative achievements. If, for example, a high-school student wants to enter a specific university, it would be helpful for him to know how his scholastic aptitude compares to that of the typical freshman of that college or what grades his test scores indicate he is likely to make in the future. Perhaps another student wants to study medicine. He can gain insight into the probability of his success by comparing his achievements in science, mathematics, and related subjects with those of other students majoring in premedical programs.

Percentile scores may be obtained by the teacher by ranking the pupils' scores from highest to lowest. Percentile scores show how a pupil compares with others of a particular group. This group, the *norm* group, may consist of students' scores from a single class, school, or national population sample. Thus, if a pupil has a percentile score of 78, he equaled or did better than 78 per cent of the pupils of the group for which norms were obtained. On the other hand, if he has a percentile score of 22, he equaled or did better than 22 per cent of the pupils of the group, while 78 per cent did better than he. In the former case we say that the pupil is in the upper one-fourth of the group or the upper quartile. In the latter case the pupil is in the lower quartile group. Many standardized test manuals provide tables for converting test scores to percentile scores. Other methods of reporting norms are available, such as grade-equivalent scores, standard scores, I.Q.'s, stanines, or deciles. These are described in test manuals.

The use of norms. Norm tables furnish a basis for comparing a student's score with the scores of others. Frequently it is desirable to compare his test scores with that of several norm groups. For example, Henry is a senior in a large high school where a relatively small percentage of students go on to college. He wants to enter Central State College. To know how he compares with other students in academic ability, comparisons must be made between his test score and norms for three distinct groups:

> Senior norms for his own school
> Publishers' national 12th grade norms
> Norms for students admitted to Central State College

It is obvious from this presentation that test scores must be interpreted through comparisons with distinct groups. For example, Henry may be one of the outstanding seniors in his class with a percentile score of 95 for his own school. On the publishers' national 12th-grade norms, however, his percentile score may be 76, and for students admitted to the college, 68.

SUMMARY

Teachers have always attempted to appraise the extent to which their students have mastered the skills and subject matter taught in the instructional program. During this century there has been a noticeable refinement in educational measurement and evaluation as well as a broadening of methods and procedures. The concepts of measurements and evaluation often are confusing to both students and teachers. Measurement, usually, is merely one facet of evaluation and pertains to the process by which the teacher assigns a given rank or quantity to a specific characteristic of the pupil. Evaluation, on the other hand, is thought of as the complex process of bringing together from a number of measures, observations, interviews, or other sources, pertinent information about a specific pupil or group of pupils. Evaluation always assumes that the teacher and the school have certain clearly stated objectives against which pupil achievements and progress are being measured.

A number of basic concepts concerning measurement must be understood before one can correctly employ the tools of measurement and evaluation. Probably the most essential concept is that of *validity* or the degree to which a test or technique actually measures what it presumes to measure. Validity is more than a characteristic of a test and should be regarded as specifically applying to a given use of the instrument in a particular situation. *Reliability,* another important consideration, pertains to the consistency with which the instrument yields results. If one is to make proper decisions concerning pupils, the test results must be relatively stable and consistent. A third concept, *usability*, is related to the usefulness of the test in a specific situation. Such factors as cost, time required to administer and score a test, difficulties encountered by pupils in taking the test or by teachers in scoring and interpreting it as well as many other practical considerations fall into this category.

The vast number of tests available often serves to confuse the teacher. Classifications of tests either by procedures and methods of testing or by the objectives and purposes of the measurement are often helpful. Classifications based on methods may include the following: individual or group tests, speed or power tests, standardized or teacher-made tests, objective or subjective tests, and performance or paper-pencil tests. Classifications based on the objectives and purposes of measurement include the following: achievement tests, mental ability tests, aptitude tests, and personality tests.

Standardized tests vary from teacher-made tests in a number of ways. Probably the most important feature of the standardized test is that it provides a basis for comparing the scores attained by a single student or group of students with those of a comparative group. The scores made by such groups are called *norms*. The use and limitations of norms were discussed in some detail.

Presently most school systems plan testing programs which provide yearly and systematic evaluation of student progress. Care must be taken to assure that all concerned understand the uses and misuses of tests. Many teachers need time allotted to them if they are to receive maximum benefits from testing. Orientation and in-service training may also be necessary.

Although standardized testing has been employed at an increasing rate in American schools, teacher-made tests and teacher-assigned grades continue to constitute the major basis for pupil evaluation. Chapter 14 is devoted to a discussion of the teacher-made tests, grading schemes, and methods of reporting pupil progress. Students wanting additional information about educational and psychological tests should consult some of the references at the end of this chapter and chapters 14 and 15. They should also read some of the critical reviews found in *The Mental Measurements Yearbook*.

Problems and Exercises

1. Examine the manuals of a number of commonly used standardized tests to determine their validity and reliability.
2. How does reading ability affect a pupil's scores on a paper-pencil test of mental ability?
3. Read the reviews in the *Mental Measurements Yearbook* devoted to the discussion of an achievement test you believe is a good measure.

4. Assume you are teaching this course. What aspects of behavior should you measure in order to evaluate pupil progress?
5. List the various methods available to teachers at various grade levels for evaluating pupil progress. Which would you use and why?
6. Explain why many aptitude tests may be regarded as measures of achievement.
7. Make a list of occasions when pupil evaluation might better be served by standardized tests than by teacher-made tests. For what purposes might teacher-made tests prove to be superior?
8. Examine the manuals of a number of standardized tests. Make a list of the various groups used in the standardization. How adequate do you think these norms are for use in the schools you are familiar with?

Selected Readings

AHMANN, J. S., and GLOCK, M. D., *Evaluating Pupil Growth* (Boston: Allyn and Bacon, 1959), Chs. 4 and 5.

BARON, Davis, and BERNARD, H. W., *Evaluation Techniques for Classroom Teachers* (New York: McGraw-Hill Book Co., 1958), Ch. 2.

BRADFIELD, J. M., and MOREDOCK, H. S., *Measurement and Evaluation in Education* (New York: The Macmillan Co., 1957), Ch. 16.

CRONBACH, Lee J., *Essentials of Psychological Testing*, 2nd ed. (New York: Harper & Row, 1960), Ch. 2.

DOWNIE, N. M., *Fundamentals of Measurement: Techniques and Practice* (New York: Oxford University Press, 1958), Ch. 5.

GREENE, H. A., JORGENSEN, A. N., and GERBERICH, J. R., *Measurement and Evaluation in the Elementary School* (New York: Longmans, Green and Co., 1953), Ch. 1.

REMMERS, H. H., and GAGE, N. L., *Educational Measurement and Evaluation*, rev. ed. (New York: Harper and Row, 1955), Ch. 1.

ROSS, C. C., and STANLEY, J. C., *Measurement in Today's Schools*, 3rd ed. (Englewood Cliffs: Prentice-Hall, 1954), Ch. 8.

THORNDIKE, Robert L., and HAGEN, E., *Measurement and Evaluation in Psychology and Education*, 2nd ed. (New York: John Wiley and Sons, 1961), Ch. 2.

TYLER, Ralph, "Evaluation in Learning," in L. D. Crow and Alice Crow, eds., *Readings in Human Learning* (New York: David McKay Co., 1963).

Evaluating the Outcomes of Classroom Instruction

In the previous chapter certain broad aspects of measurement and evaluation were discussed along with a brief description of a variety of methods for measuring pupil progress toward educational objectives. It was stressed that measurement and evaluation should be regarded as non-culminating, continuous processes involving almost all facets of the school program. This chapter is devoted to the role of the teacher in evaluation, and specifically, to the problem of measuring and evaluating the effectiveness of the teaching-learning process. We shall also consider the problem of assigning grades and the methods of reporting pupil progress.

EVALUATION AND EDUCATIONAL OBJECTIVES

To evaluate what schools achieve, the results, is not easy. Tyler has set forth certain principles, commonly followed in such attempts. These are:

1. Evaluation is based on a set of objectives. Hence objectives need to be clearly identified in the minds of the staff.
2. There should be periodic appraisals made to determine what changes are being made.
3. Samplings of students may be used in evaluation, thus making the appraisal less costly of time and effort.
4. A variety of devices may be used: tests, observation of habits, questionnaires, check lists, informal interviews, etc.
5. Ways of summarizing the results of appraisals need to be devised in order to better understand how our teaching and learning is going on.[1]

[1] Ralph W. Tyler, "Modern Aspects of Evaluation," *California Journal of Secondary Education*, Vol. 29 (1954), pp. 410-412.

Identifying educational objectives

One of the first steps in successful evaluation is the identification and formulation of educational objectives. It should be apparent that if one is to evaluate pupil progress or the effectiveness of the learning experience, he must know what the goals are. The identification of objectives is difficult because many of the most important changes sought in pupil behavior are complex and involve total personality structure. They include such broad goals as the fostering of objective thinking and satisfactory self-other relationships, the development of moral and ethical standards for productive functioning, and the development of patterns of creative thinking. Although such goals may be paramount in the educative process, their evaluation is frequently so difficult as to make actual evaluations meaningless.

To be valid, then, educational objectives should be clearly formulated prior to instruction; they should be limited in scope to real and attainable goals, and should be susceptible to evaluation. As we have previously suggested, however, many educational objectives are difficult to define precisely in behavioral terms and hence are not easy to measure. Dressel, in discussing the measurement and evaluation of instructional objectives, points out that "An educational objective which speaks of the cultivation of character is so complex that it provides very little guidance to educational planning. Educational objectives which are excessively simple and specific tend to break education into unrelated bits and pieces. On the other hand, highly complex objectives are usually ignored in instruction." [2]

School personnel have a tendency to compile long and elaborate lists of objectives. Rothney suggests that such lists can usually be reduced to such major classifications as the following:

1. The development of effective methods of thinking
2. The cultivation of useful work habits and skills
3. The inculcation of constructive social attitudes
4. The acquisition of a wide range of significant interests
5. The development of increased appreciation of music, art, literature, and other esthetic experiences
6. The development of social sensitivity
7. The development of better personal-social adjustment
8. The development of skill in effective communication
9. The acquisition of important information
10. The development of physical health
11. The development of a consistent philosophy of life [3]

[2] Paul L. Dressel, "Measurement and Evaluation of Instructional Objectives," *The Seventeenth Yearbook of the National Council on Measurement Used in Education,* 1960, p. 1.
[3] John W. M. Rothney, "Evaluating and Reporting Pupil Progress," *What Research Says to the Teacher,* Department of Classroom Teachers, American Educational Research Association of the National Education Association, No. 7 (1960), p. 6.

Methods of evaluation. Many students preparing to teach believe that the only way to evaluate the outcomes of instruction is to administer tests. Although both standardized and teacher-made tests are important tools in evaluation, a number of other valuable methods are available to the teacher. Observational techniques are often used in helping the teacher ascertain a number of pupil characteristics. In fact, it is only through observation that the teacher can obtain insight into the child's personal-social adjustments, work habits, attitudes, and motivations, and other behavioral characteristics. Interviews with parents and students can also help the teacher gain insight into the pupil's aspirations and attitudes toward his school work. They furnish another means of gaining additional information about the child not obtainable in the classroom milieu. Anecdotal records, when used together with cumulative records and other objective methods of evaluation, also furnish a good picture of the child's development in such areas as personal-social adjustment. Elementary teachers have found that the systematic filing of samples of pupils' homework or classroom work provides an excellent source of performance measures for judging pupil progress. Such self-reporting methods as inventories, checklists, autobiographies, logs, and diaries also serve to help teachers identify pupil difficulties and determine growth.

Most of these methods will be discussed in greater detail in Chapter 15, "Studying the Individual Child." It is important, however, for the teacher to recognize that evaluation consists of a great deal more than simply administering and interpreting standardized or teacher-made tests. It should also be stressed that pupils, parents, teachers, and administrative personnel must cooperate in the evaluative procedures if maximum benefits are to be obtained.

The relationship of measurement to learning. Without some sort of evaluation neither the teacher nor the learner can determine the nature or the extent of learning that has taken place. Nor can reliable judgments be made concerning the level of proficiency already attained relative to the objectives which have been set. Moreover, without testing, teachers cannot ascertain which particular deficiencies a student may have. Measurement, then, is extremely important to teachers and to the teaching process. Horrocks describes the relationship of measurement to learning as follows:

Measurement serves four important functions in teaching and learning. First, it enables teachers to make an assessment of the past learning experiences of pupils. It provides an estimate of pupil strengths and weaknesses as revealed by general capacity, special abilities and aptitudes, and state of personal adjustment. In short, measurement makes possible an analysis of a student's readiness to profit from instruction and reveals what needs to be done to bring him to the point where he may derive the greatest benefits from what is to be taught.

It indicates what instructional adaptations must be made in individual cases and to what extent given instructional objectives are practical.

Second, measurement indicates the quantity and quality of what has been learned. By examining the results of achievement examinations, teachers and learners alike may gauge what has been taught and learned. Such knowledge enables teachers to judge the effectiveness of their instructional techniques and provides data upon which to plan further instruction. It shows the pupil the extent to which his attempts at learning have been successful and gives him objective information upon which to base his future plans. The results of measurement provide an opportunity for school administrators to learn about the effectiveness of instruction in their schools and enables them to compare learning in their school with that of learning in similar schools. Parents are also provided with information about the progress of their children and help in vocational planning for them.

Third, measurement may become a valuable adjunct to learning. Selective use of tests as instructional devices makes possible more effective teaching and learning. Usually measurement is thought of as occurring either before or after learning takes place. In this sense measurement is seen as quite apart from the actual process of learning. Yet it has been found possible to integrate measurement procedures into instructional practices so that measurement becomes an aid to teaching and the process of effective learning. Many teachers have found that it is possible to teach with tests.

Fourth, measurement may lead to the improvement of teaching and learning by acting as a tool for research. Effective teaching and learning is based not only upon good instructional techniques but upon a knowledge of the nature of the learner, and upon knowledge of how learning takes place. Answers about all of these things may be provided by research either of a survey or of an experimental kind. Such research, however, requires the collection of a great deal of objective information that is susceptible to quantitative manipulation and analysis. The results of measurement procedures may provide such information.[4]

PRINCIPLES OF TEST CONSTRUCTION

Despite an increasing use of standardized tests, observational techniques, check-lists, anecdotal records, and similar procedures, the teacher-made test and grades or marks assigned by the teacher remain as the single most important form of pupil evaluation. The importance of tests in the instructional program is emphasized by Findley in his insistence that "testing must have as a central purpose helping teachers to help children to learn. . . . No matter how carefully other desirable practices in the use of tests are followed, they will fail in their effectiveness if testing is not seen as a means of helping the teacher do better what he must do anyway—teach."[5]

[4] John E. Horrocks, "What Does Psychology Indicate About the Relationship of Measurement to Teaching and Learning?" *Twelfth Yearbook of the National Council on Measurements Used in Education,* 1955, p. 36.

[5] Warren G. Findley, "Factors that Affect Test Results," *The National Elementary Principal,* Vol. 41 (1961), p. 8.

The teacher-made test should be valid and reliable if optimal results are to be obtained. A weakness of teacher-made tests is that often they are hurriedly prepared. The construction of tests which are valid and reliable measures of progress toward the objectives of a course is time-consuming and difficult. The teacher who devotes little time and thought to the task, who, for example, suddenly realizes that it is report card time, and sits down to prepare a test then and there, will not have a valid and reliable instrument.

It is sometimes helpful to think of test construction in terms of several distinct stages or steps:

planning the test
preparing the test
administering and scoring the test
evaluating the test and the results

Planning the test

Satisfactory tests result from careful and deliberate planning. The first step is to determine the objectives of the course and to state them specifically. It is generally assumed that each course in the curriculum of the school has well-developed objectives prior to instruction. The teacher should analyze his lesson plans, textbooks, work books, and other instructional media to ascertain the degree to which these sources contribute to the instructional program. The next step is to develop a broad outline from which the test will eventually be developed. Stanley states that "A well planned test will provide the means for evaluating progress toward the expected outcomes of instruction, as expressed in the educational philosophy of the particular school and as defined in the objectives of the particular course." [6]

Preparing the test

If a test is to be reliable and valid, considerable care should go into its planning and preparation. As we have already mentioned, the typical teacher often fails to devote the necessary time to its preparation. The teacher should prepare the test well in advance of the time it is to be used by composing a few items or questions either at the time he prepares his lesson plans or shortly after he actually instructs the class. The teacher will find this procedure most helpful, and he will be sure to include items that actually evaluate the instruction he gives.

Some specialists feel that a test should contain more than one type of item and that each item should be of sufficient difficulty to block

[6] Julian C. Stanley, "ABCs of Test Construction," *Journal of the National Education Association,* Vol. 47 (1958), p. 224.

about half the class. In the end, however, the teacher's purpose in testing may well determine the type and difficulty of the items. For example, if the teacher desires to ascertain whether pupils can apply what has been learned, he may decide upon an essay type of test as the best device for evaluating this objective. Similarly, if he wishes to be sure that the class knows certain basic skills, the difficulty level for certain items may vary from the fifty per cent level. It is generally considered advisable to prepare a greater number of items that will be eventually used. This procedure allows the teacher to eliminate unsuitable, duplicating, or poorly prepared items prior to constructing the final product. If possible the teacher should prepare a tentative test in advance and subject the preliminary copy of the test to a critical review a few days before it is to be used.

The essay test.   Prior to the twentieth century many teachers, particularly in the secondary schools and colleges chiefly employed oral examinations. However, this method of testing pupils was found to have serious limitations. The essay examination, found to be less time-consuming for the teacher, had an added advantage. The same questions and exercises could be given to all the pupils. The essay test has long been popular with teachers and is still widely used in the secondary schools and colleges.

In the early part of this century the essay examination came under attack by such pioneers in the measurement field as Starch and Elliott. In one study they noted that when the same set of English essay examinations was graded by different teachers, the grades ranged all the way from 50 to 98 per cent.[7] The range of grades assigned to a mathematics paper by presumably competent teachers was even greater, as Figure 14-1 shows.[8]

The essay examination is generally regarded by measurement specialists as less satisfactory than most types of objective tests. The subjectivity of scoring, referred to earlier, seriously affects its reliability. Moreover, the essay test is thought to have less validity in measuring student achievement because it rarely appraises the breadth of a pupil's knowledge. Students who possess a high degree of language facility usually have an advantage over those who have more difficulty in phrasing their answers, but who may have greater knowledge about the subject. All college students and teachers know of individuals who have developed techniques for interpreting essay questions in the light of their knowledge. Such students can often bluff their teachers into giving

---

[7] D. Starch and E. C. Elliott, "Reliability of the Grading of High-school Work in English," *School Review*, Vol. 20 (1912), pp. 442-457.

[8] D. Starch and E. C. Elliott, "Reliability of Grading Work in Mathematics," *School Review*, Vol. 21 (1913), pp. 254-259.

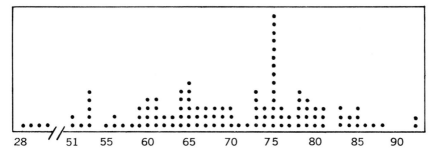

FIGURE 14-1. Grades Assigned To The Same Mathematics Paper By 115 Teachers Of Mathematics *(Starch and Elliott)*

them credit for an answer which is at best, on the periphery of the question. Also, because essay exams are time-consuming, the teacher must take a narrower sampling of pupil-achievement, thus lowering the reliability of her scores.

Critics of the essay examination also point out that studies generally show that most teacher-made essay tests tend to be just as limited to the appraisal of factual knowledge by recognition and recall as are objective tests. In spite of these findings, however, proponents of the essay examination argue that this form of testing enables the teacher to more carefully evaluate complex mental processes. They point out that many objective tests place a premium on recognition or memory. The essay examination is said to enable the teacher to determine how well a student can synthesize facts, generalize, apply what has been learned, and evaluate and interpret the contents of the course.

Weidemann [9] identified eleven different types of essay questions which elicit varying types of mental response. Arranged in order from simple to complex processes, they are:

1. What, who, when, which, where
2. list
3. outline
4. describe
5. contrast
6. compare
7. explain
8. discuss
9. develop
10. summarize
11. evaluate

It should be recognized that Weidemann's list does not automatically mean that test questions which include one word rather than another are automatically more complex. It is possible to elicit higher mental processes by the use of all of these terms.

[9] C. C. Weidemann, "Written Examination Procedures," *Phi Delta Kappan,* Vol. 16 (1933), pp. 78-83; also "Review of Essay Test Studies," *Journal of Higher Education,* Vol. 12 (1941), pp. 41-44.

Improving the essay examination. A number of suggestions have been made to assist the teacher in improving the essay test. One basic suggestion is that the teacher limit its use to the measurement of objectives it is best suited for. Whenever the objectives do not require highly complex mental processes, short-answer tests might be better employed. The reliability and validity of essay examinations can also be increased by increasing the number of items and reducing the amount of time required to answer each item. Some specialists also insist that students need to be instructed in the proper methods of taking examinations. Teaching students how to read and answer examination questions, instructing them in the criteria used in judging answers, and cautioning them in the observation of time limits will tend to help increase the accuracy of the measurement.

Probably the most serious weaknesses in the essay examination grow out of the scoring procedures teachers use. It has been pointed out previously that the teacher's conscious or unconscious biases, as well as the student's command of language often affect the grading of an essay test. Grading practices can be improved if the teacher adopts the following procedures.

1. Code test papers so that you do not know which student has written the paper being corrected.
2. Prepare a key which contains the major points which should be discussed for each item.
3. Do not take off points for misspelling or poor language structure unless correct language usage is a pertinent objective of the class.
4. Score the same question for all students; then go on to the next question. This procedure enables a closer comparison of one answer with another.
5. Utilize the full scale of points in scoring answers. For example, if 20 points is the top possible score for an answer, it should be used for the best papers. A number of teachers fail to employ the full scale because they think the student could always have written just a little more about the topic.

Teacher-made objective tests

Since World War I, teacher-made objective tests have become increasingly popular, particularly in the high school and college. Proponents of objective testing point out that because such measures consume less time and are easier to score they provide for more extensive sampling of pupil performance. Measurement specialists also stress the value of objective tests because they are less susceptible to the influence of language proficiency and expression than are essay examinations. On the other hand, critics of teacher-made objective tests claim that they tend to overemphasize factual knowledge and hence, encourage rote learning. Some teachers also believe that the short-answer test does not provide for the development of such abilities as expression, organization of facts, and applications of what has been learned. Another criticism is that most teachers lack sufficient knowledge to be able to construct good objective tests. It should be apparent that teachers find it easier to construct essay tests than objective tests.

Types of objective items. Objective test items are usually classified according to the type of mental response they elicit from students. The most commonly employed items in the classroom are the supply and selection types. The supply-type item commonly asks a question the answer to which the student must recall from his reading or classroom experience. The test item thus functions as a stimulus and the student must supply the correct response. This method of testing can be employed in a variety of subjects as shown by the following examples.

1. John had $1.50 and spent 49¢ for a notebook. How much money did he have left?
2. What two gases are the principal components of air?

Completion test. The completion test is one of the most frequently used supply-type of objective test. It is similar to the simple supply-type items shown above, but usually consists of a series of sentences from which certain words or phrases have been omitted. The task of the student is to successfully complete the sentences by supplying the proper word or phrase. The following are examples of a completion item:

Instruction: In the space provided, write the word or words which correctly complete the sentence.
The delegates met in the city of Philadelphia in May 1787   1. _____
for the purpose of amending the articles of _____. Alex-   2. _____
ander Hamilton represented New York, while _____   3. _____
and _____ represented Virginia.

or

Most of the laws on which both Democrats and Republicans chiefly depend at present to ward off major depressions were passed during the administration of President ————4———.

Specialists in measurement recommend that supply-type statements not be lifted from the text, that the omitted words represent important points rather than trivial details, and that statements be definite enough for the student to recognize what is being described. The teacher must also guard against providing the pupil with clues which can help him answer the question. An *a* or an *an* for example, immediately preceding a blank informs the knowledgeable student that the desired word starts with a consonant or a vowel. Many difficulties can be avoided if the teacher will couch supply-type items in the form of direct questions.

Alternate-response items.   The alternate-response form of classroom test is the most commonly used type of objective test. Despite its popularity, however, experts consider the true-false test to be one of the most difficult to construct because of the language itself. In an effort to avoid ambiguous statements, teachers often modify key words to make the meaning of statements clearer. However, such modifiers as *always, never, none,* and *all,* tend to serve as clues. Similarly, such qualitative words as *many, few,* and *important* tend to introduce an element of vagueness into the item which confuses some pupils.

Because true-false and other types of alternate-response tests are highly susceptible to guessing, considerable research has been devoted to the problem of discouraging guessing and to the development of correction formulas to treat the problem.

A further weakness of true-false items is that they tend to be highly factual and often emphasize the memorization of details. Many important concepts and generalizations do not lend themselves to strictly correct or incorrect answers. Also, the standard of truth or falsity differs from subject to subject. In natural science, for example, a statement is considered true only when it is always and unexceptionally true. A single exception makes it false. In social sciences a statement sometimes is considered true when it is generally true. A number of test specialists feel that the true-false test should rarely be used at the senior or graduate student level.

Multiple-choice tests.   A favorite method of testing among publishers of standardized tests is the multiple-choice type of test. The multiple-choice test is also gaining favor among teachers, particularly in the high schools and colleges. It consists of a number of items, each of which presents several responses. Only one of the choices is correct or more suitable than the others. The following are examples of an item taken from an arithmetic examination.

> If it took six men half a day to paint a house, how many days would it take the same six men to paint six houses provided they painted at the same speed?
>
>   a) six days
>   b) five days
>   c) four days
>   d) three days
>   e) two days

Which of these examples will have the same answer as the example in the box?

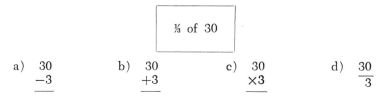

a) 30
   −3
   ——

b) 30
   +3
   ——

c) 30
   ×3
   ——

d) 30
   ——
    3

Many test specialists consider the multiple-choice test as one of the best and generally applicable forms of short-answer tests. Generally they are thought more difficult to construct than alternate-response tests. The multiple-choice item can elicit responses requiring complex mental processes as well as responses requiring recognition and recall.

A number of suggestions concerning the construction of such test items may prove beneficial. First, all responses should be plausible. Second, care must be taken to avoid furnishing grammatical clues. For example, the word *a* or *an* should be avoided as the last word in any statement preceding the foils or choices. Many teachers prefer to use a question rather than an incomplete statement to prevent the possibility of furnishing such clues. Besides, the direct question form represents a more natural type of item from the pupils' viewpoint. Third, many specialists feel that no less than four responses should be listed for each item. Five choices may even be more satisfactory. In four-choice items the probability of correct guessing is twenty-five per cent, while in five-choice items it is twenty per cent. As in the previous types of short-answer tests, considerable care must be taken to assure that the answers to a given item are not furnished in previous or subsequent items.

Matching tests. Another widely used form of the recognition test is the matching test. This test usually consists of two columns, each item in the first column being paired with a word or phrase in the second column. Generally it is considered good practice to provide a greater number of choices in the second column, so that students will be unable to answer certain items through the process of elimination. The matching test is thought to be particularly well adapted for evaluating specific associations like names and accomplishments of famous men, dates of important events, and locations of places. The following illustration is typical of matching tests.

Directions: Match a man with his contributions to the field of educational and psychological measurement by writing the letter preceding his name in the space provided.

(   ) Sociometry   A.   Karl Pearson
(   ) Genetic studies of genius   B.   Alfred Binet

( ) Original intelligence scale   C. Lewis Terman
( ) Correlation techniques   D. Jacob Moreno
( ) Factored theory of intelligence   E. Louis Thurstone
                                       F. David Wechsler
                                       G. J. McKeen Cattell

In constructing a matching test care should be taken to assure that the alternates provided are homogeneous. The test should neither be too short nor too long. If only a few items are used, guessing becomes a real problem. If more than ten to fifteen items are used, it often becomes a tedious exercise for the student.

Procedure and product evaluation. It is often beneficial for the teacher to evaluate certain procedures or sequences of movements made by pupils in undertaking complex processes or tasks. For example, the wood shop instructor might be interested in observing the procedures and methods a student employs in making a particular object. Closely related to procedural evaluation is product evaluation. The product, of course, is the finished piece of work. Teachers of industrial arts, art, business education, home economics and agriculture typically employ such methods of evaluation. Similarly speech teachers may evaluate both the content of a pupil's speech as well as his method of delivering it. Athletic coaches and physical instructors are concerned not only with the child's ability to perform a complex skill, but rate the speed, grace, and coordination displayed during the performance. Many similar educational experiences are evaluated by an examination of performance or product measurement. The *Easel Age Scale,*[10] which provides criteria for evaluating the growth and adjustment of kindergarten and primary-grade children, is an excellent example of this type of measure. The scale does not require special testing but rather provides for an evaluation of paintings normally produced in the classroom.

The use of standardized achievement tests

Although standardized tests were discussed in some detail in the previous chapter, it is well to point out that the results of standardized achievement tests often provide valuable information concerning pupil learning. It was noted previously that the present trend in school-wide testing is to provide information which is helpful to the classroom teacher. Concerning the use of such tests for assessing pupil achievements, Tyler states:

Perhaps the most common use, but certainly not the most significant, is in assessing the level of pupil achievement in the school subjects, grade by grade. One or more standardized tests in such fields as reading and arithmetic are

[10] *Easel Age Scale,* devised by Beatrice Lantz, California Test Bureau, Los Angeles, California.

given at several grade levels. Using the results, it is possible to: 1) estimate the amount of learning in these fields during the time since the same pupils were tested previously; 2) compare the indicated amount of learning (that is, the change in achievement since the previous measurement) with that indicated in previous years—this is one index of improvement in the school's educational accomplishments; and 3) compare the mean and the variability of the pupils' achievement in these fields with the mean and variability of similar schools in the city, state, region, or nation.[11]

It should be emphasized that the results of any standardized achievement test must be evaluated in terms of local conditions. In fact it is usually necessary to supplement the results of any tests with other types of information. Speaking to this point, Ebel maintains, "A teacher should not ask a standardized test to provide evidence on how well she has taught all things she has tried to teach, but only on the things that all teachers ought to have taught. For those achievements which are truly and rightly unique to a particular school or teacher, locally constructed tests are the best answer." [12]

Achievement batteries. In order to help teachers assess pupil achievements, a number of test publishers have developed coordinated series of tests (batteries), which provide a basis for evaluating pupil achievement longitudinally, or over a long period of time. The *Metropolitan Achievement Tests*, for example, are organized at five levels:

Primary I—for use in the latter half of Grade 1.
Primary II—for use in Grade 2.
Elementary—for use in Grades 3 and 4.
Intermediate—for use in Grades 5 and 6.
Advanced—for use in Grades 7, 8, and 9.

Such measures expand from grade level to grade level to accommodate the varied content and purposes of the curriculum. Table 14-1 illustrates the differences in each of the levels of the Metropolitan tests in content, number of items, and working time. The results of each child's performance on the various subtests of the battery can be profiled, as shown in Chapter 13, so that the teacher has a readily interpreted graphic presentation of the student's abilities.

Use by classroom teachers. The purpose of standardized achievement tests is to furnish dependable data about the level of the pupils' achievement in the different areas of the curriculum. Some of the most

[11] Ralph W. Tyler, "Educational Measurement, a Broad Perspective," *The National Elementary Principal*, Vol. 41 (1961), p. 8.
[12] Robert L. Ebel, "Standardized Achievement Tests . . . . Uses and Limitations," *The National Elementary Principal*, Vol. 41 (1961), p. 31.

TABLE 14-1. *Metropolitan Achievement Tests Series*: Subject Tests, Number of Items and Working Time (World Book Company)

SUBJECT	PRIMARY I		PRIMARY II		ELEMENTARY		INTERMEDIATE		ADVANCED	
	ITEMS	TIME	ITEMS	TIME	ITEMS	TIME	ITEMS	TIME	ITEMS	TIME
Word Knowledge	35	15	37	18	50	15	55	14	55	14
Word Discrimination	35	12	35	12	36	12	–	–	–	–
Reading	45	35	51	35	44	22	44	25	45	25
Spelling	–	–	30	10	40	20	55	17	55	17
Arithmetic: Concepts and Skills	63	23	72	25	–	–	–	–	–	–
Problem Solving & Concepts					35	26	48	35	48	35
Computation					47	30	48	38	45	35
Language: Usage					24	10	35	13	24	8
Punctuation and Capitalization					36	12	36	9	28	7
Parts of Speech—Grammar							10	4	20	10
Kinds of Sentences							–	–	10	4
Language Study Skills							28	16	28	16
Social Studies Information							60	20	60	20
Social Studies Study Skills							29	26	39	36
Science							55	20	55	20

important ways in which the classroom teacher uses standardized achievement test results are as follows:

1. To determine the achievement level of each student so as to plan an instructional program commensurate with his needs.
2. To compare present achievement with past achievement so as to evaluate rate of progress.
3. To ascertain the achievement level of each pupil as a partial basis for grades and reports.
4. To determine the outcome of an instructional program by comparing achievement at the beginning and end of an instruction period.
5. To serve as a basis for educational and vocational guidance.
6. To obtain data on the level and range of ability of the members of the class.
7. To help in the diagnosis of learning difficulties among the members of the class.

Some school officials and teachers tend to regard the norm as representing a level that must be achieved. In one school system the teachers, who taught in a school which drew children from the lowest socioeconomic level, felt that they failed because year after year their pupils' achievements were below the average for the city. After it was explained to them that their children were handicapped by a number of cultural deprivations which were reflected in their achievement test scores, they felt somewhat happier. Some school principals may also be unhappy when they discover that the achievement levels of the students in their schools fall below the national average as the norms on test batteries show. However, they fail to recognize that such factors as training and experience of teachers, length of instructional periods and the school year, adequacy of school equipment, and instructional materials are factors in establishing the norms.

In using a norm for comparison several important factors must be considered. The first is the type of norm available. Many achievement tests provide grade-level norms, that is, the score of a given pupil can be interpreted in terms of grade-equivalent. When this type of norm is used it is essential to know at what time of year the scores were obtained for the norm group. The writer once talked to an elementary-school principal who used an achievement test battery during the first month of the school year and then compared the scores of his pupils with norms based upon scores obtained at the end of the year. In essence he was penalizing his own students by nine months. Some tests do not provide grade-level equivalents but use special reporting devices such as standard scores, percentile ranks, decile ranks, and similar point scales. Although there is not sufficient space to discuss these questions in detail in this text, the student should learn to examine standardized tests to find out if he understands the nature of the norms provided.

Closely related to the type of norms is their comparability. Norms are often based upon a number of sampled populations. Obviously it is not very helpful to compare the algebra test scores of high school freshmen with those of college freshmen. Similarly, the teacher gains little by comparing the achievement scores of a culturally deprived youth with those of a child enrolled in an expensive private school. Unfortunately, a number of users of standardized tests fail to recognize that norms are most helpful when the populations from which they are derived are comparable to the group with which the test is employed.

Diagnostic analysis. Interpretation and diagnosis for remedial action are especially important for pupils falling below their average level of achievement in one or more sections of a standardized achievement test. Both standardized and teacher-made tests are useful to the teacher in ascertaining an individual's strengths and weaknesses as well as those of an entire class. The use of test results in diagnosing pupil weaknesses will be described in greater detail in Chapter 15. The following case study involving the reading achievements of a fifth-grade boy illustrates this use.

Harold, a fifth-grade child, seemed to enjoy arithmetic but did not like language arts. On the *Stanford Achievement Battery*, his arithmetic scores were slightly above the school mean but his reading and spelling scores were two grade levels below his grade placement. Additional informal reading tests indicated word recognition skills comparable to a second grade child's. He lacked knowledge of phonics, blends, and digraphs. His sight vocabulary was comparable to a third-grader's. With this information Harold's teacher was able to plan a remedial program using materials suited to his reading level and instructional needs.

Educational and vocational guidance. Standardized test results may be used to help pupils for instructional purposes. No less important is the use of tests in the educational guidance of pupils in junior- and senior-high school. Standardized test results are useful to teachers in selecting superior students for an enriched educational program and in selecting students for a simplified program.

Teachers and counselors can be helped in planning an educational program for each student by a knowledge of his profile on a battery of educational and psychological tests. If the achievement test is used sufficiently early, difficulties can be determined and remedial work undertaken to help the student. The test results, presented in the form of a profile chart, help the student determine his strengths and weaknesses, thereby furnishing him with useful and dependable data for making educational and vocational decisions.

The testing program

The importance of testing in the school program is well recognized by teachers, administrators, and school psychologists. However, tests should not be administered simply because "it is the thing to do." A successful testing program will require, first of all, that the tests be recognized as useful in the total educational program. Thus, teachers, as well as others concerned with the educational process must be directly concerned with the testing program. Concerning the use of tests Wrightstone states: "There is a test for almost every area of a student's life, and—properly used—these tests can be of great service in helping us answer questions about a child's ability, behavior, and special skills." [13]

Planning the program. The decision about the measuring instrument to be employed will be determined by the objectives of the school. If the purpose is to determine how well the pupil can organize learned materials and present them in writing, the essay examination should be used. However, if the purpose is to discover if pupils remember facts, then, certain short-form objective tests are most suitable. There is no one best form of test for all purposes. Thus, educational objectives must be the start of any testing program.

As is true with other aspects of the teaching and learning program, a number of factors must be considered before a school or system can achieve maximum benefits from any testing program. It is generally considered a wise practice to organize a school-wide committee on tests and measurements which will take a leadership role in planning the program. All grade levels of teachers should be represented, as well as such specialized personnel as the school counselor, visiting teacher, and principal. Similarly, all of the teachers should have a voice in planning the program. After the program is adopted the school-wide committee might well be asked to assume responsibility for it. It should be recognized that any effective testing program is time-consuming. If the teachers are to have a major role in the development and administration of the program, they must be convinced of its value. Stevenson notes that time must be spent to do each of the following:

1. To involve the classroom teacher in developing the program, selecting the tests, and establishing testing policies
2. To orient the students to the purposes and use of the test
3. To administer the test

[13] J. Wayne Wrightstone, "Tests are What They Test," *Journal of the National Education Association,* Vol. 47 (1958), p. 222.

4. To correct the test, or better still, provide for clerical help to correct the test
5. To interpret the test and analyze the strengths and weaknesses of individual students
6. To make use of the results and give students the individual attention they need as indicated by the test.[14]

Testing for guidance and evaluation. Although the standardized tests most commonly employed in public schools are designed to appraise academic achievement and scholastic aptitude, instruments are available to measure almost every phase of human behavior. Many school systems have developed well-planned, continuous programs of annual testing. Usually such systematic programs provide for a test or test battery to be administered at each grade level to furnish information about each child's educational progress. A typical program might provide for a readiness test at the beginning of first grade or at the end of kindergarten, a reading test which estimates the reading achievements of pupils at grade two, and a primary achievement battery at grade three with measures of reading, arithmetic, and spelling. At the intermediate grades the achievement batteries are broadened to sample achievement in language arts, social studies and science. At the junior-high level scholastic aptitude and achievement measures may be used to diagnose a student's difficulties and to assist him in educational and vocational planning. At the high-school level additional batteries serve to help school personnel and vocational counselors. It is now fairly common to administer scholastic aptitude tests to eleventh and twelfth graders to help them in planning programs of higher education.

Traxler has summarized the recent developments in testing for guidance and evaluation as follows:

1. Guidance and individual evaluation have become the main reasons for school testing programs.
2. A substantial degree of agreement has developed concerning the nature of and steps in this kind of program.
3. Many new measurement instruments for use in evaluation and guidance have recently been made available but as yet little is known of their relative value.
4. The use of evaluative and guidance tests is increasing at a rate so rapid as to create doubt as to whether training in the use of tests is keeping pace.
5. New methods of machine scoring and data processing are spurring the development of testing programs for evaluation and guidance.
6. Numerous schools are making a strong effort to promote greater teacher- and counselor-understanding of an involvement in testing programs.
7 There is an increasing tendency among schools to report test results to par-

[14] Margaret Stevenson, "The Role of the Classroom Teacher in School Testing Programs," *The 16th Yearbook of the National Council on Measurements Used in Education.* New York: 1959, p. 45.

ents and pupils along with explanations of the meaning of these data for future planning.

8. An especially important new development is federal participation in financial support of testing and guidance.[15]

Administering and scoring the test. At the time the test is planned and prepared the teacher should decide upon the answers which will be regarded as correct. While this is fairly easy to do with short-answer tests, it is more difficult to do with essay tests. Generally any lack of validity in the essay examination stems from the subjectivity and inconsistency of scoring procedures. Certain practices can help to control these factors. As we mentioned earlier, the teacher should plan to use the upper and lower score limits assigned to each question to be graded. Similarly, some teachers always give part credit, perhaps five points, for any answer. If this procedure is followed the scoring limits are not zero to twenty, but five to eighteen. In scoring essay tests it is often helpful to group the papers into three or five piles according to the worthiness of answers. Then the piles can be reorganized into additional categories if further refinement is desired, or simply weighted as they are. It usually is a wise practice to keep the scoring procedures as simple as possible to save time and avoid the possibility of clerical error.

In scoring a short-answer test the teacher may desire to use a "correction formula" to offset the effects of chance. Such correction formulas may function to discourage certain students from guessing but it is likely that those who are inclined to guess will continue to do so despite the penalty. Many writers feel that correction formulas complicate scoring procedures and only increase the spread of scores without changing the relative positions of pupils. Since the correction formula suggests the unfortunate implication that correct answers are largely due to guess work, and since the formula makes a difference only when individuals omit questions, it is sometimes regarded as an unprofitable refinement.

One additional word concerning the administration of the test. A teacher should decide in advance the types of questions he will answer during the testing period. Generally these should be concerned only with directions which are confusing to the student or with ambiguous items. Many students seek to get hints regarding the answers to the test itself. Again, it is generally assumed that the teacher will be generous with the time allowances for taking the test. Few teacher-made tests, then, are speed tests.

Uses and misuses of standardized tests. It is very important for teachers to know the proper procedure and ethics in administering and

[15] Arthur E. Traxler, "Testing for Guidance and Evaluation," *The 16th Yearbook of the National Council on Measurements Used in Education.* New York: 1959, p. 5.

scoring standardized tests. Each teacher should be familiar with the test or tests used at his grade level, and should analyze the tests in terms of the skills and content tested and norms provided. Assistance should be provided to help teachers to better analyze the results statistically and to construct profiles of individual and group abilities. It is also essential that teachers recognize the number of variables which may affect test performance. Such factors as a pupil's reading ability, the emotional impact of testing, the motivations of a pupil regarding the test, and numerous other variables should be understood.

Essentially, teachers must recognize that tests can be helpful tools, but cannot be panaceas. They provide an excellent basis for helping the teacher individualize instruction and for guiding the learning of her children. The following misuses or questionable uses of standardized tests, developed by Traxler, are valuable.

1. Tests are used to appraise teacher quality and effectiveness without controlling all extraneous variables. This has perhaps done more than anything else to reduce confidence in tests and retard educational-measurement programs.
2. Tests are given carelessly without meticulous following of the directions for administering under which they were standardized.
3. Tests are overemphasized and students are coached for them. Coaching is not only largely a waste of time, but it detracts from the regular course work.
4. Importance is attached to small differences in score, although a few points' change in a pupil's score from one test to another is of no significance. In connection with some of the newer tests, such as the Cooperative School and College Ability Tests and the Sequential Tests of Educational Progress, a procedure is made available for interpreting the score, not as a point but as a fairly broad band.
5. IQ's are regarded as fixed and unchangeable. Because of differences in the composition of different intelligence tests, because of differences in rate of mental growth, and because of lack of complete reliability of tests, changes of as much as 10 or 15 points in IQ from one intelligence test to another are common and normal.
6. Single scores are employed in isolation. A score on one achievement test, for example, has little meaning unless it is compared with earlier results on the same test or with results of scholastic-aptitude tests or with scores on another achievement test.
7. Test results are used authoritatively in counseling pupils. The student or his parents should never be told that the results of tests show definitely that he ought to study in a certain field or that he should enter this or that field of work. As a student matures, he should be helped to understand the results of his tests, but he should take main responsibility for his own decisions with the help of his family and the school.[16]

---

[16] Arthur E. Traxler, "Standardized Tests," *National Education Association Journal*, Vol. 48 (1962), p. 20.

Effects of tests on children. Although some evidence shows that children who are tested regularly are likely to be more motivated toward learning and tend to achieve somewhat higher levels than those who are not systematically evaluated, it should also be recognized that school progress and success represent a source of worry and anxiety to many children. Among middle class children, particularly, anxiety about school marks or the possibilities of failure is common.

It seems likely that the increased use of standardized and teacher-made tests may cause excessive anxieties in some children. Anxiety also may adversely affect the child's test performance.

Sarason studied children's reactions to tests in grades one through six as well as the results of such attitudes on test performance. His findings may be summarized as follows:

1. Test anxiety is by no means an infrequent occurrence among elementary-school children. The level of test anxiety tends to increase with grade.
2. The higher the text anxiety, the lower are the scores on conventional group measures of intelligence. This negative correlation between anxiety and intelligence-test score is significantly reduced when the intelligence test employed is more "game-like" than "test-like."
3. When pairs of children are matched for grade, sex, and IQ, but one of each pair is high-anxious while the other is low-anxious, the problem-solving performance of the high-anxious children tends to be significantly inferior to that of the low-anxious children.
4. Test-anxious children are at the greatest disadvantage when they are not sure what is expected of them and when they are expected to function independently. When the problem-solving situation partially satisfies pupils' needs for direction and dependence, there is little difference in the performance of high- and low-anxious children; in fact, the high-anxious children tend to do better than low-anxious children.
5. The test-anxious child is one who tends to be anxious about many things, has a derogatory self-picture, and has a predominant tendency to blame himself for failure. There are differences in the parent-child relationships between high- and low-anxious children. The mother of the high-anxious child is one who is much concerned with what is right and wrong and with what other people think of herself and her child. She discourages the expression of aggression in her child and tends to keep the child in a dependent relationship.
6. It has been assumed by many that test anxiety is affected by social class; that is, that as one goes up the social classes there is increasing emphasis on school performance and intellectual achievement, with a corresponding increase in the number of children who experience anxiety about tests. Our findings cast much doubt on such an assumption. Test anxiety seems to occur with equal frequency in different social classes.
7. Sex differences are significant in anxiety. Girls admit to more anxiety than do boys. Despite this, however, the predicted differences between high- and low-anxious children are found more consistently among boys than girls.[17]

[17] Seymour B. Sarason, "What Research Says About Test Anxiety in Elementary School Children," *National Education Association Journal,* Vol. 48 (1959), pp. 26-27.

Reporting pupil progress

It is generally accepted that the school and home should coordinate their efforts to assure optimal child growth and development. An essential facet of educational evaluation is reporting pupil progress. The traditional report card is generally recognized as inadequate for this purpose. The mere assigning of numerical or letter grades which presumably represent a child's progress leaves considerable to be desired as a medium of communication. It generally is recognized that some form of report cards are essential, but should be supplemented with other reports, individual letters to parents, and teacher-parent conferences.

Purposes of reporting pupil progress.   Despite a common agreement that the school should provide some means of reporting pupil progress, considerable difference seems to exist regarding the purposes, content, and nature of the reporting form. Alexander contends that of the various and conflicting purposes of reporting systems, two seem to emerge which are clear-cut and justifiable.

1. Parents should have information about their children's progress and standing in school. If this information can be given in a way that promotes understanding of home and school, all the better. But the information needs to be sufficiently factual, even if disappointing, so that the mother and father can use it to understand and help their child. Certainly such information at the high-school level should also be available to college-admission officials and prospective employers.
2. Ultimately, it is even more important that boys and girls have the best information available in understandable form about their own progress. To understand themselves, to capitalize on their strong points, and to remedy, if possible, their weaker ones, they need to know what these strengths and weaknesses are. Many types of evaluative data are needed for this purpose in addition to a six- or twelve-weeks' set of marks, but the accumulation and summary of facts at reporting time may be very useful in the pupil's own plan for continued, improved progress.[18]

Correspondence with parents.   A number of schools have developed systems of reporting which call on the teacher to write a short paragraph about the child. Often such reports are of little or no value because the teacher sits up the night before report cards are due and tries to think of suitable phrases. The writer has received a report for one of his children which said: "Betty is an asset to our group." While this is flattering to a parent, it conveys little information which can help the parents or teacher coordinate their efforts. Similarly, teachers often seem hesitant to write anything detrimental or negative about a child.

[18] William M. Alexander, "Reporting to Parents—Why? What? How?" *National Education Association Journal*, Vol. 48 (1959), p. 16.

Closely related to correspondence with parents is the interview between parent and teacher. A number of teachers shy away from frank discussions with parents because they fear unpleasantness. The interview, as well as correspondence, should be oriented to the recognition that the mutual goal of school and home is to help the child to progress within the limits of his capabilities. Teachers must recognize that parents are ego-involved in their children's success and failures, but should not hesitate to report both the "good" and the "bad." Failure to do so actually hampers the child, for an integrated and coordinated program of assistance is unlikely to be forthcoming.

Characteristics of good report cards. Regardless of how report cards have been revised or regardless of their format, they still constitute the major means of reporting pupil progress. Although educators continually discuss and debate the value of such reports, it seems safe to say that in most school systems report cards are here to stay. Generally the report card should be a realistic appraisal of student progress. It should also be sufficiently clear to parents to enable them to understand the progress their children are making.

Findley believes that the reporting form can be most helpful when it accomplishes the following:

1. emphasizes *specific* improvable skills, understandings, habits, and attitudes. Particularly in the primary grades is it helpful to list and check off the degree of success with which the child is achieving each of several goals within such broad fields as reading, arithmetic, etc. Marks in these broad areas alone convey no clear meaning.
2. is comprehensive, balanced, yet simple. It should contain some indication of meeting standards in classroom behavior as well as in scholastic achievement. This should be reported separately from scholastic grades, not mixed in with it. A separate grade or separate grades for "school citizenship" should be reported and be given equal stress with scholastic grades in discussions with parents. Such additional information should be presented simply. Elaborate systems of separate grades for absolute achievement and achievement relative to capability have been tried and discarded.
3. is positive, constructive—something the parents and child can "accept" gracefully. In the report, as well as in any conference, it should be possible to indicate some point of strength, some growth, some gleam of hope.
4. is accurate and objective. Marks need to be given in an atmosphere of honest appraisal, holding one's feelings well in hand. Do not give favorable marks for encouragement or unfavorable marks to indicate displeasure with effort. Such practices boomerang and make all uncertain.
5. involves the child in his own interest, thereby helping him mature through understanding himself and internalizing goals and standards. Get him into the act to the extent that he can take part.
6. is consistent with the school's total program of instruction and promotion and bears a recognized relationship to past and present practices. This means that marks should indicate the possibility of retention in grade. It also means

that "old fashioned" letter grades are to be preferred to newer schemes of S and U, or H, S and U. Most users move back after a time to the standard letter grades.

7. is consistent from subject to subject, grade to grade, teacher to teacher, school to school. Marks should be subject to administrative control because of their public relations ramifications. A parent is understandably confused and angered if one teacher gives A and another gives C for the same quality of work in successive grades, within a grade, between schools, or between subjects.

8. makes only reasonable demands on teachers timewise. Elaborate letters and reports have come and gone. Add a note or remark here or there. Have a space on the report for this. But let it go at that. New terms and ideas to express similar facts from report to report are hard to think up and serve no useful purpose.[19]

SUMMARY

If the teacher is to evaluate the outcomes of instruction in valid and reliable ways it is necessary that he have clear-cut definable objectives and goals against which to judge the progress of pupils. The formulation of such objectives is a difficult task. Although there have been many refinements in measurement techniques and an increased use of other methods of pupil evaluation, the teacher-made test remains one of the central methods for evaluating student progress.

In spite of its importance in education, numerous teachers at all grade levels have received no formal instruction in measurement. The intimate relationship of measurement to learning, however, makes it essential that teachers become more familiar with the principles and techniques of measurement and evaluation. Teacher-made tests can be improved if teachers devote more care to each of the following stages: (1) planning, (2) preparing, (3) administering and scoring, and (4) evaluating. Some basic considerations in each of these areas was discussed. Both short-answer and objective tests are commonly employed by teachers. A number of principles concerning each were discussed and suggestions were offered for improving these instruments.

The problems of reporting pupil progress should first take into account the purposes of reporting such progress. Correspondence with parents along with interviews are frequently used to report pupil progress; however, the report card remains the major device for reporting such progress. What characterizes a useful and helpful device for reporting progress has been presented by Findley and is summarized in this chapter.

[19] Warren G. Findley, "Report Cards," unpublished talk to Atlanta Public School teachers, 1958.

Problems and Exercises

1. Assume you are the instructor of this course. Construct five true-false, five multiple-choice, and five completion items based on the contents of this chapter.
2. Consult the Mental Measurements Yearbook edited by O. K. Buros. Select and evaluate an achievement-test battery commonly used at the intermediate grade levels.
3. Discuss the relative merits and shortcomings of the grading system used in your college or university. How would you improve the procedures?
4. What methods for evaluating the development of attitudes in science would you recommend?
5. How would you evaluate a student's progress in a teacher-education program?
6. How should a teacher provide for individual differences in ability, interests, and motivation in the evaluation of pupil achievements?
7. Discuss why teachers should or should not recognize different abilities in evaluating pupil progress.
8. Secure a copy of a report card used by some school with which you are familiar. What objectives of the school can you infer from the information given on the report card? Evaluate this report card in light of suggestions set forth in this chapter.
9. A seventh-grade pupil made the following grade level scores on a standardized test: Paragraph meaning, 6.0; word meaning, 7.5; spelling, 7.2; language, 8.2; arithmetic reasoning, 6.6; arithmetic computation, 8.0; social studies, 7.2; science, 7.5; study skills, 5.4. Prepare an educational profile, based on these scores.
10. Evaluate the results of the standardized test presented in Exercise 9. Where are the students strengths? Where are his weaknesses? What other information would be useful in better understanding the basis for this unevenness of educational development?

Selected Readings

AHMANN, J. S., and GLOCK, M. D., *Evaluating Pupil Growth* (Boston: Allyn and Bacon, 1959), Ch. 9.

BARON, Denis, and BERNARD, H. W., *Evaluation Techniques for Classroom Teachers* (New York: McGraw-Hill Book Co., 1958), Ch. 13.

BRADFIELD, J. M., and MOREDOCK, H. S., *Measurement and Evaluation in Education* (New York: The Macmillan Co., 1957), Ch. 9.

CRONBACH, Lee J., *Educational Psychology*, 2nd ed. (New York: Harcourt, Brace & World, 1963), Ch. 16.

LINDGREN, Henry C., *Educational Psychology in the Classroom*, 2nd ed. (New York: John Wiley & Sons, 1962), Chs. 14 and 15.

SMITH, Henry P., *Psychology in Teaching*, 2nd ed. (Englewood Cliffs: Prentice-Hall, 1962), Ch. 12.

THOMAS, R. M., *Judging Student Progress* (New York: Longmans, Green and Co., 1954), Ch. 13.

THOMPSON, George G., GARDNER, Eric F., and DI VESTA, Francis J., *Educational Psychology* (New York: Appleton-Century-Crofts, 1959), Ch. 4.

THORNDIKE, Robert L., and HAGEN, E., *Measurement and Evaluation in Psychology and Education* (New York: John Wiley and Sons, 1961), Ch. 11.

TRAVERS, R. M. W., *Educational Measurement* (New York: The Macmillan Co., 1955, Ch. 4.

WEITZMAN, Ellis, and McNAMARA, W. J., *Constructing Classroom Examinations* (Chicago: Science Research Associates, 1949), Chs. 2-7.

WOOD, D. A., *Test Construction* (Columbus: Chas. E. Merrill Books, Inc., 1960), Ch. 4.

CHAPTER 15

Studying the Individual Child

If a teacher wishes to accomplish her educational objectives, she usually finds that she must study the individual students in her class despite the quality of her training in educational methods and procedures, her mastery of her subject, or her eagerness to instruct. We have already pointed out that children grow and develop according to certain fundamental principles and that wide differences are to be seen in the rate of development, behavioral characteristics, and aptitudes and abilities of any group of children or adults. Despite the criteria of size, chronological age, sex, and achievements which society commonly uses in judging children, a wide range of differences must be expected. During the twentieth century significant advances were made in the scientific study of children. A better understanding of these methods should serve to help the teacher accomplish her goals. If any teacher hopes to succeed in her task, she must study the individual members of her group.

INDIVIDUAL DIFFERENCES

As a result of the interaction between the biological heredity of a child and the environmental influences which serve to foster or deter, mold and develop him, no two individuals are ever identical. Wide variations are noticeable prior to school age, and such differences tend to be maintained and even increase as the child progresses through adolescence into maturity. Often teachers tend to overgeneralize about the characteristics of an age group. For example, it is common to think that all adolescents identify closely with their peer groups. While it is undoubtedly true that most adolescents seek the approbation of their peers, a casual observation of a typical high-school class will reveal a number of boys and girls who still identify more closely with adults than with their classmates.

How children differ

Anyone who has ever visited a classroom or observed a group of children at play has noticed a wide range of individual differences in such characteristics as size, body build, coordination, and personal-social behavior. Individual differences can readily be seen in a study of the characteristics of a group of fifteen fourth-grade children. These data, selected from the files of a school located in an underprivileged area, are shown in Table 15-1. The chronological ages of the group range from 96 months to 117 months; the IQ's range from 84 to 120. Scholastic achievements reveal a wide range of abilities. Such measures of personality as the *Manifest Anxiety Test* and the *Self-Concept Scale* reveal variations in adjustment and in the way children view themselves. No child in the group can be regarded as typical or average. The concept of average is fundamentally a mathematical term, a statistical rather than a real-life child. The teacher should bear this in mind in her work. Take for example, three girls, Betty, Janice, and Sally, who comprise a group. Although each girl is enrolled in the same grade, each differs from the other in ability, achievements, interests, and other personal characteristics. Betty is the oldest of four children from a lower middle-class family background. Last summer she worked in a cannery during the vacation period to obtain money for her clothes and other expenses. Her younger siblings are all boys and she has learned to give and take in social situations. She is popular with her peers, musically talented, and active in the youth programs of her church. Her grades are average, but her teachers consider her to be emotionally stable and socially mature.

Janice, however, is an only child from a lower-class home. She often works afternoons as a baby sitter for neighbors. She receives no financial allowance from her parents. She seems to limit her friendships to two girls but is active in group activities while at school. Janice has an IQ of 98 but is achieving academically somewhat below the class average. She is considered to be somewhat emotionally immature and doesn't accept responsibility for her actions.

Sally is the youngest of five children from a lower-class family. Her parents are separated and Sally resides with her mother, who is employed in a bakery. She has average intelligence and scholastically, does average work. She is reserved and rarely enters into play activities unless invited. She seems to have developed a close relationship with another girl, but rarely interacts with other members of the class. Her teachers report that the child is emotionally stable but quiet and somewhat withdrawn.

Scientific methods of studying children

Although children have been studied and observed for many years, it is likely that the behavior of each generation of children and adolescents

TABLE 15-1. Some Characteristics of a Group of Fourth-Grade Children *

NAME	CHRONOLOG-ICAL AGE (MONTHS)	I.Q.	READING GRADE	ARITHMETIC GRADE	SPELLING GRADE	MANIFEST ANXIETY	SELF CONCEPT
Don	107	103	2.1	2.2	2.7	18	68
David	117	109	3.6	3.1	2.2	30	73
Howard	100	104	3.2	3.3	3.9	17	77
Carl	106	103	2.9	3.6	3.6	15	58
Henry	114	87	3.3	3.4	3.4	12	89
Jerry	113	100	3.4	3.1	2.5	18	61
Larry	100	119	4.2	4.1	4.0	13	79
Ronald	108	116	3.1	3.3	3.1	12	83
Speck	96	113	3.7	4.2	2.4	7	81
Betty	99	108	3.5	3.5	3.1	25	73
Jean	117	89	2.8	2.7	3.4	29	72
Gail	104	84	3.3	3.1	3.4	17	75
Janice	98	120	3.4	2.2	2.9	34	84
Peggy	106	88	2.7	3.2	2.7	24	69
Sally	101	118	3.8	3.3	3.4	20	79

* These data are taken from studies on file in the Division of Educational Psychology, University of Georgia, of children in the public schools of Athens (Georgia). The names of the children have been changed.

371

is a cause of bewilderment to adults. Throughout history numerous writers have suggested methods to train, educate, and rear children. From the time of Plato, who proposed a system of education based upon the varying potentialities of children, through Rousseau, who stressed the innate goodness of the child, writers have attempted to grapple with the problem. Despite such interest in the subject, however, the scientific study of children cannot be said to have begun very much before the latter part of the 18th century. During that period a number of books were published which reported the results of observations made of the growth and development of individual children (usually the writer's offspring or relatives). Toward the end of the nineteenth century, Sir Francis Galton studied differences found among groups of individuals and used statistics to analyze the data. As a result of Galton's statistical treatment, differences among groups of individuals could be analyzed more systematically.

In the United States, G. Stanley Hall pioneered in the study of large groups of children. In one of his early studies he employed questionnaires and checklists to ascertain what children knew when they first entered school.[1] Hall also studied adolescents at a later date and furnished a vivid description of adolescents in his writings. During the twentieth century a number of laboratories were set up to study children. These child-study laboratories have furnished valuable information about children at different stages in their development.

Various aspects of child development and behavior have received increased attention in recent decades. The methods developed to study children during the latter part of the nineteenth and early twentieth century have since been refined and new techniques have been created. A vast array of research studies dealing with school-age children are available and serve to furnish parents and teachers with insights which lead to a better understanding of child behavior and development. Although the classroom teacher is not likely to become a research worker, it is important for him to know and understand the various methods researchers employ. An understanding of the procedures employed in studying children will help the teacher evaluate the results of investigations and experiments as well as help her to increase the reliability and validity of classroom methods of studying children. It is important to recognize that the complexity of the human organism and the myriad factors which influence its growth and development have prevented any one method of child study from becoming accepted as the major or most important technique of research. Present-day studies seem to be moving away from the generalized observations of the nineteenth century, however, and it appears, more emphasis is being placed upon systematic recording of specific patterns while certain other factors are controlled.

[1] G. Stanley Hall, "The Content of Children's Minds on Entering School," *Pedagogcial Seminary,* Vol. 1 (1891), pp. 139-173.

The development of statistical methods for analyzing and interpreting data has also resulted in more precise and specific evaluation. All of the procedures described in the following pages have contributed to our knowledge of child and educational psychology.

The genetic or longitudinal method. The genetic or longitudinal method of studying children is concerned with the development of a particular characteristic or attribute throughout a given period of time. The method seeks to ascertain the day to day, week to week, or month to month relationship of some specific attribute in the individual's pattern and growth rate. This method can be utilized whether the research worker studies a single individual or a group of individuals. It has been used to investigate such factors as the development of muscular control in children, the relationship of height to weight at different chronological ages, and the relationship of the length of appendages such as legs and arms to torse size at various stages of development. Gesell's work with infants and young children, as well as the research conducted at Ohio State University in the 1930's and at the University of Iowa are excellent examples of the contributions made by studies which utilize this approach. Alfred Binet's contributions to intelligence testing, particularly with respect to the use of the mental-age concept, grew out of a recognition that differences in intellectual function and ability to differentiate can be observed in children at various stages of their development. One of the most famous examples of the genetic method of studying children is Terman's long-term investigation of a group of very bright California school children. In a series of studies extending over a period of more than twenty years, Terman followed a group of elementary-school children from childhood to maturity. As a result of this monumental work, many popularly held beliefs concerning the "intellectual genius" or "gifted" child were found erroneous and were revised.

Genetic or longitudinal studies, by their very nature, require long-term continuous study. Many research workers are unable to devote the long periods of time, often years, that are needed to make painstaking and continuing observations. Others feel that they cannot wait the long time this type of research requires for answers to their questions. In many of the problems involving children of school age, the mobility of the population and the difficulties in securing repeated and systematic observations preclude the use of this procedure.

The normative-survey method. Following the early studies of Galton in England and Hall in the United States, students of child psychology employed the normative-survey method for studying large groups of individuals. If the genetic method may be characterized as longitudinal, the normative-survey method of investigation may be characterized as cross-sectional. Essentially the normative-survey method attempts to study one or more characteristics in a group which is thought to be a representative sample of the total population. If a researcher wanted to know how the height and weight of ten-year-old girls differed from the height and weight of ten-year-old boys, he might determine these differences by obtaining a representative sample of ten-year-olds and then weigh and measure each of the selected children. Through the use of standard statistical techniques he could determine the averages and variances of each of the two groups. Similarities and differences thus could be found. Another scholar might seek to compare the mathematics achievements of fifth-grade boys and girls. A third research worker might seek to discover whether the typical six-year-old child can perform certain hand-eye coordinated tasks which are related to the mastery of hand-writing skills.

Normative-survey methods are employed in many child studies and many techniques are used to accumulate the necessary data: questionnaires, interviews, scales and tests. A criticism sometimes made of the normative-survey is that the sample which is studied rarely satisfies all of the criteria of randomness and representativeness deemed necessary for proper statistical analysis. In most of the child studies where the normative-survey is used, lack of knowledge of the characteristics of the total population (or universe) prevents the investigator from properly testing the sample to determine whether the obtained data is representative of the total group being studied. As a result of this grave limitation, normative-surveys are often criticized by other social and physical scientists. In the fields of child psychology and education the validity of the generalizations made from many studies employing the normative-survey technique are somewhat suspect.

Experimental methods. These methods have been employed in many investigations of the behavior and development of children. Two general types of experimental methods are used in studying children: the single group and the parallel group. The single-group method is used in studies of single individuals or group of individuals, while the parallel-group method is used in studies of two or more groups. Essentially the experimental methods seek to test a specific hypothesis by carefully controlling all variables except the one being studied.

Watson and Rayner [2] used the single-group method in demonstrating the conditionability of emotional responses during infancy. A single infant was used as the subject. Gordon employed a single-group method in

[2] J. B. Watson and R. Rayner, "Conditioned Emotional Reactions," *Journal of Experimental Psychology*, Vol. 3 (1920), pp. 1-4.

Individual testing is an important part of the guidance program in good educational practice

studying children's concept of the self. In the investigation by Gordon,[3] teams of observers were assigned to judge individual elementary-school children who were unaware that they were being observed. The results of these observations showed that such observers tend to agree upon the personal meaning of the behavior observed. Lippitt [4] used one-way vision screens for observing the effects of democratic and autocratic social atmospheres on the behavior of children. The parallel-group method of experimentation was employed in this study. A distinguishing feature of the experimental methods is the active role the experimenter plays

[3] Ira J. Gordon, "Inferring Children's Concepts of Self: Interobserver Reliability." Paper presented at the Southeastern Psychological Association, St. Augustine, Florida, April 24, 1959.

[4] R. Lippitt, "An Experimental Study of the Effect of Democratic and Authoritarian Group Atmosphere," *University of Iowa Studies in Child Welfare*, Vol. 16 (1940), No. 3.

as he attempts to control the variables in the environmental situation which the subjects are exposed to.

An example of a problem that could well be studied by the parallel-group method should reveal more clearly the nature of the experimental methods. Suppose a research worker hypothesized that children who have the benefits of a daily program of physical education in the primary grades would develop better muscular coordination than those who did not. The experimenter would probably select two groups of children for the study. Both groups would be equated; i.e., would be approximately equal in as many variables as are feasible or deemed necessary. The most likely variables would be sex, age, home conditions, present health condition, and muscular coordination. After the experimenter felt that he had two groups of approximately the same caliber, he would begin the study. He would hope that both groups encountered the same general treatment and experienced the same general conditions except for one thing. One group (the experimental group) would receive the planned program of physical education. The other group (the control group) would not receive physical education. At the end of the planned period of study, the experimenter would study the muscular coordination of both groups and compare the results. If the control group displays muscular coordination that is little or no different from the experimental group, the hypothesis is probably wrong. It is also possible, of course, that the criteria of evaluation were not clearly differentiated, or that important interviewing variables were not controlled sufficiently well.

The experimental method might also be used to ascertain the effectiveness of a particular method of instruction, to determine the value of more frequent tests on learning, or to discover whether students who are taught by courses which include homework learn more than those who are taught by courses without homework.

It can be readily seen that applying the experimental method is difficult because many conditions must be controlled. Even after a successful experimental study, the hypothesis cannot be accepted as true. It must be repeated many times before it can be even cautiously accepted. The experimental approach, however, is likely to become more popular in future studies of children.

The case study. The case study or clinical method of child study has developed largely as a result of the efforts of specialists to understand and to assist children who have special problems. It is widely used by child psychologists, child psychiatrists, remedial specialists, speech correctionists, counselors, and social workers. The procedure may be viewed as somewhat analogous to the genetic method in reverse; i.e., it starts from the present and delves into the past developmental history of the particular child. Essentially the case-study method seeks to study intensively a wide range of factors which may have contributed to or had some bearing upon the development of the child. Usually it is hoped that such intensive study will reveal something about the etiology of the child's difficulty besides furnishing clues for proper handling. Although complete case studies ideally require a team approach involving a number of specialists, school teachers are finding it increasingly helpful to gather more accurate and pertinent information about their pupils. The typical case study generally includes the following information.

1. *Family history.* Usually information is obtained regarding the physical and mental health of the various members of the family. The health history is often important in helping to determine whether the child's present condition might be due to genetic factors, such as heredity. Instances of mental retardation, susceptibility to heart disease, and cases of mental illness should be noted.
2. *Prenatal and birth history.* As human development begins with conception, it is important to learn something about the environmental conditions which might have affected the child prior to birth. Infections, injuries, toxemias, poor nutrition, or other complications during pregnancy may affect the post-natal development of the child. Similarly, unusual birth conditions, such as prolonged labor, prematurity, difficult delivery, may have resulted in brain damage or otherwise may have affected the child's development.
3. *Developmental history.* An understanding of the child's past developmental patterns often is helpful in understanding present problems and conditions. A knowledge of the child's motor, language, and physical development usually is valuable. Illnesses and injuries, food habits, toilet training all provide valuable clues.
4. *Personal and social history.* A knowledge of the child's social adjustments helps the clinician or teacher to better understand his present needs and behavior. Habits of eating, sleeping, playing, should be noted. Skills he has mastered should be recorded. A knowledge of the child's abilities, interests, likes and dislikes, play activities, all help to present a helpful background for understanding the immediate problem.
5. *Educational history.* The progress the child has made in his school work and the difficulties he has encountered as he progressed through kindergarten and each grade provide valuable information in diagnosing his problems. General achievement, results of standardized tests, grades attained, attendance record, special abilities or disabilities are important factors to consider.

Frequently it is necessary to obtain additional data about the child, his needs, and his condition from physical, neurological, psychological, and psychiatric examinations. However, although the case study is invaluable, it has certain limitations. First, it is time-consuming and is limited to the investigation of an individual child. It is difficult to generalize on the basis of a single case-history or even on the basis of several case-histories. Clinicians, however, constantly identify significant factors which support prevalent theories or which lead them to subsequent theorizing. Second, a complete case-study requires the services of specialists. Teachers cannot hope to function as specialists with competencies in all the different areas dealing with child behavior and development. However, as special services to aid the teacher become more prevalent in school systems, it is likely that the case-study will play an increasingly important role in the lives of children with special difficulties.

Methods employed by classroom teachers

Up to this point, the discussion has centered upon the various procedures specialists employ to study the characteristics and behavior of children. Although it is helpful for the classroom teacher to understand such methods, it is unlikely that she will use them to any extent in her own work. It is important, however, that each teacher, regardless of her grade-level or subject, learn certain methods and techniques for studying the children who comprise her classes. The nature and extent of the individual differences found among children have been stressed throughout this text. Since all teachers are expected to teach as many as twenty-five or thirty children at a time, they should realize that effective teaching implies adjusting instructional methods and subject materials to the individual needs of the members of the class. If this is to be accomplished, the teacher must study the children of the group, for one cannot know the important characteristics of any child without careful and continuous study.

It would probably be ideal if each teacher had a complete case history of every child assigned to her. Careful study of such histories would furnish valuable clues on the behavior, abilities, and motivation of each student. Unfortunately, such case studies are rarely available and are usually restricted to children who are atypical in their development or adjustment. Teachers, however, do have a number of aids available to help them understand their pupils. The child's academic record is valuable in helping the teacher judge his achievements. Teacher grades also furnish valuable clues. They may show that one child has excelled at all grade levels while another child has had difficulty in preceding grades. They also reveal relative patterns of strengths and weaknesses: John may exceed his classmates in verbal subjects but may only be mediocre or even poor in subjects requiring quantitative abilities. Sally may reveal a somewhat different pattern of achievement or even a contrasting one. Other pertinent information regarding a child's school performances can also furnish helpful leads. The record of attendance, deportment, extent of participation in club, social, or other extracurricular activities can help the teacher understand the child. The development of cumulative records discussed in Chapter 13 has been a beneficial development, for they provide the teacher with a longitudinal record of the child's educational development.

The use of school records.   Through a careful study of school records a teacher can gain considerable insight into a student's assets and liabilities at various levels of development. Most cumulative records provide the following types of information.

1. Personal data
    a. Full name
    b. Sex
    c. Date and place of birth
2. Family information
    a. Name of parents or guardians
    b. Educational level of parents
    c. Occupational status of parents
    d. Number and age of siblings
    e. Status of parents—e.g., living together, separated, divorced, father dead, mother dead
    f. With whom pupil resides
3. Academic Record
    a. Schools attended
    b. Complete grade record
    c. Attendance record
    d. Teacher comments
    e. Standardized test results
    f. Promotions and retentions
    g. Discipline reports
4. Health Information
    a. Illnesses: types and dates
    b. Physical abnormalities
    c. Sensory tests: vision and hearing
    d. Height and weight
    e. Other physical reports
5. Extra-curricular activities
    a. Sports
    b. Clubs
    c. Special talents

It should be apparent that by studying such records, a teacher can obtain valuable information about a child's growth patterns, academic achievements, family background, physical condition, and adjustment to the demands of the school. Such background information is invaluable in understanding a child's difficulties, for it provides a basis for understanding the complex and interrelated factors which operate in the individual at any given time.

Informal records.   In addition to the more standardized and formal records maintained by the entire school, many teachers find it helpful to supplement such records with informal records. Usually they contain information about the student's achievements in the given subject or grade, his work habits, attitudes toward school, and social adjustment. Elementary-school teachers often keep samples of pupil's work which provide a basis for judging his achievements and progress. Other teachers keep records of the books each pupil reads during the school year or record observed weaknesses in such tool subjects as reading, arithmetic, or spelling.

High school teachers often find it valuable to note whether students hand in homework assignments promptly. Observations concerning the care with which work is done, the student's ability to tackle assigned work quickly and efficiently, and his attitude toward the subject and study are helpful. These and similar informal records are most useful, not only in evaluating pupil progress, but in identifying sources of difficulty.

Interviews. Teachers have always talked to pupils concerning their work. The teacher-pupil interview usually serves two general purposes, to help a teacher better understand the pupil's attitudes and behavior, and to help the child better understand himself and his problems. Thus, it may lead to more satisfactory adjustments. If it is to be effective, however, an interview must have some definite purpose or purposes at hand. Often a single interview will not be sufficient. Some of the more common purposes of the interview are:

1. To improve or more firmly establish the relationships between student and teacher. Sometimes an individual interview helps the pupil to see the teacher in a somewhat different light. He learns that the teacher is genuinely interested in helping him work through his problems.
2. To obtain information about the pupil which is not readily apparent from other sources. Regardless of the elaborateness of the cumulative record, test reports, and other sources of information, many pertinent facts concerning the pupil may remain unknown. A friendly discussion with a pupil often reveals important additional or highly significant information concerning his aspirations, family situation, work habits, and other aspects of behavior.
3. To guide students in the proper directions. Individual interviews often serve to clarify the objectives of a course or to redirect the child's thinking into more productive channels. Often pupils become confused concerning the demands of the teacher, the course, or the school. A friendly exchange between pupils and teacher sometimes assists the pupil to more adequately understand the nature of the tasks he faces.
4. To motivate or reassure students. All people like to feel that their efforts are recognized and that they are significant to others. The interview often reassures the pupil that his efforts are being recognized and serves to motivate him to increased effort.

Ideally the teacher should plan systematic interviews with all the students in a class as well as their parents or guardians. Unfortunately, in many schools the teacher load is so great that this is impossible. In such cases the teacher should interview those pupils who seem to be in greatest need of special assistance: pupils who seem to have difficulty in academic achievement, pupils with physical disabilities, pupils who reveal asocial behavior patterns or who seem to be poorly adjusted, or pupils who seem to be functioning below the level of their abilities.

Teachers should keep complete notes on each interview and file these reports in each pupil's cumulative record. The school counselor can often assist the classroom teacher by interviewing pupils if time does not permit the teacher to carry out systematic interviewing.

The use of resource people. Sometimes the teacher finds it difficult to understand the problems of a given child despite the availability of test scores, interviews with the child and his parents, grades, school records, and other types of information. In such cases the teacher may find it helpful to talk to others who are more familiar with the child and his family. Teachers who have taught the child previously can often provide important facts not found in school records. Such specialized personnel as the guidance counselor, principal, school nurse, or even the librarian may be familiar with a certain phase of the child's life which is unknown to the classroom teacher.

Often such resource persons are not connected with the school. Community agencies like the child's church frequently can supply additional information. Similarly, youth groups, welfare organizations, and other social agencies may prove helpful in supplying information about a child's background. Often such sources provide clues which enable the teacher to gain insight into aspects of the child's environment affecting his classroom behavior.

Observations. It is axiomatic that teachers should try to verify information derived from a single source. One difficult feature of child study is to reconcile seemingly conflicting aspects of a child's behavior. An excellent way to verify information about a child, as well as to gain new insights into his behavior is to observe him directly. Teachers see children daily and under a number of different conditions. It is important that a teacher interpret the behaviors she sees, in terms of her understanding of child development and psychology rather than in terms of her own personal and moralistic beliefs.

Observations may either be scheduled at regular intervals, or may be unscheduled if significant characteristics are revealed. The observation, however, should always seek to provide significant information about the child. Best results are obtained when the observations are made in a variety of situations. How does the child behave when he is alone, when he is with his peer group, or when he is with children younger than he? How does he behave with older children, or with adults? How does he work? Play? How does he react to triumphs? To frustrations?

Through observational methods further insight can be gained into the child's energy and endurance, his physical coordination and body control, his social relationships and adjustment, his psychological makeup including his attitudes toward self and others, his defense mechanisms, work habits, span of attention, and a number of other characteristics which cannot be obtained from other sources.

Other informal methods of studying pupils

Closely related to the observational technique are a number of other informal methods of studying pupils. Certain of the more common procedures are discussed below.

The checklist. The checklist usually consists of a series of descriptive words or phrases designed to help the teacher in her observations of a given pupil. Such forms have proven their value in diagnosing pupil weaknesses, planning programs of remediation, or for identifying specific manifestations of pupil maladjustment. The checklist shown in Table 15-2

TABLE 15-2. Checklist of Difficulties in Basic Reading Skills

Word Recognition

    Has limited stock of sight-recognition words
    Does not recognize common phonograms
    Reverses letters
    Reverses simple common words
    Reads many words incorrectly
    Omits words
    Adds words

Word Analysis

    Hesitates to try unfamiliar words
    Recognizes word beginning and guesses rest incorrectly
    Does not use context clues
    Depends too heavily on context clues
    Does not look for recognizable parts
    Depends too heavily on phonetic analysis
    Substitutes words
    Does not recognize word errors

Phrasing, Fluency

    Ignores punctuation
    Reads word by word

TABLE 15-2, Cont'd

Habitually repeats words or expressions
Reads too slowly, ploddingly
Reads too fast, carelessly

Ocular Motor Skills

Holds book too close
Loses place
Does not have left-to-right directional habit
Return sweep to next line is too slow
Points finger
Moves head
Eye-voice span too narrow
Eye movements poor

Speech

Mispronounces certain words frequently
Enunciates poorly
Stutters or stammers
Voice weak
Voice loud

General Observations

Does not understand what he is reading
Does not show interest in reading

Other Characteristics

Unfavorable attitude toward school
Poor work habits
Emotionally disturbed
Socially immature
Low intelligence
Limited speaking vocabulary
Foreign language background
Poor home environment
Poor hearing
Poor vision
Poor motor control
Other physical handicap

was designed to help a teacher appraise the reading difficulties of an elementary school pupil.[5] In using the checklist the teacher merely checks or writes those difficulties deemed to be characteristic of a given pupil. The checklist provides a convenient and easily used method of recording pupil behavior and at the same time also serves to remind the teacher to

[5] Miriam S. Aronow and J. W. Wrightstone, *The Informal Appraisal of Reading Abilities*, Educational Research Bulletin No. 10, 1949, Board of Education of the City of New York, pp. 24-25.

note the more significant components or characteristics she is observing.

Although the majority of checklists employed by classroom teachers seem to be designed to help in the evaluation of learning problems, a number have been developed to assist the teacher in identifying other forms of behavior. The list of behaviors suggestive of emotional maladjustment, developed by Topp [6] provides a helpful and convenient guide to teachers.

BEHAVIORS TO WATCH FOR

1. Flies into fits of anger on slight provocation.
2. Shows signs of excessive "worriedness" and anxiety on such occasions as a school fire drill or a rehearsal for a play.
3. Frequently depressed appearance; almost never smiling or joking with fellow-students.
4. Repeatedly steals small articles from fellow-students despite severe punishment.
5. Frequently appears to be lost in his daydreams.
6. Exhibits habitual facial grimaces, or tics, particularly when under slight emotional stress.
7. Although of adequate intellectual ability, cannot apply his ability to his work and, as a result, does an inferior job. This is true despite the fact that he seems to be conscientiously trying.
8. Physically energetic and active to such a degree as to lack control over his actions; restless and practically unable to remain quiet even for short periods of time.
9. Very sensitive over real or imagined slights; feelings easily hurt.
10. Shows evidence of being excessively cruel to younger or smaller children or animals; enjoys seeing other creatures suffer.
11. Abnormally anxious to achieve perfection in any task; never late with an assignment, being much more concerned with perfection in work than most others his age.
12. Overconcerned about disease and germs; unusually clean physically for one his age.
13. Shows evidence of disliking or hating most people including his teachers and fellow-students.
14. Frequently expresses the idea that he is being singled out for punishment more often than others, when such is not the true state of affairs.
15. Lazy and irresponsible about completing any disagreeable or difficult task; must continually be urged to apply himself; shows little concern over failure.
16. Cannot avoid misbehaving, even though repeatedly warned and punished for identical activity on numerous earlier occasions.
17. Exhibits little or no affection for anybody whether it be his teachers, classmates, or other adults.

[6] Robert F. Topp, "Preadolescent Behavior Patterns Suggestive of Emotional Malfunctioning," *Elementary School Journal*, Vol. 52 (1951-52), pp. 341-343. Copyright 1952 by the University of Chicago.

18. Has difficulty facing a task which others accept readily because he fears he cannot do it suitably; lacking in confidence.
19. If permitted to do so, "just sits" without seeking entertainment or activity of any sort; remains passive in this manner for rather long periods of time.
20. Even though completely innocent of wrongdoing, visibly suffers or cries in sympathy when another child is being reprimanded.
21. Exhibits many reactions of timidity; fears certain animals or situations to such a degree as to call attention to himself.
22. Excessively concerned with his appearance; abnormally tidy and neat in comparison with others of his age.
23. Possesses the habit of telling lies on any occasion to suit his purposes and does so with unemotional skill.
24. Seldom or never shows remorse over injury which he has intentionally or accidentally caused another student.
25. Shows a tendency to do certain routinized acts over and over again, somewhat as though it were part of a ritual; may walk about the room a certain way each time or go through identical and unnecessary motions each time he opens a book.
26. Absents himself from school without adequate reason and shows little genuine remorse.
27. Exhibits a high degree of indecisiveness when relatively minor choices must be made; cannot make up his mind.
28. Stutters most of the time, or more obviously when attention is directed toward him; if observed carefully, will be discovered speaking normally when singing or when completely relaxed.
29. Highly restricted in emotional expression; never seems able to "let himself go" or to relax and enjoy himself.
30. On occasion has been known to lose his voice momentarily when frightened or very embarrassed, despite the fact that others do not react in that manner in the same situation.
31. Appears to be perpetually fatigued even though medical check-up discloses no physical ailment; appears to be lethargic, tired, listless.
32. Frequently has a dazed, perplexed, confused expression on his face; seems to be touching only the surface of life, with many commonplace occurrences not impressing themselves upon his consciousness.
33. Although having been checked for physical causes, occasionally faints, particularly when under stress.
34. Seems to be hostile toward any kind of higher authority—the teacher, parents, policemen, principal, student council, the president of the United States; always able to show where such people in authority are wrong or incapable.
35. Very self-punitive; appears to enjoy being injured psychologically or physically.
36. Subject to frequent headaches for which no physical cause can be found; complains of such headaches to the teacher and seems to be really suffering, yet the headaches may come at very opportune times for avoiding some difficulty.
37. One of those people to whom accidents seem to occur much more frequently than they do to most others in his group; injures himself on the playground, in the classroom, or while playing, supposedly accidentally, yet much more frequently than do others.
38. Can hardly bear being in large groups of people, as at school assemblies;

asks to be excused on some pretense or may admit fearing the situation.
39. Repeatedly destructive of material things; carves desks, writes on walls, or simply breaks things of no value, for the joy of it.
40. Shows peculiarities in dress which seem to have ritualistic or mysterious significance to him, such as wearing an unusual type of cap all the time or carrying a certain trinket with him.

An approach, somewhat related to that of the reading checklist previously described, is often employed to measure speech difficulties. The following informal test of articulation developed by Ainsworth [7] is an example of the type of measures which might be used by classroom teachers or speech clinicians in screening pupils to determine whether they have articulation problems. This test can be administered in a few minutes and allows the teacher to check nearly all of the consonant sounds which are likely to cause problems in children's speech. In this example the pupil merely reads the sentences orally while the teacher checks the correctness of articulation. A feature of this informal test is that the vocabulary employed is commonly found in most basal reading series.

Test of Articulation

Basic Vocabulary

s	1. See the pussy in the wee house.
z	2. The zoo has many surprises for us.
w, hw	3. Willie Whistles everywhere he goes.
Voiceless th	4. The three kittens did nothing but cry.
Voiced th	5. They went with their mother.
sh	6. She shall wash her face.
ch, k	7. Chicks like to catch bugs.
d, t	8. The dog went into the bedroom.
ng, m	9. The woman is coming home now.
l	10. Little Black Sambo had a yellow umbrella.
r	11. The girl wore her new red dress.
f, v	12. Father will know if the stove is very heavy.
b, g	13. Get the dog the biggest bone.
p, b	14. Spot plays with the baby kitten.

Other informal analyses. Many experienced classroom teachers have developed informal methods of appraising student abilities in the specific subject areas. Such measures usually furnish an excellent means of surveying pupil abilities in basic skills and aid in diagnosing problems. Betts,[8] for example, has demonstrated the value of informal reading analyses as a means of helping teachers to determine the proper instructional level

[7] Stanley H. Ainsworth, Chairman, Program for Exceptional Children, University of Georgia, *Test of Articulation,* 1945.

[8] Emmett A. Betts, *Foundations of Reading Instruction* (New York: American Book Co., 1957), pp. 438-487.

for working with each member of a class. A recent basal reading series has incorporated methods of informal reading analysis in its teachers' manual.[9]

The alert teacher, through careful observations of pupils having special difficulties in particular school subjects, is usually able to determine some of the factors or conditions related to the difficulty. The case of Emily illustrates how careful observations enabled the teacher to determine Emily's spelling difficulties.

Emily was in the sixth grade and had an IQ of 115. Her reading was satisfactory and she was getting along all right in her arithmetic and other school subjects. As the teacher had Emily pronounce each word carefully before she tried to spell it, she noticed that the words Emily could not pronounce gave her the most trouble. She tried to spell words by sounds. If she didn't know the correct sounds of the letters of a word she was unable to spell it. No previous teacher had bothered to attempt to locate the trouble. Once the teacher had determined the trouble she was able, through remedial procedures, to help Emily overcome her spelling difficulty.

Anecdotal records.   During the course of the school term, the teacher may note a situation which reveals significant aspects of the behavior of a given pupil. It is often helpful to make some record of the incident and to file it in the child's cumulative record. Periodic examinations of such records often help the teacher to understand more fully the adjustment problems of the pupil. Such reports are called anecdotal records, and are among the oldest and most commonly employed informal methods of child study. Essentially the anecdotal record consists of a report of some incident deemed to be typical or especially significant of a child's behavior. If the teacher systematically records such incidents it is likely that consistent patterns of behavior will be revealed. When anecdotal records are made over a period of time and in a variety of situations, it is likely that some fairly valid judgments can be made concerning the behavior of a given pupil. The incidents recorded may either be favorable or unfavorable. It is important that the teacher, however, learn to differentiate between her perceptions and interpretations of the behavior and the actual behavior itself. Often it is helpful to have the teacher merely report the child's behavior in a narrative fashion and then in a later section to try to interpret it. Such separation of the anecdote from the interpretation helps to assure greater objectivity. Anecdotal reports should contain the pupil's name, the name of the observer, the date of the incident, and the place. It often is preferable to provide a space for

---

[9] William D. Sheldon *et al., Sheldon Basic Readers* (New York: Allyn and Bacon, Inc., 1957). Section Three: *Teachers' Manual.*

comments by the observer. The following examples show typical anecdotal records of two first-grade pupils.

I.

Jack, age six years and two months, arrived at school the first day accom-
panied by his mother. Mrs. W. left immediately; however, even before she left
Jack had made himself at home by joining two other children at the sand table.
Throughout the day he appeared attentive, alert and interested.

II.

Billy, age six and five months, arrived at school the first day accompanied
by his mother. Mrs. C. practically had to drag Billy into the room. After he had
entered he clung desperately to her hand. He insisted his mother remain with
him. Even after he was assigned to a table he kept looking to the back of the
room to see if his mother was still there. At first he rebuffed all attempts to
get him involved in the group. Billy was given some art supplies which held
his interest. As he became more interested in drawing, he appeared to be more
at ease and his mother was able to leave.

Information derived from pupils. In studying pupils, the teacher
should never overlook the opportunities for obtaining pertinent information from the child himself. The value of the pupil-teacher interview
previously discussed, stems in part from the information obtained about
how the child sees himself and his difficulties. Many teachers have their
pupils write an autobiographical essay as part of their work in language
arts. Such sketches often reveal problems, or aspects of the child's life
which otherwise may not be readily apparent. Although a number of
colleges use this method as a basis for identifying students who may
need guidance, it is more commonly employed at the elementary or
secondary school levels.

Closely related to the autobiographical sketch is the practice of
having students write compositions about their problems or "ideals."
Students sometimes will write about the problems they face when they
are too shy to discuss them orally in class or in the interview. Similarly,
a theme written on a subject such as "The Type of Person I Would Like
To Be" or "The Type of Person I Admire," tends to reveal the personal
aspirations of a child as well as his concepts about himself. A number
of studies have shown that the discrepancies between the self-concept
and the ideal-self-concept may furnish helpful indices of personal adjustment.

Other samples of children's work are often helpful to teachers. The
tests children take may also have a real diagnostic value. The drawings
of primary-grade children may be used to study their dates of development and types of conceptualization. Informal interest inventories also
tend to reveal the child's hobbies, play activities, and interests.

Sociometric methods. We have emphasized that the individual functions in a social environment from birth. Therefore, the behavior of all individuals is both limited and fostered by the social experiences they have. The classroom and school consists of numbers of children who comprise a special type of society. Their many problems of adjustment are reflected in their social behavior. It is often helpful for the teacher to discover how children see and relate to each other. Although a teacher seeks to adapt her methods of instruction to the needs of various individuals, she needs to understand the structure of the group itself. An intimate awareness of the status of various pupils in the class, the interpersonal relationships among the pupils, and the typical patterns of interaction help the teacher in guiding pupils toward desired goals. Sociometric methods are invaluable for these purposes.

A number of sociometric techniques may generally be employed to determine the internal social structure of a group. By determining the group structure and the roles individuals play, the social acceptance of each member of the group can be appraised. A description of this method along with a sociogram was presented in Chapter 6 in connection with the socialization of children. Additional materials bearing on its nature and use should be of value to the teacher in studying children.

The sociometric technique is not a test in the usual sense. Rather the method is employed to analyze the social structure of a classroom group. Generally, the technique asks each member of a class to choose a given number (usually three to five) of classmates for some type of activity or social situation. In this manner the examiner gains an understanding of the way each child feels toward every other child in the group with respect to certain activities or criteria. The following examples are typical of the sort of questions which may be asked.

1. List in the order of choice, the three pupils whom you would like to have sit near you in class.
    1.
    2.
    3.
2. List in the order of choice your three best friends in this class.
    1.
    2.
    3.
3. List in the order of choice the three classmates with whom you'd like to play after school.
    1.
    2.
    3.
4. List in the order of choice the three classmates who you would like to have help you with your school work.
    1.
    2.
    3.

A similar procedure is the "guess-who" technique. Couching questions in language easily understood by the pupils in the class, a teacher seeks to discover the characteristics children see in each other. The following questions are typical.

1. Guess who is the bossiest child in the class.
2. Guess who is most ready to pick a fight with other students.
3. Guess who is the most fun to work with on a school project.

A variety of different measures can also be employed for evaluating specific aspects of the atmosphere of the classroom. As in other forms of evaluation, a teacher should have definite goals and criteria in mind prior to developing a sociometric instrument. A number of studies have shown that sociometrics are helpful in identifying pupils who are social isolates—children who appear to function on the fringe of social groups. On the other hand, leaders or popular children can also be identified. Another social pattern that often appears is the clique and minority group. Analyzing the results of sociometry in terms of cross-sex choices can also prove fruitful. Such analysis furnishes clues as to the degree of interaction between boys and girls in the various activities of the school. By careful study of the class social structure a teacher gains valuable knowledge not only of the social structure of her class but also of the behavior of individual students.

Clark summarized research findings in sociometry and drew conclusions as to how sociometrics can assist the classroom teacher. He suggested that the following eight points can be made about the present status of sociometrics.

1. A variety of sociometric devices is available for use by the classroom teacher.
2. There is considerable evidence that data for sociometrics should be obtained in an informal classroom situation.
3. Sociometric devices enable the classroom teacher to understand his pupils better.
4. It appears that sociometric devices offer less in the way of measuring social adjustment than in the determination of prestige.
5. There is a positive relationship between pupil-teacher rapport and teacher awareness of status structure within the group.
6. Many techniques are available for the simplification of sociometrics.
7. Teachers should use instruments closely related to sociometrics to add to their understanding of the classroom atmosphere.
8. A main function of sociometric devices is to measure growth in the effectiveness of the group and in the social progress of the individual child.[10]

[10] E. J. Clark, "Sociometric Techniques for Determining Classroom Atmosphere," *The Twelfth Yearbook of the National Council on Measurements Used in Education,* 1955, pp. 63-64.

Special considerations. The discussion in this chapter has centered around the scientific methods research workers use in studying children. A number of techniques commonly employed by classroom teachers have also been discussed. Teachers should remember that a variety of methods should be employed to insure that more of the important educational objectives are evaluated, as well as to help them gain better insight into the total behavior of a given pupil. The study of the individual child must entail more than the use of valid and reliable standardized and teacher-made tests described in Chapters 13 and 14. It is axiomatic that a teacher should verify information obtained from one source with pertinent information from other sources. Both formal and informal methods of child study have a definite place in the modern school. The classroom teacher should also be aware of her own personal and professional limitations and not hesitate to seek the assistance of more specialized personnel whenever such help is indicated.

Measures of physical attributes

It is commonly recognized that the child's physical well being has a direct relation to successful school adjustment. Unfortunately, most schools do not have medical personnel available to assure that every child enjoys adequate physical health. Most states require certain vaccinations and inoculations before a child may be admitted to school. Unfortunately, a number of equally important physical factors are not adequately checked. To identify problem areas many school systems have installed visual and auditory screening programs. In one system one of the writers worked in, because all first graders are administered both vision and hearing tests, a number of seriously handicapped children are identified annually. Often, teachers and parents are unaware of a child's disability. Other schools annually record the height and weight of their children. A few schools evaluate the students' posture or carriage and provide remedial exercises for those who need it.

It should be emphasized that the study of physical characteristics must be coordinated with and supervised by medical specialists if optimal results are to be attained. Unfortunately the school does not often give sufficient care to this vital area in studying children.

Studying visual acuity. The Snellen Chart is the standard measure most frequently used for measuring visual acuity. The Snellen E Test, shown in Figure 15-1, is perhaps the most common and simplest measure available for use with primary grade pupils. It is useful in detecting gross visual deficiencies, especially those related to nearsightedness, and to a lesser degree, those related to farsightedness. Other forms of the Snellen test are usually used at higher grade levels. Binocular coordination,

FIGURE 15-1. The Snellen Chart is frequently used in studying visual acuity for varying distances

muscle balance, and the effects of tension on vision are measured by more elaborate testing devices. An example is the *Massachusetts Vision Test* which can be readily used in a classroom situation. An easily portable device for such screening is here illustrated. A study by Foote and Crane,[11] as well as other studies, have indicated that the Snellen test is as reliable as more elaborate devices for screening purposes, especially among younger children. Visual screening devices are used primarily to determine what children are in need of further examination and treatment.

Visual difficulties are usually evident to the observant teacher. Some suggestive symptoms of visual difficulties may be listed as follows:

1. Blinks continually when reading or when focusing the eyes for some time on small objects.
2. Shows extreme nervousness. Displays frequent fits of temper.
3. Materials often appear blurred, and attempts may be made to brush the impediments away.
4. Holds the book in abnormal position when reading, for example, far away or very close.

[11] F. M. Foote and Marian M. Crane, "An Evaluation of Vision Screening," *Exceptional Children*, Vol. 20 (1954), pp. 153-161, 180.

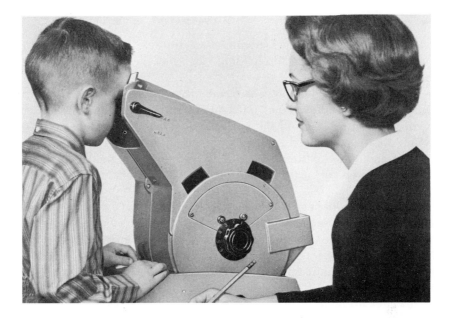

A Classroom Teacher Testing A Child's Vision With A Specially Developed
Vision Tester (Titmus Optical Co., Inc.)

5. Tilts head to one side when reading. Often looks out of side of eyes and then tries to look straight ahead.
6. Restless and irritable after using the eyes for reading or when at movies, or in other situations that require excessive use of eyes.
7. Inattentive during wall chart or map work. Does not like to try to follow other children in their oral reading.
8. Rubs the eyes frequently. The eyes may become watery from use. Frequently cries after reading.
9. Reads only a short time before stopping. Prefers play and other activities that do not tax the eyes.
10. Screws up the face considerably when reading or when looking at distant objects. Body may be very tense under such conditions.
11. Shuts one eye when reading. Confuses the letters very readily, and guesses, as it were, at a number of words.[12]

Studying auditory acuity. The teacher should be alert to behavior symptoms indicative of auditory difficulties. Methods of testing auditory acuity vary from the simple whisper test to the use of expensive precision instruments. Some suggestive symptoms are monotonous vocalizations,

[12] Karl C. Garrison and Dewey G. Force, Jr., *The Psychology of Exceptional Children* (New York: The Ronald Press Co., 1959), p. 224, See D. Kenneth Winebrenner, "Finding The Visually Inadequate Child," *Visual Digest*, Vol. 16 (1952), pp. 21-34.

misinterpretations, seeming inattentiveness, tilting of head to hear better, extensive use of gestures, discharging ears, and slow or retarded school work.

The pure-tone audiometer is frequently used for measuring hearing acuity. Hearing curves based on data from the audiometer reveal the severity of hearing loss and the loss relative to specific frequencies. Considerable data have been gathered on school children showing a wide range of audiogram patterns. Such data included in a child's cumulative record should be useful to the teacher in better understanding the child.

Studying faulty health habits. Many children have developed faulty health habits that seriously interfere with learning at school. The teacher should first of all be on the alert for symptoms indicative of poor health. This is not however, a substitute for a physical examination. There are certain symptoms indicative of poor health conditions. Some symptoms indicative of malnutrition are presented in Table 15-3.[13] Some of these the teachers are able to detect; others require the experience and training of the nurse; still others require the more careful observations of the physician.

Frequently health problems are closely related to eating, sleeping, and exercise. The possible results of faulty eating habits may be observed in overweight, underweight, and malnutrition. Through conferences with the child, with parents, or through home visits the teacher acquires information concerning faulty eating habits.

Faulty sleep habits lead to low scholarship, irritability, susceptibility to colds and fatigue, and nervousness. When these symptoms appear the teacher should strive to determine their origin. Again, home visitations and conferences with the pupil and parents should prove useful. Lack of exercise has arisen out of our changed ways of living as a health hazard. Some children spend too much time in sedentary activities like watching television. Healthy growth and development requires a balance between rest and exercise. The listless child, the overweight child, and the tense child may be getting little exercise. Through interviews, questionnaires, home visitations, and general observations the teacher will be able to determine more accurately whether or not the child is maintaining a good balance between eating, exercise, and rest. Lack of exercise may be a result rather than a cause. The malnourished child, the child with a frail constitution, and the child with a chronic disease may be listless. In either case the teacher should have an understanding of the forces and conditions producing the particular pattern of behavior symptoms indicative of lowered vitality.

[13] "Recognition of Early Nutritional Failure in Infants, Children, Adolescents, and Adults," *Journal of the American Medical Association*, Vol. 118 (1942), pp. 615-616.

TABLE 15-3. Symptoms and Signs Suggestive of Early Deficiency States in Infants and Children

Symptoms	Physical Signs
1. Lack of appetite (L)	1. Lack of subcutaneous fat (N)
2. Failure to eat adequate breakfast (L)	2. Wrinkling of skin on light stroking (N)
3. Failure to gain steadily in weight (L)	3. Poor muscle tone (D)
4. Late period of sitting, standing, and walking (N)	4. Pallor (N)
5. Aversion to normal play (L)	5. Rough skin (Toad skin) (N)
6. Chronic diarrhea (L)	6. Hemorrhage of newborn (D)
7. Inability to sit (L)	7. Bad posture (L)
8. Pain on sitting and standing (L)	8. Nasal blackheads and whiteheads (N)
9. Poor sleeping habits (L)	9. Sores at angles of mouth, cheilosis (L)
10. Backwardness in school (L)	10. Rapid heart (N)
11. Repeated respiratory infections (L)	11. Red tongue (D)
12. Abnormal intolerance to light, photophobia (L)	12. Square head, wrist enlarged, rib beading (N)
13. Abnormal discharge of tears (L)	13. Vincent's angina, thrush (D)
	14. Serious dental abnormalities (N)
	15. Corneal and conjunctival changes —slit lamp (D)

L = Those which parents or teachers might observe.
N = Those which nutritionists or nurses might observe.
D = Those which physician only would be expected to observe. The physician would take into account all other symptoms whether or not they have been previously observed.

Ways of assessing personality needs

This chapter has stressed the importance of helping pupils achieve wholesome personality integration which can aid them in learning activities. Failure in one or more developmental tasks leads to frustration with consequent detrimental effects on learning. Anything which the school can do to help pupils satisfy their basic needs will aid in improved adjustment.

In order to achieve this aim, the teacher must assess pupil needs. If personality needs are known, the teacher can help pupils achieve these through appropriate activities and through rewarding human contacts. Some commonly used methods of assessment will be discussed in this section.

The observation method described earlier in this chapter is the oldest and perhaps most widely used of all methods. A perceptive educator with a fine understanding of human nature, the dynamics of its growth and development, and with a deep insight into personality can gain much from watching the child perform in structured and unstructured learning situations, in play activities, in group activities, and in unfamiliar situations. The anecdotal record might be thought of as an aspect of the observation method. Significant incidents and occurrences in a child's life activities are recorded *as observed* by the teacher. Comment and evaluation are made separately from the recording and are labeled. This procedure adds reliability. Through the use of anecdotes the teacher seeks to evaluate the overt performance of the child so as to understand the basic needs which must be satisfied.

Information from pupil-teacher conferences is sometimes the most time-consuming to obtain. However, in short snatches of informal conversation and in informal or formal conferences, much insight into the causes of pupil behavior may be obtained. If the teacher can be accepting, if she can understand the student's viewpoint—even while disagreeing with it—and develop skill in helping young persons objectify feelings and verbalize problems, pupils will disclose more of themselves and reveal their problems. Feelings may be released that may be the start of reorientation and re-education. This method involves getting information more directly than by observation and inference. There is, however, a subjective element which is dependent upon the teacher's involvement with the pupil and which influences interpretation. The teacher, therefore, must be mature, professional and objective. He must also understand his own biases, must keep confidences, and respect the thoughts and feelings of the persons with whom he confers.

The case-study method described earlier, is especially useful in dealing with maladjusted children, children exhibiting signs of undeveloped ability, and children who are often labelled delinquents. Although such studies are often made by a specialist, teachers find it increasingly helpful to gather accurate information about their pupils in order to study carefully the past history and present status of those whose behavior suggests some problem. The case study normally comprises information about the child's past and data relative to his present status. These materials furnish a basis for understanding the child better and for predicting his future activities.

Personality inventories and questionnaires. The personality inventory, developed by Woodworth to measure neurotic tendencies, has been widely extended in number, range, and type of forms. Some questionnaires are designed for oral administration, others for group administration. Some cover a wide range of human traits or categories of behavior; others are limited to single traits, such as introversion-extroversion.

These inventories are of little value, however, if the testee knows what the normal answer is and wishes to be dishonest. Some tests have a "lie score" which gives some indications of whether the testee has been untruthful. This, however, does not always provide an adequate corrective factor. Tests and inventories of this sort are often of some use in special diagnosis of individual pupils but are not of great value in general personality measurement of classroom groups.

Projective techniques. The study of personality and its manifestations in Chapter 16 will make obvious that human personality is much too complicated to measure in its entirety. There can be no one "personality test." It is only possible to sample aspects of personality and from this, to infer certain conclusions.

Adequate theoretical and statistical principles must underlie any sampling of personality. Accurate interpretation of the results of personality sampling requires understanding and proper application of these principles as well as professional training and clinical experience in the special problems of projective techniques. The typical teacher will probably not be qualified to administer these instruments but he should know of their availability and of their referral value and limitations.

The free-association and semi-structured instruments, such as the *Rorschach Ink Blots* (see Figure 15-2) and the *Thematic Apperception Test* provide some basis for interpreting the personal and social needs of the individual. As do all projective instruments, these require the administrator to subjectively evaluate the individual's responses—hence the need for a high degree of training and an ample amount of clinical experience.

Caution should be observed, however, in attempting to arrive at a purely quantitative and objective score for all aspects of personality. Its intangible and interdependent nature makes it difficult (and perhaps impossible) to describe personality in purely quantitative terms based on some composite score. Projective techniques are of the greatest value in the area of the intangible. Present day procedures, however, do not permit complete accuracy in the measurement of personality.

It is difficult to overestimate the importance of careful and accurate assessment of personal needs by the teacher. Such assessment is invaluable to him in promoting good personal and social adjustments among the boys and girls under his guidance. To help the child overcome his difficulties, the teacher can (1) train himself to recognize early difficulties and symptoms of maladjustment, (2) take appropriate steps to treat the difficulties, and (3) cooperate with various individuals or

FIGURE 15-2. There are many tests designed to measure the free responses of individuals. The *Rorschach Test* makes use of the individual's interpretations of ink blots.

agencies in their attempt to help the child overcome special difficulties.

In this connection, it may be noted that, although referrals are not a completely valid index of the occurrence of problem behavior, they do furnish a guide for determining the types of problems observed at school —problems which indicate the need for further psychological help. The results of a survey of referral problems seen in child guidance clinics in New York City by Gilbert [14] furnishes us with useful information. For children at all grade levels the most frequent referrals were for academic reasons (45 per cent) followed by aggressive and antisocial behavior (30 per cent). A further analysis of the data by grades showed that responses of emotional insecurity were relatively more frequent in the early school years, reflecting problems related to adjustment to school.

Professional considerations

The teacher must recognize that she can never accumulate all the desirable information about a given child. She must recognize the limitations of time, skill, and validity of techniques. She must also recognize that each child is a complex organism functioning in an integrated manner. Often the causes of behavior are not readily apparent. In fact, the observed behavior may be misleading. Teachers must recognize their limitations and should obtain just enough data to help them understand specific types of problems and behaviors. These considerations will be discussed in greater detail in the following chapter.

Because some methods are regarded as more objective than others does not mean that they should be used exclusively. An important developmental trend among school psychologists is to adapt the method to the problem at hand rather than to attempt to study all problems by a proven scientific method. It is for this reason that observations are extremely important. They can be conducted by the typical teacher in a classroom situation and frequently, observation permits one to approach problems directly that can only be dealt with indirectly by more scientific methods. The use of careful scientific analysis alone, has often interfered with the process of understanding a particular child.

There is no formula that can tell a teacher which method to use and which to discard. In deciding, several factors should be considered, some of which are listed here:

1. The nature of the problem. Some difficulties are obviously more complex and more pervasive than others. Complex problems of long standing generally require more careful analysis than difficulties of a minor or transitory nature.

[14] G. M. Gilbert, "A Survey of Referral Problems in Metropolitan Child Guidance Clinics," *Journal of Clinical Psychology*, Vol. 13 (1957), pp. 37-42.

2. The amount and kind of information already available. Some school systems maintain excellent, up-to-date cumulative records. Certain school systems maintain meager and scanty records. The teacher employed in schools of the latter type probably will need to secure information about a given pupil which is readily available to a teacher in the school with adequate records.

3. The type of instruments and resource personnel available to the teacher. The typical classroom teacher may lack access to highly qualified specialists such as school psychologists, personal counselors, or similar personnel. In such cases she must do what she can without too much assistance. Similarly, her school may lack an adequate budget for standardized and specialized diagnostic tests; hence she may have to resort to teacher-made devices.

4. The training of the teacher. Some teachers have supplemented their professional training so that they are competent in the use of such clinical tools as individualized intelligence scales, projective tests, and similar instruments not often used by classroom teachers.

5. The uses to be made of the information gathered. It usually is impossible to gather all of the information desired about a given individual. The teacher should seek to gather sufficient pertinent information to help her help the pupil achieve adequate adjustments.

SUMMARY

Because children differ widely in all characteristics and attributes, it is necessary that the teacher study the various individuals who comprise the classroom group. Individual differences result from the interaction of biological heredity with environmental forces. As children age and mature, greater heterogeneity is found in any class-size group.

Scientific methods of studying children were described. The genetic or longitudinal method seeks to study a particular attribute or characteristic for a given period of time. In contrast the normative-survey investigates a characteristic or group of characteristics in a representative sample of the population being studied. Experimental methods seek to control all variables except those being studied. The case study or clinical method examines the histories of a number of individuals in an attempt to discover common factors leading to the present condition. Modification of these methods may be used by classroom teachers.

School records are valuable sources of information concerning pupils. Well-kept cumulative records help the teacher to obtain a developmental view of an individual pupil. Other informal records are also of assistance. Interviews between pupil and teacher as well as between teacher and parents often reveal important information about a given student. Many teachers find that observations, checklists, and anecdotal records reveal pertinent information concerning pupil behavior as well as provide means for systematic evaluation. Sociometric methods provide one method by which the teacher can examine the structure of the class group. Many schools employ screening tests for the early identification of sensory impairments. Check-lists and observations are also helpful in locating physical difficulties. A number of methods for discovering personal-social problems were discussed. These included inventories, interviews, questionnaires, and projective tests.

The teacher should recognize that she can never obtain all of the information she should like to have about any given pupil. Any study of a given pupil is limited by the nature of the problem involved, the amount and kind of information already available, the type of measures available, and the level of training of the teacher.

Problems and Exercises

1. Assume that you are a teacher and one of your classmates is a pupil. Conduct an interview designed to help you discover what problems, if any, the pupil is encountering with his school work.
2. What behaviors would you look for if you were observing a primary-grade child to ascertain his social adjustments? A middle-grade child? A junior-high school pupil? A high-school student?
3. Develop a sociometric test to determine the group structure of your society, fraternity, or residential hall. Make a sociogram to show the relationships discovered.
4. List the types of information you think can best be ascertained from school records. Examine some school record or records to determine the extent to which such information is available on such records.
5. Using the headings found in this chapter, make a case history of a child at the grade-level which interests you most. What are the uses that can be made of such records?
6. What are the advantages of a "check list" over ordinary observations in studying children? What uses can be made of "check lists?"
7. Study the materials presented in Table 15-1. Speck, Janice, and Betty are the youngest members of the group. What do the results indicate about their intelligence? About the school work? About their concept of themselves?
8. How would you define anecdotal records? Can you cite an anecdote about one of your friends or acquaintances that reveals something of the nature of the person?
9. How would you define projective techniques? Give illustrations of different kinds of projective techniques. Why are they frequently useful in helping to understand individuals?

Selected Readings

AHMANN, J. S., and GLOCK, M. D., *Evaluating Pupil Growth* (Boston: Allyn and Bacon, 1959), Ch. 16.

FROELICH, C. P., and DAILEY, J. G., *Studying Students* (Chicago: Science Research Associates, 1952), Ch. 17.

GARRISON, Karl C., and FORCE, D. G., Jr., *The Psychology of Exceptional Children*, 3d ed. (New York: The Ronald Press, 1959), Ch. 2.

MOULY, George J., *Psychology for Effective Teaching* (New York: Holt, Rinehart, and Winston, 1960), Ch. 15.

THORPE, Louis P., *Child Psychology and Development*, 3d ed. (New York: The Ronald Press, 1962), Ch. 1.

TRAXLER, A. E., *et al.*, *Introduction to Testing and the Use of Test Results in Public Schools* (New York: Harper & Row, 1953), Ch. 2.

WATSON, Robert J., *Psychology of the Child* (New York: John Wiley & Sons, 1959), Ch. 2.

CHAPTER 16

Children with Learning Difficulties

In spite of a teacher's training, the suitability of instructional materials, and the curriculum, we must realize that not all the children in a class will master the skills and content equally. We have already pointed out that children vary considerably in aptitudes, abilities, personality, emotion, socioeconomic level, rate of development, and other factors. All teachers can expect to have pupils with a wide range of abilities; some will have difficulty mastering certain aspects of school work. In any given elementary classroom it is not uncommon to find that the variation in student abilities is greater than three to five grade levels. In junior high-school and high-school, variability is likely to be even greater. Greater heterogeneity is usually found in language arts, social studies, and other verbal subjects, but wide differences in achievements will be found in all other subject areas. A very real problem of any teacher, then, is to adjust the learning situation to the various abilities and needs of her pupils.

This chapter will discuss the more common factors related to learning difficulties and touch on their diagnosis and remediation. In an introductory text it is difficult to provide a complete discussion of the causes, concomitants, and significance of all of the factors involved in the lack of adjustment to school learning. Although the chapter is organized so that discussion centers around physical, intellectual, linguistic, familial, and personal-social factors, it should be emphasized that rarely is merely one factor involved in the difficulties of a given child. Rather, the human organism functions in an interrelated way and the causes of any disability are usually complex and often difficult to detect.

The methods used for studying children discussed in chapters 12 and 13 are certainly applicable to the diagnosis of children with learning and adjustment problems. Standardized and teacher-made tests are often used to identify children with problems. Similarly, the informal methods of studying children discussed in Chapter 15 serve to help the teacher identify and locate special areas of needs.

Before discussing the causes of disability and the means for detecting and treating them, it might be wise to describe the nature of a learning disability. Unfortunately, no precise descriptive term that is equally applicable to all cases is available. Many children will be discovered whose achievements are not consonant with their capacities or abilities. Such children, however, are not usually regarded as "disabled" unless an obvious discrepancy is apparent. A usual rule of thumb is that the child's achievements tend to lag one to two or even more years behind his normal mental development. For example, the child with superior intelligence may be thought to have difficulties despite the fact that he makes progress typical of his age level. On the other hand, the child whose mental development is less than average may make satisfactory progress, although his achievements are somewhat less than his classmates. Learning difficulties, then, result from a variety of causes and require a variety of methods for detection and treatment.

Physical factors which contribute to learning difficulties

A number of physical factors seem to accompany learning difficulties in the classroom. The teacher should recognize that in almost all such cases the problem is organic, and that treatment and correction should largely be the concern of the medical specialist. The teacher here should simply refer the child to proper specialists; in the event of physical impairment, the teacher should seek advice on how best to deal with the child.

Physical condition. Generally a poor physical condition hampers the behavior of a child in almost every facet of his life. The classroom situation places many demands upon the pupil which require an active mobilization and expenditure of energy. Almost any physical disability or debilitating condition will adversely affect the child's performance in the learning process. It may lower his energy level, distract him from the learning task, or otherwise prevent him from marshalling his abilities to the desired level. The following case may illustrate the debilitating effects of poor physical condition upon a child's adjustment to school.

Sylvia, a third-grade child from an upper-middle class family, was regarded as a slow learner. She read at high first-grade level and her arithmetic abilities were at a low second-grade level. Sylvia appeared disinterested, listless, and irresponsible in her behavior. During a routine physical examination, the family's doctor discovered that the child had a low-grade urinary infection. She was referred to a specialist who discovered a slight blockage in the child's urethra. An operation was successfully performed. Since the operation Sylvia appears to be a different child. She is more interested in her school work, more

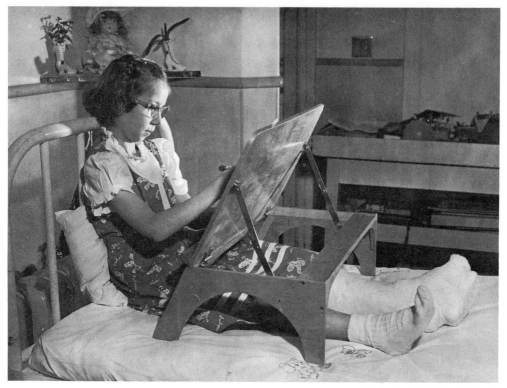

A crippling condition may be a serious handicap to a child's learning unless steps are taken to provide special instruction. This is recognized as an important part of an educational program for *all* the children

active in play activities, and generally more alert. With the aid of remedial instruction she has made noticeable improvements in her school achievements and now reads at grade level and has about caught up with her class in arithmetic.

Sylvia's case is not unusual. There are probably many children in schools who suffer from undiscovered conditions which adversely affect their school performance. It is a wise practice to suspect that the easily-fatigued child, the listless or bored pupil, or the child who must be continuously prodded into action may need medical attention. Too often teachers feel that children behave this way because they are lazy or irresponsible. A good axiom is to investigate physical factors and health before reaching any conclusions about a child's attitudes or personality.

Developmental variations. Individual differences among children in any school room are due, for one thing, to differences in their rate of development. If one were to examine a number of areas of development—physical, mental, social-emotional—for a group of children of exactly the same chronological age, a wide variation in these stages of development would be found among them. Similarly, such variations in the development of different factors would be found in a single child. One child may be mentally alert and fluent, but may lack the physical coordination one expects in children of his age. Another child of the same age may reveal a reverse pattern of development. Children who vary considerably in areas of development sometimes have difficulty meeting the demands imposed upon them by the adult world. Such children often encounter difficulty in the classroom.

Another consideration stems from the rate of a child's development. Children who mature more slowly than their peers constantly face tasks which are more difficult for them than for their fellows. Recognition of this fact has led educators to devote considerable effort to attempt to appraise the *readiness* of pupils to master such complex skills as reading and writing. This concept was discussed more fully in Chapter 9. It should be stressed, however, that the child's rate of development may be a fundamental cause of maladjustment if it functions to inhibit his ability to meet the expectations of adults and to master many of the developmental tasks he faces. For example, the child whose patterns of development are slower than average may encounter difficulties in establishing beneficial relationships with his peer group. The following case is typical.

George, a twelve-year-old boy enrolled in the sixth grade, has been slow in developing physically. He is somewhat undersized in comparison to his peers, and has not developed motor skills to the degree possessed by other boys in the class. As a result, George is poorly coordinated, plays games badly, and is unskilled in sports. His classmates think of him as awkward, rarely choose him to play such games as baseball or basketball. He sometimes is dismissed as a sissy or as being "no good." As a result of this handicap, George is not a well-accepted member of the class and lately has tried to gain recognition by disrupting the work of the classroom.

Malnutrition and other dietary problems. A number of dietary conditions can adversely affect the child's adjustment to school. One of the conditions which appears to be decreasing in the number of extreme cases, but still occurs frequently, is malnutrition. The term *malnutrition* is commonly employed to describe a condition in which essential nutrients are not fully utilized or obtained by the organism. Better dietary and health habits, and free and inexpensive school-lunch programs have alleviated malnutrition due to poverty in many sections. Teachers, however, should remain alert to spot children who lack appetite, do not gain weight, appear overly tense, seem to be listless and lethargic, or who avoid normal play activities. Such children may be suffering from dietary deficiencies. Malnutrition has been associated with retarded skeletal growth and extreme nervousness, it can also affect adversely the child's motivation in school work. Harrell [1] found that the addition of thiamine to the diet of such children resulted in greater gains in the performance of intellectual tasks.

Although poverty no longer seems to be an important factor in malnutrition, a number of American children are actually undernourished because of faulty eating habits. Many children also lack an optimally balanced diet. Some suffer a loss of appetite; others have irregular eating habits; still others overeat. Although medical diagnosis is important in such cases, we ought to recognize that many faulty eating habits have psychological bases. Furthermore, it has been frequently observed that children with the most money to spend select the poorest diets.

Other physical factors. A number of ailments can lower the natural vitality of a child. Anemia results in a loss of energy. Ear, eye, and nose and throat infections are prevalent among children and can have debilitating effects as well as cause increased absences from school. Glandular conditions such as hypothyroidism or thyroid deficiency are often manifested by sluggishness and obesity. On the other hand, certain glandular conditions cause tension, hyperactivity, irritability, and similar behavior which can hamper the child's learning in the classroom as well as his social adjustments.

The metabolism of any child as well as other of his complex processes function to provide a certain energy level which is expended by physical processes as well as various types of activities. This energy level is important in determining the child's patterns of behavior and personality characteristics. A hyperactive child tends to respond in a noticeably different way to restrictions affecting his activities than the child with a lower energy level. Many of the tasks which children face in the school room require a certain amount of sustained attention and concentration. Elementary teachers long have recognized that they must provide outlets for the physical energy built up during the instructional periods if they are to keep children from becoming too restless. Recently the writer examined a first grade child who was having difficulty learning to read. The child had a superior I.Q. and language fluency but was unable to sit still long enough to interact with his teacher. The teacher declared that she knew she could teach the child to read if he would only cooperate. She reported that she had been unable to get him to sit long enough for her to teach him, and that he could not sit at his desk long enough to complete the assigned work. His need for physical activity impeded the learning situation and disrupted the classroom.

Sensory difficulties

Two senses, vision and audition, appear to be most closely related to successful adjustment. Certainly they have important functions in school learning at each stage. As the child's ears and eyes help him to interact with his environment, it follows that any impairment in these sense organs would hamper his rate of development and learning. In the case of school learning, any disability affecting these organs becomes even more important. Almost all of the instruction in the typical classroom is largely dependent upon one or the other or both of these senses.

Visual handicaps. Visual difficulties may result because the eye itself is improperly developed or because both eyes fail to coordinate. These types of handicaps are usually classified either as *monocular* or *binocular* difficulties. The parent and teacher should be on the lookout for children with defective vision. A list of behavioral characteristics of children who may have visual difficulties is here set forth.

1. Blinks continuously while reading and at other times when the eyes are focused on small objects.
2. Holds the book either too far or too close to the eyes while reading.
3. Tilts the head while reading and often looks out of the side of the eyes and then attempts to look straight ahead to read.
4. Nervous and irritable after a period of reading.
5. The eyes become watery or red. The individual may resort to rubbing them during and after a reading period.
6. Makes peculiar facial grimaces while reading, and displays considerable tension.
7. Doesn't like to read. Reads only a short period of time.
8. Reading materials may appear blurred. The child continuously confuses letters and words that are quite similar in appearance.

A study by Leverett illustrates the importance of visual health problems among school children. Analyzing the results of visual tests administered to 6000 public school children in Bristol, Connecticut, he notes that "Apparently about the time that visual acuity matures, it begins to deteriorate. The number of children who are unable to demonstrate 20/20 acuity in both left and right eyes increases from less than 10 per cent at age five to about 39 per cent at the age of 17 years." [2] Fig-

[2] H. M. Leverett, "Visual Test Performance of School Children," *American Journal of Ophthalmology*, Vol. 4 (1957), pp. 508-519.

ure 16-1 shows the per cent of children at each grade level who failed the acuity tests in this study.

Monocular defects. A number of learning difficulties may stem from faulty eye structure. If the eye is incorrectly shaped the retina sometimes receives a distorted image. Some individuals can see adequately at distances, but have difficulty in perceiving images held two feet from them. Such persons are said to be *hyperopic* or far sighted. By contrast, some individuals have no difficulty in seeing objects a short distance from them, but have difficulty seeing objects at a distance. Such people are said to be *myopic* or near sighted. Far sighted children often find it difficult to read or study their text books for more than a short period of time because of the strain imposed by the visual task. Moreover, they cannot generally be screened by vision tests of the traditional wall-chart type.

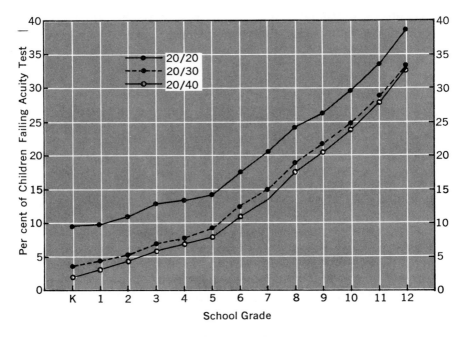

FIGURE 16-1.   Per Cent Of Children In Each Grade Failing The Acuity Tests
At the 20/20, 20/30, And 20/40 Levels

On the other hand, near sighted children do not usually suffer discomfort when they read, but have difficulty seeing demonstrations, examples, and other materials shown on chalkboards or charts. Since many elementary-school children do not know that they have visual defects, the teacher must be especially alert to identify them. Teachers often mistakenly ascribe restlessness and tension due to these difficulties to motivational or developmental factors.

A third type of visual problem results from defects in the curvature of the cornea or lens of the eye. Such defects serve to distort the visual image because the light rays are distorted. The name for this difficulty is *astigmatism*. The distorted vision astigmatism causes adversely affects the child's perceptions making it difficult for him to learn to recognize letters or numbers.

Fortunately, these three types of defects can be remedied, in most cases, by corrective lens prescribed by vision specialists. Another source of visual difficulty stems from the binocular nature of man. Such disturbances result from muscular imbalance rather than from the organic structure of the eye.

Muscular imbalance. Attached to the sclera of each eye are six muscles which control the movements of the eye. The coordinated contraction of these exterior pairs of muscles enable the eye to move in various directions. Normally, both eyes move together in a coordinated fashion. As the individual looks at objects at various distances the eyes vary their degree of convergence. Thus, the eyes will normally tend to turn more toward each other as they examine an object at a closer distance. Sometimes a muscular imbalance causes the eyes to turn inward, a condition known as *esophoria* or cross-eyedness. *Exophoria* is roughly the opposite, or the tendency of the eyes to turn outward. Another type of muscular imbalance, called *hyperphoria*, may cause one of the eyes to turn upward. Children who lack coordinated vision encounter difficulties with certain aspects of the school curriculum, notably learning to read. Probably the most serious results, however, stem from the likelihood that the child so affected may learn to suppress the vision of one eye.

Auditory impairments. After vision, auditory defects are probably the most serious handicaps to the child's learning in the school room. The child with a hearing impairment encounters difficulties at almost every turn. Not only is his learning of academic skills hampered, but his personal-social adjustments are also adversely affected. It is unfortunate that hearing disabilities are not discovered and treated before a child enters school because, too often, such children are thought to be slow learners or developers. It is difficult, however, to discover such disabilities until the infant becomes more aware of his surroundings or until he reaches the age when he should begin talking. Moreover, there are many children who have entered school with relatively serious auditory impairments that have never been discovered, or, if discovered, have never been measured. Garrison and Force [3] present a check list of symptoms to help the teacher identify children who may need a more complete hearing examination.

I. Behavior
  1. Tilts head at an angle to get better sound.
  2. Listless and inattentive.
  3. Fails to respond when questioned.
  4. Shows defects in speech, especially where phonetics are important.
  5. Peculiar voice qualities, often high pitched.
  6. Avoids people.
  7. Tends to run his words together.
  8. Has poor oral reading ability.
  9. Has poor general scholarship in relation to I.Q.
  10. Usually talks louder than necessary.
  11. Watches face (especially mouth and lips) of speaker.

II. Appearance
  1. Deformities of the outer ear.
  2. Discharging ear.
  3. Muscular tension when listening.
  4. Mouth breathing.
  5. Blank facial expression when spoken to.
  6. Chronic catarrhal condition.

III. Complaints by the child
  1. Buzzing or ringing noises in the head.
  2. Earache.
  3. Nausea or dizziness.
  4. Inability to understand directions.
  5. Headaches in the sinus area.

A further note should be made regarding the development of the structure of the ear. It is generally recognized that the auditory structure of the neonate and infant is not completely developed. There is a major difference between the ear of a child and that of an adult, especially in the proportional length and breadth of the Eustachian tube which connects the ear and the throat. The Eustachian tube of the child is noticeably shorter and wider. As a result, a child's ears are more susceptible to various infections. This structure is one reason for the prevalence of ear aches, running ears and similar difficulties found among elementary-school children. As the child matures the Eustachian tube lengthens proportionately to its breadth, and infections are less likely to occur.

[3] Karl C. Garrison and Dewey G. Force, *The Psychology of Exceptional Children,* 3d ed. (New York: The Ronald Press Co., 1959), pp. 255-256.

Intellectual factors

School learning is, of course, positively related to intelligence. The failure of certain pupils can be traced to various factors of mental ability. The child whose rate of mental development is somewhat slower than his classmates may have difficulty in keeping up with his group. Every teacher must realize that in each class at every grade level, a number of children will have difficulty because of a lesser vocabulary and lower mental ability than their peers. These factors were discussed in detail in Chapters 4 and 5.

Most teachers learn to recognize children whose rate of mental development is somewhat slower than those of other children. A number of teachers, however, fail to recognize that the overall patterns of intellectual abilities vary sharply among children of the same developmental level. One pupil may manifest a high degree of verbal ability although his ability to handle quantitative concepts is considerably less well developed. In another pupil the reverse pattern may be found. Intellectual abilities reflect academic training, motivation, and a number of other personality factors. Wide individual differences can be expected as the child progresses in school. The materials of Table 16-1, adapted from a study by Seashore,[4] illustrate how different the abilities of five superior tenth-grade boys may be.

TABLE 16-1.   Profiles of the Mental Abilities of Five Superior 10th Grade Boys in Percentiles (*after Seashore*)

PUPIL	SCHOLASTIC APTITUDE	VERBAL REASON-ING	NUMBER ABILITY	ABSTRACT REASON-ING	SPACE RELA-TIONS	MECHAN-ICAL REASON-ING
1.	90	95	65	65	70	70
2.	95	90	90	80	75	95
3.	90	95	65	80	50	90
4.	95	80	99	55	45	65
5.	90	95	55	55	75	65

Since variations in ability are sufficiently common, teachers should recognize that the child having difficulties with certain subjects may make satisfactory progress in other courses.

[4] Harold Seashore, "Aptitude Tests and Counseling the Gifted," Address given at American Psychological Association, March 28, 1961.

Readiness factors. It is a common belief among students of child development that there is an optimal period for learning and mastering certain skills and knowledge. A major problem of the school curriculum has been to introduce the teaching of certain skills at a time when the typical child is considered to be sufficiently mature to benefit from the instruction. One of the best ways first-grade teachers have of determining the time is by applying the concept *reading readiness.* Through observations and tests the teacher appraises such abilities as perceptual skills, eye-hand coordination, extent of vocabulary, speech fluency, and similar characteristics to determine whether a child is likely to have success in beginning reading instruction. Readiness measures are also employed to determine whether a child can succeed in cursive handwriting, arithmetic calculation, and similar basic tool skills.

Although readiness is most often thought of in connection with readiness for school or reading readiness, the concept should also be applied to the different educational levels and to the various areas of learning. In the high school program the question may be raised, Is the student ready for algebra or botany? Certainly the student without preparatory background learnings and experiences will not succeed in learning botany. The aptitude tests referred to in a previous chapter are designed to determine the extent to which students do have the qualities that will enable them to learn certain skills or to acquire an understanding of a particular area of knowledge. Such tests take into account a student's previous learnings.

Low intelligence. Children who show greater aptitude for one type of thought and one kind of learning are common in the classroom at all grade levels. Sally, an A student in English and social studies, barely manages to pass algebra. By comparison, Bill, a good mathematics student who never receives grades lower than B+, usually receives D's and has never received a grade higher than C in the language arts or reading. School achievement records of this sort can be accounted for by the existence of varying patterns of mental ability in given children of the same intelligence level. The interests, motivations, and aspirations of the pupils may also account for some of the variations.

Another group of children who encounter difficulty are those usually classified as *slow-learners.* Although these children are not mentally retarded in the sense of being mentally deficient, they seem unable to keep pace with the learning rate of other boys and girls of comparable age. The following case is typical.

Linda, a neatly dressed, pleasant girl of thirteen, was referred to the school psychologist for special testing by her sixth-grade teacher. Although Linda had successfully passed the primary grades, she had been retained in the fourth grade and was failing in all of the subjects of the sixth grade. The psychologist administered a battery of achievement tests and found that Linda read at a fourth-grade level and spelled at a level comparable to that of a high third-grade pupil. Her arithmetic scores were comparable to those of a high second-grade child. Her social studies and science scores also were extremely low. The *Stanford Binet Scale* indicated that Linda had an Intelligence Quotient of 85. Although Linda would not be classified as mentally retarded, it was apparent that her mental ability was sufficiently below average as to cause her some difficulties at every grade level. It was believed that the cumulative effect of being "pushed" just a bit too much at each grade level had caused her difficulties. When the instructional program was adjusted to her slower learning rate, Linda appeared to make more satisfactory progress.

There are many children like Linda in the classrooms of the nation. Unfortunately, their special needs are not often recognized, and sufficient adjustments are not made in the curriculum to help them achieve more satisfactory progress. The problem often becomes acute in the high school, where there are certain subjects which such children may be unable to master. For example, with the crowded conditions and limited time and facilities in many high schools today, it is difficult, if not impossible, to teach a student with an I.Q. of 75 sufficient algebra or physics to be of much value. It usually is the practice to provide a somewhat different curriculum more suited to the needs of these students than the traditional college preparatory one.

It should be stressed that educational retardation does not automatically disappear because teachers and parents exercise patience. Johnson points out, "Unless some type of remediation is effective, a child who is a half-year retarded at the end of the second grade will be one year retarded at the end of the fourth grade, and two years retarded, educationally, at the end of the eighth grade. Hence, educational retardation becomes more noticeable as the child grows older because of the larger discrepancy between achievement and age." [5]

Language ability. In the earlier chapters on intelligence and language and thinking, it was emphasized that language achievement is intimately related to mental ability and the ability to conceptualize. Generally language capacity and achievement appear to be significantly correlated to academic achievement. Therefore, teachers would be wise to determine the extent of a child's language capacity and achievement in reading, spelling, and oral language whenever a learning problem is encountered. Children who are bilingual or who have learned English as a second language may have difficulty in their school work because of language deficiencies. Children who come from homes where educa-

[5] G. Orville Johnson, "Here and There," *Exceptional Children*, Vol. 25 (1959), p. 228.

tional or cultural experiences are meager may also suffer because their environment provides few opportunities for learning and for verbalizing experiences.

One further caution. Many children who appear to lack adequate mental ability and whose scores on paper-and-pencil tests of intelligence seem to verify the diagnosis of low intelligence, may actually be disabled readers. Most group tests of mental ability are highly influenced by the child's reading skills. The writer once tested a boy who had an I.Q. of 65 on a paper and pencil intelligence test. On an individual intelligence scale which did not require extensive reading, this student achieved an I.Q. of 104. If a pupil has a severe disability in any one of the basic tool skills such as reading, spelling, or arithmetic, it is not wise for the teacher to assume that the child has low intelligence or is a slow learner.

A number of intellectual factors, naturally, are positively correlated to school success. A child's rate of mental development helps to determine his degree of readiness for tackling school problems. The pattern of intellectual abilities affects the likelihood of success or failure in the various subjects in the curriculum. Some children appear to be able to handle verbal tasks with greater ease than quantitative tasks. Others have greater reasoning ability but have difficulty in memorizing tasks. Such individual patterns affect school achievement because the different subjects may require different components of intelligence. However, the child who has a limited vocabulary and who lacks fluency is not likely to be highly successful in mastering most of the required subjects in the curriculum.

Children not working to capacity. Unfortunately, almost every teacher can cite cases of children whose achievement levels are not commensurate with their capabilities. Although such children may not have learning difficulties in the usual sense, educators are concerned with helping such children achieve maximum development. Often such students lack interest or motivation or may have emotional difficulties which prevent them from marshalling all of their resources. The following case is typical.

John is the middle child of three older boys. Two very young children are also in the family. His father died when John was small. His stepfather died two years ago. His mother has worked hard to support her five children, and has relied upon John to baby-sit with the younger children and to help with the housework. This John has done with compliance and seeming willingness. His brothers have duties at home also, but they are more rebellious about them. Mrs. Rogers rules the home with an iron hand, but is erratic, nervous, and exacting with her children.[6]

[6] Louise C. Spence, "Guidance Activities of the School Social Worker," *National Elementary Principal Yearbook*, Vol. 33 (1954), p. 116.

Home and family factors

It is considered axiomatic that the home and school must coordinate their efforts if the best results are to be obtained. Certainly children who come from homes which reinforce the values and instruction of the classroom tend to have fewer adjustment difficulties than children who come from homes where the reverse is true. A number of factors appear to operate concerning the home and family situation which may serve either to facilitate or to impede the child's learning at school.

Socioeconomic level. Many children enter school with a wide variety of personal experiences which serve to facilitate their learning. Such children have been read to, have had drawing and coloring materials for experimentation, and have heard correct standards of speech from birth. They have also learned a rich and varied vocabulary from their parents, siblings, and friends, and have had many opportunities for experiences which have helped them to develop concepts about themselves and their society. Despite the spread of material and cultural opportunities through our democratic way of life, however, numerous American families suffer from economic and cultural handicaps. It was pointed out in Chapter 5 that children from the lower socioeconomic homes were seriously handicapped in their language development. In homes where the cultural and educational level of the parents is low, children have limited learning experiences which place them at a definite disadvantage. Vocabulary and speech patterns are often below the levels required for successful reading and language arts. The concepts such children have are limited as well because they lack rich and varied experiences. Such children do not have opportunities to travel, and have only vague ideas about the world they live in.

The case of Willie is typical. Willie's father has a third grade education and works as a janitor. His mother, who completed the fifth grade, is a housemaid. The family lives in two rooms in a substandard section of the city. Although they own a television set, they subscribe to no magazines and do not buy a daily paper. There are no books in the home and the parents never read. Willie does not remember ever having toys except for a rubber ball and a pair of skates. He has never had coloring books or crayons. Because of his parents' work schedules the family rarely eats together and has never gone on picnics or outings together. Willie's world is bounded by the school and the neighborhood.

Obviously the experiences which Willie brings to the classroom are both meager and one-sided. Many of the experiences felt to be common to American children are missing in his life. Compare his background with Mark's, another child of the same age.

Mark's father is a college professor and his mother is a college graduate who had taught school prior to marriage. The family enjoy camping and Mark goes camping several times each year. He has his own room, and collects insects, stamps, and coins. He is given a weekly allowance with which he buys kits for making airplanes. This summer the family plans to travel throughout the far west camping in the national parks.

Not only does the socio-cultural level of the child's home life affect his readiness for school, but it continues to influence him throughout his childhood and adolescence.

Conflicts between home and school.   Unfortunately, the goals of the school and the behaviors sought by teachers may sometimes conflict with those inculcated by the home. At such times the child may find that behavioral patterns which are rewarded and reinforced at home are discouraged and disapproved in the classroom. As schools and classroom teachers tend to foster middle-class values, goals, and behaviors, the conflicts faced by pupils from lower-class homes often are greater than those faced by children from middle-class families. Evidence shows that, in general, children from middle-class homes tend to make easier adjustments and earn higher grades than children from lower socioeconomic levels. How much the difficulties encountered by lower-class children in school achievement is directly attributable to this condition is, of course, debatable. It is safe to say, however, that a number of children find the discrepancies between the expectations of home and school sufficiently great as to cause problems.

Another facet of this problem relates to the relationships of parents to the teacher. Often parents and teachers differ in the way they exercise authority. A child who has domineering, autocratic parents learns to adjust to such patterns and may find it difficult to relate to a teacher who is democratic and permissive. Often a child who experiences such diverse authority figures finds adjustment difficult. Similarly, the child who is overprotected at home may find the more carefree, permissive environment of a classroom difficult to cope with. These problems are discussed more fully in other chapters of this text which deal with personal-social and emotional adjustments. The effective teacher, however, recognizes that the child's home life plays an important role in his ability to achieve in the school environment. Whenever a child shows anxiety or disinterest, has difficulty in concentrating on a learning task or shows persistent difficulties in learning, it is wise to gain some knowledge of the emotional climate in his home, and determine the extent to which home and school are coordinating their efforts. In the sense that school adjustment and learning takes place in a social setting, a child's social adjustments are necessarily important.

Radke [7] summarized a number of studies dealing with the effects of domineering parents on the personal-social development of children. He noted a number of behavioral constellations which frequently appear among children from autocratic homes. As shown by the following list, many of these behaviors can have an adverse effect on a child's classroom behavior and on his ability to learn.

Dominating Parents	*Autocratic Parents*
Quarrelsome	Doesn't get along with
Uncooperative	other children
Tense	Non-compliant
Bold	Emotionally unstable
Disinterested	Uninhibited
Dependable	Inconsiderate
Shy, submissive	Insensitive
Polite	Nonrivalrous
Self-conscious	Unpopular

Emotional-social factors

In Chapter 6 it was pointed out that the human organism has certain needs and behaves in a way that will satisfy those needs. The typical child and adolescent desires to learn and finds that successfully mastering the learning tasks in the classroom tends to be gratifying. Continual failure to achieve success, on the other hand, creates continual tensions, frustrations, and anxieties which can seriously impede normal social-emotional developments. If he lags behind seriously, as in the case of the pupil whose achievements are two or three grade levels below those of his agemates, the emotional concomitants of the situation become noticeably severe. A number of authorities feel that the learning disability itself is symptomatic of emotional maladjustment. Certainly a cyclical relationship can be thought to exist.

Personal-social maladjustments. A pupil may have difficulty learning because personal-social maladjustments may impede concentration, block interaction between himself and his teacher, and prevent sustained effort on his part. As he lags behind his classmates, the every day failure to achieve success increases his tensions and frustrations. Under such circumstances, many children and adolescents seek to relieve their frustrations by various forms of maladaptive behavior which, in the long run, cause continual difficulties. Such evasive behaviors as failure to try hard, truancy, hostility to the learning task, teacher, or school itself,

[7] M. J. Radke, *The Relation of Parental Authority to Children's Behavior and Attitudes* (Minneapolis: University of Minnesota Press, 1946), p. 103.

giving up, rationalization, and similar defense mechanisms are typical of the nonproductive behavior certain pupils adopt.

It is important for teachers to recognize that in almost every case where a pupil has a learning disability there are likely to be severe emotional concomitants. The effective teacher uses a variety of the methods discussed in the previous chapter to gain knowledge about the personality of any child who is not making adequate progress. In the case of pupils with severe learning disabilities she seeks the helps of specialists such as remedial teachers, guidance counselors, school psychologists and similar specialized personnel. For many children the answer to learning disability will not be additional study, tutoring, exhortation, retentions, or punishment, but rather a careful diagnosis of personality and treatment designed to deal with the psychological factors of the problem. In such cases the goal must be to help the child find suitable solutions to his problems.

Although the scope of this text does not allow a full discussion of all of the psychological problems which may impede learning in the classroom, the following short illustrations may be helpful in showing the variety of problems which may arise.

1. Jimmie, an eight-year-old boy, was a nonreader. Clinical diagnosis revealed that he gained satisfaction by punishing his domineering mother through his failure to succeed in school.
2. Andrew, a nine-year-old boy, was also a nonreader. The psychologist found that Andrew had a fear of growing up because he feared it would change his relationship with his parents. By failing to read he felt that he maintained a closer relationship with them.
3. Gwenn's father was killed in an automobile accident. As a result, her mother started to work. During the next school year, the child's work became increasingly poor. The counselor found that the child suffered continual anxiety over the safety of her mother when she was away from home. Her fears concerning her own security prevented her from concentrating on any learning task.

Although these illustrations have been greatly simplified, they serve to show the variety of personal-social problems any teacher can expect to find. It is axiomatic that the teacher examine the personal-social adjustment of any child whose progress is less than expected.

In the chapters dealing with learning, the importance of motivation was stressed. Because of its importance, the following discussion is included here.

Level of motivation. Not all children are equally motivated to achieve in school. A number of children eagerly look forward to entering school. The writer's six-year-old son, for example, has made an excellent adjustment to first grade. It is readily apparent that he considers successful school work important and seeks to learn because it makes him "a big boy." On the other hand, some children regard school as work or at best, a necessary evil, and see little relationship between school and life. If parents are disinterested or indifferent to school and academic achievement it is likely that the child will reflect these attitudes. A number of writers have reported that children from lower-class homes fail to recognize that education is one of the major routes to successful vocational adjustment. Such children often fail to take advantage of opportunities the way middle-class children do. Evidence further indicates that such factors as school attendance and participation in the various extra-curricular activities are related to the social status of the child's family. Children from homes of higher social status are less likely to drop out of school. They attend school more regularly, and participate in extra-curricular activities to a greater extent than lower-class children.

Generally the typical child is interested in school because many of his needs are satisfied through school activities. Unfortunately, the school environment may not be able to satisfy the needs of some children. Such is the case with many school "drop-outs." It is probable that failure to achieve success in school learning has profound effects on the self-concepts of children and adolescents at all grade levels. Certainly failure hampers self-enhancement and goal attainment, and deprives the individual of recognition and self-esteem. Careful diagnosis is required to determine why the student lacks motivation or is disinterested.

Instructional shortcomings

A certain number of school failures result from various aspects of the school situation itself. Some teachers find themselves unable to adjust instruction and materials to the individual needs of their pupils. Such teachers may lack sufficient knowledge of child psychology or principles of learning. Others may not know the best methods of preparing materials and introducing lessons. Many teachers fail to appraise the academic growth of their pupils and to help them set realistic goals. An important factor is the increased pupil-teacher ratio. In many elementary classrooms the teacher is assigned 35 or 40 pupils. Such numbers make individualized instruction extremely difficult to achieve.

Sometimes the school situation fails to provide a challenge to the average or above average child. Such was the case of Carl.

Carl's problem was that, while he was doing moderately well in his school work, he was extremely sensitive to the feelings and attitudes of his classmates. Further, in his home school, his classmates were not interested in high academic achievement beyond their grade level. With the parents' consent, Carl was moved to another school where he received much greater intellectual challenge. The intellectual atmosphere of the home was improved by the purchase of books. The parents had always given Carl, an only child, much attention and affection. This attention took a more intellectual flavor as a result of the study.

After two years in the new school, he was one of the best achievers in the room, was well-liked, and held class offices. Moving Carl into a more adequate and challenging intellectual environment seemed to pay important dividends . . .[8]

Diagnosis and treatment

As suggested in Chapters 12 and 13, a number of methods and aids are available to assist the teacher in identifying students' difficulties. Formal and informal tests, observational techniques, careful programs of evaluation, case studies, and well-kept records will help the teacher to locate children with learning difficulties. It should be kept in mind, however, that rarely will a single factor be the cause of a given pupil's difficulties. The human is a complex organism which functions in a more or less integrated manner. Usually a number of interrelated factors function to produce any given disability.

The diagnosis. Educational diagnosis involves the identification of two elements: (1) the difficulty; and (2) the cause, or causes of the difficulty.

The first essential is to determine what the difficulty is. In George, discussed earlier in this chapter, we find a boy who is not well-accepted by his classmates and who continuously disrupts the work of the class. Certainly this is an annoying problem to his teacher, but having recognized the problem the next thing is to attempt to locate the cause or causes of his behavior.

This may be difficult because of a number of factors such as (1) inadequate school records, (2) lack of teacher training, (3) lack of trained personnel in the school system, (4) lack of cooperation from the home and others concerned with the guidance of the child, and (5) the interrelations of the different factors. The interrelation of the different factors frequently makes it difficult to distinguish between the cause and effect. In George's case it may be hard to determine whether his lack of acceptance by other members of his class was a cause or an effect of his disorderly behavior in class. It is well known that unsuccessful learning experiences often lead to emotional maladjustments. Likewise, emotional maladjustments are frequently basic to reading failures and other learning problems. It is important to make such distinctions and to gain a clear picture of the cause or causes of behavior and learning difficulties.

[8] James J. Gallagher, Margaret Greenman, Merle Karnes, Alvin King, "Individual Classroom Adjustments for Gifted Children in Elementary Schools," *Exceptional Children*, Vol. 26 (1960), p. 419.

This can best be done when use is made of all resources available for a diagnosis.

The wide variety of techniques available for diagnosing learning difficulties is illustrated by the methods employed in discovering slow-learning pupils, presented in Table 16-2.[9]

The teacher should not approach the diagnosis with preconceived ideas and seek to justify her thinking by failing to consider a variety of factors. She should not place undue confidence in her hunches and guesses or upon test results. She should seek to verify her beliefs by objective study. Generally the more she learns about the child's educational, familial, physical and social history and background, the better she can understand his behavior. A teacher must also understand her own limitations. If she suspects that the child has a physical disability which contributes to the learning difficulty she should urge the child's parents to seek competent medical advice. By the same token, if she finds that the child is suffering severe personal maladjustments she should refer him to the school psychologist or obtain other specialized help.

Remedial principles and methods. Although an extensive discussion of methods for diagnosis and helping pupils with specific learning problems is not within the scope of this book, a brief discussion of some of the basic principles may be helpful. When working with a child who has experienced considerable failure the teacher should attempt to provide numerous opportunities for him to succeed. She should recognize that the child has had few opportunities to succeed previously. Essentially this means modifying her standards and adjusting the outcomes of instruction to achievable goals. Fundamentally the teacher must accept the child where he is, rather than where she wishes he might be, and adjust instruction to his needs. The teacher must be willing to abandon instructional procedures which are not fruitful and concentrate on those which yield success. Constant modification and redirection are needed as the pupil progresses. The remedial program should not be substituted for classroom or school activities which normally motivate or attract the pupil. Remedial programs should not replace other school activities which serve to motivate or interest the pupil. Special lessons in reading or arithmetic, while the rest of the class is enjoying recreational activities on the playground, are not likely to succeed. Another general principle is that the teacher should start remedial assistance by making use of the child's resources. If he is interested in animals he will probably want to read about them. If a child works nicely with others, this asset may be utilized. Remedial training may function best if the cooperation and understanding of the home and family can be obtained.

[9] "Teaching Rapid and Slow Learners in High Schools," Bulletin No. 5, 1954, United States Department of Health, Education and Welfare, p. 17.

TABLE 16-2. Techniques Used in Discovering Slow Learning Pupils

ITEM NO. *	ITEM	TYPE OF ORGANIZATION							
		ALL SCHOOLS (814)[1]		JUNIOR HIGH SCHOOL (403)		REGULAR HIGH SCHOOL (142)		SENIOR HIGH SCHOOL (269)	
		MEAN	RANK	MEAN	RANK	MEAN	RANK	MEAN	RANK
1	2	3	4	5	6	7	8	9	10
1	Teachers' marks	1.70	1	1.09	1	1.74	1	1.09	1
2	Group intelligence tests	1.59	2	1.62	2	1.63	2	1.51	2
3	Teachers' estimates of school achievement	1.50	3	1.59	3	1.44	5	1.40	3
4	Information on physical health	1.42	4	1.50	5	1.35	7	1.34	5
5	Standardized achievement tests	1.40	5	1.52	4	1.36	6	1.25	7
6	Guidance counselor's appraisal of pupils' interests, aptitudes, and abilities	1.32	6	1.27	8	1.48	3	1.31	6
7	Information on vocational plans	1.26	7	1.14	15	1.46	4	1.39	4
8	Information on reading interests and habits	1.27	8	1.83	6.5	1.21	8	1.21	8
9	Information on home environment	1.26	9	1.33	6.5	1.18	9	1.18	9
10	Anecdotal reports and records	1.18	10.5	1.22	11.5	1.08	15	1.17	10
11	Information on personality adjustment	1.18	10.5	1.26	9.5	1.14	10	1.08	11
12	Teachers' estimates of aptitudes	1.14	12	1.20	13	1.12	12	1.07	13
13	Information on physical maturity	1.13	13	1.22	11.5	1.10	13	1.01	15.5
14	Information on social maturity	1.10	14	1.19	14	1.02	16	1.01	15.5
15	Homeroom adviser's appraisal of pupils' interests, aptitudes, and abilities	1.07	15.5	1.26	9.5	.96	18	.84	19
16	Information on hobbies	1.07	15.5	1.06	17	1.13	11	1.07	13
17	Individual intelligence tests	1.05	17	1.13	16	1.09	14	.91	18
18	Teachers' estimates of intelligence	1.03	18	1.02	18	.95	19	1.07	13
19	Standardized aptitude tests in specific fields	.89	19	.79	20	.96	17	.99	17
20	Parental appraisal of pupils' interests, aptitudes, and abilities	.75	20	.81	19	.65	20	.72	20

[1] Number of usable returns.
* Items are arranged in rank order and do not conform to original numbering on the questionnaire.

Individual help is essential in a good remedial program of instruction

Finally, a teacher should not be embarrassed by providing remedial assistance. The recognition that children have learning difficulties is an indication of good teaching and school administration. Schools which do not offer planned programs of assistance fail to recognize the needs of some of their pupils. The following guides are recommended for working with pupils with learning difficulties:

1. An effort should be made to diagnose the child's difficulties. If, for example, the child has difficulty with spelling, the teacher should seek to discover the types of errors the child makes. Does he spell phonetically or not? Does he make errors on common blends or phonograms? Does he hear the word correctly? Can he say the word correctly? How does he feel about his spelling?

2. Generally, the more the teacher can find out about the child, the more she will be able to assist him. Physical and motivational factors, family background, past history are important, as is the child's feelings about himself and his difficulties.

423

3. Recognize that the child's feelings about himself and his problems are important. The teacher should accept the child as he is and help him to gain confidence in his ability to achieve a goal he sets.
4. Enable the child to achieve success in the lessons.
5. Evaluate the growth of the pupil constantly and vary the remedial program in the light of such findings.

SUMMARY

All teachers must expect to have students who will experience difficulty in learning. Sometimes a child's failure to attain sufficient mastery of the required skills and knowledge result from a slower maturational rate than usual. Such pupils, if achieving at levels consistent with their abilities, need not necessarily be considered to have learning disabilities, although they may have difficulty mastering the tasks of the school. On the other hand a child whose achievements are normal, but who has very superior capabilities, may be laboring under a learning disability.

The causes of learning difficulty are numerous and involve all aspects of the organism. Poor general health, discrepancies in development, inadequate diet, and sensory impairments have been shown to affect school performance. Auditory and visual defects have been shown to be intimately related to many school learning tasks.

A child's behavior in the school depends in large part on the nature of his home and family life. Children from low socioeconomic homes often have difficulty adjusting to the demands of the teacher who generally represents middle-class culture. Often the child faces conflicts between home and school which must be reconciled and dealt with. The failure of certain pupils in school stems from the inconsistencies in the demands of home and classroom.

Any intellectual task requires certain personality adjustments. Many social-emotional conflicts prevent a child from interacting beneficially with a learning task or with other significant persons such as teachers and classmates. A number of emotional problems were described. The effective teacher recognizes these factors and attempts to deal with them in helping the child to solve his problems.

In the detection and diagnosis of children with learning difficulties the teacher employs a variety of methods and tools. All of the methods and techniques described in previous chapters are valuable. The teacher treats the learning difficulty as something which is complex and which affects the child's total personality. She examines all aspects of his behavior and restructures the teaching to move from the student's present needs in a systematic, planned fashion to achieve the desired goals. Constant reappraisal and evaluation are needed to assure success.

Problems and Exercises

1. What standards should the teacher employ in determining that a given student has a "learning disability"?
2. What pre-school experiences do you feel will help a child make optimal adjustments to school?
3. What methods would you employ as a teacher to determine the specific nature of a student's learning disabilities?
4. How can the teacher or the school prevent the development of learning difficulties?
5. Show how retention may help or hinder a child who has a learning disability.
6. List various methods by which a teacher may provide successful experiences for a child who has difficulties with the various subjects.
7. How can the teacher help to motivate a typical child?
8. What role does the elementary-school curriculum play in the development of learning disabilities? The high school curriculum?
9. What methods would you employ to help correct the learning disabilities of an elementary-school child? A high-school student?
10. What should the relationship be between the classroom teacher and the counselor? Between the classroom teacher and school psychologist?
11. Show how tests might be used to identify pupils with special learning difficulties. Why is the testing program an essential part of a successful correction program?
12. How may an emotional set against arithmetic occur? How may the teacher help the pupil overcome such an emotional set?

Selected Readings

BLAIR, G. M., *Diagnostic and Remedial Teaching* (New York: The Macmillan Co., 1956).

BRUECKNER, Leo J., and BOND, G. L., *The Diagnosis and Treatment of Learning Difficulties* (New York: Appleton-Century-Crofts, 1955).

D'EVELYN, Katherine, *Meeting Children's Emotional Needs* (Englewood Cliffs: Prentice-Hall, Inc., 1957), Chs. 10-11.

GABBARD, Hazel F., "How Can the Home Help a Child Make a Good School Adjustment?" in Lester D. Crow and Alice Crow, eds. *Readings in Child and Adolescent Psychology* (New York: Longmans, Green, and Co., 1961).

LINDGREN, Henry C., *Educational Psychology in the Classroom*, 2d ed. New York: John Wiley & Sons, 1962, Ch. 17.

SARANSON, Seymour B. *et al.*, *Anxiety in Elementary School Children*. New York: John Wiley & Sons, 1960, Ch. 10.

WOOD, Ernest R., "Subject Disabilities: Special Difficulties in School Learning," *Educational Psychology*, 4th ed. (Chas. E. Skinner, ed.). Englewood Cliffs: Prentice-Hall, Inc., 1959, Ch. 21.

PART V

Guiding the Child

CHAPTER 17

Personality

Terms used in psychology reflect the philosophy or the frame of reference of the psychologists who use them. Consequently, there are almost as many concepts of personality as there are individuals attempting to define them. Moreover, perhaps no other concept in psychology has been so variously defined and measured by such a variety of procedures as personality. Definitions of personality range from mystical verbiage to detailed descriptions of social acts. Efforts to measure it vary from the interpretation of reactions to ink blots to the use of rating graphs made by acquaintances. One reason for this variability in definition and measurement is that personality is such a broad and inclusive concept that it is difficult to comprehend all of it at any time, and more difficult still to measure it in its entirety.

An understanding of the nature of personality, how it develops and is integrated as a functional unit, is essential to teachers and others if they are to carry out their role in guiding learners in their development. The next three chapters will be developed as an integrated unit reflecting the principles of learning in their interaction with forces of personality, and culminating in practical applications. This integration will aid teachers in forming effective theories of personality—its development, modification, and reshaping.

ASPECTS OF PERSONALITY

There are three *phases* or *aspects* of personality which account for much of the apparent disagreement among psychologists and educators. These are really different points of view of the same thing. What is true of one aspect (viewed in isolation) may or may not be true of another aspect.

First, there is the *action* aspect of personality concerned with *how* a person acts. Using this aspect as a guide, some personalities are called *emotional* while others are considered *calm, intellectual,* and so on. Thus, personality is sometimes defined as the *sum total* of a person's action patterns. Using this definition, a person who acts in a wide range of situations with jovial and felicitous behavior is said to have a happy and jovial personality. Any personality may be described from the standpoint of the *action* or *behavioral* aspect.

Second, there is the *social* aspect, or the stimulus effect a person has on other people. "John has a good personality" in every day speech means that John has a favorable effect on one or more people. This aspect is the sum total of all those things about a person that affect other people. The social aspect of personality, then, simply describes the characteristic effect a person has on others.

A *third* aspect of personality is the *cause* or *why* aspect. This is the aspect of personality which makes a person act in *social* or *unsocial* ways and makes people react accordingly. People like a person (the *social aspect*) because his actions are interpreted as friendly (the *response aspect*) which, in turn, is the result of his positive attitudes (the *cause aspect*). *All three aspects are important.* None of them alone nor even all of them together describe the whole of personality. No aspect definition, no aspect measurement will give more than a partial understanding of personality. Our effect on others, the effect on us of things and events in life, our deepest thoughts, feelings, and attitudes are all interesting and important aspects of our personalities. But, personality cannot be identified with any one of these aspects. It is all of these and more.

The meaning of personality

Personality is the whole of man: his inherited aptitudes and capacities; all his past learnings; the integration and synthesis of these factors into characteristic behavior patterns; and his ideals, values, and expectations. Since personality is a generic term involving intelligence, emotion, motivation, learning, memory, thinking, perceiving, and other factors, some psychologists believe it would be better to drop the word *personality* entirely. These psychologists assert that explanations of these components leave nothing further to be said.

In the organic world, however, the whole is *more* than the *sum* of its parts. A synthesis of dynamic parts produces something unique. There are so many cross-relationships involved in an organic combination of living, interacting parts that very small differences can produce very great effects. Therefore, a synthesis of psychological factors into a personality, living and dynamic as it is, is not a mere assemblage of components. The whole personality becomes something quite different from the psychological factors composing it. Thus, personality can never be understood from the mere study of its components alone. Of course, the study of personality development and an understanding of its major aspects will give insight into its nature. This insight will aid the teacher in guiding the child in his educational growth.

A primary fact about personality is that each personality is *unique*. No two personalities are alike, not even those of identical twins. Of course, personalities are similar in one or another factor and can be arranged into rough classifications. But they cannot be precisely catalogued. An individual, remarkably stable at times, may act in an unstable way at other times. A similar personality trait may function differently in different personalities. It may do so even in seemingly similar personalities. The dynamics of individual personalities differ, and generalizations about them are often unjustified.

Another basic fact about personality is that it is a product of its own functioning. Today's functioning of a personality will depend, in part, on how it functioned yesterday. The experiences accumulated from today's responses will influence how the personality will function tomorrow. Personality is constantly in the process of becoming. This fact has profound significance for education. Each person develops his personality by the slow process of day-to-day learning and acting in various situations and roles. As we shall discuss later, the reactions of others to a person's behavior will have a *confirming* or *weakening* effect on his personality. Each personality pattern is shackled to its own past, yet it is the determiner of its own future, strongly influenced by the actions of significant persons in the environment.

Personality differences in early childhood. Observable differences in behavior and appearance are apparent at birth, and while particular behavior patterns do not appear at this stage, the potential qualities necessary for their development are there. The variations in behavior, apparent among infants, mark the beginnings of personality differences. Since no two individuals have the same physical and social environments, they tend to exhibit, increasingly, differences in behavior patterns as they grow older. Thus, by the time children reach school-age various personality patterns or "types" are discernible. Studies show that significant differences in personality are apparent by the age of three years.[1]

The significance of personality differences during childhood are apparent when we apply the concepts *continuity* and *unity* to a consideration of the nature of personality. Continuity refers to the similarity in appearance, speech, and emotional behavior an individual exhibits during childhood and adolescence. By *unity* we mean the relatedness present in

[1] B. Klopfer, "Personality Differences between Boys and Girls in Early Childhood," *Psychological Bulletin,* Vol. 36 (1939), p. 538.

the speech, emotional behavior, motor activities, and intellectual processes of the child. These are further related to such involuntary forms of behavior as the circulation of the blood and the secretions of the glands. *Unity* furnishes a better basis for understanding the dynamics of the individual's behavior at a particular time. The term *continuity* emphasizes passage of time in the child's development. These concepts bring to focus the consistency found in child behavior and development.

The self as personal entity. Strictly speaking, we do not say that personality does things or becomes something. It is the person or self who reacts through his capacities and powers. Combs and Snygg [2] define *self* as a conscious, thinking entity with all particular characteristics and attitudes. A person has a personality developed in accord with his natural predispositions, environment, and experiences.

A person develops his personality by acting and interacting with (objective) reality in a reasonably competent manner or by refusing to do so. The type of person he becomes depends largely upon his level of response to reality. This is clearly shown in a study of 125 sixth-grade boys who were selected from a high delinquency area. They had never experienced contact with the police or courts in their development.[3] A sample of 103 of these boys was studied four years later. The results indicate that once a favorable self-image is developed it is difficult to alter to a delinquent self-image.

We know ourselves largely through our perceptions of the reactions of others to us. Thus, the descriptions children give of themselves correspond remarkably well with those given by their mothers. This was recently observed by one of the authors in comparisons of self-descriptive statements of fourth-grade pupils with those of their mothers. One fourth-grade boy described himself as fidgety and ill-mannered, although the teacher had not observed these characteristics. When the mother was interviewed, it was noted that her description was almost identical with the boy's.

Significance of the self-concept

Many psychologists employ the terms *self* and *self-concept* to get a better understanding of the motivations and behavior of children. Perkins,[4] for example, points out that the *self-concept* is a valuable tool

[2] Arthur W. Combs and Donald Snygg, *Individual Behavior*, rev. ed. (New York: Harper and Brothers, 1959), pp. 44-45.

[3] F. R. Scarpitti, Ellen Murray, S. Dinitz, and W. C. Reckless, "The 'Good' Boy in a High Delinquency Area," *American Sociological Review*, Vol. 25 (1960), pp. 555-558.

[4] Hugh V. Perkins, "Teachers' and Peers' Perceptions of Children's Self-concepts," *Child Development*, Vol. 29 (1958), pp. 203-220.

for investigating psychological factors which influence learning and development. It has also helped teachers and parents understand child behavior. Personality theorists and other students of child psychology have made worthwhile contributions to understanding children through their studies and explorations of the *self*.

The self-concept. From the emergence of the notion of *self* or individuality, indicated by the suggestibility of the last stage of infancy to the awareness of his own identity in late childhood, the child gradually develops the power to enter into the reality of his environment. Progressively, he gains understanding of the process through practice in a number of roles (pupil, group member, team leader, member of a family, etc.) until he becomes less disturbed by changing moods. A person's self, as defined previously, is an objective reality. His ideas of himself or his understanding of himself, with all his strengths and weaknesses, however, is a learned product which is always subjective. This learned concept of self may be realistically and precisely correct, or grossly erroneous. As in the development of all concepts, knowledge gained through the cognitive activities of his life's experiences, colored deeply by his complex, individually developed emotionality, conditioned by his constitutional equipment, and determined by his personal choices relate and interrelate in the evolution of the *self-concept*. Combs and Snygg [5] describe the *self-concept* as the way a person perceives or knows himself, especially concerning the fundamental aspects that are very important and central to himself and which are involved in a great deal of his behavior. It is the very essential *me* whose loss is regarded as personal destruction and whose disorganization is vigorously resisted. These writers apply the term *phenomenal self* to the person's awareness of what he is at the precise moment of action. To an "outsider" who can never know a person as completely and intimately as he knows himself, the phenomenal self is an *inference* from the individual's behavior. It is a useful concept in *assessing personality* and *predicting probable behavior*.

An important aspect of the self, then, is that it represents the way in which the individual sees himself. Usually the individual's behavior, including his thoughts, feelings, motives, and values, tends to be consistent with this self-concept or the way he sees himself. Lecky [6] has suggested that a basic need of an organism is the need for self-consistency. In other words, the individual's behavior will tend to be consistent with his self-concept. A simple case may illustrate this point.

Tom, a six-year-old first grader, hostilely refuses help from his teacher in putting on his rubbers when preparing to go home after school.

[5] Arthur W. Combs and Donald Snygg, *Op. cit.*, pp. 45 and 128.
[6] Prescott Lecky, *Self-Consistency: A Theory of Personality* (New York: Island Press, 1955), p. 350.

Tom's teacher was motivated by kindness and a sincere desire to help the boy after watching his unsuccessful struggles. Tom, however, saw her efforts to help as a threat to his self-concept as a "big boy" who was able to dress himself and care for his dressing needs. On the other hand, Sally, a classmate, sees in the teacher's helping hand a gesture or sign of affection and welcomes such assistance.

Growth in concept of self.   It has been pointed out that the child's concept of self is influenced by a great many factors: his parents' social status and class membership; their attitudes, values, standards of behavior, and moral and ethical beliefs; the practices under which he is reared; cultural patterns which ascribe the various roles he is expected to play; personal qualities such as body size, weight, strength, agility, physical assets and defects; his sex, race, religion, and mental ability. Naturally all these factors are not developed at any one time, but result from the varied experiences he encounters throughout life. It must be emphasized that the child's self-concept, to a large extent, is the result of the reactions of others to him. In the case of Tom, for instance, perception that the other children welcomed the teacher's aid in preparing to go home could change Tom's reactions. Tom would redefine his self-concept to include help from others as part of being a "big boy." If actions of others suggest that a child is stupid, inept, insincere, etc., then it becomes difficult for the child to hold on to a self-concept of adequacy.

The developmental nature of the child's self-concept has been revealed by a number of investigators. Generally the child's experiences at home, in school, and in the community lead to fairly accurate insights concerning his abilities and achievement. Brandt[7] had a group of sixth graders and a group of eleventh graders estimate how well they expected to do in certain academic and physical tests in comparison to the group as a whole and in comparison to each classmate. He concluded from his study that self-rating accuracy may be developed and that it tends to increase with age and grade in school. Students with self-concepts of inadequacy (not good students, not good in school, etc.) which have been built up through experiences with parents, classmates, teachers, etc., often perform less well than they potentially could. They also manifest lower aspirational levels relative to tasks at school. In a study by Bledsoe and Garrison[8] fourth- and sixth-grade girls were found to have significantly higher self-concept ratings (by themselves) than fourth- and sixth-grade

[7] Richard M. Brandt, "The Accuracy of Self-Estimates: A Measure of Self-Concept Reality," *Genetic Psychology Monographs*, Vol. 58 (1958), 55-59.

[8] Joseph C. Bledsoe and Karl C. Garrison, *The Self Concepts of Elementary School Children in Relation to Their Academic Achievement, Intelligence, Interests, and Manifest Anxiety.* Cooperative Research Project No. 1008, U. S. Office of Education. College of Education, University of Georgia (1962).

boys. It was also noted that self-concepts of elementary-school pupils were related to cultural forces in their backgrounds.

In an investigation of the self-concepts of potentially delinquent and potentially nondelinquent boys from similar physical environments, Reckless, Dinitz, and Kay [9] found significant differences. Boys who were deemed nondelinquent saw themselves as obedient. They liked school, rarely played "hookey," felt that their families were as good as most families, and believed their parents to be neither overly strict nor too permissive. In most cases, their families were striving to achieve the "middle class" norms of behavior. Therefore, these boys found their actions confirmed by teachers—persons in authority—and peers whom they considered important. Such confirmations (responses of approval) strengthened their self-concepts which supported nondelinquent behavior.

Boys who were delinquent, however, saw society as set against them. Many came from broken homes; most came from homes in which parental behavior was *inconsistent*. Expectations transmitted by the parents led the boys to expect inconsistent, unfair treatment from persons in authority. The self-concept of the delinquent was one of revolt against established authority (because it was unfair and did not allow him to meet his needs).

The child is born into a particular general culture as well as subcultures. His personality is both enlarged and restricted by these cultures. As shown in Figure 17-1, these subcultures overlap the general culture and thus restrict or enlarge the child's world. The family, religious group, social group, and neighborhood make for a diversity of culture and contribute to personality differences.

The ideal-self. Some investigators have resorted to the use of the concept *ideal-self* as a means of determining the self-aspirations of children. The ideal-self is usually thought of as an expression of the type of person a child would like to be or resemble. The term *ideal-self* has been shown to be valuable in determining the relationship between how the child sees himself and what he thinks he should be like. Havighurst, Robinson, and Dorr [10] have hypothesized that the ideal-self may be developmental in nature. They suggest that the ideal-self begins when the child identifies with a parental figure. During middle childhood and early adolescence it moves through a stage of romanticism and glamor, and culminates in late adolescence as a composite of desirable characteristics which may be symbolized by an attractive, real, and visible young adult or perhaps even an imaginary person.

[9] W. C. Reckless, S. Dinitz, and B. Kay, "The Self Component in Potential Delinquency and Potential Non-Delinquency," *American Sociological Review*, Vol. 22 (1957), pp. 566-570.

[10] R. J. Havighurst, M. Z. Robinson, and Mildred Dorr, "The Development of the Ideal Self in Childhood and Adolescence," *Journal of Educational Research*, Vol. 40 (1946), pp. 241-257.

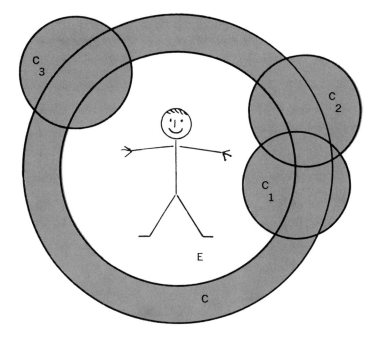

FIGURE 17-1.   Schematic Representation Of The Operation Of
Biology, Culture, and Environment. The human organism, made
up of active living cells, continuously responds to biological
forces. The nature and direction of these responses are affected
by his natural environment (E) and his culture (C) or different
cultures (C_1, C_2, C_3). These different cultures may be termed subcultures to distinguish them from the general culture.

The school-age child develops an ideal-self concept through learning.
Since these children come from diverse cultural backgrounds, significant
differences may be noted in ideal concepts of a group of children. There
is evidence, however, that the self-concepts and ideal-selves of children
become increasingly and significantly congruent through time. Perhaps
the greatest value of the ideal-self concept is that it provides an index
of the child's aspirations against which his abilities, potentialities, and
levels of development can be compared. Table 17-1 illustrates the type of
people a group of children have indicated they would like to resemble.
These results furnish valuable information regarding the types of people
who influence children's concepts regarding "ideal" or "model" behavior.
The influences of parents and relatives, glamorous adults, and attractive
and successful young adults are shown to be important for both boys and
girls. The effects of sex and socio-cultural factors may be noted in the
children's choices of the "ideal-person."

TABLE 17-1.   Classification of Persons Described as the Ideal
Self, Percentage Distribution (*After Havighurst, et al.*)

BOYS

| | | *Group* | | | | |
CATEGORY	A	B	C	D	E	F
I. Parents and relatives	7	23	11	—	16	7
II. Parent surrogates	0	0	0	—	0	2
III. Glamor adults	12	32	47	—	23	37
IV. Heroes	3	6	11	—	10	5
V. Attractive adults	53	30	23	—	21	15
VI. Composite character	25	6	8	—	28	23
VII. Age mates	0	0	0	—	2	1
VIII. Miscellaneous	0	3	0	—	0	5

GIRLS

	A	B	C	D	E	F
I. Parents and relatives	6	32	14	6	11	7
II. Parent surrogates	2	0	2	0	4	12
III. Glamor adults	16	17	27	23	21	37
IV. Heroes	2	3	3	6	1	7
V. Attractive adults	36	13	25	18	25	18
VI. Composite character	33	22	23	29	35	18
VII. Age mates	3	8	6	12	3	1
VIII. Miscellaneous	0	5	0	6	0	0

Description of groups:
   A. Ten-, eleven-, and twelve-year-olds in a typical midwestern community.
   B. Sixth graders (age 11-12) in an industrial section of Chicago.
   C. Fifth and sixth graders in a war industry community.
   D. Girls at a Chicago Settlement House, mostly Italian.
   E. Seventh and eighth graders in a war industry community.
   F. Middle-class Negro children (age 12-14) in Baltimore.

Sex differences. Some interesting sex differences have been noted
in a comparison of the ideal self. In the previously mentioned study by
Havighurst and others, boys and girls were asked to tell something
about the character, appearance, and activities of the person listed as
their ideal self. The frequency of mention of the different character and
personality traits is listed in Table 17-2. The boys listed material things
such as money and property more frequently than girls, while the girls
frequently listed good looks, cooperativeness, and helpfulness as the
most desirable characteristics. Both boys and girls regarded honesty,
industriousness, and responsibility as very desirable character and personality traits. It has constantly been noted that secondary-school-age
pupils will accept almost any qualities in their teachers as long as they
feel that they are fair and sincere in their relationships.

TABLE 17-2.   Comparison of Character and Personality Traits Mentioned by Boys and Girls (*After Havighurst, et al.*)

	BOYS N = 158	GIRLS N = 168
Material values—money, clothes, property	34	3
Good looks, good appearance, neat, clean	21	51
Good personality, stereotypes, popular	21	20
Friendly, lots of friends, courteous, polite, can take a joke	31	22
Honest, responsible, industrious, church-goer, kind	42	51
Cooperative, helpful, patient	5	18
Self-sacrificing, working for social justice, human brotherhood, altruism	4	3

Realization of the self

A human being possesses dynamic capacities that are organized or patterned in an organic unity. These have the *potential* power to grow in and through integrated activity to full maturity. It will be recalled that an educational program which fails to emphasize self-realization will tend to constrict potential growth capacities.

Many personality theories consider the internal and external stimulations to the maturing and life activities of an organism as drives. Under the influence of Hebb,[11] many psychologists have postulated the presence of a basic state (which Anderson calls *activation*) as a property of the very nature of a living being. Anderson observes that, using Hebb's analogy, "human mechanism is more like a steam engine with some steam always in its boilers than like an automobile engine which starts from a complete stop." [12]

Needs and drives.   As we pointed out in Chapter 3, behavior patterns evolve as a result of efforts on the part of the organism to satisfy needs. In the discussion of needs in Chapter 3, you will recall that the major needs related to the developmental tasks of childhood and adolescence in American culture are (1) need for affection, (2) need for independence, (3) need for approval, and (4) need for self-esteem. It was further pointed out that personality integration is dependent, in large measure, on the manner and extent to which the individual is successful in satisfying these needs constructively.

[11] Donald O. Hebb, "Drives and the Central Nervous System," *Psychological Review,* Vol. 62 (1955), pp. 243-254.
[12] John Anderson, "Dynamics of Development: System in Process," *The Concept of Development,* ed. by Dale Harris. Minneapolis: University of Minnesota Press (1957), p. 31).

The tendency of an organism to realize an unfulfilled need, psychological or physical, may be termed *drive*. Just as there is a hierarchy of powers with man, so there is a corresponding hierarchy of needs. Combs and Snygg resolve the hierarchy of needs to just one basic need—that of developing and enhancing self. Other writers have drawn up very elaborate lists. The student is well advised to avoid either oversimplification or over-fine categorization.

Drives are the dynamic element in human nature which urge the person on to goal-seeking activities. Some of these, described as they related to learning in Chapter 7, are an example of bipolarity or contradictory drives. The drives tend basically to dispose to action which must be balanced by effective controls. Happiness and effective living depend to a great extent on the person's achieving a balance between the drives pressing for action and the controls which direct these drives. Lack of control (sometimes mistakenly thought to reflect permissiveness) and over-rigid controls are both harmful.

Frustration. *Frustration* or *thwarting* is a blocking of or interference with an aroused drive by some barrier or obstruction. Some degree of frustration, of course, is a universal force in the life of an organism and a goal to self-realization and achievement. In fact, the ordinary process of growth, mentioned earlier in the concept of self-consistency and imbalance, is normally achieved by:

1. A *drive* serving as a motivating factor to realize the satisfaction of a basic *need*.
2. A *thwarting* or *frustrating* factor entering to demand a solution. A problem has been created.
3. A *response stage* in which past experience, habit, rational thought, emotional impulse, insight, and conditioning interact to produce some action.
4. *Attainment of solution.*

There are varying degrees of frustration, from slight frustration where the usual response is ineffective and the drive is also weak to severe frustration arising from a serious threat to one's self-concept posed by failure of the adaptation system.

Usually *conflict* involves frustration, aroused by the necessity to make a choice between two equally strong or appealing goals or two equally repelling objectives. If the conflict remains chronically unresolved, personality growth may become inhibited through unhealthy or irrational responses, such as those of avoidance and escape. Such maladjustive techniques will be discussed in the next chapter.

Frustration occurs especially at every new stage of personality development, the period when new developmental tasks appear. The individual develops new abilities or powers to which he is not yet adjusted; and new experiences occur for which there are no ready-made or habitual responses. Frustration may also result from

1. physical factors in the environment
2. social factors and conditions, particularly restrictions imposed by authority figures
3. economic conditions or factors
4. personal defects or limitations
5. incompatible goals (which produce internal conflict)
6. conflicts between personal values and physical or emotional needs.

Personality development

Personality formation is a complex task beginning in infancy or perhaps even before birth. Materials bearing on factors involved in personality development were presented in earlier discussions of developmental tasks, basic and acquired needs, and the socialization process. Earlier chapters have pointed out that biological and cultural forces operate to produce differences in personality. A consideration of the development of some of the most striking aspects or facets of personality follows. The discussion will take account of their development and of the influence which may be constructively exerted by the teacher.

Concepts of human nature. According to one important concept, human nature resides in those human qualities that are universal. Another interesting and useful concept of human nature maintains the uniqueness of each individual. Each person who begins life is a unique human being who grows up in a culture where others are present, and where he is expected to learn to play his assigned roles. Although the socialization process was described in Chapter 6, we will discuss it further in this chapter. Learning to play the sex role, class role, and the role based upon parental expectations appears early in life. The socioeconomic status of the home, proximity to playmates, the mores and customs of the home and community, and the leisure activities of children and adolescents have important bearings on the nature of socialization.

Constitutional elements of personality. Total personality development, even in its psychological aspects, involves both the *physical* and *constitutional* elements of human nature. It also involves the basic hereditary endowment. Scott points out that heredity, while not predetermining the behavior of an organization, influences it at every stage through maturation and differentiation:

> As we see its role in relation to other determinants, heredity tends to promote variability of behavior, both within an individual, where adaptability is dependent upon variability, and between individuals, where it increases the variety of social organization. All modern knowledge of heredity tends to emphasize the inevitability of variation and hence of individuality.[13]

Maturation as a process of organization and differentiation is largely controlled by *biological* and *physiological* processes although, as a number of authorities have shown, psychological processes are also involved. In her list of the processes affecting growth (heredity, environment, personal interaction, and self-directing principles), Dolores [14] outlines the physical factors underlying behavior in children. In the preschool child, the finer muscles are so developed by age 4 or 5 that he engages in physical activity such as running and jumping through sheer delight. Pikunas [15] has shown that, when a readiness for a new set of task skills has developed, the person seems to have a pressing need to utilize them for sheer pleasure. In doing this, he develops a proficiency in one set of tasks which prepares him for the next developmental stage. Dolores takes note of the preschool child's acuity of sense perception and fine discernment of response which makes him so ingenious in observing and imitating even the slightest mannerisms of adults, often unnoticed by the adults. This ability forms the readiness for the *learning by identification* discussed earlier in this book and in Chapter 6.

In childhood, from ages 7 to 10, the rate of growth seems to reach a plateau, remaining about the same for boys and girls. Since the brain centers through which the higher thought processes are often not yet fully developed, rote memory and imitation are the main channels of learning available to many children. Concrete examples and analogies secure the best retention. Dolores' concept of functional learning compares with Piaget's *operational reasoning*. Operational reasoning will be discussed later in relation to the intellectual aspect of personality. Children at this age like repetitive activities so that drill of many kinds is acceptable. By the end of this period, the child's consciousness of and pride in his motor skills and motor co-ordination leads him to such activities as chasing, tagging, pushing, pulling, and wrestling which may continue into adolescence.

[13] J. P. Scott, "The Genetic and Environmental Differentiation of Behavior," *The Concept of Development,* ed. by Dale Harris. Minneapolis: Univ. of Minn. Press (1957), p. 76.

[14] Sister Marian Dolores, S.H.N., "Physical Factors Underlying Behavior Patterns in Children," *Education,* Vol.   (1951), pp. 267-271.

[15] Justin Pikunas and Eugene Albrecht, *Psychology of Human Development* (New York: McGraw-Hill Book Co., Inc., 1961), pp. 61 et. seq.

By the time a child reaches late adolescence, his physical abilities are essentially the same as those of an adult. His brain and glandular system is almost fully developed. His developmental tasks now consist in refining his feelings and processes of thought, and in determining his own activities. Thus, physical factors that determine readiness affect every aspect of personality development.

Many psychologists suggest that there are certain constitutional *tendencies* underlying behavior. Although these tendencies *do not determine* behavior, they may have considerable educational implications. Findings in this area of research, although not conclusive, indicate that some basic individual differences in personality traits are based on *constitutional elements* which make it easier for the child to seek need satisfaction in some ways rather than in others. These predisposing constitutional elements affect personality development in other ways also, i.e. in the amount of energy available and in tendencies to adopt roles which society may or may not approve.

It is important for the teacher to be aware that children have differing constitutional tendencies which may manifest themselves in specific personality traits. Furthermore, teachers need to be perceptively insightful into their own personality structures and their relations to students. This aspect will be discussed in Chapter 19.

The role of learning in personality formation. The basic needs inherent in man's nature "drive" him to the realization of his natural potentialities through a continuum of maturational and developmental stages. The nature and direction of their development is that aspect of personality which is learned. It is what we call personality that makes a person "personal" and unlike any other human being. It adds a note of uniqueness and worth to the dignity of his inherited nature.

One may raise the question, How is personality learned? As we shall see, in a certain sense, it is *caught.* The process of directing and guiding this "self-directed" growth is called *education.* According to the thesis and theme of this text, this kind of education reaches beyond the intellectual development to that of the entire personality or the whole person. Ruskin [16] called this guidance "painful, continual and difficult, to be done by kindness, by watching, by warning, by precept, and by praise, but above all—by example."

The normal personality is formed by learning, primarily in a favorable atmosphere or climate. The quality of human change that takes place is affected by the physical and social forces encountered in daily living. However, one must not overlook the dynamic nature of the individual in personality integration. In Chapter 2 it was noted that a

[16] John Ruskin, *Educational Digest,* Vol. 21 (1956), p. 33.

child is born into the family where he is normally accepted with love. Learning begins at birth and changes progressively, but in a continuum as the various needs manifest themselves at each maturational stage. From the beginning and throughout life the child is a member of a group learning chiefly through interpersonal relationships. Each person within most groups has a status which implies certain rights and obligations. He is also expected to behave according to a *role*. There will be the dependency role, leadership role, parental role, sex role, and so on ad infinitum even to a scape-goat role. Role-playing is implicit in almost any group situation.

From early childhood the human being learns adequate emotionality, language, and religious sentiment by imitation. A child's emotional control (or the lack of it) is greatly influenced by association with the people around him. This imitation, by which a person learns so much early in life and all through life, is called *role identification*. Identification is one of the most imperative qualities of human nature. At first it is unconscious and spontaneous. Even the child, (and certainly the adult), does not identify with just anyone nor with everyone. Identification models are persons who are psychologically close to him—persons who accept and love him, and whose personalities offer him something to respect and admire.

The identifying child *feels* at one with this person. The first identification models for the infant are normally the mother and father. Identification with each in infancy seems to be basic to the child's future understanding of his own sex role as well as to the adequacy of his adult relationships with members of either sex. When the child first leaves the family group, he may strongly identify with other adult authority or status figures such as his teacher. In later childhood, a person will tend to identify with like-sex peer groups which enables him to further learn and practice his sex-role skills, perfect his communication skills, and develop increasingly his independence, self-direction, and social skills. In adolescence, a youth identifies with both sex groups and defines his self-concept through his acceptance. He tends to refine his social skills through experiences until he finds the one person with whom he can identify as a life partner, developing a beautifully balanced independent-dependent relationship that may even tend to liken their physical appearance after many years of intimate association.

As maturation proceeds, the type and quality of identification models change. For example, in late childhood and preadolescent gang-age (and beyond), there is a strong tendency to "hero-worship," to identify with a hero. The model may be a local status person, a national, historical, or religious figure—anyone possessing an admirable quality that may be related to a personal need or to a level of aspiration in life. Often these models of identification serve the purpose of *confirming* the child's self-concept.

Love and loyalty may easily be transferred from the quality or model to the person himself to produce total identification. For example, qualities of kindness, self-possession, optimism, fairness, and enthusiasm may make a teacher a hero or a heroine to a young person who internalizes these desirable qualities through identification so that they become part of his self-concept.

Finally, a person who is a friend, who respects the younger or older person's integrity, who can permit the expression of feelings and the exploration of personal problems with the understanding and support of a completely trustworthy ally can become an identifying figure strong enough to reorient a negative learning process in personality development.

Learning through identification is sometimes called *spontaneous learning*. Another kind of learning which is involved in personality development and modification is called *associative learning*. This learning is associated with pleasant or unpleasant emotional or feeling tones. This type of learning, together with learning by example, is in large measure the source of personality habits, attitudes, values, ideals, etc. It is responsible for much of the negative and undesirable direction of personality development. Authority figures may, consciously or unconsciously, use associative learning in such forms as the reinforcement of reward and punishment (in terms of discipline or limit-setting) to produce behavior changes. *Associative learning*, if supported by affection and acceptance, is necessary for establishing reality limits to adequate socialization, for providing basic inner security and social acceptance, and for laying the foundation for self-direction and self-restraint.

Personality is continuously learned both *consciously* and *unconsciously* in gradual increments which shape the whole. It should be remembered that each person's capacities are so interrelated and interdependent that it is impossible to separate them for schematic conceptualization except artificially. This schematic separation can be used to facilitate the understanding of the integrated whole. In reality, personality is an *entity* entirely different from the sum of its parts. A 13-year follow-up study of 28 adolescents who were given the *Symonds Picture-Story Test* and the Rorschach in 1940 and again in 1953 lends support to the persistence of certain personality characteristics.[17] The themes in the stories of the adolescents and in the stories related thirteen years later showed a marked persistence of certain features, "including aggressiveness in response to the interview situation and to tests, in nervous signs,

[17] P. M. Symonds and Arthur R. Jensen, *From Adolescent to Adult* (New York: Columbia University Press, 1961).

in hobbies, and in attitudes." Behavior ratings indicated a high degree of consistency in overt personality. No firm predictive relationship, however, was found between educational and vocational intentions during adolescence and actual educational and vocational experiences thirteen years later.

Educational implications. Personality, the learned product, is very important to the educator as a counselor, for it is here where personality change, insight, and integration can take place. Knowledge motivates the self-directing dynamism which is designed to control even as it is spurred on to the goal-achievement of personal enhancement or learning. With each change the individual undergoes (and through all the maturational stages), he constantly redefines his self-concept.

The good, normal, healthy feeling a child has that he counts for something, that he is worthy enough to be accepted and worthy of self-acceptance with security and esteem is achieved through his experiences in the way others, especially those who are psychologically important to him (parents, siblings, peers, and esteemed acquaintances), treat him. They accomplish this by emphasizing his strengths, accepting his weaknesses without withholding love, and by allowing reasonable scope for the exercise of his continually emerging abilities. If he finds acceptance, he will react in the circumstances of his life's experiences with the confidence and joy of an adequate personality. If, however, he experiences rejection, threat, and insecurity, he will almost surely develop the personality problems of an emotionally disturbed and maladjusted person. A person's self-concept affects all that he is, all that he does, and all that he becomes, whether criminal, little man, sage, or saint.

Guiding pupils in the achievement of personality integration

The needs, developmental tasks, and character development of children and adolescents were presented in preceding chapters. The nature of personality, the development of personality, and products of personality were described earlier in this chapter. Since personality refers to the *total* person, we cannot separate these different aspects of the growing individual. An important task of parents, teachers, and other adults concerned with guiding children and adolescents is to help them satisfy their basic needs and accomplish their developmental tasks in a personally and socially constructive manner.

Components of a healthy personality. The Midcentury White House Conference on Children and Youth set forth the components of a healthy personality as follows:

This member of the Future Farmers of America displays his prized
accomplishment. The feeling that one can carry real tasks through
to successful completion is an important component in the development of a healthy personality structure

1. sense of trust: a short-cut expression which conveys the characteristic flavor of all the child's satisfying experiences with others.
2. sense of autonomy: the feeling that one is an independent human
   being who is still able to use the help and guidance of others in
   important matters.
3. sense of initiative: individual's employment of learning, imagination, and enterprise to events of daily living.
4. sense of accomplishment: feeling that one can carry real tasks
   through to successful completion.

5. sense of identity: increasingly clarified feeling of continuity, sameness and meaning of life.
6. sense of intimacy: rewarding interpersonal relations in the form of love, friendship, and inspiration from others.
7. parental sense: ability to regard one's children as a trust of the community, rather than as an extension of one's own personality or as persons with whom one lives by accident of contiguity, relationship, or force of circumstances.
8. sense of integrity: love of one's parents which is free from the wish that they had been different and one's acceptance of the reality that life is the responsibility of the individual.[18]

Meeting frustrations and conflicts. It was suggested earlier that frustrations and conflicts in life are inevitable. Parents and teachers cannot hope to protect children at all times from all frustrations. Children need help in meeting frustrations, but not protection from all frustration. Every child needs to learn that he cannot always have his own way, that he cannot always be the winner, and that he cannot control all the forces about him. As an antidote to the notion that the well-adjusted child does not meet frustrations and conflicts Thompson states:

. . . Every child suffers some anxiety, displays some behavior that is unacceptable to others, fails to reach some goals that are extremely important to him, and experiences some periods of what he calls unhappiness. However, the child whose psychological adjustment can be considered within normal range "bounces back" from these disappointments and depressions. He continues to orient his behavior toward goals that promise to satisfy his needs, and he adjusts his goal-setting to the social demands of the culture.[19]

The extent to which frustrations and conflicts lead to personality difficulty depends upon a number of factors, such as:

1. the *dynamic nature* of the basic need which is blocked—whether it is a privation (never having been satisfied) or a deprivation (having once been satisfied)
2. *extent of blocking*
3. possibility of finding substitute goal
4. extent to which other basic needs of affection, security, and acceptance have been and are being satisfied.

[18] Helen Witmer and Ruth Kotinsky (Editors), *A Healthy Personality for Every Child: A Digest of the Fact Finding Report to the Midcentury White House Conference on Children and Youth.* (1953). Washington: Health Publications Institute, Inc., pp. 8-24. Definitions of the various components have not been quoted exactly but paraphrased in the interest of the purpose of this chapter.
[19] G. C. Thompson, *Child Psychology: Growth Trends and Adjustments* (Boston: Houghton Mifflin Co., 1952), p. 183.

It is through satisfactory solution of problems that the self is adequately realized and that personality achieves full maturity at each stage of development to complete personality integration. If, as has been said, life is warfare, then the battleground is the stability of human nature. *Realization* in education makes possible self-change that can release potential powers and capacities previously unknown. On the other hand, coercion and exhortation result in restriction of potential growth powers.

Self acceptance. In order to be able to accept himself, a person must have a self-concept which is realistic and which is not too different from his ideal of what he should be. The self-accepting person is familiar with his weaknesses. He recognizes those that he cannot change and those he must accept and live with. Such a person approves himself while he recognizes his deficiencies.

The person who accepts himself is guided by his own standards. He has insight and understanding into his ability, worth, and relations to others. Sheerer [20] has written that the self-acceptant person believes that he can deal with life; is confident that he is as worthy as others; does not expect rejection or scorn from others; assumes responsibility for his own behavior; follows his standards in preference to external standards; is objective in assessing praise or blame; neither denies his feelings nor condemns himself for experiencing them; and realistically appraises his limitations and superior qualities.

The individual with a healthy concept of himself sees himself as adequate. Adequacy, however, is not thought of here in terms of ability. As Soper points out:

It has to do with whether a person sees himself as worthy of respect, understanding and love; whether he sees himself as having the right to be himself and to communicate himself to others. [21]

Self-adequacy is closely related to self-acceptance, which involves a realistic appraisal of the self.

Accomplishing the developmental tasks. Important developmental tasks of childhood and adolescence were presented in Table 3-3 of Chapter 3. The accomplishment of these developmental tasks is closely related to the development of an integrated personality. Teachers and

[20] Elizabeth Sheerer, "An Analysis of the Relationship between Acceptance of and Respect for the Self and Acceptance of and Respect for Others in Ten Counseling Cases," *Journal of Consulting Psychology*, 13 (1949), 169-175.
[21] Daniel W. Soper, "Guiding Your Students toward a Realistic Appraisal of Worth," *Journal of the National Education Association*, Vol. 49 (1960), p. 22.

Mental and physical activities are important for
wholesome personal and social development
(From Teacher's Edition, *Think-and-Do Book*, 1962,
Scott, Foresman and Company)

other adult leaders should help adolescents accomplish tasks in ways that
are socially acceptable and personally satisfying.

For a child to develop an appropriate independence-dependence pattern of behavior, he must be allowed to make repeated choices of action
and to experience the consequences of these choices. At the same time
(often in connection with the choice-making) he must learn some of
the boundaries of self-determination.

Another important developmental task is achieving an appropriate
affectional pattern. It will be seen that a fairly well developed sense of
trust, identity, and autonomy are basic to the achievement of adequate
affectional relationships. Chapter 3 commented on the difference in
class expectations in this area. It was pointed out that middle-class expectations are mainly those conveyed by the school. Witmer and Kotinsky
also point out the role which cultural factors play in sustaining or discouraging the individual's development.

> American culture is unusually successful in encouraging the development
> of the feelings of independence, initiative, industry, and identity. It is some-
> what less successful in the area of intimacy, for the culture's ideal is the subor-
> dination of sexuality and sensuality to a life of work, duty, and worship.[22]

Consequently, if the teacher is to assist students in achieving this
important developmental task, she will have to understand different
social-class expectations. She will have to construct situations to enable
students to experience spontaneous and warm interpersonal relationships
which are rewarding. Teachers themselves will strive to *accept* each student in a way which maximizes his autonomy, reinforces his sense of
trust, and permits initiative. This is impossible without self-acceptance

[22] *Op. cit.*, p. 22.

on the part of the teacher. She needs a highly developed sense of integrity. Teachers who have had a wide range of experiences with people of different backgrounds have empirical understandings that are most helpful in this connection. To the extent that the teacher is able to integrate experiences with theoretical understandings, she will be able to deal more effectively with pupils from diverse cultural backgrounds.

A third developmental task is that of achieving a sense of belonging. This requires the child to learn how to behave with friends, with members of peer groups, with adults, with parents and authority figures, with close relatives (as opposed to strange adults), and with all other kinds of groups. The child must learn appropriate ways for dealing with different social and interpersonal relationships. He may experience conflict between the standards of the peer group, the school, and the home.

The teacher supports the child as he begins to make the essential differentiations between expected, allowable, and forbidden in interpersonal relationships. She will understand that identifications are established with children's groups. Thus she will expect the child to give weight to peer group standards. She will understand that adolescent cliques and fads are part of the struggle for identification. With this understanding, she will work to present the students with positive activities through which they can achieve these ends. She will avoid pat diagnoses and will understand the cultural realities. Trust must be developed or sustained; doubt, guilt, and feelings of inferiority must be overcome or lessened. The teacher helps the student cope with others, and with others' feelings toward him. She helps him to meet the social demands which are properly made and helps him to find socially acceptable outlets for his feelings. Previous chapters of this book have discussed devices, such as the sociometric techniques, which are helpful in this regard.

Another developmental task is that of acquiring an appropriate sex role. This task involves (as shown in Chapter 3):

1. learning to identify the self with male or female roles
2. identifying with peers of the same sex
3. learning one's role in heterosexual situations
4. becoming attached to a member of the opposite sex and preparing to accept one's future sex role in a wholesome and integrated fashion.

It has been pointed out that boys and girls often use each other's company to examine verbally each other's ideals, plans, and life outlooks. As children grow toward adulthood, they select models from significant adults and from their peers to aid them in achieving a well-defined sex role. If the models are inadequate, the child is likely to fail in his attempts at role definition.

The teacher, therefore, needs to present a well defined model to her students. She must be aware that if students are to achieve their proper self roles, they must first achieve feelings of trust, identity, intimacy, and parental sense. The school must offer the students situations in which they can mingle with their peers in socially constructive, like-sex and heterosexual activities where they can meet appropriate masculine and feminine adult leaders whom they can accept as models.

The child will be guided toward matter-of-fact acceptance of its proper sex role. The boys will learn to cultivate the actions the culture considers appropriate for males. Similarly, the girls will pursue feminine activities. The accomplishment of this task is a life-long process.

A fifth important developmental task is that of developing intellectual skills and concepts. Achievement of this task, of course, requires careful training in appropriate use of cognitive thinking, practice in concept formation, and application as well as acquisition of background knowledge and experiences. A number of writers, however, have pointed out the effect of inadequate personality integration on this task. Anxiety has been found to cause poor decision-making through use of "all or nothing" approaches. One of the authors found that an inappropriate self-concept resulted in reading disability because the children expected to fail.

Teachers, therefore, will avoid stereotyping pupils on the basis of tests which may only reflect inadequate behavior caused by poor personality integration. They will be sensitive in presenting situations to a child so that he can experience a genuine feeling of success. Such teachers will understand that, as a child genuinely achieves in tasks suited to his readiness level, he will be prepared for developing further intellectual skills. The teacher will plan experiences suited to differing levels of conceptual abstraction, varying her methods so that each child learns to master the intellectual skills and methods of concept formation appropriate for his stage of development. To do this, she should be familiar with conceptual levels. A good summary may be found in Paul McKee's *The Teaching of Reading*, pp. 59-95.[23]

Another major developmental task is that of developing conscience, morality, and a sense of values. This task involves the following learnings:

1. understanding of the needs and rights of others on both the abstract and concrete levels.
2. control of social effects of behavior through compliance with authority when the authority figure (parent or teacher) is present.

[23] Paul McKee, *The Teaching of Reading* (Boston: Houghton-Mifflin, 1949), Chapter 3.

3. internalization of moral values (conscience replaces the monitory adult).
4. learning social rules of behavior in a number of roles: student, team member, family member, etc.
5. resolution of conflicts arising from observation of flouting of laws, codes of conduct, and moral principles with his conscience and moral imperatives warning against such behavior.

With each of the personality components described and with each of the developmental tasks discussed, it is not "all or nothing," not as Witmer and Kotinsky point out a matter of "trust *or* mistrust, autonomy *or* doubt and so on. Instead, each individual has some of each. His health of personality is determined by the preponderance of the favorable over the unfavorable, as well as by what manner of compensations he develops to cope with his disabilities." [24]

The teacher who has an adequate understanding of the assets of a well integrated personality in education will see that attitudes and ways of life are learned in combination with knowledge and skills. Conversely, unfavorable personality integration will inhibit intellectual learning.

SUMMARY

In order to carry out their tasks most effectively, teachers need to understand the interaction between learning and personality forces. Three aspects of personality were discussed: the *response* aspect (how); the *social* aspect; and the *cause* aspect. It was pointed out that over-emphasis on one or two of these aspects was responsible for much of the seeming disagreement among educational and psychological writers.

In response to principles of personality development, a child builds meanings into his life. These meanings, in turn, become a selective influence in determining further learning. Thus, learnings and experiences tend to become organized in an organic unity. This chapter has pointed out the importance of emphasizing self-realization in the educational program to facilitate growth toward full maturity.

Behavior patterns were shown to evolve in response to the efforts of the child to satisfy needs. It was also shown how frustration of important needs can lead to thwarting of educational, social and psychological growth. Causes of frustration were discussed and degrees of frustration were examined. It was seen that some frustration is unavoidable at major stages of personality development but that teachers need to guide the child to constructive responses.

Personality development is a complex task beginning in infancy and

[24] H. Witmer and R. Kotinsky, *op. cit.,* p. 8.

continuing throughout life. It involves physical and constitutional elements of human nature, maturation processes in interaction with the physical and social environment, imitative learning, associative learning, and unconscious learning.

Among the products of personality development is the self-concept. This is very important in determining the child's approach to problem situations. It is useful to the teacher in assessing the child's probable behavior and in preparing aids to help him develop.

Thus, personality integration is self-directed for good or ill. To aid that integration toward a high-value, flexible response of self-realization, educators in the home, church, and school need to *integrate* their efforts in wise partnership. There is presently a tendency toward fruitful articulation among the levels of education to provide a continuity of philosophy, aims, and structured subject matter consonant with the stages and tasks of the human developmental cycle. The various disciplines in all fields of human learning are beginning to *integrate* and synthesize their basic findings for the effective education of the *whole man*. The great minds, moreover, on the frontiers of the various fields of learning are coming to the direct aid of the teacher and educator in planning the "meat" that men may truly "grow big."

Problems and Exercises

1. What are the educational implications of the concept presented in this chapter that "each personality is unique"?
2. Look up several definitions of the *self*. How does one's notion of the *self* affect his personality development? How does one acquire his self-concept? What is the importance of the pupil's self-concept to the teacher?
3. How are needs related to drives? To personality development? To achievement? (See also chapters 7 and 8).
4. List the major sources of frustration. What are some frustrations frequently met by elementary pupils? by high school students? by college students?
5. Show how differences in constitutional elements have affected the personality development of two children of your acquaintance.
6. Review the pertinent sections of Chapter 8, along with those of this chapter that deal with attitudes and values. What conclusions would you draw relative to the relationship of attitudes and values to personality integration? To retention and transfer?
7. What is meant by self-acceptance? Why is this important in connection with personality integration? What are factors facilitating the development of a self-acceptant attitude?
8. Study the developmental tasks set forth in this chapter together with the chart presented in Chapter 3. Show how the home, the school and the other community agencies, such as the church, work together in helping boys and girls achieve these developmental tasks.
9. What are five important components of a healthy personality? List some *overt* signs and acts which might be clues to the presence of each of these components in a person.

10. (a) Miss Dudek is in her first year of teaching. She teaches a 7th grade class. During an examination, she continually walks around the room, peering intently at each child. If a child looks up, she quickly rushes to his desk. What self-concept type is she betraying by her actions?

(b) Miss Dudek harshly reprimands any pupil who contradicts one of her statements (no matter how courteously the difference of opinion is presented). She praises those girls who sit quietly and nod assent to her statements. An analysis of her marks reveals that the high grades all went to pupils who conformed; the only failing marks were received by boys who were known as creative and independent thinkers. What type of personality development is she encouraging by her procedures? What can you say about her self-concept?

Selected Readings

BRECKENRIDGE, Marian E., and VINCENT, E. Lee, *Child Development*, 4th ed. (Philadelphia: W. Saunders, 1960), Ch. 12.

CRONBACH, Lee J., *Educational Psychology*, 2nd ed. (New York: Harcourt, Brace & World, 1963), Ch. 18.

HAVIGHURST, Robert J., "Social-class Influences on American Education," *Sixtieth Yearbook of the National Society for the Study of Education, Part 1, Social Forces Influencing American Education* (Chicago: University of Chicage Press, 1961), Ch. 5.

HAVIGHURST, Robert J., and TABA, Hilda, *Adolescent Character and Personality* (New York: John Wiley and Sons, Inc., 1949).

McCLELLAND, D. C., *Personality* (New York: Holt, Rinehart, and Winston, 1951).

McDONALD, Frederick J., *Educational Psychology* (San Francisco: Wadsworth Publishing Co., 1959), Ch. 12.

STEPHENS, J. M., *Educational Psychology: The Study of Educational Growth*, rev. ed. (New York: Holt, Rinehart, and Winston, 1962), Chs. 7, 8, 10, 16, and 17.

TRYON, Caroline, and HENRY, W. E., "How Children Learn Personal and Social Adjustment," *Forty-Ninth Yearbook of the National Society for the Study of Education, Part 1, Learning and Instruction* (Chicago: University of Chicago Press, 1950), pp. 156-182.

CHAPTER 18

Adjustment Problems of the Child

M any children who are emotionally disturbed or socially maladjusted cannot fit into normal situations. They become a problem to themselves as well as to the home, school, and community. Such disturbances often have their roots in early childhood experiences, but may also arise from improper teacher-child relationships in an inadequate class situation. These points should constantly be kept in mind even though most of the materials of this chapter are concerned with disturbances of school-age children.

ADJUSTMENT

Adjustment involves the ability to solve one's personal problems in a socially acceptable and constructive way. Too often, unfortunately, the concept *adjustment* has been twisted to mean the degree to which a student *conforms* to expected social norms. For this reason, the term *self-actualization* has sometimes been substituted. Regardless of which term is used, the adjusted person is able to handle interpersonal relationships with insight and understanding. Since human dynamics are organismically related to the whole personality, adjustment is most adequately conceived of as the smooth, harmonious functioning of the whole individual—physical, psychological, sociological, and ethical—to achieve fulfillment of his potentialities.

It is important for the teacher to realize, however, that adjustment does *not* mean freedom from problems, conflicts, frustrations, or even from all personality deviations. Rather, it means the ability to deal with life *effectively* so as to satisfy personality needs in *constructive* ways. Hilgard points out that the goal of education is not to stifle creativity through the production of "very uninteresting normal and contented people." [1] He remarks that there is some truth in the popular conception about creative people deviating from the "social norms." He concludes:

> . . . For one thing, artists and writers who come to analysis are those who find that they are *afraid* to practice their arts. For them psychotherapy may give back their creativity. *Again, the end of therapy is not necessarily to get rid of conflicts but to find ways of living with them.*[2]
> [Italics are ours.]

Thus, the teacher is concerned with aiding the individual to achieve an adequate personality. Combs and Snygg [3] have characterized such personality adjustment as (1) an essentially positive view of self, (2) the capacity for acceptance of self and of others, and (3) the ability to identify broadly with his fellow man.

Personal and social adjustment problems

Each child is unique. Positive guidance and help in teaching children to adjust to their problems, and in developing individual traits and personality patterns will go far to produce very different but adequate and happy children. An individual's learning and development are, in every sense, his own. Treating boys and girls as individuals who are aware, according to their maturity, of their needs, rights, and obligations, will help them understand what self-adjustment means.

It has been stressed that schools should provide each pupil with every possible opportunity to think of himself as a worthy and responsible citizen. Education, therefore, should be geared to developing future citizens who will feel accepted, and be acceptable to, society.

The complex nature of the human being has been consistently stressed in this text. The responses on all levels of reaction—sensing, feeling, thinking, choosing, and doing—need to be coordinated, controlled, and integrated to enable the person to function effectively in all his intrapersonal and interpersonal relationships. It may be said that maladjustment can be explained by the underdevelopment, misdirection, or abuse of any one or more important aspects of personality.

Adjustment and maladjustment are patterns of response which are learned; they are patterns of a person's response to reality. Irala [4] considers departure from reality as the root of personal disturbance. He categorizes the types of such departure as (1) false interpretation of

---

[1] E. R. Hilgard, *Theories of Learning* (New York: Appleton-Century-Crofts, 1956), p. 310.

[2] *Ibid.*

[3] Arthur W. Combs and Donald Snygg, *Individual Behavior: A Perceptual Approach to Behavior,* rev. ed. (New York: Harper & Row, 1959), p. 377.

[4] Narciso Irala, S.J., *Achieving Peace of Heart,* trans. by Lewis Delmage, S.J. (New York: Joseph F. Wagner, 1957).

The adults in the child's world contribute to his security (From Teacher's Edition, *Think-and-Do Book*, 1962, Scott, Foresman and Company)

reality, (2) failing to accept reality, and (3) building up an absurd reality.

Just as personality connotes a bipolar concept of *self* and *others*, so adjustment has a personal and social aspect. The individual adjusts himself to reality in a social milieu in a fast changing society. The reality of the world of objects and events, of people, and their needs and wishes, sets limits to self-expression—limits that may challenge, frustrate, and crush the individual. We will briefly consider some of these forces at different periods in a child's life.

Types of frustrating factors. External factors, including all obstructions originating in the environment, influence adjustment. The degree of the frustrating quality of these external forces depends upon the individual's response to them. In early childhood there will be geographical restrictions and restrictions of exploratory activity. Some are necessary for the child's personal welfare and some are needed to teach him to set realistic limits. There is much need for wisdom and love in setting them and in guiding intelligent adjustment to them.

In addition to the frustrations which may arise from a sudden change in family setting or in family constellation, there are the restrictions of sex-patterning and age patterning in the American culture. In a study of five- and six-year-old children, Koch reported the following findings:

Males were rated by teachers as more active, expressive of anger, quarrelsome, revengeful, given to teasing, extrapunitive, insistent on their rights, alibi-building, exhibitionistic, uncooperative with teachers and peers, and given more to stammering than were females. Girls were rated as more affectionate, obedient, responsible, and tenacious of purpose than boys . . .

First-borns were judged as showing more anger, as being more intense emotionally, more upset by defeat. Second-born males with an older sister were judged more sissyish, on the average, than were first-born males.[5]

Language handicaps frustrate the small child until he has mastered the understandings and skills to converse adequately with adults. Language handicaps of a different type plague the adolescent even more until he has gained the poise and acceptance of adult status. Finally, there are the external frustrations of privation—a lack of things he has never had but deeply feels the need for, such as clothes—and deprivation or loss of goods which the child has known or experienced.

Frustrating factors of privation and deprivation also become internal or psychological forces when they involve the love bestowed or withheld by parents. The loss of a parent—by death or functionally, by separation—and physical or mental defects, actual or imagined, can create painful adjustment problems. In addition, there are the ideological adjustments required throughout the course of personality development. These become crucial during the critical period of adolescent transition involving as they do, attitudes, values, ideals, religious beliefs, moral judgments, and social insights.

Finally, there are the social adjustments and accompanying problems requisite to family living, peer-, group-, or gang-identification, and vocational choices. Children will have to face these problems both as students and as adults in life-time jobs or occupations.

In all of these adjustments related to the basic needs of human nature or involved in mastering the developmental tasks in the cumulative stages of growth, there are challenges and hazards to the adequate adjustment patterns sought. The kind of adjustments a person makes at any level of development is powerfully influenced by the kinds of adjustments he learned to make at each previous level of growth. As has been indicated, the human personality is characterized by *unity* and *consistency*. Besides the intimate personal and social problems of a maturing human being, there are factors within the home and school which are within the direct or indirect control of educators guiding human growth.

Self-acceptance and adjustment. A number of investigations have shown that there is a relationship between self-acceptance and adjustment. Taylor and Combs [6] found that children who were better adjusted

[5] Helen L. Koch, "Some Personality Correlates of Sex, Sibling Position, and Sex of Sibling Among Five- and Six-Year-Old Children," *Genetic Psychology Monographs*, Vol. 52 (1955), p. 47.

[6] Charles Taylor and Arthur Combs, "Self-acceptance and Adjustment," *Journal of Consulting Psychology*, Vol. 16 (1952), pp. 89-91.

tended to see themselves in a more matter-of-fact manner than did those who were less well-adjusted. Walsh [7] compared a group of middle-class low-achieving boys from the second, third, fourth, and fifth grades with a group of adequate achievers. The groups were matched on the basis of intelligence, grade placement, age, and socioeconomic grouping. Using the *Driscoll Play Kit* she discovered significant differences in the performance of the two groups. Low achievers consistently portrayed the boy doll as restricted, unable to express his feelings appropriately and adequately, and as acting defensively. Similarly, low achievers more frequently depicted the boy doll as being criticized, rejected, or isolated.

The importance of self-acceptance to personal adjustments is well recognized by students of human behavior. The purpose of psychology, especially as it relates to mental health, has been stated by Meerloo as follows:

. . . to free man from his internal tensions by helping him to understand what causes them. Psychology seeks to liberate the human spirit from its dependence on immature thinking so that each man can realize his own potentialities. Psychology teaches man to communicate freely and to express himself, unhampered by prejudices and taboos. It seeks to help man to face reality with its many problems and to recognize his own limitations as well as his possibilities for growth. [8]

Hazards to adequate adjustments

There are hazards to personal development which are neither natural nor normal but to which growing boys and girls are too often unwittingly exposed. A fairly large percentage of children present serious adjustment disorders which lead to marked antisocial activities. An even larger percentage suffer from neurotic difficulties which manifest themselves in phobias, obsessions, and learning difficulties of various types, especially reading. This situation causes real concern to insightful educators. Education should make a difference in the kind of people children become.

The family crisis. The failure of the home to guide children in making adequate personal and social adjustments has become a pressing problem. The American family is in transition. It is losing its cohesiveness through response to extra-familial roles, through mobility of the family and its members, and through "outer-directed" orientation.

Concerning the family crisis Vaughan states:

The many agencies and institutions in our cities are not strong enough to make up the lacks in such things as security, love experiences, direction, disci-

[7] Anne M. Walsh, *Self-Concepts of Bright Boys with Learning Difficulties.* Bureau of Publications, Teachers College, Columbia University, (1956), p. 38.

[8] Joost A. M. Meerloo, "The Psychology of Democratic Freedom," *Mental Hygiene,* Vol. 45 (1961), p. 274.

pline and control and identification models. Children, who comprise our future adult society, live in the midst of a paradoxical situation—a life with material comforts and perquisites never before known to man, but a life with a dearth of meanings, of direction, of clear and definite purpose.[9]

Parental attitudinal patterns. Within the family there is a wide range of attitudinal patterns. These attitudinal patterns are extremely important to the development of favorable or unfavorable behavior patterns in children. The results of a study by Peterson and others show that "the attitudes of fathers are at least as intimately related as maternal attitudes to the occurrence and form of behavior problems in children." [10] This thought is worthy of consideration, especially in view of the prevalent tendency to offer help to mothers with unfavorable attitudes and give little or no consideration to fathers with similar attitudes. It was found further that both mothers and fathers of children who displayed adjustment difficulties were judged to be less well-adjusted and sociable than the parents of children who manifested no adjustment problems. Personality problems of children with adjustment difficulties were found to be relatively independent of maternal attitudes, but appeared to be related to autocratic attitudes and lack of parental concern by the fathers. Conduct problems, on the other hand, were more closely associated with general maladjustments among the mothers, and with evident permissiveness and disciplinary ineffectuality on the part of the fathers.

Parent-child relationships. Within the family constellation, there are some parent-child relationships that may be damaging to the wholesome development of the child, and often the parents unwittingly victimize one or all members of the family.

Overprotection may result either from domination or indulgence by one or both parents. In either case, the child is shielded from situations which might challenge his initiative and aid him in gaining skill in the use of his powers for self-direction. He is deprived of the opportunity to engage in highly competitive physical and motor activities. He is not permitted to make mistakes, nor is he guided to new learning through the mistakes he does make. Very often, parents are so overconcerned about the child's health and general well-being that they watch his diet and every daily activity too closely. Overprotective parents expect little from the child and protect him from all adventurous undertakings. Such parents often show much inconsistency in their relations with the child. They are afraid to say "no" to him (which "no" needs to be said), since

[9] Warren T. Vaughan, "Children in Crisis," *Mental Hygiene,* Vol. 45 (1961), p. 355.
[10] Donald R. Peterson, Wesley C. Becker, Leo A. Hellmer, Donald J. Shoemaker, and Herbert C. Quay, "Parental Attitudes and Child Adjustment," *Child Development,* Vol. 30 (1959), pp. 1-30.

they fear this might keep him from loving them. They are not unwilling to say "no," however, when the child wishes to do something which they regard as dangerous.

Children who are overprotected manifest certain characteristics. First of all they are *immature* in many of their reactions since they have not been given the opportunity to grow up. They lack self-reliance. They seek almost exclusive activity with their parents, usually the mother, who shields them from frustrations and other difficulties. Such children are likely to be submissive, obedient, and withdrawing when faced with difficulty. The personality of the "spoiled" child (one suffering from over-indulgence) is likely to be egocentric and selfish. He responds poorly to tasks when he cannot have his own way.

What has been said of parents in the home may also apply to other educators in their respective areas of influence. The hazard is greater with parents, however, because they have the child first for a longer period of time and in a closer and more constant relationship.

Rejection is a phenomenon which may be overt or covert, conscious, but more often, unconscious. The rejected child is unwanted. Oftentimes, the parent displays outright hostility. Interviews with such parents indicate that they frequently have no plans for the child's future, but are anxious for him to grow up and "get on his own." In homes of good financial circumstances, the rejected child is sent to camp—probably to a boarding school—and to other places where he will not interfere with the activities of the parents. There is little companionship with the parents, and such children mention no help received from their parents.

Anxiety states, and conditions associated with them, are found most frequently among children from homes in which there is considerable tension or outright rejection. Children who lack affection or who have been rejected are difficult to help. The disappointment which Tommy received in not measuring up to his father's ideal of a son indicates the serious effects of rejection.

Tommy was almost eleven years old when his mother brought him to the psychological clinic. By then he was a defeated child, suffering from a feeling of complete inadequacy. He did not think he could do anything successfully, and didn't want to try. He was doing poorly at school, afraid to take part in activities involving his peers, and fearful of attempting anything that could be evaluated by others. When asked to express three wishes very important to him, he gave the following: "I wish I had never been born." "I wish I was different, but that's no use." "I wish I didn't have to go to school."

Very early Tommy failed to satisfy his father's desire for a son who would be a good athlete. His father, a successful athlete in high school but unable to participate in athletics in college because of responsibilities at home, had hoped to have his ambitions fulfilled through the activities and interests of Tommy. Thus, when Tommy did not respond favorably to his efforts to make an athlete of him when he was barely three years of age, he was much disappointed.

The mother admitted quite freely the father's disappointment in Tommy. The father laughed at his efforts at school, at his interests in things of a non-athletic nature, and referred to him as a "softy and a sissie."

Covert rejection may take the paradoxical form of overprotection or of "smothering" love. Parents who covertly reject their children sometimes go to absurd extremes to provide them with every material luxury and to pamper their every whim. This reaction-formulation of rejection can confront any other educator also. Could some "disciplinary problems" be children who have learned to expect rejection—overt or covert—from adults? Perhaps some are children who sense rejection by the teacher.

Overattentiveness is one feature of the composite picture of the over-ambitious parent who is domineering. The parents have set up their own special standards and expect their children to accept them and measure up to them. Thus, the child is likely to be *forced* to move ahead in school from an early age. Parents of this type take the attitude that play on the part of the child is largely a waste of time (unless, of course, play will aid the child in reaching some goal set up by the parents for him— such as making the football or baseball teams). Too often parents attempt to satisfy their own unsatisfied aspirations or needs through the achievements of their children.

The results of the study by Hattwick and Stowell,[11] presented in Figure 18-1, indicate that children who were babied and pushed by their parents had many more social-adjustment difficulties than children from homes with better familial relationships. The researchers found that the kinds of behavior most characteristic of these children (in the order of its frequency of occurrence) were: social immaturity, lack of a sense of responsibility, nervousness, dependence on others, self-con-

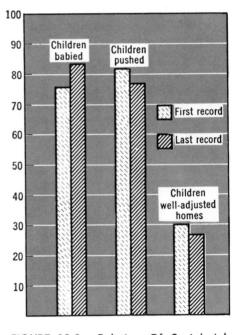

FIGURE 18-1.   Relation Of Social Adjustment Difficulties To Certain Home Factors

[11] L. W. Hattwick and M. Stowell, "The Relation of Parental Over-Protection to Children's Work Habits and Social Adjustments in Kindergarten and the First Six Grades of School," *Journal of Educational Research*, Vol. 30 (1936), pp. 169-176.

sciousness, a play for attention, day dreaming, teasing and annoying others, withdrawal from the group, inability to meet new situations well, contrariness, insistence on own ways, and lack of self-reliance.

Parental expectations. Differences in low-class and middle-class parental expectations were pointed out in Chapter 3. A real problem exists for the child from a lower-class family who often must adjust to the middle-class standards imposed by the school and the teacher. All children, however, face the problem of living up to the expectations of their parents who sometimes overestimate and often underestimate the capabilities of their children. Langford and Alm [12] compared the judgment of a group of parents with the feelings of their twelve-year-old children regarding their self-adjustments and social adjustments. They found that parents tended to underestimate children's feelings and concepts concerning self-adjustments in such areas as self-reliance, sense of personal worth, feelings of belonging, and freedom from nervous tension. Similarly, the parents tended to overestimate ideas and feelings concerning the children's social adjustment in such areas as adherence to social standards, extent of social skills, freedom from antisocial tendencies, and adjustment in family and school relations.

The importance of parental satisfactions with the child's development is shown in a study reported by Elkins.[13] The results, presented in Figure 18-2, show that eighth-grade children whose parents express greatest satisfaction are more frequently chosen by their classmates as friends than children whose parents express least satisfaction. Too high parental expectation lead to frustrations, with their accompanying results, while too low parental expectations lead to low standards of achievement and conduct. Neglected and unwanted children and adolescents are likely to be inadequate in their social relations. These children perceive themselves as unworthy of affection since they have not received affection from their parents. Likewise, they tend to show a lack of kindness toward other children. Although not necessarily hostile toward other children, they are inconsiderate of the feelings of others and tend to compete for whatever attention they get.

Class culture. Class culture may present hazards from the home, the school, and the community to the personal adjustment of the maturing personality. The conflict of class culture has long been recognized as

[12] Louise M. Langford and O. W. Alm, "A Comparison of Parent Judgments and Child Feelings Concerning the Self-Adjustments and Social Adjustments of Twelve-Year-Old Children," *Journal of Genetic Psychology,* Vol. 85 (1954), pp. 39-46.
[13] Deborah Elkins, "Some Factors Related to the Choice-Status of Ninety Eighth-Grade Children in a School Society," *Genetic Psychology Monographs,* Vol. 58 (1958), pp. 207-272.

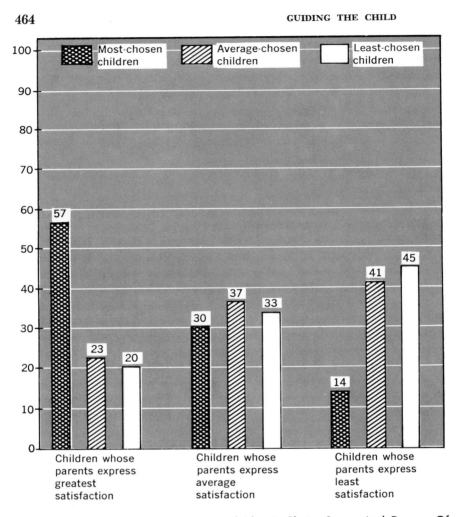

FIGURE 18-2. Relationship Between Children's Choice-Status And Degree Of
Parents' Expressed Satisfaction With Their Children *(Elkin)*

an important source of personality difficulties. The educator's task is
that of guiding boys and girls into improved ways of living and successful adjustment. When the experiences of boys and girls vary from the
teacher's own early childhood experiences in certain respects, the pupils
may experience unhappiness owing to the lack of harmony between expectations in the educational environment and their earlier established
interests, habits, and ideals.

A study reported by Rezinkoff and Rezinkoff [14] showed significant

[14] Marvin Rezinkoff and Helga R. Rezinkoff, "The Family Drawing Test: A Comparative Study of Children's Drawings," *Journal of Clinical Psychology,* Vol. 12
(1956), pp. 167-169.

differences between the family drawings of second-grade children from low- and middle-income families. As noted in Table 18-1, children from the low-income group more often made themselves the smallest figure in the family group and drew the members of their families as if they were floating in air. It is suggested that this difference may reflect the greater feelings of insecurity and inferiority of the children from the lower class. The children from the lower class omitted the mother more often, also, and drew the oldest sibling as the largest figure in the family group. This may reflect the authority pattern of the home in which the older members are given considerable responsibility in caring for the younger members of the family. Likewise, the irritating effect of a specific social environment can be so great as to affect a child's behavior in another social group. For example, negative home conditions involving interpersonal relations can affect the child in such a way that he displays neurotic behavior at school.

TABLE 18-1. Comparison of Children's Family Drawings from Low- and Middle-Income Families (*Rezinkoff and Rezinkoff*)

	PER CENT OCCURRENCE	
FACTORS	LOW INCOME	MIDDLE INCOME
Self smallest figure	24	0
Figure off the ground	62	37
Mother figure omitted	21	0
Sibling largest figure	24	3
Father without arms	25	6

Pope discovered socioeconomic differences in the prestige values of the peer cultures of twelve-year-olds in a number of sixth-grade classrooms. Differences based on sex were also found within each socioeconomic level. Using the Guess-Who technique, he found:

1. Restlessness was less acceptable to high than to low socio-economic status boys. Although boys from both high and low status groups tended to value a boy's ability to fight, it seemed to be more vital to low-status boys than to high.
2. Boys of low socio-economic status who fight also go out with girls. In the high group, fighting is a liability to social relationships with girls.
3. In high socio-economic groups, boys, while not necessarily accepting "good students" as leaders, do not reject them. With low groups, "good students" tend to be rejected.
4. Girls manifest similar value judgments. In addition, the "tomboy" was unpopular with girls from high socio-economic groups.

Pope concluded that:

The high groups of both sexes expect their members to show an appropriate tendency to conform to adult standards within the classroom. They also
show a positive evaluation of certain conventional rules of decorum when attending parties and dances with the opposite sex. These qualities are not at all
stressed by the low socio-economic groups.[15]

Social-class influences. The social class of a child's family determines not only the neighborhood in which he lives and the group with
whom he associates and plays, but also—to a very large extent—the goals,
aspirations, and social skills of the individual child. This was emphasized
in Chapter 6. There is evidence from many sources that children from
low socioeconomic neighborhoods are likely to have feelings of insecurity
and display hostility to a much greater extent than children from more
privileged neighborhoods.[16] A recognition of the operation of these
forces should help teachers and others to guide children from underprivileged homes and neighborhoods.

Closely related to this problem are the problems encountered by
children from minority groups. The prejudice of one group toward another, the variations in the patterns of living, the values of the different
cultural groups, and the straining of the less privileged to be accepted by
the more privileged present difficult adjustment problems to children
in the elementary school. Recent research in child development has produced considerable evidence to show that class and cultural tensions
are sources of many adjustment problems among children. Children of
foreign-born parents are often caught in the conflict of trying to gain
the acceptance of their classmates without losing the support and affection of their parents. Children of some minority groups often find themselves friendless and unwanted by their classmates from the majority
group.

Consider the following example. Joan was a tenth-grade student in a
high school attended mainly by children from upper middle-class families. Joan's family had recently come to the community. Her father was
a tenant farmer on the large farm of one of the school student leaders.
Plainly but neatly dressed, Joan was ignored by her classmates. Perceptive and careful guidance by the class adviser enabled her to put to
use her interest in music so that she became the person in charge of
playing records for the after-school dances. She also secured fifteen
minutes on Saturdays on one of the community radio stations for a "Teen-

[15] Benjamin Pope, "Socio-Economic Contrasts in Children's Peer Culture Prestige
Values," *Genetic Psychology Monographs,* Vol. 48 (1953), pp. 157-220.

[16] Arnold Goldstein, "Aggression and Hostility in the Elementary School in Low
Economic Areas," *Understanding the Child,* Vol. 24 (1955), pp. 20-21.

There is no one absolute set of cultural values in the American way of life. Because of this, the need for insight into and acceptance of values different from the teacher's own is of immense importance in aiding adequate personality development

Age Request Spin" program. Soon, aided by talent and hard work, Joan was a valued member of her peer group organizations.

Another example was Tómas. His family were recent immigrants from Latin America. Speaking English with a marked accent, he found himself rejected by his classmates in a high school populated by children from a high socioeconomic stratum. Tómas conceived of plans to enable the student organization to raise money to buy needed sports and audio-visual equipment. Adroitly aided by the student adviser and his teachers, he gradually secured student organization consent to try his plans. As they began to bear results he found himself more and more a part of student life until, after a year, he was elected to the Student Council.

It should be emphasized that these examples are only summaries which capsule a long series of events drawing on teacher guidance and encouragement and which involved students with initiative, ability and industry. Nevertheless, many children, even though lacking these assets, may be helped to acceptance in a school where the teacher-student relationship is conducive to good personal adjustment.

Hazards in the school to personal adjustment

The teacher's attitude toward children, toward the class, or toward individual students can (as illustrated above) help pupils grow and develop in the direction of their potentials or it can stunt that growth and cripple personal adjustment. Lack of proper teacher guidance may sometimes be the cause of a pupil's misplacement in the school program. Often, too, there is nobody to whom the pupil can turn for help, no one especially interested in him. Methods of teaching which do not enable

Many teachers have not developed sound techniques of dealing with problem behavior at school

children to achieve success, recognition, and a sense of security, regardless of their cultural and social backgrounds, can be devastating to personal development and to adequate adjustment. Some other factors which can injure maturing personalities are curricular materials not in keeping with the needs or the maturational levels of the children (whether superior, average, or retarded); lack of coordination between the various levels of teaching between the successive grade-levels; over-intense competition, and excessive use of extrinsic incentives.

Interpersonal relationships in the classroom. The teacher's understanding, acceptance, and facilitation of the attitudes, values, and strivings of the child are not the only influence on his adjustment. It is, perhaps, not even the most important. His relationships with the other children and his evaluation of his position in the class social-structure powerfully affect his psychological outlook. Elkins found that children chosen as best friends most often tended to be more active, engaged in a greater number and variety of activities, and were more flexible in role-performance than were children who were seldom chosen. Parents of the frequently chosen children also tended to be better satisfied with their children. The influence of peers in the school situations and the use of sociometric techniques by the teacher was discussed at some length in Chapter 6.

The stability of stars (those frequently chosen) and neglectees (those seldom or never chosen) in four sixth-grade classes was studied by Thompson and Powell.[17] They found that between 66 and 100 per cent of the stars maintained their high sociometric rating over one- and five-week intervals. The low sociometric rating of the neglectees ranged from 59 to 90 per cent during this interval. Such stability suggests the relative permanence of the interpersonal relationships in the classroom.

Interpersonal relationships within the school not only affect the child's personal adjustment, but also, when maladaptive, affect his achievement, measures of his performance, and measures of intelligence. In this connection, Commoss found that second grade children who were rejected by their classmates showed inadequacy in interpersonal relationships, in ability to communicate verbally, and in eye-hand coordination. She concludes:

. . . The anxiety engendered by mistakes due to misconceptions may lead to failure to clarify concepts through open discussions and hence to further misconceptions. Other studies suggest that a similar relationship (as that found between isolation and eye-hand coordination) also exists in respect to general motor development (p. 42).[18]

Intelligence and social acceptance. Closely related to the problem of the relation of social acceptance to educational achievement is that of the relation of social acceptance to intelligence. Based on a

---

[17] G. C. Thompson and M. Powell, "An Investigation of the Rating-scale Approach to the Measurement of Social Status," *Educational and Psychological Measurement*, Vol. 11 (1951), pp. 440-455.

[18] Harriet Commoss, "Some Characteristics Related to Social Isolation of Second Grade Children," *Journal of Educational Psychology*, Vol. 53 (1962), pp. 38-42.

rather complete review of the literature bearing on this problem, Lindzey and Borgatta [19] concluded that measures of intelligence are positively related to social acceptance. In a study by Gallagher [20] 355 children enrolled in Grades 2 through 5 were used as subjects. These children came from 12 classrooms in a midwestern community of superior socioeconomic status with a population of under 100,000. Intelligence test scores were obtained by using group tests of intelligence. Table 18-2 shows the rela-

TABLE 18-2. Average Number of Choices as Best Friend Received by 332 Pupils in Grades II-V According to Intelligence Test Scores (Gallagher)

GRADE AND INTELLIGENCE TEST SCORES	NUMBER OF PUPILS	NUMBER OF CHOICES	AVERAGE NUMBER OF CHOICES
Grade II (79 pupils)			
70 and above	8	63	7.88
60-69	19	91	4.79
50-59	27	106	3.92
40-49	22	63	2.86
30-39	3	4	1.33
Grade III (76 pupils)			
70 and above	4	16	4.00
60-69	35	166	4.74
50-59	28	106	3.78
40-49	7	18	2.57
30-39	2	1	0.50
Grade IV (90 pupils)			
70 and above	4	29	7.25
60-69	26	131	5.04
50-59	46	218	4.74
40-49	13	60	4.62
30-39	1	2	2.00
Grade V (87 pupils)			
70 and above	2	6	3.00
60-69	15	75	5.00
50-59	46	187	4.06
40-49	19	79	4.16
30-39	5	24	4.80

[19] Gardner Lindzey and E. F. Borgatta, "Sociometric Measurements," in *Handbook of Social Psychology* (Lindzey, Editor). Cambridge: Addison-Wesley Publishing Co., (1954).

[20] James J. Gallagher, "Social Status of Children Related to Intelligence, Propinquity, and Social Acceptance," *Elementary School Journal*, Vol. 58 (1958), pp. 225-231.

tion of the intelligence test scores to the number of times a child was chosen by his classmates.

A study of the results indicates that pupils with higher intelligence-test scores tended to receive more friendship choices than those with lower measured levels of ability. This trend was quite consistent through Grades 2-5, although in Grade 5 it was not so marked. A further analysis of the choices by the individual pupils showed that there was no pronounced tendency for the intellectually bright children to choose bright children as friends or for intellectually average children to select their best friends from their own range of intellectual ability.

Age and social acceptance. Closely related to the problem of achievement in relation to social acceptance is that of the acceptance of the overage child. It has been suggested by a number of students of child psychology that the overage child in the classroom is not accepted. Morrison and Perry [21] conducted independent studies of this problem among elementary-school children. They divided each class into four sociometric quarters and computed the percentage of overage pupils who fell into each sociometric quarter for each of the class groups. Three criteria were used and three choices were allowed for each criterion in determining the sociometric status of each child. The score for each child was determined by totaling the number of choices he received. The results for the two studies, presented in Table 18-3, show that of the total of 21 overage children in the different class groups, none was found in the highest sociometric quarter of his class. Eighty-six per cent of these overage children were found to be below the medians of their respective classes in sociometric status. The investigators concluded from their studies:

. . . The overage child was found to have a significantly lower choice status than his peers. These data further support the findings from studies of promotional policies which have emphasized the importance of keeping the child with his own age group in order to avoid detrimental effects to his personality and his educational progress.[22]

Emotionally disturbed children in the classroom. It is recognized that the school population varies as much in emotional behavior as it does in intellectual behavior. Ewald [23] points out that developments in school mental hygiene have not kept pace with developments in intelligence testing and classification of scholastic abilities. In the first place, many teachers fail to recognize emotional problems in the children with whom

[21] Ida E. Morrison and Ida F. Perry, "Acceptance of Overage Children by their Classmates," *Elementary School Journal,* Vol. 56 (1955-56), pp. 217-220.

[22] *Ibid.,* p. 220.

[23] Marguerite O. Ewald, "The Emotionally Disturbed Child in the Classroom, *Education,* Vol. 76 (1955), pp. 69-73.

TABLE 18-3. Distribution of Sociometric Status of Overage Children by Quarters of Their Class (*Morrison and Perry*)

GRADE	FIRST QUARTER NUMBER OF CHILDREN	PER CENT	SECOND QUARTER NUMBER OF CHILDREN	PER CENT	THIRD QUARTER NUMBER OF CHILDREN	PER CENT	FOURTH QUARTER NUMBER OF CHILDREN	PER CENT
Morrison study:								
V–VI	0	0	3	14	6	29	12	57
Perry study:								
V–VI	0	0	1	10	5	50	4	40
IV–VI	1	4	5	20	11	44	8	32
VII–VIII	11	23	12	25	9	19	16	33

they work; and secondly, they fail to attach due significance to the problems which present themselves.

A distinction should be made between problem behavior which interferes with normal classroom activities and that kind of problem behavior which leads to serious personal and social maladjustments. Such a distinction was made in the study by Sparks.[24] A comparison was made between traits rated by one group of teachers as most detrimental to the future of the child and those rated by another group of teachers as most troublesome in the classroom. The teachers were given the 55 problems to rate from the Wickman list. The ten traits rated by the teachers as most serious to the child and the ten traits rated as most troublesome to the teacher are presented in Table 18-4.

TABLE 18-4. Teacher Ratings of Serious and Troublesome Traits (*After Sparks*)

RANK	SERIOUS TO THE CHILD	TROUBLESOME TO TEACHERS
1	Stealing	Interrupting
2	Untruthfulness	Carelessness in work
3	Unreliableness	Inattention
4	Cruelty and bullying	Restlessness
5	Cheating	Silliness, smartness, etc.
6	Heterosexuality	Whispering and note taking
7	Impertinence	Tattling
8	Impudence	Thoughtlessness
9	Selfishness	Disorderliness
10	Laziness	Inquisitiveness

It seems evident from the results of this study (which are congruent with the findings of the original Wickman research) that teachers tend to consider those traits which are contrary to our social and moral code the most detrimental to future adjustments of the child.

Beilin's reexamination of the studies of Wickman and others suggests that, in recent years, there has been a shift in the attitudes of at least some teachers. His appraisal [25] indicates that teachers' attitudes about detrimental traits now more closely approximate those of clinicians. He also suggests that the attitudes of clinicians in this matter have changed somewhat. Beilin points out that more boys are identified as maladjusted

[24] J. N. Sparks, "Teachers' Attitudes toward the Behavior Problems of Children," *Journal of Educational Psychology*, Vol. 43 (1952), pp. 284-291.

[25] Harry Beilin, "Teachers' and Clinicians' Attitudes Toward the Behavior Problems of Children: A Reappraisal," *Child Development*, Vol. 30 (1959), pp. 9-25.

than girls. He also found that the sex of the teacher doing the rating affected, in part, the teacher's attitude toward children's problems. Beilin concluded that because teachers tend to be oriented to the task of teaching, while clinicians are more directed to the task of aiding children achieve more constructive adjustment, complete agreement between the two groups is not likely to be reached.

Of prime importance is the early recognition and appreciation of emotional problems, however minor they may seem. It has already been suggested that many teachers are likely to pick out those pupils who create classroom problems as the "problem" children. These children, however, at least have a "vent" for their frustrations. The really serious problems usually occur among the overly quiet, withdrawn children who seldom create classroom disturbances. Such children have found no constructive satisfying way of reacting to the social situation, so their response is simply to withdraw. Left unnoticed by the teacher and their classmates, they receive no help for their increasingly severe maladaptive behavior.

Symptoms of maladjustment

Symptoms of personal and social maladjustments are not the same for all children. There are, however, some symptoms which appear frequently among different groups of maladjusted children. Some symptoms are also more readily observed than others. Jane, for example, may be quiet in school but given to fantasy. On the other hand, her cousin Mary may be aggressive and given to lying, showing-off, and quarreling. The inexperienced teacher, in particular, is likely to think Mary a seriously maladjusted person while overlooking the withdrawn child (Jane) or regarding her as a model pupil.

The roots of personality disorders among adults can usually be traced to childhood experiences. Many types of mental and emotional disturbances first appear, or their symptoms first display themselves, during the early years of life. If these children can be identified during the beginning stages of these disturbances and if measures can be taken to help them, much can be done to prevent emotional and social maladjustments at a later period.

Recent studies show that it is the frequency and patterning of the appearance of certain symptoms that is especially important in evaluating personality maladjustments. These symptoms have been classified by different investigators in various ways. They are so interrelated that no clear-cut classification can be presented. The writers have attempted a three-fold classification involving (a) physical signs, (b) behavior deviations, and (c) emotional manifestations. These are presented in Table 18-5.

TABLE 18-5. Symptoms of Maladjustment

Physical signs

facial twitching	rocking feet
nervous spasms	drumming with fingers
stuttering	twisting hair
biting nails	restlessness
scratching self	fidgeting
vomiting	rapid, nervous speech
enuresis	crying easily
digestive disturbances	

Behavior deviations

aggressiveness	retiring
negativism	easily embarrassed
night terrors	sleep disturbances
bullying	walking in sleep
lying	masturbation
voluntary mutinism	stubbornness
poor school work	regression
oversensitiveness	

Emotional manifestations

given to excessive worry	disposition to hate
feelings of inferiority	resentful
abnormal fears	temper tantrums
pouting	extreme timidity

Maladaptive responses related to volition or self-direction. One aspect of personality implying self-direction, self-control, responsibility, freedom, decision-making, and goal-seeking involves the basic need to "will" or to "choose." The fundamental human need satisfied through the adequate exercise of these activities is that of a fine balance between the bipolar principle of independence-dependence. Inadequacies in this area of personality development are also closely connected with excessive or exaggerated negative emotionality.

Emotional impulsiveness is natural in some situations. When it becomes a habitual form of response, it is often indicative of immaturity or maladjustment. An impulsive reaction is indeliberate; it may be instinctive and is usually very forceful and chaotic. A victim of his own impulses is not truly and humanly free. This difficulty is often related to uncontrolled emotionality which has not been corrected by adequate socialization and moral development.

Indecision and personal inefficiency is another indication of deficiency or maladaptive response in the area of personal direction. Some causes for indecision may be:

1. underdevelopment of ability to make choices because of lack of opportunity to do so or because of fear of making mistakes;
2. lack of intellectual concentration or attention to set effective goals or to incorporate personal values;
3. the simultaneous existence of equally strong motives for and against an action;
4. actually or apparently conflicting motives.

The teacher's approach to this problem is education or re-education in the thinking and choosing aspects of personality discussed in the last chapter. The educational task of providing opportunities to satisfy this human need in an accepting, supporting, but educationally sound situation will be developed in Chapter 19.

Closely related to indecision is the inability of the child to say "no" or to set limits upon outside pressures, especially those arising from requests made by "prestige" figures. Such inability may arise from an undeveloped aggressivity, an inadequate self-concept, or from neurotic guilt (which will be discussed later in this chapter). Refusals are a part of intelligent choice-making. Resistance, which is usually considered an aspect of emotional aggressivity or a "fighting response," is the opposite side of this coin. It is an unsaid reaction of habitually thinking "no" when another wants "yes." When such responses are subconscious and impelling, they are maladaptive, bringing neither the adequate satisfaction of needs nor resultant happiness.

Compulsion is closely allied with impulsive reactions. It is an uncontrollable drive impelled by intense, negative emotions, usually of anxiety, to perform a particular act. Compulsion may cause a person acute distress if, for example, he carries out his plans with the slightest deviation.

Dependency is an unwillingness, usually not conscious, to accept responsibility in general or a specific responsibility in particular. It is a deficiency in the development of the ability to make decisions and to accept the responsibility for them. The individual may never have had the opportunity to make intelligent choices. Given experiences to learn to decide on a progressively independent plane, he can be guided in developing the *habit* of directing his energies into creative living so that he will not exercise his choices negatively through dependency.

Dependent behavior seems to result from very different kinds of experience. The backgrounds include overprotective homes and indifferent ones. Children of overprotective parents often feel hopelessly incapacitated in solving their own problems without help from stronger personalities, whereas those from neglected or perhaps rejected homes seem insecure and preoccupied with being cared for and loved.

Adjustment problems related to various levels of consciousness. *Consciousness* refers to the individual's cognitive aspects. The term means the knowledge, truths, values, and realities of which he is aware as well as the realities of his experiences, which he can become aware of, at a given moment of action.

Concentration may be defined as the ability to apply attention to one idea to the exclusion of other ideas. Often persons with problems of maladjustment complain of inability to concentrate. Children who cannot concentrate on school activities such as reading or arithmetic may not be consciously aware of their deficiency. The need to know, to think, to solve problems, and to achieve in mental activity may be blocked by negative feelings of anxiety, hostility, fear, etc. These ideas or distracting forces, interrupting and interfering with concentration on school work, sap energy, cause fatigue, and inhibit performance. Wrightsman[26] has shown that stressful situations interfere with performance of highly anxious students on complex tasks. He concludes that actual test performances of extremely anxious individuals are not good indicators of their actual ability.

Meeting difficulties

The term *frustrations* used in connection with human adjustment, refers to any control or limitation imposed upon the individual that interferes or blocks the satisfaction of a need or drive. The child learns during the process of growing up that he cannot satisfy all his needs or wants. He meets at an early age boundaries set forth by nature. He finds that he is not big and strong and is unable to do many of the things which his father can do. He meets boundaries defined by his parents and other members of his family. At a later date he meets reality in the boundaries defined by the community and other children. When he enters school he finds limitations placed upon his behavior by the general school program. There are some who believe that frustrations are in themselves harmful. It is inconceivable that healthy growth could occur in the complete absence of frustrations. There are, however, desirable as well as undesirable ways of meeting frustrations. When these boundaries are narrowed and autocratically imposed the development of the ability to meet frustrations through rational choices is seriously endangered. Again, when these

[26] Lawrence S. Wrightsman, Jr., "The Effects of Anxiety, Achievement Motivation, and Task Importance upon Performance on an Intelligence Test," *Journal of Educational Psychology*, Vol. 53 (1962), pp. 150-156.

boundaries melt away before the child's demands, the development of self-discipline on the part of the child is rendered null and void.[27]

Frustrations and conflicts result in tension. The individual strives to reduce this tension. One of the striking differences in the personality of individuals is the way they react when certain needs are thwarted or conflicts appear in the satisfaction of their needs. The way an individual reacts to such situations or conditions is primarily a result of the manner in which he has met difficulties and frustrations during the early years of life. This is clearly implied in the statement by Frank: "From psychiatric studies it is becoming clear that what is called mental health, or wholesome, well-balanced personality development depends in a large measure upon how the individual from birth onward meets the unavoidable tasks of life." [28]

A mental or overt adjustment becomes necessary when an individual is faced with a barrier to the attainment of a goal. Several possibilities are then open to him: he may resort to some form of *aggressive* behavior, either in an attempt to overcome the barrier or as a subterfuge; he may *compromise* by falsification, identification, or projection; or he may use some withdrawal or *escape* device, either in actuality or by subterfuge. The method used by an individual in meeting a barrier to the satisfaction of a need will depend primarily on what has proved fairly effective to him in the past and the nature of the present situation. Most people develop fairly effective methods for meeting difficulties, although they may not always be regarded as most desirable.

Aggression. Aggression has previously been discussed as a manifestation of negative emotionality. When it is direct and in proper proportion, aggression seems to be conscious and not essentially a maladaptive device. Counter-aggression and displacement, however, are covert and maladaptive devices of aggression.

A more subtle form of aggression may manifest itself in the form of common gossip against the person connected either directly or indirectly with frustration. Deception, if compulsive, unconscious, and impulsive, is a mechanistic device used by children when faced with seemingly insoluble frustrations.

Aggression sometimes takes the form of retaliation and revenge is likely to appear in this form when the individual feels that he has been wronged and believes that he will be unable to secure justice. Through recognizing the worth of each individual child and according him fair treatment, the teacher can considerably reduce occasions for resentment

[27] Frederick H. Allen, "Aggression in Relation to Emotional Development, Normal and Pathological," *Mental Hygiene,* Vol. 34 (1950), pp. 353-363.

[28] Lawrence K. Frank, "Working for Healthy Personalities," *Educational Leadership,* Vol. 3 (1946), p. 308.

and retaliation. A positive program of discipline which places the emphasis upon desirable forms of behavior rather than on "don'ts" and "no's" and which accepts the expression of a certain amount of anger, hostility, etc., will tend to reduce frustrations and their accompanying aggressive behavior.

Ego-centrism. Closely related to aggression is ego-centrism. The "show-off" and the exhibitionist, examples of the operation of ego-centrism, are forms of behavior motivated by the desire for attention, a need which is denied at home or in other situations of importance to the child. Ego-centrism indicates inadequacy and insecurity, and generally points to arrested development—a form of immaturity in anyone beyond the primary grades. The ego-centric person looks for attention, even in undesirable and harmful forms. Behavior problems similar to those of aggression may be symptoms: disobedience, running away, lying, petty thievery, etc.

Hypersensitivity. Hypersensitivity, which may verge on paranoia, is a maladaptive defense mechanism related to aggression. The person feels and reacts with the conviction that other people are willfully blocking him. Others (he thinks) "have it in for him." This feeling may be unwittingly promoted in some adolescents by encouraging youth to put undue blame unrealistically on persons in positions of authority.

The extent of aggressive behavior observed among elementary school children has increased during the past two or more decades.[29] This is quite likely a result of the increased permissiveness in the American home, and the emphasis upon competition in so many aspects of children's lives. Children can be aided in learning friendly and cooperative behavior if parents and teachers will guide them in the development of their abilities and in the pursuance of useful activities that will help them feel worthwhile and that will help them secure social approval.

It should be pointed out that aggression is not always maladaptive. Certainly, when there is a good chance of success in overcoming a difficulty through an aggressive approach, such aggressiveness should be encouraged. On the other hand, maladaptive aggressiveness is self-defeating and should be discouraged by guiding the child to more constructive ways of meeting his needs. For example, immature outbursts, aggressive attacks against others, or intrapunitive attacks (such as hypersensitivity) should be replaced with understanding, adequate problem-solving techniques, self-restraint, and the ability to face and deal with

[29] Eleanor Redwine and Letitia Wainwright, "The Development of a Power Contest," *Journal of Individual Psychology,* Vol. 11 (1955), pp. 172-177.

reality. Chapter 19 discusses ways in which the teacher may achieve these ends.

Compensation and sublimation.   In general, *compensation* refers to the tendency to make up for a weakness or deficiency in one trait by excelling in another. *Sublimation* is a substituted reaction which may be classified as a form of compensation. If compensatory reactions are realistic and deliberate, they can be healthy and helpful responses to insurmountable obstacles to a goal. When one approach does not lead to a desired goal, when impassable obstacles frustrate its attainment, "detour" or compensation may be the way to circumvent the problem. It may be a way, also, of substituting a higher level of response, on the rational or spiritual level, in place of a response on the sense or impulse level.

Sublimation involves those reactions, performed, perhaps unconsciously or with no particular plan about the matter, by which the individual takes advantage of opportunities about him for satisfying a frustrated need. This represents a higher level of development and may be noted in the behavior of children as they grow toward maturity. The individual's desire for adventure may appear in the form of camp life, a theme at school, or in some dramatic performance in school plays. The possibilities for sublimation will depend largely upon the opportunities offered by the child's environment and upon the experiences of the child in meeting difficult situations.

Compensation, as is true of almost all forms of defenses, is useful within limits. If tension can be reduced in socially acceptable ways not damaging to the personality while attention is drawn from a defect or deficiency, it has value. Compensation becomes maladaptive when it is used to build up a false reality, when insight into the reaction is lost. If the compensation is not rewarding, if the person finds himself in a situation of continuing inadequacy, the result may be physical or mental collapse.

Identification.   A form of compensation in which an individual lives vicariously through others to reduce tension from his own inadequacy or insecurity is known as identification. Identification as a *defense device* must not be confused with *role identification*. The latter is a natural developmental requisite for personality formation and learning in the early years (and through adolescence). Role identification has been discussed in earlier chapters. When there is no *true* identification, there is psychological isolation. All group therapy is dependent, to some extent, upon identification. The sense of identification makes a person defend individuals, places, and things of importance to him. In adolescence, peer group identification is very strong and is a means of learning social skills and fine group loyalties.

Identification becomes a maladaptive device when the individual has no other way of gaining adequacy or self-respect. As a defense mechanism it may be classified as a form of fantasy. The characteristics of some real or imaginary persons are appropriated by the inadequate personality. The exploits and successes of this hero give the individual a stature which tends to exalt him.

The prime danger involved in identification is that it may become a habitual mode of reacting to frustration, leaving the person's problems unsolved. He may become fixated at an immature level. Parents and teachers who seek to relive their youth and fulfill unsatisfied needs through the achievements of their children may harm those children.

Projection. A common form of defensive response, projection, in its many forms, transfers blame for an individual's troubles and shifts unacceptable drives onto others. He thus may accuse another person of the sin which really tempts him. Projection guards self-esteem by either shifting the guilt to another person or by creating a belief in the hostility of another person to permit the individual to feel justified in his own aggression. Projection provides unsatisfactory solutions and can cause considerable harm. Its forms represent maladaptive responses to thwarting, frustration, conflict, and other problems.

Perfectionism. Another form of compensation, perfectionism, is a morbid dissatisfaction with what one is or does. It is characterized by a tremendous drive toward absolutism. The child may need to think in wonderful and grandiose terms to save himself from his own cruel self-criticism. Alternatively, he may have learned that a person has to be *all good* and *always good* to be a lovable, worthwhile person. Since such perfection is impossible in the real world, the individual constantly perceives himself as a failure.

One reaction to this on the part of the pupil may be procrastination until such a short time is left for completing the task that he is freed from the crushing burden of having to do it perfectly. A final escape may be the "laziness" of desperation, the resignation of withdrawal.

Rationalization. Rationalization is a response to reality that falsifies circumstances to some extent. By rationalizing, a person finds sound and worthy reasons for an action which he intends to take. These are really pseudo-reasons, however, and do not correspond to reality because the real reasons for the action might be painful or uncomfortable to the individual. Rationalization is maladaptive insofar as the device involves self-deception. Like fantasy, however, it is inevitable to a certain extent. But, there are usually strong emotional concomitants involved in true rationalization.

Withdrawal or evasion. Some people react to life's problems by refusing to face them. There are many manifestations of this kind of behavior, and, as with the other maladaptive devices, much overlapping and interrelating. To describe its different manifestations, educators use various expressions, such as: *withdrawing into a private world, leaving the field, wishful thinking, day-dreaming, truancy, laziness, indifference, being bored, uninterested, absent-minded, solitary.* Excessive eating, drinking, illness (as a consequence of unresolved emotional conflicts), erratic behavior, overwork, "joining," sulkiness, pouting, and excessive worry are also ways of escaping reality situations. The extreme manifestation of withdrawal is resignation, complete apathy, and loss of all contact with reality.

Habitual withdrawal responses to life's problems are serious for several reasons. Because children who withdraw do not cause social annoyance, their problems may go unnoticed and unsolved until they have become so numbed by life's shocks and disappointments that they resign themselves to a world of inner living. Teachers should be alert to early symptoms, since the younger the child, the more easily can he be helped to tear down the wall between himself and others. The case of Joan illustrates some characteristics of many withdrawn children and some problems they face.

Joan was in the fourth grade of a village school. The teacher noted that she was an unusually quiet child; she did not speak to the other children; she did not play with them. The children ignored her because she so successfully pulled within herself. In an endeavor to help Joan, the teacher tried giving her special tasks or "privileges" such as watering the plants, going on errands, passing the paper, etc. Joan did these things mutely and with no show of interest.

When the teacher decided the treatment was not helpful, she invited the mother for a conference. The mother told the teacher that Joan was the oldest of four children and as such she was given much responsibility at home. The mother leaned on Joan to help watch the younger ones, to dust, to wash the dishes, and to run errands to the store. No wonder Joan did not see the teacher's "privileges" as such; this was more of the same work she had at home! The teacher talked to the mother about her concern over Joan's withdrawing, silent behavior, and together they wondered if perhaps Joan was too burdened for a nine-year-old. She probably felt the others were getting much more than she was from the parent. They were free and taken care of while Joan was always asked to be helpful and had to take care of herself.

Teacher and mother tried to plan ways to help Joan be more carefree and childlike. The mother planned to give Joan less responsibility and more "fun." . . . By the end of the year, Joan was still "shy" but no longer the silent, solitary child she had been in the fall.[30]

---

[30] Katherine E. D'Evelyn, *Meeting Children's Emotional Needs* (Englewood Cliffs: Prentice-Hall, Inc., 1957), p. 77.

Suppression. Feelings and thoughts which run counter to social standards are hidden by the process called *suppression.* Cultures teach their members to suppress certain kinds of feeling. For instance, the American middle-class culture frowns on fighting, swearing, improvidence, and sexual curiosity. Emotional control has traditionally been taught by punishing emotional expression. When a child, however, learns to suppress an emotion, he is learning to feel guilty. Children who are very cautious are likely to deny themselves all forms of emotional expression to avoid any danger of social disapproval. As a consequence, their lives lack spontaneity and flexibility. Suppression also leaves tensions unresolved that could erupt in new situations with the possibility of even greater conflicts arising.

Daydreaming. A form of escape frequently found among adolescents and preadolescents is daydreaming. Many boys and girls, unsuccessful at school or at play, find refuge in a "dream world"—a world of fantasy. Lewin has referred to personalities as varying along a dimension of reality-irreality. The distinction between fact and fantasy is not always clear to the child. With increased mental maturity and education, the child becomes better able to distinguish fact from fantasy. On many occasions, however, he may find his dream world a more pleasant one than the real world. Through fantasy he is able to shape the world and the happenings according to his liking.

Joseph and Zern,[31] among others, caution that it is not necessarily pathological for a child to have an imaginary playmate. They point out that this may be the result of a child's loneliness, unhappiness or boredom. The child creates a companion with whom he shares his joys and sorrows. This may happen among preschool-age children and usually ends when they enter school.

Fixation. Fixation is a type of escape response in which an individual's behavior remains fixed at a lower level of development than is normal at his particular maturation stage. Hilgard gives two means of the term as it is used psychologically:

1. that of arrested development so that an adult may be fixated at an infantile or adolescent level of psychological functioning. This usually implies an object choice (the mother: a like-sexed person) appropriate to the level of fixation and the statement is made that the person is fixated at such-and-such a level and is fixed on such-and-such an object.

[31] Harry Joseph, M.D. and Gordon Zern, *The Emotional Problems of Children* (New York: Crown Publishers, 1954), pp. 175-184.

2. a second meaning is that of fixed habits leading to preferred modes of problem-solving, such as fixation upon a particular mechanism of defense. The
habit fixations discussed as compulsions are fixations of this kind. The two
meanings are not clearly distinguished in psychoanalytic theory because the
stage of arrested development is so intimately related to the style of life.[32]

Regression. An unconscious "back-tracking" either in memory or in
behavior to an earlier adjustment which may have been successful in
the past without regard to its appropriateness at the present time is
called *regression.* It is sometimes regarded as a form of fixation. The old
man who tells of the successful achievement of his earlier years or the
woman who cries like a child when her slightest wants are denied are
examples of regression. Regression explains many manifestations of
infantile behavior on the part of adolescents and adults. Whenever they
face difficult adjustments, they simply regress to forms of behavior that
worked when they were children.

Figure 18-3 gives, in schematic summary, the adjustment approaches
which we have discussed.

Facing and solving life problems

Constructive adjustments are made by the conscious, rational uses of
a person's powers to overcome an impeding difficulty. To meet a frustrating situation successfully, a person must recognize it as a problem situation which requires a rational approach. The problem must be isolated
and sufficiently defined so that steps can be taken to solve it or handle it.
A variety of tentative solutions will then come to mind. The consequences
of each are elaborated mentally and the inadequate ones are rejected.
This process implies the mental activities of attention, concentration, and
deliberation necessary for any serious thinking and problem-solving. The
one or several "best" solutions are tested empirically and the final decision determined by the evidence.

The power of individual choice in behavior, usually termed *will
power,* underlies the hope of help from educators, counselors, psychologists, or psychiatrists. A study by Rechters and others [33] indicated
the effect which expectation and self-image have on behavior. Thirty
teachers were asked to nominate boys they thought were potentially
delinquent and boys who were well "insulated" against delinquency.
The researchers' check on court records revealed that 8 per cent of
"insulated" boys as compared to 23 per cent of potential delinquents had
been in contact with the courts.

[32] E. R. Hilgard, *Theories of Learning* (New York: Appleton-Century-Crofts,
1956), p. 302.
[33] Walter G. Rechters, Simon Dinitz, Barbara Kay, "The Self Component in
Potential Delinquency and Potential Non-Delinquency," *American Sociological Review,* Vol. 22 (1957), pp. 566-570.

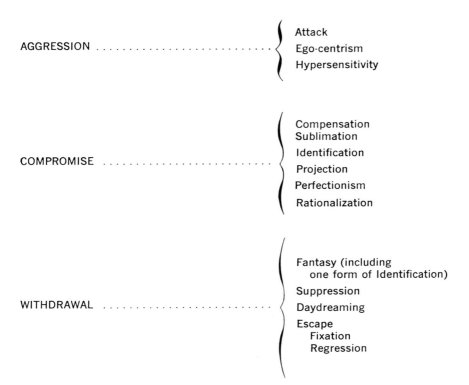

FIGURE 18-3. Adjustment Approaches Of Varying Defense Mechanisms

The researchers point out:

An analysis and comparison of the "insulated" and potentially delinquent nominees revealed significant differences in the self images of members in the two groups. The "insulated" boys, unlike the potentially delinquent, did not ever expect to have to be taken to juvenile court or to jail. They indicated a desire to avoid trouble at all costs and they had rarely engaged in any form of theft, and they had few, if any, friends who had been in trouble with the law. They like school and rarely played "hookey." They conceived of themselves as obedient sons who did not frequently behave in a manner contrary to their parents' wishes. They evaluated their families as being as good or better than most families and the relationships in the home as harmonious and cordial. They felt that their parents were neither overly strict nor lax and certainly not unnecessarily punitive. In all of these respects they differed from the boys nominated as being potentially delinquent.[34]

Whether a response or a solution is adjustive or maladaptive depends upon the nature and results of the behavior as viewed in a particular personality setting. Some positive indicators of adjustive responses are:

[34] *Ibid.*, p. 569.

1. The response is always satisfying. One of the results of a constructive decision is peace.
2. The response is a form of learning which contributes to a person's stability and maturity.
3. There is reduction or removal of tension. Satisfaction of need reduces drives in a constructive fashion which will *not* lead to secondary anxieties.
4. There is an economy of response. The solution is consonant with personal resources: e.g., abilities are consistent with chosen goals. It is also consistent with personal behavior, habits and values.

Balancing and compromising with problems.   Life's problems sometimes cannot be directly solved or completely disposed of. Compromises are inevitable, but they may either be adjustive or maladaptive. The child requires guidance in facing *reality* so that he deals with conditions as they really are rather than as he would like them to be.

Constructive approaches sometimes require the exertion of more effort to reach the desired goal or to meet the problem. It may be useful or essential to seek more information or to obtain help from a trustworthy and competent person (friend, teacher, counselor, or specialist). The person may also utilize alternative means to the same goal or consciously work out a substitute goal or sublimate to a higher one. (For example, a woman who is unable to have children of her own might consciously sublimate her maternal energies in nursing or in teaching).

Escaping from life problems.   There are persistent nonadjustive responses to life problems which get a person nowhere. Such responses neither reduce tension nor bring an adequate solution with its concomitant satisfaction. Once learned, responses to life problems tend to become habitual and automatic. If these responses are adequate and healthy they are termed adjustive mechanisms. If they consist in a refusal to face a reality situation, a fear of the solution of a problem, or a withdrawing or running away, it is a maladaptive device. Responses of this type usually result from ego loss or from some threat to self which the person cannot meet with the behavior he has learned.

As an example, Richard, a sixth grader, was a disabled reader. Severely handicapped because he lacked fundamental reading skills, the reading period presented a severe threat to him. Furthermore, his mother frequently bemoaned his poor marks and compared them to his sister's excellent scholastic achievement. Richard complained of stomach pains and headaches for which no organic basis was discovered. At length, the school nurse discovered that Richard became ill just before reading period. Often, his illness culminated in vomiting so that he had to be sent home for the day. This response to frustration, while it protected him from daily reading embarrassment, was maladaptive because it was intensifying his reading weakness while producing other undesirable results (ridicule from his peers, etc.).

When a person finds that he cannot adequately solve a problem or face a situation without loss of self-respect or damage to his self-concept, intense emotionality is aroused. This emotionality usually involves the whole complex of negative emotions related to anger or to a "fighting" defense, or to those of fear or "avoiding" defenses. Primitive defense reactions increase, and pressures upon the person build up. In the intensity or duration of the conflictual situation, faulty habits or personality traits may inadvertently be developed and unconsciously experienced and learned. This makes the person feel increasingly inadequate, insecure, afraid, and even desperate. Combs and Snygg [35] term the habitually severely frightened person *neurotic,* and the habitually, unconsciously desperate one *psychotic.* The human need for adequacy is insatiable. If problems become a threat of such proportions which the person cannot reasonably bear, there will be a "crushing of one's psychological bones, of one's true inner nature."

While it will always be necessary for the psychological specialist to take care of special maladaptive disorders, it is expedient for educators to recognize the nature of threatening problems and to be aware of maladaptive devices in order to refer seriously maladjusted children for professional care and to be able to guide and aid the incipient or temporary ones.

The teacher should help the child to develop sound goals, to cope with obstacles, and to attain the selected goals or to substitute other goals.

SUMMARY

Many children, because of emotional disturbances or social maladjustments, are unable to function adequately in normal home, school, and community situations. These children are problems to themselves as well as to the adults concerned with their proper development. Such disturbances usually have their roots in early interpersonal and home experiences and have a growth dynamism which is in accord with the laws of learning.

The chapter described an *adjusted* person as one who achieves his fullest potentialities through smooth and harmonious functioning of physical, psychological, sociological, and ethical aspects of self. The stu-

[35] Arthur W. Combs and Donald Snygg, *Individual Behavior: A Perceptual Approach to Behavior* (New York: Harper and Row, 1959), p. 267.

dent was cautioned that adjustment did *not* imply the absence of difficulties, problems, or frustrations. The adjusted person, however, makes *minimum* use of maladaptive devices to solve such problems.

In meeting his needs and seeking to approach his problems, the person can (1) face and constructively solve life problems; (2) balance and compromise with such problems; or (3) seek to escape from life problems. The nature of responses characteristic of these types of approaches were discussed together with positive indicators of adjustive responses.

The role of the home, the school, the class culture, interpersonal relations within the classroom, the teacher's understanding of and attitude toward children who deviate from the mythical norm, and the impact of physical and mental attributes were discussed in light of their impact on children's ability to achieve adjustive responses.

The chapter emphasized that symptoms of personal and social maladjustment were not the same for all children. It was noted, however, that some symptoms appeared frequently among different types of maladjustments and that some symptoms are more readily observed than others. The frequency and patterning of the appearance of certain symptoms is of major importance in evaluating personality maladjustments.

A number of maladaptive responses to problems, conflicts, and frustrations were discussed. The student was cautioned that most children seem to manifest some of the symptoms accompanying such responses at irregular intervals. Certain children display them often and quite regularly. The persistence of such symptoms and their patterning should receive thoughtful evaluation with a view to corrective action by the school specialists or corrective action within the classroom.

Problems and Exercises

1. Show how principles of child dynamics are related to emotional and social adjustment. What factors determine the seriousness of a frustrated or thwarted need? Why was it said that adjustment does not mean the *absence* of conflict or frustration?
2. Ask some of your college friends (who are not taking teacher preparatory courses) to rank the ten traits (shown in Table 18-4) in the order of their seriousness to the child and their troublesome nature in the classroom. How do these ratings compare with Sparks' list? With Beilin's more recent findings?
3. What are some of the major hazards encountered by a child from a minority group as he strives to achieve adequate personality adjustment?
4. Study the symptoms of maladjustment presented in Table 18-5. What other symptoms have you observed in children you believed to be having adjustment difficulties? How many of them have you observed in children who seemed to have adequate adjustment?
5. What difference will it make in the teaching-learning situation if a teacher

conceives of certain forms of behavior as *symptomatic* rather than as *acts* to be dealt with?

6. Consider some problem-child of your acquaintance. What symptoms of maladjustments are manifested by this child? What do these symptoms suggest relative to possible causes of the maladjustment?

7. Why is it important for the teacher to have information regarding the child's behavior in a number of different behavior situations: home, school, peer-group play, formal play, church, etc.?

8. Why is peer conformity so important at the fourth-grade level? How is this often closely related to adjustment problems among fourth-grade children?

9. Discuss the following incident in the light of this chapter:

> Miss Jones, a sixth-grade teacher in an elementary school located in a high socioeconomic suburb, frequently warns her pupils of the moral evils of cheating. She "puts them on their honor *never* to lie or copy." She tells her colleagues that she has never had a pupil lie or cheat in her classes. One day she sees a boy apparently copying from his neighbor. The boy is the son of a father whose social position, income, and education are much lower than that of the community. Miss Jones takes the paper, lectures the boy at length on the evils of his crime, tears up the paper and records a failing mark. The boy's protests of innocence go unheeded. Miss Jones then assigns the boy to a seat by himself in the rear of the room.

Selected Readings

BRUCE, William F., "Personality and Children's Adjustment Problems," in Chas. E. Skinner, ed., *Educational Psychology*, 4th ed. (Englewood Cliffs: Prentice-Hall, 1959), Ch. 5.

CRONBACH, Lee J., *Educational Psychology*, 2nd ed. (New York: Harcourt, Brace, and World, 1963), Ch. 17.

HENRY, Nelson B., ed., *Mental Health in Modern Education*, Fifty-fourth Yearbook of the National Society for the Study of Education (Chicago: University of Chicago Press, 1955).

KLAUSMEIER, Herbert J., *Learning and Human Abilities: Educational Psychology* (New York: Harper & Row, 1961), Chs. 9 and 10.

LAZARUS, R. S., *Adjustment and Personality* (New York: McGraw-Hill, 1961).

SMITH, Henry P., *Psychology in Teaching*, 2nd ed. (Englewood Cliffs: Prentice-Hall, 1962), Ch. 14.

SHAFFER, L. F., and SHOBEN, E. J., *The Psychology of Adjustment* (Boston: Houghton Mifflin Co., 1956).

STRANG, Ruth, *Helping Your Gifted Child* (New York: E. P. Dutton & Co., 1960).

CHAPTER **19**

Pupil-Teacher Relationships

PERSONALITY RELATIONSHIPS

The human being develops primarily through relationships with other people. Through the satisfaction of basic and acquired human needs, he matures and changes throughout his life under the influence of dynamic, vital drives toward self-realization. The fulfillment of these needs involves the cognitive abilities of sensing, perceiving, and knowing; it also involves the dynamic drives of emotional relationships and the drive for independence through choice-making.

The adult leader who understands the nature of the relationships an individual tends to form in the various maturational stages will be able to guide interpersonal development with greater perception and insight. Moreover, this understanding can help the teacher to use developmental forces to influence the integrated growth of the child.

Childhood and adult relationships

The nature of the child's identification with his parents was discussed in Chapter 6. This extensive identification with the parents, and later, with other adult authority figures, has an important bearing on the child's development and learning. It especially influences the acquisition of habits, attitudes, values, ideals, and other personal characteristics and traits. Children learn by imitating those whom they admire and love and whose reaction to themselves they *interpret* as loving and accepting. This identification tends to be transferred to all authority figures, such as the teacher in the primary grades, as long as their previous experiences with these adults has been satisfying and positive. If it has not been so, children may reject the efforts of those perceived as authority

490

figures to teach them. This positive (or negative) child-adult relationship will continue into late childhood when there is a gradual detachment of authority-figure identification due to the partial transference of personal relationships to peers.

The perceptive educator who is aware of these phenomena will utilize the advantages and strengths of his influence inherent in his relationship with young boys and girls. He will be able to understand, accept, and counterbalance the child's resistance by providing for constructive ways to satisfy his basic, individual, and personal needs. Most of all, he will be aware that his influence will be positive to the degree that he *is* a mature, integrated personality. Anderson points up the implications of the educator's attitudes for personality growth and learning:

Give the child good models of behavior by showing enthusiasm for activities. Attitudes are readily communicable and apparently much more so through indirect rather than direct stimulation. If persons about the child are interested and enjoy activities, the child readily falls into the pattern, whereas if persons are half-hearted, listless, uninterested, and look upon their activities as invasions of rights, the likelihood of interest on the part of children is much lessened. When children are approached from the point of view, "You should, must, ought to, be interested," instead of the point of view, "What fun it is to do this," "Isn't it interesting?" positive orientation is destroyed. But active participation by the adult with obvious gestural, postural, and vocal indications of interest make the outcome almost a foregone conclusion. This is particularly true of younger children who are unusually responsive to the attitudes of those about them and are somewhat less concerned with the objective features of the activity in question. With older children competence is also involved. There must be not only enthusiasm but also some recognizable skill and ability in performing the activity since the more sophisticated children look for and perceive the results as well as the enthusiasm of their teachers and co-workers. Because of this sophistication, older children more readily detect assumed rather than genuine interest.[1]

Ryans studied the relationships between trained observers' assessments of several classrooms of pupils and the teachers of those pupils in regard to selected types of behavior. He found:

For elementary school classes, *high* positive relationships were noted between observers' assessments of "productive pupil behavior" (pupil alertness, participation, confidence, responsibility, self-control, etc.) and assessments of patterns of teacher behavior which seemed to refer to understanding, friendly classroom behavior; organized, businesslike classroom behavior, and stimulating, original classroom behavior.[2]

[1] G. Lester Anderson, "Theories of Behavior and Some Curriculum Issues," in L. D. Crow and Alice Crow, eds., *Readings in Educational Psychology* (Ames, Iowa: Littlefield, Adams, Co., 1956), p. 278.

[2] David G. Ryans, "Some Relationships between Pupil Behavior and Certain Teacher Characteristics," *Journal of Educational Psychology*, Vol. 52 (1961), p. 90.

For the child, then, the influence of the adult is direct and that of an authority figure. The perceptive educator will strive to utilize this natural relationship positively, effectively, and consciously in guiding the educational development of the child.

Adolescent and adult relationships

A new aspect of the dependence-independence human need begins to manifest itself at the maturational stage of preadolescence when the child begins to transfer his relationships both of dependence and identification to his peer group. This transference, which seems to become dominant in adolescence, can become the source of much conflict, frustration, and distressing personality problems if it is misunderstood or denied by adults. When, in the normal process of maturing, boys and girls begin to align themselves with their peer groups, the teacher may facilitate the simultaneous working-out of peer and adult identifications by recognizing, accepting, and supporting adolescents in these needs. This need for peer group status begins in late childhood and extends through life. It is culturally saturated in its tone.

It has been pointed out that young people choose as friend, hero, or confidant, an adult who respects their individuality and can communicate detached interest and warm support. This adult may be a teacher, community leader, religious leader, parent, or any ideal—contemporary, historical, or literary. Group models and their influence depend upon the needs and values of the group members and upon the cohesiveness of the group. The educator, as an adult, has a twofold responsibility in his relationship to the adolescent in view of the personality needs of students at this particular age. The teacher's *first* task is to be an acceptable model in American culture and to utilize group processes within the educative process for the complete education and personality integration of the adolescent. Overton further defines this first responsibility:

We refer to the need for the teacher to be an appropriate model for the youth he teaches. But what is an appropriate model? After all, the teacher is also subject to choice in our culture. This being the case, we can hardly expect the teachers to be of the same stamp. It seems to me in answering the question, we should consider two points: first that it is appropriate to have a range of models among those who teach, for this increases the possibility of active choice among students; second, even though the range of teacher models does exist and the sanctions for holding their values vary, there is need for agreement among teachers of America on the basic values that they are to demonstrate in the action of their lives. These values, it seems to me, should not be relative to any place or time, but should be those values which have enabled us to rise in human experience above animal experience. They are the values that have made us significantly human. These are value choices such as honesty over deception, fair play over foul, courage above cowardice, compassion above brutality, love above hate. In other words, these are the choices teachers must make in order to qualify them to teach.

Ultimately, what values youth accept in America is a problem of choice. The choice is in their hands. This is as it should be. For us who are concerned with how our youth will turn out, this is fundamentally a problem of faith—faith that if we as adults can serve as moral models and encourage and guide our youth to think for themselves, they will come up with answers that are right for them. It seems to me that is the only course consonant with the American creed.[3]

The *second* responsibility of the educator is to recognize that relationships change at different age levels and to adjust his reactions, as an adult, to these changes. Lindgren points out this need:

> The truth seems to be that much of the time we in education are unaware of the fact that people tend to act differently as members of groups from the way they act when they are not members of groups. Even if we are aware of this, we often appear to ignore it. We treat students as though we expect them to behave the same within groups as they do away from them. We easily fall into the error of assuming that since Mike Moreno who sits in class is physically the same student with whom we "had an understanding" in our office, he should be the same student psychologically. Hence when Mike Moreno displays personality traits as a class member that are different from those displayed when alone with us, we feel frustrated and inadequate. Sometimes we are equal to this feeling and recover quickly, but at other times our resentment at being let down disturbs our relationship with our class or with our family and friends . . .[4]

The teacher, as an adult, must recognize the adolescent's continuing dependency needs directed toward him, his increased need for independence, and his need for self-direction and choice-making even in the matter of his dependency. The teacher must also understand the influence that an accepted adult can have upon the individual teen-ager and his group, and the nature of peer-group dynamics in order to utilize their potential for full personality integration.

Peer relationships

The psychological and maturational aspects of individual- and peer-group relationships have been defined in previous chapters. These range from the parallel play activities of the young child through like-sex peer groups to the strong urges of adolescents to be with their peers and become identified with their peer-group.

---

[3] Harvey Overton, "Youth and Their Values," *The Clearing House*, Vol. 35 (1961), p. 411.

[4] Henry C. Lindgren, "The Effect of the Group on the Behavior of the Individual," in L. D. Crow and Alice Crow, eds., *Readings in Educational Psychology* (Ames, Iowa: Littlefield, Adams, Co., 1956), p. 384.

Group cohesiveness, especially in the younger ages, is increased by activities in which all members of the group contribute to the achievement of a successful group activity.

The perceptive educator will know enough about peer groups at each level of psychological maturation, will understand the characteristic relationship of boys and girls (with adults and with each other) at each stage—and the influence of these relationships in the educative process—to be able to direct their energies. As a leader he will guide the group toward its goals, will develop its leadership, and will influence individual attitudes, values, and ideals for the development of integrated personalities. By virtue of his mature insight he will respect the unique individuality of each person in the group. Furthermore, he will recognize the value of and work for a positive classroom relationship while utilizing constructive subrelationships within the class, such as "chum" groups, cliques, and groups of friends from neighborhood, church, club, etc. Recent investigations have indicated that, in the elementary grades, group cohesiveness is increased by some form of activity in which all members feel successful in the experienced success of a common group activity.

494

Some of the variables that will affect the quality of the individual pupil's personal relationships are:

1. The extent to which he has been accepted and respected as an individual by adults and by peers in his group.
2. The extent to which he has experienced democratic guidance and a rationally permissive atmosphere in which to exercise his developing need for reasonable decision-making and self-direction.
3. The extent to which his relationships with the adult in his life have been need-fulfilling, insightful, and psychologically satisfying.
4. The degree to which he has been permitted to think for himself, to make judgments and mistakes, and to take the consequences in a supportive learning situation.
5. The degree to which he has positively interpreted his experiences and constructively responded to their influences.

Thus the child grows to the fullness of human personality through the satisfaction of his basic needs in his social or personal relationships.

The social structure of the classroom

Although a child's contacts with peer groups have been somewhat limited prior to school age, they become important to him even before he enters school. After he enters school, they tend to play an even more important part in influencing his development.

The classroom may be viewed as a social organization where children tend to gain certain prestige and status from the roles they achieve within the group. Much of the interaction, and many of the interpersonal relationships grow out of the group structure which the teacher plays a part in directing. A knowledge of group structure, therefore, is valuable to the teacher, since it helps her to understand the relationship of each child to the total group. She can also direct and guide the class more effectively if she understands its power structure.

Teachers appear to vary in their ability to determine the sociometric structure within their classes. Gronlund [5] correlated the accuracy of the judgments of the sociometric status of their classmates made by a group of student teachers with their judgments of the sociometric status of the children whom they were teaching. He felt that the correlation of +.49 indicated the presence of a general ability to judge the sociometric status of others.

A number of studies have shown that a relationship exists between

[5] N. E. Gronlund, "The General Ability to Judge Sociometric Status: Elementary Student Teachers' Sociometric Perceptions of Classmates and Pupils," *Journal of Educational Psychology*, Vol. 47 (1956), pp. 147-157.

the pupil's sociometric position within the group and his personal adjustment, academic achievement, and the social status of his home and family. In a study of boys and girls enrolled in the kindergarten through sixth grades, Gold [6] found a relationship between the values of children and their positions in the power structure. He concluded, "The results of this study suggest that the values of the children do reflect a great deal of the situation in which they interact. Further, these values seem to play an important role in transforming certain properties of the children into resources which in turn determine the relative power positions of the children in the classroom groups." [7]

Children's reactions to teachers. The attitudes which children display toward school often reflect their attitudes toward their teacher. Often children will comment positively or negatively on the personality

"When I'm through with this
assignment what do I do next?"

[6] Martin Gold, "Power in the Classroom," *Sociometry*, Vol. 21 (1958), pp. 50-60.
[7] *Ibid.*, p. 59.

characteristics of a teacher. One of the writer's children, a second grader, commented at dinner one night, "I don't like Miss X because she never smiles." A first-grade child stated, "I like Mrs. T. because she's fun." Often children comment on the behavior of the teacher as she reacted to a situation. "Miss X made me cry because she made me stay in at recess. She said I was talking to John, but I only asked him for my pencil which I dropped on the floor."

Comments such as these tend to reveal the way the child sees the teacher. While it is to be expected that the child of elementary-school age often will misinterpret or confuse the purpose of certain actions on the part of an adult, or will not comprehend the necessity of certain disciplinary actions, such comments tend to reveal the child's emotional reactions to a situation or toward an authority figure. Since affective or emotional factors are of prime importance in all behavior, it is essential that they be considered in school learning situations. Generally the teacher who has been successful in gaining the cooperation of her pupils has also gained their respect and admiration.

A number of studies have indicated that students at all grade levels have certain expectations about their teachers and react to their behavioral characteristics. Tiedeman [8] obtained opinions from about 8,000 junior-high-school pupils concerning things their teachers had done that they either liked or disliked. The data revealed that pupils tended to like teachers who were kind, friendly, cheerful, helped pupils gladly, explained their materials clearly, had no favorites, were neat and tidy, had a sense of humor, understood children and their problems, allowed children to do things for them, and were friendly and polite when they met their pupils outside the school. On the other hand, the students disliked autocratic, domineering teachers, teachers who used ridicule, sarcasm, threats, fear, or punishment to secure discipline, and teachers who failed to provide for individual differences, showed partiality, or had disagreeable or peculiar personal characteristics.

Leeds [9] administered a questionnaire designed to reveal certain aspects of their teachers' behavior, to approximately 1,000 fourth-, fifth-, and sixth-graders. He noted that a pupil's liking of a teacher was intricately related, if not determined, by factors that were essentially affective, personal, and human. It is likely that when the elementary-school child tells his family that he likes school, he is probably stating that he likes his teacher.

The attitudes of pupils toward teachers, once they are developed,

[8] S. Tiedeman, "A Study of Pupil-Teacher Relationship," *Journal of Educational Research*, Vol. 35 (1942), pp. 657-664.

[9] C. H. Leeds, "Teacher Behavior Liked or Disliked by Pupils," *Education*, Vol. 75 (1954), pp. 29-37.

tend to remain fixed and constant. Smith [10] investigated the attraction and repulsion of 184 elementary-school children to their student teachers. In a retest three months later he found remarkably constant acceptance or rejection. As the teacher's ability to relate with children depends at least in part on her own personality, the adjustment of the teacher is an important factor to be considered in the education and selection of future teachers. If a teacher is personally insecure, has unresolved needs, is tense or is functioning under pressures, she will have difficulty providing for the social-emotional needs of children. Similarly, a rigid teacher who has strong moral convictions or who feels that her judgments are always right has a tendency to stifle individual opportunities for self-expression. It is interesting to speculate about the reactions of pupils who detest school but who may be reflecting an intense dislike for their teachers. The fact that most children enjoy elementary school and are attracted to their teachers speaks well for the adjustment and personality of the majority of teachers.

The feminine character of the elementary school. One of the difficulties encountered in the elementary-school environment is the predominantly feminine characteristic of the elementary school. Despite a slight increase in the number of men who prepare for elementary teaching positions, the majority of elementary-school teachers are women. If the teacher is to serve as a model for the child to identify with, it would seem to follow that more male models should be furnished, especially for boys. Unfortunately, many elementary schools are completely staffed by women; in many other schools the only male in the institution serves as principal and deals directly with the pupils only on rare occasions.

Some writers have noted that many teachers perceive boy students to be more difficult to manage, less motivated by school, and generally more troublesome to deal with. In one of her investigations, Koch [11] noted that teachers of five- and six-year-olds tended to rate boys more active, more expressive of anger, quarrelsome, revengeful, given to teasing, extrapunitive, insistent of their rights, and uncooperative with teachers and peers. Girls were rated more affectionate, obedient, responsible, and tenacious of purpose than boys. Whether differences in behavior are due to sex or to different adult expectations and standards, or whether such behavioral differences reflect different maturational patterns has not yet been satisfactorily explained.

[10] W. D. Smith, "Social Attraction between Elementary-school Children and Student Teachers: Sociometric Analysis, *Journal of Educational Psychology,* Vol. 44 (1953), pp. 113-125.

[11] Helen L. Koch, "Some Personality Correlates of Sex, Sibling Position, and Sex of Sibling among Fve- and Six-year-old Children," *Genetic Psychology Monographs,* Vol. 52 (1955), p. 47.

Harris [12] asked a group of student teachers to supply behavior descriptions of the most and least responsible children in their classrooms. A marked tendency on the part of the teachers to nominate boys the least responsible was noted.

THE TEACHER

All that has been said previously about the nature of personality, its integration and adjustment, and the dangers of its maladjustment can be applied to the teacher as a human being. What the educator, the teacher, *is* in the totality of his own personality—all the qualities he has in common with other persons, but uniquely and specially developed and integrated—constitutes his primary influence on maturing personalities under his direction, for good or ill.

The teacher as an integrated personality

Social realities, cultural values, environmental pressures, relationships, and conflicts exert their primary force on the educative process as they are incorporated into the personalities of those directing educational development, and, as such, influence the daily reactions and decisions of teachers. These reactions and decisions may stimulate or inhibit the realization of children's potentialities.

An extremely important part of a teacher's personal history is his cultural background. Consequently, he must face it realistically and understand it in the context of American culture. He must also understand that his background may make it difficult for him to adequately perceive the differences and needs of children from different cultural backgrounds.

Research, for instance, has shown that many teachers are from middle-class families. These teachers, however, are called on to teach children from every social and cultural level. On each cultural level, the nature of the human personality and its development is essentially the same. The experiences which make each child unique—environment, past experiences, and direction of goal seeking—will be radically different (although not necessarily superior or inferior). The attainment of insight, perceptiveness, acceptance and warmth in the teaching relationship is dependent to a large measure on the teacher's awareness and realistic acceptance of his own personal and cultural history and its relationship to the other cultural levels.

The personal aspect of the educator involves his personal appearance, grooming, voice, mannerisms, speech, physical features, expression, and

[12] D. B. Harris, "How Student-Teachers Identify Responsibility in Children," *Journal of Educational Psychology,* Vol. 45 (1954), pp. 233-239.

reflection of attitudes. These, together with his own attitude toward them and their relation to his self-concept, are basic factors in the type of interpersonal relationships he can establish and the rapport he can elicit in his work with human personalities. Most of these manifestations of the personal aspect are subject to change, control, or sublimation. Thus, they need not, generally, be handicaps to the teacher's adequacy as a person.

The teacher will be psychologically adequate as a person to the extent that:

1. He *is* himself, accepting his strengths and weaknesses realistically. He is not smug nor complacent nor unreasonably conforming.
2. He has realistic goals, aspirations, and ideals for himself and others. He has a vision which keeps him dynamic, alive, alert, and positive.
3. He can adequately satisfy his need "to know": to know himself; to understand human personality in its psychological aspects; to know the elements of his profession, its subject matter, techniques, and purposes; and his ability to find satisfaction in continuing to be a learner relative to himself, his profession, his students, and the entire environment of his universe.
4. He can feel adequately about his relationships with himself, the learner, his fellow teachers, his family and community associations, with his fellowman and his Creator.
5. He can be finely balanced in his independence-dependence relationships. This balance involves the handling of negative emotions and maladjustments, the self-respect that can combine conformity with creative professional contribution, and the freedom and security that is basic to flexibility of personality pattern.
6. He can love adequately. This involves respect for human dignity, sincere acceptance of individuals in personal relationships, ability to create a warm and constructive partnership with each student, and the synthesis of all these in levels of motivation corresponding to the levels of integration consonant with an adequate and mature personality as defined in Chapters 6, 11 and 16.

In this connection, the personal needs of teachers assumes considerable importance. Garrison and Scott [13] investigated the validity of the hypothesis that personal needs of college students preparing to teach differ according to the area of teaching chosen. Their results showed that prospective women teachers manifested a need for achievement, for

[13] Karl C. Garrison and Mary H. Scott, "A Comparison of the Personal Needs of College Students Preparing to Teach in Different Teaching Areas," *Educational and Psychological Measurement*, Vol. 21 (1961), pp. 955-964.

nurturance, for order, and for succorance. Differences were found between prospective elementary, secondary, and special teacher groups. In general, these findings are congruent with Ryans' factors determining the effective elementary teacher.

Influences of emotional factors. Normal and adequate emotional adjustment is important for success as a teacher. Retan [14] made a study of the relation between emotional stability and ability as a teacher. In his investigation, he secured ratings of teacher competence for 152 teachers on which he had complete data. The ratings presented in Table 19-1 indicate that emotional instability, as measured by the tests

TABLE 19-1. A Comparison of the Ratings Given by Superintendents to Teachers Listed as Stable with Those Listed as Unstable

	GOOD TO EXCELLENT PER CENT	FAIR TO POOR PER CENT	TOTAL PER CENT
Emotionally stable	75.8	24.2	48
Emotionally unstable	51.9	48.1	52

used, is not conclusive evidence for unfitness for teaching. There is no one pattern of traits which designates the excellent teacher. Rather, there appear to be several patterns. Likewise, there are many patterns of traits which make poor teachers. Emotional instability is most harmful when combined with other factors which adversely affect the educational and personal development of the children.

There are, nevertheless, subtle influences of negative emotionality which, because of their power, should become a part of the effective teacher's awareness. The following elaborates some of these:

His feelings about the learner, about parents or about fellow teachers are interwoven with feelings about himself. What he sees to praise or encourage or to condemn and punish will be influenced, not simply by what is objectively there, but by what he projects from his own values, his own needs and past experiences. All of his own conflicts, his anxieties, his readiness for various classroom experiences, his compulsions as to what must and must not be done become part of this interpersonal relationship. More than manipulation of the environment, and methods of studying children—or the use of newer methods of teaching—is required. No amount of the external will touch upon the internal drives of the teacher unless he is willing to examine himself. He must struggle

[14] George A. Retan, "Emotional Instability and Teaching Success," *Journal of Educational Research,* Vol. 37 (1943), pp. 135-141.

to understand himself if he is to understand students and to function in a wise and sympathetic, and constructive way. The study of children or the tryout of new materials or new methods, therefore, is of value when it assists the teacher to re-examine himself and his own drives and compulsions. Through such re-examination he rebuilds and improves his relationship with others.[15]

Sister Amatora studied the personalities of teachers and their pupils in a group of city and rural schools in grades four through eight. She found a significant similarity between the pupil and teacher personality in over half of the scales employed.[16] Long term studies of the effects of teacher personality on the behavior patterns of pupils show that this influence persists beyond the period of contact with the teacher. This finding is extremely important, since teachers are entrusted with responsibilities that have such an important bearing on the character and personality of pupils. It should be emphasized that teachers, parents, and others teach by example as well as by precept. It has been observed constantly, for example, that students in a science laboratory become very careless in the use and care of science materials and equipment when the science teacher displays such attitudes and habits.

A study conducted in 55 fourth-, fifth-, and sixth-grade elementary school classes in Brooklyn revealed that children's achievements depend mainly upon teacher personality and the interaction of such personalities with the personalities of the children being taught.[17] The materials presented in Figure 19-1 show the relative achievement gains for different kinds of teachers and different kinds of children. The achievement gains shown are adjusted for IQ scores and school differences. The study showed that, generally, self-controlling teachers with their ordering, limit-setting, and work-oriented characteristics obtain more total achievement gains than teachers classified *turbulent*, or *fearful*, whose main characteristics were vacillation and uncertainty. It should also be noted that the study showed that pupils classified as *strivers* made the greatest achievement gain and that their gain was *unrelated* to the teacher personality.

Because of the interrelatedness of teacher personality and pupil behavior and achievement (as indicated by studies previously cited), the maladjusted teacher will have a detrimental effect upon the lives of a large number of growing boys and girls. An important mental health hazard among teachers is an attitude of negative valuation toward teach-

[15] *Creating a Good Environment for Learning.* Yearbook of The Association for Supervision and Curriculum Development (1954), p. 154.

[16] Sister Mary Amatora, "Similarities in Teachers and Pupil Personality," *Journal of Psychology,* Vol. 37 (1954), pp. 45-51.

[17] Louis M. Heilm, Marion Powell, and Irwin Feifer, *Characteristics of Teacher Behavior and Competency Related to the Achievement of Different Kinds of Children in Several Elementary Grades.* Cooperative Research Project, U.S. Office of Education, 1960.

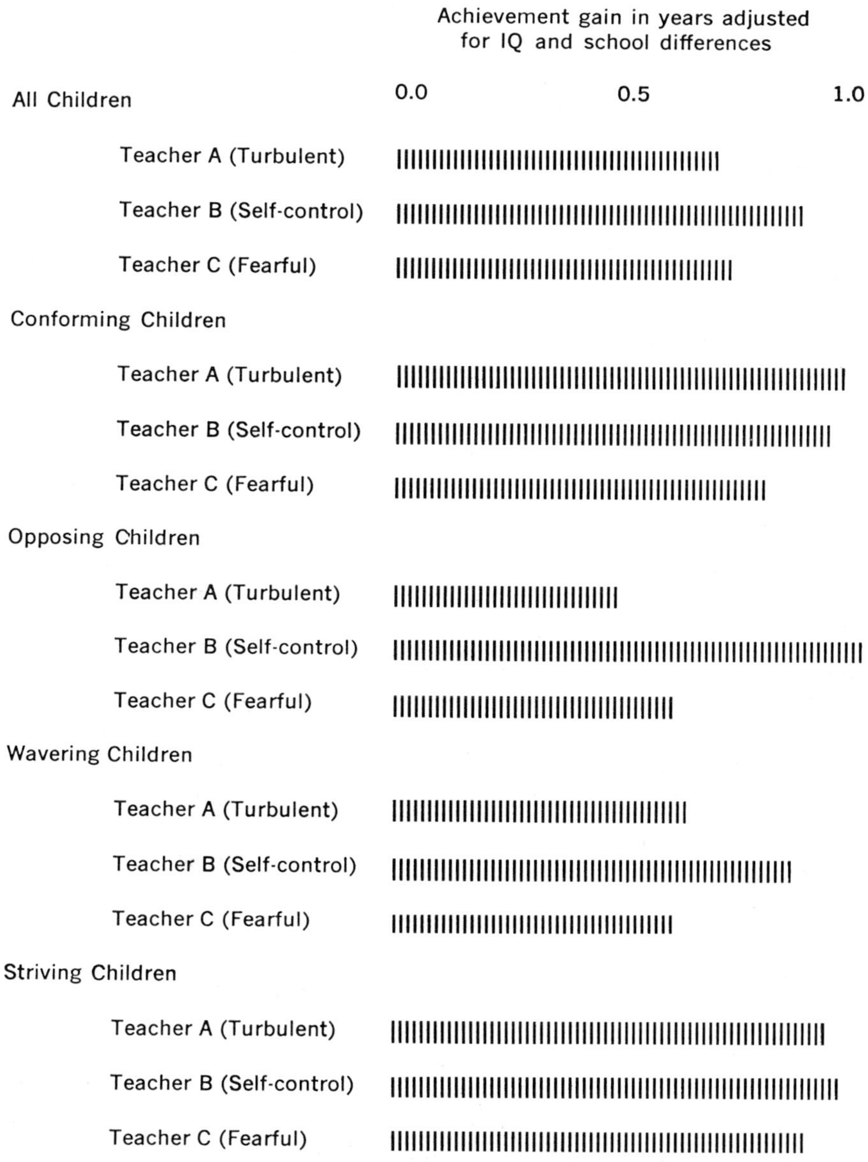

Achievement gain in years adjusted
for IQ and school differences

All Children	0.0	0.5	1.0

Teacher A (Turbulent) |||||||||||||||||||||||||||||||||||||||

Teacher B (Self-control) ||||||||||||||||||||||||||||||||||||||||||||||||||||||

Teacher C (Fearful) |||||||||||||||||||||||||||||||||||||||||||

Conforming Children

Teacher A (Turbulent) |||||||||||||||||||||||||||||||||||||||||||||||||||||||||||||||

Teacher B (Self-control) ||||||||||||||||||||||||||||||||||||||||||||||||||||||||||||||

Teacher C (Fearful) ||||||||||||||||||||||||||||||||||||||||||||||||||||||

Opposing Children

Teacher A (Turbulent) |||||||||||||||||||||||||||||||

Teacher B (Self-control) ||||||||||||||||||||||||||||||||||||||||||||||||||||||||||||||||||||

Teacher C (Fearful) ||||||||||||||||||||||||||||||||||||||

Wavering Children

Teacher A (Turbulent) |||||||||||||||||||||||||||||||||||||||||

Teacher B (Self-control) ||||||||||||||||||||||||||||||||||||||||||||||||||||||||

Teacher C (Fearful) |||||||||||||||||||||||||||||||||||||

Striving Children

Teacher A (Turbulent) ||||||||||||||||||||||||||||||||||||||||||||||||||||||||||||

Teacher B (Self-control) |||||||||||||||||||||||||||||||||||||||||||||||||||||||||||||||

Teacher C (Fearful) |||||||||||||||||||||||||||||||||||||||||||||||||||||||||||

FIGURE 19-1.   Relative Achievement Gains For Different Kinds Of Teachers and Different Kinds Of Children (Heilm, Powell, and Feifer).

ing—in some cases, a stifling self-pity. Deprecation of the value of their work, complaints about salaries, difficulties of working with children, supervisors and parents, the unreasonable demands made by community authorities, and complaints about restrictions on their activities accompany such a negative attitude.

Bernard has listed certain action patterns which are conducive to good mental health and the maintenance of positive attitudes:

1. Maintain sound physical health.
2. Seek to gain understanding of your own conduct.
3. Achieve security through developing skills.
4. Seek improved relationships with others.
5. Maintain confidential relationships with selected individuals.
6. Face strain and stress with poise.
7. Substitute planning for worry.
8. Give both work and play a place in your life.
9. Give attention to the present situation.
10. Just do the best you can.
11. Capitalize on the mental health value of religion.
12. Learn to enjoy living.[18]

These statements present, in action form, a summary of the constructs and theory relative to personality.

The teacher as an educator. It was pointed out in Chapter 2 that the role of the teacher as a professional educator has gradually changed during the course of the past century or more. The professional educator today not only teaches the whole student but accepts him with his complete background of experience, respects him for what he is and what he may become, tries to see the field of learning from the student's viewpoint, and thinks of his relationship with the student as *we* instead of *I* and *they*. He continues to be a learner—to learn more of his specialty through research and professional reading, to learn more of the learner as he develops each new relationship in the partnership of learning, and to learn ever more of the intangibles of learning that will keep him alive, alert, and developing professionally.

Investigators have asserted that professional training and preparation enlarges the individual's cognitive framework so that he has more and better criteria with which to evaluate possible actions. A study by Runkel and Damrin [19] strongly supports this hypothesis. They found that teachers with low levels of knowledge perceived students' problems erratically and inadequately. Teachers with high levels of knowledge, on the contrary, manifested specialized and differentiated perceptions of students' problems. Teachers with "average knowledge" were found to possess relatively low variability of criteria which the researchers inter-

[18] Harold Bernard, *Mental Hygiene for Classroom Teachers* (New York: McGraw-Hill Book Co., Inc., 1952), Chapter 19.

[19] Philip J. Runkel and Dora E. Damrin, "Effects of Training and Anxiety upon Teachers' Preferences for Information About Students," *Journal of Educational Psychology*, Vol. 52 (1961), pp. 254-261.

preted as "indicative of the restricted simplicity of the partially trained individual." For male teachers, the study indicated that feelings of anxiety narrowed perception to only a few elements of the environment. (The investigators express the belief that more reliable measures of anxiety would show more extensive application of this phenomenon.)

In the sphere of professional teaching excellence, there is, as in all areas of human experience, individual differences in ability. Enriching experiences and educational opportunities among teachers can also be as varied and as fruitful as the unique individuality of learners. Hundreds of items have been used at various times to evaluate professional teacher excellence: the consensus of expert raters, ratings made while in teacher-preparation and in practice teaching by supervising teachers, in-service supervisors, fellow teachers, and pupils. Self-ratings (singly or in combination with ratings by fellow teachers), and measured pupil change have also been used. Ackerman[20] considers change in pupil behavior as the ultimate criterion of teacher effectiveness. He asserts that effectiveness is a multi-dimensional factor which must include all-around pupil growth. Such a concept includes the teacher's physical, mental, social, and moral qualities as he has developed these in his total life experiences, and especially, in his specific, professional training and preparation to guide the education of tomorrow's men and women. This guidance implies *leadership* of the young in group situations and a certain kind of acceptance and understanding which we shall define subsequently in this chapter as the *counseling role* of the teacher.

The teacher as a leader. Leadership connotes going somewhere; it connotes purpose, goals, values, ideals, and human destiny. All that has been said of these in the preceding chapters is a frame of reference for the educator in his role as a leader. More specifically, educators in America are preparing children to exercise or accept leadership in a democracy. There is no one type of leadership for all teachers, nor one type for the same teacher all the time. The kind of leadership the teacher exerts should accord with his own personality first of all. It should also be consonant with the maturity, needs, experiences, and size of the group he is guiding, and be in accord with the type of learning and outcomes he wishes to see. To do this successfully, the teacher needs training and experience in group activities and in democratic processes and procedures, as well as in the principles of group dynamics.

Synthesizing a number of research studies, Petrullo and Bass[21] assert that leadership exists in an interactional situation. The group is a system

[20] W. I. Ackerman, "Teacher Competence and Pupil Change," *Harvard Educational Review,* Vol. 29 (1954), pp. 273-289.

[21] L. Petrullo and B. M. Bass (editors), *Leadership and Inter-Personal Behavior* (New York: Holt, Rinehart and Winston, 1961).

by which its members *reward* each other: effective leadership is shown when changes in behavior of group members occur leading to more rewards for all. Effective leadership provides two types of activities: *planning* and *motivating*. The effective leader will have a good understanding of the motivating forces operating within the group. Sometimes the psychological distance between the leader and the members making up the group is too great for effective leadership. Much research and study is being conducted relative to the conditions and factors that contribute to effective leadership in the classroom and other educational situations.

What are the different kinds of leadership one can exert? Lippitt and White describe three plans for three types of leadership roles or three types of leadership situations to which each of several groups of boys in club activities were subjected experimentally:

Plan for authoritarian leadership role. Practically all policies as regards club activities and procedures should be determined by the leader. The techniques and activity steps should be communicated by the authority, one unit at a time, so that future steps are in the dark to a large degree. The adult should take considerable responsibility for assigning the activity tasks and companions of each group member. The dominator should keep his standards of praise and criticism to himself in evaluating individual and group activities. He should also remain fairly aloof from active group participation except in demonstrating.

Plan for the democratic leadership role. Wherever possible, policies should be a matter of group decision and discussion with active encouragement and assistance by the adult leader. The leader should attempt to see that activity perspective emerges during the discussion period with the general steps to the group goal becoming clarified. Wherever technical advice is needed, the leader should try to suggest two or more alternative procedures from which choice can be made by the group members. Everyone should be free to work with whomever he chooses, and the divisions of responsibility should be left up to the group. The leader should attempt to communicate in an objective, fact-minded way the bases for his praise and criticism of individual and group activities. He should try to be a regular group member in spirit but not do much of the work (so that comparisons of group production can be made between the groups.)

Plan for laissez-faire leadership role. In this situation, the adult should play a rather passive role in social participation and leave complete freedom for group or individual decisions in relation to activity and group procedure. The leader should make clear the various materials that are available and be sure it is understood that he will supply information and help when asked. He should do a minimum of taking the initiative in making suggestions. He should make no attempt to evaluate negatively or positively the behavior or productions of the individuals or the group as a group, although he should be friendly rather than "standoffish" at all times.[22]

[22] R. Lippitt and R. K. White, "An Experimental Study of Leadership and Group Life," in E. E. Maccoby, T. M. Newcomb and E. E. Hartley, eds. *Readings in Social Psychology* (New York: Holt, Rinehart & Winston), p. 498.

Rarely has classroom leadership been so clearly described as in this study. The reactions to the three types of leadership in the investigation just cited depended upon the previous experiences with leadership which the individuals had had with their parents or other adults. In general, however, the research showed that democratic leadership elicited better work productivity and resulted in more individual satisfaction. In a more recent reappraisal of this research, White and Lippitt [23] caution that genuine democracy emphasizes constructive leadership, involves some authority and discipline, rests on realistic usage of majority opinion, and continually requires a realistic adaptation of methods to the teaching circumstances. They point out that some faults attributed to "democratic classrooms" really are the result of laissez-faire approaches.

Crow, among many others, placed an obligation on those training teachers to give student-teachers actual experience in democratic group processes to enable them to develop the ability to guide this type of educational process:

> Free discussion has value, and teachers should be trained to function through its process. But the success of the procedure must inevitably rest upon evaluation. Just to permit learners to talk for the sake of free discussion may, in the long run, do as much harm as good. Individual learners should be encouraged to express their opinions freely, candidly, and openly with the assurance that the teacher has the leadership qualities and insight that will enable him to evaluate competently what is being said. When the teacher demonstrates that he is able to accept those ideas that are erroneous or do not apply, he gives positive, dynamic stimulation toward sound thinking.[24]

The teacher as a counselor. Although the term *counselor* is not the exact word for the concept to be developed here, it seems to be the closest term available to express the relationship of warmth, insight into personality need, acceptance, a friendliness that can still remain empathic yet personally uninvolved, and a general psychological orientation in personal and professional teacher-pupil relationships. Strictly defined, counseling refers to professional use of special techniques designed to aid a person in the solution of personal problems. When the problems of pupils are serious, chronic, or beyond his ability to help, the professional teacher, recognizing the limits of his training and experience, will refer the cases to the appropriate resource persons.

There is, however, an aspect of the successful, effective teacher which implies more than what he *is* through his own personality integration, his professional training, and his leadership ability. This aspect presup-

[23] Ralph K. White and Ronald Lippitt, *Autocracy and Democracy: An Experimental Inquiry* (New York: Harper & Row, 1960).

[24] Lester D. Crow, "The Teacher and the Educative Process," *School and Society,* Vol. 77 (1953), pp. 276-278.

poses the interaction of each of these factors in a helping relationship with the pupil. Klausmeier has termed this "the teacher as a helpful person" and observes that

. . . . it is surprising to find the large number of teachers in the intermediate grades, high school and college who make no attempt to be helpful to the student in overcoming learning difficulties directly connected with the subject matter. . . . Much teacher leadership yet is confined to knowing the subject matter moderately well and then telling students what to learn and when to have it learned.[25]

In studies of teacher behavior and the productive behavior of pupils, Cogan[26] appraised the competence of teachers by taking into account what he termed "inclusive, preclusive, and conjunctive" measures of behavior. The "inclusive" and "preclusive" behavior related to the ability of the teachers to take account of the pupil's feelings and goals, whereas the "conjunctive" behavior related to classroom procedures. Cogan found that inclusiveness, or acceptance, is an observable and measurable trait in teachers and that it is significantly related to the amount of required work and self-initiated work pupils produce. The effectiveness of the teacher's "inclusiveness," however, is dependent upon the pupils' perception of his behavior as such.

This psychological orientation of the educator in his relationship with the learner implies a certain amount of rapport or an ability on the part of the teacher to build a warm and accepting relationship inspiring confidence and cooperation while minimizing fear and resistance. The nature of the relationship will vary with the individuality and needs of the particular person as well as with his age and level of maturity. Rapport of this nature is not only an important element present in personal interviews or contacts but is a vital aura in the actual learning situation.

The relationship between a teacher and his pupils will vary because of differences in teacher personality and teaching situations. Each teacher should teach in ways harmonious to his own personality. A quiet teacher who creates a calm, relaxed atmosphere, a vivacious teacher who stimulates children, a strong teacher whose self-reliance and assurance conveys a feeling of security may each get good results in spite of their different approaches.

Children know when they are accepted and they also have a keen sense of the hypocritical. The teacher who doesn't accept a child usually cannot help him permanently (and perhaps not even temporarily). A

[25] Herbert J. Klausmeier, *Learning and Human Abilities: Educational Psychology* (New York: Harper & Row, 1961), pp. 144-145.
[26] Cogan, Morris L., "The Behavior of Teachers and the Productive Behavior of Their Pupils: I. Perception Analysis; II. Trait Analysis." *Journal of Experimental Education*, Vol. 27 (1958), pp. 89-124.

disabled learner's problems go beyond being accepted, however. He feels hurt, discouraged, and angry. The teacher who understands these feelings, has insight into his own personality, and can accept the child, may be able to help him put these emotions in the service of learning.

Many psychologists have pointed out that the perceptive teacher, as an educator who is psychologically oriented, will not feel threatened by the negative emotional reactions of a student, will not need supporting statements from the learner to bolster his professional security or self-concept of worth, will not be frightened, embarrassed, or threatened by the child's expression of emotion, positive or negative, toward him. When the pupil at the beginning of a relationship is defensive and resistant, it may be difficult (or even impossible) for the teacher to remain objective. The teacher who can reflect hostile and critical attitudes toward himself in a sincere but professional manner will be giving effective assistance to the learner by that very reaction. Understanding and accepting hostile impulses in himself will aid the teacher in accepting pupils who are hostile and aggressive. Teachers have a greater contribution to make to the learning process than merely assigning study tasks, lecturing, hearing recitations, and keeping order.

The learning atmosphere or climate in the classroom

It was pointed out in Chapter 17 that one basic personal need is for adequate self-realization and transcendance of self to others in a social environment. Every classroom has an intangible atmosphere or climate which affects learning in a positive or negative way along a continuum of influence. This classroom atmosphere is fostered by the teacher—by what he is in the totality of his own personality, by his relationship to the particular class being taught, by the aids, methods, and teaching approaches he uses, and by his reaction to the physical features of the room. Since the learning climate is largely created by the teacher, it ought to be consciously designed (insofar as this is possible) to facilitate personal development toward maturity and integration.

A major force in this learning climate consists of that emotional rapport or understanding and insightful acceptance that a teacher shares with each learner because of his native human dignity. This force involves the teacher in a psychological orientation related to his role as a counselor. It is also akin to the type of leadership the teacher employs generally. Bernhardt has described it in terms of domination or participation:

That intangible but very real characteristic of the classroom sometimes called "atmosphere" becomes a very important consideration. This in turn places a very heavy responsibility on the teacher for it means, in effect, that the easy technique of threat and bribery are not only inadequate but detrimental. In a classroom dedicated to the above goal the teacher loses his role as a dominating, directing, and restricting authority and becomes a true leader and guide who creates a permissive atmosphere conducive to active participation by all children in meaningful experiences.

Wise and intelligent behavior requires choice and self-direction. This is possible only when the child is capable of anticipating the possible consequences of his activity. This is the product of experience in which the child has sufficient freedom to explore for himself. But this does not mean that the child has to discover everything for himself. Obviously, he need not discover personally that poison kills, or water drowns. There are some things he can take on faith. When the atmosphere is such, however, that he does not feel threatened or restricted he has confidence in the teacher such that he accepts willingly and with confidence the necessary direction and guidance the teacher provides. And he can accept equally the necessary and sensible rules which the group formulates. But there is a very important difference in atmosphere between the group that develops its own rules and the one in which the rules are determined by one autocrat who imposes them on the group.

The teacher-leader has much to do with the development of a classroom atmosphere conducive to the self-development of the students. Perhaps the most important single factor is his attitude toward his role as a teacher and his understanding of himself as a part of the educative process. Naturally, he must have knowledge and skills, but unless he is free from a desire to master and dominate his students he will not be able to create the atmosphere necessary for the healthy growth of his students. This means that the basic qualification of a good teacher is the possession of a happy, healthy, mature personality.[27]

From the viewpoint of the learner, the atmosphere involves interaction with all he is as an individual and with all he hopes to be. Shostrom and Brammer [28] have shown that this interaction comprises the forces of the "I am" (his nature), the "I can" (his capacities), the "I should not" or "I should" (his values), and the "I want to be" (his aspirations).

The realization of these forces cannot be obtained in a lecture or in direct response to a verbalized wish. They must be experienced. An individual learns to respect and value himself when he finds that, although he has weaknesses and handicaps as well as strengths, he is still worthy of the attention and friendship of an adult whom he can learn to value. If the teacher can see the positive and the adequate in the learner; is able to find the good in him and help him to discover and experience it, a primary condition for readiness conducive to lasting learning has been achieved.

The learning climate of the classroom, however, involves more than just the teacher—important though he is. A study made by Astin and Holland [29] indicates that the character of a social environment is

[27] Karl S. Bernhardt, "Motivation in the School Age Child," *Education,* Vol. 72 (1951), p. 266.

[28] Everett L. Shostrom and Lawrence M. Brammer, *The Dynamics of the Counseling Process* (New York: McGraw-Hill Book Company, 1952).

[29] Alexander W. Astin and John L. Holland, "The Environmental Assessment Technique: A Way to Measure College Environments," *Journal of Educational Psychology,* Vol. 52 (1961), p. 308.

dependent upon the typical characteristics of its members. "If, then, we know the character of the people in a group, we should know the climate that group creates."

An atmosphere conducive to true learning will be an emotionally secure environment. Some of the factors contributing to this type of climate may be listed as follows:

1. A relationship of understanding, cooperation, and participation between the teacher and individual students, between teacher and the class as a group, and among the individual pupils.
2. Limits, in the form of rules, regulations, standards, purposes, and sanctions, defined, understood, and mutually accepted in the light of fairness and effectiveness of class activity.
3. Genuine acceptance of pupils as individuals with personal worth, involving rapport, recognition of individual differences, weaknesses and strengths, impartiality and respect in instances of correcting lapses.
4. Provision for constructive emotional release of negative personality forces and for expression of positive and pleasant emotions.
5. Provision for instances of success, of challenge, and also of possible failure (but with safeguards against frustration, useless conflict, or damaging anxiety).
6. Opportunities for development of skills and approaches to give confidence in new situations and in new learning.

Relations in the classroom

Teacher-pupil relationships. The relationships which develop between pupil and teacher are important indications of the adjustment of both the child and the adult. However, let us concentrate on the effects which such instructions have upon the child. One important part of the socialization process is learning to modify one's behavior so that it meets the expectations of others. Throughout his life the child will learn to play various roles in accordance with the standards and patterns of his culture. His teacher is one representative of that culture and the child learns that when he behaves as she desires he is rewarded. When he fails to behave as expected, his behavior is not rewarded. Unhappily, his teacher is not merely typical of all adults as she has individual standards, attitudes, and values which affect her expectations and behavioral patterns. By the same token, it should be recognized that the interactions of the child with his teachers reflect his previous learning. If he has been overprotected and sheltered at home he will strive to obtain a similar relationship in the school. If he has learned to function within the sphere of a rigid or autocratic atmosphere at home, he will encounter difficulties in a freer, more permissive classroom. While most children are able to make the adjustment from the home environment to the school situation without too much difficulty, a few may find it so difficult as to need special help.

In previous chapters, it was suggested that many children encounter difficulties in school because of their social and cultural backgrounds. Many children develop behavioral patterns which conflict with standards imposed by the typical classroom teacher. Since the majority of public school teachers come from middle-class backgrounds, their attitudes and standards tend to reflect such cultural conditioning. Children of the lower-social class often encounter difficulty in adjusting their behavior to the standards imposed by the teacher. The problems encountered by a number of such children become intensified by the apparent conflict between family and school.

Environmental control. Although the classroom teacher plays an important role in determining the social climate within the classroom, she is limited, of course, by the general atmosphere found within the whole school situation. Within the various classrooms of any school many differences can and do exist. Teacher A imposes rigid standards of classroom conduct. Her pupils must raise their hands to speak. They may not leave their seats without permission and are strongly discouraged from conversing with each other. There is a businesslike atmosphere which is almost grim in her room. The interactions of pupils are limited in kind and number. The behavioral patterns of children are restricted but they are oriented to the tasks at hand. On the other hand, the classroom of teacher B across the hall is quite different. Teacher B does not impose such rigid standards. Children are freer to move around. They often talk in low tones to each other, compare their work, and seek help from each other. The number and variety of interactions between pupils is much greater in her classroom than in Teacher A's room. The pupils in each room have a different social atmosphere.

By the standards they impose, the opportunities they furnish for pupils to relate with each other, and the situations they provide for children to assume various roles, teachers profoundly influence the emotional and social development of their students. The classroom environment should be sufficiently free so that each child has an opportunity to try out a number of roles. At times he should be a leader, a follower, a competitor, and a collaborator. He should learn to respect the rights of others and develop a recognition of the importance of individual and group effort. He learns these things, not as a result of mere verbal instruction, but by living and working in an atmosphere where they prevail.

Problems of discipline. Przychodzin [30] has pointed out that classroom discipline is, in general, the most difficult problem for the inexperienced teacher as well as for the experienced teacher. One of the fundamental questions considered by administrators in evaluating qualities of applicants for teaching positions is "Can this individual handle the disciplinary needs of the classroom?" The question is of prime importance because it lies at the heart of the teacher's ability to create a constructive learning atmosphere in the classroom. As Przychodzin observes, "weakness in discipline accounts for 25 per cent of all teacher failure."

One reason for the difficulty in handling disciplinary problems in the present day school is the changed concept of discipline. In the past, disciplinary measures were well defined and applied in the form of whippings, ridicule before the class, and special janitorial duties. The basis, of course, for such discipline was fear. As we have seen, an atmosphere charged with fear and anxiety is detrimental to real learning. Consequently, the fear or "whipping" form of discipline has been largely abandoned. More constructive methods are now employed, methods which place emphasis upon guidance rather than punishment.

Ausubel has outlined the rationale for the modern discipline as follows:

> The proponents of democratic classroom discipline believe in imposing the minimal degree of external control necessary for socialization, personality maturation, conscience development, and the emotional security of the child. Discipline and obedience are not regarded as ends in themselves but only as means to these latter ends. They are not striven for deliberately, but are expected to follow naturally in the wake of friendly and realistic teacher-pupil relationships. Explicit limits are set . . . only as the need arises, i.e., when they are not implicitly understood or accepted by pupils.
>
> Democratic discipline is as rational, nonarbitrary, and bilateral as possible. It provides explanations, permits discussion, and invites the participation of children in the setting of standards whenever they are qualified to do so. Above all it implies respect for the dignity of the individual and avoids exaggerated emphasis on status differences and barriers between free communication. Hence it repudiates harsh, abusive, and vindictive forms of punishments, and the use of sarcasm, ridicule and intimidation.
>
> . . . . democratic discipline does not imply freedom from all external constraints, standards, and direction, or freedom from discipline as an end in itself. [31]

Przychodzin [32] lists some attributes which apply to good classroom discipline:

[30] Joe Przychodzin, "Discipline," *Clearing House,* Vol. 32 (1958), pp. 411-414.
[31] David P. Ausubel, "A New Look at Classroom Discipline," *Phi Delta Kappan,* Vol. 43 (1961), p. 28.
[32] *Op. cit.,* pp. 412-413.

1. *Keep the students well informed concerning what is expected of them.* The initial class period is the time to orient the students concerning your (the teacher's) policies. At this time they should be informed about classroom courtesy, assignments, classroom responsibility, study habits, and work with others. "The teacher's directions should leave no uncertainty in the minds of the pupils."

2. *Be firm and consistent in dealing with all pupils.* Students will soon recognize the teacher who is half-consistent, punishing at one time for an incident and failing to punish for a more serious action at another time. This will confuse the student as to the consequences he must pay for what he does, and may likely be the tip-off for actions to try the teacher concerning various forms of behavior.

3. *Be courteous and fair in dealing with pupils.* Students can quickly sense evidence of kindness and courtesy as opposed to unfairness and discourtesy. In general, students respect the teacher who shows absolute fairness when dealing with all people, and lose respect when the teacher tends to "play favorites." In addition, the courteous teacher will be kind, generous, and helpful to his students; he will not need to display authority unnecessarily because his students will recognize his authority.

4. *Avoid using threats.* Obedience in the classroom is essential but it is not necessarily the result of threats and commands. Often, gentle persuasion in the form of suggestions or discussion can be more effective than the most dire threat. The teacher who makes threats is very likely to find students testing his intentions. The result will be the creation of new and often more difficult disciplinary problems.

5. *Praise pupils when they deserve it.* Students resent ridicule and censure (just as teachers do!). When a teacher uses such methods he is likely to lose any personal rapport he has with his students. In general, students appreciate praise and will respond much more quickly when their work is praised and their improvement encouraged by constructive suggestions. If it is necessary to censure students, private discussions are usually more effective.

6. *Be active, not passive, when trouble is developing.* One of the most important assets a teacher has is his ability to sense and avoid trouble *before* it can develop. It is recognized that if no disciplinary problems are allowed to rise, then no disciplinary action will be needed. This, however, is difficult to achieve. The teacher cannot always detect incipient trouble before it becomes overt, nor can he always "overlook trouble." It becomes necessary to judge which little disturbances may be taken as acceptable and which must be dealt with as disciplinary problems. The students will respect the teacher who uses sound judgment in the exercise of his authority respecting disciplinary actions.

7. *Put yourself in the pupil's place.* The students are the individuals with whom you work. How would you feel if you were in their shoes?

What would you expect of the teacher under similar circumstances? How would you accept and react to similar authority? Success in handling students is most probable for the teacher who can accurately envision and analyze the students' position.

Teacher-pupil planning. To guide his planning, whether it is related to subject matter or to personal problems, the teacher must have very clear and definite aims and a sense of direction with which to inspire the student through cooperative planning. This sharing of aims with the students by cooperative goal-setting is a source of intrinsic motivation in the learning that is to follow. The teacher can guide learning through purposeful, reasonable, and flexible assignments geared to the students' capacities, in which they can see the means to their goals. Assignments should also be related to the maturational and developmental level of the pupils. The teacher can guide pupil-participation in self-learning activities by encouraging pupils to think, to use their initiative, and to use their knowledge of concepts and meanings. The teacher can encourage them to take no meaning or experience for granted and can supply direct or vicarious experiences to permit the *growth* of meaning and understanding. This development, as with all growth, takes time. By involving the growth of the whole personality with the learning of a subject and growth in skill, the teacher will insure student participation and the self-activity basic to education and self-realization. That kind of teaching will not end with tests or grades, or with the finality of a record report; but will become a part of the life of the student and the basis of future learning.

Teacher-pupil evaluation. Pupils learn better when they have definite goals toward which they are working cooperatively with their teacher and peers. Pupils learn still better and become even more intrinsically motivated when they have knowledge of the results. Often, children do not have a true and realistic knowledge of themselves. They see themselves through the eyes of other people, adults and peers, especially those psychologically close to them. The pupil will gain a healthier concept of himself, a sounder outlook on life, and will have a dynamic motive for making the most of his potentialities when he can see his own strengths and weaknesses relative to those goals toward which he is progressing.

Knowledge of one's success as a vital motivating factor was emphasized in Chapter 7. Besides knowing the goals of classroom activities or personal activity, the pupil needs help, opportunity, and guidance in passing judgment on his achievement toward those goals. Atmosphere conducive to learning, teacher efficiency, effective leadership, and mature insight are factors in the effectiveness of a teacher-pupil evaluation program. Widened into the concept of an educator-learner program of learning, this cooperation in evaluating progress will include the parents in a shared communication and comprehension of goals, participation in setting these goals, responsibility for achieving them (with a knowledge of applicable methods and means), as well as understanding of progress toward the goals. All of this involves judgment or comparison with some soundly based norms used constructively. Kingsley and Garry [33] list three common norms:

1. comparison with the performance of others, which may be the present class or individuals who are well known;
2. comparison with the potential performance of the individual himself in the light of his strengths and weaknesses;
3. comparison with some absolute, external standard, as national norms.

Self-evaluation using reliable and valid norms under teacher guidance will give the learner more realistic knowledge of the results of his efforts. Such evaluation will be the basis for intrinsic motivation and may also pave the way for an effective counseling relationship with both learner and parent. The pupil will not only learn to understand himself but will appraise his assets and deficiencies more realistically when such appraisals of his growth and progress are made in a nonpunitive, accepting, objective atmosphere. This is one way to achieve a productive educator-learner relationship.

Cooperative evaluation will eliminate to some extent, at least, the fear of judgment and threat which may come from arbitrary teacher grading. It contributes to a better understanding of the self, and to a more realistic self-concept.

Building wholesome relationships through meeting basic human needs

The teacher as an adequate, mature, professional, insightful person can establish a wholesome relationship with the pupil which facilitates development toward maturity. This relationship, which has been described as a *learning climate,* can be consciously cultivated to meet basic personality needs through adaptations of the learning process directed by the teacher. In a study of 6000 teachers in 1700 classrooms, Ryans [34] found that teachers who best achieved such a learning climate were warm, understanding, friendly, and stimulating as they introduced pupils to new areas of learning, new ideas, or new concepts. They were also more responsible, systematic, and businesslike in their relationship with

[33] H. L. Kingsley and R. Garry, *The Nature and Conditions of Learning,* 2d ed. (Englewood Cliffs, N.J.: Prentice-Hall, Inc., 1957), Ch. 8.
[34] David G. Ryans, *Characteristics of Teachers: Their Description, Comparison, and Appraisal.* Washington, D.C.: American Council on Education (1960).

their pupils. Effective teachers were found to stimulate creativity and imagination in their pupils.

The personality needs of pupils were presented earlier in Chapter 3. Some of these needs will now be viewed in the light of their significance in the learning process.

The need to be. The need for an adequate self-concept is the core and all-pervasive need of humans, embracing all an individual is and hopes to be. It has been pointed out previously that a person learns to respect himself and accept himself in the measure that he is respected and accepted by those he loves. The teacher not only helps a student satisfy this basic need by accepting him in a relationship, but also by helping him to understand how the group perceives that relationship and accepts the individual. Flanders and Havumaki found in a study of data collected from 330 tenth graders that ". . . after they had interacted with a teacher who praised the participation of some of them individually and the participation of others as a group . . ."[35] the sociometric choice value of students was increased, indicating greater peer acceptance, by supportive and constructive praise.

In an atmosphere of acceptance a learner can feel that he is understood without being judged. He feels that he can safely express himself, be creative and original without risking rejection and disapproval. He learns that he can be himself and still be loved and accepted by a teacher who respects his right to have feelings while not necessarily agreeing with his manner of expressing them.

In such an atmosphere, the teacher can build the student's confidence by maintaining a positive, optimistic attitude toward him which will enable the student to reflect confidence and to profit from it. Helping students, especially adolescents, to discover that basically their hopes, fears, difficulties, weaknesses, and strengths are not much different from other peoples' can instill tremendous confidence in them and can give them a boost toward greater self-adequacy.

The need to become. This need is an extension of the one previously discussed. When satisfied, the need for achievement nourishes the self-esteem basic to the feeling of adequacy and to a healthy self-concept. Its realization, moreover, is synonymous with self-realization and personal integration. Success experiences are needed to offset the effect of failure and frustration. Success can be regulated by an insightful educator who knows the capability of the learner, the general rate of his intellectual growth, and the approaches that will insure it. A feeling of success in

[35] Ned A. Flanders, and Sulo Havumaki, "The Effect of Teacher-Pupil Contacts Involving Praise on the Sociometric Choices of Students," *Journal of Educational Psychology,* Vol. 51 (1960), pp. 65-68.

one subject can often generalize to motivate the student to perform other more difficult tasks.

A shift in the level of performance in one area may stimulate a shift in the general level of aspiration. The ease with which a student is permitted to achieve and the difficulty of the tasks attempted need to be carefully planned and arranged according to the abilities and the personality needs of the student. This relationship between motivation and task difficulty is called the Yerkes-Dodson law.

Justified, sincere praise for effort and accomplishment is an important technique in fostering further success. Evidence of success—or of growth—(such as graphs or records to make it tangible and cumulative) is likewise helpful. Undue pressures to achieve, however, should be avoided.

Thompson and Hunnicut [36] found that different children react differently to praise or blame. The results of their study suggest that praise as well as blame may be used unwisely by the elementary-school teacher if he does not fully appreciate and understand the different personalities in the classroom. The investigators found that, when introverts and extroverts are grouped together, praise or blame are equally effective in motivating the work achievement of fifth-grade pupils. The results presented in Table 19-2 indicate that either praise or blame was more effective in increasing the work output of the students than was no ex-

TABLE 19-2. Comparison of the Mean Gains in Cancellation Scores of the Praised, Blamed and Control Groups (*Thompson and Hunnicut*)

EXPERIMENTAL GROUPS	MEAN GAINS				
	TEST 2	TEST 3	TEST 4	TEST 5	TEST 6
Total Blamed Group	18.1	16.3	17.9	20.3	21.1
Total Praised Group	18.3	16.2	16.6	19.6	19.9
Control Group	11.6	11.4	11.2	12.5	14.9

ternal incentive. The study showed that, if repeated often enough, praise increases the work output of introverts until it is significantly higher than that of introverts who are blamed or extroverts who are praised. If repeated often enough, blame increases work output of extroverts more

[36] George G. Thompson and Clarence W. Hunnicut, "The Effects of Repeated Praise or Blame on the Work Achievement of 'Introverts' and 'Extroverts'," *Journal of Educational Psychology*, Vol. 35 (1944), pp. 257-266.

than work by extroverts who are praised or introverts who are blamed.

In evaluating this study, one should bear in mind that "praise," "blame," difficulty," and "success" are meaningful only in the frame of reference of the student. "Difficult" means, then, "something which a particular student finds difficult" *not* something which is hard for an "average" student or which the teacher judges difficult.

Even as blame may be used effectively and wisely at times, so may failing marks be used, on occasion, to foster personality development. Failing, at times, may be a revelation for the student that the goal he pursues is false, or that his means to a goal are inadequate. Failing can also represent a challenge which goads the person on to higher achievement.

Basic to the effectiveness of failure, however, is the interpretation which the individual, and adults psychologically close to him, place upon it. The insight and wisdom of the educator is vitally important here. The perceptive teacher will foster self-realization through achievement and success. She will insure growth in self-realization while developing, at the same time, a realistic approach to difficulties, to challenges, and to failure as stepping stones to mature, integrated, courageous personalities. It has been observed that some parents try desperately to shield their children from the hardships and challenges which helped the parents themselves to become the mature persons they are.

Need to feel adequately. The nature of emotional problems and the need to release negative feelings to objectify, understand, and control or re-educate them has been treated in Chapter 17. In a favorable, warm, learning climate, negative emotions can give way to positive ones. Some students need the opportunity to reorient their perceptions of adults in authority or to experience success in learning situations which have previously frustrated them.

In a constructive learning climate, students will understand that life has its inevitable ups and downs, that there are times, for example, when one feels discouraged, hostile, fearful, jealous, inadequate, resistant and ambivalent. The child will learn from the insightful teacher how to cope with these emotions and how to continue an overall progress toward emotional maturity. The teacher must perceive and understand the student's difficulty, must maintain a steady faith in the child, must be a sympathetic listener, must adapt the pace of activities to the child's readiness, and must help the child to set his own limits.

"Setting limits" basically means disciplining, but *without* the harsh authoritarian connotation which was discussed previously in this chapter. Learning to set one's own limits is essential to emotional adequacy and to the development of personal responsibility and self-direction. Limits should be minimal in number, basic in importance. They should be

The needs of pupils are best met in an educational situation that promotes good pupil-pupil relationships and stimulates pupils in different activities at school.

established as the need arises—cooperatively whenever feasible. Limits should be viewed as guides to behavior and the pupils should be helped to replace teacher limits with cooperatively planned behavioral guides.

In a secure relationship, the educator can show disapproval without rejection, can sympathetically recognize and reflect negative feelings, can wisely permit conversation or discussion, can lengthen, shorten, or change activities and can introduce appropriate new stimuli in the classroom. Such a relationship reduces anxieties so that the student can take greater advantages of learning situations and utilize his abilities more productively.

The need to know. The need for self-direction together with the need to think critically and creatively, to judge soundly, to form essential concepts and meanings—especially in relation to human nature and human destiny—make the realization of self essentially human. The adequate satisfaction of these needs is the source of human happiness. The adult who can convey understanding and appreciation of student needs in these areas and who provides opportunities for students to exercise the power to know and to choose in an accepting and supporting atmosphere will have a relationship with boys and girls which facilitates true learning. Youth tends to follow leaders who invite it to *discover* meanings and to *judge* values under its own power, with the aid of teacher guidance as needed.

Through science, through the social sciences, and especially through literature where are found the verities which have engrossed man through the centuries, new avenues and new opportunities can continuously be opened to boys and girls. Religious leaders also have a significant contribution to make, not only in developing personalities in the classroom but also in developing educators in the home and in the school at all levels of education.

The need to will wisely. If acceptance is basic to feelings of adequacy and the core value of acceptance is human dignity, then the basis of that human dignity is precisely the person's power of independent, responsible choice. It has been suggested that in reading, for instance, (as it would be in all areas of human life) the integrity of the learner's right to learn or not to learn cannot be violated. In view of the basic need and right to learn discussed in this chapter, however, this concept may well be limited to a "learner's right to learn this particular thing or that thing." If the learner does not recognize his need to learn a particular subject, for instance, and is not convinced that it will help him, there is every reason to believe that he will resist learning it. In a warm, accepting learning climate, the perceptive teacher will evaluate realistically, the student's need to learn that specific subject at that particular time, give attention to the individual's felt cultural needs, his orientation and motivations, and secure the learner's voluntary participation—perhaps in the goal-setting, in the planning, and in the evaluating.

Permitting a person to become fully involved in solving his own problem is sometimes the clue to its real solution. The purpose of a warm, supporting atmosphere, besides relieving emotional pressure, is to place responsibility on the student and to give him experience in making wise choices, according to his level of maturational development. The intrinsic dynamism in each person is this need for self-assertion, for freedom and independence, and the bipolar concomitant of adequate, mature dependence or compliance. With behavior limits set cooperatively or personally, the learner is free to choose and the educator can be more permissive.

Duncan, considering the problem, "how a teacher can insure that a learner accepts responsibility for learning," made the following suggestions:

. . . We must help the student arrive at a *point of view* toward that which he is going to learn. We give him an opportunity to take a real attitude toward it (e.g. the Revolution—a period in history).
. . . The self-propelled learner has more than an attitude toward the content. He is in addition oriented toward it. This orientation is nothing more than getting that which he knows "shaken" into some kind of relation to that which he is about to learn . . . He needs a chance to talk about what he knows already in the light of that new point of view . . .
Point of view and orientation go hand in hand. As we strengthen one, we strengthen the other. But sometimes they are not sufficient. The student needs an opportunity to explore that which he is to learn. If it is important, as we assume it is, it is worth exploring. The *exploration* clarifies the topic under consideration.
If we put *point of view, orientation,* and *exploration* together in an effective manner, the student should know what it is that he is trying to learn . . . This takes more time than we often think it will. It certainly takes more time than we often give it. To help insure that the learner knows what he is trying to learn, it is worth all the time it takes.
Not only does the motivated learner know what he is trying to learn, but he has somehow miraculously accepted the responsibility to learn. What is the secret?
Part of the answer is in his seeing what it is that he has to learn. He can nevertheless reject the challenge, and if he does, he will not take the responsibility for learning.
It is a truism that no one can learn for the learner. He simply must do it himself. He must commit himself. He will not commit himself wholeheartedly except on his own terms. He needs, therefore, to clarify and define the problem as he sees it.
The *clarification* process extends the exploration, but it is student directed. We may ask provocative questions, encourage the use of particular sources, but basically we should be demanding of the student that he find his own problem and begin to develop his own ideas about how to deal with it.
By encouraging the student to clarify the problem on his own, we encourage him to accept it. Good questions, helpful leads, suggestive ideas give guidance to the quest without directing. As clarification continues, students will, one-by-one, catch hold of a problem that they believe is theirs—and it will be theirs. At this stage each of them will have defined his problem.
Defining the problem sometimes calls for *verbalization* and sometimes it does not.
When he has defined his problem, the student should have the essential characteristics of a motivated learner—that is, he knows there is something to be learned and he has "gotten" with it.[37]

[37] James K. Duncan, "The Motivated Learner," *The Clearing House,* Vol. 35 (1961), pp. 273-275.

SUMMARY

The human personality develops under the influence of dynamic vital drives toward self-realization. These are actuated by the attempts to satisfy basic and acquired human needs. Knowing and making choices imply goals, purposes, and activity which lead to the total expression of personality in habits of choice, in responsibility, and in values indicative of character.

Since humans develop primarily through relationships with others, development can be guided in a positive direction when the teacher understands the nature and working of interpersonal relationships.

The implications for personality growth and learning posed by the mature integrated teacher were discussed. It was shown how the teacher could structure a learning climate conducive to personality growth and to mental and intellectual growth by consciously planning the educator-learner relationship, by keeping the orientation pupil-centered to meet basic human personality needs for adequacy, for achievement and success, for emotional control, for a fine independent-dependent self-expression in an integration of personality.

In structuring a facilitating learning climate, aspects of the teacher which came into play were discussed and described. The changing concept of discipline and some recommendations for achieving democratic discipline consonant with a sound learning climate were outlined.

Approaches to assessment of personality needs of students were discussed. Several types of group dynamic situations were outlined with their implications for personality development. It was pointed out that the teacher needs to have very clear definite aims together with a sense of direction and an adequate understanding of the students if he is to be successful in cooperative planning and evaluation. Cooperative planning and evaluation permits students to develop more realistic goals and substitutes intrinsic motivation for extrinsic incentives.

Since affectivity and oblativity are the height of human fulfillment, the whole concept of the educator-learner relationship in which each finds his personal fulfillment and completion might be, in the words attributed to Kahlil Gibran, "Work is Love made Visible."

Problems and Exercises

1. Give five personal-experiential variables which will affect the quality of a pupil's personal relationships.
2. Name several attributes of the psychologically adequate teacher.
3. Show how children's achievements depend upon the teacher's personality and the classroom atmosphere.

4. List several action patterns which are conducive to mental health according to Bernard. Discuss ways in which a classroom teacher could aid pupils in developing these.
5. Discuss the implications for the teacher which arise from the Lippitt and White study of leadership. What aspects of genuine democracy are sometimes overlooked?
6. Name several factors which contribute to the establishing of a classroom atmosphere conducive to true learning. Give some specific ways in which you would put these into effect if you were a teacher (1) of high school students, (2) of junior high school students, (3) of elementary pupils.
7. Give examples of several commonly used methods of assessing pupil needs. What caution is given regarding their use?
8. What materials should be included on a cumulative record to help the teacher in the continuous guidance of the individual child?
9. What are some actions a teacher can take to provide conditions conducive to a productive counseling session with a pupil?
10. What is the difference between "setting limits" and arbitrarily restricting action?
11. Discuss the following questions from the ethical standpoint and in light of this course:
    a. Are you released from keeping a student problem in confidence (when you have promised to do so) if you learn that someone else has the same information?
    b. Should you discuss with another teacher what a student has told you in confidence if you believe you can help the student by doing so?
    c. Should all teachers have access to records containing information about a pupil's personal problems and discipline and behavior infractions?

Selected Readings

CRONBACH, Lee J., *Educational Psychology,* 2nd ed. (New York: Harcourt, Brace and World, 1963), Ch. 18.

KLAUSMEIER, Herbert J., *Learning and Human Abilities: Educational Psychology* (New York: Harper and Row, 1961), Ch. 4.

LINDGREN, Henry C., *Educational Psychology in the Classroom,* 2nd ed. (New York: John Wiley & Sons, 1962), Ch. 18.

PRESSEY, Sidney L., ROBINSON, Francis P., and HORROCKS, John E., *Psychology in Education* (New York: Harper and Row, 1959), Ch. 19.

STEPHENS, J. M., *Educational Psychology,* rev. ed. (New York: Holt, Rinehart and Winston, 1956), Chs. 21 and 22.

THOMPSON, George G., GARDNER, Eric F., and DI VESTA, Francis J., *Educational Psychology* (New York: Appleton-Century-Crofts, 1959), Chs. 22 and 23.

TROW, William C., *Psychology in Teaching and Learning* (Boston: Houghton Mifflin Co., 1960), Chs. 14 and 15.

WHITE, Ralph K., and LIPPITT, R., *Autocracy and Democracy: An Experimental Inquiry* (New York: Harper and Row, 1960).

APPENDICES

Appendix A

A Selected Annotated Bibliography of Recent Textbooks in Educational Psychology

CRONBACH, Lee J., *Educational Psychology*, 2nd ed. (New York: Harcourt, Brace & World, 1963). In this revision the author attempts to give the student an understanding of the learner as a person, emphasizing that intellectual learning is a developmental process.

DREIKAUS, R., *Psychology in the Classroom* (New York: Harper and Row, 1957). This book offers an abundance of examples of problems actually encountered in the classroom. Much of its interpretation is in line with that of recent work in the field of social psychology.

FRANDSEN, Arden N., *Educational Psychology* (New York: McGraw-Hill, 1961). The concepts of educational psychology have been organized around the major functions of teaching and the conditions regarded as essential to effective learning.

GATES, Arthur I., JERSILD, Arthur T., McCONNELL, T. R., and CHALLMAN, Robert C., *Educational Psychology* (New York: Macmillan, 1948). The important problems in the area of educational psychology have been selected and presented in terms of their values to students preparing to teach.

LINDGREN, Henry C., *Educational Psychology in the Classroom,* 2nd ed. (New York: John Wiley & Sons, 1962). This text attempts to relate psychological principles to classroom activities. Extensive use is made of pictures, illustrations, case studies, and cartoons.

LOVELL, K., *Educational Psychology and Children* (London: University of London Press, 1958). This text deals with motivation, learning, child development, mental measurement, adjustment and maladjustment, and related topics. The relevance of psychological research to teaching is presented.

MACDONALD, F. J., *Educational Psychology* (San Francisco: Wadsworth Publishing Co., 1960). This is a more difficult text to read than many texts in educational psychology. Maintaining a consistent point of view, the author aims to encourage teachers "to analyze critically the bases for the decisions they make."

McFARLAND, H. S. N., *Psychology and Teaching* (London: Harrap, 1958). This is a standard text in educational psychology. It deals with such topics as learning, child development, psychological assessment, personality, and mental health.

MOULY, George J., *Psychology for Effective Teaching* (New York: Holt, Rinehart and Winston, 1960). A text which treats the traditional topics of educational psychology in a goal-oriented manner toward school practices. The materials are organized around determinants of human behavior, introduced in the second chapter of the text.

PRESSEY, Sidney L., ROBINSON, Francis P., and HORROCKS, John E., *Psychology in Education* (New York: Harper and Row, 1959). The first part of this text treats development as a process. The second part deals with the nature of learning and the ways of fostering learning. The third part emphasizes working with the individual pupil.

SKINNER, Charles E. (ed.), *Educational Psychology*, 4th ed. (Englewood Cliffs, N. J.: Prentice-Hall, 1962). Twenty-two well-known students of educational psychology have contributed to the twenty-five chapters of this fourth edition. Personality and adjustment, growth and development, learning, and evaluation and measurement comprise the larger topics around which most of the materials are organized.

SMITH, Henry P., *Psychology in Teaching*, 2nd ed. (Englewood Cliffs, N. J.: Prentice-Hall, 1962). In this second edition the author continues to emphasize the role of psychological theory and research in the teaching process.

STEPHENS, J. M., *Educational Psychology*, rev. ed. (New York: Holt, Rinehart and Winston, 1956). The emphasis throughout this text is on educational growth or development. Special attention is given to the teacher's role in the educational growth process, with the emphasis on the teacher as a theorist.

STROUD, J. B., *Psychology in Education*, rev. ed. (New York: Longmans, Green and Co., 1956). This text draws heavily upon sociology and cultural anthropology. It also furnishes a historical perspective to many problems and presents an abundance of research materials on problems relating to the educative process.

THOMPSON, George G., GARDNER, Eric F., and DI VESTA, Francis J., *Educational Psychology* (New York: Appleton-Century-Crofts, 1959). Principles of learning and problems of adjustment are presented and interwoven with classroom practices and educational procedures.

TROW, W. C., *Psychology in Teaching and Learning* (Cambridge, Mass.: Houghton Mifflin, 1960). Teaching is regarded as helping children develop their potentialities. Much space is given to photographs of children, teachers, and related subjects.

VALENTINE, C. W., *Psychology and Its Bearing on Education*, 2nd ed. (London: Methuen, 1960). The results of much research are included in this text, making it a valuable source book for advanced students as well as a standard text. Materials from Gestalt psychology and data from animal experiments are prominent in this revised edition.

Appendix B

A Selected Annotated Bibliography of 16 mm. Films Correlated with the Materials of the Various Chapters

Part I: Psychology in Education

Bridges for Ideas (U. S. Calif., 20 min.). The use and techniques of language, motion pictures, radio and television, and other means of communicating information and ideas are examined and demonstrated.

Design for Growing (U. W. F., 33 min.). Individual and group activities in the Cleveland public school, intended to develop creative potentials of each child, are presented. The integration of the arts with other features of the school program is shown.

The Great Challenge (C-F, color, 28 min.). Portrays the influence a Sunday School teacher's life has upon the lives it touches in the development and enrichment of Christian character.

The Teacher as Observer and Guide (Tchrs. Col., 20 min.). Ways are indicated whereby teachers can help pupils meet problems, improve their learning, and develop desirable character traits.

Preparation of Teachers (U. W. G., 20 min.). The need for teachers who are trained and possess desirable personality traits is stressed.

See How They Learn (Indiana U., 29 min.). Explains how learning experiences at school and elsewhere contribute to the development of special skills.

Part II: The Child and His Development

Growth: A Study of Johnny and Jimmy (I. F. B., 43 min., sil.). The interdependence of maturation and practice is clearly illustrated in this comparative study of twins, who were the subjects of a special study.

Developmental Characteristics (M-H, 18 min.). The behavior problems of eight- and nine-year-old children are presented as a basis for curriculum planning.

Heredity and Environment (C. I. F., 10 min.). Examples of the operation of heredity and environment are given. An overview is presented of cultural inheritance, environmental influences, and genetics.

Children Growing Up with Others (U. W. F., 30 min.). The importance of social relations in the development of self-reliance is shown.

Perceptual and Motor Development (P. S. C., 18 min.). This film supplements three previous productions. It continues a boy's growth to show physical and behavioral characteristics at ages 3, 4, and 5 years. The development of motor coordination is well illustrated.

Principles and Development (M-H, 17 min.). The fundamentals of growth and change are outlined and six basic principles of development presented.

Social Development (E. B. F., 16 min.). Materials bearing on social development collected over a period of 15 years in Yale University Clinic of Child Development are here shown.

Part III: Learning and the Educative Process

Children Learning by Experience (U. W. F., 30 min.). The relation between interests, learning, and experiences around problems of daily living are brought forth.

The Children Must Learn (N. Y. U., 2 reels). This film points the way to the necessity of developing learning experiences around problems of daily living.

Experimental Studies in Social Climates of Groups (I. F. B., 30 min.). A comparison of the effects upon boys' behavior of different forms of group organizations is presented.

How We Learn (C. I. F., 10 min.). The main principles basic to learning are condensed and presented.

Learning from Class Discussion (C. I. F., 10 min.). The values of well designed questions presented in class are shown as they tend to promote effective learning.

Making Learning More Meaningful (M-H, 19 min.). This film shows how a teacher helps pupils to develop skills in arithmetic through their attainment of a better understanding of certain economic pursuits.

Importance of Goals (M-H, 19 min.). The importance of goal-seeking behavior is emphasized through the presentation of an episode in school contrasting the in-school and out-of-school behavior of a teen-age boy.

Motivating the Class (M-H, 19 min.). Bill, a young enthusiastic teacher, at first finds his class bored and restless. Through class motivation he is able to increase interest and learning.

Part IV: Evaluating Pupil Growth

Discovering Individual Differences (M-H, 25 min.). Show how the teacher comes to know and understand each of the pupils and how the teacher adapts the teaching program to meet individual needs.

Children are Creative (I. F. B., 33 min.). This film shows motivation, creative work, and evaluation of the final product in an elementary art class.

Learning to Understand Children: Part I, A Diagnostic Approach (M-H, 21 min.). Presents diagnostic techniques useful to the teacher in discovering the causes of emotional and social maladjustment of individual pupils.

Learning to Understand Children: Part II, A Remedial Program (M-H, 23 min.). The remedial measures used by the teacher in helping one of her pupils is shown.

Individual Differences (M-H, 23 min.). Roy is different from his older brother who made a good scholastic record at school. The teacher, after successive failures with Roy, comes to understand him and is thus able to deal with him in terms of his abilities and personality characteristics.

Testing Intelligence with the Stanford-Binet (P. S. C., 18 min.). Shows the administering of the Revised Stanford-Binet Scale to four children. An explanation of mental age and the calculation of the intelligence quotient are also shown.

Part V: Guiding the Child

Angry Boy (I. F. B., 33 min.). The story of ten-year-old Tommy Randall, sent to a child guidance clinic when he is caught stealing, reveals the importance of emotional and social adjustments during childhood.

A Class for Tommy (B. F., 20 min.). The problem of teaching mentally and physically handicapped children are revealed in this film.

Emergence of Personality (E. B. F., 30 min.). Indicates the role of heredity and environment in the development of the individual personality.

Guidance Problems for School and Home (Tchrs. C., 18 min.). An attempt is made to give parents and teachers an understanding of some of the forces that contribute to poor adjustments at home and at school.

Maintaining Classroom Discipline (M-H, 14 min.). Different classroom situations are presented. Emphasis is given to the development of desirable behavior controls.

Problem Children (C. O., 20 min.). This is the story of two school boys, one a shy, withdrawn type, the other an aggressive anti-social type. The story shows how the school may be able to help such problem children.

Problem of Pupil Adjustment, Part I—The Dropout: A Case Study (M-H, 20 min.). Shows some of the causes and consequences of dropping out of school.

Problem of Pupil Adjustment, Part II—The Stay-In: A School Study. (M-H, 19 min.). Shows how the school program built around the needs and interests of pupils with a good guidance program tends to hold pupils in school.

Sources of the Films Used in the Appendix

A F C—American Film Center, Brandon Films, Inc., 200 West Street, New York.

B F—Bailey Films, Inc., Hollywood 28, Calif.

C F—Cathedral Films, 2921 A. Alameda Avenue, Burbank, California.

C I F—Coronet Instruction Films, 65 East South Water Street, Chicago, Ill.

C O—Ohio Division of Mental Hygiene, Columbus, Ohio.

E B F—Encyclopaedia Britannica Films, 1150 Wilmette Avenue, Wilmette, Ill.

I F B—International Film Bureau, 57 East Jackson Blvd., Chicago, Ill.

Indiana U—Audio-visual center, Indiana University, Bloomington, Indiana

Iowa—State University of Iowa, Iowa City, Iowa

Kan U—University of Kansas, Bureau of Visual Instruction, Lawrence, Kansas

Mahnke—Carl F. Mahnke, 215 East 3rd Street, Des Moines, Iowa

M-H—McGraw-Hill Book Co., 330 West 42nd Street, New York

N F B C—National Film Board of Canada, 1270 Avenue of the Americas, New York

N Y U—New York University Film Library, 26 Washington Place, Washington Place, New York

P S C—Pennsylvania State University, Psychological Cinema Register, State College, Penn.

Tchrs Col—Teachers College Bureau of Publications, Columbia University, New York

U S Calif—University of Southern California, Los Angeles, Calif.

U W F—United World Films, Inc., 1445 Park Avenue, New York

U W G—United World Government, U. S. Office of Education, Washington, D.C.

Index of Names

Abel, L. B., 170, 171
Ackerman, W. I., 208, 505
Ahmann, J. S., 342, 367, 401
Ainsworth, S. H., 386
Albrecht, E., 441
Alexander, W. M., 364
Allen, F. H., 478
Alm, O. W., 136, 463
Amatora, M., Sr., 502
Ames, E. W., 57
Ames, L. B., 226
Anastasi, A., 25, 118
Anderson, G. L., 5, 22, 491
Anderson, Gladys, 151
Anderson, H. H., 151
Anderson, J., 438
Aronow, M. S., 383
Arthur, G., 83, 84
Astin, A. W., 510
Ausubel, D., 183, 214, 269, 513

Baker, C. T., 80, 81
Barnett, L., 9
Baron, D., 342, 367
Bass, B. M., 505
Bayley, N., 52, 80, 83, 95
Becker, W. C., 460
Beilin, H., 473
Beller, E. K., 63
Benedict, R., 27
Bennett, G. K., 336
Berkowitz, L., 39
Berlyne, D. E., 172
Bernard, H. W., 342, 367, 504
Bernhardt, K. S., 510
Bersch, O. F., 85
Betts, E. A., 386
Biderman, A. D., 196
Binet, A., 70, 73, 74, 373
Birch, H. G., 10, 283
Blair, G. M., 425
Blake, E., 183
Bledsoe, J. C., 434
Bloomers, P., 74
Boll, E. S., 135
Bond, G. L., 425

Bonney, M. E., 138
Borgatt, E. F., 470
Bossard, J. H. S., 135
Bouchard, J. B., 178
Bradfield, J. M., 342, 367
Bradley, N. C., 259
Bradshaw, J., 308
Brammer, L. M., 510
Brandt, R. M., 434
Breckenridge, M. E., 454
Brotherton, D. A., 262
Brown, A. W., 306
Bruce, W. F., 187, 489
Brueckner, L. J., 420
Bruner, J. S., 40, 206, 221
Buhler, C., 95
Burt, C., 84
Burton, A., 192
Burton, W. H., 268, 291
Buswell, G. T., 232

Carlson, B. R., 134
Carlton, L. E., 106
Carlton, T., 106
Carpenter, A., 234
Carpenter, F., 256, 257
Castaneda, A., 166
Center, S. S., 34
Church, J., 151
Clark, E. J., 390
Clymer, T., 96, 98
Cogan, M. L., 508
Coladarci, A. P., 22
Cole, L. E., 187
Combs, A. W., 432, 433, 456, 458, 487
Commoss, H., 469
Conrad, H. S., 96
Cooper, R., 315
Cordora, F., 118
Couch, G. B., 306
Cox, P. H., 35
Crandall, V. J., 130, 131
Crane, M. M., 392
Cronbach, L. J., 22, 40, 61, 69, 151, 155,
    221, 247, 268, 315, 342, 367, 454,
    489, 524

534

Index of Subjects